JOHN DANIEL

Scarlet and the Beast

I

A HISTORY OF THE WAR BETWEEN ENGLISH AND FRENCH FREEMASONRY

OMNIA VERITAS.

JOHN DANIEL

Scarlet and the Beast I
A history of the war between
English and French Freemasonry

First Edition, 1993 JKI Publishing Tyler, TX

© Omnia Veritas Limited - 2018

*O*MNIA VERITAS.

www.omnia-veritas.com

Portrait of 33rd degree Freemason Albert Pike as pictured in the front of his book, *Morals and Dogma*. Pike, from 1859 until his death in 1891, occupied simultaneously the positions of Grand Master of the Central Directory of Scottish Rite Freemasonry at Washington, D.C., Sovereign Grand Commander of the Supreme Council of Scottish Rite Freemasonry, Southern Jurisdiction at Charleston, S.C., and Sovereign Pontiff of Universal Freemasonry.

Below are actual photocopies of pages from *Morals and Dogma*, a Masonic book written in 1871 by the world's most esteemed Mason, 33rd degree Albert Pike.

The January 1990 issue of the *New Age* magazine, a monthly publication by the Southern Jurisdiction of Scottish Rite Freemasonry at Charleston, S.C., states that Pike's *Morals and Dogma* is a "Mason's guide for daily livings."

Albert Pike writes with sarcasm, and *Morals and Dogma* must be read with that understanding. Below, Pike says on P. 321 of Morals and Dogma that Lucifer is the light of this world, blinding "feeble, sensual, or selfish Souls", which are Pike's sarcastic words for defining Christians.

The Apocalypse is, to those who receive the nineteenth Degree, the Apotheosis of that Sublime Faith which aspires to God alone, and despises all the pomps and works of Lucifer. LUCIFER, the *Light-bearer!* Strange and mysterious name to give to the Spirit of Darkness! Lucifer, the Son of the Morning! Is it *he* who bears the *Light,* and with its splendors intolerable blinds feeble, sensual, or selfish Souls? Doubt it not! for traditions are full of Divine Revelations and Inspirations: and Inspiration is not of one Age nor of one Creed. Plato and Philo, also, were inspired.

Why do most Masons not know the truth about Freemasonry? Albert Pike tells you on P. 819 of *Morals and Dogma*.

[The Blue Degrees are but the outer court or portico of the Temple. Part of the symbols are displayed there to the Initiate, but he is intentionally misled by false interpretations. It is not intended that he shall understand them; but it is intended that he shall imagine he understands them. Their true explication is reserved for the Adepts, the Princes of Masonry. The whole body of the Royal and Sacerdotal Art was hidden so carefully, centuries since, in the High Degrees, as that it is even yet impossible to solve many of the enigmas which they contain. It is well enough for the mass of those called Masons, to imagine that all is contained in the Blue Degrees; and whoso attempts to undeceive them will labor in vain,

Notice the symbol of the Baphomet around Albert Pike's neck (upper left) and on the Fez of Henry C. Clausen (upper right), the past Sovereign Grand Commander of the Supreme Council of Scottish Rite Freemasonry, Southern Jurisdiction at Charleston, S.C. Upper center is the same symbol used by Satanist and 33rd degree Freemason Aleister Crowley when he signed his name "Baphomet X."

GENERAL ALBERT PIKE 33°

SYMBOL OF BAPHOMET

PAST SOVEREIGN GRAND COMMANDER HENRY C. CLAUSEN, 33°

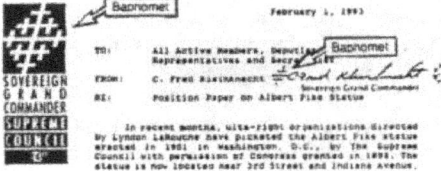

Notice the symbol of the Baphomet on the letterhead of the current Sovereign Grand Commander, C. Fred Kleinknecht.

HERMAPHRODITIC GOAT OF MENDES

Albert Pike defines "Baphomet" in *Morals and Dogma* (p. 734) as "the hermaphroditic goat of Mendes." The goat head of Mendes is also pictured in the upsidedown Eastern Star. The Baphomet is a universal symbol of Satan.

GOAT OF MENDES IS THE "GOD OF LUST"

PREFACE

> *Woe to those who call evil good and good evil, who put*
> *darkness for light and light for darkness, who put bitter*
> *for sweet and sweet for bitter.*
>
> Isaiah 5:20[1]

What began quite by accident turned into a 20-year research and writing project.

In 1972, while taking courses on the Bible at a university in Texas, I happened upon a book that related certain Biblical prophecies I was interested in to what is generally today called "conspiracy" theories of history.

I come from a strong conservative, evangelical Protestant family. Both by religious upbringing and from study of the events and direction of modern history, I have long been convinced that we live in the "last days" prophesied in the Bible.

Like all believing Christians I understand history as a battle between the forces of good and evil, between God and Satan - from the Garden of Eden to the Second Coming of Christ.

As a Christian I also believe that Almighty God is the victor in this great battle, for He is sovereign over all events. He alone will permit the developments of the Apocalypse to mature within His providence and predestination. As Daniel 2:21 tells us, God "removeth kings, and setteth up kings."[2]

But to return to that long-ago day in 1972.

In a prayerful attempt to relate Bible prophecy to current events, I asked for God's special guidance as I searched for the meaning of God's sealed vision of Daniel 12:9. The prophet Daniel wrote of the progression of world governments, which would end with the kingdom of the Beast. In the last chapter of Daniel's book, God tells him, "Go thy way, Daniel: for the words are closed up and sealed till the time of the end. Many shall be purified, and made white, and tried; but the wicked shall do wickedly: and none of the wicked shall understand; but the wise shall understand."

Pondering this verse from Daniel about the end-times, I recalled the burden of living in the last days, when Almighty God is revealing to "the wise" what He forbade Daniel to communicate. And I found myself drawn over and again to Revelation, chapters 17 and 18, which delineate in symbolic language the nature of the end-times.

How will this great battle between good and evil, God and Satan play itself out, I asked. How are these Biblical prophecies related? If it is true that Scripture provides clues to interpret history, is there a definite political or historical shape to the drama of the end-times?

These were just some of my questions. Perhaps they are yours too.

SCRIPTURAL CLUES TO THE "MYSTERY OF INIQUITY"

The apostle Paul in 2 Thessalonians 2:3a, 7, 8a, 9-12 talks about the "mystery of iniquity" (emphases mine):

Let no man deceive you by any means... For the mystery of iniquity doth already work: only he [the Holy Spirit] who now letteth [hinders] will let, until he be taken out of

---

[1] Bible, New International Version (NW).

[2] All Bible citations are from the King James Version (KJV) unless otherwise indicated.

the way. And then shall that Wicked [One] be revealed... Even him, whose coming is after the working of Satan with all power and signs and lying wonders, And with all deceivableness of unrighteousness in them that perish; because they received not the love of the truth, that they might be saved. And for this cause God shall send them strong delusion, that they should believe a lie: That they all might be damned who believed not the truth, but had pleasure in unrighteousness.

As Paul tells us in this passage, the Wicked One, Antichrist, who is indwelt by Satan, works by lies - by "lying wonders" and "deceivableness." And those who follow him have no "love of the truth": they abide in "strong delusion," believing "lies." In fact, Satan's human minions will attempt to "deceive" others by "any means."

It should come as no surprise that Satan, the Adversary, is the father of lies. For Satan has been active in the corruption of human affairs since he tempted Adam and Eve from righteousness in the Garden of Eden.

How far back can we trace the "mystery of iniquity" of which Paul speaks? Paul gives us a clue about its duration when he says that it "doth already work." Turning to the Old Testament, in Genesis 11:1-9, we find the first Scriptural account of the first organized attempt of "iniquity," when humanity tried to unite the known world in defiance against God:

Now the whole earth had one language and few words. And as men migrated from the east, they found a plain in the land of Shinar [Babylon] and settled there. And they said to one another, "Come let us make bricks... then they said, "Come, let us build ourselves a city, and a tower with its top in the heavens, and let us make a name for ourselves, lest we be scattered abroad upon the face of the whole earth." And the Lord came down to see the city and the tower, which the sons of men had built. And the Lord said, "Behold, they are one people, and they have all one language; and this is only the beginning of what they will do; and nothing that they propose to do will now be impossible for them. Come let us go down, and there confuse their language, that they may not understand one another's speech." So the Lord scattered them abroad from there over the face of all the earth, and they left off building the city. Therefore its name was called Babel, because there the Lord confused the language of all the earth; and from there the Lord scattered them abroad over the face of all the earth.[3]

From this passage in Genesis, we can conclude that the Adversary, for millenniums, has had a blueprint to throw off the yoke of God's authority. Satan's plan from the start has been to gather mankind under the banner of a global government - what we call today *globalism* or the *New World Order*. Of course, as I have suggested, the primary prophetic guide for understanding the historical shape and drama of the end-times is Revelation 17-18. If you are not familiar with these two chapters from the New Testament, I suggest you read them now, since they are too long to reproduce here.

In chapters 17-18 of Revelation, John describes two powers as active in the last days. Initially these two powers are allied in some way, for John tells us that the harlot called MYSTERY, BABYLON THE GREAT, THE MOTHER OF HARLOTS, is riding the Beast (Rev. 17:3).

Although seemingly united, Scripture reveals that the two powers are in conflict, each struggling to dominate the other. In fact that the Harlot rides the Beast is a figurative portrayal of her initial dominion. But "the beast will hate the harlot" and in the end he will conspire with ten kings, who burn the Whore (Rev. 17:16). The Beast will triumph over the Whore.

But the question remains, Who or What in historical terms is MYSTERY, BABYLON THE GREAT, THE MOTHER OF HARLOTS? And Who or What is the Beast?

---

[3] Bible, Revised Standard Version (RSV).

Prophecy scholars have generally identified the Beast as a political power, the Harlot as a spiritual force or power.

Twenty years of exploring and researching these questions have further persuaded me that the two powers described by John are initially allied in a one-world government, in which the Whore controls the Beast.

But we must remember that both powers are also in conflict. They battle for world dominion.

I have identified MYSTERY, BABYLON THE GREAT, THE MOTHER OF HARLOTS, as a system that is idolatrous and pantheistic. The other power, the Beast, appears to be atheistic and humanistic. Both powers are anti-Semitic and anti-Christian.

At first, the Whore (who throughout this book I call Scarlet) controls the Beast. But in the end, the Beast destroys Scarlet, the Whore.

SCRIPTURE, HISTORY AND CONSPIRACY

When I first read the book which presented a conspiratorial view of history some twenty years ago I was so shocked and disturbed by its contents and claims, I found it difficult to believe. My reactions were the same as many with whom I have discussed this subject since:

You must be out of your mind! What do you mean "conspiracy"? How could an intrigue run through all of history?

Many non-Christians especially ridicule any suggestion of such an intrigue. They maintain that all events 'lust happen."

For someone to suggest that a thread of conspiracy is woven through past and current political events and that such a conspiracy is shaping future events provokes hostility. Why? Because to accept such a view requires a radical change of perception of world history. My doubts however were short-lived.

As a Christian, I accept the fact that Satan is the ancient Adversary and Deceiver of humanity. I also know that because Satan is a spirit, he must rely upon and perfect his work through mortal men.

I also believe Paul's statement in 2 Thessalonians that "the mystery of iniquity doth already work." I discovered that the Greek word "mystery" in this verse means "a secret through the idea of silence imposed by initiation into religious rites."[4]

In Revelation 17, we find the same Greek word, "Mystery, Babylon the Great," referring to the future Babylon which will be destroyed by the Beast's end-time government.

If we connect the *mystery* in these two passages, can we not conclude that the "Wicked One" will gain power by clandestine means through a mystery religion? A mystery religion which millenniums ago first attempted to unite the known world in defiance of God at Babylon. A mystery religion that Revelation reveals will command the Beast's global empire before her destruction by fire.

But when will this all come about? According to 2 Thessalonians the Wicked One cannot secure power until "he [the Holy Spirit] be taken out of the way." Protestant theologians hold that the exiting of the Holy Spirit from the world will coincide with the Rapture of the Church.

My earthly father, a prophecy teacher, taught that the Rapture or removal of Christians from the world before the Great Tribulation would cause international chaos.

---

[4] James Strong, *Strong's Exhaustive Concordance of the Bible,*(1890; Nashville: Abingdon, 1980) Selected words from the King James Version, Greek #3466.

He held that when Christians are taken out of this world, a wicked man, called the Beast, will instantly form a global government. The Beast will then rule with brutal force.

I still accept this scenario of the last days, but with some reservations as to the sequence of events. Even as a child I wondered how a kingdom so vast and complex as that described in Revelation 17 and 18 could suddenly appear overnight. No power on earth had ever advanced so rapidly. Why should this power be an exception? I reasoned that such an empire must be conceived and gestate. After birth would follow stages of growth, requiring time and patience. Only then could such a government or empire flex its power. To my understanding, the development of such a power would need decades, if not centuries to complete.

If my assumption were correct, I could search history and find the beginning of the Adversary's empire. I began to explore recent conventional histories, searching for answers. But none were forthcoming in generally accepted historical works. They seemed strangely silent. It was then I stumbled upon my first "conspiracy" book.

REVISIONIST HISTORY

The intrigue outlined in the "conspiracy" history I read in 1972 conformed to my Scriptural understanding that the Adversary's plan for an end-time government would be housed within a secret mystery religion and that it would mature by clandestine means.

The thesis of this ''conspiracy'' or ''revisionist'' history, as books on this subject are often called, was that a definite conspiracy has been active in the events of the last 200 years. The author further claimed that the conspiracy was a continuation of Satan's age-old plot against God and humanity. It was this convergence with Scriptural understanding that frankly shocked me and caused me to review my own skepticism regarding "conspiracy" theories of history. To maintain my intellectual honesty, I felt compelled to examine this view of history further.

The book I read, as well as the hundreds of other books and documents I have accumulated on the subject since, proposes that a conspiratorial group has been active through the last two centuries, working to unite the world under one global government.

It was the shattering experience of World War I that began throughout Europe and America a major re-thinking or revising of world history - thus the term "revisionist" history was coined in America in 1921 - although the first of this genre appeared as long ago as 1798.

In my examination and study of these materials I found general agreement on one fact. Each author describes and attempts to expose an organization, a secret society, cloaked in mystery, born over two and a half centuries ago. According to revisionist historians, this organization - operating a single conspiracy - attempts to control or alter world politics toward its goal of world domination.

Veiled in mystery, this society has an enormous membership, with over 9,000 operating centers worldwide. A select group within a central directory commands all centers with local agents working from each. Tens of thousands of individuals across the nations can be activated at any given time by the collective voice of the central directory.

I discovered, however, that no author could with certitude name which individuals or group comprised the "collective voice" within the secret society. Thus they coined the term "hidden hand" to describe the ultimate power or decision-makers driving the conspiracy.

A GENERAL OVERVIEW: THE OCTOPUS THEORIES

The literature of revisionist or conspiracy history has developed no less than eight theories to explain the purposes and activities of the single conspiracy each describes. I call these *The Octopus Theories*.

Some write that the Jesuits (the Society of Jesus, a powerful military priesthood in the Catholic Church) are the organizers and propagators of the conspiracy. Others claim the Illuminati, a secret society dedicated to the overthrow of absolute rule, arising in the age of enlightenment. Still others propose Freemasonry, the Jews, the Communists, world bankers, and multinational corporations.

Most recently, the intrigue has been credited to the Oligarchy, the Pretenders to the old European thrones. This group consists of members of the wealthy families descended from the absolute monarchs of Europe who were dethroned during the numerous revolutions of the last 300 years. Initially I was baffled by so many conjectures and apparent contradictions in the accounts of the conspiracy. I raise one objection, as a typical example, regarding the oligarchy theory: the revolutions which convulsed Europe cast out kings and their wealthy cohorts. Why would the same class be involved in the intrigue which eliminated them in the first place?

In spite of these difficulties, I found that each of these entities described and investigated by various authors were, in some way, involved in a plot. In fact, an author exposing any one of the eight groups could present so much convincing evidence, that without knowledge of the peculiar role played by each of the others in the whole, he or she could present plausible proof that the entity was indeed the "hidden hand" in control of the conspiracy to establish a one-world government.

I struggled with two more questions, however, in evaluating these accounts of the conspiracy. First, How can such a diverse group cooperate? Second, What keeps these men and women working their entire lives from one generation to the next without seeing the fruit of their labors?

Some authors propose that the conspirators have been motivated by greed for power. Others suggest they are driven by an insatiable desire for wealth.

Undoubtedly the conspirators have obtained wealth and power as the intrigue broadens. As a unifying factor, however, pursuit of wealth and power seldom brings cooperation. Instead it wreaks division.

Another seeming obstacle in the way of cooperation would be the professed, opposed religious dogmas and political theories of the eight groups. How could Jesuits, Jews, communists, aristocratic world bankers, members of the business elite, royalty, and even members of the Protestant clergy work toward a common ideal?

What could sustain this kind of enterprise, when its ambition is not realized in one generation? Conspiracy researchers have in fact coined the term "gradualism" to describe the slow progress by which the conspirators are achieving their goal. But how could these diverse groups work together without destroying each other in the process?

I found the answer to these questions, as I have already suggested, by turning to Scripture. Recalling Paul's statement in 2 Thessalonians, that "the mystery of iniquity doth already work," I perceived that *harmony among these groups could only be achieved through the unifying bonds of a mystery religion.*

This mystery religion is the brotherhood of Freemasonry. I discovered that all conspiratorial players have been or are members of either the Masonic Lodge or its affiliate secret societies. The largest and most powerful mystery religion, or secret society as it is known today, on earth, Freemasonry permits all faiths and political parties within all nations to join its ranks without discrimination.

In my years of research into and evaluation of these books and documents, I also discovered that the controlling mechanism of the conspiracy, the so-called Hidden Hand was, and still is concealed within the highest degree of Freemasonry, the 33rd degree Supreme Council, whose members include Jesuits, Jews, communists, aristocratic world bankers, members of the corporate elite, royalty, and sad to say, many pastors of Protestant churches.

A BIBLICAL INTERPRETATION: ONE CONSPIRACY OR TWO?

Revisionist authors, as we have seen, lay the conspiracy at the door of the above-mentioned groups. All authors agree, however, that while there may be *one conspiracy, two conflicts* can be traced throughout modern history.

The first conflict, originating some 200-300 years ago, was the struggle of democracy against monarchy. The second conflict, in our century, has been that of communism against democracy. Revisionist authors claim that both struggles or conflicts were and still are manipulated by the same conspiracy. "Divide and conquer is the conspirator's tactic," they write.

Here I faced the same contradiction as I did in my evaluation of the "oligarchy" theory: Why would a single group of people - the monarchy, for instance - who controlled the Old World Order, chance their own destruction to reach a goal of globalism? Why not set up a world government using the old system?

As I have said, most revisionist authors ascribe the direction and control of the plot to an inner circle, called the Hidden Hand. Only a few of these authors relate their data to Scripture, and then only in part. Fewer still examine their evidence thoroughly in relation to Apocalyptic prophecy.

A few see the conspiracy as a struggle between the forces of good and evil. The majority regard it solely as man's struggle against man for world dominion. Many claim that the original plotters, along with their successors, are on schedule with a pre-designed, precise blueprint.

However, I believe that it is humanly impossible and Scripturally inaccurate to assign such complete control of history to mortal men and women. No human being can know the future, much less manipulate it. Such an enterprise can be planned only gradually, stage by stage, and then only as the conspirators are "enlightened" by unseen powers. We must further remember that God is in sovereign control of all events and He alone will permit the Apocalypse to develop within His own time frame.

My conclusion, reached after many years of investigation, research and study - and always in conjunction with Scripture - is that the groups described by the octopus theory were and are allied in Freemasonry. Each group or entity has its role and task.

What allies the conspirators is their intense hatred of the Old World Order, and their mutual desire to establish a New World Order in its place.

The Old World Order is embodied religiously by Jews and by Christians (both Protestant and Catholic). Politically, the Old World Order is a term which describes the system by which Europe was governed before the modern revolutions. In the Old World Order, the Crown and Church ruled, with the Crown usually answerable to the Church.

In contrast to the Old World Order, the New World Order is associated with the "new world" of the Western Hemisphere and the Americas. The New World Order is a term that designates the political system of democracy, the rule of the people. The political goal of the New World Order, however, is not simply national democracies, but rather the manipulation of such toward a global government. The New World Order will be marked by a universal government. The goal in religion of the New World Order is to totally separate Church and State, with the purpose of destroying the Church.

The conspirators' hatred of the Old World Order has overshadowed any ideological differences between them. They cooperate to destroy the powerful obstacle hindering globalism - the Church.

As I have suggested, the view of history as shaped by a single conspiracy leaves too many unanswered questions. Here again we need to recall Revelation 17 and 18.

Scripture does not indicate a single mortal conspiratorial group manipulating history. To the contrary, there are two separate conflicts, two separate conspiracies.

One is called MYSTERY, BABYLON THE GREAT, THE MOTHER OF HARLOTS, representing a system which is pantheistic and idolatrous. The Whore of Babylon stands for the Old World Order. The other is called the BEAST, which appears to be atheistic and humanistic. The Beast represents the New World Order, which will destroy the Whore and usher in the Apocalyptic holocaust of tomorrow.

I have uncovered both plots in Freemasonry.

THE TWO POWERS OF FREEMASONRY

My research has revealed that there are two separate and opposing powers in Freemasonry. One, headquartered in London, subscribes to and promotes an idolatrous and pantheistic view of the world. It is monarchist, capitalistic, wealthy, right-wing. The other, in Paris, is atheistic and humanistic in origin and outlook. It is republican, socialist, poor, left-wing.

One is Scarlet. The other, the Beast. The breakthrough theory which I have developed with Scripture as my guide makes sense of the massive literature I have collected on Freemasonry as well as its apparent contradictions. My library includes books written by members of and defectors from both English and French Freemasonry.

At the beginning of my research, like many other revisionist authors, I thought revisionist authors were reporting one single plot. I gradually realized that many authors were exposing what in reality were often the machinations of one group of conspirators against the other. The devices of both wings of Masonry were so similar that without Scripture as a guide, one could easily perceive only a single intrigue.

This interesting twist in the historical drama, confirmed again and again by my research, points to the existence of a struggle between the two powers in Freemasonry. Although revisionist authors are supposedly concerned about one plot, I noticed that all exposes pointed to Paris as the center of an intrigue before World War I. After the War, however, evidence points to the shift of intrigue to London.

I will explain this shift in the course of this book.

THE PURPOSE OF THIS BOOK

Thousands of books have been written to expose the workings of a conspiracy in human history. But all these books have done little to impede its progress.

Only a few people are aware of the truth. As Daniel prophesies in 12:3, the wise have listened, and turned many to righteousness. Yet to most people, this conspiracy, or, as I will show, these conspiracies, remain a mystery.

I am not addressing unbelievers. For those without Christ as Savior, maintaining peace of mind requires mocking the frightening evidence I shall present in these pages. To these people God has sent a "strong delusion," and I will pray for them.

I am writing instead to bring deceived Christians and Jews out of Freemasonry. A disturbing and sad discovery to me has been how many Christians there are, Protestant and Catholic, who have been beguiled by Masonry.

As I will later show in detail, Freemasonry in its present form was created during the Protestant Reformation - organized for the express purpose of eliminating the Catholic Church. Hence, many Reformers joined Freemasonry to fight the common enemy. Freemasonry is rife with Protestants to this day.

In contrast, the Catholic Church until Vatican II has been more vigilant. Catholics have been forbidden to enter Freemasonry. For self-preservation, Rome maintained investigators who were well-versed in this intrigue, and historically, she has been aware of the deadly animosity of Freemasonry toward the Christian churches.

Why is it so important that Christians and Jews be warned about Freemasonry?

Revelation 17:6 reveals that Scarlet is both anti-Semitic and anti-Christian, for she is "drunken with the blood of the saints, and with the blood of the martyrs of Jesus..." The "blood of the saints" she drinks is the blood of the Jews, and the "blood of the martyrs of Jesus" is the blood of Christians. Both Christians and Jews will be devoured by Scarlet and the Beast.

The Apostle Paul warns Christians against allying with false religion and its followers: "Be ye not unequally yoked together with unbelievers; for what fellowship hath righteousness with unrighteousness? And what communion hath light with darkness?" (2 Cor. 6:14).

Through John, Christ warns both Christians and Jews who have joined Mystery Babylon to "Come out of her, my people, that ye be not partakers of her sins, and that ye receive not of her plagues" (Rev 18:4).

For it is a terrible fact, as I will show, that Freemasonry is a pagan religion. And although its leaders will openly deny it, its ultimate goal includes the ritual slaughter of all Jews, the destruction of all Christianity (Catholic and Protestant), and the inauguration of a godless one- world government. It will bring about this globalism or New World Order, according to Revelation 18:23 by the deception of "sorceries," which I shall show involve the use of magic, witchcraft, and drugs.

Some Christians are aware of the dangers of Freemasonry. One of them, Rev. Wayne Poucher, a Church of Christ minister and founder of the famous 1950s conservative radio program *Lifeline,* warned me over ten years ago that few people would heed my discoveries. "You will not be able to tell the whole truth," he said. "If you attempt to, it will be so unbelievable that you will make yourself incredible."

THE HISTORIC CONFLICT

There are many Christians who are aware of the Satanic undertow of Freemasonry.

Some Masons (though not all, as I will show) are fully cognizant actors in bringing the New World Order into being through covert activities, just as Christians are aware of their own overt activity in winning the world to a saving knowledge of Jesus Christ.

Scripture teaches that God's salvation has a two-fold purpose. Not only does He offer us eternal life in the hereafter, He wants us to carry the Gospel of Jesus Christ to the ends of the earth.

God has a blueprint for each Christian to fulfill. We must complete His commission here and now. God's strategy is not vague. If we seek God's will, the Holy Spirit will confirm in our hearts what our part is in God's plan. With confidence in and love for Him, we risk all to accomplish this task. Are we conspirators? No! Our activity is in the open for the world to see.

Satan too has servants. They are driven by their intense hatred of Jesus Christ and His Church. Whether they are conscious that their actions further the Adversary's goal of world domination is of no consequence.

What is clear is that they consciously oppose all that is Biblically righteous. Masonic publications state that the God of Christians is evil. They accuse Him of opposing every human effort to advance in science. The flood in Genesis, the destruction of Babel, and the Catholic Inquisitions during the Middle Ages are all cited as prime examples of God's revulsion toward both science and other religions.

In order to avoid persecution, Freemasons claim they must remain a secret society.

Unlike Freemasons, righteous men and women of God desiring to reform Catholicism fought their battles in the open. They did not hide like cowards in secret societies.

I am writing this book for them, because some in ignorance, during the Reformation, joined Freemasonry to fight the common enemy. As a result, Protestant Christians fill Masonic Lodges to this day.

On the other hand, Satan's cowardly henchmen dare not affect their machinations overtly, lest they be directly opposed by sovereign governments and the Roman Church. They allied themselves politically, though not spiritually, with the Protestant Reformation for the purpose of destroying the old alliance of Crown and Church. But they hid in the shadows of secret societies in order to bring about their political revolutions.

Neither Christian nor Jew should be involved in this plot, for Freemasonry is the vehicle the Beast of the Apocalypse will ride to his universal inauguration. This book is dedicated to *bringing God's people out of Freemasonry.*

John Daniel
Summer 1993

Do you have a question about the King James Bible versus Modern Translations?
For the author's opinion see Appendix 11.

INTRODUCTION
WHAT IS FREEMASONRY?

A WORD ABOUT SOURCES

In this introduction I will first examine Freemasonry as religion. I shall trace the history of Masonry's powerful ancestors, Rosicrucianism and the Knights Templar, and outline the development of Masonry and its various offshoots and branches. Next I will review the degrees of Masonry and the knowledge and secrets of Masonry available to members in the various degrees, and discuss its appeal, deceptions, and methods. But before proceeding, I should like to say something about my sources.

Although the history of Masonry is admittedly difficult to construct, ample historical references exist from which its development can be traced.

Valuable information can be found in materials written by former adherents to Masonry. Also quite illuminating are those works by "insiders," who while remaining loyal to the goals of Freemasonry, have felt that this conspiracy toward a one-world government should not remain secret. They want "benevolent" Freemasonry to receive credit for what it has been doing. Included in my source materials are also many books by Roman Catholic investigators as well as investigations by Protestants. Again I must reiterate the inestimable value of those books, documents and publications, past and present, authored and used by Masons themselves. Throughout the text, I have attempted to document sources with concise but thorough footnotes and appendices.[5]

Biblical texts cited throughout the three volumes are from the King James Version of the Holy Bible unless otherwise noted.

THE UNIVERSAL RELIGION OF FREEMASONRY

Masons often try to present Masonry as a Judeo-Christian brotherhood, while in fact it is a universal, pagan religion. We have only to turn to the Masons themselves, in particular to the "High Masons" of the 32nd and 33rd degrees, to discover the beliefs and tenets of the Masonic religion.

In *Morals and Dogma* (1871), a book still considered a Mason's "daily guide for living," 33rd degree Freemason Albert Pike writes that "Masonry is a search after Light... Every Masonic Lodge is a temple of religion; and its teachings are instructions in religion."[6]

---

[5] Book Distributors may purchase these Masonic books from Charles T. Powner Co., 7056-38 W. Higgins, Chicago, IL 60656. Individuals may purchase them from Ezra A. Cook Publishers Ltd., 6604 W. Irving Park Road, Chicago, IL 60634. Write Powner or Ezra for a book list, prices and order form.

[6] Albert Pike, *Morals and Dogma* (1871; Richmond, VA: L. Jenkins, 1942) 741, 213. The Southern Jurisdiction of Scottish Rite Freemasonry, of which Pike was its Grand Commander from 1859 until his death in 1891, publishes the monthly magazine entitled *New Age* (name changed in 1991 to *The Scottish Rite Journal*). In the January, 1990 issue of the *New Age,* the current Grand Commander of Freemasonry, C. Fred Kleinknecht, 33rd degree, told all Masons that Albert Pike's *Morals and Dogma* was to be their daily guide for living - their "Bible."

Albert Mackey, also a 33rd degree Mason, in his *Textbook of Masonic Jurisprudence*, affirms that Masonry is "undoubtedly a religious institution."[7] And in his *Manual of the Lodge* he states, "As Masons we are taught never to commence any great or important undertaking without first invoking the blessing and protection of deity, and this is because Masonry is a religious institution.[8]

To the unsuspecting Christian, Freemasonry would appear to be a Christian institution, for upon joining the Lodge, he finds the Holy Bible placed upon the altar.

Masonic publications suggest that Masonry is a Christian and patriotic institution. For example, the inquirer reading the brochure, *To a Non-Mason: You Must Seek Masonic Membership,* will find a referral to a medieval poem, the Regius poem, which the text says "set[s] forth articles and fifteen points and rules of behavior at church, teaching duties to God and Church and Country, and inculcating brotherhood."

The non-initiate, or the member in the lower degrees of Masonry, will seek and find in Masonry whatever he wishes it to be. However, the truth is otherwise.

As Freemason Robert Morris writes in *Webb's Monitor*, "So broad is the religion of Masonry, and so carefully are all sectarian tenets excluded from the system, that the Christian, the Jew, and the Mohammedan, in all their numberless sects and divisions, may, and do harmoniously combine in its moral and intellectual work with the Buddhist, the Parsee, the Confucian, and the worshipper of Deity under every form."[9]

Thus Albert Pike in *Morals and Dogma* reveals the real purpose of the placement of the Bible on the Masonic altar: "The Bible is an indispensable part of the furniture of a Christian Lodge [meaning Lodge in a Christian nation], only because it is the sacred book of the Christian religion. The Hebrew Pentateuch in the Hebrew Lodge, and a Koran in a Mohammedan one, belong on the Altar."[10]

Unlike Christianity, Freemasonry does not offer humanity one saving, universal creed. Instead, says 32nd degree Freemason Dr. J.D. Buck in his *Mystic Masonry* (1925), Masonry is a "universal science" and "a world wide religion, and owes allegiance to no one creed, and can adopt no such sectarian dogmas as such, without ceasing thereby to be Masonic... Masonry is the universal religion only because and only so long as it embraces all religions."[11]

According to 33rd degree Mason Delmar Duane Darrah in his book *History and Evolution of Freemasonry* (1954), Masonry publicly tailors itself to the prevailing faith or moral system of the nation within which it operates. "The original plan of Freemasonry," he states, "was intended to give to the world a thoroughly tolerant institution. And the recognized book to be used was to be that volume which was accepted as the basis of the religious belief of the country or nation wherein Masonry might propagate."

While Darrah states that Masonry "tells no man how he should worship God but leaves the method to his own selection," he also insists that Masonry transcends the particular faiths of its members: "Those early founders of Masonry conceived a system of moral religion at whose shrine all men might worship, the Christian, the Catholic, the Protestant, the Confucian the Buddhist, the Mohammedan, as well as all others who are willing to acknowledge a supreme being... Thus there has evolved a religious society,

---

[7] Albert G. Mackey, *Textbook of Masonic Jurisprudence* (Chicago: P.R.C. Publications, n.d.) 95.
[8] Albert G. Mackey, *Manual of the Lodge* (Chicago: P.R.C. Publications, n.d.) 40.
[9] Robert Morris, *Webb's Monitor* (USA: N.p., n.d.) 280.
[10] Pike 11.
[11] J.D. Buck, *Symbolism of Mystic Masonry* (1925; Chicago: Charles T. Powner, n.d.) 113-114.

which has been charitable enough to recognize good whether it be found in the Bible or the Koran, or in the Moral Code of those who have sought the higher things of life."[12]

SALVATION WITHOUT CHRIST

We should ask ourselves at this point, What god accepts the worship of adherents of all religions? Certainly not the God of the Holy Bible. When Christians in Freemasonry are confronted with the syncretic, universal claims of Masonry, such as those I have just presented, some justify their affiliation by saying their membership gives them the opportunity to witness for Jesus Christ in the Lodge.

The doctrine of Freemasonry, however, strictly forbids Christian witness within the Lodge. Dr. Mackey in his *Lexicon of Free masonry* makes this prohibition explicit: "The religion then of Masonry is pure theism on which its different members engraft their peculiar opinions, but they are not permitted to introduce them into the lodge or to connect their truth or falsehood with the truth of Masonry... A Christian Mason is not permitted to introduce his own peculiar opinions with regards to Christ's mediatorial office into the Lodge."[13]

In fact, a Christian, upon pain of death, is not even permitted to pray in the name of Jesus Christ inside the Masonic Temple. According to Edmond Ronayne, a Master Mason who authored the *Masonic Handbook* and who later renounced Masonry, "whenever a minister prays in the name of Christ in any of our assemblies, you must always hold yourself in readiness, if called upon, to cut his throat from ear to ear, pull out his tongue by the roots and bury his body at the bottom of some lake or pond."[14] (Since this truth has been exposed, the *Masonic Handbook* has been revised, deleting this and other incriminating evidence.)

Rev. Jim Shaw, a 33rd degree member who renounced Freemasonry' after becoming a Christian, tells of a pastor initiated into the first degree of Masonry, who was asked to pray at a Masonic gathering. The pastor, in ignorance, closed his prayer in the name of Jesus. Shaw reports that the pastor was later taken aside and gently reprimanded with these words: "We don't want to offend our Brothers who are of other Faiths by ending our prayers in Jesus' name. From now on, end your prayers 'in thy name, amen,' or use an abrupt 'amen'."[15]

Masonic authorities insist that the name "Jesus Christ" is not to be uttered in the Masonic temple. If the Christian Mason does make a slip of the tongue, his anti-Christian programming will begin.

A FALSE RELIGION OF WORKS

It is a logical conclusion that if the founder of Christianity cannot be mentioned in a Masonic Lodge, Freemasonry cannot be a Christian institution. Indeed, Dr. Mackey confirms this in his *Encyclopedia of Freemasonry*. "Freemasonry is not Christianity," he states. "Its religion is that general one of nature and primitive revelation - handed down

---

[12] Delmar Duane Darrah, *History and Evolution of Freemasonry* (1954; Chicago: Powner, 1979) 292, 294, 300.

[13] Albert G. Mackey, *Lexicon of Freemasonry* (Chicago: P.R.C. Publications, n.d.) 404.

[14] Edmond Ronayne, *Handbook of Freemasonry* (1943; Chicago: Charles T. Powner, 1973) 74.

[15] Questions and answers on Freemasonry, narr. Jim Shaw, Tape Ministry of Rev. Jim Shaw (audio cassette).

to us from some ancient and Patriarchal Priesthood - in which all men may agree and in which no men can differ."[16]

But if Freemasonry does not worship Christ as the Son of God and our Savior, what god, if any, does it worship? What kind of religion is it?

Again, the Masons provide the answer. They refer to God as the Great Architect of the Universe, a god who is a personification of humanity' Dr. J.D. Buck in *Mystic Masonry* states that "the only personal god Freemasonry accepts is humanity in total. God, the Great Architect of the Universe, personifies himself through man. Humanity, therefore, is the only personal god there is."[17]

Freemason and past Grand Master Daniel Sickles elaborates in his book *Ahiman Rezon:* "If we with suitable true devotion maintain our Masonic profession, our faith will become a beam of light and bring us to those blessed mansions where we shall be eternally happy with God, the Great Architect of the Universe."[18]

Likewise says Dr. Mackey in his *Lexicon of Freemasonry:* "A Mason who lives in strict obedience to the obligations and precepts of the fraternity is free from sin."[19]

To a Christian, the Masonic equation of God with humanity recalls the lie of the Serpent in the Garden of Eden, when the Serpent told Adam and Eve, "Ye shall be as gods" (Gen. 3:5). As we know, humanity again attempted to become like God at Babylon after the Great Flood, whence Mystery Babylon was born. Freemasonry has adopted the belief of Mystery Babylon that God and man are the same.

Freemasonry is also a religion of works, for it teaches that man can obtain his salvation outside the mediatorial work of Jesus Christ. This is plainly contrary to the teaching expressed by the apostle Paul in Ephesians 2:8-9: "For by grace are ye saved through faith; and that not of yourselves, it is the gift of God: Not of works, lest any man should boast"

Symbolic representation of the religion of "works" of the Masons is found in the most prominent emblem of Universal Freemasonry: the Square and Compass.

The Square and Compass represent the tools used to create the heavens and the earth by the Masonic Great Architect of the Universe. In America, the letter "G" in the center of the Square and Compass is said to represent God. The emblem of English Freemasonry, however, more powerfully illustrates the Masonic god and religion of works. In the center of their Square and Compass is a human arm holding a hammer in its hand. The curvature of the arm and the position of the hammer shape the letter "G" to represent God. This emblem of English Freemasonry displays the Mason's god as "man at work" building his own temple in heaven.

French Freemasonry displays the same symbology as American and English Freemasonry. In 1877, declaring that "There is no god but humanity," French Masons incorporated the Hammer and Sickle as their symbol. However, the French Masons reversed their design so that it is shaped like the letter "G" backwards, which in Masonic symbology means the negation of God, or the declaration of atheism.

---

[16] "Christianization of Freemasonry," *Mackey's Encyclopedia of Freemasonry* (Chicago: The Masonic History Company, 1946) vol.1.

[17] Buck 216.

[18] Daniel Sickles, *General Ahiman Rezon* (N.p.: n.p., n.d.) 79.

[19] Mackey, Lexicon of Freemasonry 16.

What deity accepts the worship of "good works" from the Egyptian, Hindu, Buddhist, Zoroastrian, Confucian, Mohammedan, Mormon, Voodooist, Christian Scientist, Spiritist, or adherent to any other religion? Certainly not the God of the Holy Bible!

Obviously Freemasonry is a religion but not one compatible with Christianity. Christians are obliged to have no part in it.

Yet deceived Christians remain in the Lodge for two reasons. One, either they are not diligent students of God's Holy Word, which forbids fellowship in false religions; or two, they have not been exposed to the truth of Masonry as revealed in Masonic books.

FREEMASONRY AND MYSTERY BABYLON: A PAGAN RELIGION

The Tower of Babel and Solomon's Temple

The Masons trace their spiritual ancestry all the way back to Nimrod, whom Genesis identifies as the founder of the Kingdom of Babylon (Gen. 10:10). The Masons see in the destruction of the Tower of Babel the destruction of ancient Freemasonry. So too in their writings and rituals, they see Solomon's Temple as symbolic of their rebirth and progress. Likewise their rites and symbols contain many pagan elements reminiscent of Babylonian mystery religions.

Dr. Mackey, in the *Encyclopedia of Freemasonry* quotes the *York Manuscript, No.1*, which contains Old Charges of Freemasonry on parchment dated in the year 1560. Written in doggerel, the *York Manuscript* locates Masonry's origins at Babylon: "At ye makeing of ye Toure of Babell there was Masonrie first much esteemed of, and the King of Babilon yt was called Nimrod was A Mason himselfe and loved well Masons."[20]

Mackey also cites the *Cooke Manuscript*, which is sometimes called "The Legend of the Craft."[21] It is the second oldest Masonic manuscript, dated at the time of its discovery (1450), but is believed to have been penned in 1420."[22] Also written in doggerel, it repeats the claim of the *York Manuscript:* "And this same Nembroth began the towre of babilon and he taught to his werkemen the craft of Masonrie, and he had with him many Masons more than forty thousand. And he loved and cherished them well."[23]

Mackey explains the significance and use of these texts in Freemasonry:

[T]he old instructions speak of the lofty tower of Babel as the place where language was confounded and Freemasonry lost... So, when the neophyte, being asked "whence he comes and whither is he travelling," replies, "from the lofty tower of Babel, where language was confounded and Masonry lost, to the threshing-floor of Ornan the Jebusite

---

[20] "Nimrod," *Mackey's Encyclopedia*, vol.11.
[21] "Legend of the Craft," *Mackey's Encyclopedia*, vol.1.
[22] "Legend."
[23] "Nimrod."

[where Solomon's Temple was later built], where language was restored and Freemasonry found."[24]

That King Solomon's Temple is of extraordinary importance to Masons is confirmed by numerous Masonic texts. *The Masonic Library* asserts: "Solomon's Temple is one of the most sublime symbols in the order of Freemasonry."[25] And Mackey concurs: "Tradition informs us that Masonic Lodges were originally dedicated to King Solomon, because he was our first Most Excellent Grand Master."[26]

While Masons borrow the image of Solomon's Temple from the Jews (and put it to their own use as we shall shortly see), they also cite another source of Jewish inspiration, which actually derives from Babylon: The Jewish *Cabala*.

According to the *Encyclopedia of Free masonry,* the Masonic Lodge drew much of its initial inspiration from the *Cabala,* the rabbinical book of concealed mystery, which Mackey acknowledges is a development of Persian Zoroastrianism.[27] The *Cabala* is an apostate, occult form of Judaism, an ancient esoteric tradition which the Jewish rabbis acquired while in captivity at Babylon. Mackey remarks on its use: "Much use is made of it in the advanced degrees, and entire Rites have been constructed on its principles. Hence it demands a place in any general work on Freemasonry."[28]

In fact, the Scottish Rite of Freemasonry is called the Jewish Rite, not because it was founded by the Jews, but because the Masons derived its doctrine from the *Cabala.* Moreover, the ritual in the Blue Lodge (the first three degrees of Masonry) centers around the allegory of building Solomon's Temple.

Masonry imbibed dualistic, eastern mysticism through the *Cabala.* But while the Jews may have looked forward to the literal rebuilding of Solomon's Temple as a restoration of their religion, Freemasonry imported from Rosicrucianism and the Knights Templar allegorical speculations on Solomon's Temple. Solomon's Temple was used symbolically in Masonic initiation ritual to signify the spiritual rebuilding or restoration on high of the Tower of Babel. Again Mackey explains:

If the tower of Babel represents the profane world of ignorance and darkness, and the threshing- floor of Oman the Jebusite is the symbol of Freemasonry, because the Solomonic Temple, of which it was the site, is the prototype of the spiritual temple which Freemasons are erecting, then we can readily understand how Freemasonry and the true use of language is lost in one and recovered in the other, and how the progress of the candidate in his initiation may properly be compared to the progress of truth from the confusion and ignorance of the Babel builders to the perfection and illumination of the temple builders, which Temple builders all Freemasons are.[29]

Mackey further states that "Each Lodge is and must be a symbol of the Jewish Temple; each Master in the chair representing the Jewish King; and every Freemason a personation of the Jewish Workman."[30]

The Masons, however, are far from equating Solomon and his temple with historical, Biblical reality. In fact, that King Solomon signifies to Masons the sun god is proposed by Martin L. Wagner in *An Interpretation of Freemasonry,* where he explains how the Masonic meaning of the name, Solomon, differs from any Biblical understanding:

[T]his name Solomon is not the Israelitish king. It is the name in form, but different in its meaning. It is a substitute which is "externally" like the royal name. This name is a

---

[24] "Babel," Mackey's Encyclopedia, vol.1.
[25] C.F. McQuaig, *The Masonic Report* (Norcross, GA: Ahswer Books and Tapes, 1976) 13.
[26] "Dedication of a Lodge," *Mackey's Encyclopedia,* vol.1.
[27] "Cabala," *Mackey's Encyclopedia,* vol I. (See Appendix 5).
[28] "Cabala."
[29] "Babel."
[30] "Temple of Solomon," *Mackey's Encyclopedia,* vol.11.

composite, Sol-om-on, the names of the sun in Latin, Indian and Egyptian, and is designed to show the unity of several god-ideas in the ancient religions, as well as with those of Freemasonry. It is a glyph which indicates the unity of the god-ideas of these various cults, a coordination of their deities, and expresses the Masonic idea of the "unity of God" as it was conceived of in these religions.[31]

Wagner's analysis is supported by Masonic literature. Dr. Mackey in *Manual of the Lodge,* confirms the Masonic preoccupation with an orientation to the sun:

The orientation of the lodges or their position east and west is derived from the universal custom of antiquity...The primitive reason for this custom undoubtedly is to be found in the early prevalence of sun-worship... Freemasonry retaining in its symbolism the typical reference of the lodge to the world and constantly to the sun in his apparent diurnal revolution, imperatively requires when it can be done that the lodge should be situated due east and west, so that every ceremony shall remind the Mason of the progress of that luminary.[32]

As rites developed in the Masonic religion of "works," Masons were taught that as they advanced through the various degrees, they were symbolically climbing "Jacob's Ladder" to the Celestial Lodge on high. Again *Mackey's Encyclopedia of Freemasonry* explains the connection between the Masonic corruption of a Biblical image and the ancient mystery religions:

As to the modern Masonic symbolism of the ladder, it is a symbol of progress, such as it is in all the old initiations.[33] Its three principal rounds, representing Faith, Hope, and Charity, present us with the means of advancing from earth to heaven, from death to life - from the mortal to immortality. Hence its foot is placed on the ground floor of the Lodge, which is typical of the world, and its top rests on the covering of the Lodge, which is symbolic of heaven.

The similarities between Freemasonry and the ancient mystery religions are many. One example can be seen in the pattern of initiation in the Lodge, which retraces the pattern of initiation into a mystery religion. As Freemasons are well aware, Babylonian mystery religions conducted their initiations underground, at night, in the dark. Freemasons Pierson and Mackey in *Traditions of Freemasonry,* and *Symbolism of Freemasonry* respectively, reveal how Freemasonry draws upon and reenacts the ancient customs:

In every country under heaven, the initiations, i.e. into the mysteries, were performed in caverns, either natural, or artificial.[34]

Darkness like death, is the symbol of initiation. It was for this reason that all the ancient initiations were performed at night. The celebration of the mysteries was always nocturnal. The same custom prevails in Freemasonry and the explanation is the same.[35]

Likewise, the structure and customs of the Lodge imitate the ancient mystery religions. As Freemason Daniel Sickles in *General Ahiman Rezon* reports, "Lodge meetings at the present day are usually held in upper chambers...[because]...[b]efore the erection of temples the celestial bodies were worshipped on hills and the terrestrial ones in Valleys."[36]

It is an established fact of ancient pagan religions that where mountains were plentiful, pagans worshipped the sun on mountain peaks. Where there were not mountains, they built pyramids. In Mesopotamia these pyramids were called ziggurats.

---

[31] Martin L. Wagner, *Freemasonry: An Interpretation* (Dayton, OH: privately printed, 1912) 97.
[32] Mackey, Manual of the Lodge 55.
[33] "Jacob's Ladder," *Mackey's Encyclopedia,* vol.1.
[34] McQuaig 16; quoting Pierson in *Traditions of Freemasonry* 31.
[35] Albert G. Mackey, *Mackey's Symbolism of Freemasonry* (Chicago: Powner, 1975) 157.
[36] Sickles 75.

As archaeologists and Biblical scholars confirm, the ziggurat was called by the pagans, "mountain peak, hill of heaven, mountain of God, or high place."[37]

The differences between the God of the Israelites and the god of the Masons are obvious and instructive. First, although the Israelites some-times fell into idolatry, the God of the Israelites was never identified or confused with created nature, e.g., the sun. Second, Almighty God never spoke from secret. God, speaking through the prophet Isaiah (45:19) says, "I have not spoken in secret in a dark place of the earth: I said not unto the seed of Jacob, Seek ye me in vain: I the Lord speak righteousness, I declare things that are right."

Freemasonry and Anti-Semitism

Although Freemasons appropriate Biblical or Christian symbols or objects (such as Solomon's Temple, the Bible, and the Cross) and use them in their ceremonies, their doing so makes their brotherhood neither Jewish nor Christian, as we shall see time and again. So, too, the Masonic use of the term "Gentile" to refer to non-Masons far from proves that Masonry is a Jewish conspiracy. I would like to suggest the contrary: that Freemasonry is in fact deadly in its anti- Semitism.

The Masonic practice of referring to non-Masons as Gentiles has led many conspiracy researchers to the erroneous conclusion that Freemasonry is a Jewish conspiracy bent on the destruction of Christianity and all Gentile governments. Even a brief examination of Masonic rituals will reveal the profound anti-Semitism of Freemasonry. For, as Mackey says, from Masonic rituals "a modern Freemason can learn more than facts about the backgrounds of the Masonic Lodge.'"[38]

Stephen Knight in *The Brotherhood* (1984) recounts that when a meeting is called at the Masonic Temple, Masons converge on the Lodge from all directions. "Once inside the Hall, each turned his steps towards the Crypt, which was cordoned off so that no intruder could make his way down the stair and report the going-on to any 'Gentile'."[39] Knight further reveals that the Master Mason ceremony (the third degree of the Blue Lodge) "involves the mimed murder of Hiram [Abif] by three Apprentice Masons, and his subsequent resurrection. The three Apprentices are named Jubela, Jubelo and Jubelum - known collectively as the *Juwes* [Masonic spelling for Jews]. In masonic [sic] lore, the Juwes are hunted down and executed..."[40] The Master Mason ceremony then concludes with the mimed, ritual slaughter of the three Jewish ruffians.

To understand the horrifying significance of this ceremony, we must first discover who Hiram Abif is. We again turn to *Mackey's Encyclopedia of Free masonry* for an answer: "There is no character in the annals of Freemasonry whose life is so dependent on tradition as the celebrated architect of King Solomon's Temple."[41] Mackey reports that in Masonic lore, Hiram Abif is identified as the Syrian architect of Tyre who was hired by King Solomon to build his temple. In four pages of explanation, Mackey gradually moves beyond Solomonic tradition, revealing instead that Masonry's Hiram Abif is not, after all, the Tyrian builder. "Hiram," says Mackey, "represent[s] a popular Syrian god against whom the champions of Jehovah [the Jews] strove ceaselessly."[42]

---

[37] Merrill F. Unger, *Archaeology and the Old Testament* (Grand Rapids: Zondervan, 1954) 104.

[38] "Rituals used by ancient Greeks," *Mackey's Encyclopedia*, vol.111.

[39] Stephen Knight, *The Brotherhood: The Secret World of the Freemasons* (New York: Stein and Day, 1984) 216.

[40] Knight 54.

[41] "Hiram Abif," *Mackey's Encyclopedia*, vols. I & III.

[42] "Hiram Abif."

Freemason Daniel Sickles offers another explanation, identifying Hiram instead with an Egyptian god. In *General Ahiman Rezon*, Sickles states that the legend of Hiram Abif "is thoroughly Egyptian."[43] Pierson's *Traditions of Freemasonry* confirms without doubt that the Hiram Abif of the Master Mason ritual represents all pagan sun-gods:

The legend and Traditions of Hiram Abif form the consummation of the connecting link between Freemasonry and the ancient mysteries... We readily recognize in Hiram Abif the Osiris of the Egyptians, the Mythras of the Persians, the Bacchus of the Greeks, the Dionysius of the Fraternity of the artificers, the Atys of the Phrygians, whose passion, death and resurrection were celebrated by these people respectively.[44]

Mackey's *Lexicon of Freemasonry* agrees that the legend of Hiram Abif is purely astronomical and symbolic - that Masonry's Hiram is, in reality, equivalent to the pagan sun-gods.[45]

If the Masonic figure of Hiram Abif is an esoteric representation of the sun-god, then Freemasonry is ritually teaching its initiates that the sun-god is the true builder of Solomon's Temple. The Masonic Solomon's Temple thus cannot be equated in any way with the Jewish Temple at Jerusalem. (Recall what Wagner in *An Interpretation of Freemasonry* said: "This name is a composite, Sol-om-on, the names of the sun in Latin, Indian and Egyptian...")

Albert Pike confirms the hidden meaning of Solomon's Temple in *Morals and Dogma:* "The Temple of Solomon presented a symbolic image of the Universe; and resembled, in its arrangements and furniture, all the temples of the ancient nations that practiced the mysteries."[46]

Allen Douglas, in his article "Solomon's Temple: a pagan crusade against Israel" for the *Executive Intelligence Review*, confirms the buried anti-Semitism of the Hiram Abif ritual: "The Masons regard their spiritual forebears to be, not the Jews, but the Baal worshipping Phoenician masons, led by Hiram, who were builders of the first Solomon's Temple in the 10th century B.C."[47]

In summary, the Masonic Hiram Abif, who allegedly built Solomon's Temple, is equivalent to the pagan sun-god. Solomon's Temple is not representative of the Jewish Temple at all, but is according to Masonic authorities, an esoteric symbol of ancient pagan temples, with each local lodge an instance of Solomon's Temple, a pagan high place, dedicated to the sun-god.

Without doubt, Freemasonry in our day is a resurrection of the old pagan religion of sun-worship, and thus the meaning of the Master Mason ritual is clear. The initiate takes the place of the sun-god, Hiram Abif. Jubela, Jubelo and Jubelum, known collectively in Freemasonry as the Juwes, are those Israelites who killed the sun god Hiram Abif and his religion. In ritual retaliation Freemasonry acts out genocide of the Jews.

The reason for Freemasonry's theological animosity toward the Jews and Judaism should be clear. Historically, the Jews destroyed the religions of the sun-gods. The five books of Moses and the book of Joshua tell the story of that engagement. In the *Supplement to Mackey's Encyclopedia of Freemasonry*, under the heading "Anti-Semitism and Freemasonry," H.L. Haywood justifies Jewish genocide with these sarcastic words: "[T]he record of Jewish persecutions of Gentiles is a long one and they

---

[43] McQuaig 24.

[44] McQuaig 28, 29.

[45] McQuaig 29.

[46] Pike 208.

[47] Allen Douglas, "Solomon's Temple: a pagan crusade against Israel," *Executive Intelligence Review* 22 May 1984, 22.

have sometimes been carried out with unspeakable cruelty; the Old Testament itself is in some chapters obviously antiGentile."[48]

I will show throughout *Scarlet and the Beast* that Freemasonry is not a Jewish conspiracy bent on the destruction of Christianity and all Gentile governments. On the contrary, Freemasonry is a Gentile order, calling itself Jewish as a decoy. I will show how Jews have been used as fronts in this conspiracy toward the following end: in the case of exposure of the conspiracy, Jews will be the scapegoats. The frightening Jewish Holocaust of World War II is a horrifying example of what Freemasonry can inflict upon a people when it backs a demented individual such as Adolf Hitler. Freemasonry itself is anti-Semitic.

Modern Freemasonry: an historical overview

Freemasonry in its present form is only 300 years old. Prior to the organization of several loose-knit Masonic Lodges into a Grand Lodge at London in 1717, "masonry" did not exist in any form comparable to what we see today.

The original "masons" were stone masons, carpenters, draftsmen, workmen, and others who traveled throughout Europe and England building the massive cathedrals of the Roman Church, as well as various fortifications, abbeys, castles, etc. A conglomerate of workingman guilds, equivalent to unions today, these masons date their origin to the first millennium after the birth of Christ. Masonic workmen lodged together while building cathedrals, hence the term "masonic lodge."

Freemasonry adopted the trade names - such as Workmen, Craftsmen, Builders, Carpenters, and Masons - of the workingman guilds out of which it developed. In their rituals, the guilds used titles such as Travellers, Fellows, Brothers, Companions, and Comrades. Freemasonry today retains these various names: the Craft, the Lodge, the Order, the Fraternity, the Fellowship, and the Brotherhood.

Additionally, the names of the first three degrees - "Entered Apprentice," "Fellow Craft," and "Master Mason" - as recorded in the oldest rite of England, the York Rite[49], reflect the origins of Masonry in the guilds.

The Catholic Church required that those building the churches adhere to the Christian faith. Jews or pagans were thus excluded from the guilds. The masons further protected their jobs and the secrets of their trade by disallowing any man entry to their quarters who was unable to document membership in the guild. To expose imposters they devised an elaborate system of grips and passwords, which are still in use within the first three degrees of modern Masonry, known as "Blue Lodge Degrees."

With the rise of Protestantism beginning in the 1500s, and the decline of grand church building in Europe, the number of "operative" or working masons - brick layers, carpenters, etc., - began to decline. Meanwhile, Rosicrucians were infiltrating the operative guilds. The Rosicrucians were aristocrats or members of the new middle class. They called themselves "speculative" masons and eventually took over the guilds. By 1717 the "operative mason" was non-existent.

The Rosicrucians

A century before the Masonic Lodges united in London in 1717, the workingman guilds were infiltrated by a secret society called Rose Croix (Rose Cross), or the

---

[48] "Anti-Semitism and Freemasonry," *Mackey's Encyclopedia,* vol.111.

[49] Mackey, *Lexicon* 16.

Rosicrucians. Rosicrucians distinguished themselves from the "operative" or working masons, calling themselves "speculative" masons, because of their understanding of esoteric or speculative theory. Soon these speculative masons outnumbered the operative masons, taking control of hundreds of loose-knit masonic lodges throughout England.

The *Encyclopedia Americana* provides us with a conventional, if generally accurate, summary of Rosicrucian doctrine:

Rosicrucians generally believe that everything in the universe is permeated by the Divine. Once man is initiated into awareness of the divinity within himself, he as the microcosm of the universe can control its forces. So empowered, he can lessen the evils of suffering and ignorance. These lofty pantheistic and humanistic doctrines are often mixed with elements of alchemy, astrology, and the occult.[50]

The Rosicrucians emerged in Europe during the upheaval of the Reformation and Counter- Reformation. While actually a gnostic association ("gnostic" from the Greek, meaning "knowledge seekers"), Rosicrucianism was associated with Protestantism, and in fact helped fund the Protestant movement.

The Rosicrucians developed a deceptive blend of Christianity with their paganism to attract Protestant Reformers to their Order. Weak in Scriptural doctrine, the newly emerging Protestants had no conviction against affiliation with the Rosicrucians. Some of these Reformers joined in alliance with the Rosicrucians to fight what they saw as a common enemy - the Catholic Church. Theological differences were overlooked and gradually syncretized.

The Rosicrucians, however, were less interested in religion than they were in politics.[51] For example, in England they attracted to their ranks members of the gentry, the newly rich of the middle and upper classes in British society. The new class wanted a political voice, without which they would lose through greedy taxation what they had gained.

Their ultimate goal was "to reform the human race by the extermination of kings and all regal powers."[52] What they settled for was a constitutional monarchy and an elected parliament, through which they would have a political voice and by which they could protect their worldly goods from excessive taxation. "Absolute Monarchy must be changed to a Constitutional Monarchy for our protection," they demanded.[53]

In England they achieved their goal with the "Glorious Revolution" of 1688, which will be examined at length in Chapter 2. In this revolution, the Stuart dynasty, which succeeded the unmarried and childless Elizabeth I, was overthrown.

The Rosicrucians are important for being the first to plant the seeds of revolutionary thought in Masonic Lodges. The Rosicrucian order in Great Britain saw the chance for rapid expansion of their secret society through the operative masonic guilds of Protestant England. Nesta Webster, in *Secret Societies and Subversive Movements*, quotes a lecture given in 1883 by 33rd degree Mason, John Yarker, who in turn quotes from a Masonic book, *History of Freemasonry*, by Robert F.Gould:

"It is evident therefore that the Rosicrucians... found the operative Guild conveniently ready to their hand, and grafted upon it their own mysteries... also, from this time Rosicrucianism disappears and Freemasonry springs into life with all the possessions of the former."[54]

---

[50] "Rosicrucians," *The Encyclopedia Americana*, 1991 ed.

[51] Nesta H. Webster, *Secret Societies and Subversive Movements* (1924; Hawthorne, CA: Christian Book Club of America, 1979) 92.

[52] "Cromwell," Mackey's Encyclopedia, vol.1.

[53] See Chapter 2.

[54] Webster 122.

After the Glorious Revolution, Englishmen became free, that is, they were entrusted with certain rights. Masons took the name Freemasons, which means "Free and accepted Masons."[55] Mackey elaborates in the *Encyclopedia of Freemasonry:*

In reference to the other sense of free as meaning not bound, not in captivity, it is a rule of Freemasonry that no one can be initiated who is at the time restrained of his liberty. The Grand Lodge of England extends this doctrine, that Freemasons should be free in all their thoughts and actions...

As noted above, Rosicrucianism is an hermetic religion. "Hermetic," a word derived from the Greek god Hermes, messenger of the gods and god of many trades, is a term that indicates the mystical, magical or occult sciences. The Rosicrucians were heavily involved in occult sciences, and in alchemy they were noted leaders.[56]

Nesta Webster, again in *Secret Societies and Subversive Movements,* when discussing three centuries of occultism in Europe and England leading up to the formation of Masonic Lodges as we know them today, remarks on the Rosicrucians' reputation of hiring poisoners and assassins:

[T]he intellectual chiefs [Rosicrucians] from whom the poisoners derived their inspiration were men versed in chemistry, in science, in physics, and the treatment of diseases... [T]hey included alchemists and people professing to be in possession of the Philosopher's stone...[57]

Like Masonry, Rosicrucianism reveals its occult character by its use of occult, pagan symbolism. For example, the god of the Rosicrucians is symbolized by the "zero": a circle created by the serpent swallowing its own tail. This symbol was superimposed on the Christian cross with a sunburst surrounding the circle. The circle also represented the sun, as well as the "eye" of Osiris, the Egyptian sun-god.

The most prominent emblem of Rosicrucian belief is a red rose twined around the base of the standing cross. The rose is the phallic occult symbol of the serpent. Together, the rose and the cross became known as the "Rosy Cross," or "Rose-Croix," hence the name Rosicrucian.

The Rosicrucian cross will of course be unsettling to any Christian who is aware of its true significance.

Rosicrucian and Freemason Carl Gustav Jung (1875-1961), founder of analytic psychology, reveals the meaning of this symbol in an analogy he drew between the Rosicrucian symbol and his family's coat-of-arms. (Jung's grandfather, by the way, was an ardent Freemason and Grand Master of the Swiss lodge Alpina, the supreme Masonic Lodge of Switzerland.)[58] "The symbolism of these arms is Masonic, or Rosicrucian," said Jung. "Just as cross and rose represent the Rosicrucian problem of opposites, that is, the Christian and Dionysian elements, so cross and grapes are symbols of the heavenly and chthonic [infernal] spirit."[59]

The Templars

The second great stream of Freemasonry finds its origins in the Templars, or Knights Templar as they were officially known. A military priesthood in the Catholic Church, the Templars were formally organized in 1118 by Hugh de Payens, their first Grand Master, who, following the Crusades, derived the name from the Temple of Jerusalem.

---

[55] "Free," Mackey's Encyclopedia, vol.1.
[56] J.R. Church, *Guardians of the Grail* (Oklahoma City, OK: Prophecy Publications, 1989) 87.
[57] Webster 95.
[58] C.G. Jung, *Memories, Dreams, Reflections* (New York: Vintage Books, 1965) 232.
[59] Jung.

The Templars were the first religious community to yoke the cross to the sword. The Templars' initial stated purpose was to guard and guide pilgrims to the Holy City of Jerusalem. Gradually, the Templars' duties expanded to defend the Holy Land against all infidels and "any force menacing Jerusalem of their religion."[60]

The nucleus of the Templars consisted of nine men. As the order grew, de Payens created 13 degrees within it.[61] Why he chose to stop at "thirteen" is not known. Perhaps it represented the tribes of Israel (eleven full tribes and the two half tribes of Joseph - Ephraim and Manasseh). Maybe it stood for the twelve disciples and Jesus Christ.

What is significant about the number "13" is that it identifies the Templar headquarters of our day.

Another symbol that identifies the Templars is the emblem of their order. They adopted the famous splayed red cross of the Merovingian kings of France, placing it on their mandes, swords, buildings, and gravestones. This symbol is also important in tracing their movements to their present-day headquarters, which will be discussed in detail in the final chapter of this book.

After founding their order in Jerusalem in 1118, the Templars headquartered themselves in a fortified abbey above the ruins of Solomon's Temple on the Temple Mount in Jerusalem, hence the name Templars. Their domicile is of great significance, for somewhere beneath it was allegedly buried the unfathomable wealth of Solomon. As the Templars' fame increased, so did their wealth. According to standard histories, one source of their wealth was gifts from kings and princes grateful for their services. Although it is said that many of the nobility joined their ranks[62], we shall later learn why so few did at the beginning.

As their wealth and influence grew, the Templars "developed into an efficient military organization that adopted absolute secrecy to cover all internal activities."[63]

The Templars also made powerful enemies, among them King Philip IV (the Fair), who ascended the throne of France in 1268, his country near bankruptcy. The Templars possessed both money and land in abundance.

The failure of the Templars to defend Jerusalem against the Moslems in 1187, their extensive banking and financial interests in both London and Paris, their rich establishments, and the rumors of heretical practices within the order gave Philip the ammunition he needed to launch a successful campaign to destroy the order throughout Europe. The association of the Templars with the heretical sect of the Cathars (or Albigensians as they are also known) is of especial interest, as this association helped fuel the charge of heresy against them. For the Cathars were gnostics, replacing faith with knowledge. Knowledge to them was firsthand religious or mystical experience.

The Knights Templar imbibed the doctrines of gnosticism from the Cathars, but also further elaborated Cathar heresies. From their long tenure in the Holy Land, they had also been exposed to eastern mysticism. Like the Cathars, they practiced meditation - in their case Hindu Yoga - to reach an altered state of consciousness to open the "third eye." This was known as white magic.

There is also evidence, which shall be discussed in chapter 1 which fully addresses the convoluted history of the Templars and their involvement with drugs.

Suffice it to say that eventually the Templars took on the Satanic symbol of the skull and crossbones, the symbol of death. In Free-masonry, the skull and crossbones became

---

[60] G. Grosschmid, "Templars," *New Catholic Encyclopedia* (1967) XIII, 992.

[61] Edith Starr Miller, *Occult Theocrasy* (1933; Hawthorne, CA: Christian Book Club of America, 1980) 143.

[62] Grosschmid 992.

[63] Grosschmid 993.

the symbol of the Master Mason, but was dropped after World War II because Hitler had used it for his 55.[64]

But to return to Philip IV's campaign against the Templars: On Friday, October 13, 1307, Philip ordered the arrest of all Templars in France. Following the French Inquisition of the Templars, in 1314 on Philip's order, then Grand Master Jacques de Molay and other dignitaries of the Templars were burned at the stake. During these years a remnant of the order fled to Scotland, allying themselves with Scotland against England.

Michael Baigent, co-author of *Holy Blood, Holy Grail,* confirms this history: "Many English, and it would appear, French Templars," he states, "found a Scottish refuge, and a sizable contingent is said to have fought at [King] Robert Bruce's side at the Battle of Bannockburn in 1314. According to the legend - and there is evidence to support it - the order maintained itself as a coherent body in Scotland for another four centuries."[65]

In Scotland the Knights Templar left their mark - an octagonal pattern with the splayed cross in the middle (see Appendix 2, Fig. 6). Sometimes the mark was only the octagon. This symbol, along with the skull and crossbones, and the number 13, imprinted on dated gravestones, has assisted researchers in tracing the migration of the Templars.

A descendant of Robert Bruce, the Catholic James Stuart *VI,* reigned in Scotland from 1567 until he ascended the British throne as James I in 1603. He succeeded the unmarried Elizabeth I (r. 1558-1603), who enforced Protestantism by law, but who, because of her lack of an heir, designated James her successor on her deathbed. During James I's reign (1603-1625) we received the King James Version of the Bible, the first official English translation of the Bible.

Like their ancestors, the Stuarts had been initiated into the Order of the Knights Templar, and James was more Templar than Catholic. James arrived in England with a contingent of Scottish Templars, and their first lodge opened at York in northern England at the turn of the 17th century.

During James Stuart's reign the embryos of both the Scottish and York Rites of Freemasonry developed in England. At that time it was called Jacobite Freemasonry, in memory of the martyred Templar Grand Master Jacques de Molay. James and his descendants were members of the Royalist Jacobite Lodges, which practiced Templar rituals. Later these rituals became known to Masons in England and America as the York Rite, and in France and America as the Scottish Rite.

French and English Freemasonry

London, England, can rightly be called the birthplace of both branches of Masonry, since both Rosicrucian and Templar Masonry developed there. After the Glorious Revolution of 1688, which had the backing and support of the emergent gentry of English or Rosicrucian Freemasonry, English Freemasons remained divided in loyalty between the new Hanoverian monarchy (established in 1714) and the deposed Stuart pretenders. On January 4, 1717, the Scottish Stuarts were sent to France in permanent exile. With them went Jacobite (Templar) Freemasonry. On June 24, 1717, six months after the exile of the Stuarts, four lodges in London (names not given) met at Apple-Tree Tavern and united English Freemasonry under the name "United Grand Lodge," which has been nicknamed the Mother Grand Lodge, or Grand Mother Lodge.

The first French Templar Lodge was founded in 1725 by a contingent of exiled Stuart sympathizers. In 1745 Prince Charles Edward Stuart, the Young Pretender, attempted to

---

[64] Intercessors for America (Oct.1988) 4.
[65] Michael Baigent, Richard Leigh, and Henry Lincoln, *Holy Blood, Holy Grail* (New York: Dell Books, 1982) 77.

regain his Scottish throne and was soundly defeated in less than a year. Upon returning to France, the Scottish Templars founded the Ancient and Accepted Scottish Rite of Freemasonry, quickly developing it to 32 degrees by 1755. In 1801 all French lodges accepted the Templar Scottish Rite degrees. That same year the Scottish Rite of Charleston, S.C., created the 33rd and final degree in Templar Freemasonry.

On the continent of Europe, French Freemasonry is known as Scottish Rite, Grand Orient, French Grand Lodge, Continental, or Latin Freemasonry. The Templar York Rite in England was transported to America, where it remains to this day. English Freemasonry continued with the three Craft Degrees until 1860, when it adopted the thirty additional degrees of the Scottish Rite, but for competitive reasons refused to call it "Scottish."

After the expulsion of the Stuarts to France, the Church of England and the British monarchy became subservient to Rosicrucian Freemasonry. Since 1737, every male monarch in Great Britain has been a Mason, while the head of the Anglican Church (Church of England) is a member of the Masonic hierarchy. Masonry in England since has controlled both Church and Crown. Even today we see this alliance in effect. For example, Geoffrey Fisher, the past Archbishop of Canterbury, was a Mason. Likewise, Queen Elizabeth II, the reigning monarch, is the Patroness of English Freemasonry, while her consort, Prince Philip, is a Freemason.[66]

THE SPREAD OF FREEMASONRY FROM THE MOTHER LODGE

The York and Scottish Rites in America

English Freemasonry was first known as York Masonry after the oldest known Lodge, founded by the Templars, in the city of York.[67] Mackey, in the *Encyclopedia of Freemasonry,* confirms that the York Rite "is the oldest of all the Rites, and consisted originally of three Degrees: (1) Entered Apprentice; (2) Fellow Craft; and (3) Master Mason." After the Stuart Templars were deposed and exiled to France, the York Rite was practiced in the Constitutional Grand Lodge of England for fifty years before spreading to America.[68]

Sometime before our Revolutionary War (possibly in 1767), the York Rite was established in Virginia, where it retained the original three degrees. As it spread to other colonies, Americans added 10 additional degrees, the 13th being called the Knights Templar degree. Today, York Rite Masonry is practiced only in North America, and because of its Templar degrees, is known as the Christian Rite.

Scottish Rite Freemasonry had already been developed to 32 degrees by the time it arrived in America. Its degrees were derived from the Jewish *Cabala,* and hence is sometimes called the Jewish Rite.[69] The Scottish Rite in America "derived its authority and its information from what are called the French Constitutions" of 1786.[70] The Scottish Rite established headquarters in Charleston, South Carolina, because of that city's

---

[66] William R. Denslow, *10,000 Famous Freemasons,* vol.11 (Trenton, MO: Missouri Lodge of Research, 1958) 51; Knight 211-215; and Martin Short, *Inside The Brotherhood: Further Secrets of the Freemasons* (New York: Dorset Press, 1989) 55. On p.55 of Short's book, he quotes Marius Lepage, a French Mason, as saying, "It is absolutely useless for a Frenchman to try to understand English Masonry unless he realizes that the Crown, the Anglican Church, and the United Grand Lodge of England are one God in three persons."

[67] "American System, The," *Mackey's Encyclopedia,* vol.111.

[68] "York Rite," *Mackey's Encyclopedia,* vol.11.

[69] "Cabala."

[70] "Supreme Council," *Mackey's Encyclopedia,* vol.11.

geographic location on the 33rd degree parallel. By 1801, Americans had added the 33rd and final degree, and the Ancient and Accepted Scottish Rite of Freemasonry at Charleston became known as the Mother Supreme Council of the World.[71]

English Masonry remained with only the three Craft Degrees until 1860. Then it added the other degrees developed by French and American Masonry, to bring its total to 33 degrees. The British, for competitive reasons, refused the word "Scottish" and called its 33 degrees the "Ancient and Accepted Rite of Freemasonry."

The 33rd degree is the "controlling" degree of Freemasonry. Masons of this rank, approximately 5,000 in all worldwide, are known as "Sovereign Grand Inspectors General," and are authorized to sit at any Masonic Lodge meeting in the world. Thirty-third degree Masons are also members of the "Supreme Council," the ruling body of Masonry. According to Ronayne's *Handbook of Freemasonry*, Supreme Councils originally met once a year. Current practice is to hold meetings once every other year.

Just before the War of 1812, the British clandestinely organized several Scottish Rite Lodges in the northeast with headquarters at Boston. After the War they were discovered by Charleston, and following some negotiations, were permitted to operate under the English Masonic obedience (obedience meaning "constitution"). The Boston headquarters became known as the Northern Jurisdiction of Scottish Rite Freemasonry and has since been nicknamed the "Eastern Establishment." The Charleston headquarters became known as the Southern Jurisdiction of Scottish Rite Freemasonry. As stated earlier, the Southern Jurisdiction followed the French Masonic obedience.

The Southern Jurisdiction Supreme Council operates its "Grand East" or spiritual headquarters from Charleston. In 1870 it moved its "Secretariat" (political office) to Washington, D.C.[72] An indication of Masonry's influence is the fact that of the two parades permitted to march down Pennsylvania Avenue in Washington D.C., one is the Inaugural Parade and the other the Shriner's Parade.

Shriners are sometimes referred to as thirty-second and a half degree Masons. The Shriners operate children's hospitals. (See Appendix 7 for their history).

All Masons in America must travel through the first three "Blue Lodge" degrees before choosing York or Scottish Rites, both of which are Templar Rites. The 13th degree York Mason and 32 degree Scottish Mason unite in the Shrine. (See Appendix 2, Fig. 3.)

We can make some general observations regarding the Northern and Southern Jurisdictions of American Freemasonry. The Northern Jurisdiction, which we can identify in American politics with the Eastern Establishment, is right-wing or moderate. It is the headquarters of America's aristocracy and is primarily Republican. The Southern Jurisdiction is left-wing or liberal, more or less comprised of the working middle class and common laborer, and usually Democrat. There are crossovers in both Jurisdictions, and when voters in America take sides on issues, we are caught up in this Masonic struggle of conservative versus liberal, right-wing versus left-wing, big business versus labor, free enterprise versus socialism, etc.

A BITTER CONFLICT

English Freemasonry Versus French Freemasonry

---

[71] "Supreme Council."

[72] "Sovereign Grand Inspector-General," and "United States of America," *Mackey's Encyclopedia*, vol.11.

After the union of lodges in England under the Grand Mother Lodge in 1717, the formation of other lodges were then "warranted," or certified by the Grand Mother Lodge. English Masonry spread rapidly throughout the world during the colonial expansion of the British Empire. It is believed that English Freemasonry exerted covert influence on and even control of her colonies largely through these lodges.

Today there are over 9,000 Masonic Lodges warranted by the Grand Mother Lodge at London. Three thousand are in the British Isles alone. Great Britain and the United States have more registered Masons than the entire world combined!

English Freemasonry made its first attempt to control French Freemasonry in 1743 by certifying or "warranting" as the French Grand Lodge the existing Jacobite lodge founded in 1725 by the Stuart sympathizers. Remember that the Stuarts had been exiled to France from England and had already reestablished Templar Masonry with this Lodge at Paris.

There were those, however, who opposed British domination of Continental lodges, and in 1772 they founded the Grand Orient Lodge in Paris. This was the first "irregular" or "clandestine" lodge - meaning a lodge unwarranted by the English Grand Lodge, and considered to be operating illegally. Soon the Grand Orient infiltrated the French Grand Lodge, and took control of the impending French Revolution. The French Grand Lodge, however, remained a separate entity, still "warranted" by the Grand Mother Lodge at London.

The French Grand Orient Lodge became the most powerful of the clandestine or irregular Masonic lodges. In 1801 it adopted the 33 degrees of Scottish Rite Freemasonry. The French Grand Lodge also contains the Scottish Rite degrees.

It is clear that rites and degrees are universal to and overlap in the various lodges and sub lodges, warranted and unwarranted. What is significant is that the powers behind the lodges - French and English Masonry - are in bitter and sustained conflict.

The Grand Orient Lodge of Paris is English Freemasonry's primary rival and most bitter enemy. Although English Freemasonry maintained fellowship with the Grand Orient until 1877, 1801 marks the year that English and French Freemasonry began the rivalry that was to develop into a war with each other for world dominion. The bitterness of the rivalry can be surmised from the writing of French and English Freemasons.

Freemason George H. Steinmetz states the claims of English Free-masonry in *Freemasonry, Its Hidden Meaning:* "A Lodge can be formed without a charter from a Grand Lodge [meaning from English Freemasonry], but it would be clandestine and not 'recognized' by 'regular Masons,' [those with English charters], and it will not prosper because it operates 'illegally.'"[73]

English Freemasonry would have the Masonic world believe that it is in total control of all Masonry. The contrary however is true. "Clan-destine" Lodges have been formed and have prospered for two centuries. It is important for the reader to understand at the outset that these two distinct Masonic institutions - the French and English - are in full operation today. They are at odds. And their refusal to recognize each other, does not cancel either's power or longevity.

In 1963 Grand Orient Freemason, J.C. Corneloup, Grand Commander of Honor of the Grand College of Rites at Paris, chronicled the persistent claims and ambition of English Freemasonry to control all Freemasonry, especially the French. In his *Universalisme et Franc-Maconnerie,* he documents the division between English and French Freemasonry that still exists today:

London [English Freemasonry] claims the right to lay down Masonic law; the United Grand Lodge of England claims to dominate the Masonic world, to be the sovereign judge

---

[73] George H. Steinmetz, *Freemasonry, Its Hidden Meaning* (Richmond: Macoy Publishing and Masonic Supply, 1976) 82.

of the authenticity of the different Masonic powers, and to impose its law upon them. Confident in its powers of intimidation, which it has skillfully cultivated, and owing to the pusillanimous ignorance of the leaders of the different obediences, who are afraid of the least suggestion of a rupture, it arbitrarily fixes the criterion for regularity in such a way that it can always, in the last resort, make a decision according to its sole good pleasure.

But what is their aim, or rather, their dream?

They want to make the Mother Grand Lodge the unique sovereign authority over the whole of Masonry throughout the world, in order to condemn every group suspected of being able to overshadow it, to qualify every independent obedience as irregular and schismatic, and above all, to destroy, or at the very least to isolate enemy number one: the Grand Orient of France, which for 190 years has been regarded as a dangerous rival.

The bitterness [between the two Freemasonries] clearly reveals that London considered that it was the Mother Grand Lodge, and that all the others were subsidiaries whom it wanted to keep in its dependence, the sign of a strong desire to set up universality to its exclusive profit.

Two hundred years after this struggle broke out, we still find as lively a spirit of hostility, though couched in less truculent terms, on the part of the Grand Lodge of England with regard to French Masonry, apparently concentrated against the Grand Orient of France, but equally apparent against the Grand Lodge of France.

The fact is that we are confronted with two organizations, sprung from the same stock [operative Masonry], and palpably born at the same time and in the same country, but which have evolved differently because one developed in powerful middle-class, intellectual and aristocratic surroundings, and the other in a much more democratic climate.[74]

As Corneloup remarks and as we have observed, English Freemasonry's membership consists primarily of the middle and upper classes - aristocrats, professionals and business owners. French Freemasonry, on the other hand, is primarily made up of the working class. As in American Freemasonry, crossovers occur. However, the middle class suffers most in the battle between the French and English Lodges. The French system wants the middle and upper class destroyed, while the English system wants the middle and lower classes subdued.

Throughout the rest of this Introduction, I will use the word "clandestine" when referring to Lodges not warranted by the English Grand Lodge. These clandestine Lodges oppose constitutional monarchical English Freemasonry. On the continent of Europe, they are generally known as Continental Lodges, and specifically as Grand Orient Lodges. Also throughout the book, you will find the usage of "London," referring to English Freemasonry, and "Paris," referring to French Freemasonry.

The Spread of French Freemasonry

During the final quarter of the 18th century, French Freemasonry developed the idea or theory of our modern democracy or republic. The results were the American Revolution of 1776 and the French Revolution of 1789. In 1794, following the Reign of Terror in France, the Revolution was floundering and needed a strong leader. The Grand Orient backed one of its own, Napoleon Bonaparte, to solidify what it had earlier gained, but was now in danger of losing. In 1799 Napoleon came to power.

---

[74] Vicomte Leon de Poncins, *Freemasonry and the Vatican*, trans. Timothy Tindal-Robertson (N.p.: n.p., 1968) 106-109.

The subsequent Napoleonic Wars exported Grand Orient lodges throughout continental Europe and Russia. Later they spread to Africa by way of Italy, and to Latin and South America via Spain, although English Lodges were scattered in these territories as well. English Freemasonry was dominant in England, the Arab countries and Oriental nations. When contemplating the geography of Freemasonry, we can understand how the world has divided into two warring Masonic factions that vie for political and economic dominance.

In 1840, the clandestine or Continental lodges went atheistic, spawning socialism and communism. Thirty-second degree Grand Orient Freemason Karl Marx became their spokesman, planning under Masonic guidance the replacement of all monarchies with socialistic republics, with the next step conversion to communistic republics.

In order to survive, English Freemasonry, which supports constitutional monarchy, once again found herself in an unwanted, secret political war. Finally in 1877, French Freemasonry declared what it had held for some time - that there is no god but humanity. English Freemasonry, which demands at least an ostensible belief in deity, broke fellowship completely with the French.

Although these two fraternities continue to war with each other, they are still brothers - and brothers stand together when fighting a common enemy. Freemasonry's common enemy was initially the Catholic Church. Today it is all Christendom. As each Masonic order tries to dominate the other, Scarlet and the Beast will always unite against the Church.

Sub-Masonic Lodges

Both Masonic powers have established lodges whose names are designed to disguise Masonic affiliation. Such lodges are either directly or indirectly controlled by one of the two Masonic powers.

In the mid-1960s, Italian Grand Orient Freemasonry organized the clandestine and infamous Propaganda Two (P-2) Masonic Lodge. The Italian Grand Orient also founded the Mafia in 1860. Trafficking heroin is the Mafia's job, strangely enough, for the hierarchy of English Freemasonry. P-2's job is to launder the Mafia's drug money. David Yallop's book *In God's Name*, as well as other publications, document these facts, which I will discuss in Volume III of this three book series.

In the Far East we find clandestine oriental drug-dealing lodges called Triads, which furnish heroin to the Mafia. The rituals of the Triads, according to Fenton Bresler's *The Chinese Mafia*, are identical to those of Freemasonry. The Triads, much older than Western Freemasonry, were obviously not founded by the British. But they were used by English Masonry during the British Opium Wars against China in 1840 and 1860. The vicious Triads continue their illegal drug activity to the present day.

Like the Triads in the Orient, which protect British Masonic drug running from the East, the clandestine Shining Path terrorist Masonic Lodges protect the Grand Orient drug cartel in South America.[75]

Quatuor Coronati, the most secret of Masonic Lodges, was founded in London on January 12, 1886. Its function was and is to research the roots of Freemasonry. Today every Grand Lodge jurisdiction in the world has its own research lodge, which funnels data on archaeology, history, and ancient religion to the Quatuor Coronati Mother Lodge of Research.

---

[75] Konstandinos Kalimtgis, David Goldman and Jeffrey Steinberg, *Dope, Inc.* (New York: The New Benjamin Franklin House, 1978) entire.

When English Freemasonry severed fellowship with the Grand Orient in 1877, it was the Quatuor Coronati Lodge that linked their activities at the turn of the 20th century through various licentious and homicidal sub-societies.

The Quatuor Coronati founded several sub-lodges, including the drug and sex Order of the Golden Dawn. In 1888, the Quatuor Coronati Lodge backed 33rd degree English Freemason William Wynn Westcott and 32nd degree English Freemason and Cabalist MacGregor Mathers in organizing the Golden Dawn. At the beginning of the 20th century, 33rd degree Freemason Aleister Crowley (1875-1947) became a member of the Golden Dawn, and ultimately its leader. Crowley, a drug addict and avowed Satanist, is the idol of many rock and roll artists today, some of whom are members of his Golden Dawn.

A cousin of the Golden Dawn is the drug-dealing Ordo Temple Orientis (O.T.O.). While the Golden Dawn is licentious, the O.T.O. is homicidal. Originally, the O.T.O. was housed within the 33rd degree Grand Orient. The O.T.O. was infiltrated by the Golden Dawn in Germany, and organized on its own in 1902. An early member of the O.T.O. was Freemason Louis Constant (alias Eliphas Levi). He was a major influence on Aleister Crowley, who also headed the English chapter of the O.T.O. Crowley himself allegedly performed at least 150 human sacrifices on the unholy altars of the O.T.O. (Read Crowley's instructions for human sacrifice in the O.T.O. Masonic lodges in Appendix 6).

According to investigative journalist Maury Terry, who published *The Ultimate Euil* in 1987, Aleister Crowley's organization became the most powerful and lasting chapter of the O.T.O., which chapter extends to the United States. Today, says Terry, it operates a network of assassins in this country, two of whom were Charles Manson and "The Son of Sam," David Berkowitz. Terry also claims that the O.T.O. is responsible for many of the child kidnappings and ritualistic Satanic murders in North America. The O.T.O. has centers in North Dakota and Texas, and California and New York. When lines are drawn on a map from their geographic centers north to south, and east to west, they blasphemously form a cross.

Another spin-off of the Golden Dawn was the Thule Society. It too was homicidal. Both the O.T.O. and the Thule Society were used as breeding grounds for the inner core of the Hitler movement. This will be fully documented in Chapter 22.

Further spin-offs of Masonry include the Theosophical Society, or Co-Masonry, founded and headquartered in New York City in 1875 by Helena Petrovna Blavatsky, a Russian who joined both French and English Freemasonry. Her society is the mother of the New Age Movement. In 1887 Blavatsky moved to London. After Blavatsky's death in 1891, the Theosophical Society operated as the recruiting agent for the O.T.O. According to Maury Terry, the present-day recruiting agent for the O.T.O. is Freemason L. Ron Hubbard's Church of Scientology. Crowley initiated Hubbard into the O.T.O. in 1944. Twenty years later, says Terry, Charlie Manson was recruited by Scientology before he was initiated into the O.T.O.[76]

At the turn of the century, in a schism with the Theosophical Society, 33rd degree Grand Orient Freemason Rudolph Steiner founded the Anthroposophical Society. Conspiracy researchers have linked the Anthroposophical Society with the Masons and with the Bolshevik Revolution.

For the black race, a negro lodge called Prince Hall (named after a black man by that name) Freemasonry was founded at Boston, Massachusetts, in 1775. Prince Hall is considered clandestine by the Southern Jurisdiction of Freemasonry. Never has a black man been allowed to join Southern Jurisdiction Lodges. However, blacks are welcome in the Northern Jurisdiction, and in other lodges throughout the world.

---

[76] Maury Terry, The Ultimate Evil: An Investigation into America's Most Dangerous Satanic Cult (New York: Dolphin Books, 1987) 181, 245.

Other descendants of Freemasonry today wield political and spiritual power on their own. In 1830, a Master Mason named Joseph Smith founded a new rite at the Masonic Lodge in Nauvoo, Illinois, and named it the Mormon Rite. Smith planned to make Mormonism a superior rite in Freemasonry. Mormonism began to take over the Masonic Lodges in Illinois, and many researchers believe that Joseph Smith was killed to stop his movement. Whether or not this speculation is true, the Illinois Grand Lodge did revoke the charter of the Mormon Masonic Lodge.

After Smith's murder, Freemason Brigham Young took the Mormons to Salt Lake City and established The Church of Jesus Christ of Latter Day Saints, now known as the Mormon Church. Young was succeeded by Freemason John Taylor. All "apostolic" successors since have been Freemasons: Wilford Woodruff, Lorenzo Snow, Joseph Fielding Smith, and Herbert J. Grant.[77]

Masonic membership is still a requirement for members of the Mormon Church's "apostolic" hierarchy. According to Tom McKenney, co-author of *The Deadly Deception*, the Mormon hierarchy must be members of the Masonic Blue Lodge.[78] In *Scottish Rite Masonry illustrated*, Dr. J. Blanchard states of Mormonism and Masonry: "The two institutions are morally and legally the same."[79]

Not only is the Mormon hierarchy required to join the Masonic Lodge, other institutions in America have the same requirement. In the May 1972 issue of the Scottish Rite monthly magazine *New Age*, Freemason Stuart Parker pointed out that "there are at least 160 organizations that require their members to also be initiates into the Masonic Fraternity."[80] As a result, *according* to the *New Age*, *it* is estimated that "between one in five and one in 10 of the adult thinking population [in America] come directly within the circle of Masonic influence..."[81]

One example of this "Masonic influence" is seen in yet another religion founded in America. During the latter half of the 19th century, Freemason Charles Taze Russell became disillusioned with the Lodge and began studying the Bible. His Bible study was somewhat biased by his Masonic background, and he found no religion to his liking. He became "Pastor" to his own International Bible Student Movement, which he began with his own peculiar Bible study teachings. This movement became known as the Russellites. In 1879 he started *The Watch Tower* magazine, of which he was sole editor. Today the Russellites are known as Jehovah's Witnesses.[82]

In a later chapter, J will discuss in more detail two other sects that developed out of Freemasonry: the Christian Scientists and the present day anti-Semitic, anti-Black Ku Klux Klan (not to be confused with the Klan of Civil War days, which was also Masonic. See Vol.111.).

Space does not permit naming all the arms of the Masonic conspiracy. In the United States alone there are hundreds, if not thousands of secret and semi-secret organizations which either derive from or are controlled directly or indirectly by the Lodge. Each has its function in the conspiracy toward one-world government. This network is commonly known today as the *New Age Movement.*

---

[77] Miller 464.
[78] Tom McKenney spoke at a church in Texas in July, 1989, where he said that the hierarchy in the Mormon Church must be Blue Lodge Masons. He offered no documentation.
[79] J. Blanchard, *Scottish Rite Masonry illustrated,* vol.11 (1944; Chicago: Charles T. Powner Co., 1979) 373.
[80] Paul Fisher, *Behind The Lodge Door* (Washington, DC: Shield Publishing, 1988) 248, 339.
[81] Fisher 248.
[82] Miller 539.

The Benevolent Deception of Freemasonry

In the July 1950 issue of the *New Age* magazine, 33rd degree Freemason Harry L. Baum wrote:

> *"This nation [United States] was nurtured on the ideals of Freemasonry... [M]ost of those who are today its leaders are also members and leaders of the Craft. They know that our American Democracy, with its emphasis on the inalienable rights and liberties of the individual, is Freemasonry in government..."*[83]

Members of the Masonic Lodge are some of the most prominent people in the United States of America. Most of our founding fathers, almost half our presidents, many federal judges, the majority of Supreme Court justices of the last fifty years, one fourth of our politicians, key people in the United Nations, and over fifty percent of pastors of the largest mainline churches in America are Masons.

Most are good men, unaware that their particular assignment is one small part of a "Great Plan" to re-establish a one-world government - a government that Masons claim was destroyed by God at Babylon.

To the world at large, however, and in particular to Christians, the Masons present a benevolent face. The Masonic brochure, *To a Non-Mason: You Must Seek Masonic Membership*, illustrates this:

Masons practice charity and benevolence and strive to promote human welfare. All over the world Masons care for their indigent Brethren, widows and orphans; maintain homes: support their mother countries in great wars; aid medical research, gerontology, blood banks, youth programs, military rehabilitation; contribute scholarships and practice character building.

Is it any surprise that Masonry should use philanthropy as a protective shield to conceal their other, covert purposes? If the integrity of Masonry is ever questioned, Masons have only to appeal to their benevolent activities to silence doubters.

An example of this "benevolent strategy" in action is recorded in the *Congressional Record - Senate*, September 9, 1987.[84] The nomination of a judge to the federal judiciary was questioned in the Senate Judiciary Committee on the basis of the nominee's membership in the Masons. Some asked, "Could this Judge, while on a federal bench, make an unbiased decision when he belongs to a Masonic Lodge that forbids membership to a certain race of people?"

The Masons in the Senate were strangely silent until debate seemed to be moving in their favor. Then they came out of the woodwork, defending Masonry on the basis of philanthropy.

Several of the Masonic senators spoke. Senator Simpson of Wyoming said, "It is my pleasure to hold the 33rd degree in Masonry... [Senator] Byrd holds that distinction... Forty-one members of the Federal judiciary are presently Masons... I just say that Masonry in this country is the bedrock."

Then Senator Byrd of West Virginia spoke. "I am proud to be a Mason. I have been a Mason since 1958 or 1959... I am a 33rd degree Mason...I hope that this ugly head of prejudice against Masons will not rear itself again."

---

[83] Fisher 249, 339.

[84] *Congressional Record - Senate* (Washington, D.C.: Library of Congress, 9 Sept.1987) n.p.

Finally Senator Thurmond of South Carolina spoke. "I guess about half of the members of the Judiciary Committee are members of the Masonic order. I have been a member since 1924 and as was stated by the able assistant leader here, Senator Simpson, it simply means people who believe in God and love their fellow man. In short that is what it stands for."

Thurmond continued. "I commend the majority leader, who is a 33rd degree Mason and Bob Dole, who is a 33rd degree Mason... I think the Masons have done a lot of good in the world. You have to be a Mason before you become a Shriner and the Shriners are maintaining hospitals throughout the nation to treat little crippled children and to cure burns, a most worthy cause.

"So I hope the question about Masonry being raised to try to keep one from becoming a judge is now finally settled, that will be the end of it and we will not hear any more on it."

The benevolent strategy worked. The stunned non-Masons in the Senate dropped their objections. The question of race bias in the Masons was dropped. And Masonic Judge Sentelle was unanimously appointed to the federal judiciary.

Among blacks, the membership of prominent members of their communities in black lodges is enough to dissuade many from any suspicion of or doubt about what may lie behind the publicly promoted purposes of Freemasonry.

Black Muslim Mustafa El-Arnin in *Freemasonry, Ancient Egypt, and the Islamic Destiny* (1988), published the following list of contemporary black Freemasons: "Jesse Jackson, Democratic Candidate for President of the United States; Andrew Young, Mayor of Atlanta, Georgia: Kenneth Gibson, former three-term Mayor for the City of Newark, New Jersey; the late Harold Washington, former Mayor of Chicago, Illinois; State Senator Julian Bond; [former] Supreme Court Justice Thurgood Marshall; and finally Marion Barry, (former] Mayor of the District of Columbia."[85]

In his foreword, El-Amin also identifies as black Masons, NAACP Executive Director Benjamin Hooks; Mayor Thomas Bradley (Los Angeles); Congressman Louis Stokes; Mayor Coleman Young (Detroit); and John A. Johnson, publisher of *Ebony* and *Jet* magazines.

When I have discussed my research with people who are neither Masons nor Christians, I have discovered that most know of Freemasonry only through the Shriner's Circus and Children's Hospitals. If humane activities are the sole purpose of Freemasonry, however, why are Masonic meetings always shrouded in secrecy and mystery?

An answer to this question was suggested in 1954 by British Air Commodore G.S. Oddie in the foreword to Dr. Meyrick Booth's book, *Rudolph Hess: Prisoner of Peace:* "It is well nigh impossible for the ordinary citizen to become sufficiently acquainted with facts to judge a case. He does know however, that secrecy has never been and will never be a weapon of Good while more often than not it is the distinguishing mark of Evil."[86]

Degrees of Initiation and Knowledge

As was indicated, it has been discovered that Freemasonry's mysteries have nothing to do with philanthropy. Freemasonry's cloak of benevolence is a diversion to conceal secrets known only to high degree initiates.

---

[85] Mustafa EI-Amin, *Freemasonry, Ancient Egypt, and the Islamic Destiny* (Jersey City: New Mind Productions, 1988) 67.
[86] Meyrick Booth, *Rudolph Hess: Prisoner of Peace,* Trans. Frau Isle Hess, ed. George Pile (Torrance, CA: Institute for Historical Review, 1954) entire.

I have discussed my research with a few business clients and friends who are Masons. Because I had learned their Masonic grips and passwords, some talked freely, believing I too was a Mason. All were sincere, honest and patriotic men. Most did not believe what I had discovered, since most were Blue Lodge Masons. They consider their involvement with the Lodge a wholesome fellowship, not placing much import on the secrets, claiming the blood-curdling oaths are all in fun. The initiate also believes that he is entering into a Christian fellowship. This understanding is encouraged not only by the Bible upon the altar, but also by the Masonic claim that Jesus Christ was a Mason. One of the nicknames given a Mason is "Carpenter," which American Masonry uses as proof that Jesus was a Mason. In fact, Blue Lodge Masons are told that Jesus, the carpenter, kept his Masonic obligation (or oath) when He refused to answer the questions put to Him by Pontius Pilate.[87]

In the first three degrees - what is called the Blue Lodge - the initiate is told that everything in Freemasonry has been handed down orally for millenniums. Nothing, it is said, is in writing. This of course is far from the truth. What Masons use in their lengthy ceremonies to perpetuate this myth of oral transmission is something called a "coded memory aid" book. The "codes" used in these books are made up of various glyphs and abbreviations, and are so childish that anyone can break them in a matter of minutes.

If any of the initiates or members of the Lodge were to walk into the Masonic library in his own lodge, his education would begin, for he would discover that everything about Freemasonry from its inception has been written down by Masonic authors.

Blue Lodge Masons who tell you with all honesty and sincerity that Freemasonry is a Christian institution, are confounded when shown in their own books that they are in a pagan religion. What they do not at first realize is that they have been intentionally deceived. Thirty. third degree Freemason Albert Pike, in *Morals and Dogma*, states that this deception of members in the early degrees is deliberate.

The Blue Degrees are but the outer court or portico of the Temple. Part of the symbols are displayed there to the Initiate, but he is intentionally misled by false interpretations. It is not intended that he shall understand them; but it is intended that he shall imagine he understands them... and who so attempts to undeceive them will labor in vain...

Pike confirms Freemasonry's deliberate deception of its members. The two photographs of Masonic ceremonials in Appendix 2 (figs. 1 & 2) vividly illustrate the deception in action. To convince a Mason that he is not a member of a genuinely Judeo-Christian institution is nearly impossible. The Masonic Supreme Council believes their deception of the lower degree Masons is so powerful that no one can "undeceive them," forgetful of or even denying the power of Almighty God, Who can "undeceive them" if they study the written Word.[88]

In fact, we can turn to Scripture, John 18:20, for a repudiation of the Masonic heresy that Jesus was a Mason, where Jesus says, "I ever taught in the synagogue, and in the temple, whither the Jews always resort; and in secret have I said nothing." In other words, Jesus *never* took the Masonic oath!

The bloody oaths that bind initiates in the lower degrees to silence are in reality meaningless, because the secrets these oaths conceal are trivial. The real purpose of the lower degrees is to maintain a reserve from which to select tested men, who are then entrusted with the deeper secrets of subversion and revolution taught only to those in the higher degrees. Those in the lower grades are used only to disseminate propaganda for the purpose of altering public opinion.

---

[87] Confirmed by the author with conversations with several Masons in and out of the Lodge.
[88] Pike 819.

The Masonic Hierarchy and Conspiracy

Research has revealed that only the Hierarchy in Masonry - a select group within the 33rd degree Supreme Council - has full knowledge of the Masonic conspiracy. It has always been essential to this Hierarchy to increase Masonic membership in the low degrees, while at the same time keeping the novice ignorant.

Freemasonry realizes that a man's spiritual conscience is soothed when he joins a benevolent cause. The smoke screen of charitable activities aids the conspirators. With such a beautiful, yet deceptive presumption that Freemasonry works good for mankind, the initiate can be kept ignorant as he is led deeper into the mysteries of Free-masonry.

Beginning with his first initiation, the novice is compelled to unquestioning, blind obedience of his unseen superiors. Past Grand Master Robert Morris confirms in the Masonic book *Webb's Monitor* that "Right or wrong, [the initiate's] very existence as a Mason hangs upon his obedience to the powers immediately set above him."[89]

Former 33rd degree Mason Jim Shaw, coauthor of *The Deadly Deception,* states in his taped testimony *Degrees of the Adepts,* that "As one progresses in Freemasonry, or shall we say the Scottish Rite, or the York Rite, you are narrowly watched, and you are told this in the Blue Degrees."[90]

With the oath of secrecy taken by members in each degree, the conspirators are assured that silence is maintained in and out of the Lodge.

At first the Mason obeys his obligation to secrecy with love and loyalty to the Order. As he moves up the degrees and is gradually "enlightened," he keeps his oaths because he is privileged to know a secret only the "worthy" are entitled to know.

Finally, Masons keep their oath of silence for fear of reprisal should they expose the truth. Such fear often silences those Masons who have turned away from the Lodge (some of whom I know). In either case, a Mason maintains silence upon penalty of death, so states the oath by which he obligates himself.[91]

The majority of Masons are of course insensible of being manipulated. Some as high as the 32nd degree remain ignorant of the intrigue of Freemasonry, especially those who pass through the higher degrees in one to three days. How can these men possibly realize they are being deceived? These Masons usually remain "card carrying" members, rarely frequenting the Lodge, yet paying their annual dues.

A few High Masons, those members of the 30th to the 32nd degree, betray some knowledge of the conspiracy through their own words and actions. They are not "card carrying" Masons. They have worked their way through the "chairs," a process by which they become rulers, priests, or wise men in the Lodge. This process may take as long as twenty years, enough time to enlighten them to the "truth" of Freemasonry.

That "truth," however, may be one of ten interpretations of Freemasonry - an interpretation that their higher-degree instructors had previously determined for them while they were yet in Blue Lodge. You recall that 33rd degree Mason Jim Shaw said that each Mason is "narrowly watched" in Blue Lodge. Shaw means that each initiate is observed at the very beginning to determine which interpretation he might accept. If none, he stays in Blue Lodge. But, if the initiate shows interest in advancing to higher degrees, it is determined beforehand what he will be taught.

For example, if the initiate is a clergyman, he will be taught a spiritual interpretation, whereas one aspiring to be a politician will be taught a political interpretation. If the initiate is a Jew, Hindu, or Christian, he will be taught an interpretation compatible with

---

[89] Morris 169.
[90] *Degrees of the Adepts,* narr. Jim Shaw (audio cassette).
[91] Ronayne, *Handbook* 70, 123, 173. (Read Masonic oaths in Appendix 4.)

his particular religion. And if the initiate is a communist, he will be taught an interpretation different from that of a democrat.

There are ten interpretations of Freemasonry. And once the Mason arrives at the 33rd degree, the interpretation he has been taught remains with him for life. Therefore, the Hierarchy in Freemasonry (the 33rd degree Supreme Council - approximately 5,000 in all) are not of one mind as to the true interpretation of Freemasonry. In fact, as we shall learn later, within the Supreme Council is yet another secret society made up of approximately 300 men, who actually rule the world of Freemasonry, and ultimately the world as a whole. It is they who possess the true interpretation - an interpretation that will be discussed in a future chapter. These men are the real "Hidden Hand." They are believed to be spiritually in tune with the Great Architect of the Universe, who, as we have seen, is not the God of Christians. Thus the Adversary works in the spiritual realm much in the same manner as does Almighty God - through mortal men and women. The only difference is that the Adversary's activity is unrighteous activity.

Masonic Preaching and Propaganda

Ceremonies in the lodge meetings - excluding initiations - are similar to the services of the Protestant churches. Masonic hymns are sung and a sermon given.

The sermon has a special place in Masonic life, for it is the means by which Masonic thought is inculcated in members. It is also the means by which Masonic thought is disseminated through the larger community in which each lodge exists.

The importance of Masonic sermons is explained by Copin Albancelli, a French Freemason and expert on occultism. Albancelli is quoted by Cardinal Caro y Rodriguez, Archbishop of Santiago, Chile, in his book *The Mystery of Freemasonry Unveiled:*

"What have I done in Masonry? It is a question which the reader ought to ask me. It is, in effect, what one always hears:

What is done in Masonic meetings?

> *"The reply is so simple, that it always amazes those who hear it for the first time. In the Masonic meetings one begins by listening to sermons, and later one gives them."Their lodges are places where one is preached to and where one preaches, and nothing more."If this reply has been able to surprise the reader at the beginning of our study, it should not do so now. One who tries to understand the suggestions of the occult power residing in the spirit of Masonry has only one medium at his disposal, namely, the sermon."Upon what are these sermons based? Upon two principal themes which revolve unceasingly for every purpose and for no purpose."First theme: Freemasonry is a sublime, holy and sacred institution. It is the eternal initiator of all that is upright, good and great in humanity."Second theme: This association, so lofty, so respectable, so venerable, has one enemy. This enemy is Christianity. How does one arrive at this conclusion? Since Christianity is the enemy of Masonry, it is the enemy of all the great causes to which the latter claims to dedicate itself. Consequently, if they [the Masons] truly love these great causes, it is necessary to combat Christianity."Such are the two embryonic ideas which serve as a hinge for Masonic teachings. Such are the two suggestions which the Occult Power wishes at all costs to implant into the minds of the members, the two ideas which it is intended to impose upon them for good or evil, until such a point that those who refuse to accept them are definitely cast out of Masonry. That, above all, must serve as a base for all the rest."Around this there are studies in common, in the*

form of lectures and discussions, in which the members are encouraged and which deal with political and social questions, etc."[92]

As reported by Albancelli, the two themes of Masonic sermonizing can be reduced to one: the exaltation and veneration of Masonry over Christianity, which is regarded as the "enemy." Such a theme or understanding is truly the product of an "Occult Power." And it is clear that his theme then informs all studies, lectures on and discussions of "political and social questions."

The sermon process of Masonry is, in fact, a very pragmatic and effective way of spreading propaganda - a propaganda that is demonic in origin.

The obligation of the ordinary Mason to disseminate Masonic teachings in his community is embodied in Masonic ceremony. For example, in the concluding remarks given the candidate upon the completion of the 13th and final degree, the Knights Templar degree of the York Rite, the Mason is instructed to spread Masonic propaganda in his community. The following passage from *In-Hoc-Signo-Vinces, a* coded memory aid booklet authored by C. Gavitt in 1894, sets forth this obligation:

On this occasion permit me, Knight, to remind you of your mutual engagements, our reciprocal ties; for whatever may be your situation or rank in life, you may find those in similar stations, who have dignified themselves and been useful to mankind. You are, therefore, called upon to discharge all your debts [to Masonry] with fidelity, and patience, whether in the Field [military person], in the Senate [politician], on the Bench [judge], at the Bar [lawyer], or at the Holy Altar [pastor][93]

This sample of a Masonic "charge" confirms that Masons are obligated ("in debt") to carry Masonic thought into their vocation whatever it may be. Thus the "message" heard at the Lodge is quickly disseminated throughout the community as Masons return from meetings to their daily occupations. Since each Mason has taken an oath of secrecy never to divulge what transpires within the Lodge meeting, no outsider is aware from whence these "opinions" originate. Masonic thought thus influences, infects, and shapes "public opinion."

Just as deadly as the sermons preached in Masonic Temples is the century-old Masonic Scottish Rite Supreme Council's monthly publication, *New Age Magazine,* which title was changed in 1990 to *The Scottish Rite Journal* after it was exposed by Paul Fisher in *Behind The Lodge Door* (1988), as being anti-Christian, anti-Church, and antifamily."[94] According to an article, "The New Age Dawns," of October 1959, the *New Age* monthly magazine is "generally recognized as the most influential and widely read Masonic publication in the ~ In the January 1980 issue, the article "Report of the Committee on Publications,"[95] stated that "The monthly issues of the *New Age,* if combined, would present a fine summary of Scottish Rite philosophy in action."[96] The faithful Masonic reader imbibes the Masonic philosophy on a regular basis.

And what is the philosophy that the journal promotes? In the article "Why Stand Ye Here Idle?" published in the *New Age,* March, 1959, we learn that every Mason becomes

---

[92] Cardinal Caro y Rodriguez, *The Mystery of Freemasonry Unveiled* (1957; Hawthorne, CA: Christian Book Club of America, 1971) 67-68.

[93] *In-Hoc-Signo-Vinces* (New York: Allen Publishing, 1912) 190. I have several of these coded books in my possession, some old and threadbare, some current publications. With slight variations, all say the same thing.

[94] *New Age* magazine, see front cover in Appendix 2, Fig. 14.

[95] Paul Fisher, *Behind The Lodge Door* (Washington, DC: Shield Publishing, 1988) 16; quoting J. Allen, "The New Age Dawns," *New Age* magazine (Oct.1959) 553.

[96] Fisher 16; quoting "Report of the Committee on Publications," *New Age* (Jan.1980) 16.

the teacher of "Masonic philosophy to the community," and that Freemasonry is "the missionary of the new order - a Liberal order...in which Masons become high priests."[97]

When a local, state, or national issue is before the public, the Masonic newspaper journalist, judge, lawyer, legislator, politician, businessman, or (God forbid) Christian pastor has been programmed in the Masonic Lodge, and by his consistent reading of the *New Age Magazine,* how to react to the issue at hand.

By using loyal Masonic "knights," the Masonic Supreme Council disseminates its attitude- shaping agenda as its members carry Lodge-inspired and -formed opinions back into their communities through their daily jobs and vocations. Thus desired information or opinions pervade every level of society. Non-Masons, swayed by the tide of "public opinion," begin to parrot the same doctrines. Finally, the Masonic opinion or version of events is accepted by the public as "truth," for truth today is measured by what is perceived to be the belief of the majority.

The Deception of Christians

That Christians, even pastors, can be deeply deceived or compromised by Freemasonry is indicated by the number of pastors of Christian Churches who are High Masons.

The following defense of Masonry offered by the Rev. Forrest D. Haggard, a 33rd degree Mason and author of the book *The Clergy and the Craft,* illustrates how Masonry can co-opt the Christianity of its members, and use self-proclaimed Christians for its own ends. Haggard's Masonic credentials are impressive and he is a respected Masonic speaker. In the following he addresses the subject "Masonry Under Attack." The text appeared in the *Texas Mason* (Summer, 1990):

> *Over the past two years, I have listened to, watched on TV or read every program, article and item concerning the modern day anti-Masonic movement that has been called to my attention.It has been good for me. I have reexamined my own membership in all of my "other than Church" commitments.I have reached a considered decision that Freemasonry is not now and never has been detrimental to my Christian faith and doctrine. In fact, my fraternal relationships have strengthened and assisted me in my ministry as well as in my personal faith and life.We [Masons] have no "one voice," nor one leader, nor one ritual. Our critics pick and choose their quotes or dramatizations from any era, source or supply that meets their particular needs.They can always justify their stance on the basis of their own interpretation of their Source, such as the Word.It is disturbing that the opponents of Freemasonry are, in effect, attacking that which is supportive of the Christian faith.The "Christian" anti-Masonic leaders are not only inaccurate in their attack on Freemasonry but they are, in my opinion, making a far more serious attack on the basic Christian faith under whose banner they claim to operate.Where Freemasonry has instructed its candidates in its history, purpose, and intent and where a local lodge is going about its business with pride and dignity, there is very little that anti-Masonic groups can do to destroy the Craft.*

The most interesting fact of this witness to Masonry from a Christian pastor, is that Rev. Haggard never testifies to his faith in Jesus Christ, nor mentions our Savior's name,

---

[97] Fisher 56; quoting Dr. James D. Carter, "Why Stand Ye Here Idle?" *New Age* (Mar.1959) 155.

nor His mediatorial role. Haggard states adamantly that Masons "have no one voice, nor one leader, nor one ritual!"[98]

Christianity, on the other hand, does have one voice, one leader, and one ritual! All three are centered in Jesus Christ. And fellowship with our Savior is in the body of believers within the Church, not in a pagan temple with those who worship other gods. Rev. Haggard also speaks of a "personal faith," yet gives no clue as to who or what that faith is in. He claims Freemasonry is not detrimental to his Christian belief, but fails to articulate what that belief is. Furthermore, he slams those critics who appeal to the Word of God.

We must, in all devotion to Christian charity and truth, ask the Rev. Haggards of this world how they would interpret the following Word from Deuteronomy 13:6-8: "If thy brother, the son of thy mother, or thy son, or thy daughter, or the wife of thy bosom, or thy friend, which is as thine own soul, entice thee secretly, saying, Let us go and serve other gods, which thou hast not known, thou, nor thy fathers; Namely, of the gods of the people which are round about you, nigh unto thee, or far off from thee, from the one end of the earth even unto the other end of the earth.

Thou shalt not consent unto him, nor harken unto him..."

It matters not how eloquently a Masonic pastor defends the Lodge. when it is clear from God's Word that Freemasonry is a false religion of secrecy and secrets, deceptions and false gods, it is clear that communion with people from this religion is strictly forbidden.

The person who fails to heed God's warning may be deceived into worshiping false gods.

Scarlet and the Beast: In Three Volumes

Scarlet and the Beast will examine fifteen hundred years of political, financial and spiritual intrigue between two conspiratorial powers. As a seasoned investigative trainer, I have examined circumstantial evidence, evaluated it according to hard evidence, and combined what is worthy with the hard facts to develop a story that has intentionally been hidden for a millennium and a half.

You have the opportunity to evaluate this evidence and compare it with what Bible prophecy confirms will happen in the last days.

Volume I is subtitled *A History of the War between English and French Freemasonry*. This book will trace each occult power as it labors separately for world dominion. We will examine the four great political revolutions each spawned: the Glorious Revolution in Great Britain (1688), the American Revolution (1776), the French Revolution (1789) and the Russian Revolution (1917). We will address as well their activities through the two World Wars. Finally, we will examine God's Word to see what His prophets say about Freemasonry and the Beast empire it will erect in the last days.

Volume II is subtitled *English Freemasonry, Mother of Modern Cults, vis-a-vis Mystery Babylon, Mother of Harlots.* We will journey back to the patriarchs of ancient Babylon, from whence are Freemasonry's roots. We will discuss Ham, Cush, Nimrod, and his wife Semiramis, and examine how Freemasonry's ceremonies are linked to Babylon's fertility worship of male and female gods. We will learn why the Babylonian religion hid itself and why it continues today in secret societies such as Freemasonry.

Volume III is subtitled *English Freemasonry, Banks, and the illegal Drug Trade.* This volume places the Harlot's cup of abomination squarely in the hands of English Freemasonry. We will learn how and why drugs have been used in all eastern mystery

---

[98] Forrest D. Haggard, "Masonry Under Attack," Texas *Mason* (Summer 1990) 5.

religions, and trace Freemasonry's involvement in drugs to the British Opium Wars against China. This book will examine English Freemasonry's role as the world's drug financier and money launderer, and French Freemasonry's role as the world's drug trafficker. We will examine the horrifying prospect of the nuclear destruction of London by the Beast, and how afterwards the Beast will mark the world.

Scarlet and the Beast

VOLUME I

The adversary of Almighty God is manipulating events to bring about his long-desired universal government of Antichrist. His fight for world dominion began at Eden, where he whispered his plans to Adam and Eve. Within two millenniums Satan had captured all but eight of the Human race - Noah and his wife, his three sons and their wives. God stopped Satan's attempt toward globalism with a universal flood. After the Great Flood, Satan tried at Babylon to reestablish globalism, but God stopped him again. Satan then took his conspiracy underground. It became known as Mystery Babylon.

The adversary's clandestine plan is still being directed from behind the lodge doors of mystery religions today, the most powerful of which is Freemasonry. Here we can find the Babylonian plans to inaugurate a godless one world government. Freemasonry plans a Universal Empire, the same spoken of by the prophets Daniel and John. We will reveal their plans in this book.

SCARLET

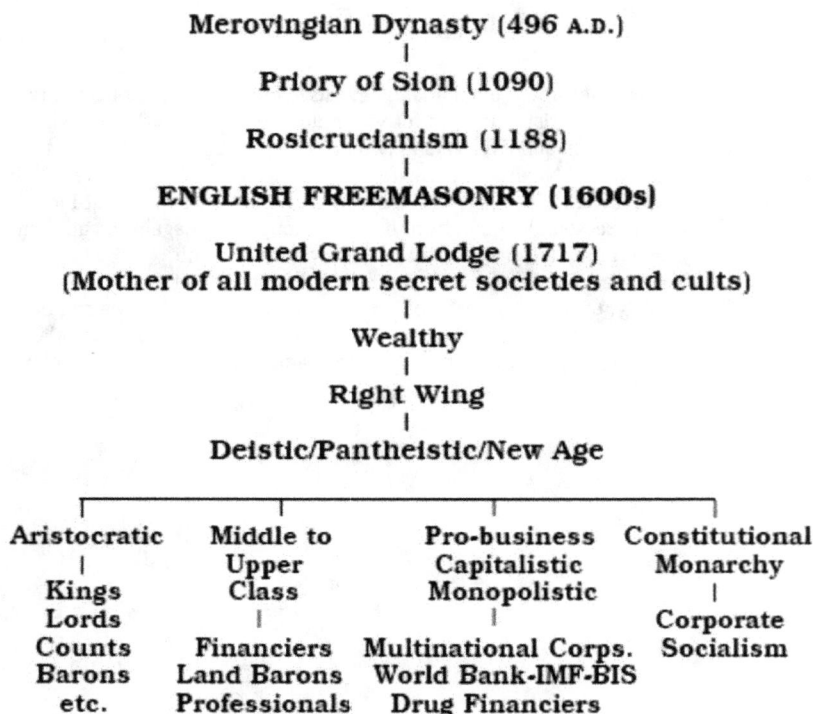

Merovingian Dynasty (496 A.D.)
|
Priory of Sion (1090)
|
Rosicrucianism (1188)
|
ENGLISH FREEMASONRY (1600s)
|
United Grand Lodge (1717)
(Mother of all modern secret societies and cults)
|
Wealthy
|
Right Wing
|
Deistic/Pantheistic/New Age

Aristocratic	Middle to	Pro-business	Constitutional
	Upper	Capitalistic	Monarchy
Kings	Class	Monopolistic	
Lords			Corporate
Counts	Financiers	Multinational Corps.	Socialism
Barons	Land Barons	World Bank-IMF-BIS	
etc.	Professionals	Drug Financiers	

Dominates:
> Great Britain, Canada, Northeast USA (Eastern Establishment), most oriental countries, Hong Kong, Australia, and South Africa.

THE BEAST

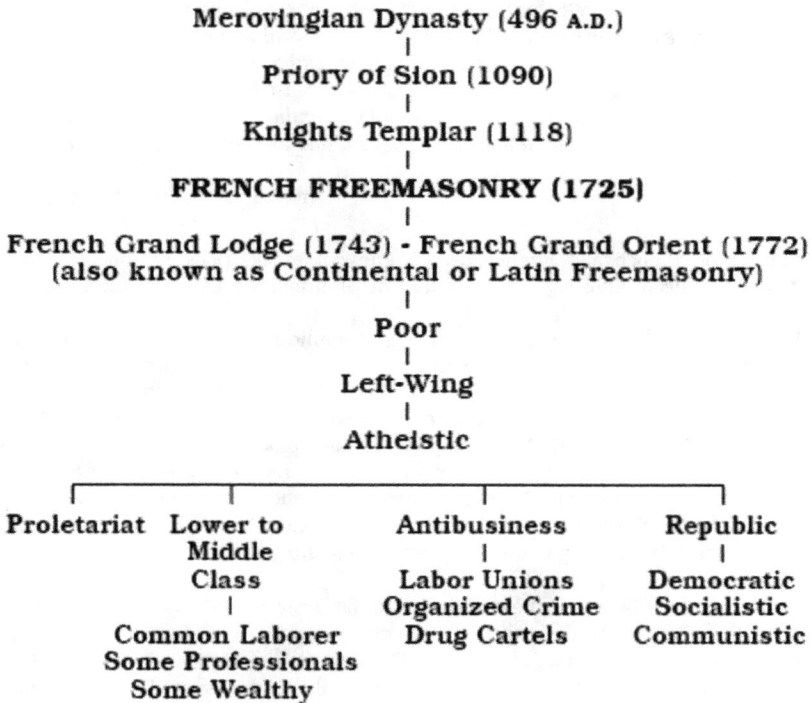

Merovingian Dynasty (496 A.D.)

|

Priory of Sion (1090)

|

Knights Templar (1118)

|

FRENCH FREEMASONRY (1725)

|

French Grand Lodge (1743) - French Grand Orient (1772)
(also known as Continental or Latin Freemasonry)

|

Poor

|

Left-Wing

|

Atheistic

Proletariat	Lower to Middle Class	Antibusiness	Republic
	|	|	|
	Common Laborer Some Professionals Some Wealthy	Labor Unions Organized Crime Drug Cartels	Democratic Socialistic Communistic

Dominates:
Continent of Europe, Southern and Western U.S.A.,
former U.S.S.R., Communist China, Pacific Islands,
Philippines, Latin and South America, Africa (during
1990s has taken over South Africa).

1. THE CONFLICT: PRIORY OF SION VERSUS KNIGHTS TEMPLAR

Secret societies by virtue of their very secrecy have often kept historians at bay, and the historians, reluctant to confess their ignorance, prefer to diminish the consequence of their subject. Freemasonry... is of vital importance to any social, psychological, cultural or political history of eighteenth-century Europe, and even to the founding of the United States; but most history books don't even mention it. It is almost as if an implicit policy obtained: If something cannot be exhaustively documented, it must be irrelevant and thereby not worth discussing I at all.

Investigators of the Holy Grail[99]

Freemasonry, French and English, as we know it today, finds its loots in two organizations of the Middle Ages - the Priory of Sion and the Order of the Knights Templar.

What follows is the fascinating, if sometimes complicated and obscure history, of how these two modern, anti-Christian secular secret societies - English and French Freemasonry - developed from two groups that themselves had roots in the occult. We will see how the Priory of Sion desired to rule the world from the throne of David in Jerusalem through its counterfeit Jewish Merovingian bloodline, and how its own creation, the Knights Templar, moved beyond its role as police and protector of Sion to financial masters of medieval Europe. We will trace the alliance of Sion and the Templars, their dispute over the discovery of Solomon's treasures, and the terrible intrigues which followed that led to the undoing of the Templars in their struggle over wealth, power, and politics.

We will reveal the beliefs of these two groups: that Jesus fathered children by Mary Magdalene; that a spiritual god of good (Satan) battles a material god of evil; that Lucifer, not Jesus, deserves worship; that a "Spear of Destiny" (later sought and possessed by Hitler) allows the holder to rule the world. We will also present data about the whereabouts of King Solomon's wealth, the plan to one day return it to Jerusalem, and reveal that the ultimate goal of these two groups is world government, and that their descendants, English and French Freemasonry, desire the same.

THE HISTORICAL TRAIL: THE PRIORY OF SION AND THE HOLY GRAIL

In 1982 and 1986 three secular revisionist authors, Michael Baigent~ Richard Leigh, and Henry Lincoln published *Holy Blood, Holy* Grail followed by *The Messianic Legacy*. These two books dramatically reveal a secret order structured in the manner of Freemasonry, and founded in Europe twelve centuries before the Grand Lodge was officially formed in 1717. This order protects both the Holy Grail and the Merovingian bloodline, which bloodline carried Mystery Babylon into the Catholic Church in 496 A.D.

---

[99] Baigent et al, *Holy Blood* 19.

The Holy Grail, of course, is the so-called cup from which Jesus drank at the Last Supper. The Merovingians, owners of the Holy Grail, teach that Jesus fathered children by Mary Magdalene. The Merovingians claim to be the offspring of that "holy" union, and as such, assert they are Jews of the Davidic line.

In Revelation 17:3-5 the apostle John describes a vision, which Rev. J. R. Church in *Guardians of the Grail* believes is fulfilled in the Grail legend. The Whore of Babylon is holding in her hand a golden cup full of blasphemy. Church believes the cup is the blasphemous Holy Grail Another element of the Grail legend is the spear supposed to have pierced the side of Jesus, also known as the Spear of Longinus or the Spear of Destiny. Whoever possesses this spear, so the legend goes, will rule the world. The Merovingians, whose descendants are the Habsburg pretenders to the Austrian throne today, are in possession of the spear. It is on display in the Habsburg museum in Vienna, Austria~ No one, however, knows the location of the Holy Grail. At least no one is telling.

Although heretical, this secret society should not be discounted, for it is alive and well today. In fact, in 1956, an Order calling itself the Prieure de Sion, or Priory of Sion, registered itself publicly for the first time with the French government. (Sion is French for Zion.) It is from this Order that the legend of the Holy Grail originated five centuries after Christ's death.

Rev. Church remarks of this organization:

This mysterious group is presently made up of over 9,000 men, including Protestants, Roman Catholics, Jews, and Moslems. The members of this secret sect should be considered unfaithful to their respective beliefs, for in reality they are neither Christian nor Catholic, they are neither Jew nor Moslem. Their doctrine sidesteps the basic tenets of those beliefs and replaces them with the teachings of their greatest prophet - whom they believe to be Buddha.[100]

From this secret order J. R. Church believes will come the Anti-Christ, for he writes, "Their ultimate goal is world government!"[101]

DOCUMENTATION: ANCIENT PARCHMENTS OF THE PRIORY OF SION

Sion's ruling adepts are known as "Nautonniers," meaning navigators, pilots, or helmsmen. Their duty is to steer the course plotted by the Priory of Sion. One Nautonnier is alive at all times and another is always being prepared to take his place. We shall refer to these Nautonniers as Grand Masters.

> *"1982, the Grand Master of Sion was a man named Pierre Plantard, according to the authors of Holy Blood, Holy Grail. In The Messianic Legacy these authors interviewed Plantard, who told them the Priory of Sion "actually possessed the lost treasure of the Temple of Jeru- salem. It would be returned to Israel, he said, 'when the time is right."*[102]

---

[100] Church 11.Buddhism is the 500 B.C. reformation of Brahmanism (Hinduism today), which in turn is believed to be the original Babylonian harlot religion founded by Nimrod. (See vol. II of *Scarlet and the Beast.)*

[101] Church.

[102] Michael Baigent, Richard Leigh and Henry Lincoln, *Messianic Legacy* (New York: Dell Books, 1986) XIII.

Before 1956 no "outsider" had ever heard of the Priory of Sion. Yet, as the authors of *Holy Blood, Holy Grail* in 1982 wrote:

> Since 1956 a quantity of relevant material has been deliberately and systematically "leaked" in a piecemeal fashion, fragment by fragment. Most of these fragments purport, implicitly or explicitly, to issue from some "privileged" or inside'' source. Most contain additional information, which supplements what was known before and thus contributes to the overall jigsaw. Neither the import nor the meaning of the overall jigsaw has yet been made clear, however. Instead, every new snippet of information has done more to intensify than to dispel the mystery. The result has been an ever-proliferating network of seductive allusions, provocative hints, suggestive cross-references and connections. In confronting the welter of data now available, the reader may well feel he is being toyed with - or being ingeniously and skillfully led from conclusion to conclusion by successive carrots dangled before his nose.

And underlying it all is the constant, pervasive intimation of a secret - a secret of monumental and explosive proportions.[103]

The authors of *Holy Blood, Holy Grail* embarked on a ten-year investigation that took them throughout Europe. The results of their investigation caused astounding repercussions. One example is the Hollywood "Indiana Jones" trilogy, based upon their research. Moviegoers will recognize *Raiders of the Lost Ark, The Temple* of Doom, and *The Last Crusade.*

The most important documents discovered by the authors concerning the Priory of Sion came from the Grand Lodge Alpina, the supreme Masonic Lodge of Switzerland - the Swiss equivalent of the Grand Lodge in London and the Grand Orient Lodge in France. These documents called the *Dossiers secret* told of a Catholic priest named Berenger Sauniere, who was also a Freemason. But this Freemasonry, note the authors "differed from most other forms in that it was Christian, Hermetic, and aristocratic."[104]

This description matches that of a Rosicrucian Order founded in 1873, which Sauniere had joined. On June 1, 1885, Sauniere was posted to a little parish in the tiny village of Rennes-le- Chateau in southern France. Eight centuries earlier, in 1059, the village church of Rennes-le-Chateau was consecrated to Mary Magdalene, the patron saint of southern France.

At the time of Sauniere's assignment, the church was in need of repair, and in 1891 Sauniere embarked on a modest restoration. Report the authors of *Holy Blood, Holy Grail,* "In the course of his endeavors he removed the altar stone, which rested on two archaic Visigoth columns. One of these columns proved to be hollow. Inside the priest found four parchments preserved in sealed wooden tubes. Two of these parchments are said to have comprised genealogies, one dating from 1244, the other from 1644."[105]

THE BLOODLINE OF ANTICHRIST

These parchments contained a list of Grand Masters of both the Knights Templar and the Priory of Sion, as well as a history of the Merovingian bloodline. The heading of one

---

[103] Baigent et al, *Holy Blood* 96-97.
[104] Baigent 197.
[105] Baigent33.

of the documents was in cipher. When translated it read: "To Dagobert II King and to Sion belongs this treasure and he is there dead."

The research undertaken by the authors of *Holy Blood, Holy Grail* primarily centered around authenticating these genealogies. They discovered that the *Secret Dossiers*, cataloged in the Alpina Masonic Lodge, were amazingly accurate. Their investigations revealed what secular history has forgotten, or has intentionally withheld.

MYSTERY BABYLON ENTERS THE CATHOLIC CHURCH

A complimentary and corrective Christian evaluation of what these researchers have discovered is provided by Rev. J.R. Church in his *Guardians of the Grail*. Church writes:

> *According to the tenets of the organization [Priory of Sion], Jesus Christ did not die on Calvary - but merely pretended to die, was taken from the cross, stolen from the tomb, and was believed to have married Mary Magdalene and even produced children.*
>
> *They claim that when the Romans destroyed the Temple at Jerusalem in 70 A.D., the Magdalene fled with her sacred children by boat across the Mediterranean to France. There she found refuge in a Jewish community. Future generations of her offspring were said to have married into the royal Frankish family and by the fifth century produced a king.*
>
> *His name was Merovee. He was the first in a series of kings called the Merovingian bloodline. It is said that the offspring of Merovee were noted for a birthmark above the heart - a small red cross. This symbol eventually became the emblem of the Guardians of the Grail.*
>
> *Merovee, king of the Franks from 447 to 458 A.D., was an adherent of the religious cult of Diana. His son, Childeric I (458-481 AD.) practiced witchcraft. His son, Clovis I (481-511 A.D.) adopted Christianity in 496 A.D.*
>
> *In 496 A.D., the Bishop of Rome made a pact with Clovis, the grandson of Merovee, and king of the Franks, calling him the "New Constantine," giving him authority to preside over a "Christianized" Roman empire. (The term "Holy Roman Empire" was not officially used until 962 A.D.)*
>
> *The so-called offspring of Mary Magdalene were thus established as leaders of the empire.[106]*

Rev. Church believes that the Merovingian bloodline and its protector, the Priory of Sion, is an arm of Mystery Babylon, if not Scarlet herself. Their religion is not new, but rather, the revival of the old religion at Babylon, altered to deceive the Church.

Initially the Vatican was ignorant of the "Holy Blood" heresy that had entered the Church. In time it would be discovered, and an excise attempted. But the Merovingians would secretly buy their way back into the Roman Church through simony, the practice of buying or selling ecclesiastical appointments, pardons, and benefits. The word simony" derives from Simon Magus, a Samaritan who tried to purchase from the apostles Peter and John the power of conferring the Holy Spirit (Acts 8:18-19).

J.R. Church traces the lineage of these Merovingian kings documenting that most European royalty descends from this bloodline, including the Habsburg dynasty and the present royalty of Spain.[107]

---

[106] Church 11-13.
[107] Church 13-22.

Today, twelve royal families in Europe have Grail blood.[108] Claiming to be descendants of Jesus Christ and Mary Magdalene, they believe themselves Jews of the line of David. Among their many noble names is the title "King of Jerusalem," which title was given them at the successful conclusion of the First Crusade. Rev. Church believes this title, of course, blasphemous. In fact, they are usurpers of the Davidic line.[109]

Jesus Christ speaks to such a heresy in Revelation 3:9, where He admonishes the Philadelphia Church, representing Church history from approximately 1750 to the 1900s: "Behold, I will make them of the synagogue of Satan, which say they are Jews, and are not, but do lie; behold, I will make them to come and worship before thy feet, and know that I have loved thee."[110]

THE SECRET LIFE OF DAGOBERT II

In 1891, when Freemason Sauniere discovered the Priory of Sion *Dossiers secret* parchments at Rennes-le-Chateau, one was headed with the inscription: "To Dagobert II King and to Sion belongs this treasure and he is there dead."

History speaks of Dagobert I and Dagobert III, but remains silent on Dagobert II. Who is he? And why has he been removed from historical records? What secret did he possess that caused European royalty and the Vatican to fear him to the extent of excising his name from memory, if in fact he ever existed?

Research by the authors of *Holy Blood, Holy Grail* unveiled Dagobert II. Clovis was succeeded by his son Dagobert II, born in 651 A.D. Clovis ruled the Franks and Gauls from France, and died when Dagobert was age five. A struggle broke out for ascendancy to the throne. Five-year-old Dagobert II was reported to have been killed. But the fact is he was kidnapped by a Catholic priest and spirited away to Ireland where he was raised and protected at the Irish monastery of Slane, "not far from Dublin; and here, at the school attached to the monastery, he received an education unobtainable in France at the time."[111]

In 666 A.D., Dagobert married a Celtic princess, fathering three daughters, but no sons. Soon he moved to England, establishing residence at York. His first wife died in 670 A.D., and Dagobert II returned to France. He married his second wife, Giselle de Razes, daughter of the count of Razes and niece of the king of the Visigoths in southern France. The marriage was celebrated at Rennes-le-Chateau, a Visigoth bastion, the same village where Sauniere found the secret geneologies in 1891. With this marriage the Merovingian bloodline was now allied with the royal bloodline of the Visigoths, who had strong gnostic tendencies. Dagobert II was in fact converted to the religion of his wife, turning away from his Catholic heritage. For three years Dagobert bided his time at Rennes-le-Chateau, watching the changes made in his domains to the north. Finally, in 674 A.D., with the support of his mother and her advisers, the long-exiled monarch announced who he was, reclaimed his realm, and was officially proclaimed king of Austrasia, which took in the territory of northwestern Europe and parts of what are now Germany and Austria.[112]

---

[108] Church 62.

[109] J.R. Church's hypothesis of who this bloodline really is has been well documented by him, and his book should be read by those interested in Bible prophecy. For the purpose of my book I need not go back that far, therefore, I do not mention his hypothesis.

[110] J.R. Church's hypothesis of who this bloodline really is has been well documented by him, and his book should be read by those interested in Bible prophecy. For the purpose of my book I need not go back that far, therefore, I do not mention his hypothesis.

[111] Baigent et al, *Holy Blood* 247.

[112] Baigent 250.

Dagobert II established a coat of arms for Rennes-le-Chateau consisting of two triangles interlaced, one white and upright, the other black and up-side-down, forming a six-pointed star.[113] This emblem has enabled researchers to trace the migration of the Priory of Sion over the centuries, for it is a dominant symbol used in Freemasonry. *Mackey's Encyclopedia of Freemasonry* defines the six- pointed star as representing the good and evil powers in life[114], a division of powers which was held by the gnostic Visigoths. In fact, this star is in mosaic on the lobby floor of many Masonic Lodges today.[115] From it has developed the Square and Compass. (See Figs. 4 & 5, Appendix 2.)

ASSASSINATION OF DAGOBERT II

Dagobert was a worthy successor to Clovis. Austrasia had been broken up into small principalities. Anarchy prevailed, so he set about asserting and consolidating his authority, reestablishing order. His firm rule broke the various rebellious nobles who had mobilized sufficient military and economic power to challenge him. He drew upon his substantial treasury at Rennes-le-Chateau, using these resources to finance the reconquest of Austrasia.[116] Dagobert II also set himself against the Roman Church. His newly acquired gnostic beliefs left him no room for Christianity. On every front he curbed the expansion of the Vicar of Christ. By this time Rome was knowledgeable of the Merovingian heresy, and could not permit it to continue. On December 23, 679 A.D., while resting under a tree during a hunt in the Arteries forests of northern France, Dagobert was assassinated. His assassins then returned to his northern palace, intent on exterminating the rest of the royal family.

SURVIVAL OF THE MEROVINGIANS

Before the discoveries of the authors of *Holy Blood, Holy Grail*, Dagobert's assassination was regarded as the end of the Merovingian dynasty. At least this is what the Catholic Church wanted the world to believe. In its place in 754 A.D. Rome established the Carolingian dynasty with Pepin II. The name "Carolingian" derives from Charles Martel, grandfather of Charlemagne, the first designated "Holy Roman Emperor." This title, by virtue of the pact with Clovis three centuries before, should have been reserved exclusively for the Merovingians.

The authors of *Holy Blood* discovered, however, that Dagobert's son (Sigisbert IV) by his second wife had survived. His sister had rescued him and smuggled him southward to the domain of his mother, the Visigoth princess Giselle de Razes. Arriving in the Lanquedoc (southern France) in 681 A.D., he shortly thereafter inherited his uncle's titles - Duke of Razes and Count of Rhedae. Sigisbert also adopted the surname "Plant-Ard" (subsequently Plantard), which means "ardently flowering shoot" of the Merovingian vine. Under this name, and under the titles acquired from his uncle, he perpetuated his lineage. By 886 A.D. one branch of that lineage culminated in a certain Bernard

---

[113] Baigent 396.

[114] "Triangle and Square," Mackey's Encyclopedia of Freemasonry, vol.11.

[115] See six-pointed star in mosaic on the lobby floor of Masonic Lodges in Appendix 2, Fig. 4.

[116] Baigent et al, *Holy Blood* 251.

Plantavelu (which name is a derivative of Plant-Ard or Plantard), whose son became the first Duke of Aquitaine.[117]

GUIFLEM: FATHER OF THE GRAIL FAMILY

For 100 years after the murder of Dagobert II, the Merovingian bloodline was protected by an unnamed secret society. Then in 790 A.D., one Guillem de Gellone assumed "the title of count of Razes - the title Sigisbert is said to have possessed and passed on to his descendants He was to direct the reestablishment of the Merovingian line.

Guillem was one of the most famous men of his time. So much so, report the *Holy Blood* authors, "that his historical reality...has been obscured by legend. Before the epoch of the Crusades there were at least six major epic poems composed about him, *chansons de geste* similar to the famous *Chanson de Roland*. In *The Divine Comedy* Dante accorded him a uniquely exalted status. But even before Dante, Guillem had again become an object of literary attention. In the early thirteenth century he figured as the protagonist of *Willehalm*, an unfinished epic romance composed by Wolfram von Eschenbach - whose most famous work, *Parzival*, is probably the most important of all romances dealing with the mysteries of the Holy Grail... Wolfram stated in another poem that the 'Grail castle,' abode of the 'Grail family,' was situated in the Pyrenes [southern France], in what, at the beginning of the ninth century, was Guillem de Gellone's domain."[118]

POWER MARRIAGES AND THE GRAIL BLOOD

Guillem maintained a close rapport with Charlemagne of the Carolingian dynasty. His sister married one of Charlemagne's sons, thus establishing once again the Merovingian bloodline in European royalty. "By 886 A.D. the line of Guillem de Gellone culminated... in [Bernard Plantavelu-Plantard], precisely the same individual as...Sigisbert IV and his descendants."[119] The authors of *Holy Blood, Holy Grail* believe that Guillem de Gellone was in fact Sigisbert VI, grandson of Sigisbert IV, thus making him the great grandson of Dagobert II.

Sigisbert VI was also known as Prince Ursus. *Ursus* in Latin means an echo. As subsequently became apparent, he was indeed an echo of Dagobert II. Between 877 A.D. and 879 A.D. Prince Ursus was officially proclaimed King Ursus. He undertook an insurrection against Louis II of France in an attempt to reestablish the Merovingian dynasty. The insurrection, however, failed. Prince Ursus and his supporters were defeated at a battle near Pointiers in 881 A.D. With this setback, the Plantard family lost its possessions in the south of France. Ursus died in Brittany (northwest France), his line allied by marriage with the Breton ducal house. By the turn of the ninth century the Merovingian blood had flowed into the duchies of both Brittany and Aquitaine.

Approximately two centuries before the Crusades the Plantard family sought refuge in England, establishing an English branch of the family called Planta. From this line came Bera VI, nicknamed "the Architect." It is interesting to note that he and his descendants, having found a haven in England under King Atheistan, practiced "the art of building." The authors of Holy *Blood* state that "Masonic sources date the origin of

---

[117] Baigent 259.You recall that the Grand Master of the Priory of Sion in 1982 was a Frenchman named Pierre Plantard. He traces his family tree to the Merovingian bloodline.
[118] Baigent.
[119] Baigent 26l.

Freemasonry in England from the reign of King Athelstan. Could the Merovingian bloodline... in addition to its claim to the French throne, be in some way connected with something at the core of Freemasonry?"[120]

THE CRUSADES AND A SECRET SOCIETY

"The Crusades," writes Rev. J.R. Church, "played an important part in the promotion of the Merovingian bloodline. Many of the Crusaders were French who went to Palestine to liberate the Holy Land from the Moslems. The Catholic Crusaders had conquered the city of Jerusalem and established Godfroi de Bouillon on the throne of Jerusalem. Claiming to be of the lineage of David, Godfroi de Bouillon organized a secret society called the Ordre de Sion."[121]

SION: CULT OF THE HOLY GRAIL

The authors of *Holy Blood, Holy Grail* elucidate the byzantine political and family ambitions of the Merovingian clan which lie behind Godfroi de Bouillon's participation in the Crusades.

A half century before the completion of the First Crusade of 1099, Godfroi reigned in the vicinity of the Ardennes Forest in northern France where Dagobert II had been assassinated five centuries earlier. As we have noted, three centuries after this murder, Dagobert's great grandson, Prince Ursus (Sigisbert VI) was defeated near Pointiers in 881 A.D. Upon this setback, the Merovingians established and funded a foundation of monks in Calabria, in southern Italy, to alert them of any Vatican developments against their bloodline. For the next 200 years the Holy Grail bloodline continued the practice of simony, while the monks in Calabria waited, watched and listened. In 1070 a pope ascended Peter's throne who might cause problems for the Mero- vingians. This was three decades before the First Crusade.

THE MEROVINGIANS PLOT AND PLAN

The Calabrian monks immediately embarked on a journey to northern France to visit Godfroi de Bouillon. They were aware of his so-called Holy Blood heritage. Their leader was one named Ursus, a name, as we have seen, associated with the Merovingian bloodline. When the monks identified themselves to Godfroi as the protectors of the Holy Grail, they were given the tract of land at Orval where Dagobert II was assassinated. There they built an abbey. Traveling with them was also the man subsequently known as Peter the Hermit.

The purpose of the monks' journey was two-fold. First, they warned Godfroi of the whisperings in the Vatican. Pope Alexander II (1061-1073) was promoting the abolition of simony. Since the usurpation of the throne of the Holy Roman Empire by the Carolingians, simony had been the primary means by which the Merovingians for centuries had penetrated the Vatican in an attempt to regain their ascendancy. Apparently,

---

[120] Baigent 265.
[121] Church 23.

the pope was aware of their methods and aims. Therefore, the second purpose for the monks' journey was to present a plan to preempt the pope.

TO RULE THE WORLD FROM THE THRONE OF DAVID

The Merovingian cult of the Holy Grail needed the Catholic Church to establish its legitimacy: not only to regain the coveted position of Holy Roman Emperor, but also to legitimize its claim to the throne of Israel. The Merovingians' ultimate goal was to rule the world from the Davidic throne at Jerusalem. The papal plan to eliminate simony would eliminate the Merovingians main avenue into the Church and its power.

Therefore, the monks encouraged Godfroi de Bouillon to start a Holy War against the Muslims for the conquest of Jerusalem, deport the Muslims, and establish himself as King of Jerusalem on David's throne before Pope Alexander could make any headway in once again excising the Merovingians.

Pope Alexander died three years after the monks' meeting with Godfroi. The next Pope, Gregory VII, took up Alexander's cause and in 1073 began his series of reforms, of which Malachi Martin has written in his book *The Decline and Fall of the Roman Church* (1981). Martin says that Gregory continued the abolition of simony, forbidding "under the direst penalties all and every and any investiture of any cleric (bishop, priest, abbot, deacon, sub deacon) by any lay ruler from the Holy Roman emperor down to the most impotent village squire in Haddam-Haddam, England."[122] His papal order was also meant to free the enormous real estate holdings of the church from control and possession by kings and princes. This was to strike at the very feudal system itself, the only system Europe at that time knew.

Gregory apparently was appraised of Alexander's suspicion - that there was still a Merovingian "echo" of Dagobert II about. The confiscation of royal land holdings, in addition to the abolition of simony, would keep Dagobert's descendents from becoming too powerful.

Gregory's plan, if successful, would have been as disastrous to the long-nurtured ambitions of the Merovingians as Alexander's. Hence, revolt against Gregory boiled over everywhere.[123] Meanwhile, the Calabrian monks continued to encourage Godfroi de Bouillon toward Jerusalem.

A KING OF JERUSALEM

Gregory died without achieving his goal of reform. In 1086, Victor Ill ascended the papal throne. He was no better than Gregory. He died mysteriously within a year. The next pope, however, was a Merovingian, according to the *Secret Dossiers*. The Merovingians through simony had achieved one of their goals. Urban II ascended the throne of Peter in 1088, just one decade before the First Crusade.

Meanwhile, Peter the Hermit tutored Godfroi de Bouillon on his selected appointment to become the King of Jerusalem. In 1090, Godfroi founded the "Order of Sion" in preparation for his mission. On that same date the Calabrian monks departed northern France, their destination Jerusalem.

---

[122] Malachi Martin, *The Decline and fall of the Roman Church* (New York: Bantam Books, 1983) 117-119.

[123] Pope Gregory's order set the stage for the Protestant Reformation, the withdrawal of Mystery Babylon from the Catholic Church, and the founding of English Freemasonry, the home of Mystery Babylon today. These events are fully discussed in chapter 25.

In 1095, Peter the Hermit, along with Pope Urban II, prepared Europe to mobilize against Palestine by preaching the need for a crusade -"a holy war that would reclaim Christ's sepulchre and the Holy Land from the hands of the Muslim infidel."[124] The Crusaders began to march toward Jerusalem. Ursus and Peter the Hermit were already there when the Crusaders arrived.

In 1099, Godfroi de Bouillon, with three other European potentates, conquered Jerusalem. Immediately the Calabrian monks convened in secret conclave with Ursus and Peter the Hermit to elect a King of Jerusalem. Godfroi de Bouillon was offered the throne.

At Godfroi's behest, an abbey was built on Mt. Zion which housed the Order of Sion. When Godfroi died one year later in 1100, his younger brother Baudouin, accepted the tide and throne of King of Jerusalem.

THE KNIGHTS TEMPLAR: PROTECTORS OF THE ORDER OF SION

To protect the new King of Jerusalem and his Sion cult, the Order of Sion backed Hugues de Payens in founding the Knights Templar, officially organized in 1118. De Payens, as the first Grand Master, created 13 degrees for the Templar Order, an important esoteric number that has enabled conspiracy researchers to track the movements of the Templars to the present.[125]

"The secret purpose for the Knights Templar," according to J.R. Church, "was to preserve the Merovingian bloodline in hopes of one day establishing a world government and putting their king upon the throne - a king who could claim to be the offspring of Jesus Christ and Mary Magdalene."[126]

The Knights had unofficially been in operation since 1114. At that earlier date they were known as milice du Christ, soldiers of Christ. In March, 1117, King Baudouin I, who owed his throne to the Order of Sion, took the constitution of the Knights Templar to the Order of Sion for approval. The Order of the Knights Templar was approved in 1118.

The Templars became the military and administrative arm of the Order of Sion. Their name derives from their quarters in Sion's fortified abbey above the ruins of Solomon's Temple. The specific site of the Knights' domicile, the wing of the royal palace on the Temple Mount, is believed to be of great significance, for somewhere beneath it was allegedly buried the unfathomable wealth of Solomon.

SOLOMON'S WEALTH

We are told in the New International Version of the Bible about King Solomon's tremendous wealth. I Kings 10:14 informs us that 25 tons of gold bullion came into Solomon's treasury every year for 40 years. Based on a modern standard of $400 an ounce, Solomon would have amassed almost $13 billion in gold bullion during his reign. I Kings also informs us that this wealth does not include "the revenues from merchants and traders and from all the Arabian kings and the governors of the land." According to I Kings, there was so much gold that silver was considered worthless during the days of Solomon.

---

[124] Baigent et al, *Holy Blood* 114.
[125] Miller 143.
[126] Church 25.

Solomon's gold came from a place called Ophir. He had built a navy to bring back the gold from this legendary place. There is also evidence in I Kings that the ships of Tarshish brought gold to Solomon from his mines at Ophir.

When Solomon died, his kingdom divided. Scripture makes no mention of hoards of gold being carried away by conquering kings. Only the gold used in building the Temple was taken, and that is far short of what Scripture indicates Solomon amassed.

The authors of *Holy Blood* trace the dispersal of Solomon's wealth centuries later: "In 70 A.D. the temple that then stood... was sacked by Roman legions under Titus. Its treasure was plundered and brought to Rome, then plundered again and perhaps brought to the Pyrenees [southern France]."[127] But these plunderings would still not exhaust the abundance of wealth described in Scripture. Where could Solomon's treasure have been hidden?

The Dead Sea Scrolls, discovered in 1949, provide a clue. One of the scrolls, the Copper Scroll, "deciphered at Manchester University in 1955-1956, makes explicit reference to great quantities of bullion, sacred vessels, additional unspecified material, and 'treasure' of an indeterminate kind. It cites twenty-four different hoards buried beneath the temple itself."[128]

THE WEALTH OF THE WARRIOR MONKS

According to the *Holy Blood* authors, "the fledgling order" of the Knights Templar, "almost immediately after its inception, undertook excavations beneath the temple."[129]

This "fledgling order," consisting only of nine men, had quartered their horses in the so-called Stables of Solomon directly beneath the temple mount itself and may at first have stumbled across Solomon's ancient treasury. Apparently, something had been found by 1104, because Hughes de Payens, soon-to-be first Grand Master of the Knights, sent word back to the Count of Champagne, his vassal lord in France. The count met immediately and secretly with certain high- ranking nobles, one of whom had already returned from Jerusalem with information of the discovery.

Shortly after this secret meeting the Count of Champagne departed for the Holy Land and remained there four years, apparently as an observer, returning to France in 1108. In 1114 he made a second journey to Palestine, intending to be initiated into the Knights Templar, still called the milice *du Christ*. He stayed only one year, however, returning hastily.

THE TEMPLAR INTELLIGENCE NETWORK

Apparently, while the count was in Jerusalem that year, the Knights, still consisting of nine men, found all the treasure beneath the temple. Returning to France in 1115, the Count began to prepare a depository.

---

[127] Baigent et al, *Holy Blood* 88.

[128] Baigent.Whether or not there were twenty-four different hoards of treasure still buried beneath Solomon's Temple, and whether or not it was successfully excavated by the Templars is not of consequence. What is of consequence is the fact that the conspirators "believe" it was there, and they believe it "was" excavated and carried to southern France, and there buried in man-made underground vaults. A "belief' can be perpetuated whether or not it has any basis of truth. Meanwhile, this "belief' has been woven into the esoteric doctrine and ritual of secret societies to this day. In the end, they can create a treasure when necessary.

[129] Baigent 89.

It was during this time that the Templars developed an intelligence support service to protect the transport of the treasury. John J. Robinson, author of Born *in Blood: The Lost Secrets of Freemasonry* (1989), informs us of the extent of the Templar intelligence network:

> *The Templars were known to maintain intelligence agents in the principal cities of the Middle East and the Mediterranean coast, and they would necessarily have employed covert means of communication. International financial dealings required total secrecy, naval operations required it to hide shipping information from Moslem or pirate forces, and military administration over two continents would certainly require it. As a matter of record, the Templars gained a reputation, and not a good one, for their dedication to secrecy, even in the meetings and councils of the order.*[130]

In the ten years that followed, the Templars became immensely wealthy. History informs us that they acquired their wealth from the Crusaders in payment for protection. What is not revealed is that there were only nine Knights to protect and collect from tens of thousands of Crusaders - an impossible task. Even the authorities of the day knew better. They questioned the Knights about the source of their wealth, especially their gold, and were told they had discovered the alchemical secret of the transmutation of metal.

PROPAGANDA AND INFLUENCE

Saint Bernard, the foremost spokesman for orthodox Christianity and a dominant influence in the Cistercian monastic order, was a major propagandist for the Templar image and reputation. This, of course, would be the appropriate response of a man who benefited from their wealth. The *Holy Blood* authors report that "By 1115 money was already flowing back to Europe and into the coffers of the Cistercians, who, under Saint Bernard and from their new position of strength, endorsed and imparted credibility to the fledgling Order of the Temple."[131]

A decade after the official founding of the Order of Knights Templar, however, there still were only nine members. By then Bernard was working for their establishment as a religious military priesthood in the Church. In one of his tracts he lauds their virtues and qualities, declaring the Templars to be the epitome and apotheosis of Christian values. In 1127, all nine had returned to Europe to a triumphal welcome, orchestrated in large part by Saint Bernard. In January 1128, a Church council convened at Troyes, and the Knights were officially recognized and incorporated as a religious-military order. Hughes de Payens was made Grand Master of the order.

Following their approval as an official religious-military order of the Church, the Knights Templar truly became warrior monks. By means of Templar wealth, Bernard guided the Cistercians to spiritual ascendancy in Europe, while Hughes de Payens and Andre de Montbard attained for the Templars a military and administrative ascendancy in the Holy Land, the fame of which quickly spread to Europe.

The next pope, not surprisingly, was a Cistercian monk. A protege' of Bernard of Clairvaux, Innocent II ascended the throne of Peter in 1130. In 1139, Innocent issued a papal bull that the Templars would owe allegiance to no secular or ecclesiastical power

---

[130] John J. Robinson, *Born in Blood: The lost secrets of Freemasonry* (New York: M. Evans & Company, 1989) 77.

[131] Baigent et al, *Holy Blood* 91.

other than himself. The authors of *Holy Blood* quite rightly note that the Templars "were rendered totally independent of all kings, princes, and prelates, and of all interference from both political and religious authorities. They had become, in effect, a law unto themselves, an autonomous international empire."[132]

In 1146, the Templars adopted their famous insignia: the splayed red cross of the Merovingians, placing it on their mantles, swords, buildings, and gravestones. The design changed somewhat over the years, but the cross always remained splayed. Researchers also trace the Templar movements across Europe, Scotland, and England by examining cemeteries for the gravestones displaying this insignia.

With the splayed cross emblazoned on their mantles, the Knights accompanied King Louis VII of France on the Second Crusade. "Here they established their reputation for martial zeal coupled with an almost insane foolhardiness and fierce arrogance as well," report the authors of *Holy Blood*. "On the whole, however, they were magnificently disciplined - the most disciplined fighting force in the world at the time."[133]

HERESY, PERVERSION AND BLOODSHED: TEMPLARS AND THE CATHARS

In 1153, Bertrand de Blanchefort, a nobleman from a Cathar family, became fourth Grand Master of the Knights Templar. The Cathars were a gnostic sect, also known as the Albigensians, a name derived from the town of Albi in southern France where an ecclesiastical council condemned them for heresy in 1165.

The ancestral home of Bertrand de Blanchefort was situated on a mountain peak a few miles away from Rennes-le-Chateau, where, it is alleged, the Templar treasure is buried. We can date the Templars' seeming descent into paganism from the ascension of Bertrand de Blanchefort to the position of Grand Master in 1153.

The Cathars held the gnostic doctrines that Freemasonry would embrace 500 years hence. For example, the Cathars replaced salvation by "faith" with salvation through "knowledge." They received their gnostic doctrines from the Jews, who preserved ancient esoterica in their *Cabala*. And they practiced religious tolerance, as does Freemasonry.

ANTI-PROCREATION

The practices of the Cathars reflected their dogmas. In seeking knowledge they practiced meditation. They were also strict vegetarians, although the eating of fish was allowed. They held the doctrine of reincarnation and recognized the feminine principle in religion. To control their population growth, their priesthood frowned upon any type of sexual union that would result in childbirth. Hence, they were the first known population controllers, experimenting with various methods of birth control, including abortion.

Sex for procreation was tolerated only for sustaining their race. Realizing that the lower elements in their society would not be able to eliminate their animal drives entirely, the Cathar priesthood introduced the practice of homosexuality and unnatural acts of sodomy, including intercourse with animals as a means of birth control.[134]

The Cathars' most serious heresy however was their denial that Christ was the Son of God. They considered Him a prophet no different from any other, a mortal being. They

---

[132] Baigent 68.
[133] Baigent 69.
[134] Arthur Lyons, *Satan Wants You* (New York: Mysterious Press,1988) 31.

vehemently repudiated the significance of both the crucifixion and the cross. They also denied the validity of such sacraments as baptism and the Catholic sacrament of Holy Eucharist.

A local council of the Roman Church, as we have noted, had condemned the Cathar, or Albigensian heresy in 1165. But by 1200, Rome itself had grown distinctly alarmed at the heresy of the Cathars. The Papacy charged them with "unnatural sexual practices," which was taken to mean homosexuality and bestiality. Although these charges were true, their purpose was to incite the northern nobles against them.

On January 14, 1208, one of the papal legates to southern France was murdered, but not by the Cathars. Some suggest the murder was a set-up by Rome - to create a martyr. At any rate, Rome did not hesitate to blame the Cathars. At once Pope Innocent III ordered a crusade. The heresy was to be extirpated once and for all. A bloodbath ensued, which went unequalled until World Wars I and II in our 20th century. Thus began the Inquisitions.

It was into these Cathar communities in southern France that the Knights Templar, founder of French Freemasonry, settled in the early and mid-1100s.

MONEY, POWER AND POLITICS: SOLOMON'S WEALTH

Bertrand de Blanchefort is credited with transforming the Knights Templar into the superbly efficient, well-organized, and magnificently disciplined hierarchical institution it eventually became. Under his administration, the Knights in 1156 imported to the area of Rennes-le-- Chateau a contingent of German-speaking miners. According to the authors of Holy *Blood*, "Their alleged task was to work the gold mines on the slopes of the mountain of Blanchefort - gold mines that had been utterly exhausted by the Romans nearly a thousand years before."[135]

The truth is otherwise. The German workers were not mining. Later investigations reveal they were "smelting, perhaps, melting something down, constructing something out of metal, perhaps even excavating a subterranean crypt of some sort and creating a species of depository."[136]

THE TEMPLARS:
INTERNATIONAL BANKERS AND POWER BROKERS

The German workers are believed to have been digging great underground vaults in which to store the vast wealth discovered by the Templars beneath Solomon's Temple - wealth the Templars had smelted down. Almost immediately afterward, report the authors of *Holy Blood*, the Templars "created and established the institution of modern banking. By lending large sums to destitute monarchs they became the bankers for every throne in Europe... With their network of preceptories throughout Europe and the Middle East, they also organized, at modest interest rates, the safe and efficient transfer of money for merchant traders... Money deposited in one city, for example, could be claimed and withdrawn in another by means of promissory notes inscribed in intricate codes. The Templars thus became the primary money changers of the age, and the Paris preceptory

---

[135] Baigent et al, *Holy Blood* 93.
[136] Baigent.

became the center of European finance. It is even probable that the check as we know and use it today was invented by the order."[137]

No medieval institution did more for the rise of capitalism than the Templars:

> During the next hundred years the Templars became a power with international influence. They were constantly engaged in high-level diplomacy among nobles and monarchs throughout the Western world and the Holy Land.
> We can turn to England for an example of how pervasive Templar influence was in Europe. So powerful was the Master of the Temple, that he was regularly called to the King's parliament and was regarded as head of all religious orders, taking precedence over all priors and abbots in the land.[138]

At one point England even stored part of the crown jewels with the Templars.[139] When King Richard the Lion-Hearted took his English army on a Crusade to the Holy Land, he lived with the Knights Templars at Acre in 1191. In June 1215, when King John signed the Magna Carta, a document constituting a fundamental guarantee of rights and privileges, the master of the Knights Templar stood by.

On almost every political level the Templars acted as official arbiters in disputes, and even kings submitted to their authority. So powerful had they become that they could make or depose monarchs at will.

THE FALL OF JERUSALEM: PLOT OR HAPPENSTANCE?

Within seven decades of their founding, instead of being the protector of Sion's Merovingian "King of Jerusalem" cult, the Templars began to neglect that role. While attaining prosperity and notoriety in Europe, they permitted the situation in the Holy Land to deteriorate seriously. The Order of Sion, for which the Knights had taken a blood oath to defend and obey, was weakened. The authors of Holy *Blood, Holy Grail* tell the story:

> In 1185 King Baudouin IV of Jerusalem died. In the dynastic squabble that followed, Gerard de Ridefort, grand master of the Temple, betrayed an oath made to the dead monarch and thereby brought the European community in Palestine to the brink of civil war. Nor was this Ridefort's only questionable action. His cavalier attitude toward the Saracens precipitated the rupture of a long-standing truce and provoked a new cycle of hostilities. Then, in July 1187, Ridefort led his knights, along with the rest of the Christian army, into a rash, misconceived, and as it transpired, disastrous battle at Hattin. The Christian forces were virtually annihilated; and two months later Jerusalem itself, captured nearly a century before, was again in Saracen hands.[140]

Apparently the abandonment of Jerusalem was planned, for after obtaining the 24 hoards of wealth beneath Solomon's Temple and transporting it to secret underground vaults in southern France, the Templars' loyalty to the Order of Sion and its Merovingian

---

[137] Baigent 71.
[138] Baigent 69.
[139] Robinson 74.
[140] Baigent et al, *Holy Blood* 72.

kings turned to animosity. Perhaps the Knights viewed the Order of Sion as a rival to be eliminated.

THE "CUTTING OF THE ELM" AT GISORS BY THE FOUNDERS OF TWO MODERN FREEMASONRIES

A text in the *Dossiers secret* from the Priory of Sion parchments found at Rennes-le-Chateau does suggest that the Knights were planning the destruction of the Order of Sion. As the *Holy* Grail investigators state, "It speaks not of Gerard's impetuosity or ineptitude, but of his 'treason' - a very harsh word indeed. What constituted this 'treason' is not explained. But as a result of it the 'initiates' of Sion are said to have returned en masse to France - presumably to Orleans [in northern France]."[141]

Gerard de Ridefort's "treason" of 1187, whatever it was, resulted in the loss of Jerusalem, and precipitated a disastrous rift between the Order of Sion and the Knights Templar. According to the *Dossiers secret,* the following year witnessed a decisive turning point in the affairs of both orders. In 1188 a formal separation occurred when the Order of Sion, which had created the Knights Templar, washed its hands of its celebrated protégé. This rupture is recorded in the *Dossiers secret* as a ritual or ceremony of some sort, and is referred to as the "cutting of the elm." The event took place at Gisors, a city close to the coast of northern France, and under the control of the English monarchy.

The Priory documents cloak in allegory and symbology what happened at Gisors. Some sort of bloody battle between King Henry II of England and King Philippe II of France, however, did occur there in 1188. Apparently, at the end of the battle a truce was made, and a huge elm tree was cut down as a symbol of that truce. The *Holy Blood* authors suggest that both the Knights Templar and the Order of Sion were involved in the conflict. The "cutting of the elm" was therefore symbolic of their division and truce as well. Their truce, as we shall see, apparently was to allow each to operate independently of the other.

At Gisors, when the King of England took sides with Sion, London became its new protector. From 1188 on, the Order of Sion remained headquartered in northern France under its English protectors, while the Knights Templars remained headquartered at Rennes-le-Chateau in southern France, where their wealth is alleged to have been hidden. Sion would eventually give birth to Rosicrucianism and English Freemasonry as we know it today. From the Knights Templar would emerge its revolutionary offspring - French Freemasonry.

SION AND ENGLAND

"Following the battle at Gisors, the Order of Sion underwent a major administrative restructuring of its own, changing its name to the Priory of Sion, and selecting as its first Grand Master, Jean de Gisors, a vassal of the King of England. The Grand Master also possessed property in England."[142]

The Priory of Sion went by another name as well - "Ormus." Secret societies are known to change names for the purpose of concealment when embarking on some clandestine activity. The Priory of Sion was planning such an activity. Although Sion had agreed to permit the Templars to operate independently, Sion did not intend to leave the

---

[141] Baigent 120.
[142] Baigent 120.

Templars their wealth. Instead her initiates prepared to penetrate their adversary's Order for the purpose of reclaiming Solomon's wealth.

CULT ELEMENTS OF SION

The word *Ormus* contained within its spelling the history of Sion. Its symbol was shaped like a capital M. Within the frame of the M were four letters - OR and US - which together with the M spell "Ormus." These letters combine a number of other key words and symbols important to Sion. *"Ours* means 'bear' in French. *Ursus,* or echo in Latin, suggested, as subsequently became apparent, Dagobert II and the Merovingian dynasty. *Orme* is French for 'elm.' Or, of course, is 'gold.' And the M that forms the frame enclosing the other letters is not only an M but also the astrological sign for Virgo - connoting, in the language of medieval iconography, Notre Dame"[143] - which in France is not commemorative of the Virgin Mary, but of Mary Magdalene.

The name *Ormus* also represents Sion's religion. Ormus was the name of an Egyptian sage and mystic who was supposedly converted to Christianity in 46 A.D. In reality he was a gnostic adept of Alexandria, blending Christianity with Masdaism, which was the Greek-Roman form of Zoroastrianism. Zoroastrianism was a modification of Brahamanism (now Hinduism) at a time when Buddhism was a reformation of the same. As was common practice in the eastern mystery religions, the Priory of Sion often used mind-expanding drugs in their ceremonies.

The Priory of Sion set out to emulate the Knights Templar by using the religion of the Egyptian, Ormus. Ormus and his initiates had taken the red cross as their identifying symbol four centuries before Merovee (founder of the Merovingian Holy Grail dynasty) was born with the red cross birthmark above his heart. The Knights Templar adopted Merovee's red cross six centuries later. To emulate the Templars, the Priory of Sion took the red cross of Ormus as its own emblem, then adopted the title *l'Ordre de la Rose-Croix Veritas,* which means "The Order of the mie Red Cross." This additional name was added at the behest of Sion's Grand Master, Jean de Gisors.[144] Thus, Jean de Gisors is considered the founder of the Rose-Croix, or Rosicrucians.

At that time, Sion adopted the "eye" of the Egyptian god Osiris as its symbol. The same "eye" is known as the "third eye" of knowledge in the Hindu religion, which was adopted by the Templars. In Freemason~ it is known as the "All-Seeing Eye."

With so many similarities to the Knights Templar, the Priory of Sion had no difficulty penetrating their adversary's ranks.

SATANISM AND "SACRAMENTAL" DRUGS IN SECRET SOCIETIES: THE TEMPLARS EMBRACE THE DEVIL AND DRUGS

Following their schism from the Order of Sion at Gisors, the Knights Templar plunged into Satanism. They had encountered eastern mysticism in part from their stay in the Holy Land, and partially through integrating with the Cathars. From the Cathars they had imbibed the secret doctrines of gnosticism.

As in the Priory of Sion rituals, drugs had an important role in Templar rituals. The *Holy Blood* authors tell us that the Knights acquired their knowledge of drugs from their close association with the "Hashishim, or Assassins [Medieval Mafia], the famous sect of

---

[143] Baigent 122.
[144] Church 86-87.

militant and often fanatical adepts who were Islam's equivalent of the Templars. The Hashishim paid tribute to the Temple and were rumored to be in its employ."[145]

The founder of the Hashishim was a Persian by the name of Hasan Saba. The drug "hashish" and the name "assassin" are both derived from Hashishim. Before performing an assassination, Hasan's adepts took this addictive drug to give them courage. From them the Templars acquired the knowledge of manufacturing hashish and using it for their own wounded in battle - eventually incorporating its use into their pagan rituals.

The Templars were also well-versed in Hindu doctrine. They practiced Yoga to reach an altered state of consciousness to open the "third eye." This was known as white magic. When they practiced black magic they reached the same altered state of consciousness more rapidly through the use of mind-expanding drugs.[146]

Drug use by both the Templars and the Sionists was carried into the degenerate lodges of both Freemasonries. In future chapters and in volume three of *Scarlet and the Beast,* we shall learn how our modern drug traffic flows through, and is protected by these sub-lodges.

As the Templars descended deeper into drugs and witchcraft they saw Jesus Christ as their enemy and began to hate the Catholic Church. Gradually they abandoned Catholicism, becoming worshipers of the Baphomet, a pagan symbol of Satan pictured as a goat head within an upside- down star. The Templars also adopted the Satanic symbol of the skull and crossbones, which symbol of death would follow them throughout their migrations, even to the city where they are presently headquartered. The use of the skull and crossbones persisted in Freemasonry, where it became the symbol of the Master Mason until after World War II. It was dropped because Hitler used it as an emblem for his SS.[147]

According to the gnostic dualism of Templar doctrine, God had two sons - Jesus and Satan. Jesus was the younger brother. From their Catholicism, the Templars understood Jesus was good and Satan was evil. Yet, they taught that "The elder son of God, Satanael or Lucifer alone has a right to the homage of mortals; Jesus his younger brother does not deserve this honour."[148] Perhaps this doctrine developed because of the animosity of the Templars toward the Merovingians, the so- called offspring of Jesus and Mary Magdalene.

The Templars' most fervent worship was addressed to this god of evil, who alone could enrich them, and indeed he had. No doubt they understood the Lucifer of eastern myths, of whom in the 1930s British author Warren Weston wrote in *Father of Lies:*

> *In his conceit, he pretends to have inspired in man all the inventions of the human reason. "He is Prometheus, the friend of men, who gave them fire, taught them all the crafts, showed them the rich ore and precious stones buried in the earth, and so forth. It is for these countless benefactions conferred on humanity that the jealous spirits who claim to be true gods have combined against him and wronged him. He is [to the pagan] the brightest angel unjustly cast out of heaven, Lucifer, son of the morning."[149]*

---

[145] Baigent et al, *Holy Blood* 71.

[146] Church 46, 134.

[147] *Intercessors for America* (October 1988) 4. Today it is the symbol of a century old secret society on the campus of Yale University. The society is called "Skull and Bones." President George Bush became a life-time member when he was a student at Yale.

[148] Webster, *Secret* Societies 64.

[149] Warren Weston, *Father of* Lies (London: N.p., 1930s) 29.

DESTRUCTION OF THE KNIGHTS TEMPLAR

If the Priory of Sion knew of the riches beneath the Temple Mount at Jerusalem, and was aware that the Templars had found them, as the authors of Holy *Blood, Holy Grail* suggest, the "treason" of the Knights may have been that they absconded with the treasure. Sion, now devoid of funds and unprotected, was compelled to find and retrieve Solomon's vast wealth if she was to further her cause of world dominion.

Within two generations after the Priory of Sion and the Templars parted company at Gisors in 1188, European royalty was once again Merovingian through intermarriage. Yet, Sion's monarchs, instead of holding the gold from beneath Solomon's Temple were borrowing it. More and more they found themselves financially indebted to their own Templar creation.

A SECRET INTELLIGENCE NETWORK

King Philip the Fair of France (Philip *W)* was one of the Merovingian beggar monarchs. History tells us that at the turn of the 14th century he became alarmed at Templar power and coveted their wealth. He decided to act. What ensued was the immediate, and almost perfectly accomplished destruction of their order. So swift was the collapse of the Templars, it seems doubtful to have been the work of a single monarch. Yet it was nearly impossible for other kings to have assisted Philip. The Templars dominated royal courts throughout Europe and England. They themselves were well-seasoned subversives, operating an intelligence network second to none, with spies everywhere.

Yet, in an atmosphere of unequaled secrecy King Philip completely destroyed the Templars. We must therefore assume that he had a superior intelligence force which history does not record. For Philip to have accomplished what he did necessitated, at the least, the assistance of a society equal in secrecy and subversion to the Templars - one that had the same symbols, that knew their grips and passwords - to infiltrate their ranks. This could only have been the Priory of Sion.

There are certain Priory documents that imply Sion oversaw the demise of the Templars. Although the authors of *Holy Blood* do not commit themselves to this hypothesis, they make a statement which can be so interpreted. They report that "after the formal separation in 1188, Sion did in fact continue to exercise some clandestine control over Temple affairs."[150] This "clandestine control" could have been subversive, exercised by infiltrators, spies, and double agents not necessarily that of accomplices.

THE KIDNAPPING AND DEATH OF A POPE

King Philip realized the Vatican had to be brought into the intrigue. The Knights Templar, regardless of its blasphemy, was still an arm of the Catholic Church. So wealthy were the Templars that no pope dare agree to their destruction - unless he realized gain for the Church, or for himself. Therefore, Philip planned for his own pope to sit on the throne of Peter, one that would do his bidding. This meant getting rid of the existing pope.

Between 1303 and 1305 the French King, along with his ministers, engineered the kidnapping and death of Pope Boniface VIII, and quite possibly poisoned Pope Benedict XI. In 1305 the archbishop of Bordeaux ascended the papal throne, taking the name

---

[150] Baigent et al, *Holy Blood* 127.

Clement V. He was King Philip's own candidate - one with Merovingian blood. The authors of *Holy Blood* inform us, "Indebted as he was to Philippe's influence, he could hardly refuse the king's demands. And these demands included the eventual suppression of the Knights Templar."[151]

RECOUPING THE HOLY GRAIL

While Philip the Fair's main objective was acquiring the Templar wealth, the Priory of Sion was concerned with retrieving something more significant than Solomon's riches. The Templars apparently had in their custody the Holy Grail, supposedly the cup used at the Last Supper by Christ before His crucifixion. According to legend, Joseph of Arimathaea, Mary Magdalene's alleged uncle, held the cup at the foot of the cross, filling it with Christ's Holy Blood. In her flight to southern France in 70 A.D., Mary Magdalene had carried the cup and blood with her. Some believe it was taken to the vicinity of Rennes-le-Chateau. The Priory of Sion wanted to retrieve the cup from the Templars, as well as the wealth alleged to be stored there.

Rev. Church provides a clue to the cup's location today. In *Guardians of the Grail*, he says, "Some accounts say that Joseph took the Grail on to England, while other accounts hold that Mary Magdalene kept the Grail in France."[152]

These speculations about the Grail's whereabouts may have developed after the persecution of the Knights. Mary Magdalene, or some imposter claiming to be the Magdalene, may have taken the so-called Holy Grail to southern France in the year 70 A.D. At some later date, perhaps at the beginning of the 14th century, it was removed by someone, or some institution, and taken to England. If the Priory of Sion was that institution, it would naturally hide its action behind the "Joseph of Arimathaea" allegory. Therefore, both legends would have some basis in truth.

A SUDDEN, SWIFT AND LETHAL BLOW

King Philip, as a Merovingian attempting to acquire the Templar wealth, most certainly solicited help from the Priory of Sion, which had its own motives for assisting him. With such superior assistance he planned his moves carefully. The *Holy* Blood authors inform us that "A list of charges was compiled, partly from the king's spies [possibly Sionist] who had infiltrated the order, partly from the voluntary confession of an alleged renegade Templar. Armed with these accusations, Philippe could at last move; and when he delivered his blow, it was sudden, swift, efficient, and lethal."[153]

Before the king took action against the Templars in 1307, the Priory of Sion made one of the most debilitating moves in intelligence operations, one that polarized the Knights Templar. In 1306, the Priory of Sion lifted its veil, exposing its true identity by dropping the cover "Ormus." The Knights were confounded when suddenly they realized their persecutors were not the King and Pope, but rather, their century-old enemy. How many from the Priory of Sion had infiltrated their ranks was impossible for the Templars to know. To fight would be futile.

---

[151] Baigent 75.
[152] Church 76.
[153] Baigent et al, *Holy Blood* 75.

CONVENTIONAL HISTORY PERPLEXED

Conventional history is perplexed by the Knights' failure to offer resistance. A revisionist perspective, however, can account for their sudden collapse: they were psychologically and militarily unprepared against their foes. The authors of *Holy Blood* describe it this way: "In a security operation worthy of the SS or Gestapo, the king issued sealed and secret orders to his seneschals throughout the country. These orders were to be opened everywhere simultaneously and implemented at once. At dawn on Friday, October 13, 1307, all Templars in France were to be seized and placed under arrest by the king's men, their preceptories placed under royal sequestration, their goods confiscated."[154]

FRIDAY THE 13TH

"Friday-the-13th" has since entered the culture as a "bad omen" day. The Priory of Sion did not in ignorance choose Friday-the-13th for their attack upon the Templars. Well aware of the significance the Templars placed on the esoteric value of this number (its Order contained 13 degrees), the Priory must have realized the debilitating effect an attack on this day would have. King Philip, on the other hand, was probably less discerning. All he wanted was the Templars' immense wealth, which eluded him. It was never found, which is strange indeed, for in Paris was the Templars' central bank for all Europe. The preceptory there would have stored the largest cache of gold, second only to that which was allegedly hidden at Rennes-le-Chateau.

ANOTHER DOUBLE-CROSS?

Had the Priory of Sion double-crossed King Philip, too? Circumstantial evidence supports this conclusion. For instance, throughout the period of this intrigue, Guillaume Pidoye - one of the king's men and guardian and administrator of the Templar goods at the Paris preceptory after the arrest of the Templars - was also a colleague of Guillaume de Gisors, the Grand Master of Sion. If Pidoye was himself a Sionist, which seems to have been the case, he would certainly have been more loyal to his Grand Master than to the King.

The *Holy Blood* authors also suggest that Pidoye acted as a "double agent," warning the Templars of their impending arrest at the Paris preceptory. This would appear to have been an act of treason against both the king and Sion. According to legend, sometime before Fridaythe- 13th, the treasury in the preceptory, together with almost all its documents and records, was transported to the Templar naval base at LaRochelle, and loaded into eighteen galleys, which were never heard of again.

Why would Pidoye warn the Templars? It is unlikely he would warn the enemy of his Sionist Grand Master. He would more likely inform Guillaume de Gisors of the King's impending move against the Templars.

The authors of *Holy Blood* hint at another explanation when they suggest that the Grand Master of Sion "might have been partially responsible for... the unexplained disappearance of its treasure."[155]

---

[154] Baigent 127.
[155] Baigent.

Alerting the Templars would then be part of an intricately woven plan. Pidoye may not have been a "double agent" as has been suggested, but a "triple agent." Pidoye knew Sion had no means of transporting Templar gold to the coast. Nor had they any ships. Only the Knights Templar had means of transport, with a fleet at La Rochelle. If tipped off in advance, the Knights could reach the port city in time. Pidoye, as representative of the king, would feign sympathy toward the Templars, warning them of impending danger, suggesting they transport their wealth out of the country before Friday-the-13th. As a triple agent, he would then inform the Grand Master of Sion of the gold transport. The Priory in turn would instruct its protector, the English navy, to intercept and scuttle the ships after confiscating the gold. The gold would then be taken to England.

ENGLISH COMPLICITY AND NEW POWER

Although this hypothesis can never be proved, it is interesting to note that England, over the next century, rapidly became the dominant power in the old world. The wealth of the Templars could most certainly lie at the heart of what was eventually to become the British Empire.

Another indication that the English may have assisted the Priory of Sion is the fact that the Knights Hospitaller of St. John, or the Hospitallers as they came to be known, acquired the holdings of the Templars after their 1314 persecution. The Hospitallers were the 12th century English competitors of the Knights Templars during the Crusades.[156] After the Saracens regained Jerusalem from the Crusaders in 1187, one group of Hospitallers landed on the island of Rhodes, changing its name to the Temple of St. John of Jerusalem, and the other landed on the island of Malta, changing its name to the Knights of Malta. British journalist Stephen Knight, author of *The Brotherhood* (1984), states that both orders are today English Masonic Military Orders.[157] Moreover, the authors of *The Messianic Legacy* state that the Knights of Malta are also today viewed as an ideal conduit for English Masonic intelligence gathering.[158]

A third indication that the British may have assisted the Priory of Sion at La Rochelle is the fact that the Templars fled to Scotland soon after their suppression and there fought alongside King Robert Bruce, who was at war with England. Why would the Templars travel to such a remote place and take arms against England, unless it was related to the disappearance of their galleys at La Rochelle and the confiscation of all their holdings by the English controlled Hospitallers?

MYSTERY AT RENNES-LE-CHATEAU: GRAIL AND GOLD

In the seizure of the Templars, their property and wealth, that Templar stronghold, Rennes-le- Chateau, would not have been overlooked. Hidden in man-made vaults in the hills above the chateau was the Holy Grail and the alleged wealth of Solomon. Investigation into the activities at Rennes-le-Chateau reveal, however, that of all the Templars arrested, those stationed at this small hamlet in southern France went untouched, causing the *Holy Blood* investigators to suggest that Pope Clement was a double agent, working for the Templars instead of the king. But why? Had Clement not

---

[156] Michael Baigent and Richard Leigh, *The Temple and The Lodge* (New York: Arcade Publishing, 1989) 95, 99.
[157] Knight, The Brotherhood 44.
[158] Baigent et al, The Messianic Legacy 360.

agreed to the assassination of two of his predecessors in order to obtain the throne of Peter. Why protect the Templars now?

The authors of *Holy Blood* suggest several reasons: (1) Pope Clement's family was from that area; (2) the Pope still knew many people there, even those guarding the chateau; and (3) history reveals he was slow to prosecute the Templars, although hand-picked by the king to do so.

A slightly different reading of these facts, however, offers a more plausible reason for the protection of Rennes-le-Chateau. The failure of authorities to move against such a significant stronghold might have been because the garrison was not manned by Templars. Because the Pope was a Merovingian, he would not be likely to protect guards who were Templars. What if the guards were imposters - imposters dressed like Templars, who, perhaps, were Sionist? This suggestion is not without merit, since the "Joseph of Arimathaea" legend states that the Holy Grail was taken to England.

History does not record what happened to the Templar wealth, either at the Paris depository, or at Rennes-le-Chateau. Yet we do well to listen to the claim made in 1981 by Pierre Plantard, the contemporary Grand Master of the Priory of Sion, to the authors of *The Messianic* Legacy: "The Order actually possesses the lost treasure of the Temple of Jerusalem. It will be returned to Israel when the time is right."[159]

One thing is certain: when the Templars were crushed, all mention of what happened to their wealth was purged from history.

Rennes-le-Chateau remains an enigma. History has forgotten the untouched Templars stationed there. Their fate remains a mystery to this day. Meanwhile, England rose rapidly during the next four centuries to become the most powerful and the most wealthy nation on earth. Today London is the financial center of the world. Is it because of Templar wealth?

THE CURSE OF THE KNIGHTS TEMPLAR: OCCULT POWERS?

The year 1307 did not complete the Inquisition of the Templars. Jacques de Molay, Grand Master of the Knights Templar, was still at large. When he was captured seven years later in 1314, he was tried and burned at the stake.

The authors of Holy *Blood* describe the aftermath of Jacques de Mo. lay's execution: "As the smoke from the slow fire choked the life from his body, Jacques de Molay is said to have issued an imprecation from the flames. According to tradition he called his persecutors - Pope Clement and King Philippe - to join and account for themselves before the court of God within the year.

Within a month Pope Clement was dead, supposedly from a sudden onslaught of dysentery. By the end of the year Philippe was dead as well, from causes that remain obscure to this day. There is, of course, no need to look for supernatural explanations. The Templars possessed great expertise in the use of poisons..."[160] For that matter, we must remember, so did the Priory of Sion. They too had reason to eliminate the king, whom they double-crossed, and the pope, who knew too much.

Nevertheless, the apparent fulfillment of Jacques de Molay's curse lent credence to belief in the Templars' occult powers. Furthermore, according to legend the curse did not end there. It was to cast a pall over the French royal line far into the future.[161]

---

[159] Baigent et al, XIII.
[160] Baigent et al, *Holy Blood* 79.
[161] Baigent.

JACQUES DE MOLAY AND THE "THIRD DEGREE"

The Templars would never forgive Crown and Church for their destruction. There would be a day of reckoning. To keep vivid their memory of this atrocity, the Templars who fled to Scotland adopted the legend of the death of Hiram Abif- the alleged builder of Solomon's Temple in Freemasonry - as symbolic of the destruction of their order, the loss of their wealth, and the death of their Grand Master, Jacques de Molay.[162]

Today the legend of Hiram Abif is acted out during initiation into the Master Mason degree, called the 3rd degree. From then until now, when someone says, "He gave me the third degree," the person is unaware of using an expression which derives from the inquisition of Jacques de Molay.

THE TEMPLARS FLEE TO SCOTLAND

When the Templars were suppressed throughout Europe and England during the early 14th century, they fled to Scotland, which was at war with England at the time. In Scotland alone were the Templars protected. The authors of Holy *Blood, Holy Grail* state that "Many English and, it would appear, French Templars found a Scottish refuge, and a sizable contingent is said to have fought at [King] Robert Bruce's side at the Battle of Bannockburn in 1314. According to the legend - and there is evidence to support it - the order maintained itself as a coherent body in Scotland for another four centuries."[163]

THE TEMPLARS AND FRENCH FREEMASONRY: INTERNATIONAL BANKING

A descendant of Robert Bruce, James Stuart VI, reigned in Scotland from 1567 until he ascended the British throne in 1603 at the request of childless Queen Elizabeth I. The Stuarts, and their ancestry, were all initiated into the Order of the Knights Templar in Scotland, bringing to London a contingent of Scottish Templars. The Knights who traveled from Scotland to reside in London purchased property there, which they Still own today. A fascinating fact is that built upon this land is the financial district of London, which currently clears most international banking transactions daily.

THE BIBLE AND SION

AS we know, during James Stuart's British reign (1603-1625), the Christian world received the first English translation of the Bible - called the King James Version (KJV). Among the conclave of scholars who presided over the translation was Robert Fludd Grand Master of the priory of Sion.[164] Interestingly, throughout the translation of the New Testament, when reference is made to Zion the spelling is found in its French form - Sion!

SCOTTISH RITE MASONRY

---

[162] Webster 110.

[163] Baigent et al, *Holy Blood* 77.

[164] Baigent 426.

During the reign of James Stuart the embryo of Scottish Rite Freemasonry began to develop in England. At that time it was called Jacobite Freemasonry in memory of Jacques de Molay. James and his descendants were all members of the Royalist Jacobite Lodges, which practiced Templar rituals. The Templars also infiltrated the "operative" or working man's lodge at York. Later its rituals became known to Masons as the York Rite.

The Templar-Stuart reign in England was short-lived. Sion once again uprooted the Templars. Robert Fludd, the first British Grand Master of Sion, was appointed for that express purpose. The Stuart expulsion was swift and complete, and as we have seen, they were exiled to France following the Glorious Revolution of 1688. The Priory of Sion then united the scattered lodges of English Freemasonry under one Grand Mother Lodge in 1717. Sion has remained in control of the British Brotherhood to this day.[165]

The Scottish Templars of course returned to France with the exile of Prince Charles Edward Stuart and founded French Freemasonry in 1725. By 1755 it was known as the Scottish Rite, with 32 degrees. In France, as in Scotland, the Templars have left behind the symbols of their presence: the octagonal symbol and their number "13."

TEMPLARISM = FRENCH FREEMASONRY

Today French Freemasonry is Templarism. Since the Templars never retrieved their wealth from England, French Freemasonry remains financially destitute to this day. The war between the Knights Templar and the Priory of Sion, which began at Gisors with the "Cutting of the Elm" in 1188, still rages between English and French Freemasonry.

Freemasonry honors the Templars in various degrees in both the Scottish and York Rite. The Order of DeMolay in America is the secret society for sons of Masons in honor of the Templar Grand Master, Jacques de Molay. It is easy to see the ideals of the early pagan Templars in modern Masonry.

Mackey's Encyclopedia of Freemasonry confirms the evolution of Templarism into Freemasonry: "From Larmenius came the French Templars. From Aumont, the German Templars of Strict Observance. From Beaujeu, the Swedish Templars of the rite of Zinnendorf From the Protestant Templars of Scotland and the Ancient Lodge of Stirling, the Scotch Templars. From Prince Charles Edward [the Stuart King who fled to France when deposed in 1688] and his adherents, the Templars of the Ancient and Accepted Scottish Rite."[166]

SION AND ENGLISH FREEMASONRY

We have followed the Templars from the "Cutting of the Elm" at Gisors in 1188 to the creation of French Freemasonry in 1725. Now we will return to Gisors and trace the activity of the Order of Sion to its creation of English Freemasonry.

After the "Cutting of the Elm" in 1188, while the Templars were developing their Order into an international banking institution, the Order of Sion modified its name to the Prieure de (Priory of) Sion. To conceal more deeply the name "Sion," the Priory took the name "Ormus," also adopting the title *l'Ordre de la Rose-Croix Veritas,* or The Order of

---

[165] Do not confuse Sion, which is not Jewish, with true Jewish Zionism.
[166] "Knights Templar, Masonic," *Mackey's Encyclopedia,* vol.1. Most of these men are famous only to Freemasonry and are not known to the general historian.

the True Red Cross. This additional name was added at the behest of the Priory's first Grand Master Jean de Gisors. It was he who founded the *Rose-Croix, or Rosicrucianism.*

ROSICRUCIANISM

Four centuries later another Grand Master of Sion, Johann Valentin Andrea (GM 1637-1654), popularized the Rose-Croix as Rosicrucianism in the legend of Christian Rosenkreuz - with his famous *Chemical Wedding of Christian Rosenkreuz.* According to this legend, Rosenkreuz founded Rosicrucianism near the time that the Priory of Sion, Pope Clement V, and King Philip the Fair persecuted the Templars. The Grand Master of the Priory of Sion at that time was Guillaume de Gisors, the same Grand Master who assisted in the confiscation of the Templar wealth. He is credited by Andrea with organizing the Rosicrucians into a type of Hermetic Freemasonry. He probably is the fictitious model for the Christian Rosenkreuz.

SATAN VERSUS JESUS

We have discussed many of the pagan elements of Rosicrucianism in the Introduction, but now will return to one in particular that illustrates the similarity of doctrine held by the Templars and the Rosicrucians: a gnostic belief in a dualistic universe.

As noted before, the Rosicrucian-Freemason Gustav Carl Jung remarked that the "[Christian] cross and [Rosicrucian] rose represent the Rosicrucian problem of opposites, that is the Christian and Dionysian elements..." In his explanation of the meaning of the cross and rose intertwined in the Rosicrucian emblem, Jung confirms the Rosicrucian belief that Satan has the same redemptive qualities as does Jesus Christ - the same belief held by the Rosicrucians' gnostic adversaries - the Templars. The name *Christian Rosenkreuz* (Christian rose-cross or snake-cross) itself illustrates the Rosicrucian belief in dualism. And the Rose-Croix is the red cross of Satan - a blasphemous insult to the cross of Christ.

PROTESTANTS AND ROSICRUCIANISM

As we have seen, many Protestants joined the Rosicrucian movement in order to fight the Catholic Church - which they viewed as a common enemy. The Reformation embodied by these Protestants, however, was a "reformation" in name only, for they were spiritually dead, having drunk a deceptive and deadly mix of Christianity and paganism.

Again Scripture prophesies this period of church history in the book of Revelation. The period of the Reformation, according to Clarence Larkin, is signified by the Church at Sardis. The word Sardis means *those escaped.*[167] These Christians were escaping the Thyatira Church age, in other words Roman Catholicism. Jesus, through the apostle John, speaks to their weakened condition in Revelation 3:1-3:

> *I know thy works, that thou hast a name that thou livest, and art dead. Be watchful, and strengthen the things which remain, that are ready to die: for I have*

---

[167] Bible, Pilgrim Edition, footnote on Church of Sardis, Revelation 2.

not found thy works perfect before God. Remember therefore how thou hast received and heard, and hold fast, and repent.

Rosicrucians, having recruited the support of Scripturally weak Protestants, achieved their political goals with the Glorious Revolution of England by planting the seeds of revolutionary thought in the Masonic Lodges. The Rosicrucians expanded their secret society through the operative masonic guilds of Protestant England.

FOUNDER OF ENGLISH FREEMASONRY

Thus we can see how the Priory of Sion, via the Rosicrucians, founded English Freemasonry. Since both streams of Freemasonry were born in London, we again see both English and French Masonry commemorating Rosicrucianism in their Masonic rituals. *Mackey's Encyclopedia of Freemasonry* lists the Rosicrucian degrees in various rites of Masonry: "The Seventh Degree of the French Rite. The Seventh Degree of the Philalethes. The Eighth degree of the Mother Lodge of the Philosophic Scottish Rite. The Twelfth degree of the Elect of Truth. The Eighteenth Degree of the Mother Scottish Lodge of Marseilles. The Eighteenth Degree of the Rite of Heredom, or of Perfection."[168]

We will now turn to the cause of the first Masonic revolution called the Glorious Revolution of 1688 in England, which was a civil war between Sion and the Templars.

---

[168] "Rose Croix," *Mackey's Encyclopedia of Free masonry*, vol.11. You will notice that Rosicrucianism and Templarism continually mix, although adversarial. The reasons are two:(1)Although enemies, they are Brothers; (2) They crave to learn each other's occult secrets. These facts have confused conspiracy historians, who subsequently write of only one conspiracy.

2. ENGLISH FREEMASONRY AND REVOLUTION

When the Grand Lodge was founded (1717), George I had been on the throne only three years. The prominent in Masonry were poised to have a hand in the manipulation of the new Hanoverian dynasty.

British journalist, Stephen Knight[169]

In the 17th century, a redistribution of political power was required to protect the newly rich of the British Isles, who had grown wealthy during the expansion of the British colonies. This new elite were Freemasons, who gave England the Glorious Revolution of 1688 - our modern world's first experiment with representative government.

British journalist Stephen Knight documents in his book *The Brotherhood* that English Freemasonry after the rebellion was involved in every walk of life. Affiliation with the Lodge was a prerequisite for anyone, including the king, who wanted to achieve prominence and influence. Knight's most significant point is that from that day until now English Freemasonry has been deeply involved in British politics.[170]

Prior to the Glorious Revolution of 1688, ecclesiastical persecution had fueled the fires of rebellion. For instance, during the reign of Edward III (r.1327-1377), the church in England had become corrupted by error and superstition. The light of the Gospel of Christ was greatly eclipsed by human inventions, burdensome ceremonies, and gross idolatry. John Wycliffe (1330- 1384), desiring to expose these errors, translated the Bible into English. When many began to follow his teachings, the clergy prevailed upon the king to permit a bill to be brought before parliament to settle the issue. The bill passed in 1401. It read in part: "whatsoever they were that should read the Scriptures in the mother-tongue [which was then called 'Wycliffe's learning'], they should forfeit land, cattle, body, life, and goods, from their heirs for ever, and so be condemned for heretics to God, enemies to the crown, and most arrant traitors to the land."[171]

Religious persecution convulsed England for the next century and a half- not subsiding until the reign of Elizabeth I (r.1558-1603). The most bloody slaughters occurred during the reign of Elizabeth's half-sister Mary I (r.1553-1558), nicknamed Bloody Mary. John Foxe[172] (1517-1587) wrote of the sufferings of Protestants during her

---

[169] Knight, *The Brotherhood* 22.

[170] Stephen Knight's primary purpose for publishing *The Brotherhood* was to reveal that the KGB had penetrated the intelligence agencies of the West by joining Freemasonry, after which, the "good old boy" club promoted them into high places. In the case of the KGB agents, they were given high position in British intelligence by their Masonic brothers. It is interesting to note that after the publication of *The Brotherhood*, 15 US citizens were caught spying for the KGB. Perhaps Knight's book alerted our government to investigate Freemasonry, because never in the history of the USA have this many spies been caught in such a short period of time. I have no proof, but I firmly believe that if this topic were researched it would be discovered that these spies were recruited by the KGB in Masonic lodges, as suggested by Stephen Knight's investigations of British Intelligence. Why? Because spies in the 40s and 50s got the death penalty - but not these 15. Could it be that Masonic Judges are looking after their own?

[171] John Foxe, *Foxe's Book of Martyrs* (1569; Chicago: The John C. Winston Co., 1926) 196.

[172] John Foxe was born a Catholic in England in 1517. The Reformation had commenced shortly before his birth. Educated at Oxford, Foxe was chosen "Fellow" of Magdalen College, which was considered a great honor in the university. He studied Greek and Latin, and had acquired a competent skill in the Hebrew language. His obedience to the Catholic Church was shaken by the Reformation,

reign. A story taken from *Foxe's Book of Martyrs* (1569) will demonstrate the horrors suffered by British Protestants who lived under Mary.

PROTESTANT MARTYR: MARTYRDOM OF JOHN HOOPER

About eight o'clock, on February 9, 1555, he was led forth, and many thousand persons were collected, as it was market day. All the way, being straitly charged not to speak, and beholding the people, who mourned bitterly for him, he would sometimes lift up his eyes towards heaven, and look very cheerfully upon such as he knew; and he was never known, during the time of his being among them, to look with so cheerful and ruddy a countenance as he did at that time. When he came to the place appointed where he should die, he smilingly beheld the stake and preparation made for him, which was near unto the great elm tree over against the college of priests, where he used to preach.

Now, after he had entered into prayer, a box was brought and laid before him upon a stool, with his pardon from the queen, if he would turn. At the sight whereof he cried, "If you love my soul, away with it!" The box being taken away, Lord Chandois said, "Seeing there is no remedy; despatch him quickly."

Command was now given that the fire should be kindled. But because there were not more green fagots than two horses could carry, it kindled not speedily, and was a pretty while also before it took the reeds upon the fagots. At length it burned about him, but the wind having full strength at that place, and being a lowering cold morning, it blew the flame from him, so that he was in a manner little more than touched by the fire.

Within a space after, a few fagots were brought, and a new fire kindled with fagots, (for there were no more reeds) and those burned at the nether parts, but had small power above, because of the wind, saving that it burnt his hair and scorched his skin a little. In the time of which fire, even as at the first flame, he prayed, saying mildly, and not very loud, but as one without pain, "O Jesus, Son of David, have mercy upon me, and receive my soul!" After the second fire was spent, he wiped both his eyes with his hands, and beholding the people, he said with an indifferent, loud voice, "For God's love, good people, let me have more fire!" and all this while his nether parts did burn; but the fagots were so few that the flame only singed his upper parts.

The third fire was kindled within a while after, which was more extreme than the other two. In this fire he prayed with a loud voice, "Lord Jesus, have mercy upon me! Lord Jesus receive my spirit!" And these were the last words he was heard to utter. But when he was black in the mouth, and his tongue so swollen that he could not speak, yet his lips went until they were shrunk to the gums; and he knocked his breast with his hands until one of his arms fell off, and then knocked still with the other, while the fat, water, and blood dropped out at his fingers' ends, until by renewing the fire, his strength was

---

of which he was partial. When he stated his opinions at Oxford, he was tried by the university, convicted, condemned as a heretic, and expelled. During the reign of Henry VIII, Foxe kept himself concealed. When Queen Mary (Bloody Mary) ascended the throne, Foxe was under the protection of the Duke of Norfolk, but soon had to flee toSwitzerland. There he wrote *History of the Acts and Monuments of the Church,* which was first published in Latin at Basel in 1554, and in English in 1563.When Queen Elizabeth ascended the throne in 1558, Foxe returned to England. The Duke of Norfolk brought him into his home and paid him a salary. When the Duke died, Foxe inherited a pension bequeathed to him by the Duke.On his resettlement in England, Foxe began to write his book on "Martyrology." He wrote every line of this book with his own hand, and transcribed all the records and papers himself. He completed this celebrated work in eleven years.Queen Elizabeth held him in respect and referred to him as "Our Father Foxe."Foxe enjoyed the fruits of his work while he was yet alive. *Foxe's Book of Martyrs* passed through four large editions before he died in April, 1587.

gone, and his hand clave fast in knocking to the iron upon his breast. Then immediately bowing forwards, he yielded up his spirit.[173]

Many British Protestants suffered in the flames during the Reformation. Throughout these years the monarchs of England, driven by the Church, slaughtered or imprisoned thousands who did not adhere to Church doctrine. Some of the most imaginative methods of torture were used - all in the name of God!

Suppressing spiritual opposition was only part of the responsibility of the Inquisition. Scientific experimentation was tried as well. Ignorant kings and clergy had conceived certain superstitions that the earth was flat and that the sun orbited the earth. They forbade any scientific discovery that refuted their doctrine. All across Europe the Inquisition ruled that inventors be burned at the stake for practicing witchcraft.

While it is true that many Rosicrucian alchemists at the time were practicing witchcraft, the Church suppressed solid scientific theory as well. The story of Galileo, recalled in *Foxe's Book of Martyrs*, is a prime example:

> The most eminent men of science and philosophy of the day did not escape the watchful eye of this cruel despotism. Galileo, the chief astronomer and mathematician of his age was the first who used the telescope successfully in solving the movements of the heavenly bodies. He discovered that the sun is the center of motion around which the earth and various planets revolve. For making this great discovery Galileo was brought before the Inquisition, and for a while was in great danger of being put to death.
>
> After a long and bitter review of Galileo's writings, in which many of his most important discoveries were condemned as errors, the charge of the inquisitors went on to declare, "That you, Galileo, have upon account of those things which you have written and confessed, subjected yourself to a strong suspicion of heresy in the Holy Office, by believing, and holding to be true, a doctrine which is false, and contrary to the sacred and divine Scripture - viz., that the sun is the center of the orb of the earth, and does not move from east to the west; and that the earth moves, and is not the center of the world."
>
> In order to save his life, Galileo admitted that he was wrong in thinking that the earth revolved around the sun, and swore that - "For the future, I will never more say, or assert, either by word or writing, anything that shall give occasion for a like suspicion." But immediately after taking this forced oath he is said to have whispered to a friend standing near, "The earth moves, for all that."[174]

Is it any wonder that the many revolutions connected with political, economic, religious, and scientific enlightenment, separating Church from State, finally plunged men into a time of terror and blood? When the revolutions took hold, England was the first to fall.

A TEMPLAR KING FOR ENGLAND

The conspiracy behind the Glorious Revolution began in London in 1603, after the death of childless Queen Elizabeth I. As we have seen, she had provided an heir by

---

[173] Foxe 215.
[174] Foxe 85-86.

appointing the Templar king of Scotland to ascend the British throne upon her death. King James Stuart VI of Scotland became King James Stuart I of England.

PRIORY OF SION AND THE LOST KING

The Priory of Sion of course could not allow the Templars to capture so powerful a throne.

For the third time Sion found herself battling her adversary. Sion's duty was to protect the interests of the Merovingian bloodline. As the Priory documents state, "Without the Merovingians, the Prieure de Sion would not exist, and without the Prieure de Sion, the Merovingian dynasty would be extinct."[175]

To make sure Merovingian interests were protected, the Grand Masters of Sion were given assignments that, if properly carried out, would guarantee the perpetuation of the Grail bloodline. The Grand Masters were and are carefully selected by the Merovingian monarch currently holding the title "King of Jerusalem." Priory documents confirm that a secret Merovingian King of Jerusalem exists at all times, reigning from one of the thrones in Europe: "The King is shepherd and pastor at the same time." He is revered as a god, and the "temporal sovereigns are aware of his existence, acknowledge him, respect him, and fear him."[176]

Although invisible to the world, his elevated position is known to the Merovingian monarchs. To the initiated, the "King of Jerusalem" is regarded as the "Lost King."

SPYMASTERS AND CONSPIRATORS:
THE GRAND MASTERS OF SION

Grand Masters of Sion were privy to the identity of the Lost King. Selected for their ability to advance the conspiracy, their occupation in life was determined by their assignment. Some were, or became famous men, such as Leonardo Da Vinci, Sir Isaac Newton, and Victor Hugo. Others remained obscure. Many achieved fame in the performance of their assignment, unless they met failure - then history seems to have forgotten them.[177]

Sion's Grand Masters were always headquartered close to their assignment. Although the Lost King chose their task, the Grand Master designed what action to take to complete it. No one made that decision for him. He could operate alone, or employ as much help as required.

Every action of a reigning Grand Master appears to have revolved around one of two assignments: (1) the protection of the "Lost King" and his immediate bloodline; or (2) the protection of the confiscated Templar treasure. The successful conclusion of each assignment was to further advance the ultimate goal of Sion: that of moving toward a universal government ruled by the King of Jerusalem himself.[178]

These assignments made the Grand Masters' lives precarious, requiring brilliance, cunning, subversiveness, and expendability. Should they accept their assignment, they were either victorious, or they were destroyed - giving tremendous incentive for success. If their goal was achieved, they could become famous - perhaps wealthy.

---

[175] Baigent et al, *Holy Blood* 206.
[176] Baigent 206-207.
[177] Baigent 206-207, 423, 429, 435.
[178] Church, entire.

Explaining what awaits the Grand Master for success or failure, one of the Priory documents states: As "Custodians of a secret, one can only exalt them or destroy them." The document further states that upon the death of a Grand Master his "wake is attended by a perfume of magic in which sulphur is mingled with incense - the perfume of the Magdalen" - indicating, of course, both the glory and the suffering which he carries in accepting and carrying out the assignment.[179]

GRAND MASTERS (GM) OF SION VS. THE STUARTS

Robert Fludd (GM 1595-1637):
Father of Rosicrucian-English Masonry

The Merovingian kings reigned on the Continent of Europe protected by the British crown. But when a Templar monarch ascended the British throne in 1603, the Lost King took action by appointing Robert Fludd Grand Master of the Priory of Sion.

Robert Fludd was England's leading exponent of esoteric thought. Although he never claimed to be a Rosicrucian, which movement was causing a sensation in Germany, Fludd warmly endorsed it, declaring that the "highest good" was the "Magia, Cabala and Alchymia of the Brothers of the Rosy Cross."[180]

The *Encyclopedia of Freemasonry* claims that Fludd was "a prominent member of the Rosicrucian Fraternity... Rosicrucianism was perhaps indebted more to Fludd than to any other person for its introduction from Germany into England, and it may have had its influence in molding the form of Speculative Freemasonry..."[181] Quoting the London *Freemason Magazine* (April, 1858, p.677) the *Encyclopedia of Freemasonry* further reports that "Fludd must be considered as the immediate father of Freemasonry..."[182] The *Encyclopaedia Britannica* concurs by reporting that Fludd's writings were "a principal source of the symbolic ideas of freemasonry [sic]."[183]

When the Stuarts appeared certain to ascend the throne, Fludd devoted his life to writing and researching Rosicrucianism. In all England there were only the masonic workingman guilds, but as yet no esoteric society available to subvert the Templars. Apparently Fludd's assignment was to prepare the ground for receiving the Rose-Croix from Germany to conspire against the Templar throne at some future date.

Meanwhile, Fludd worked his way into the good graces of James I, and according to the authors of *Holy Blood, Holy Grail*, he "was among the conclave of scholars who presided over the translation of the *King James* Bible."[184] Fludd's presence may explain why an English translation of the Bible contains the French spelling of "Sion" in every location found in the New Testament (KJV only).

Johann Valentin Andrea (GM 1637-1654):
Creator of Secret Societies

---

[179] Baigent 2o6.
[180] Baigent 426.
[181] "Robert Fludd," *Mackey's Encyclopedia of Freemasonry*, vol.1.
[182] "Robert Fludd."
[183] "Robert Fludd," *Encyclopaedia Britannica: Micropaedia*.
[184] Baigent 426.

Valentin Andrea, son of a Lutheran pastor and theologian from Wurttemberg, Germany, was unscathed by the chaos of the Thirty Years War. His primary assignment appears to have been the same as his predecessor: to popularize Rosicrucianism by writing the *Chemical Wedding of Christian Rosenkreuz*. After Fludd had prepared the masonic workingman guilds in England for its reception, Andrea imported Rosicrucians from Germany. *Holy Blood, Holy Grail* confirms that amidst the turmoil raging around him Andrea created a network of more or less secret societies known as the Christian Unions. According to Andrea's blueprint, each society was headed by an anonymous prince, assisted by twelve others divided into groups of study. The original purpose of the Christian Unions was to preserve threatened knowledge - especially the most recent scientific advances, many of which the Church deemed heretical. At the same time, however, the Christian Unions also functioned as a refuge for persons fleeing the Inquisition - which accompanied the invading Catholic armies and was intent on rooting out all vestiges of Rosicrucian thought. Thus, numerous scholars, scientists, philosophers, and esotericists found a haven in Andrea's institutions. Through them many were smuggled to safety in England - where Freemasonry was just beginning to coalesce. In some significant sense Andrea's Christian Unions may have contributed to the organization of the Masonic lodge system.[185]

The Creation of Masonic Lodges in England

Once in England these refugees from the Inquisition infiltrated the guilds Fludd had prepared, while continuing correspondence with Andrea on the Continent. Within a half century they had completely taken over operative masonry and formed what they called Speculative Masonry, keeping the first three degrees of the workingman guilds, and superimposing on them Rosicrucian rituals. They inducted many of the newly rich into their society.

They also made contact with one Elias Ashmole (1617-1692), a celebrated antiquarian, expert on chivalric orders and author of the well-known *History of the Order of the Garter,* initiating him into their Rosicrucian Masonic Lodges in 1646. They became intimate with the young, precocious Robert Boyle, who was destined to be the next Grand Master of the Priory of Sion. And they inducted into their form of Masonry a rebel by the name of Oliver Cromwell (1599- 1658), directing him to the forefront of the revolution.[186] (Ashmole would later turn Masonry against Cromwell.)

Cromwell and Rosicrucian Freemasonry

While the invisible arm guiding Cromwell was Rosicrucian Masonry, he, as a former Unitarian turned Puritan, was a recognized Protestant, making his rebellion in England look like a Protestant movement. Yet a careful study of Unitarianism will reveal that its religious dogma is identical to deistic Freemasonry. In fact, Oliver Cromwell was first and foremost a Mason, as were many of the Puritans. His Masonic affiliation was confirmed years later by French Freemasons, whose ceremonies originated with the Templars he ousted. Frenchmen claimed Cromwell was a high initiate of Masonic mysteries and used the system for his own elevation to power.[187]

---

[185] Baigent 143-144.
[186] Baigent 144.
[187] Webster, *Secret Societies* 126.

Abbe Larudan, a Catholic expert on Masonry from Amsterdam, in his book, *The Freemasons Crushed* (1746), claims that Oliver Cromwell "established the Order [of Freemasonry] for the furtherance of his [own] political designs," and that "Freemasonry was organized, its Degrees established, [and] its ceremonies and ritual prescribed" by Cromwell and several of the adherents he initiated. Larudan further alleges that "The Institution was used by Cromwell for the advancement of his projects, for the union of the contending parties in England, for the extirpation of the monarchy, and his own subsequent elevation to supreme power."[188]

Mackey's Encyclopedia of Freemasonry attempts to discredit Larudan: "[Larudan] writes with seeming fairness and mildness. But it is hardly necessary to say that this theory of the origin of Freemasonry finds no support either in the legends of the Institution, or in the authentic history that is connected with its rise and progress."[189]

However, another Masonic publication, *History and Evolution of Freemasonry*, affirms Oliver Cromwell's links to Masonry. Cromwell, it says, regularly met at the Masonic Lodge in the tavern called Crown. This was a Lodge for the aristocratic Rosicrucian gentry, the new elite who were the newly rich.[190] Cromwell was supposed by

---

Some individuals, after having read the first edition of this book, have rejected my claim that Oliver Cromwell was a Unitarian, showing me in current Christian literature that he is said to have been a Puritan. Further research has revealed the following.

As a young man in his 20s, Oliver Cromwell was a Unitarian. In his 30s he repented and in 1638 gave this testimony: "You know what my manner of life hath been. Oh, I have lived in a loved darkness, and hated light; I was a chief, the chief, of sinners. This is true: I hated godliness; yet God had mercy on me. Oh, the riches of His mercy! Praise Him for me - pray for me, that He who hath begun a good work would perfect it in the day of Christ." (Will and Ariel Durant, *The Story of Civilization:The Age of Reason Begins*, vol. VII, 208)

History records that Cromwell "spoke in terms of Puritan piety" (Durant 208). As a member of Parliament in 1628 under the Independent Party, a Party heavily membered by Puritans, naturally Cromwell would speak in Puritan terms. And his close political association with Puritans during his first decade in parliament may have had something to do with his conversion (Durant 208). Moreover, as a general during the first Civil War (1641-1645), he led a band of Puritans in battle, and never once were they defeated (Durant 215).

The Presbyterians, the most powerful Christian sect in the House of Commons, in 1648 successfully lobbied to pass a bill "punishing with life imprisonment the opponents of infant baptism, and with death those who denied the Trinity, or the Incarnation, or the divine inspiration of the Bible, or the immortality of the soul" (Durant 214). But not Cromwell and his party of Puritans, who moved for toleration, a Masonic dogma which makes them suspect. And indeed they were, for Edith Miller reports that "the Rose Croix had spread rapidly among the Puritans" (Miller, *Occult Theocrasy* 157). We know that during Cromwell's Protectorate (1653-1658), he surrounded himself with Rosicrucian Masons (Baigent, *Holy Blood, Holy Grail* 144). Moreover, we know from Masonic sources that during the Civil War, Cromwell frequented a Rosicrucian Masonic Lodge called "Crown," which he could not have done unless he were a Rosicrucian Mason himself (Darrah, *History and Evolution of Freemasonry* 174). We also know that in exchange for financial support from Amsterdam Jews, Cromwell promised to symbolically rebuild Solomon's Temple for them in Freemasonry (see note 32).

Cromwell, therefore, is typical of many Protestant Reformers who joined Freemasonry to win political freedom. If the Sardis Church Period of Revelation 3:1-6 is a prophecy of the Reformation Church, as some theologians believe, Christ was not pleased with their political involvement. What I have discovered, and still maintain, is that Cromwell's revolution was more Masonic than Protestant.

[188] "Cromwell," Mackey's Encyclopedia of Freemasonry, vol.1.

[189] "Cromwell."

[190] Darrah 174.

many to be a Rosicrucian himself, since he was on the best of terms with them.[191] This view is endorsed by the *Encyclopedia of Freemasonry.*[192]

Although Cromwell was indirectly selected by the Grand Master of the Priory of Sion to foment revolution, there is no evidence that the Protector was personally associated with Sion. There is ample evidence, however, that he was surrounded by Rosicrucians and that his revolution was plotted in Rosicrucian Masonic Lodges. English Masonry, however, had a second house - the Templar Masonic Lodges.

A Masonic House Divided

During Cromwell's day Masonry in England was not yet united. Each lodge operated independently. Some backed Cromwell, while others supported the Stuarts. Cromwell gained control of the government because his Masonic sect was more powerful. Less than a decade after Cromwell's Protectorate began in 1653, an opposition Masonic sect, the Levellers - whose symbols were the square and compass - supported the Royalists and shifted the balance of power back to the dethroned Stuart kings. English Lodges by the end of the 17th century were once again Royalist.[193]

On the surface, embryonic Masonry seems to have consisted of several splintered factions trying to wrest power from each other, when in fact their conflicts were a continuation of the division between the Knights Templar and Sion's Rosicrucians. The Masonry to which Cromwell belonged was Rosicrucian. Stuart Freemasonry, known as Jacobite Freemasonry after 1688, and later as Scottish Rite Freemasonry on the Continent, was of Templar origin, hearkening back to Jacques de Molay.

Cromwell's Revolution: The Triumph of Rosicrucian Masonry

A century before Cromwell's revolution, John Hooper, and many more Protestants like him, were burned at the stake. When Protestantism was protected by Queen Elizabeth in 1558, the Reformers were no better than their persecutors, for they punished Catholics as severely. Consequently, many Catholics fled to Ireland, where they were protected by "The Defenders," an Irish Catholic order founded by Roger Moore in 1562 to protect Crown and Church against the Protestant Reformers. Behind Moore were French and Spanish Jesuits. In 1641, The Defenders rose and massacred many Irish and English Protestants, but were crushed by Cromwell in 1649.[194]

Oliver Cromwell, the political standard-bearer of triumphant Protestantism, became Lord Protector of England four years after he had the Stuart king, Charles I, beheaded on January 30, 1649. The historians Durant, in *The Story of Civilization, Vol. WI,* describe the executions:

> *Prince Charles dispatched from Holland a sheet bearing only his signature, and promised the judges to abide by any terms they would write over his name if they would spare his father's life. Four nobles offered to die in Charles's stead; they were refused. Fifty-nine judges, including Cromwell, signed the death sentence. On January 30, before a vast and horror-stricken crowd, the King went quietly to his death. His head was severed with one blow of the executioner's ax.*

---

[191] Webster 126.
[192] "Cromwell."
[193] Miller 159-160.
[194] Miller 320.

"There was such a groan by the thousands then present," wrote an eyewitness, "as I never heard before and desire I may never hear again."[195]

Was the execution legal? Of course not. On the basis of existing law, the Parliament progressively and rudely appropriated royal rights sanctioned by the precedents of a hundred years. By definition a revolution is illegal; it can advance to the new only by violating the old. Charles was sincere in defending the powers he had inherited from Elizabeth and James; he was sinned against as well as sinning; his fatal error lay in not recognizing that the new distribution of wealth required, for social stability, a new distribution of political power.[196]

The newly wealthy of whom the Durants speak were in fact the Rosicrucian gentry who had co- opted one of the opposing factions of Operative Masonry. Many of this class were shareholders in the monopolistic British East India Company. They accumulated their riches through trade with the colonies, i.e., cotton trade from the new world in exchange for African slaves; opium, tea, and spices from the Orient. Others became prosperous through scientific inventions during the Renaissance, which provided the means for manufacturing saleable goods from these raw materials, again traded by the East India Company.

The nouveau-rich wanted a political voice. Without it they were subject to lose, through greedy taxation without representation, what they had gained. "Absolute Monarchy must be changed to a Constitutional Monarchy for our protection," they demanded.

Masonic Lodges afforded protection. There they could meet and plan a strategy to gain a political foothold. Once in government, Masonry remained a covert political force to assure that their voice survived. As British journalist Stephen Knight writes in *The Brotherhood*, Eng- lishmen saw "the need to preserve the gain of the Civil War of 1642-1651 - the limitation of the power of the King... Whether Lodges as such or Masons as Masons took part in the initiative to invite William of Orange and his consort Mary to become joint sovereigns in 1688 is not known, but the suggestion is plausible."[197]

Funding Cromwell's Revolution

When Cromwell had dethroned the Stuart monarchy, he dissolved all Crown-protected monopolies, including the British East India Company (BEIC). For three years the BEIC ceased to exist as a chartered corporation. In October 1657, however, short of capital for his new government, Cromwell granted the company a new charter in return for financial aid.[198] The BEIC stockholders rushed to join Cromwell's now ascendant Masonic Lodge.

Cromwell and Jewish Financing

The Jews of Amsterdam also helped to finance Cromwell's government. As the most persecuted and destitute of all people, they would buy their freedom if necessary. Will and Ariel Durant, in *The Story of Civilization: The Age of Reason Begins*, tell of the

---

[195] Will Durant and Ariel Durant, *The Story of Civilization: The Age of Reason Begins*, vol. VII (New York: Simon and Schuster, 1961) 220.

[196] Durants, vol. VII.

[197] Knight 21-22.

[198] "Cromwell, Oliver: Foreign and economic policies," *Encyclopaedia Britannica: Macropaedia*.

Jewish misery. The Durants write that the Christians of Europe, in order to protect their faith, sought to isolate the Jews with geographical barriers, political disabilities, intellectual censorship, and economic restraints. Nowhere in Christian Europe before the French Revolution - not even in Amsterdam - were they allowed full citizenship and its rights. They were shut out from public office, the army, the schools and universities, and the practice of law in Christian courts. They were heavily taxed, they were subject to forced loans, they might at any time suffer confiscation of their property. They were excluded from agriculture by restrictions on the ownership of land, and by the haunting insecurity that forced them to put their savings in currency or movable goods. They were ineligible to the guilds, for these were partly religious in form and purpose, and required Christian oaths and rituals. Limited to petty industry, to commerce and finance, they found themselves harassed even in these occupations by special prohibitions varying in place and changeable at any time: in one district they could not be peddlers, in another they could not be shopkeepers, in another they must not deal in leather or wool. So most Jews lived as small tradesmen peddlers, dealers in secondhand goods or old clothes, tailors, servants of their richer fellow men, craftsmen making goods for Jews. From these occupations, and the humiliations of the ghetto, the poorer Jews developed those habits of dress and speech, those tricks of trade and qualities of mind, that were distasteful to other peoples and higher ranks.[199]

Masonic Promise to Rebuild Solomon's Temple

Thus when Cromwell guaranteed the Jews he would relieve their plight, they agreed to bankroll his revolution. In appreciation, Cromwell invented the allegory of the Temple of Solomon and promised the Jews that Masonry would one day rebuild their Temple.[200]

Monsignor Dr. George E. Dillon, in *Freemasonry Unmasked*, writes:

> *The building of the Temple of Solomon was the dream of their lives. It is unquestionable that they wished to make common cause with other bodies of persecuted religionists. They had special reason to welcome with joy such heretics as were cast off by Catholicity. It is, therefore, not at all improbable, that they admitted into their secret conclaves some at least of the discontented... burning for revenge upon those who dispossessed and suppressed [them]...*[201]

Some Jews also looked to Cromwell as a possible Messiah. As the Durants remark, "To the Jews so dispersed, and so often destitute and maligned, the prop of life was the faith that someday soon the real Messiah would come to raise them out of misery and ignominy to power and glory.[202]

Nesta Webster elaborates: "Now, just at this period the Messianic era was generally believed by the Jews to be approaching, and it appears to have occurred to them that Cromwell might be fitted to the part. Consequently emissaries were despatched to search the archives of Cambridge in order to discover whether the Protector could possibly be of Jewish descent. This quest proving fruitless, the Cabalist Rabbi of Amsterdam,

---

[199] Durants, vol. VII, 469-70.
[200] George E. Dillon, Grand Orient Freemasonry Unmasked as the Secret Power behind Communism 13.
[201] Dillon 14.
[202] Will Durant and Ariel Durant, *The Story of Civilization: The Age of Louis* XIV, vol. VIII (New York: Simon and Schuster, 1963) 471.

Manasseh ben Israel, addressed a petition to Cromwell for the readmission of the Jews to England."[203]

Partial Emancipation of English Jews

Cromwell did win partial emancipation for his Jewish friends, but not without opposition. The Anabaptists, a radical Protestant sect that advocated rebaptism for church membership and promoted the separation of church and state, denounced Cromwell as the Beast of the Apocalypse because of the Messianic way in which he presented himself to the Jews.[204] (Scripture indicates that the Jews will worship the Beast as their Messiah during the Tribulation - see chapter 27.) Edith Starr Miller, in *Occult Theocrasy*, tells us of the disaster which later renewed anti-Jewish sentiment in England:

> *After the death of Charles I, Cromwell appointed an assembly of lawyers and divines to consider the petition of Manasseh ben Israel demanding the abolition of the legal exclusion of the Jews from England. In December 1655 the legal prohibition was removed. Eleven years after occurred the great fire of London.[205]*

The commercial center of the city was almost wiped out. But the political heart of the city, Westminster, was saved. Altogether two-thirds of London was destroyed.[206] Of course, the fire was blamed on the Jews, but there was no proof to substantiate the charge.[207]

The Jews Switch Sides and Back Templar Rivals

Not satisfied with Cromwell's partial success in winning them freedom, the Jews financially backed the Stuart cause to regain the British throne for Templar Freemasonry. The Jews anticipated that the Stuarts would give them full emancipation for their financial services.

The Jews also turned to Elias Ashmole, who had been inducted into Rosicrucianism in 1646, and through him turned the Rosicrucian Masonic system against Cromwell, so that towards the end of the 17th century that Order also rallied to the Stuart cause.[208]

Without Jewish financial support, Cromwell's government faltered and collapsed, plunging the nation into depression. The British began calling for the return of the Stuarts, in hopes that a change of administration would better their desperate condition. To avoid another civil war, the Rosicrucians permitted the Stuart Templar King, Charles II, to reclaim the throne of England eleven years after his father was beheaded.

Robert Boyle (GM 1654-1691): Masonry Founds the Royal Society of England

---

[203] Webster 179. Nesta Webster's information came from two Jewish sources, *Anglia Judaica* (p.275) and the *Jewish Encyclopaedia* in its article on Manasseh ben Israel.
[204] Durants, vol. VIII, 194.
[205] Miller 160.
[206] Durants, vol. VIII, 263.
[207] Miller 161.
[208] Webster 126 and Baigent 144.

Robert Boyle, a Rosicrucian alchemist, was at the head of the Priory of Sion when Cromwell was still in power, but before Templar Charles II ascended the throne. In his letters, Boyle speaks repeatedly of the "Invisible College," which the authors of Holy *Blood, Holy Grail* suggest was a secret code name for the Priory of Sion, or at least for the Grand Master's activity.

Robert Boyle appears to have been preoccupied with alchemy. His voluminous correspondence with the Continent deals extensively with alchemy and alchemical experimentation. More important, his letters confirm his membership in a secret hermetic society - probably the Rosicrucians.[209]

Boyle's interest in alchemy, however, masked his main occupation. With another Stuart king on the throne, his primary task was to control Charles II. He accomplished this through the Royal Society of 1660, created the same year Charles II ascended the throne. Its founders were solely Rosicrucian Masons, including the Grand Master of Sion, Robert Boyle, and the next Grand Master, Isaac Newton. They graciously appointed the Templar king as patron and sponsor of the Society.[210]

Young and naive Charles II could hardly resist such a prestigious appointment, one that associated him with scientific minds. Consequently, Charles took advice from Rosicrucian Sionists, instead of from the Templars who brought him to power.

The Durants have called King Charles' 25-year-long reign (1660-1685) incompetent. But he was incompetent because his advisors assured it. Sion had played this game for 800 years![211]

Sion's Plot to Rid England of the Templar Stuarts

In 1660 the Priory of Sion could have easily assassinated Charles II. The decapitation of Charles I eleven years earlier, however, had turned too many subjects against the revolution. Any move against the young monarch would mean civil war, which would not be in Sion's best interest. With a faltering economy, and Cromwell's death in 1658, Sion was determined to preserve its advances, even if that meant returning a Stuart to the throne - for a while, at least. If Charles II were kept incompetent, Stuart enthusiasm would gradually weaken, reversing the Masonic royalist trend.

Twenty-five years passed before the strategy worked. James II, brother of Charles II, ascended the throne in 1685. Great Britain, however, had enough of incompetency. James' reign only lasted three years before he was dethroned by the Glorious Revolution of 1688.

Again the Jews were in the financial forefront of revolution. In 1688 they helped their cause by funding William of Orange against James ~ By this time, as the Durants write, the Jews were heavily involved in British commerce: "The Jewish mind, sharpened by hardship, oppression, and study, developed in trade and finance an acquisitive subtlety never forgiven by their competitors. The activity of Jewish exporters and importers played a significant part in the prosperity of Hamburg and Amsterdam. One twelfth of England's foreign trade passed through Jewish hands in the first half of the seventeenth century."[212] As a result Jewish merchants and bankers rapidly became wealthy. They were so wealthy,

---

[209] Baigent 427-428.

[210] Baigent 144.

[211] Webster 179-180. Webster documents this through the writings of a Jewish author named Lucien Wolf in *Transactions of the Jewish Historical Society of Eng land,* vol.11, p.18, as well as from articles Wolf wrote in 1894 and 1901. Other sources she uses are the *Jewish Encyclopaedia, Anglia Judaica,* and writings by Mirabeau in 1787.

[212] Durants, vol. VIII, 470.

in fact, that from Cromwell on we will witness some prominent Jews heavily involved in funding revolution through secret societies in an effort to bring about the one-world government of the Priory of Sion.

Throughout the British insurrections, Jews were continually shifting loyalty, not to gain power or wealth, but to guarantee and increase their freedom. Thus, Jews were not directing the Glorious Revolution, as some conspiracy authors would have it, but rather were taking advantage of an opportunity for freedom, as any downtrodden people would do if found in the same untenable circumstances.

Knight maintains the revolution was not Jewish but purely Masonic when he writes that Englishmen saw "the need to preserve the gain of the Civil War of 1642-1651- the limitation of the power of the King... Whether Lodges as such or Masons as Masons took part in the initiative to invite William of Orange and his consort Mary to become joint sovereigns in 1688 is not known, but the suggestion is plausible."[213]

Sir Isaac Newton (GM 1691-1727): Religious Sceptic and Masonic Fellow Traveller

Robert Boyle was close friends with the next Grand Master of Sion, even teaching him the secrets of alchemy. His name was Isaac Newton.

Reigning as Grand Master from 1691-1727, his assignment was that of caretaker of a perfected revolution.

Newton was educated at Cambridge and elected in 1672 to the Royal Society. During this time he was intimate with a young French Protestant refugee, Jean Desaguliers, also an alchemist and one of the Royal Society's two curators of experiments. So close was their friendship that according to the *Encyclopedia of Freemasonry*, Newton stood godfather to Dr. Desaguliers's daughter.[214] In the years that followed, Desaguliers became one of the leading figures in the astonishing proliferation of English Freemasonry throughout Europe. He was also instrumental in initiating into Freemasonry the Duke of Lorraine, a Merovingian whose younger brother would become a future Grand Master of the Priory of Sion on the Continent.

There is no record that Isaac Newton himself was a Mason. Certain of his attitudes and works, however, reflect interests shared by Masons. For example, like the Masons he "ascribed great significance to the configuration and dimensions of Solomon's temple. The dimensions and configuration of the temple he believed to conceal alchemical formulas; and he believed the ancient ceremonies in the temple to have involved alchemical processes."[215]

Mackey's: Encyclopedia of Freemasonry indicates the Masons' desire to claim Newton as one of their own, at least by association: "The Royal Society was the apple of Newton's eye; Newton in turn was the leader, inspiration, and glory of the Royal Society; and the membership of the Royal Society was wholly Masonic; Newton was therefore in a Masonic circle."[216]

Holy Blood, Holy Grail declares that "If Newton's scientific interests were less orthodox than we had at first imagined, so were his religious views. He was militantly, albeit quietly, hostile to the idea of the Trinity... He questioned the divinity of Jesus and avidly collected all manuscripts pertaining to the issue. He doubted the complete authenticity of the New Testament, believing certain passages to be corruptions

---

[213] Knight 21-22.
[214] "Newton, Sir Isaac," Mackey's Encyclopedia of Freemasonry, vol. III.
[215] Baigent 430.
[216] "Newton."

interpolated in the fifth century. He was deeply intrigued by some of the early Gnostic heresies and wrote a study of one of them."[217]

Charles Radcliffe (GM 1727-1746)

There seems to be no personal relationship between Isaac Newton and Charles Radcliffe, who was a known Mason and the final British Grand Master of the Priory of Sion. After Oliver Cromwell's British revolution was solidified, after the Glorious Revolution of 1688 permanently dethroned the Stuarts, and after English Freemasonry was united in 1717 and the Templar Stuarts exiled to France - Charles Radcliffe went with them. His assignment was to make sure they did not return.

The Birth of French Freemasonry

French Freemasonry was born, as we have seen, with the arrival of the exiled Stuarts in France. Newly established French Freemasonry, as might be expected, altered the Temple of Solomon myth to reflect its own origins and political aspirations. Nesta Webster notes that "when the revolution of 1688 divided the Royalist cause, the Jacobites who fled to France with James II took Freemasonry with them. With the help of the French they established lodges in which, it is said, masonic [sic] rites and symbols were used to promote the cause of the Stuarts. Thus the land of promise signified Great Britain, Jerusalem stood for London, and the murder of Hiram [which originally was symbolic of their Templar Grand Master Jacques de Molay] represented the execution of Charles I."[218]

Webster reports the consequent shift in English Freemasonry:

> "Freemasonry in England did not continue to adhere to the Stuart cause as it had done under the aegis of Elias Ashmole, and by 1717 is said to have become Hanoverian."[219]
>
> Knight concurs with Webster's assessment: "When the Grand Lodge was founded [1717], George I [of Hanover] had been on the throne only three years. The prominent in Masonry were poised to have a hand in the manipulation of the new Hanoverian dynasty."[220]

With English Freemasonry thus firmly in the grip of Sion's Rosicrucians, Charles Radcliffe, the next Grand Master of the Priory of Sion (GM 1727-1746), was free to "flee" to France with the Stuarts. The "Lost King" could not have made a better choice than Radcliffe, who, as a high initiate in the Knights Templar, was a double agent for the Priory of Sion.

English Masonry Unified and De-Christianized

With the Protestant Hanover dynasty securely in power, and the empire under Masonic control, it was time to unify Masonry, which had been divided between Templarism and Rosicrucianism. On June 24, 1717, four London lodges of Rosicrucian

---

[217] Baigent 431.
[218] Webster 126.
[219] Webster 126-127.
[220] Knight 22.

Freemasons met together at the Apple Tree Tavern in Charles Street, Covent Garden, and with the oldest Master Mason as chair, they constituted themselves a Grand Lodge. Rabbi Manasseh ben Israel, the Jewish Mason from Amsterdam, had before his death designed the coat of arms that was adopted as the symbol of the Grand Lodge Assembly in London.

Seven Gnostic Gentiles, Magi of the English Rose Croix, the Order founded by the Priory of Sion, were the primary organizers of the United Grand Lodge. Who were these men? Dr. James Anderson, an Oxford graduate and known as a freethinker, was also a Presbyterian minister and preacher to the King of England. Dr. John Theophile Desaguliers (one of Isaac Newton's closest friends) was a lawyer, a Fellow of Sion's Royal Society, a natural philosopher and French Protestant; he had taken holy orders in England and was named Chaplain to the Prince of Wales by King George II. Desaguliers was also regarded as an occultist and an accomplished alchemist inventor. Then there was the lesser known: George Payne, a Modernist (a Masonic term denoting those who modified or changed from the so-called ancient workings of Freemasonry) who, as the second elected Grand Master, introduced the Bible into the Lodge on the pretext that Masons should take their oath on it. Finally, there were James King, Calvert, Luinden-Madden, and Elliot.[221]

Dr. James Anderson was selected to draw up a constitution, which in Anderson's hands began the de-Christianization of the Lodge. In the new constitution, titled *Charges of a Free-Mason*, Anderson, following the Modernist line, writes, "Tis now thought more expedient only to oblige them [members of the Brotherhood] to that Religion to which all men agree, leaving their particular opinions to themselves."[222]

Concerning the Anderson Constitution, Edith Starr Miller states:

> *"Masonry, which as a secret association had maintained its existence for years, had uncovered itself and become an avowed organization with the proclamation of the Anderson Constitution. Once in the open it was to be the universal screen behind which all secret societies, whether theurgic or political, would operate clandestinely. Masonry, with its proclamation of three philanthropic and altruistic degrees, with no apparent real secret, declaring itself Christian and non-political, would become the centre in which ignorant men, recruited and duped, could act like puppets animated by unseen hands pulling unseen strings. Thus it came about that all blows dealt to Christianity and States were prepared by the secret societies acting behind the veil of Masonry."[223]*

Anderson's Constitution opened the door to men of any and all faiths to fellowship in Freemasonry. The de-Christianizing of the Lodges, however, took nearly 100 years. Prayers in the English Lodges concluded with the name of Christ until 1813 when the Lodge again changed formulas under the "Ancients" Grand Master and freethinker, the Duke of Sussex, who made the order purely Deistic. The "Ancients" claimed that their ceremonies had come down from the ancient or operative lodges without change. By that

---

[221] Miller 34, 175; Webster 130-131; Knight 25-28; de Poncins, *Freemasonry and the Vatican* 108, 115, 126; Jack Harris, *Freemasonry; The Invisible Cult in our Midst* (Orlando, FL: Daniels Publishing, 1983) 23.Jack Harris was a Master Mason, rising to the position of Worshipful Master, the highest elected office in the Blue Lodge.He also passed through all the degrees of the York Rite. In October, 1970, he accepted Jesus Christ as his personal Savior. After two years of Bible study he renounced Freemasonry in May, 1972.

[222] Knight 27.

[223] Miller 161-162.

time, Turks, Jews, Jacobites, non-jurors, Protestants and Catholics (primarily Jesuits) were admitted into the order.

Importing Pagan Elements

Throughout the eighteenth century, more and more pagan elements were brought in to replace the discarded faith of the Modernists. For example, Gnosticism was considered the Mother of Freemasonry and by it all religions would be unified; the name of Christ ending each prayer gradually died out; in Masonic quotations of Scripture (e.g. I Peter 2:5; II Thessalonians 3:2 and 13) the name of Christ was pointedly deleted from the text; and finally, eastern mysticism entered their rituals.[224]

The Name of Jesus Christ Is Forbidden

To this day the sacred name of Jesus Christ is forbidden to be uttered in any Masonic assembly, as the Masons claim, "For fear of offending their non-Christian brethren." This "offense" perpetrated by Sionist Freemasonry may be the one prophesied by Paul in Romans 9:33: "As it is written, Behold, I lay in Sion a stumbling stone and a rock of offence..."

By excluding the name of Christ from the Lodge, the Ancients succeeded in introducing the undeniably occult - notably the invocation of the "lost name" of God. If the Deity was not to be identified as the Trinitarian Christian God, God then could only be defined as the Great Architect of the Universe - a name associated with the English branch of the Merovingians in the 10th century - Bera VI, known as the Architect. The authors of *Holy Blood, Holy Grail* suggest that the Masonic Great Architect of the Universe generally refers to the Merovingian bloodline, and specifically to the "Lost King" himself.[225]

Therefore, the "lost name" of God would be the name of the secret reigning king of the Merovingians, the usurper of the Davidic line, who blasphemously claims the title, "King of Jerusalem."

The Oligarchy Conspiracy and English Freemasonry

The Durants assess England's new Parliamentary "Bill of Rights" following the Masonic revolution of 1688: "This historic proclamation expressed the essential results of what Protestant England called the 'Glorious Revolution': the explicit assertion of the legislative supremacy of Parliament, so long contested by four Stuart kings... 'absolute' monarchy by 'divine right' had been changed into a territorial oligarchy characterized by moderation, assiduity, and skill in government, cooperating with the princes of industry, commerce, and finance, and generally careless of the artisans and peasantry. The upper middle classes benefited substantially from the revolution. The cities of England recovered their freedom [only] to be ruled by mercantile oligarchies."[226]

The Durants clearly recognize the wealth, influence, and political power of the mercantile oligarchies of England. Only conspiracy researchers, however, have recognized the union between wealthy industrialists, merchants, bankers and monarchs

---

[224] See footnote 53.
[225] Baigent 264-265.
[226] Durants, vol. VIII, 298-299.

through their association in the brotherhood of aristocratic English Freemasonry. This "association" is what has been called the Oligarchy conspiracy.

It is true that only the upper middle classes benefited from the English revolution. Just as the Templar Stuart kings had failed to recognize and grant the aristocracy a voice in their government, so too the new Masonic Oligarchy failed to recognize the needs of those beneath them - poor workingmen. More than 100 years passed before the common laborer won recognition. His success, however, came through a more sinister Templar Masonic revolution then brewing on the continent of Europe. That which the aristocrats won in their capitalistic English Masonic revolution, they were destined to lose in the socialist French Masonic revolution.

Summation

Five of the eight "octopus theories" have been addressed in this chapter. We have learned that the oligarchy is made up of royalty, **world bankers and multinational corporations. We have seen how** and why the Jews were involved - financing the Revolution only for the purpose of gaining their own freedom. We have discovered that these four theories are housed within the fifth theory, Rosicrucian English Freemasonry.

3. THE RELIGIOUS WARS OF FRANCE

> *There could be no greater fallacy than the theory that underground conspiracies are carried on only by poor, the downtrodden, and revolutionaries. The French Royal war against the Huguenots began as an underground movement.*
>
> Mackey's Encyclopedia of Freemasonry[227]

The Religious Wars of France started after the reign of King Henry II of Valois (r.1547-1559) and during the regency of his placable queen, Catherine. The underlying cause of the Religious Wars was not the Reformation; nor was it a conflict between Sion and the Templars. It was an internal struggle between competing Merovingians. This chapter will focus on the intrigues surrounding the second and third Religious Wars, which plunged the Holy Grail royalty into a bloodbath that lasted from 1562 to 1594.

THE MEROVINGIAN "GREAT PLAN"

As noted in chapter 1, the Merovingians had a "Secret Doctrine" (also called the "Great Plan"), which in part called for the creation of a Universal Throne in Europe. Three esoteric properties would be required for the holder of the Universal Throne to be legitimate: (1) he must possess the Spear of Destiny, as described in chapter 1; (2) he must also be the Holy Roman Emperor; and (3) he must hold the title, "King of Jerusalem." The Merovingian king with these three properties in his possession would not only be the ruler of the world, he would be the Lost King of the Merovingians, or in Holy Grail eschatology - the Messiah of Israel.

The Plan began in earnest at Gisors shortly after the Priory of Sion officially separated from the Templars in 1188. To initiate the Plan, the existing Carolingian thrones of Europe were to be subverted or otherwise overthrown. This not only involved marriage with Carolingian royalty, but sometimes necessitated covert political intrigue, assassination, or an overt seizure of power. Once the Carolingians were removed, the Merovingians would cooperate in combining, through intermarriage, various Holy Blood families to create in one line the three esoteric properties required to establish world government.[228]

PLANNING THE DESTRUCTION OF THE CHURCH

To maintain political legitimacy and esoteric control, the Merovingians initially relied on the Church. Eventually, however, Rome proved a liability and had to be weakened or removed. The Merovingians planned to diminish the influence of the Church through psychological warfare - a clandestine tradition intended to erode the spiritual hegemony of Rome - a tradition that found expression in Hermetic and esoteric thought, such as in Rosicrucian and Freemasonic secret societies.[229]

---

[227] "Knigge, Baron Von," Mackey's Encyclopedia of Free masonry, vol.111.
[228] Baigent et al, Holy Blood, Holy Grail 403.
[229] Baigent.

MANIPULATING BOURBON PROTESTANTS AND GUISE CATHOLICS: CIVIL WAR FOR A MEROVINGIAN UNIVERSAL THRONE

History tells us that the Reformation in the 16th century divided old France between Protestants and Catholics. The accepted historical consensus is that a group of warlike Protestants, calling themselves Huguenots, precipitated the events that ended with their massacre on St. Bartholomew's Day, August 24, 1572. We are not told of the Priory of Sion conspiracy that manipulated both sides of the conflict - a conflict that was fought to create for the Merovingians a Universal Throne.[230]

PLAYERS IN THE DRAMA

Conspiring for dominance, or survival, in the midst of France's Religious Wars were three royal families: (1) the pro-Protestant House of Bourbon: (2) the ardent Catholic House of Guise (subordinate to the House of Lorraine); and (3) the amiable Catholic House of Valois. The Houses of Valois and Guise were Merovingian, whereas the Bourbons were not. Not yet.

Bourbon royalty, protecting the Huguenots, ruled southwest France under a loose form of republicanism. The House of Guise, fighting viciously to annihilate the Huguenots, were the cadet branch or military arm of the Merovingian House of Lorraine, then ruling the Netherlands. Most powerful was the House of Valois, ruling northern France. Valois kings, more or less, desired peace rather than civil war between Protestants and Catholics. Their attitude only weakened an already rapidly eroding dominant Catholic position.

The Valois dynasty began with Charles of Valois (1328-1350), nephew of Merovingian Philip IV; also known as Philip the Fair. He was the same Philip who attempted the destruction of the Knights Templar and had Jacques de Molay burned at the stake in 1314. Charles of Valois became King Philip VI and held the Merovingian title *King of Jerusalem*.[231] In 1483 the title passed to the House of Lorraine through marriage, remaining there until 1735.

A century after the Valois dynasty was born, the Bourbon dynasty to the south joined the Protestant movement. Valois kings, already trying to contain the nominally Protestant Bourbons, were also having difficulty outside their borders. Austria's House of Habsburg (or Hapsburg) had sons on the thrones surrounding France. The Habsburg goal was to capture the French throne, then force a marriage with the House of Lorraine to obtain in one or two generations the "King of Jerusalem" title. Already the title of Holy Roman Emperor was attached to the Austrian throne, which throne also possessed the Spear of Destiny. The Habsburgs were well on their way to fulfilling the conditions of the Secret Doctrine for the Merovingians long-desired one-world empire!

Not willing to surrender the title "King of Jerusalem," the House of Lorraine conspired with their cadet House of Guise to take the powerful French throne for themselves, hoping thereby, to curb the Habsburg plan. Their strategy was to weaken the Valois dynasty through civil war, which meant exacerbating the existing strife between Protestants and Catholics.

---

[230] Will Durant, *The Story of Civilization: The Reformation,* Vol. VI (New York: Simon and Schuster, 1957) 61.
[231] Church 94.

To preserve their kingdom against this turmoil, the House of Valois was forced to continual appeasement when wars broke out between the Bourbon Protestants and Guise Catholics. These conflicts became known as the Religious Wars of France.

PRIORY OF SION AND THE RELIGIOUS WARS: SION'S GRAND MASTERS BACK BOURBON HUGUENOTS

Substantial evidence confirms that the Priory of Sion was manipulating both sides in the Religious Wars. The dukes of Lorraine, holding the title "King of Jerusalem," deployed two Grand Masters to France, both from the Guise clan. They were Ferdinand de Gonzague, better known as Ferrante de Gonzaga (GM 1527-1575), and Louis de Nevers, also known as Louis de Gonzaga (GM 1575-1595). Louis was the nephew of Ferrante. Their apparent assignment, which met with partial success, was to exterminate the Merovingian House of Valois in favor of the Merovingian House of Guise.[232]

Evidence supports the claim that to accomplish their task, the two Grand Masters of Sion backed the Bourbon Huguenot armies in order to weaken both the Valois dynasty and the Catholic Church. According to *Holy Blood, Holy Grail*, during the second and third quarters of the 16th century, Grand Master Ferrante "seems to have been covertly in league with the duke of Guise, who [in 1563] came within a hair's breadth of seizing the French throne."[233] In the last quarter of the 16th century, Grand Master Louis de Nevers "effectively exterminated the old Valois dynasty of France and nearly obtained the throne for the [House of Guise]."[234]

NOSTRADAMUS: PROPHET OR SECRET AGENT OF SION?

According to the "Prieure documents," the Guises and the Lorraines found an ally in a Jew named Nostradamus (1503~1566). Nostradamus was well aware of the history of the Priory of Sion and the Knights Templar. As the authors of *Holy Blood, Holy Grail* note, many of his writings "referred, quite explicitly, to the past - to the Knights Templar, the Merovingian dynasty, the history of the house of Lorraine... to the Razes - the old comte of Rennes-le- Chateau... In any case there is abundant evidence to suggest that Nostradamus was indeed a secret agent working for Francois de Guise and Charles, cardinal of Lorraine."[235]

The House of Valois, in ignorance, hired Nostradamus as court physician and astrologer. Not surprisingly, one of his first prophecies was that the Valois dynasty would soon be extinct.

Before embarking on his career as prophet to the French throne, however, Nostradamus spent considerable time in Lorraine where he was initiated into some portentous secret. An arcane book on which to base his prophecies was supposedly presented to him at the Abbey of Orval, the same Abbey where the Priory of Sion got its start in 1070.

---

[232] Baigent 166-171, 424-426.
[233] Baigent 424.
[234] Baigent 425.
[235] Baigent 170.

Holy Blood, Holy Grail claims that "as late as the French Revolution and the Napoleonic era, books of prophecies purportedly authored by Nostradamus were [still] issuing from Orval."[236] Holy Blood concludes:

> *"Many of Nostradamus' prophecies, in short, may not have been prophecies at all. They may have been cryptic messages, ciphers, schedules, timetables, instructions, blueprints for action."[237]*

Implementing these coded messages was one of the assignments of the Grand Masters of Sion. Francois, Duke of Guise, and his brother Charles (Cardinal of Lorraine) were related to both Grand Masters and may well have taken their orders directly from them. For example, the reputedly Catholic Guises and Lorraines funded the Protestants from time to time, while the Cardinal himself secretly gave money to certain Protestant groups. Again, on March 7, 1560, the Cardinal proposed amnesty for the Huguenots.[238]

The House of Guise has been stigmatized by historians as "rabidly bigoted and fanatic Catholics, intolerant, brutal, and bloodthirsty."[239] Yet, as the authors of *Holy Blood* state, "there is substantial evidence to suggest that this reputation is to some extent unwarranted, at least so far as adherence to Catholicism is concerned. Francois and his brother appear, quite patently, to have been brazen, if [not] cunning opportunists, courting both Catholics and Protestants in the name of their ulterior design."[240]

TROUBLE IN THE MEROVINGIAN BLOODLINE: THE VALOIS STIGMA

In 1533, young Henry de Valois (Henry IV) was wed to Catherine de Medicis, of the old royal Medici family of Italy. Both were age fourteen. Catherine was the niece of Pope Clement VII. Rumors of disease and mental illness started when for ten years no children were born to this young royal couple. Some blamed an inherent disability in Catherine, since both her parents had died of syphilis within twenty-two days of her birth. Yet, after ten years, children came almost annually - ten in all. Three died at an early age. Three became kings. Two were queens. Although Catherine outlived her husband and three successive royal sons, her children were all diseased or mentally ill.[241]

FRENCH THRONE FOR THE HOUSE OF GUISE

Disease in a Merovingian dynasty could not be tolerated by the Priory of Sion, whose duty it was to keep pure the so-called "Holy Bloodline." Consequently, there was added justification to terminate the Valois dynasty in behalf of the House of Guise.

---

[236] Baigent.
[237] Baigent.
[238] Baigent 459.
[239] Baigent 167.
[240] Baigent.
[241] Baigent 139.Cosimo de' Medici is credited with starting the Renaissance after having contact in 1439 with the Grand Master of the Priory of Sion, Rene d' Anjou [GM 1418-1480].

SION ATTEMPTS TO ENTHRONE THE HOUSE OF GUISE

When Henry died in 1559, Catherine's son, Francis II, was crowned at age sixteen. Within a year he died. Her second son, Charles IX, upon ascending the throne in 1560 at age 10, accepted the regency of his mother.

The historians Durant comment on Charles: "The sickliest of the sons, Charles IX, might have been a lovable youth except for occasional fits of cruelty and temper that blazed out at times into a passion verging on insanity. Between such storms he was a reed in the wind, seldom having a mind of his own."[242]

With the ascension of Charles IX, Ferrante de Gonzaga, Grand Master of Sion, gave orders to the House of Guise that now was the time to capture the weakened French throne. Anticipating a change of administration from the House of Valois to the House of Guise, the Council of Trent was convened in 1562 in preparation for bringing peace to France. Ferrante also intended for the Council to weaken the power of Rome in France, using the Cardinal of Lorraine to launch "an attempt to decentralize the papacy - to confer autonomy on local bishops and restore the ecclesiastical hierarchy to what it had been in Merovingian times."[243]

Grand Master Ferrante gave Francois, Duke of Guise, covert aid to seize the throne. In 1563 Francois was preparing to declare himself king of France when he fell to an assassin's bullet. On September 15 of that year, Charles IX, who was not yet fourteen, was declared of age. Catherine, while surrendering her regency, did not, however, give up her leadership.

MOVING AGAINST THE HUGUENOTS COLIGNY AND CONED: PROTESTANT WARRIORS

In 1564 pressure began mounting on the Crown to use forcible measures against the Protestant Huguenots, whose leaders were Admiral Gaspard de Coligny and Prince of Condé (Louis I of the House of Bourbon).

Prince Conde' had converted to Protestantism as a means of gaining support from his Huguenot subjects. Coligny, on the other hand, was a devout Christian, who studied Scripture and prayed every morning and evening. He detested the worldliness of the Catholic Church and was uneasy with the pomp of Royalty, yet found no difficulty in his political lobbying with a Catholic monarchy. He did not drink, was opposed to dancing, and lived a virtuous life. His only weakness was his military disposition, which lured him into many bloody battles with Catholics for the right to worship in peace. John Calvin warned him against such action.

Conde' controlled southwestern France. Coligny, presumptuous and fearful of no man, roamed all France. Fortunately for both, Catherine had often used her influence to protect them against the duplicitous House of Guise. She continued to do so now, even under great pressure.

To aid in constraining the Guise opposition, Catherine hired mercenaries from Switzerland. Misunderstanding her motives, the two Huguenot leaders, with armed followers, tried in September, 1567, to seize the young king and the queen mother.

---

[242] Durants, vol. VII, 346.
[243] Baigent 167.

Although the queen mother foiled their attempt, Catherine now feared the two men she once protected.

A SECOND RELIGIOUS WAR

To add more tension to the conflict, the young and vigorous Society of Jesus (the Jesuits), founded only thirteen years earlier had entered France in 1564. Although this new military priesthood was pledged and devoted to the papacy, it did not take up arms as did the Templars five centuries earlier. Jesuit sermons were, to the House of Guise at least, a welcome match to the warlike Huguenots. Agitated by Jesuit messages of hate, the Catholics repeatedly violated the edicts of toleration signed by the House of Valois, and barbarity reigned. Coligny felt that another attempt on the Throne was needed to restore the limited rights of the Huguenots. France subsequently entered her Second Religious War.[244]

PIUS V

In 1566 62-year-old Antonio Ghislieri, Dominican friar and Grand Inquisitor, became Pope Pius V. Historian Will Durant describes his personality: "He excommunicated Elizabeth of England and released the English Catholics from her allegiance. He urged Charles IX of France and Catherine de Medicis to prosecute war against the Huguenots till these should be utterly and mercilessly destroyed."[245]

TOLERATION AND PEACE WITH THE HUGUENOTS

The religiously tolerant Catherine refused. Peace was made with the Huguenots on March 23, 1568, restoring modest toleration. But the Catholic Guises, realizing the Protestants were becoming too powerful, denounced the treaty and refused to implement it. Coligny protested to Catherine, but remembering his earlier attempts on her life, she turned a deaf ear.

THIRD RELIGIOUS WAR AND TERMS OF RELIGIOUS PEACE

In May, 1568, Pope Pius finally convinced the House of Valois to assassinate both Coligny and Conde'. When the two Protestant leaders received this information, they formed a new Huguenot army. A fleet was assembled. Sympathetic Rosicrucian Englishmen offered their private vessels to serve under Conde's command.

The Durants explain Catherine's reaction to these events: "Catherine looked upon this Third Religious War as revolution, as an attempt to divide France into two nations, one Catholic, the other Protestant."[246] On March 3, 1569, the Third Religious War broke out. The Huguenots were defeated and Conde' died of wounds.

Catherine next offered Coligny a renewal of the original treaty. He refused it as inadequate and continued his advance. Then suddenly on August 8, 1570, the youthful Charles IX asserted his authority and signed a peace treaty. The treaty gave the oft-

---

[244] Durants, vol. VII, 238, 333-342.
[245] Durants, vol. VII, 239.
[246] Durants 345.

defeated Huguenots more than they had ever bargained for. They were granted "freedom of worship except in Paris or near the court, full eligibility to public office, and, as a guarantee that these terms would be honored in practice, the right to hold four cities under their independent rule fortwoyears."[247]

In September, 1571, Coligny joined the Valois court at Blois. Charles IX clung to him as weakness clings to strength, but Coligny began making strong demands of him. Catherine was warned of the King's secret councils with Coligny and took Charles aside to reproach him for having surrendered his mind to Coligny. He asked her forgiveness and promised obedience to her.

DYNASTIC MARRIAGE OF CATHOLIC TO PROTESTANT FOILS SION

That same year, Catherine made her last and boldest attempt to bring peace to France, a plan which ultimately could foil Sion's plan of establishing the House of Guise on the French throne. She decided to offer her daughter Marguerite in marriage to Henry III, Protestant King of Navarre, of the House of Bourbon, who, following the death of Conde', was head of the Huguenot empire. The marriage took place August 18, 1572, six days before St. Bartholomew's Day. This union, if Henry lived, would effectively bury Sion's plan for a speedy universal monarchy.

Little did Catherine realize the far-reaching consequences, destructive and beneficial, of this alliance. It was destructive to her royal House because it would end the Valois dynasty, as prophesied by Nostradamus. It would be destructive to all of France two centuries hence, since the marriage linked the House of Bourbon to Philip the Fair, the murderer of Jacques de Molay - an event which was an underlying cause of the French Revolution. It was beneficial to France because Henry III of Navarre would become Henry IV, the first Bourbon king to unite all France - and ultimately he would bring religious tolerance and peace to France for nearly a century, by signing the Edict of Nantes in 1598.

HOUSE OF GUISE AND SLAUGHTER OF THE HUGUENOTS

Meanwhile, the Netherlands revolted against the House of Lorraine. This pleased Coligny, who began pressing King Charles to give open aid to the revolting Netherlands. While Coligny anticipated approval of his request, the hammering of anvils throughout France revealed the hurried forging of weapons. Seeing a chance to forever rid France of Coligny and his Protestant followers, the House of Guise warned Catherine that the battle preparations were another attempt to kidnap her and the boy king. Catherine gave her consent to assassinate Admiral Coligny. Approval by King Charles was desirable, but not necessary.

Catherine and her Guise counselors surrounded the young ruler. According to the Durants, the insecure sovereign was informed that thirty thousand Huguenots were planning to seize him on the morrow and carry him off to some Protestant stronghold, where he would be captive and impotent; had they not twice before attempted such a move? Charles became agitated with them, and Catherine recognizing her son's hesitation, threatened to withdraw to Italy and leave him to his fate. His agitation turned to excitement, bringing him close to insanity. The boy king of 23 was told to choose

---

[247] Durants.

between his mother and Coligny. If he refused his mother, he would be set aside as a coward and a fool. Finally, in a fit of nerves and rage, Charles shouted, "Kill them all! Kill them all!" Cursing, he fled and shut himself up in his room.[248] The Durants conclude:

> If the conspirators had plotted to kill only a few, they now took advantage of the King's mad order to make the slaughter of the Huguenots as thorough as possible. Catherine insisted on protecting [her new son-in-law], Henry of Navarre...word was sent out to the district captains of Paris to arm their men and be ready for action at the tolling of church bells at three o'clock in the morning August 24, St. Bartholomew's Day. Carte blanche was given the Guises to execute their long-delayed revenge upon the Admiral. Henry of Guise sent word to the officers of the militia that at the tocsin's sound their men were to slay every Huguenot they could find.[249]

Nearly the entire race of Huguenots became extinct. Seventy thousand were killed during the weeks following August 24, 1572. Many thousands escaped and sailed to the New World, settling in America. All in all - and in the name of God - about 100,000 Protestants were slain in different parts of the kingdom.

HOUSE OF BOURBON VS. HOUSE OF GUISE

The twenty years of civil war which followed determined what noble house would replace the House of Valois in France. Would it be the House of Bourbon or the House of Guise?

In 1584 a fresh assault against the throne was attempted by the new duke of Guise and new cardinal of Lorraine. At their side was Louis de Gonzaga, Duke of Nevers, Grand Master of Sion since 1575. The banner of the conspirators was now the Cross of Lorraine, a Rosicrucian symbol.

Holy Blood records the results of this battle: "The feud continued. By the end of the century the Valois were at last extinct. But the house of Guise had bled itself to death in the process and could put forward no eligible candidate for a throne that finally lay within its grasp."[250]

TOLERATION AND FLEXIBILITY

Henry III, King of Navarre, who had wed Marguerite of Valois, daughter of Catherine, at last gained the throne through a succession of wars. He became King Henry IV of all France in 1593. Henry was the first of a long line of Bourbon kings, whose dynasty would span two centuries.

France remained Catholic, but Henry persuaded Parlement (French spelling) to accept six Huguenots into their assembly. Tolerance was restored, and the terror subsided.

Toleration was maintained, however, only so long as a lenient sovereign was persuasive of Parlement, and politically nimble enough to accept advice from it, while maintaining his power. Unlike the elected English Parliament, the French Parlement was

---

[248] Durants 350.
[249] Durants 351.
[250] Baigent 167.

appointed by the king. Should the sovereign be displeased with or threatened by this assembly, he simply disbanded it. Thus, Parlement could only be as tolerant as the king.

Henry displayed flexibility with his court of justice. In 1598 the Edict of Nantes was approved by Parlement and signed by the king bringing peace to France for nearly a century. After Henry's death, however, Parlement became a volatile institution.

SION AGAINST THE STUARTS

With the extinction of the Valois dynasty a fate accompli, Sion looked across the channel to the Scottish Templar Stuarts in line to ascend to the English throne (see chapter 2). Queen Elizabeth was old and childless. On her deathbed in 1603 she formally acknowledged James VI of Scotland her successor. James VI of Scotland became King James I of England.

A Templar throne in England was a more serious problem for Sion than the new Merovingian Bourbon throne in France. Hence, the next five Grand Masters of Sion concentrated on deposing the Templar Stuarts - a goal which took nearly a century to accomplish.

SION AGAINST THE BOURBONS:
SION ENCOURAGES THE HOUSE OF GUISE TO TOPPLE THE BOURBONS

The deposition of the Bourbons, however, would wait two hundred years, although one attempt at subversion was made during Robert Fludd's reign as Grand Master of Sion in England. In 1602, one year before James Stuart I ascended the British throne, Fludd made a lengthy trip to France. He had received a commission "to Marseilles to act as personal tutor to the sons of Henry of Lorraine, particularly Charles, the young duke of Guise. His association with Charles appears to have continued as late as 1620."[251]

Although there is no record as to what his tutoring entailed, it would certainly have included the history of Sion and the Merovingian dynasty in connection with Sion's attempt to capture the French throne for the House of Guise during the Religious Wars. It even possibly included a scheme for an overt seizure of the Bourbon throne. This theory is lent credence by the later actions of the Duke of Guise. For example, in 1610 the Duke married Henriette-Catherine de Joyeuse, whose possessions included Couiza at the foot of the mountain on which Rennes-le- Chateau is situated. In 1631 the Duke of Guise unsuccessfully conspired against the French throne and went into voluntary exile.[252]

CARDINAL RICHELIEU:
A POLICY SUITED TO ROSICRUCIAN TASTES

From 1610 to 1643 the throne of France was occupied by Louis XW, who was married to Anne of Austria. Louis paid little attention to his queen, who was lonely and desirous of male companionship.

The real power behind the throne was Cardinal Richelieu, the king's prime minister. Richelieu, if not a member of the Priory of Sion, was definitely a hireling. While the rest

---

[251] Baigent 426.
[252] Baigent.

of Europe flamed in the throes of the Thirty Years War, Richelieu established an unprecedented stability in France - until 1633. Prior to 1633, the Protestants in Germany were being financed by Sionist Rosicrucians from England and the Continent. Richelieu continued a precedent set by Sion during the Religious Wars of France: in 1633 he began financing the German Protestants.

Holy Blood explains this apparently bizarre policy: "In 1633 Cardinal Richelieu embarked on an audacious and seemingly incredible policy. He brought France into the Thirty Years War - but not on the side one would expect... A Catholic cardinal, presiding over a Catholic country, dispatch[ing] Catholic troops to fight on the Protestant side - against other Catholics... No historian has ever suggested that Richelieu was a Rosicrucian. But he could not possibly have done anything more in keeping with Rosicrucian attitudes, or more likely to win him Rosicrucian favor."[253]

LOUIS XIV ASCENDS THE THRONE

Louis XIII (r.1610-1643) and Anne remained childless. Suddenly, in 1638, after twenty-three years of sterile marriage, Anne produced a child. Few people at the time believed he was legitimate. Gossip had the child's father Cardinal Richelieu, or perhaps a surrogate employed by Richelieu, maybe Cardinal Mazarin, Richelieu's protégé' and successor. Both Louis XIII and Richelieu died in 1642. Some historians claim that Cardinal Mazarin afterwards secretly married the Queen Mother Anne.[254]

After the death of Louis XIII, the boy king ascended the throne in 1643. Louis XIV was age five. The queen mother took the regency for her son. Cardinal Mazarin was prime minister. At the queen mother's behest, the young king embraced Catholicism.

SION'S "COMPANY": PRECURSOR OF FREEMASONRY

According to the "Prieure documents," the Priory of Sion dedicated itself to deposing both Mazarin and the young king.[255] To accomplish this task, Sion founded a highly organized and efficient secret society named "The Compagnie du Saint-Sacrement." The Compagnie (or Company), meeting only with marginal success, was headquartered at Saint Sulpice, and established an intricate network of provincial branches. Similar to the operations of the Illuminati a century later, its members remained ignorant of their directors' identities. In short, the Company comprised a hydra-headed organization with a "hidden hand."

The Company was in fact a precursor of Freemasonry. As far as its lower level initiates were concerned, it was ostensibly devoted to charitable work, especially in regions devastated by the wars of religion. "It is now generally accepted," say the authors of *Holy Blood*, "that this 'charitable work' was merely a convenient and ingenious facade, which had little to do with the compagnie's real purpose. The real purpose was twofold - to engage in what was called pious espionage, gathering intelligence information, and to infiltrate the most important offices in the land, including circles in direct proximity to the throne"[256]

---

[253] Baigent.
[254] Baigent 172.
[255] Baigent 173.
[256] Baigent 174-175.

THE COMPANY'S REVOLUTIONARY INFLUENCE

By the mid-1600s the Compagnie du Saint-Sacrement wielded power through the aristocracy, the French Parlement, the judiciary, and the police - so much so, that on a number of occasions these bodies openly defied the king.[257] Actually, the Compagnie desired to control the monarchy through Parlement, but found an absolute monarchy resistant to parlementary control. For example, in 1648 Parlement addressed several demands to the King and his mother that must have seemed to them revolutionary. At the Queen Mother's rebuff, thirteen months of civil war, called the *Fronde*, broke out.

LOUIS' INITIAL TOLERATION

On September 8, 1651, when Louis XIV was thirteen, he announced that he was ending the regency of his mother and taking the government into his own hands. Even at this young age, Louis' justice, leniency, generosity, and self-control impressed the court. In 1652 Louis confirmed the Edict of Nantes. He expressed his appreciation of Huguenot loyalty and allowed them to hold their synods in peace.

Although King Louis was willing to open his reign to some tolerance, he was still an absolute monarch. He forcefully acted as such when in 1665, Parlement wishing to discuss some of his unsatisfactory decrees, he immediately ordered the disbanding of the assembly and outlawed the Compagnie du Saint-Sacrement.

LOUIS ABANDONS TOLERATION:
REVOKES THE EDICT OF NANTES

Meanwhile, as part of the Counter-Reformation of the Catholic Church, the Jesuits had maneuvered themselves into royal courts all over Europe as king's confessors. In reality they also functioned as advisors, as did the ancient Knights Templar.

King Louis too had his Jesuit confessors. This boy King was grieved that France was not united under Catholicism. When distress turned to distrust, his Jesuit advisors saw their chance to fuel the king's misgivings, suggesting the Huguenots were subversive - that they defied him in the Compagnie. Over the next two decades (from 1665 to 1685) freedoms were gradually taken from the Protestants. On October 17, 1685, 104 years before the Masonic French Revolution, Louis revoked the Edict of Nantes - the very document he had once confirmed.[258] *Foxe's Book of Martyrs* details the consequences:

> *Instantly the dragoons were quartered upon the Protestants throughout the realm, and filled all France with the like news, that the king would no longer suffer any Huguenots in his kingdom, and therefore they must resolve to change their religion. Hereupon the intendants in every parish (which were popish governors and spies set over the Protestants) assembled the reformed inhabitants, and told them they must, without delay, turn Catholics, either freely or by force. The Protestants replied, that they "were ready to sacrifice their lives and estates to the king, but their consciences being God's they could not so dispose of them."*

---

[257] Baigent 175.
[258] Durands, vol. VIII, 5-15, 69.

Instantly the troops seized the gates and avenues of the cities, and placing guards in all the passages, entered with sword in hand crying, "Die, or be Catholics!" In short, they practiced every wickedness and horror they could devise to force them to change their religion.

They hanged both men and women by their hair or their feet, and smoked them with hay until they were nearly dead; and if they still refused to sign a recantation, they hung them up again and repeated their barbarities, until, wearied out with torments without death, they forced many to yield to them.

Others, they plucked off all the hair of their heads and beards with pincers. Others they threw on great fires, and pulled them out again, repeating it until they extorted a promise to recant.

Some they stripped naked, and after offering them the most infamous insults, they stuck them with pins from head to foot, and lanced them with penknives; and sometimes with red-hot pincers they dragged them by the nose until they promised to turn. Sometimes they tied fathers and husbands, while they ravished their wives and daughters before their eyes. Multitudes they imprisoned in the most noisome dungeons, where they practiced all sorts of torments in secret. Their wives and children they shut up in monasteries.

Such as endeavored to escape by flight were pursued in the woods, and hunted in the fields, and shot at like wild beasts; nor did any condition or quality screen them from the ferocity of these infernal dragoons; even members of parliament and military officers, though on actual service, were ordered to quit their posts, and repair directly to their houses to suffer the like storm. Such as complained to the king were sent to the Bastille, where they drank the same cup. The bishops and the intendants marched at the head of the dragoons, with a troop of missionaries, monks, and other ecclesiastics to animate the soldiers to an execution so agreeable to their Holy Church, and so glorious to their demon god and their tyrant king.

Later this dreadful example of bigotry employed the pen of Voltaire (1694-1778) in deprecation of the horrors of superstition; and though an infidel himself, his essay on toleration does honor to his pen, and has been a blessed means of abating the rigor of persecution in most European states.[259]

VOLTAIRE, SION AND FREEMASONRY

Voltaire (1694-1778) was a revolutionary whose liberal philosophy helped prepare the French mind to revolt. Born nine years after the revocation of the Edict of Nantes, Voltaire grew up with these horrors impressed upon his young mind. With pen in hand he became embroiled in rebellion against Crown and Church.

Dr. George E. Dillon provides a brief childhood history of Voltaire: "His real name was Francis Mary Arouet, but, for some reason which has never been clearly explained, he chose to call himself Voltaire. He was the son of good parents, and by position and education should have been an excellent Catholic. He was trained by the very Jesuits whom he afterwards so hated and persecuted."[260]

Voltaire was age 20 when the Templar Stuarts were exiled to France and age 32 when he himself was "exiled" to England from France. From 1726 to 1728, while residing in London, Voltaire met nearly every prominent citizen in English letters or politics, including King George I, England's first Masonic king. From then on Voltaire believed

---

[259] Foxe 53-54, 59.
[260] Dillon 4-5.

that the best prospect for social reform would be through an "enlightened monarchy," meaning a monarchy whose king was a Mason.[261]

Voltaire's mentor in England was Freemason Alexander Pope[262], the famous English poet, who was a member of a rather obscure institution called the Gentleman's Club of Spalding.[263] This club was comprised of Rosicrucians, including Freemason Desaguliers, who helped organize the Grand Lodge, and Sir Isaac Newton, Grand Master of the Priory of Sion.

Voltaire was introduced to Newton when he met members of Sion's Royal Society. He attended Newton's funeral a year later. Afterward he read all the late Grand Master's work, as well as the books of Freemason John Locke[264], who before his death in 1704, had been intimate both with Newton and the previous Grand Master of Sion Robert Boyle. Finally, in 1728, just before returning to France, Voltaire joined English Masonry.[265]

There is no record of what transpired in Voltaire's two-year association with Sion's Masonic hierarchy - though, it appears Voltaire was an agent of the Priory of Sion. For example, when he returned to France from his English exile, he praised and imitated Alexander Pope's *Essay on Man*. He carried the books of the English deists home with him, including those of Isaac Newton and John Locke. All supplied him with ammunition he was to use in his war against the infamous French throne.[266]

Voltaire returned to France in 1728, the year after Charles Radcliffe (already in France) became Grand Master of the Priory of Sion. Although there is no evidence that Voltaire and Radcliffe knew each other, both were working for the Sionist conspiracy. Radclyffe's assignment was to make sure that the Templar Stuarts would not return to England. Voltaire's assignment was to foment revolution in the minds of Frenchmen.

As an English Freemason, Voltaire had the credentials to enter French Masonic Lodges, where he was protected. His writings also inflamed the Templars, who longed to avenge the murder of Jacques de Molay, a murder ordered by a French king, a king whose blood now flowed in the veins of the Bourbons.

Voltaire also became a confidant of the head of Scottish Rite Freemasonry, 32nd degree Frederick the Great, King of Prussia - a Templar king. Voltaire's commitment to a Masonic monarchy was so overpowering that when sent to Frederick's court in 1750, he spent three years there, encouraging the king to destroy not only the Catholic Church, but all Christianity. Voltaire continued correspondence with Frederick as late as 1767. Just before his death Voltaire was initiated into French Freemasonry.[267]

A CONSPIRACY MYSTERY: ALLIES OR ENEMIES?

Strangely, Voltaire and Radcliffe were both involved with the Templars and the Priory of Sion. For example, while Radcliffe was a Knights Templar fighting on the side of the Stuarts, he was appointed Grand Master of the Priory of Sion upon the death of Isaac Newton. Likewise, Voltaire had joined Sionist English Freemasonry, yet collaborated with Frederick the Great, the Templar King of Prussia. Either Sion and the

---

[261] Will Durant and Ariel Durrant, *The Story of Civilization: The Age of Voltaire*, vol. Ix (New York: Simon and Schuster, 1965) 245-248.

[262] "Pope, Alexander," Mackey's Encyclopedia of Free masonry, vol.11.

[263] Durants, vol. IX; 245-248.

[264] Durants.

[265] Dillon 6-7.

[266] Durants, vol. IX, 245-248.

[267] "Voltaire," *Mackey's Encyclopedia of Freemasonry*, vol.11.

Temple had reconciled to unite their efforts in dethroning the Bourbons, or Radcliffe and Voltaire both were double-agents for the Priory of Sion.

4. FROM ENGLAND TO FRANCE

The Order of the Illuminati was the greatest single misfortune ever to befall European Freemasonry because it became at once the pattern and the point of departure for a succession of secret, underground, political conspiracies which divided Masonry and brought disgrace upon its name.

Mackey's Encyclopedia of Freemasonry[268]

SION FAILS TO WIN THE FRENCH CROWN: BEYOND MONARCHY, TOWARDS REVOLUTION

Sion failed to capture the French throne for the Merovingian House of Lorraine during the Religious Wars of France. As we shall see in this chapter, Sion continued its scheme to secure the French crown, having successfully brought the British crown under its dominion through England's Glorious Revolution.

We will review Sion's intrigue, carried out by Grand Master Charles Radcliffe, to prevent the return of Templar Charles Edward Stuart to the throne of England. These plans also involved the creation and spread of Sionist-inspired Masonic lodges across Europe, which will figure later in our history.

Of the crowned heads of Europe, one in particular arose to thwart Sion's designs on the French throne - Frederick the Great of Prussia, a powerful military leader and 32nd degree Templar Freemason. Opposing Frederick was the Grand Master of Sion after Radcliffe's death, Charles of Lorraine, who although defeated by Frederick, helped select Adam Weishaupt as founder of the Illuminati - a secret society which would eventually penetrate and ultimately transform French Freemasonry on the Continent into a revolutionary power and shape the creation of a new world power in North America.

SION CONTROLS BRITISH MONARCHY

When Sion's Rosicrucians united the splintered factions of English Freemasonry in 1717, they embarked on a course to control the British monarchy permanently. The ease with which they accomplished this is indicated by the following three facts. First, the king was a Mason. Second, His Majesty's royal court was staffed with Masonic fellow travellers. Third, beginning in 1737, the firstborn son of every reigning monarch, except one, has been titular head of English Freemasonry.

SION TURNS TO THE CONTINENT

With British kings under Masonic obedience, Sion's Grand Masters were no longer required in England. After the death of Isaac Newton in 1727, we find Sion shifting her attention to the Continent where the Stuarts were in exile. The new Grand Master of Sion

---

[268] "Knigge, Baron Von," *Mackey's Encyclopedia of Freemasonry*, vol.111.

appears to have had a two-fold assignment: (1) direct the Templars against the French throne: and (2) thwart any Stuart attempt to reclaim the British crown.

SION AND TEMPLARS: ALLIES OR ENEMIES?

Sion shrewdly selected as the new Grand Master Charles Radcliffe (GM 1727-1746), himself a Knights Templar. Either the hierarchy of the Priory of Sion and the Knights Templar had united to link the organizations in this one man, or it is possible that Radcliffe was a double-agent in the cause of Sion.

Subsequent events and Masonic symbology suggest both scenarios. Radcliffe seems to have been a double-agent, but only Sion's hierarchy was aware of his commission. Lower grade initiates who hobnobbed with the Grand Master were unwavering Templars. To them he would appear loyal to their cause.

Radcliffe's involvement in and support of the Stuart cause had long been established. He and his brother James participated in the Scottish rebellion of 1715. Both were captured and imprisoned, and James executed. Radcliffe made a daring escape and found refuge in the Jacobite ranks in France. So far as the Jacobites were concerned, he was one of them.

Radcliffe had additional and unusual credentials which endeared him to the Stuarts. His mother was an illegitimate daughter of Charles Stuart II by the king's mistress, making him a grandson of the monarch and cousin to the exiled (Bonnie) Prince Charles Edward. Radcliffe could have won the Young Pretender's confidence through kinship alone, even had he not built his reputation as a Jacobite supporter.

Radcliffe was in Paris in 1727 when he humbly accepted the appointment of Grand Master of the Priory of Sion. Evidence reveals that he was aware of the dangers he faced working as a double- agent. Radcliffe, for example, kept a low profile, operating to a significant degree through intermediaries. Not surprisingly, his tactics proved clever, even when facing execution. More important to him than life was the success of his mission. Radcliffe may well have been the most brilliant of Sion's Grand Masters. Yet he remains an obscure personality.

PLANTING ENGLISH MASONRY ON THE CONTINENT

Meanwhile the seeds of English Freemasonry were being sown throughout the Continent by Dr. Desaguliers, one of the Rosicrucian founders of the United Grand Lodge. Desaguliers visited The Hague in 1731 to initiate the Merovingian Nicolas-Francois, duke of Lorraine, into Masonry.[269] Francois, holder of the title "King of Jerusalem," became head of English Freemasonry on the Continent.

Desaguliers' timing was no accident. Two years earlier, in 1729, Francois had begun a lengthy stay in England, for which there has been given no explanation. His contacts, however, deserve mention for they tell us what may have transpired there. He became a member of the Gentleman's Club of Spalding, whose members consisted of a number of Rosicrucians, among whom were Desaguliers himself, Isaac Newton, and Freemason Alexander Pope, Voltaire's mentor during the years 1726-1728.[270]

---

[269] Knight, *The Brotherhood* 25-26.
[270] Baigent et al, *Holy Blood* 147.

TEMPLAR CHARLES RAMSAY: MASONIC SPOKESMAN OF HIS AGE

Another of Desaguliers' contacts in London was a Templar, Chevalier Ramsay. Ramsay, who had been exiled with the Stuarts returned to join the Gentleman's Club of Spalding at precisely the same time as did Francois. More significant is Ramsay's prompt appointment to the Royal Society, without any apparent credentials. The Royal Society, led by Desaguliers and Newton, was, as you may recall, Sion's controller of the British monarchy before English Freemasonry was united.

No record of what transpired during Francois' encounters with the English Sionists is forthcoming. Yet we can speculate, based upon subsequent events. Francois and Ramsay both returned to the Continent in 1730 with separate assignments to move against the French throne. If one failed, the other would succeed.

RADCLIFFE: POWER AND VOICE BEHIND RAMSAY

When Ramsay returned to France he became increasingly active on behalf of Templar Freemasonry. On March 21, 1737, he made a famous Masonic speech before the Grand Lodge of France in Paris, on the basis of which he became the preeminent Masonic spokesman of his age. *Holy Blood, Holy Grail* authors conclude, however, that another figure hovered behind Ramsay: "the real voice behind Ramsay was that of Charles Radcliffe - who presided over the lodge at which Ramsay delivered his discourse and who appeared again, in 1743, as chief signatory at Ramsay's funeral."[271]

PROPOSED: A FRENCH (REFORMED) MASONRY

Mackey's Encyclopedia of Free masonry records Ramsay's famous speech as having been Masonry's seventh historical address. Ramsay "discussed Freemasonry and the Crusaders and traced an imaginary history of its course through Scotland and England into France, which was to become the center of the reformed [Templar] Order."[272]

Based upon the content of his speech (obviously intended for the ears of his Templar companions), Ramsay's assignment was to steer the Templar Stuarts away from the Scottish and British thrones to a permanency in France, "the center of the reformed Order." His speech, however, failed in its purpose.

SIONIST RADCLIFFE: THE PRETEND PRETENDER

In 1742 Charles Radcliffe, who was now personal secretary to the Young Pretender, Charles Edward Stuart, learned that the Prince was planning an attempt on the British throne by way of Scotland. Immediately Radcliffe went into action to thwart his Majesty's scheme. He employed an adventuresome nobleman, a Protestant and German Mason in the English Masonic Obedience, who would be able, if need be, to communicate with London. His name was Baron Karl Gottlieb von Hundt, or Hund.

Hund had just arrived in Paris from London. While at the Paris lodge, he learned of the existence of the Order of Knights Templar in Scotland. Fascinated by the Knights, he

---

[271] Baigent 147.
[272] "Addresses, Masonic," *Mackey's Encyclopedia,* vol.1.

sought membership and was initiated into the higher degrees of the Order just before he embarked for Germany. The man who presided over his initiation was thought by Hund to have been the bonnie Prince Charlie himself. Proof has since been given that the initiation was not under the leadership of the Pretender at all, but was Charles Radcliffe in disguise.[273]

HUND'S MISSION:
TO SPREAD TEMPLAR FREEMASONRY IN GERMANY

Impersonating the Young Pretender, Radcliffe told Hund of his intent to reclaim the British crown, hoping the disclosure would somehow reach Protestant London via the German Protestant Hund.

Hund was then given the mandate to take to Germany with all haste the high degrees of Jacobite Freemasonry and establish there an aristocratic lodge, which would be descended directly from the Knights Templar. There he was to await further instruction from "Unknown Superiors." Before Hund departed, he was given a list of Knights Templar Grand Masters from Hughes de Payens.

Mackey's Encyclopedia of Freemasonry picks up the story: "Von Hund returned to Germany possessed of powers, or a Deputation granted to him in Paris by which he was authorized to disseminate the advanced Degrees in that country. He was not slow to exhibit these documents, and soon collected around him a band of adherents. He then attempted what he termed a reform in primitive Freemasonry on the simple English system of the three Symbolic Degrees, which alone most of the German Lodges recognized. The result was the establishment of a new system, well known as the Rite of Strict Observance."[274] Its name derived from the oath it demanded, an oath of unswerving, unquestioning obedience to the mysterious Unknown Superiors.

The Rite of Strict Observance was comprised of Germans drawn entirely from the intellectual and aristocratic classes, per Radcliffe's instructions. On its membership roster were princes, dukes, barons, Prussian and German ministers, all of Protestant stock.[275] Freemason Gould, in *History of Freemasonry*, observes that "[n]o trace of Jacobite intrigues ever blended with the teaching of the Strict Observance"[276] - which means that no further instruction came down to Hund from his Unknown Superiors.

POLITICAL CONSEQUENCES OF HUND'S "INSTRUCTIONS"

The lack of further "instruction" may well have been Radcliffe's intent. Endless waiting for further orders would frustrate the adventuresome Hund, even embarrass him - maybe force him to talk. Indeed, he began to complain that his Unknown Superiors had abandoned him. In his defense, he revealed that his initiation had been conducted by the Bonnie Prince - and that the Young Pretender intended to reclaim the British crown. Such politically indiscreet and inflammable talk would, by its nature, reach London.

Meanwhile, the Young Pretender planned to invade Scotland in 1745. Radcliffe, expected to follow, delayed several months. No one knows why. We can only speculate. Perhaps Radcliffe awaited confirmation from London that it knew of the Bonnie Prince's

---

[273] Baigent 147.
[274] "Hunt, Baron Von," *Mackey's Encyclopedia* vol.1.
[275] Webster, *Secret Societies* 154.
[276] Webster.

plans. Perhaps he delayed to "leak" to England his own departure date. At any rate, to maintain his cover, Radcliffe finally set sail for Scotland.

Holy Blood, Holy Grail, provides details of the entire ill-fated venture:

> *"In 1745 the [Young Pretender] landed in Scotland and embarked on his quixotic attempt to reinstate the Stuarts on the British throne. In the same year Radcliffe, en route to join him, was captured in a French ship off the Dogger Bank. A year later, in 1746, the Young Pretender was disastrously defeated at the Battle of Culloden Moor. A few months thereafter, Charles Radcliffe died beneath the headsman '5 ax at the Tower of London."[277]*

Charles Radcliffe, Grand Master of Sion, paid the greatest price for the defeat of the Stuart cause. In a eulogy to him, the authors of Holy *Blood* state, "It is probable that Scottish Rite Freemasonry was originally promulgated, if not indeed devised, by Charles Radcliffe. In any case Radcliffe, in 1725, is said to have founded the first Masonic lodge on the continent, in Paris. During the same year, or perhaps in the year following, he seems to have been acknowledged grand master of all French lodges and is still cited as such a decade later, in 1736. The dissemination of eighteenth-century Freemasonry owes more, ultimately, to Radcliffe than to any other man."[278]

VICTORIOUS SION AND CHARLES STUART: THE PRETENDER ADMITTED INTO TEMPLARS

Mackey's Encyclopedia of Free masonry reveals that a few months after Prince Charles Edward arrived in Scotland, "[o]n September 24, 1745, he was admitted into the Order of Knights Templar, and was elected Grand Master, an office which it is said that he held until his death [in 1788]."[279] During his initiation, the Young Pretender apparently learned of the Sionist-Rosicrucian plot that would defeat his bid for the Scottish throne. He alludes to these opponents upon his return to France, where he founded in 1747 the Scottish Jacobite Chapter of Freemasonry, better known as the Scottish Rite. In its three-paragraph charter the Prince wrote: "our sorrows and misfortunes [came] by that of Rose Croix..."[280]

Realizing a power mightier than the Templars caused his downfall, Prince Charles turned his back on England and directed his attention toward the French throne to avenge the death of Jacques de Molay. *Mackey's Encyclopedia of Freemasonry* confirms that the Scottish Templars were the ones who "invented the Degree of Kadosh, which represents the revenge of the Templars."[281]

CONFIRMING HUND'S CLAIMS

Meanwhile, Baron von Hund was still awaiting orders from his Unknown Superiors. For ten years, and to his own embarrassment and subsequent disgrace, Hund had received no further instruction. As a result, his contemporaries dismissed him as a charlatan and

---

[277] Baigent 145.
[278] Baigent 146.
[279] "Stuart Masonry," *Mackey's Encyclopedia*, vol.11.
[280] "Arras, Primordial Chapter of," *Mackey's Encyclopedia*, vol.1.
[281] "Stuart Masonry."

accused him of having fabricated the story. In defense he could only reply that his Unknown Superiors had abandoned him. Until his death he affirmed his integrity.[282]

The authors of *Holy Blood, Holy Grail* credit the veracity of Hund's claim: "By 1746... Radcliffe was dead. So were many of his colleagues, while others were in prison or exile - as far away, in some cases, as North America. If Hund's 'Unknown Superiors' failed to reestablish contact with their protege, the omission does not seem to have been voluntary. The fact that Hund was abandoned immediately after the collapse of the Jacobite cause would seem, if anything, to confirm his story."[283]

The most convincing evidence to confirm Hund's story, the authors continue, "is a list of grand masters of the Knights Templar, which Hund insisted he had obtained from his 'Unknown Superiors.' On the basis of our own research, we had concluded that the list of Templar grand masters in the *Dossiers secrets* was accurate - so accurate, in fact, that it appeared to derive from inside information. Save for the spelling of a single surname, the list Hund produced agreed precisely with the one in the *Dossiers secrets*. In short, Hund had somehow obtained a list of Templar grand masters more accurate than any other known at the time... This would seem to confirm that Hund's story of 'Unknown Superiors' was not a fabrication. It would also seem to indicate that those 'Unknown Superiors' were extraordinarily knowledgeable about the Order of the Temple - more knowledgeable than they could possibly have been without access to privileged sources."[284]

A SION-MEROVINGIAN MARRIAGE:
IN HOPES OF A FUTURE MESSIAH OF ISRAEL

The Merovingian Nicholas-Francois, Duke of Lorraine, returned to France from England in 1730 to activate his Sionist assignment. He first planned to wed the Merovingian Empress Maria Theresa von Habsburg of Austria. The alliance would for the first time merge in one "Holy Blood" family the titles King of Jerusalem and Holy Roman Emperor, with the Spear of Destiny in its possession. In one or two generations the Messiah of Israel (known to the Holy Grail bloodline as the Lost King) would be born. To the Merovingians, the Lost King would combine awesome esoteric, political, and military powers - and be a personage to be feared and obeyed.

CONSOLIDATING POWER:
TAKING FRANCE BY MARRIAGE

In 1731 Francois was initiated into English Freemasonry at The Hague by Dr. Desaguliers. Four years later he married Maria Theresa von Habsburg. When Francois moved his court to Vienna, it became the European capital of Sionist English Freemasonry.

Francois' younger brother by four years was Charles of Lorraine, a skilled military commander. In 1744 Charles married Maria Theresa's sister, Marie Anne, and became commander-in-chief of the Austrian army, putting the Austrian military at the service of Merovingian-Sionist aims. In 1746, upon the death of Charles Radcliffe, Francois appointed Charles of Lorraine Grand Master of the Priory of Sion. Indeed, the royal court

---

[282] Baigent 148.
[283] Baigent 149.
[284] Baigent.

at Vienna had become the most powerful esoteric- political body on earth. To become the greatest military power, Vienna would only have to occupy the powerful French throne. To achieve this, the Grand Master of Sion had three choices at his command - take France by force, marriage, or subversion.

Taking France by force was out of the question, however. The historians Will and Ariel Durant describe the power of France:

> [T]he French state was the strongest in Christendom, confident in its natural resources, the skills and loyalty of its people, the strategy of its generals, the destiny of its King.
>
> One reason for French domination was manpower. France had a population of 20,000,000... while Spain and England had 5,000,000 each, Italy 6,000,000, the Dutch Republic 2,000,000. The Holy Roman Empire, which included Germany, Austria, Bohemia, and Hungary, had some 21,000,000; but it was an empire only in name... and divided into over four hundred jealously 'sovereign' states, nearly all small and weak, each with its own ruler, army, currency, and laws, and none with more than 2,000,000 inhabitants. France... was a geographically compact nation, united under one strong central government...[285]

To secure the French throne by marriage, Francois and Maria gave their daughter Marie Antoinette in marriage to the Bourbon king of France, Louis XVI. This royal marriage brought the Merovingian's final ambitions within grasp. As *Holy Blood, Holy Grail* observes: "It was in the eighteenth century... that the Merovingian bloodline probably came closest to the realization of its objectives. By virtue of its intermarriage with the Hapsburgs [or Habsburgs], the house of Lorraine had actually acquired the throne of Austria, the Holy Roman Empire. When Marie Antoinette, daughter of Francois de Lorraine, became queen of France, the throne of France, too, was only a generation or so away. Had not the French Revolution intervened, the house of Hapsburg-Lorraine might well, by the early 1800s, have been on its way to establishing dominion over all Europe."[286]

SION'S POWERFUL RIVAL: FREDERICK THE GREAT, TEMPLAR KING OF PRUSSIA AND HEAD OF HIGH MASONRY

According to *Mackey's Encyclopedia of Freemasonry*, "the exiled House of Stuart exercised an important part In the invention and extension of what has been called the High Masonry."[287] We know that by 1755 the Templar Scottish Rite had advanced to 32 degrees. At the head of High Masonry was Frederick the Great (Frederick II), the powerful military leader of Prussia. *Mackey's Encyclopedia of Freemasonry* tells us that Frederick "was initiated as a Freemason, at Brunswick, on the night of August 14, 1738, not quite two years before he ascended the throne."[288]

Frederick's initiation took place with haste following Ramsay's famous speech. Frederick had sensed that Templarism was being developed to topple the French throne. He wanted to use it to further Prussian supremacy. Upon ascending the throne in 1740, he became even more active in Freemasonry, initiating two of his brothers, a brother-in-

---

[285] Durants, vol. VIII, 3.
[286] Baigent 404.
[287] "Stuart Masonry."
[288] "Frederick The Great," *Mackey's Encyclopedia*, vol.1.

law, and a duke into the Templar Rite. That same year he called an urgent conference with Voltaire. Two remarkable events followed: (1) additional degrees were added to Templar Freemasonry; and (2) instructions for a revived Order of Templarism were taken to Paris.

By 1746 Frederick's initiates had founded fourteen Masonic Lodges. That same year, after Radcliffe's death, Frederick became the acclaimed head of Continental Freemasonry. He then used the Scottish Rite for his own independent bid for the French throne, by trying to destroy the alliance between France and Austria. Time and again he created discord between Versailles and Vienna through his Masonic agents.

Sion was taken by complete surprise and forced to counter Frederick's political and military ventures. In 1750 Voltaire was deployed the second time to Prussia, to persuade the King to redirect his efforts toward the Catholic Church. Charles of Lorraine, the new Grand Master of Sion, took Austria's armies into several battles against the Templar king. Charles fought the monarch in a final battle in 1757 (called the Battle of Leuthen) and lost. "And yet Frederick regarded Charles as a worthy and 'redoubtable' adversary and spoke of him only in glowing terms."[289]

In consequence of Charles' defeat, Empress Maria Theresa von Habsburg relieved him of his command, and Charles of Lorraine retired to his capital at Brussels.[290] From there he worked through intermediaries, as did Radcliffe. For example, Charles apparently had something to do with the selection of a renegade Jesuit named Adam Weishaupt to further the goals of Sion. Weishaupt, in turn, was founder of the Illuminati.

THE ILLUMINATI: A CONVENIENT ALLIANCE

Sion and the Templars both had their sights set on the French throne, but were not yet united in their efforts. For example, Frederick the Great, as head of the Templar Scottish Rite on the Continent, wanted to take the French throne by intrigue, while Sion planned to absorb it through marriage.

As we have observed, Sion had several simultaneous programs to reach its goal of world government. The Illuminati, although short lived by that name, appears to have been the one program most successful. Its assignment was to develop an alternate form of government at Paris - a democratic republic involving a coalition with the Templars should the impending French Revolution overthrow the Bourbon dynasty.

The first worldwide exposure of the Continental conspiracy involving the Illuminati was published in 1798, nine years after the French Revolution had begun. Authored by John Robison, professor of Natural Philosophy at Edinburgh University, *Proofs of a Conspiracy against all the Religions and Governments of Europe* was, among other things, a written warning to Great Britain and her oligarchic Brotherhood.

John Robison, a Master Mason in English Freemasonry, was a man of unquestionable character. He exposed the *illuminati* as an order housed within French Freemasonry bent on the destruction of the Roman Catholic Church, the dethroning of all monarchies, and the confiscation of businesses and land.[291] Its ultimate aim was to inaugurate a New World Order governed by an initiated few.

For several years prior to the French Revolution, Robison traveled throughout Europe, frequenting many Continental Lodges. Being a Scotsman, he naturally wanted to receive the high degrees in the Scottish Rite. During his travels he learned of the Illuminati. Appearing sympathetic to their cause, Robison was entrusted with Illuminati

---

[289] Baigent 432.
[290] Baigent.
[291] John Robison, *Proofs of a Conspiracy* (1798; Boston: Western Islands, 1967) entire.

documents. After the French Revolution and its atrocities, he studied these Illuminati documents and for the first time realized that republican French Masonry was in total opposition to the designs and directions set forth by monarchist English Masonry. He therefore felt he was not infringing on his Masonic obligation of silence by unmasking this clandestine Order.

Mackey's Encyclopedia of Freemasonry describes Robison's book as "a history of the introduction of Freemasonry on the Continent, and of its corruptions, and... to a violent attack on the Illuminati. But while recommending that the Lodges in England should be suspended, he makes no charge of corruption against them, but admits the charities of the Order, and its respectability of character."[292]

Mackey in his final comment seems to concur with Professor Robison's evaluation of French Freemasonry during the Revolution:

> "So that, after all, [Robison's] charges are not against Freemasonry in its original constitution, but against its corruption in a time of great political excitement."[293]

WEISHAUPT AND THE ILLUMINATI

Mackey's Encyclopedia of Freemasonry describes the Illuminati as: "A secret society, founded on May 1, 1776, by Adam Weishaupt, who was Professor of Canon Law at the University of Ingolstadt. Its founder at first called it the Order of the Perfectibilists; but he subsequently gave it the name by which it is now universally known... Weishaupt, though a reformer in religion and a liberal in politics, had originally been a Jesuit... To give to the Order a higher influence, Weishaupt connected it with the Masonic Institution, after whose system of Degrees, of esoteric instruction, and of secret modes of recognition, it was organized... The character [or symbol drawn as a rectangle], now so much used by Freemasons to represent a Lodge, was invented and first used by the Illuminati [as was the point within a circle, by which the Illuminati was symbolically and universally identified]... [I]t cannot be denied, that in process of time abuses had crept into the Institution and that by the influence of unworthy men the system became corrupted."[294]

Conspiracy researchers have mixed opinions about who was behind the Illuminati. A "Miss Stoddard," author of *Trail of the Serpent* and writing under the pseudonym "Enquire Within," views the Illuminati as "The Knights Templar...gathering again."[295] Many Templars did join the Illuminati. Just as evident, however, is that Rosicrucians were represented in the Order as well. Edith Starr Miller, in *Occult Theocrasy*, states that the Illuminati was as much Rosicrucian as it was Templar.

Each author calls the Illuminati "short-lived"; each concurs that initially its "Great Plan" was pure, but that corruption set in; and each states that its membership consisted of Templars and Rosicrucians.[296]

---

[292] "Robison, John," *Mackey's Encyclopedia,* vol.11.

[293] "Robison, John."

[294] "Illuminati of Bavaria," *Mackey's Encyclopedia,* vol.1.

[295] Miss Stoddard, *Trail of the Serpent* (1935; Hawthorne, CA: Christian Book Club, n.d.) 283. Miss Stoddard was discovered to be the unnamed author of this book and of another, *Light- bearers of Darkness*. She had good reason for wishing to remain unnamed. As a Ruling Chief of the Mother Temple of the Stella Matutina and R.R.et A.C., she was placing her life at jeopardy by exposing the secrets of this homicidal Masonic Lodge, a lodge co-founded by Satanist and 33rd degree Freemason Aleister Crowley.

[296] Miller 371.

The plan of the Hierarchy in Sion and in the Templars remained so secret, however, that even the highest degree Masons were perplexed as to the real function of the Illuminati. The Illuminati appears to have been a cooperative venture to inaugurate the New World Order long dreamed of by both the Priory of Sion and the Knights Templar.

SION AND WEISHAUPT

Mackey's Encyclopedia of Freemasonry gives Weishaupt's birth date and states his hostility toward the Jesuits: He "adopted the characteristic or Order name of *Spartacus,* was born on February 6, 1748, at Ingoldstadt, and was educated by the Jesuits, toward whom, however, he afterward exhibited the bitterest enmity, and was equally hated by them in return."[297]

When Weishaupt formed the Illuminati, he used the Jesuit structure as guide, yet employed the Egyptian rites of Ormus in his ceremonies, the same rites exercised by the Priory of Sion. Rev. J.R. Church agrees that probably Weishaupt was a Sionist, and concludes: "The Illuminati, then, may be simply another name in the ongoing development of the Priory of Sion..."[298]

Church also compares the ceremonies, symbols and theology of the Illuminati with Sion and the Rosicrucians and finds them identical, all three deriving from Egyptian mysticism.[299] For example, the point within a circle (a form of the All-Seeing Eye of the Egyptian sun-god Osiris), is a symbol in all three orders.[300] Weishaupt's goal was also identical to Sion's: a New World Order controlled by an initiated few.

The *Encyclopedia Britannica* (1984) indirectly connects the Illuminati with Sion via the Rosicrucians, observing that "[t]he name illuminati is also given... to the Rosicrucians."[301] This fact is documented in the *Rosicrucian Manual* itself:

> *Members who attain and complete the psychic instruction of the ninth degree or those above it may enter the Illuminati, which is a higher organization of the order wherein the worthy members continue to carry on specialized work and studies under the direction of the imperator of their jurisdiction and the personal cosmic masters. Members cannot ask for admission to the Illuminati, but must wait until they have been found ready and are invited in this additional work.*[302]

One of Weishaupt's first initiates was a traitor to his own royal house - Louis Philippe Joseph, Duke of Orleans, cousin to the Bourbon king of France. The Duke had already been initiated into French Grand Lodge Freemasonry, and according to *Mackey's Encyclopedia of Freemasonry,* he "was elected Grand Master in the year 1771, upon the death of the Count de'Clermont."[303]

The Duke of Orleans broke from the Masonic turmoil in France, which centered around British obedience in the French Grand Lodge, and founded the clandestine French Grand Orient Lodge in 1772. The Duke, according to *Mackey's Encyclopedia of*

---

[297] "Weishaupt, Adam," *Mackey's Encyclopedia,* vol.11.
[298] Church 169.
[299] Church 157-169.
[300] Church 165.
[301] "Illuminati," Encyclopaedia Britannica: Micropaedia.
[302] Harve Spencer Lewis, *Rosicrucian Manual* (N.P.: Supreme Grand Lodge of AMORC, 1955) 74.
[303] "Orleans, Duke of," *Mackey's Encyclopedia,* vol.11.

Freemasonry, also held the position of Grand Master in this opposition Lodge until he was guillotined during the Revolution in 1793.

WEISHAUPT'S BRILLIANT CAREER

In 1772, Weishaupt at age 24 was a brilliant religionist. Dr. Mackey reports that he became that year Extraordinary Professor of Law, and in 1775, Professor of Natural History and Canon Law, at the University of Ingoldstadt.[304] On May 1, 1776, at age 28, he officially organized the secret society he had started in the university five years earlier. Students at Ingolstadt University were his first initiates. After graduation they scattered throughout the Continent, working in their various professions where Weishaupt engaged them in furthering his revolutionary goals.

According to *Mackey's Encyclopedia of Freemasonry*, "It was not until 1777 that Weishaupt was initiated in the Lodge Theodore of Good Counsel, at Munich. Thence forward, Weishaupt sought to incorporate his system into that of Freemasonry, so that the latter might become subservient to his views and with the assistance of a staunch Templar, Baron Knigge, who brought his active energies and genius to the aid of the cause, he succeeded in completing his system of Illuminism."[305]

THE ILLUMINATI AND MASONRY

By 1785, nine years after Weishaupt had officially recorded the Illuminati as operative, Illuminati doctrines had sufficiently penetrated the French Grand Lodge and the French Grand Orient that they changed forever the direction of these two Continental Brotherhoods, ultimately reshaping International Freemasonry.

Mackey's Encyclopedia of Free masonry condemns the influence of Weishaupt's Illuminati upon Freemasonry: "The Order of the Illuminati was the greatest single misfortune ever to befall European Freemasonry because it became at once the pattern and the point of departure for a succession of secret, underground, political conspiracies which divided Masonry and brought disgrace upon its name"[306]

Not surprisingly, the authors of *Holy Blood, Holy Grail* fall to mention Adam Weishaupt. Their research, restricted to individuals named in the "Priory documents," would not find Weishaupt among them. They do, however, name a Rosicrucian Sionist who figured in the Illuminati plot, and who may well have been the "controller" of Weishaupt. He is mentioned along with two Grand Masters of Sion, although he himself was never a Grand Master. His name was Joseph Balsamo.[307]

Balsamo worked as a double-agent for Sion by joining the Templar Strict Observance. Soon afterwards, Adam Weishaupt ordered the Illuminati to absorb into its ranks the best of the initiates in the Strict Observance. Nesta Webster confirms that "The first Masonic body with which the Illuminati formed an alliance was the Stricte [sic] Observance..."[308]

ILLUMINATI: A CONTINGENCY PLAN

---

[304] "Weishaupt, Adam."
[305] "Weishaupt, Adam."
[306] "Knigge, Baron Von."
[307] Baigent 206.
[308] Webster 233.

Our research concludes that the Illuminati was initially formed as a cooperative venture between the hierarchies of Sion and the Templars to finish the task of two centuries ago - that of dethroning the Bourbons. The Templars were seeking revenge for the death of Jacques de Molay. Sion was seeking the French throne for the Merovingian Lorraine-Habsburg dynasty. Should Sion fail in its bid for a universal monarchy, it would transform its strategy to bring about a New World Order of republicanism. In either case the British crown was no longer necessary for the protection of the Merovingian kings. The Templars would again assume that function, for Templar military lodges were already forming throughout the French forces.

WEISHAUPT'S HANDLER:
KOLMER OR CHARLES OF LORRAINE?

Nesta Webster reports that Weishaupt did not receive the inspiration on his own for forming the Illuminati. In 1771, she claims, a mysterious Jutland merchant named Kolmer, who supposedly had spent many years in Egypt, returned to Europe to initiate Weishaupt into the Rose-Croix rites of Egyptian mysticism. On his way to Germany from Egypt, Kolmer stopped at Malta, where a remnant of the English competitors of the Knights Templar existed under the name Knights of Malta. There Kolmer rendezvoused with a famous Freemason and magician named Cagliostro. Together they displayed their magic to the crowds, nearly bringing about an insurrection among the people. Both men were driven off the island by the Knights of Malta and Kolmer promptly went to Germany for a rendezvous with Adam Weishaupt. During the next five years, Kolmer initiated Weishaupt in all the mysteries of his secret doctrine, ending his instruction in the spring of 1776. On May 1, 1776, Weishaupt founded the Illuminati.[309]

Kolmer is not mentioned in the Priory documents. In fact, Nesta Webster says he is the most mysterious man in this whole plot. Before he met Weishaupt, there was no previous history of him, other than his encounter on Malta with Cagliostro. Afterwards he disappeared. Yet, Cagliostro described Kolmer with respect and admiration, calling him "this universal genius, almost divine."[310]

Subsequent events suggest that Kolmer was none other than the Grand Master of the Priory of Sion - Charles of Lorraine. But who is this mysterious Freemason, Cagliostro?

CAGLIOSTRO AND EGYPTIAN FREEMASONRY

Mackey's Encyclopedia of Freemasonry acknowledges the importance of Cagliostro in the spread of Freemasonry throughout Europe:

> *"The history of Freemasonry in that century would not be complete without a reference to this personage. To write the history of Freemasonry in the eighteenth century and to leave out Cagliostro, would be like enacting the play of Hamlet and leaving out the part of the Prince of Denmark."[311]*

Cagliostro established more Masonic Lodges throughout Europe than did any single man then or since. On Malta he was appointed by Charles of Lorraine (disguised as the

---

[309] Webster 199-200.
[310] Webster 200.
[311] "Cagliostro," *Mackey's Encyclopedia*, vol.1.

Jutland merchant Kolmer) to act in his behalf - as the link between the Grand Master of Sion and Weishaupt. *Mackey's Encyclopedia of Freemasonry* says Cagliostro's real name was Joseph Balsamo[312], the man mentioned in the Priory documents as a figure in the Sionist conspiracy along with several Grand Masters of Sion. This man had the power of a Grand Master of Sion, yet, was never a Grand Master himself. The Priory documents say of such men:

> "Custodians of a secret, one can only exalt them or destroy them. Thus people like...Joseph Balsamo, the dukes of Nevers and Gonzaga, whose wake is attended by a perfume of magic in which sulphur is mingled with incense- the perfume of the Magdalen."[313]

Five years after Joseph Balsamo/Cagliostro met Kolmer at Malta we find Cagliostro in London where he becomes connected with Rosicrucian English Freemasonry. According to *Mackey's Encyclopedia of Freemasonry,* in April, 1776, one month before Adam Weishaupt officially founded the Illuminati, Cagliostro was initiated as an English Mason "in Esperance Lodge, No.289, which then met at the King's Head Tavern."[314] In 1777, the year Weishaupt was initiated into French Grand Orient Freemasonry, Cagliostro "was subsidized," according to Mackey, "by several extremely wealthy men, who, themselves dissatisfied by the state of affairs in Europe, did not hesitate to place their riches at his disposal for the purpose of undermining the tyrannic powers which then wielded sway."[315]

The "tyrannic powers" in Europe undoubtedly refer to the French throne. And the wealthy men in England may well have been Sionist Rosicrucians. Since Mackey does not mention them by name, we cannot positively connect them with Sion, nor can we speculate on who these individuals may have been. Yet, with substantial funds from England, Sionist Cagliostro returned to the Continent and founded Egyptian Freemasonry, which played a significant role in the Sionist plot against France, not only in the French Revolution, but for a century and a half beyond. The coat of arms Cagliostro adopted for his Order was the six pointed star, identical to that created by the Merovingian Dagobert H at the Rennes-le-Chateau, and later adopted by the Priory of Sion. This six-pointed-star later became the herald of the future genuine Jewish Zionist movement, which insignia has mistakenly led many conspiracy researchers to believe the conspiracy of Jewish origin.

Nesta Webster tells us that when Cagliostro returned to the Continent, he joined the Illuminati. She reports that "Cagliostro had also been initiated into the [Templar] Strict Observance near Frankfurt and was now employed as agent of the combined order. According to his own confession his mission 'was to work so as to turn Freemasonry in the direction of Weishaupt's projects'... Cagliostro also formed a link with the Martinistes who [followed] in the footsteps of the Rosicrucians..."[316]

Cagliostro received orders from and acted in behalf of Charles of Lorraine, the reigning Grand Master of Sion, who was relieved of his military command for failing to defeat Frederick the Great. Disguised as the Jutland merchant Kolmer, the Grand Master met Cagliostro on Malta where they planned their strategy. Cagliostro was to join the Illuminati with two conspicuous goals in mind: (1) turn French Freemasons into

---

[312] "Cagliostro."
[313] Baigent 206.
[314] "Cagliostro."
[315] "Cagliostro."
[316] Webster 233.

insurrectionists through drug addiction, prostitution, and witchcraft; and (2) unite Rosicrucian and Templar Freemasonry on the Continent. The ostensible purpose of the latter will not be evident until later. Yet from Cagliostro's day forward we find a mixture of Rosicrucian and Templar ceremonies in both Masonic orders.

It is undeniable that the frenzy leading up to the French Revolution was created by Cagliostro's esoteric Egyptian Freemasonry. At the same time, Weishaupt and his Illuminati operated in the political arena.

A SUMMARY

Sion had not altered its plan to capture the French throne for the House of Lorraine since its failure during the Religious Wars. It met only with partial success under Weishaupt. The French Revolution did dethrone the Bourbons, as Sion desired. The King of Jerusalem dynasty, however, was unable to ascend the French throne after the Revolution destroyed the monarchy.

This intrigue, with its counter-intrigues, seemed to blend Rosicrucianism and Templarism. Hence, conspiracy researchers have not understood the dual conflict within the French Revolution and they have misconstrued the French Masonic conspiracy as a continuation of Adam Weishaupt's Illuminati plot. On the other hand, opponents of conspiracy theory view the Illuminati as non-existent after 1785, since in that year it was exposed by the Bavarian government and ordered to disband. What actually happened is not immediately apparent. Sion and the Temple, however, had other plans for the Illuminati on another continent in a new world.

5. REJECTING CHRISTIANITY: PAGAN SYMBOLS OF FREEMASONRY AND THE ILLUMINATI

> *We must constantly bear in mind this fact, of the primary existence and predominance of symbolism in the earliest times, when we are investigating the nature of the ancient religions, with which the history of Freemasonry is so intimately connected. The older the religion, the more the symbolism abounds.*
> Mackey's Symbolism of Freemasonry[317]

SYMBOLS AND ALLEGORIES

All religions use symbolism, including Judeo-Christianity. Through-out the Bible, symbols, object lessons, figurative speech and parables are used to both conceal and reveal. Ezekiel saw the "wheel." Zechariah observed "mountains of brass." Daniel wondered at the "horns." John described God's judgments as "seals" and "trumpets."

God has used symbols to conceal His future plans from the prophets' generations, mystifying the prophets themselves. For example, God told Daniel in 12:9, "Go thy way, Daniel: for the words are closed up and sealed till the time of the end." Jeremiah used object lessons (Jeremiah 13-19) to symbolize God's judgement on Israel. In the New Testament figurative speech illustrates the various attributes of our Savior: Christ is the Lamb of God and the Lion of Judah. And Jesus taught spiritual truths in parables. For example, in Mark 4:1-10, when our Lord tells His disciples the parable of the "sower," they ask Him the meaning, and He replied, "Unto you it is given to know the mystery of the kingdom of God: but unto them that are without, all these things are done in parables: That seeing they may see, and not perceive; and hearing they may hear, and not understand...

The only symbols God forbade were those that were said to represent Him. In Deuteronomy 4:12, Moses reminds Israel that when the Lord spoke to them at Horeb, they "heard the voice of the words, but saw no similitude [symbol]; only ye heard a voice." In 4:15-16 and following, Moses explains the injunction against figures or images: "Take ye, therefore good heed unto yourselves; for ye saw no manner of similitude [symbol] on the day that the Lord spake unto you in Horeb out of the midst of the fire: Lest ye corrupt yourselves, and make you a graven image, the similitude of any figure, the likeness of male or female...lest thou lift up thine eyes unto heaven, and when thou seest the sun, and the moon, and the stars, even all the host of heaven, shouldest be driven to worship them, and serve them...

Symbols, figures, or images of God were of pagan origin and usage, leading to the worship of creation or even to the worship of demons in place of God. Therefore, God forbade His people of such practice.

The pagan gods were, of course, divided into male and female deities, who in turn were identified with cosmological phenomena - such as the moon, the sun, the stars, or other natural phenomena or forces - rain, sky, mountains, caves, ocean, etc. And

---

[317] A.G. Mackey. *Mackey's Symbolism of Freemasonry* 74.

humanity, in a state of idolatry, would appeal to these gods as powers, forces, or arbiters of fertility, life, and death.

The rest of this chapter will explore the use of pagan symbolism, including that of pagan fertility cults, in the symbols and emblems of Freemasonry and the Illuminati, and show how these symbols and the religion which they represent - predicted by the books of Zechariah and Revelation - are of blasphemous, anti-Christian origin and intent.

SEX SYMBOLS

The overt geometric symbols of pagan deities represent both male and female gods. Their covert meaning is most reprehensible, for they, as we shall see, represent man and woman in a procreative act to reach godhood.

Today, Masonic symbols are used in the same manner and for the same reason. The covert and actual meanings of Masonic symbology are withheld until initiates are found "worthy" to receive them. Freemason J.D. Buck reveals this progression of Masonic revelation in his book *Mystic Masonry:*

> It should be borne in mind that in modern Freemasonry there is always an exoteric portion given out to the world, to the uninitiated, and an esoteric portion reserved for the initiated, and revealed by degrees according as the candidate demonstrates his fitness to receive, conceal, and rightly to use the knowledge imparted.[318]

Freemason W.L. Wilmshurst also confirms the existence of overt and covert meanings in Masonic symbols and ritual in *The Meaning of Masonry:*

> Our teaching is purposely veiled in allegory and symbol and its deeper import does not appear upon the surface of the ritual itself. [Concealment is] partly intentional also, so that only those who have reverent and understanding minds may penetrate into the more hidden meaning of the doctrine of the Craft. [Meanings] are disclosed only to those who act upon the hint given in our lectures.[319]

Martin L. Wagner discusses in his book *Freemasonry, An Interpretation* the deliberate and self- proclaimed strategy of deceit by Masons in the presentation of their rituals and symbols:

> Masonic writers all agree that the doctrines of Freemasonry are presented to the Mason not in an open, direct and dogmatic manner, but in a veiled form either in allegory, or by means of hieroglyphs, ideographs, ciphers, symbols, and in ambiguous language of which misleading interpretations are purposely given so that if the Mason apprehends the real meaning it is solely through his own wit and power of discernment.
>
> That the institution may be perpetuated from generation to generation, and its integrity be maintained, it is imperative that its essential secret doctrine be communicated from the Mason to the neophyte in a manner that makes it secure

---

[318] Buck 69.

[319] W.L. *Wilmhurst. The Meaning of Masonry* (New York: Bell Publishing, 1980) 50.

from discovery by the uninitiated. This is effected by means of symbols and art speech which are made to carry under disguise a complete system of the Masonic ideas of the deity, nature and man. This teaching must be by symbols, for only by these can the doctrine be promulgated Masonically. All explanations that are given of these symbols are designedly misleading interpretations the more completely to defeat the interpreter, to hide their Masonic meaning and to prove the candidate's ability to catch the Masonic doctrine.[320]

In the Introduction you may recall that Albert Pike in Morals *and Dogma* confirms that initiates in the Blue Lodge are deliberately deceived.[321] A reasonable person would here object that no one would join Freemasonry if told beforehand he was going to be intentionally misled. And no decent person would join Freemasonry if apprised in advance of the true meaning of these symbols. Take, for example, the Square and Compass with the letter "G" at its center. This is Free masonry's chief symbol. Would or indeed should a Christian wear it on his lapel or ring finger if told it represents something contrary to Holy Scripture? Of course not.

What, if known, would a Christian object to in this central symbol of Masonry? Thirty-third degree Mason H.L. Haywood instructs us in the method to uncover its meaning in *The Great Teachings of Masonry:*

> *There can be no dogmatic and official interpretation of a symbol to compel the unwilling assent of any mind; the symbol's message is, by virtue of its very nature, fluid and free, so that every man has a right to think it out for himself. Of Masonic teachers and scholars there have been many - Oliver, Preston, Pike, Mackey, and others equally as honourable to our history - and these have given us noble interpretations of Masonry, but no Mason is ever compelled to accept them unless he chooses to.*
>
> *After studying the philosophy of symbolism under the leadership of the foregoing hints it will be well for the student to investigate a further question: What rule shall we go by in trying to interpret Masonic symbols? What was said of each member's right to think out the symbols for himself did not imply, of course, that he ever has a right to interpret a Masonic symbol without thinking, or that he can ever discover a true interpretation without due regard for what others have thought of it. That procedure would be not free thought but an absence of thought... If we ask ourselves, for example, what is the meaning of the square and compass, we should try to discover when that symbol came into use in the Fraternity; why it thus came into use; what it then meant, and then we should try to learn what the Fraternity has understood by this symbol during the subsequent centuries. This would save us from an inter- pretation based on ignorance, or arbitrariness, or our own crotchets, and it would also throw new light for us on what Freemasonry as a whole means.[322]*

---

[320] Wagner 148-149. In 1912 Martin L. Wagner (not a Mason) was Pastor of the St. John English Evangelical Lutheran Church in Dayton, Ohio. His interpretation comes strictly from his study of Masonic books. He writes in the Preface, "The writer offers this Interpretation as his testimony against this modern effort to hold down the Truth in unrighteousness."
[321] Pike 816.
[322] Harry LeRoy Haywood: *The Great Teachings of Masonry* (1921; Richmond, VA: Macoy, 1971) 26-27.

THE SQUARE AND THE COMPASS

To uncover the true meaning of the Square and Compass, we will follow Haywood's instructions, and examine several of the "honorable~authors he suggests all Masons investigate to avoid "ignorance" and "arbitrariness" of interpretation. First we learn from 32nd degree Freemason, J.D. Buck, in *Symbolism of Mystic Masonry*, that the Square and Compass have a significance that transcends the practical order:

> *Perhaps the most familiar symbol of a Mason is the Square and Compass, found in every Lodge, worn as a badge of fraternal recognition. We are told in the Lodge that the Square is an instrument with which the practical Mason measures and lays out his work, but we as free and accepted Masons are taught to make use of it for the more noble and glorious purpose... So also the Compass; the practical use is made symbolical of the higher moral obligation, to circumscribe our desires and keep our passions within due bounds... In a general sense, the square is a symbol of matter, and the earth; the Compass, of Spirit and the heavens.*[323]

Freemason George H. Steinmetz in *Freemasonry, its Hidden Meaning*, agrees with J.D. Buck: "Symbolically, the Square represents the earth, and the Compass the heavens." But Steinmetz expands their meaning: "Both the Square and Compass are symbolical of Man."[324]

As we can see, Freemasonry not only believes man has something in common with heaven and the earth, but further identifies, reduces and divides the Divinity into cosmological male and female sexual powers. Thirty-third degree Mason Albert Pike elaborates this scheme in *Morals and Dogma*:

> *The Compass, therefore, is the Hermetic [gnostic] Symbol of the Creative Deity, and the Square of the productive Earth or Universe... As the procreative and generative agents, the Heavens and the Sun have always been regarded as male; as the generators that fructify the Earth and cause it to produce... The Faith, therefore, the great Producer, was always represented as a female.*
>
> *These two Divinities, the Active and Passive Principles of the Universe were commonly symbolized by the generative parts of man and woman... [t]he Phallus [male sex organ] and Cteis [female sex organ], emblems of generation and production, and which, as such, appeared in the Mysteries.*
>
> *The Brahmins of India expressed the same cosmogonic idea by a statue, representative of the Universe, uniting in itself both sexes. The male sex offered an image of the sun, centre of the active principle, and the female sex that of the moon, at the sphere whereof, proceeding downward, the passive portion of nature begins. The Lingam, unto the present day revered in the Indian temples, being but the conjunction of the organs of generation of the two sexes, was an emblem of the same.*[325]

---

[323] Buck 130.
[324] Steinmetz 60-61.
[325] Pike 401, 656, 851; Appendix 2; Figs. 8 and 9 in *Scarlet and the Beast*, vol.1.

Thirty-third degree Freemason Albert G. Mackey in *Symbolism of Freemasonry* offers the same interpretation of the Square and Corn pass as does Pike, linking it to the worship of procreative powers in pagan religion:

> *The Phallus (or Lingam of the Indians) was a sculptured representation of the membrum virile, or male organ of generation. . the Cteis of the Greeks, and the Yoni of the Indians, a symbol of the female generative principle, of coextensive prevalence with the Phallus... The union of the Phallus and Cteis, or the Lingam and Yoni, in one compound figure, as an object of adoration, was the most usual mode of representation.*[326]

Finally, 33rd degree Freemason Delmar Duane Darrah, in *History and Evolution of Freemasonry*, spells out the meaning of Masonic symbols, including its most prominent symbol, the Square and Compass: "The symbolism of Masonry then is simply human life in pictures... a complete compendium expressive of man's constant duty [procreation] to the God who made him and his fellow traveler [sex partner] in life's journey."[327]

A Mason reading Darrah's "noble interpretation" can have no doubt of its meaning. The "honorable" in Freemasonry explain that the Lingam in Hinduism represents nature's intercourse with itself, and compare it to the Square and Compass, which symbol represents the Active forces in nature above (meaning the heavens) on the Passive forces beneath (meaning the earth). The Square and Compass is thus said to represent man in his duty of procreation.

Notice that the Compass is in the Active sexual position with its two legs spread downward, representing the legs of the male. The Square is in the Passive sexual position with its two legs spread upward, representing the legs of a female. Joined together, they symbolize man and woman interlocked in the position of continual sexual intercourse, which act, when literally performed, is a sacrament to the demon-god of Masonry.

Pagan religions do not merely represent their fertility gods in the act of procreation in statuary or other forms. Ancient pagans emulated their gods in temple worship by cohabiting with temple prostitutes.

Henry H. Halley, in *Halley's Bible Handbook*, informs us that such was the case in Babylonian religions. The mother goddess, he says, "was the deification of the sex passion; her worship required licentiousness; sacred prostitution in connection with her sanctuaries was a universal custom among the women of Babylonia. In connection with her temples were charming retreats or chambers where her priestesses entertained male worshippers in disgraceful ceremonies. In addition to these prostitute priestesses, every maid, wife or widow had to officiate at least once in her lifetime in these rites."[328]

God knows what wickedness is behind pagan symbols. For this reason He forbade Israel making a likeness of Him. Yet, in our day, Freemasonry commemorates and portrays these shameful practices in the Square and Compass. Even more corrupt is their notion of God, vulgarly represented by the letter "G," positioned in the center of the Square and Compass where the male and female sex organs unite. There is no doubt that a Christian should abstain from fellowship with men who worship as a god such a vulgar and base deity, which is presented in symbolic form as the act of sexual intercourse.

---

[326] Mackey, *Mackey's Symbolism of Freemasonry* 113.
[327] Darrah 289.
[328] Henry H. Halley, *Halley's Bible Handbook* (1924; Grand Rapids, MI: Zondervan, 1964) 97.

Do you now understand why Freemasonry thus must present different layers of symbolic meaning to initiates than to adepts if it is to acquire membership? Once a seeker is accepted for membership, he is deceived in each Blue Degree initiation. Blue Lodge Masons are told "G" is a symbol of God, which, of course, can mean any God-concept. After advancing in degrees above the Blue Lodge, the "G" becomes Gnosis, the worship of knowledge. Gnosis is then expanded to mean the knowledge of creation - more specifically, the creation of heaven and earth by the union of the sexual forces of nature. Finally, it dawns on a few high initiates that man perpetuates God's creation by emulating nature. These Masons are found worthy of being taught the loftier act behind this disgusting symbol - that it is man's duty to emulate his god through the worship of his own procreative activity. We see clearly that Masonry's chief symbol hearkens back to and commemorates the ancient fertility religion. The Square and Compass reveals mankind as gods.

Mackey's Encyclopedia of Freemasonry makes a statement which all Christians should heed when deciding whether or not to dismiss the matter of Masonic symbology: "Withdraw from Freemasonry its Symbolism, and you take from the body its soul..."[329]

THE ASSIGNMENT OF THE ILLUMINATI IS HIDDEN IN SYMBOLISM

Adam Weishaupt, founder of the illuminati, used symbolism to conceal both the god and the assignment of his organization. To start with a simple example, we see that the word *illuminati* is simply a Latin plural noun meaning *enlightened ones*. By itself it appears quite harmless. Yet when we research its use in mystery religions, we discover a disturbing truth. The ancients called Lucifer the *enlightened one*, or the *light-bearer*. Venus, goddess of love, was also known as the *light-bearer*. Venus, the planet, was called the *Lucifer* star, or the *morning star*. In Hebrew Lucifer means *morning star,* or *shining one*.[330] A thorough look at etymology reveals that *illuminati* means *those who emulate Lucifer, or followers of Lucifer.*

We can legitimately expect that the language and symbols used by the Illuminati will not only reveal their religious doctrine, but even unveil the assignment given Weishaupt.

MAY DAY: SYMBOL OF REVOLUTION

When Weishaupt was chosen by the Grand Master of Sion to augment the next step toward Sion- Templar unification, he was given the freedom to choose how he should accomplish his task. At first he elected to remain obscure. Only six individuals within the Illuminati knew him as Head. One of them would prove to be a Judas.

In the spring of 1776, Weishaupt's five-year indoctrination was completed by the illusive Jutland merchant, Kolmer, who we have suggested was the Grand Master of Sion in disguise, or his agent. Weishaupt was then given his assignment: to destroy the French throne through revolution, then unite Sion and the Templars in a New World Order. On May 1, 1776, Weishaupt founded the Illuminati.

May 1st, 1776. That day Weishaupt chose the color "red" to represent the human blood soon to be shed in honor of his benevolent revolution. Thirteen years later - the

---

[329] "Symbolism, Science of," *Mackey's Encyclopedia,* vol.11.
[330] Strong, Hebrew #1966 and 1984.

number is significant - the new French Constituent Assembly of 1789, consisting of 300 illuminated Master Masons[331], chose "red" as their national color.[332]

May 1st, 1776. That symbolic day was remembered in 1917 when Lenin inaugurated Weishaupt's "red" revolutionary system in Russia, choosing May 1st as a Communist national holiday. Until its recent collapse, the U.S.S.R. annually flaunted its military might under thou- sands of red banners. Awesome weapons, created to spill man's blood into rivers of red, rumbled through "Red Square."[333]

May 1st, 1776. That infamous day, so subtly interwoven into our societal conscience that revolution will never be forgotten.

May 1st, 1776. That catastrophic day is symbolically remembered as "May-day! May-day!" when transmitted along radio waves as the international signal for distress. That day became the focal point around which all revolutions since have rallied.

On that day Weishaupt's illuminated system, a Satanic strategy of universal dominion, designed in a fashion similar to that of communism today, became the "butterfly effect"[334] which gently stirred the revolutionary air until it became a violent storm. One day it will end in horrific savagery "such as was not since the beginning of the world to this time, no, nor ever shall be" (Matthew 24:21).

ILLUMINATING MASONRY

Weishaupt was to bring to maturity the impending French Revolution, which had been brewing for several decades without direction. This involved three steps: (1) found the Illuminati, which we have already discussed; (2) illuminate the various Templar Masonic Orders; and (3) illuminate the French Grand Lodge.

The first Templar order illuminated was the idle Strict Observance. A member of its hierarchy was a staunch Templar, Baron Adolph von Knigge. Von Knigge had been initiated into the Strict Observance in 1770, one year before Kolmer began indoctrinating Weishaupt. In 1780 the Sionist Weishaupt sought out Templar von Knigge after he had heard that he had been initiated into the Illuminati. That year the Strict Observance came under Illuminati control when Weishaupt gave orders to the Baron to "draw the best amongst them to us."[335] The Unknown Superiors, who were to give guidance to the Strict Observance three and a half decades earlier, were then declared by Weishaupt to be the Illuminati.

The Hierarchy in the Illuminati assumed code names, a practice continued to this day by the Hierarchy of Freemasonry. Its purpose is to protect identities in what is a dangerous enterprise. Weishaupt's code name was Spartacus. His close associate, Herr von Zwack, was secretly known as Cato. Baron von Knigge was Philo. We have record of their plot due to an unusual expose' and to the publication of their coded letters (discussed in chapter 9).

---

[331] Miller 337.

[332] In subsequent French revolutions the Flag has evolved to red, white, and blue.

[333] Gerald B. Winrod: *Adam Weishaupt: A Human Devil* (N.p.: n.p., 1935) 48. Following the Bolshevik Revolution, the "Reds" extended their anarchy outside Russian borders. In Germany, the "Reds" were known as Spartacists, using the code name of their founder, Weishaupt.

[334] James Gleick, *Chaos: Making a New Science* (New York:Viking, 1987) 8.In science, the "butterfly effect" means a "sensitive dependence on initial conditions." In a joking application to weather, as example, is the notion that a butterfly stirring the air today in Peking can transform storm systems next month in New York.

[335] Webster, *Secret Societies* 226.

Under the pseudonym Spartacus, Weishaupt wrote to Cato (von Zwack), "I should remain hidden from most of the members as long as I live. I am obligated to do everything through five or six persons."[336]

In another letter he further outlined the structure of his organization:

> *"I have two immediately below me into whom I breathe my whole spirit, and each of these two has again two others, and so on. In this way I can set a thousand men in motion and on fire in the simplest manner, and in this way one must impart orders and operate on politics."*[337]

Not only did orders rapidly descend from the Illuminati Hierarchy through this chain of command, but communication ascended to Weishaupt just as quickly through an elaborate system of internal espionage. As Salem Kirban explains in *Satan's Angels Exposed*, "Every member spied on every other member. Each month the Novice had to deliver to Weishaupt a sealed letter which revealed every aspect of his relationship with his superior."[338] Such informants enabled Weishaupt to command events by keeping abreast of the results leading up to the French Revolution. Secrecy was paramount to the operations of the Illuminati, as Spartacus says to Cato: "The great strength of our Order lies in its concealment; let it never appear in any place in its own name, but always covered by another name, and another occupation. None is fitter than the three lower degrees of Free Masonry; the public is accustomed to it, expects little from it, and therefore takes little notice of it."[339]

Weishaupt hid the Illuminati in the first three degrees of Grand Orient Freemasonry, previously organized in 1772. Dr. George E. Dillon, in *Grand Orient Freemasonry Unmasked*, records that the Grand Orient Lodge was founded because "the French Masons in the English obedience desiring independence of the Mother Lodge of England, separated, and elected the duke of Orleans the first Grand Master of the since celebrated Grand Orient of France."[340]

Like the Illuminati, the name of the Grand Orient Lodge has a sinister paternity. We turn to the story of Julian the Apostate, to explain.

Before Julian became emperor of Rome (361-363 A.D.), he was initiated into the Mysteries - one of the hydra-heads of Babylonian religion - by the theurgist, Maximus of Ephesus. As the subterranean ceremony progressed, Maximus directed his initiate, asking:

> *"Wouldst see the Rebel? Look!..."*
>
> *Above the head of the spectre shone the Morning Star, the Star of Dawn; and the Angel said:*
>
> *"In my name deny the Galilean." (Thrice demanded and thrice denied.) "Who art thou?"*
>
> *"I am the Light, I am the Orient, I am the Morning Star!" "How beautiful thou art!"*
>
> *"Be as I am."*
>
> *"What sadness in thine eyes!"*

---

[336] Webster 222.

[337] Winrod 34.

[338] Salem Kirban, *Satan's Angels Exposed* (Rossville, GA: Grapevine Book Distributors, 1980) 147.

[339] Robison 112.

[340] Dillon 19.

"I suffer for all living; there must be neither birth nor death.

Come to me, I am the shadow, I am peace, I am liberty' [R]ebel,I will give thee force... break the law, love, curse Him and be as I am."[341]

Notice that the apparition of Lucifer said, "I am the Orient." So, too, in the veiled language of Masonry, Orient actually means Lucifer! This fact was crucial to Weishaupt's success. He could indoctrinate his initiates under the cloak of harmless three-degree Grand Orient Freemasonry, progressively teaching them that the god of both the Illuminati and the Grand Orient was the same - Lucifer. Weishaupt would then send forth his illuminated Master Masons to organize additional Grand "Lucifer" Lodges under other names.

The next Templar body to illuminate was the Scottish Rite. This was not difficult, since many Scotch Masons flocked to join the Grand Orient, and subsequently, the Illuminati. Penetrating the French Grand Lodge with illuminism was more difficult, yet most crucial. With the Grand Lodge remaining obedient to monarchist English Freemasonry, it was imperative to reverse its attitude before dethroning the Bourbon dynasty.

THE PYRAMID AND THE ALL-SEEING EYE

The founding of the Illuminati in the year 1776 has significant esoteric and numeric implications. Likewise, the Seal of the Illuminati is esoterically important in that it symbolically communicates to the initiated the assignment given this Luciferian order.

The Seal is pictured as a 13-layered unfinished pyramid with its capstone missing. Hovering above is a sun-rayed triangle, as if waiting to be lowered to complete the structure. In mystery religions the triangle symbolizes power, such as a throne or kingdom, and is sometimes pictured as a horn. The triangle is also a symbol of the dwelling place of the pagan higher power, representing a mountain top in hilly country, a pyramid in Egypt, or a ziggurat in Mesopotamia. The ancients called the ziggurat Hill of Heaven, or Mountain of God.[342] Numbers 22:41 and Deuteronomy 12:2 refer to these pagan shrines as "high places."

When Weishaupt designed the sun-rayed triangle, he placed in it an eye like the eye of man - known to Masons as the All-Seeing Eye. This symbol is a rendition of the Egyptian eye of Osiris.[343] *Mackey's Encyclopedia of Freemasonry* explains how Masonry adopted this symbol from ancient pagan religion:

> *All-Seeing eye: An important symbol of the Supreme Being, borrowed by the Freemasons from the nations of antiquity... [T]he Egyptians represented Osiris, their chief deity, by the symbol of an open eye, and placed this hieroglyphic of him in all their temples. His symbolic name, on the monuments, was represented by the eye accompanying a throne, to which was sometimes added an abbreviated figure of the god, and sometimes what has been called a hatchet, but which may*

---

[341] Stoddard, *Light-bearers of Darkness* 170; quoting Dmitri Merejkovsky, the Russian historical writer, in his book, La *Mort des Dieus.*

[342] Unger 104.

[343] Webster 202. The All-Seeing Eye is also shown in its modest form as "a point within a circle." This form of the Eye originated in Egyptian mysticism millenniums before the Priory of Sion adopted it. When incorporated by the Illuminati, "the point within the circle" became the symbolic code in all correspondence between its Hierarchy.

as correctly be supposed to be a representation of a square [the symbol of a Masonic Lodge].[344]

That the eye is positioned in a triangle hovering above an unfinished pyramid has symbolic significance to the Illuminist conspiracy. First, the eye represents Weishaupt. Salem Kirban in *Satan's Angels* Exposed explains that "Weishaupt's mutual spying system was an integral part of his program to keep his associates in line. The eye symbolized a Big Brother controlling his domain."[345]

Second, the eye represents the Priory of Sion (Sion had taken the same symbol from the Egyptians), and the triangle the power of the European Merovingian thrones. The thirteen- stepped unfinished pyramid commemorates the work assigned the Knights Templar. In Masonic symbology, the Seal of the Illuminati simply means the Templars have been given the task of building a world government under the watchful eye of the Priory of Sion. When Sion, protector of the Merovingian thrones, lowers the sun-rayed Merovingian capstone in place, the world government will be complete.

Strangely, the Seal of the Illuminati was adopted by American Freemasonry two months after it was created. Stranger still - it became part of the Great Seal of the United States. The Illuminati was founded in 1776 apparently to coincide with the American Revolution. Equally apparent, Weishaupt was instructed to design the Seal of the Illuminati as part of the Great Seal of the United States.

Since 1934 the Illuminati Seal has adorned the left-reverse side of our one dollar bill. Above the pyramid are the Latin words (with a count of 13 letters) *Annuit* Coeptis, meaning *Announcing the Birth.* Below is *Novus Ordo Seclorum,* meaning *New Secular Order,* also translated *New World Order.* Superimposed in Roman numerals on the bottom layer of bricks is the year 1776, the year the Illuminati was founded, as well as the year the American colonies declared independence.

The thirteen layers of brick in the pyramid are obviously symbolic of the 13 American colonies. Thirteen is also the most sacred number of the Knights Templar, representing its 13 degrees of initiation and commemorating the day Templar persecution began - Friday the 13th, 1307. The Masonic symbology in the Seal of the Illuminati, when incorporated as part of the Great Seal of the United States, put the world of secret societies on notice that the Templars were beginning to build in America the base of Sion's long desired New World Order.[346]

THE ILLUMINATI IN AMERICA

Professor Charles Eliott Norton (1827-1908) lectured at Harvard from 1874 to 1898 concerning the Illuminati's unfinished pyramid and its All-Seeing Eye, which our forefathers, he said, laminated on the reverse side of one of our great national symbols, the Flying Eagle, which is on the front of the Great Seal of the United States. Professor Norton was not a Mason, although he befriended many of them, including Emerson, Ruskin, Longfellow, and Lowell.[347] Nor was he opposed to their conspiracy. In one of his repeated lectures he made an interesting statement about the Illuminati's involvement in the American Revolution, which sheds light on the unprecedented drive our leaders today are demonstrating in using our nation as the catalyst for the success of the New World

---

[344] "All-Seeing Eye," *Mackey's Encyclopedia*, vol.1.
[345] Kirban 154.
[346] Raymond E. Capt, *Our Great Seal: The Symbols of our Heritage & our Destiny* (Thousand Oaks, CA: Artisan Sales, 1979) 56-59.
[347] "Norton, Charles Eliott," *Encyclopaedia Britannica:Micropaedia.*

Order. The professor said, "Not only were many of the founders of the United States Government Masons, but they received aid from a secret and august body existing in Europe, which helped them to establish this country for a peculiar and particular purpose known only to the initiated few."[348]

That "secret and august body" was the Illuminati. Author Salem Kirban informs us that by 1785, "15 lodges of the Order of the Illuminati had been established in the 13 colonies. This was before the Colonies were united and the Constitution adopted. In 1785, the Columbian Lodge of the Order of the illuminati was established in New York City. Its members included Governor Dewitt Clinton, Clinton Roosevelt [ancestor of Franklin D. Roosevelt], and Horace Greeley. A Lodge in Virginia was identified with Thomas Jefferson."[349]

Ben Franklin, Thomas Jefferson and John Adams were the men most responsible for bringing the Illuminati to America. Rev. J.R. Church writes of the Masonic and Illuminati association of the Founding Fathers in *Guardians of the Grail:*

> It is reported that Benjamin Franklin was a Rosicrucian. Thomas Jefferson, John Adams, and George Washington were Masons. It is interesting to note that though these men were a part of these orders, George Washington warned the Masonic Lodge in America of the dangers of the Illuminati, while Thomas Jefferson and John Adams later disagreed over the use of the Masonic Lodge by the Illuminati. John Adams, who is reported to have been the founder of the Masonic Lodges in New England, accused Jefferson of using the lodges that he himself had founded, for subversive Illuminati purposes. The three letters of Adams which deal with this problem are in the Wittenburg Square Library in Philadelphia. Many today are becoming convinced that Franklin, Adams, and Jefferson were manipulated by the Illuminati until John Adams became alerted.[350]

Mackey's Encyclopedia of Freemasonry reports on Franklin's extensive Masonic affiliations. Franklin was associated with American Freemasonry as far back as 1730. Prior to the American Revolution, he visited London where he was initiated a Rosicrucian and given membership in the Sionist Royal Society. He was also a member of several French lodges at Paris during and after our Revolution. In 1777, for instance, he was initiated in the Grand Orient Lodge of Nine Sisters; in 1779 he was elected its Worshipful Master; in 1782 he became its Venerable Master. He helped officiate in the initiation of Voltaire in that same lodge on April 7, 1778. November 28, 1778, he is listed as one of the founders of the Lodge of Sorrows in honor of Voltaire, officiating there at Voltaire's Masonic funeral. That same year he became a member of Templar Freemasonry's Respectable Lodge of Saint John of Jerusalem. In 1782, he joined a more elusive and mysterious Templar lodge called the Royal Lodge of Commanders of the Temple West. Finally, after a long and illustrious Masonic career, Dr. Mackey reports that "On April 17, 1790 Benjamin Franklin passed to the Grand Lodge above."[351]

Benjamin Franklin and Thomas Jefferson, two of the three patriots credited with the design of our Great Seal of the United States, were adamant defenders of the Illuminati - so much so that they adopted its Seal as part of our own.

According to the *Journals of Congress,* 1776, Vol.1, pages 248 and 397, on July 4, 1776, Thomas Jefferson, John Adams and Benjamin Franklin were appointed by the

---

[348] El-Amin 10.
[349] Kirban 151.
[350] Church 163-164.
[351] "Franklin, Benjamin," *Mackey's Encyclopedia,* vol.1.

Continental Congress to prepare the seal. This was thirteen years before John Adams became concerned about a conspiracy. The Seal includes not only the Flying Eagle on the front side, but on its reverse, the Illuminati seal designed by Weishaupt. The Great Seal of the United States appears to be an Illuminati masterpiece.

We can only speculate that Franklin received his orders from both London and Paris. Subsequent events, presented in chapter 27, confirm he was a double-agent, apparently working for the Priory of Sion, as had Voltaire, Nicholas Francois, and Chevaller Ramsay. Like them, he too traveled to England. From 1757 to 1762 he was in London on a "diplomatic" trip and was there made a Rosicrucian. (Five years earlier Franklin had been honored by Sion's Royal Society for discovering that lightning and electricity were the same.) He went back to London in 1764, returning to America in 1775, just before revolution broke out. In 1776 he went to Paris to seek military and financial aid for the colonies. Apparently, while there, Franklin met Weishaupt, or some other agent of the Illuminati. When he returned to America, he carried in his baggage the republican doctrine of the Illuminati, along with its unfinished pyramid Seal.

Benjamin Franklin, Thomas Jefferson and John Adams met on the summer afternoon of July 4, 1776, and pondered the design of the Great Seal of the United States. Franklin convinced the two patriots that the Roman numeral 1776 on the base of Illuminati Seal signified the year America declared independence. The thirteen layers of brick on the unfinished pyramid simply represented the thirteen colonies. All three patriots accepted the Seal of the Illuminati without change.

What they themselves actually designed is the Flying Eagle Seal. It contains thirteen stripes on the eagle's breast shield, thirteen berries and thirteen leaves on the olive branch in the eagle's right talon, thirteen arrows in its left talon, thirteen letters in the Latin words *E Pluribus Unum*, and thirteen stars above its head. Exoterically, thirteen represents the thirteen original colonies. Esoterically it suggests that the Knights Templar played a significant role in the founding of the United States.[352]

Two of the three founding fathers were sincere in their patriotic zeal. Ben Franklin, however, was in complete compliance with the "Great Plan" of the Priory of Sion. Circumstantial evidence suggests his complicity. For example, Franklin was the only founding father who was a member of all three Masonic obediences - American, English and French - as well as an initiate in Sion's Rose-Croix, a member of Sion's Illuminati, and a Knights Templar. He alone was in the unique position to learn the "Secret Doctrine" from both sides. There is no other explanation for the peculiar, yet significant arrangement of the thirteen stars hovering in the Glory Cloud above the Flying Eagle, which also appears on the back of our dollar bill. There thirteen Templar stars in the Glory Cloud form the six-pointed star of the Priory of Sion.

Symbols and their placement are of great significance to Freemasonry. They reveal the "Secret Doctrine" of the Priory of Sion. The thirteen Templar stars arranged to shape Sion's six-pointed star sent a clear message to the initiated few that Sion and the Temple were united in founding the United States of America. The sacred symbols of Sion and the Temple united in one design peering through the glory cloud hovering above the Great American Eagle, signifies that both Sion and the Temple oversee the direction of our nation. We shall learn the ramifications of this esoteric truth in chapter 27, where we find that the Great Seal of the United States of America was seen in the visions of both the apostle John and the prophet Daniel.

THE UNITED STATES: DAUGHTER OF BABYLON?

---

[352] A.J. Langguth, *Patriots* (New York: Simon and Schuster, 1988)436.

When the thirteen colonies won their independence from mother England, there was a shift in world power. Great Britain, home of modern Mystery Babylon, surrendered her prestige to her offspring. The question arises whether this makes America the "daughter of Babylon" mentioned in Jeremiah 50:42; 51:33, and Zechariah 2:7. Rev. J.R. Church thinks so. He quotes Jeremiah in 50:12 speaking to a nation that is not Babylon, but the daughter of Babylon: "Your mother [Babylon] shall be sore confounded"

Rev. Church comments: "Should the United States be the end time nation in view in this prophecy, then Britain, by the simplest deduction, would be the mother, and, to be sure, today Britain is 'sore *confounded'* The word *confounded* in this verse means 'to pale, to become dry, or to lose strength."[353]

Did the Priory of Sion engineer the weakening of Great Britain? Was the United States selected as the new protector of the King of Jerusalem cult, when Sion and the Temple reunited under Grand Master Charles Radcliffe? These events surely would make England "sore confounded," as the prophecy above suggests. The answers to these questions are forthcoming in chapter 27.)

THE ALL-SEEING EYE: REJECTING THE CORNERSTONE

Of the three interpretations given the All-Seeing Eye, we have discussed two: in the first, Kirban says the Eye represents Adam Weishaupt in his position as a "Big Brother" controlling his domain of the Illuminati. In the second, it symbolizes the Priory of Sion overseeing her Templar project. In the third, and most blasphemous, the eye within the hovering capstone symbolizes the Masonic rejection of Jesus Christ, the Chief Cornerstone. For *Cornerstone* in Greek, as we know, can also mean *top stone* or *capstone.*[354]

As we have seen, centuries before Adam Weishaupt rejected Jesus Christ, the Priory of Sion had rejected the Cross of our Lord and Savior and replaced it with the Rosicrucian cross of Satan. Christ had become a rock of offence to Weishaupt, as had our Savior previously been a stumbling stone to Sion. Scripture itself, in the prophecy of I Peter 2:6-8, reminds us of the conflict between Christ and the "disobedient" followers of Sion:

> *Behold, I lay in Sion a chief corner stone, elect, precious: and he that believeth on him shall not be confounded. Unto you therefore which believe he is precious: but unto them which be disobedient, the stone which the builders disallowed, the same is made the head of the corner, And a stone of stumbling, and a rock of offence...*[355]

Adam Weishaupt, as a one-time minister of God's Word, of course knew that Ephesians 2:20 referred to Christ's Headship of the Church in the following terms: "Jesus Christ... the chief corner stone." Weishaupt would also have studied the prophetic words of our Lord Himself in Luke 20:17: "What is this then that is written, The stone which the builders rejected, the same is become the head of the corner?" From Acts 4:10-11, Weishaupt would have taught Peter's declaration of Jesus Christ "whom God raised from

---

[353] Church 242.
[354] Strong, Greek #206.
[355] We know that this Scripture refers to the nation of Israel. However, the authors of *Holy Blood, Holy Grail* suggest (p.185-187) that the Priory of Sion changed the English spelling of Zion to its French form, thus enabling Sion to teach its initiates that the chief corner stone broadly refers to their Grail bloodline, while it specifically implies their "Lost King", who will one day rule the world. Masons know him as the "Lost Word" or "Lost Name" of God. Christians know him as the Antichrist.

the dead, even by him doth this man stand here before you whole. This is the stone which was set at nought of you builders, which is become the head of the corner."

When Weishaupt apostatized, he determined to design an emblem which symbolized the rejection of Christ as the capstone or cornerstone. The unfinished pyramid with the capstone missing is that emblem. To this day, on the inside of the Masonic Bible in every nation where God's Word is blasphemously placed under crossed swords on the Masonic "altar of sacrifice" are written these words of mockery:

"The Stone the Builders Rejected!"[356]

In some states of our nation, such as Mississippi, the Lodge piously gives the Master Mason, upon completion of his 3rd degree, a King James Version of the Bible, which it calls, oddly enough, the "Masonic Bible."[357] John Hall, a former Master Mason from Mississippi, in an interview on a radio talk show quoted the blasphemous introduction to the Bible given him by the Masons of his Lodge, which introduction explicitly states the Masonic rejection of the Capstone:

THE STONE THE BUILDERS REJECTED

What were the peculiar characteristics of this stone? It was neither oblong nor square, and has reference to the keystone or the capstone. According to the Masonic legends the builders of the Temple of Solomon became bewildered when they received a particular stone that was neither oblong nor square, as they were used to receiving. Thus, subsequently they thrust it aside.[358]

To fully understand the import of this passage, we must know that in Freemasonry, rectangles and squares are symbolic of the stones required for building a perfect, spiritual temple on high. According to *Mackey's Encyclopedia of Freemasonry,* these two geometric symbols, the oblong and the square, represent the Masonic Lodge[359], and signify Freemasonry's belief that it is building the perfect religion. Conversely, an odd-shaped stone such as a wedge-shaped keystone or capstone used only at the pinnacle of an arch or pyramid to complete the structure is rejected while building the base of the structure.

Mackey's Encyclopedia of Freemasonry further explains why the wedge-shaped keystone or cornerstone is rejected by the Mason while building his spiritual temple on high: "In Masonic symbolism [the Chief Cornerstone] signifies a true Freemason, and

---

[356] In Appendix 2, Fig. 16, see the picture of the Masonic Bible on the "Altar of Sacrifice" with crossed swords on top of the Bible. This symbolizes not the protection of Christianity, but its planned destruction.

[357] Freemasonry claims the King James Version as its own because it was translated into English during the reign of the Templar-Masonic King of England, James Stuart I. You may recall that its translation was silently overseen by the Grand Master of the Priory of Sion, Robert Fludd. In all New Testament passages which speak of the nation of Israel as Zion, the English spelling has been rendered Sion, its French form. The Priory of Sion was created in France at Gisors in 1188 A.D., after the King of Jerusalem cult separated from its progeny, the Knights Templar, at the "Cutting of the Elm." The Priory of Sion was founded as the new protector of the blasphemous Holy Grail bloodline, which falsely claims to be Jewish. In fact, it is anti-Semitic and anti-Christian, and is believed by those Christians who have studied it, to be the medium by which the Beast will enter world politics.

[358] Marlin Maddoux: *Magic, Mormonism & Masonry,* Point of View tape ministry, #740- Kay Trimble & John Hall.

[359] "Oblong Square," *Mackey's Encyclopedia,* vol. II.

therefore it is the first character which the Apprentice [1st degree] is made to represent after his initiation has been completed."[360]

In other words, in the religion of Freemasonry, Jesus Christ, the Chief Cornerstone is rejected as Savior and the lowest degree Mason, the Apprentice, becomes his own savior. The method by which he works out his own salvation is illustrated in *Mackey's Encyclopedia of Freemasonry.* Pictured are three laborers (representing the *Entered Apprentice, Fellow Craft* and *Master Mason)* building a structure of square stones. As they work, they gaze into heaven where they faintly see the fruits of their labor - an unfinished pyramid with the keystone missing. Hovering above is the All-Seeing Eye. The caption reads, "Onward to the Heights."[361] In another picture the three Masons rest from their labor. The caption reads, "Labor Is Worship."[362]

As Mackey's definition states and the pictures illustrate, the Entered Apprentice Mason (the first degree initiate) usurps the position of Jesus Christ when he accepts himself as the keystone. He is taught that his labor on earth is never finished. His entire life is spent worshipping his own good works in the Masonic Lodge, hoping that when he arrives at the Great Lodge on high he will have acquired enough bricks to build his new abode, enabling him to stand as capstone or keystone on its pinnacle.

Manly P. Hall, a 33rd degree Mason, explains the spiritual vocation of the first three degrees in Blue Lodge Masonry in his book The Lost Keys of Freemasonry. Facing page 52 is a picture with the caption "The Master Mason" (3rd degree). The Master Mason is standing atop his pyramid in heaven taking the position of the capstone. Following the caption is written, "In this picture is concealed the allegory of the Lost Word. The Master Mason, having completed his labors, becomes a worker on a higher plane than the one in which the ordinary builder list and 2nd degree Mason] is permitted to work. The Master Mason becomes the capstone of the Universal Temple."[363]

In this religion of "salvation by works," a Mason would never accept the finished work of Jesus Christ, the Chief Cornerstone, since Christ's labor as our Savior conflicts with the first ritual in the Lodge. On the other hand, should a Mason come to the realization that he is unable to gain his own salvation through good works, and accepts Christ as his "peculiar" or "particular" cornerstone for salvation, he ceases to be a Mason and must exit the Lodge. Most disturbing, however, is the Christian, who, after accepting Christ as Savior, takes the first degree and accepts himself as the Chief Cornerstone. By implication he has rejected Jesus Christ.

Weishaupt was such a person. He symbolized his rejection of Christ by designing the "unfinished pyramid" with the capstone missing. In its place he created the hovering capstone and placed in it, not the seven eyes of the Lamb of God in Revelation 5:6, but the All-Seeing Eye of the Egyptian sun-god Osiris.

BIBLE PROPHECY AND THE ALL-SEEING EYE

An interesting passage of Scripture in the fifth chapter of Zechariah describes the All-Seeing Eye of pagan religions. The same chapter also contains an astounding prophecy of illuminated Freemasonry. Before discussing the All-Seeing Eye in this passage, we will first establish that while Zechariah's vision is descriptive of Mystery Babylon, it specifically prophesies the Masonic Lodge in our day.

---

[360] "Comer-Stone, Symbolism of the," *Mackey's Encyclopedia,* vol.1.

[361] *Mackey's Encyclopedia,* vol.1, facing p.254.

[362] *Mackey's Encyclopedia,* vol.1, facing p.558.

[363] Manly P. Hall, *The Lost Keys of Freemasonry* (1923; Richmond, VA: Macoy, 1976) facing p.52.

At the beginning of Zechariah's vision (verses 1-5), the prophet sees a "flying roll" (scroll in some translations) with the dimensions of a rectangle. The rectangle, of course, is a symbol of the Masonic Lodge. The word flying in Hebrew means "to cover with obscurity."[364] Together, the words "flying roll" describe a mystery religion, or secret society, such as Freemasonry.

In verse 3, the angel speaking to the prophet reveals that the flying roll "is the curse that goeth forth over the face of the whole earth..." In Hebrew the word *curse* means "to take an oath, usually in a bad sense."[365] Housed in the flying roll is a basket containing a woman. The basket is borne by two other women, which in Hebrew are two harlots. We shall discover that these two harlots are descriptive of Rosicrucian (English) and Templar (French) Freemasonry.

In verses 10-11 Zechariah inquires to the destination of the basket:

> *"Then said I to the angel that talked with me, Whither do these [two harlots] bear the ephah [basket]? And he said unto me, To build it a house in the land of Shinar [Babylonia]: and it shall be established, and set there upon her own base."*

As we have seen, the "flying roll" suggests a mystery religion, and the destination of the basket within the roll is Babylon. Without doubt the woman inside the basket is the Whore of Mystery Babylon, for in verse 8 the angel reveals her identity as "wickedness." Her "wickedness" is described in Revelation 17:2-4. In verse 6 of Zechariah 5 is a most baffling and significant exchange between the prophet and the angel. When the prophet was shown the basket concealing the harlot religion, he asked 'What is it? And he [the angel] said, This is an ephah [basket] that goeth forth. He said moreover, This is their resemblance through all the earth" (emphasis mine).

But *resemblance* to what? Resemblance to whatever was presented in the two previous chapters of Zechariah. For example, in the third chapter of Zechariah, the prophet views a heavenly scene in which furniture surrounds the throne of God - furniture that Zechariah was to duplicate in rebuilding Solomon's Temple at Jerusalem. We know of course that Freemasonry had intended, from its beginning, to be a "resemblance" of Solomon's Temple - even to the construction and arrangement of its furniture in the Lodge, as pictured in *Mackey's Encyclopedia of Freemasonry*.[366] It is no far-fetched conclusion to understand the basket containing the Whore of Babylon as a reference to Freemasonry, which announces itself a resemblance of Solomon's Temple.

In Zechariah 4:2 the prophet describes another piece of the furniture as a candlestick with seven lamps. In verses 4b-6a and 10b, the prophet asks about the seven lamps: "What are these, my lord? Then the angel that talked with me answered and said unto me, Knowest thou not what these be? And I said, No, my lord. Then he answered and spake unto me, saying... those seven... are the eyes of the Lord, which run to and fro through the whole earth."[367]

---

[364] Strong, *Hebrew* #5774.

[365] Strong, *Hebrew* #423 referring to 422.

[366] *Mackey's Encyclopedia*, vol.11, facing p.1050. See also Appendix 2, Fig. 2 in *Scarlet and the Beast*, vol. I.

[367] Bible, Pilgrim Edition, footnote to Zechariah 4:10. Bible commentators, Dr. E. Schuyler English and Marian Bishop Bower, state that "Certain scholars believe that the rest of this verse (Zechariah 10b), belongs after the first part of the sixth verse, so that that verse should read: 'Then he answered and said to me, These seven [speaking of the seven lamps] are the eyes of Jehovah which sweep through the whole earth.' After this, go to the 11th verse and read to the end, then go back to verse 6."

The apostle John had a similar vision in Revelation. In the first chapter he saw seven stars and seven candlesticks. It was revealed to John by Christ in verse 20b that "The seven stars are the angels of the seven churches: and the seven candlesticks which thou sawest are the seven churches." Inverse 3: 1 the seven stars are said to be "Seven spirits of God." In verse 5:6 Jesus Christ is seen as "a Lamb as it had been slain, having seven horns and seven eyes, which are the seven Spirits of God sent forth into all the earth."

John and Zechariah both saw the "seven eyes" of the Lord, which were seven ruling angels (possibly archangels) of God, whose duty it is to protect the Judeo-Christian Faith. In Zechariah's vision the seven eyes of God were headquartered at the Jerusalem temple, and from there ran "to and fro through the whole earth." In John's vision they were headquartered in the seven churches, and from there were "sent forth into all the earth."[368]

That Freemasonry sees the seven eyes of the Lord as seven archangels is found in Albert Pike's *Morals and Dogma.* "It was not without a secret meaning," Pike writes, "that John addressed his rebukes and menaces to the *Seven* churches, the number of the Archangels...

In Revelation 5:6 John informs us that the seven eyes, or Spirits of God, are under the command of our Lord Jesus Christ. So too said Zechariah: "they are the eyes of the Lord." On the basis of these passages we can reasonably conclude that Mystery Babylon in Zechariah 5:5-11 resembles not only Solomon's Temple in the Old Testament, but also the seven churches in the New Testament. There can be no doubt to what this implies, for Freemasonry, which is Mystery Babylon in our day, claims a Jewish and Christian "resemblance" in the French Templar Scottish Rite and the English Rosicrucian Rite. (See Appendix 2, Figs. 1 and 2.)

A further disturbing meaning of the word resemblance emerges when we examine its Hebrew root. *Resemblance,* a word used no place else in Scripture, refers not only to a "resemblance" to Solomon's Temple and the seven churches, but a "resemblance" to the "seven eyes of the Lord" as well. This Hebrew word, "resemblance," is ayin, a prime root, which can be translated *"outward appearance or resemblance."* However, its primary meaning is literally and figuratively a *singular eye.*[369]

All pagan religions have their "singular eye." For example, in Hinduism it is called the "Third Eye." In Egypt it is the "Eye Osiris." And in Freemasonry it is the "All-Seeing Eye."

That Freemasonry views Lucifer as the highest authority in heaven is found in the blasphemous positioning of the All-Seeing Eye on George Washington's Masonic apron. The design is obviously taken from the description of Lucifer's fall in Isaiah 14:12-13: "How art thou fallen from heaven, O Lucifer, son of the morning! [How] art thou cut down to the ground, which didst weaken the nations! For thou hast said in thine heart, I will ascend into heaven, I win exalt my throne above the stars [seven archangels] of God: I will sit also upon the mount of the congregation, in the sides of the north..."

---

[368] Pike 233.
[369] Strong, *Hebrew* #5869.

Almighty God carefully chose the word "resemblance" - the only word that could tie Freemasonry to Mystery Babylon. Mystery Babylon, the Mother of Harlots, which in the end-days has found its home in the Priory of Sion, the Rose-Croix, English Freemasonry, and now the Illuminati, has its *resemblance* - the All-Seeing Eye of the Illuminati, which is the Eye of Lucifer.

THE ALL-SEEING EYE IN AMERICA

Americans little suspect the pervasive influence of Freemasonry in America and the world. For an example we can look once more at the unfinished pyramid and the All-Seeing Eye on the back of our dollar bill.

Thirty-second degree Freemason President Franklin D. Roosevelt ordered the emblem there in 1934 after reading *The History of the Seal of the United States*. His Vice President, Henry A. Wallace, also a 32nd degree Mason, shares the story:

> *Roosevelt, as he looked at the colored reproduction of the Seal, was first struck with the representation of the "All Seeing Eye," a Masonic representation of the Great Architect of the Universe. Next he was impressed with the idea that the foundation for the new order of the ages [New World Order] had been laid in 1776, but that it would be completed only under the eye of the Great Architect. Roosevelt, like myself, was a 32nd degree Mason. He suggested that the Seal be put on the dollar bill...*[370]

President Roosevelt received inspiration for his New Deal policy from this Masonic symbol.[371] It is significant that part of the New Deal included founding the United Nations, for which President Roosevelt labored to see incorporated. Forty-six years later, on February 6, 1991, at the height of the Persian Gulf War, President George Bush spoke

---

[370] Capt 39.
[371] Capt.

before the Economic Club of New York City and described the United Nations as the catalyst behind the success of the New World Order.[372]

Today the All-Seeing Eye of the Illuminati can be seen in the meditation room of the United Nations in New York. When viewing the room from above, it is shaped like Weishaupt's unfinished pyramid. The All-Seeing Eye is at the narrow end of the room, in the position of the capstone.[373] That Weishaupt's Illuminati Seal has been adopted by the United Nations signifies it too is under the watchful eye of Lucifer and his counterfeit Priory of Sion.

A CALL TO CHRISTIANS

Christian brother in Freemasonry, you are contributing to a one world government which will end in the Apocalyptic Beast of Revelation. If you can remain in the Lodge after these revelations, perhaps you are like Weishaupt - an apostate. In his rebellion Weishaupt knowingly and defiantly shook his fist in the face of Almighty God, arrogantly saying of himself, "I am proud to be known to the world as the founder of the Order of Illuminati... I have gone through the whole circle of human enquiry. I have exorcised spirits - raised ghosts - discovered treasures - interrogated the Cabala... In 1830, however, when his day of reckoning arrived, Weishaupt begged to be reinstated in the Church, but he died a miserable apostate, unable to renew repentance.

Brother in Christ, you were deceived by Freemasonry the moment the "hoodwink"[374] was placed over your head in the Entered Apprentice (1st degree) initiation.[375] Do not in your pride defend the Lodge. You can no longer justify your continued affiliation with this Satanic order by claiming ignorance, for you now know the truth about Freemasonry. Jesus pleads with you, "Come out of her, my people, that ye be not partakers of her sins, and that ye receive not of her plagues" (Rev.18:4).

To withdraw from Freemasonry, there are three steps you as a Christian must take. The first step is important only to you. Confess to the God of the Bible that you have been deceived and have sinned by joining this pagan religion. Then ask His forgiveness. He is merciful and promises to forgive.

The second step is important to both you and your family. The prophet says in Zechariah 5:4 that when a man joins the Babylonian religion of Freemasonry, a curse "shall remain in the midst of his house, and shall consume it with the timber thereof and the stones thereof." House in Hebrew can be translated "family," while stones can be translated "children."[376]

The "curse" is understood to mean demonic activity, for anyone who joins a Satanic order subjects himself and his family to such activity. The curse can be removed by the power of the shed blood of Jesus Christ. Renounce Freemasonry and ask Jesus to cleanse you and your household of this curse. Then apply in your daily walk with God, Ephesians 6:11-18 - "Put on the whole armour of God, that ye may be able to stand against the wiles of the devil." If you are not a Mason, but are a Christian with a father or grandfather who

---

[372] "Point of View Radio Broadcast," Larry Abraham interviewed by Marlin Maddox, Dallas, TX, 11 Feb.1991.

[373] Kirban 156.In Appendix 2, Fig. 17, you can follow the picture story of the United Nation's All-Seeing Eye, excerpted from the book, The Cult of the All-Seeing Eye, by Robert Keith Spenser, 1964.

[374] Robison 80-81.

[375] "Hoodwink," *Mackey's Encyclopedia*, vol.1.

[376] Strong, *Hebrew* #1004, 6086, 68 from 1129.

is (or was) affiliated with the Masonic Lodge, you as their offspring are affected by this curse. Renounce the generational curse by the shed blood of Jesus Christ.

The third step is important to you and to those deceived who remain in the Lodge. Renounce Freemasonry in writing. Send your letter of renunciation to the warden in your Lodge. By Masonic Law, the warden must read your letter to those assembled. It is your testimony to them that you have received the true Light, Jesus Christ. (See sample letter "Petition for Withdrawal," in Appendix 8.)

6. MUSIC AND REVOLUTION

> *Music is a curiously subtle art... it can be soothing or invigorating, enobling or vulgarizing, philosophical or orgiastic. It has powers for evil as well as good.*
>
> American composer - Dr. Howard Hanson[377]
>
> *Music is a spiritual thing of its own. You can hypnotize people with music, and when you get them at their weakest point you can preach into their subconscious whatever you want to say.*
>
> Rock star - Jimi Hendrix[378]

Before and during the French Revolution, illuminated Freemasonry used anti-Christian music to spread revolution throughout Europe. One of Weishaupt's recruits, for example, a latecomer to Freemasonry, was the famous Swabian doctor Frederic Antoine Mesmer (1733-1815). Mesmer originated the "science" of Mesmerism - a forerunner to hypnotism. Nesta Webster describes how Mesmer used a form of music to mesmerize:

> *Mesmer himself - stirring the fluid in his magic bucket, around which his disciples wept, slept, fell into trances or convulsions, raved or prophesied... Freemasonry, eager to discover the secret of the magic bucket, hastened to enroll him in their Order, and Mesmer was received into the Primitive Rite of Free and Accepted Masons in 1785.*[379]

Mesmer's "magic bucket" was in fact a musical instrument. Pianist Leonard J. Seidel, in *Face the Music,* explains how Mesmer used music to alter the emotional and mental states of his patients: "Mesmer, a close friend of Mozart, treated several patients with music played on the piano or a glass harmonica fashioned of rotating glass cylinders which produced tones when rubbed by wet fingers. He related how a change of key or meter could cause spasms."[380]

The same key or meter-induced spasms are generated with rock and roll music today and puts rock artists and their audience into what they call "the state." From the Doors biography *No One Here Gets Out Alive,* keyboardist Ray Manzarek explains:

> *When the Siberian shaman gets ready to go into his trance all the villagers get together and shake rattles and blow whistles and play whatever instruments they have to send him off. There is a constant pounding, pounding, pounding... It was the same way with the Doors when we played in concert.*
>
> *We knew the symptoms of the state, so that we could try to approximate it. It was like Jim was an electric shaman and we were the electric shaman's band pounding away behind him. Sometimes he wouldn't feel like getting into the state, but the band would keep on pounding and pounding, and little by little it would take him over. God, I could send an electric shock through him with the organ. John could do it with his drum beats. You could see every once in a while - twitch.*

---

[377] Leonard J. Seidel, *Face the Music* (Springfield, VA: Grace Unlimited Publications, 1988) 23-24.
[378] *Life* 3 Oct.1969: 74.
[379] Webster, *Secret Societies* 175.
[380] Seidel 20.

I could hit a chord and make him twitch. And he'd be off again. Sometimes he was just incredible. Just amazing. And the audience felt it too![381]

Mesmer, the Ray Manzarek of yesteryear, was encouraged by Freemason Wolfgang Amadeus Mozart to join Freemasonry. The Lodge that Mesmer joined was that of illuminated Egyptian Freemasonry founded by Sionist Cagliostro. Mozart is most likely the person who taught Mesmer how to use music to control people, since Mozart composed for the Masonic Lodge certain pieces designed to incite revolution in the hearts of the populace.[382]

Mackey's Encyclopedia of Freemasonry confirms that Mozart's "works are supposed to have been intended for Masonic use."[383] For example, Mozart's famous opera, *The Magic Flute*, was a Masonic masterpiece. *The Magic Flute* was composed in the Perfect Union Masonic Lodge, a Viennese Lodge dedicated to the Masonic use of the arts. Mozart's mentor was the new Grand Master (GM) of the Priory of Sion, Maximilian of Lorraine (GM 1780 - 1801), the previous Grand Master's nephew. Maximilian's assignment appears to have been the development of liberal music to incite anti-Christian sentiment.

Masons and Masonry are essential to the creation of *The Magic Flute*. For instance, Grand Master of the Perfect Union, Ignaz von Born, "gave Mozart the material and the inspiration for his opera 'The Magic Flute.'Schikaneder, who wrote the libretto for 'The Magic Flute' and Giesecke, his assistant, were Masons. The character, Sarastro, in the opera, was Born."[384]

Dr. Mackey summarizes the opera's content: "The plot of the *Magic Flute* is now generally believed to be a book published in 1731 by the Abbe Terrasson named *Sethos,* described as a history of life drawn from the monuments of ancient Egypt. It contains a description of the initiation of *Sethos,* an Egyptian priest, into the mysteries of Egypt."[385]

Masonic sources confirm that *The Magic Flute* was designed to turn the populace away from the Catholic Church and toward occult mysticism, just as rock music is designed to do today. Thirty- third degree Mason Dr. Mackey gloated over the Perfect Union's success in using the arts for promoting spiritual rebellion. "It was the very success of this Lodge," writes Mackey, "that moved the Roman Church to launch its crusade against Austrian Masonry for reasons understandable enough to any man who knows how deadly free and genuine enlightenment is to the Vatican's program."[386]

THE PHYSICAL EFFECTS OF MUSIC

Before Freemasonry discovered that music could be used in revolution, others had long before proven its effect on the human body. Seidel writes:

A 16th century composer, Gioseffo Zarlino, experimented with what he called the four humors of the body and the four modes of music. Athanasius Kircher demonstrated in the 17th century how musical tones could move each of the four humors, building upon what Zarlino had discovered. Kircher used several

---

[381] Mark Spaulding, *The Heartbeat of the Dragon: The Occult Roots of Rock & Roll* (Sterling Hts., MI: Light Warrior Press, 1992) 11-12.

[382] Neal Wilgus, *The Illuminoids* (1978; New York: Pocket Books,1979) 117.

[383] "Mozart," *Mackey's Encyclopedia of Freemasonry*, vol.11.

[384] "Perfect Union, of Vienna," *Mackey's Encyclopedia,* vol.111.

[385] "Mozart," *Mackey's Encyclopedia*, vol.11.

[386] "Perfect Union," *Mackey's Encyclopedia,* vol.111.

glasses, each filled with a different liquid which corresponded to each of the four humors. As a moistened finger was rubbed around the rim of the glasses, producing a musical tone, each fluid was set in a different frequency of motion which resulted in each humor being moved by a particular tone.

In the 18th century, E. A. Nicolai described muscles, nerves, and arteries as fibers that were either dissonant or consonant. He demonstrated that music could alter the condition of those fibers. H. W. Albrecht, professor of anatomy at Gottingen wrote that the fibers [muscles], when they were too loose or tight, could be retuned by music.[387]

Less than a century after Freemasonry successfully used Mozart's music to incite revolution, music was scientifically proven to alter physiological states. Seidel writes:

The first accurate measurements of the physical effects of music were recorded in the 19th century by German scientist, Hermann von Helmholtz. In his work, Die Lebre von den Tonempfindungen, published in 1863, he described the components of a musical tone and the physical basis of our perception of consonance and dissonance. Many others built upon his findings, discovering that pulse, blood pressure, and breathing were measurably affected by the various musical elements of rhythm, dissonance and consonance, and pitch and loudness.[388]

As science has proven, music is not neutral. It can be used for good or evil. The shepherd boy, David, who later became king of Israel, played his harp to sooth the evil spirit in King Saul. According to Seidel, music is similarly used in mental institutions today for treatment of the mentally ill.[389]

As we all know and have experienced, music also brings out the emotions in people. Music can cause tears and joy. Military music incites vigor. Lullabies produce drowsiness. Love songs generate sensual feelings. Hollywood uses background mood music on a grand scale to create excitement, fear, suspense, etc.

Recent experiments in the subliminal use of music in retail stores have proven to cause customers to buy more. The Musak corporation has cashed in on this mind-influencing aspect of music. Now there is New Age music, which puts some people into a trance.

Sound alone, without music, will cause the same effect. An electronics and sound genius from Kansas City, who wishes to remain anonymous, explained it to the author. We will refer to him as Clark. Clark and the author were meeting to discuss their mutual interest in a security project in which they were planning to invest. Clark's discovery makes use of high frequency sound inaudible to the normal range of the human ear. He said that success with inaudible subliminal mind control has been proven so effective that it was contested in 1983 and ruled illegal in the private sector.

Clark discovered that a certain frequency beyond the reach of the human ear stops shoplifting. The demonstration for the author occurred in a supermarket known for its shoplifting problem. Clark stood close to, yet obscured from the drug section, the most vulnerable area for theft. Soon a customer stuffed some health and beauty aids inside his jacket. Simultaneously Clark pressed a button on a small box he was holding, activating

---

[387] Seidel 20.
[388] Seidel 21.
[389] Seidel.

the inaudible sound. The shoplifter stopped dead in his tracks, reached inside his jacket, and after placing the item back on the shelf, bolted from the store!

Many tests were made in this supermarket - all with the same positive results.

As this anecdote shows, sound and music are not neutral! They do affect the mind, nervous system, and emotions. Music can be used for good, as many scientists realize. Others, however, are aware that it can be used for evil.[390]

SUBVERSIVE MUSIC

Helping to compose revolutionary music appears to have been the assignment of the Grand Master of the Priory of Sion, Maximilian de Lorraine (GM 1780-1801), favorite nephew of Charles de Lorraine. Maximilian was Maria Theresa's youngest son, keeping the steering committee of Sion in the imperial court at Vienna.

Maximilian's sister, Marie Antoinette, was queen of France. She had been given in marriage to the French King Louis XVI, to produce in one or two generations a Habsburg-Lorraine heir to the French throne. Although the impending French Revolution was a threat to her life, Maximilian dared not show anxiety. While feigning sympathy toward the original objectives of the Revolution (i.e., the deposition of the Bourbon dynasty), he provided a haven for aristocratic refugees. When the storm broke, Maximilian did not panic.[391]

Four years after Maximilian accepted his assignment as Grand Master, he "turned his energies to the Church, becoming, in 1784, bishop of Munster, as well as archbishop and imperial elector of Cologne."[392] This move also appears to have been a clandestine effort to mask his Masonic activity. Maximilian, for example, was known to have consorted openly with Freemasons, although he declared he was not one himself. The authors of *Holy Blood, Holy Grail*, however, believe that he was. His denial is understandable, since, being a Freemason would jeopardize his position as archbishop, a position vital to his assignment. For, as a subversive inside the church, he could better measure the effect of his revolutionary music on Christians.

Maximilian became an assiduous patron of the arts. Not only was Mozart his protege', so were Haydn and the young Beethoven. Haydn and Mozart were both members of the same Masonic Lodge.

According to *Mackey's Encyclopedia of Freemasonry*, there are musicians' Masonic lodges in England today, identical to those on the Continent that were used by Mozart and others, where artists meet to discuss their mutual objectives.[393]

Mark Spaulding, former drummer for a rock and roll band, connects these English Masonic lodges with the modern outbreak of anti-Christian rock and roll. In his book, *The Heartbeat of the Dragon: The Occult Roots of Rock & Roll* (1992), Spaulding writes:

> *Through the late 1800's... many British based, occult organizations were formed. The Theosophical Society, The Hermetic Order of The Golden Dawn, The Order of The Silver Star, Freemasonry, and Rosicrucianism were but a few of the many esoteric societies that found their homes in England... The early 1960's*

---

[390] Seidel 23-24.

[391] Baigent, *Holy Blood* 433.

[392] Baigent.

[393] "Class Lodges"; "Musicians, Worshipful Company of'; and "Perfect Union," *Mackey's Encyclopedia,* vol.111.

> *witnessed England suddenly filled with people who were caught up in the occult;*
> *and British rock and roll was about to follow suit.*[394]

Like the music of Mozart, Spaulding confirms that rock and roll "was specifically designed to instigate REBELLION in the listener... as well as undermining their inborn God-ordained moral Code."[395]

Spaulding's book is the result of an extensive research on the occult origins and Satanic design of rock and roll. He said, "I have discovered evidence which clearly exposes an incredible interconnectedness between rock and roll, Hinduism, Shamanism, Satanism, and Voodoo... On the surface, these ideologies may seem to be quite diverse but deep within their core they are unmistakably identical."[396]

The fascination that rock and roll stars have for Freemasons and things that are Masonic is seen in their album jackets and heard in the lyrics to their songs. Following are a few examples:

1. Britisher Lord David Sutch, or Screaming Lord Sutch, as he was affectionately called by his band, the Savages, had a passion for shocking horror show theatrics. For example, in one concert he entered stage in a black coffin borne by hooded monks. He emerged from the coffin with three spine chilling screams - headless and bloody with grotesque hands. This is how Sutch introduced his album entitled *Hands of Jack the Ripper*. In chapter 20 we shall learn that the Ripper slayings were actually Masonic ritual murders.

2. On the front cover of The Beatles' album *Sgt. Pepper* is what appears to be a group portrait. Some are known Freemasons of yesteryear, including Aleister Crowley, a 33rd degree Grand Orient Mason and Grand Master of three degenerate British Masonic orders; Karl Marx, a 32nd degree Grand Orient Mason; Carl Jung a Rosicrucian Freemason; and H.G. Wells, an English Mason. When Ringo Starr was asked in an interview why they picked these people, he said, "We just thought we would like to put together a lot of people we like and admire."[397]

3. Ozzy Osbourne said that Freemason Crowley was "the phenomenon of his time."[398] Osbourne wrote a song about this Satanist entitled "Mr. Crowley."

4. Sting spent many hours reading Crowley's and Jung's occult books.

5. Jim Morrison posed with a bust of Crowley for a band promo picture, which was used on the back of the *Doors 13* album cover.

6. Grahm Bond claimed to be Crowley's son. When he formed his "Holy Magick" band dedicated to Crowley, he spelled "Magick" in the Crowley fashion.

7. In Led Zeppelin's song "Stairway to Heaven" are the words to the initiation ceremony of the Masonic Order of the Golden Dawn, an English Masonic order headed by Crowley.[399]

8. In an early W.A.S.P. stage show, Blackie Lawless drank blood from a human skull[400], which is part of the initiation ceremony in the 30th degree of Scottish Rite Freemasonry.[401]

---

[394] Spaulding 57.
[395] Spaulding 63.
[396] Spaulding 19.
[397] Spaulding 69.
[398] Spaulding 98.
[399] Spaulding 92-93.
[400] Spaulding 120.
[401] J. Blanchard, *Scottish Rite Masonry illustrated*, vol.11, (1944; Chicago: Powner, 1979) 285.

9.In the Rush album *Hemispheres,* Geddy Lee sings the "brotherhood" doctrine of Freemasonry. In Rush's "Witch Hunt," lyricist Neil Peart pens the Masonic terms "ignorance and prejudice" to reference Christianity.[402]

10.In Venom's *At War With* Satan album, the lyrics define and praise the Masonic Russian Revolution of 1917 (see chapter 19): Damnation has sunk its talons deep into the womb of utopia spilling forth great streams [of blood] of virginal purity and bliss. The golden throne of tetragrammaton [red star] is ablaze. His majesty [Satan] sits proud, the joyous drones of celebrations enact scenes of blasphemy, lust and destruction raping the Holy Trim ty.[403]

11.Paul Kantner of Jefferson Airplane wrote lyrics like "Jesus had a son by Mary Magdalene."[404] As we know, this doctrine comes straight from the lore of the Priory of Sion, founder of English Freemasonry.

12.Jimi Hendrix also sings of the Priory of Sion legend: The story of Jesus so easy to explain after they crucified him, a woman, she [Mary Magdalene] claimed his name The story of Jesus the whole Bible knows went all across the Desert and in the middle, he found a rose [Rosicrucians] There should be no questions there should be no lies He was married ever happily after for all the Tears we cry.[405]

Not only are Rock stars fascinated with Masonic symbols on their album covers, Masonic doctrine sung in their lyrics, and Masonic initiation ceremonies staged in their theatrics, many are themselves Freemasons. For example, Jimmy Page, lead guitarist for Led Zeppelin, in the early 1970s was initiated into the English Masonic order called the Hermetic Order of the Golden Dawn by Freemason Kenneth Anger. Anger was Aleister Crowley's disciple. Crowley, until his death in 1947, was Grand Master of the Golden Dawn.[406]

Page had become so enamored with the potential of mixing Crowley's magical powers with rock and roll that he purchased Crowley's old mansion, located on the shores of the famous Loch Ness. After the purchase he had a Satanist decorate the inside with occult symbols and then assumed occupancy.

On the *Led Zeppelin HI* album, scratched into the vinyl band just outside the record's center label, is the phrase, "DO WHAT THOU WILT."[407] This phrase is the whole of the "Law" of the Ordo Templi Orientis (O.T.O.), the most degenerate Masonic Lodge founded by English Freemasonry - a lodge that performs human sacrifices to this day. (See chapter 15 and Appendix 6.) Its English chapter was headed by none other than Aleister Crowley.

On the inside cover of the *Led Zeppelin W* album is the figure of a hermit. The hermit symbolizes occult power and the light of truth. In the hermit's hand is a lantern. The light from within the lantern is in the shape of the six-pointed star (hexagram) of the Priory of Sion. The hexagram is also known as the Star of Lucifer.[408]

Two other famous English Masonic rock stars are Mick Jagger and Keith Richards of the Rolling Stones. Freemason Kenneth Anger initiated both men into Crowley's Order of the Golden Dawn.[409]

After his heroin arrest Richards admitted, "There are black magicians who think we are acting as unknown agents of Lucifer.

---

[402] Spaulding 135.

[403] Spaulding 140.

[404] Spaulding 146.

[405] Spaulding 156.

[406] *Executive Intelligence Review* 31 Aug.1982: 45-46.

[407] Spaulding 90.

[408] Spaulding 91.

[409] *Executive Intelligence Review* 31 Aug.1982: 45-46.

The Rolling Stones' anthems to Satan, "Sympathy for the Devil" and "Dancing with Mr. D" (the Devil), bear out Richards' comment. And like Mozart's revolutionary propaganda in music two centuries ago, the Rolling Stones spread revolutionary propaganda today through their song "Street Fighting Man."[410]

LUCIFER - GOD OF EVIL MUSIC

How did Freemasonry discover that music could be used to provoke revolution? From their god, of course! Scripture suggests that the Fallen Angel was created a musician. The prophet Ezekiel, in 28:13, says of Lucifer's musical personality: "Thou hast been in Eden the garden of God... the workmanship of thy tabrets [drums] and of thy pipes [flutes] was prepared in thee in the day that thou wast created."[411]

Strong's Concordance defines pipes as a bezel for a gem[412]; and tabrets as a tambourine; from the primative root to *drum, i.e. play (as:) on the tambourine: - taber, play with timbrels.*[413] The same Hebrew word is used in Genesis 31:27:1 Samuel 10:5; and Isaiah 24:8 in context with other musical instruments.

As we have seen, the name Lucifer means "morning star," apparently a titled position of the angelic hierarchy. In Job 35:4-7, "the morning stars sang together" when God "laid the foundation of the earth!"[414] - while all other creation shouted fonoy. Morning stars, or archangels, were apparently created with the ability to make music. When Lucifer became corrupt, so did his music! He has passed this corrupt knowledge of mind-altering music to the Masonic Hierarchy. Volume III of *Scarlet and the Beast* will expand on this fact - that rock music today is Masonically created and designed to (1) incite world revolution and (2) market illegal drugs for English Freemasonry.

---

[410] William Josiah Sutton, *The New Age Movement and The Illuminati* 666. (U.S.A.: The Institute of Religious Knowledge, 1983) 218-219.

[411] Various translations state it differently. American Standard Version (1901) translates it tarlets, pipes; New King James Version translates it timbrels, pipes; New English Bible translates it jingling beads and spangles; Revised Standard Version takes a different view and translates it as settings and engravings; Likewise, New International Version - settings and mountings.

[412] Strong, *Hebrew* #5345.

[413] Strong, *Hebrew* #8596 from prim. root 8608.

[414] Bible, *New American Standard Bible* (NASB).

7. THE JEWISH CONNECTION

[During the French Revolution] Jewish Masons were no larger in number than their proportion to the Jewish population; and most of the Jewish Masons of the period were either Spanish or French.

Mackey's Encyclopedia of Freemasonry[415]

Many revisionist authors have assumed that the Masonic conspiracy and its various offshoots are of Jewish origin because Weishaupt, the father-founder of Illuminism, was a Jew. As support for this hypothesis they point out that many of Weishaupt's operatives were of Jewish descent. For example, Gerald B. Winrod in his short book, *Adam Weishaupt, A Human Devil*, writes, "Confiscated documents of the organization disclose that of the thirty-nine chief sub-leaders of Weishaupt, seventeen were Jews."[416]

It is true that many of Weishaupt's most ardent adherents and lieutenants were Jews. One of the most dependable disciples was Joseph Balsamo (alias Cagliostro), a Rosicrucian of Jewish birth.

Balsamo, you recall, figures in the Priory documents as equivalent to a Grand Master of the Priory of Sion. Balsamo/Cagliostro was a sorcerer and magician who performed his witchcraft throughout Europe. He founded more illuminated lodges than did any individual Freemason then or since. He is the father of the existing rite of Misraim, which is the Egyptian rite in Masonry. Its symbol is the same six-pointed star created as the coat of arms for the Rennes-le-Chateau by the Merovingian king Dagobert II.[417] The Englishman Monsignor Dr. George E. Dillon provides explicit details of Cagliostro's witchcraft:

In Paris he established lodges for women of a peculiarly cabalistic and impure kind, with inner departments horribly mysterious... He was an inveterate sorcerer, and in his peregrinations in the East, picked up from every source, the secrets of alchemy [which included the manufacture of mind bending drugs], astrology, jugglery, legerdemain, and occult science of every kind... [In the lodges he established] he used rites and ceremonies exactly resembling the absurd practices of spirit mediums, who see and speak to spirits, etc. He claimed the power of conferring immortal youth, health, and beauty, and what he called moral and physical regeneration, by the aid of drugs and Illuminated Masonry.[418]

A century later *Mackey's Encyclopedia of Freemasonry* recalls Cagliostro's importance to the Brotherhood: "The history of Free masonry in that century would not be complete without a reference to this personage. To write the history of Freemasonry in the eighteenth century and to leave out Cagliostro, would be like enacting the play of Hamlet and leaving out the part of the Prince of Denmark."[419]

---

[415] "Anti-Semitism and Masonry," *Mackey's Encyclopedia of Freemasonry*, vol.111.
[416] Winrod 43.
[417] Baigent et al, *Holy Blood, Holy Grail*, facing p.336, Fig. 36 and Fig. 34.
[418] Dillon, *Grand Orient Unmasked* 28-29.
[419] "Cagliostro," *Mackey's Encyclopedia*, vol.1.

Nesta H. Webster, in *Secret Societies and Subversive Movements*, describes how Illuminist-inspired occultism affected France before the Revolution:

> *Under the guidance of these various sects of Illumines a wave of occultism swept over France, and lodges everywhere became centres of instruction on the Cabala, magic, divination, alchemy, and theosophy; masonic [sic] rites degenerated into ceremonies for the evocation of spirits - women, who were now admitted to these assemblies, screamed, fainted, fell into convulsions, and lent themselves to experiments of the most horrible kind.*
>
> *The Baron de Gleichen, in describing the "Convulsionists," says that young women allowed themselves to be crucified, sometimes head downward, at these meetings of the fanatics. He himself saw one nailed to the floor and her tongue cut with a razor.*[420]

Another member of the Illuminati sect was Cagliostro's mentor, Daniel Wolf (alias Saint-Germain), son of a Jewish doctor from Strasburg. He delighted the King of France and Madame de Pompadour with his magic.

Saint-Germain made many outrageous claims, for one that he was the Grand Master of Continental Freemasonry at a time when that position was held by Frederick the Great, King of Prussia. He also declared he had discovered the secret of retaining his youth, displaying himself as an example. When he was only fifty, for example, he said he was seventy-four. Dr. Mackey confirms that St. Germain "laid claim to the highest rank of Freemasonry, the Order being at that time strong in France, claiming also that he was over five hundred years of age, had been born in Chaldaea, [and] possessed the secrets of the Egyptian sages..."[421] At his death he had increased his age to 1,500 years, maintaining he had gone through several incarnations. Although he died in 1784, his admirers upheld that he was in some remote corner of Europe.[422]

Not all the promoters of illuminism were Jews. A non4ew who figures in the Priory of Sion's Illuminati plot is Louis Claude de Saint Martin. In 1775 this man reformed the Martinist Order founded in 1754 by a Spanish Jew, Martinez Paschalis. (Paschalis, if not directly connected to the Priory of Sion, is indirectly connected in two ways: (1) he was a Rosicrucian, creating the higher degrees in the Martinist Order with Rose-Croix ceremonies; and (2) the symbol he designed for the Martinist Order consisted of six dots arranged in such a manner that when the Priory of Sion's six-pointed star is superimposed over the dots, each dot falls on the point of the triangles.)

When Saint Martin reformed the Order in 1775, he became closely associated with the Illuminati. He was on intimate terms with Illuminatus Jean Willermoz, who presided at two of the great Masonic conventions leading up to the French Revolution.[423] One of Saint Martin's most significant tasks was the protection of ancient documents the Martinist Order possessed - documents believed to have come from an area around Rennes-le-Chateau in southern France.[424]

Paschilis, St. Germain, as well as other less important Jews, were sub-leaders in the Illuminati plot. Most were employed only to propagate anarchy and licentious living. Such was the assignment of Scottish Rite Freemason Moses Mendelssohn, whose role

---

[420] Webster, *Secret Societies* 170.
[421] "Saint Germain, The Count of," *Mackey's Encyclopedia*, vol.11.
[422] Webster 173-174.
[423] Miller, *Occult Theocrasy* 353.
[424] Webster 310.

within the Illuminati begins with Freemason and Illuminatus Gotthold Ephraim Lessing (1729-1781).

LESSING AND MENDELSSOHN

Lessing was a rebel son of the head Lutheran pastor in Kamenz, Germany. Against the tide of popular sentiment, he was a great admirer of the Jews. His affection was not for their race as much as for a segment of liberal Jews known as Frankists, who were willing to bring down the Church in writing diatribes against it. He defended them only for the greater Illuminati cause - the total destruction of both Christianity and Judaism.

Will and Ariel Durant write that "Lessing's heresies, and his occasional truculence in controversy, left him lonely in hi~ final years." While his adversaries denounced him throughout Germany as a monstrous atheist, his admirers - Freemasons Kant, Schiller, Goethe, etc. - "looked up to Lessing as the great liberator, the father of the German Enlightenment." The Durants quote Goethe as saying of Lessing, "In life we honored you as one of the gods; now that you are dead your spirit reigns over all souls."[425]

Mackey's Encyclopedia of Freemasonry explains Lessing's assignment in the Masonic conspiracy: "Brother Lessing's dramatic poem, *Nathan the Wise*, is vigorously Masonic. The author was convinced that the stage would prove... useful in circulating the good doctrine [of Freemasonry]...and he strove in this play to preach universal brother-hood."[426]

Lessing was the founder of modern German literature and, as such, lent his powerful support to the anti-Christian League.[427] Lessing was willing to edit and distribute anything published of an irreligious nature. This led him in 1754 to the liberal Jew, Moses Mendelssohn (1728-1786), who later joined an illuminated Grand Orient Ledge in Germany.

Orthodox Rabbi Marvin S. Antelman, in *To Eliminate The Opiate*, reports that "Moses Mendelssohn is regarded by many as the father of the Haskala movement."[428] Haskala is the name given those early Jewish liberals who were known as the "enlighteners" and later called the Jewish Reform Movement.[429] These Jews were the followers of a false Messiah, Shabbetai Tzvi or Sabbatai Zevi (1626-1676), and were in Mendelssohn's day known as Frankists, named after Jacob Frank (1726-1791), who, we shall see, resurrected the Sabbatai movement for the express purpose of destroying Orthodox Judaism.

Prior to the founding of the Illuminati in 1776, Moses Mendelssohn, who was a Scottish Rite Freemason, was known as the leader of this subversive Jewish sect, the Haskala. Freemasonry, however, was his vehicle to prominence. With Freemason Lessing's help, his Jewish friend was welcomed, writes the Durants, "into the not quite 'serene brotherhood of philosophes' in Berlin."[430]

This "not quite serene brotherhood" was made up of the illumines who lived a licentious lifestyle, while spreading anarchy in the minds of the people. Meeting at various taverns throughout Germany, Lessing introduced Mendelssohn to this

---

[425] Will Durant and Ariel Durant, *The Story of Civilization Rousseau and Revolution,* vol. X (New York: Simon and Schuster, 1967) 516-517.

[426] "Lessing, Gotthold Ephraim," *Mackey's Encyclopedia,* vol.1.

[427] Miller 372.

[428] Rabbi Marvin S. Antelman, *To Eliminate the Opiate* (New York:Zahavia LTD, 1974) 67.

[429] "The Jewish Enlightenment Movement," *Encyclopedia of Jewish History* (Israel: Massada Publishers, 1986) 98-101.

[430] Durants, vol. X, 638.William R. Denslow's *10,000 Famous Masons* informs us that Mendelssohn was a Scottish Rite Mason (vol.111, 193).

brotherhood, many of whom were later to become members of the German branch of the Illuminati, perversely known as the Tugendbund, or, in English, Union of Virtue.

The first Tugendbund Lodges were founded in 1786 as Illuminati fronts. As we know, Grand Orient Master Masons were sent out by Weishaupt to organize illuminated Lodges under various names. The Tugendbunds, according to Nesta Webster, were "directed by the secondary chiefs of the *Illumines*."[431] Mendelssohn, although illuminated long before Weishaupt was born, joined the Tugendbund just before his death. No evidence exists that the two men ever met; yet there is record that Weishaupt was inspired by Mendelssohn.[432]

JACOB FRANK AND THE ASSAULT ON JUDAISM

As noted above, Jacob Frank revived the Sabbatai movement for the purpose of undermining and destroying what we today call Orthodox Judaism. Rabbi Antelman rightly calls the Frankists anti-Semitic. He also claims that the Frankists gave birth to what we know as modern Biblical Criticism - a liberal view of Scripture that diminishes the authority of God's Word.[433]

Sabbatai Zevi was a licentious Turkish Jew born in Smyrna, who, incidentally, married one of the many harlots with whom he was intimate. The *Encyclopedia of Jewish History* states that "[h]e did not hesitate to pronounce the ineffable name of God (a practice forbidden to the religious Jew) and claimed that he himself was the Messiah."[434] About this time (1650s) he was officially excommunicated by the rabbis of his generation. For several years he wandered around the Jewish communities in the Balkans and in 1662 moved to the Holy Land. The Sabbatean movement was launched on May 31, 1665, when a young cabalist "soul healer" announced Sabbatai Zevi as the Messiah.

Sabbatai, a handsome man with a magnetic voice, gained a tremendous following when he announced he would march against Constantinople to oppose the Sultan. His movement disintegrated, however, when the Sultan captured him in September, 1666, and offered him life if he converted to Islam, which he did. His followers who condoned this act maintained that temporarily the Messiah must bury himself in sin in order "to save the 'spark' of sanctity."[435]

A century later Jacob Frank resurrected the Sabbatean messianic movement, refining the concept of the Messiah sinning as the "doctrine of reversal." Frank then urged "members of the movement to sin, reasoning that if salvation could be gotten through purity, it could also be achieved through sin."[436]

Rabbi Antelman notes that "[o]ne of the ways that the Frankists indulged in their sin was to engage in sexual orgies."[437] Antelman also sees the Frankists as precursors of the modern women's liberation movement because they encouraged women to forsake their husbands and join their orgies. Another sin allowed by the Frankists was that their adherents could join any religion, especially Catholicism. Rabbi Antelman points out that "their conversion to these religions was for the purpose of imitating the Sabbatean role models as well as for subverting and destroying these faiths."[438]

---

[431] Webster 265.
[432] Webster 229-230.
[433] Antelman 93-94.
[434] "Shabbateanism," *Encyclopedia of Jewish History* 92.
[435] "Shabbateanism," 92-93.
[436] Antelman 94.
[437] Antelman 95.
[438] Antelman.

The Rabbi summarizes the five distinguishing beliefs of radical Sabbatianism:

1. Apostasy of the Messiah is a necessity.
2. Real Torah is not the real Torah and must be violated by conforming to another superior, alien mystical Torah called the Torah of Atzilut.
3. First Cause and the God of Israel are not the same, the former being the God of rational philosophers and the latter the God of religion.
4. Godhead takes human form which allowed for leaders of the sect to be incarnated into that Godhead, from Shabbetai Tzvi through to Frank and others.
5. A "Believer" must not appear to be as he really is.

This last belief especially justified its followers to live a double life. Antelman, quoting Gershom Scholem in *The Messianic Idea* in *Judaism,* says that although the Frankists were outwardly religious, "they still cherished as their goal 'the annihilation of every religion and positive system of belief,' and they dreamed 'of a general revolution that would sweep away the past in a single stroke so that the world might be rebuilt." [439]

Antelman states that to foment revolution:

> *Jacob Frank preached the "Religious Myth of Nihilism" in more than two thousand dogmatic sayings. One of the Frankist cult's publications that has come into our possession is a book entitled Book of the Words of the Lord, which [the agnostic Jewish Professor, Gershom] Scholem characterizes as "a mixture of primitive savagery and putrescent morals." The Frankists had a way of turning around old homilies and sayings that were common among the people, twisting them in their nihilistic "Torah of Atzilut." For example, religious Jews at the beginning of the morning service start their prayers with a series of thirteen benedictions in which one thanks God for providing the necessities of life, for clothing the unclothed, etc. Among these benedictions is one that praises God for freeing those in captivity. The Hebrew for this is matir asurim. In the Frankist cult the benediction was pronounced, praising God as matir isurim, which means permitting the prohibited.*
>
> *Similarly, they twisted around other sayings. They would say, "the subversion of the Torah can become its true fulfillment," and "great is a sin committed for its own sake."[440]*

How did the Orthodox Rabbis attempt to eradicate the anti-Semitic Frankist Jews? Quoting from the *Jewish Encyclopedia,* Rabbi Antelman writes: "[I]t was obligatory for every pious Jew to search and expose them."[441] The Frankists were excommunicated by the Orthodoxy on the 20th day of the Hebrew month of Sivan in 1756. Thereafter adherents to the Frankist-Reform movement built their own synagogues, established their own schools, and consecrated their own Rabbis.

In judgment of the Frankist-Reformers, Rabbi Antelman says:

> *"Judaism has no branches. There is one Torah and one God, and our Torah teaches that each Jew on his Day of Judgment, regardless of affiliation, will be individually asked to give an accounting of himself... Once anyone embraced*

---

[439] Antelman 96.
[440] Antelman 97-98.
[441] Antelman 99.

these ideologies [of the Frankists] he ceases to be a Jew, being Jew only by birth or becoming a Jew in name only (JINO)."[442]

JINO Jews were ripe for illuminated Freemasonry to exploit. The Masonic Lodge did not create them, but certainly used them. Antelman traces the Reform Movement from the time it was absorbed by the Illuminati to the 1848 Masonic-Communist uprisings that swept Europe. The most prominent Frankist in 1848 was a German Jew and Grand Orient Mason, 32nd degree Karl Marx, whose real name was Levi Mordechai. Rabbi Antelman reports that although, "[t]he first Reform service [was] conducted by Illuminati Bundist Israel Jacobson in 1807,"[443] Frankist Jews became officially known as the Jewish Reform Movement only in the 1850s. Their leader was the so-called "Father of Communism" - Karl Marx.

In 1843, New York Reform Jews founded the exclusively Jewish Masonic Lodge, B'nai B'rith. Their institutions and influence grew. At the turn of the 20th century, the B'nai B'rith founded the Anti-Defamation League, the American Jewish Congress and Federations of Jewish Charities. According to Rabbi Antelman, Reform Jews who became lawyers were, and still are, active in the subversively oriented National Lawyers Guild.[444] In addition these lawyers were instrumental in founding the American Civil Liberties Union (ACLU).

Once the Frankist-Reform Jews were well established in the illuminated Masonic Lodges, they pushed for civil rights for the downtrodden, primarily for Blacks, according to Antelman, "to exploit them for their own ends."[445] He further remarks on their influence on the events of the 1960s:

> *I have found their descendants in the United States to be very active in Marxist-Leninist and Third World activities. They have attempted to convert the Civil Rights movement into a Black revolution, and are attempting to further polarize this country by promoting women's liberation. Their children who are prominent in the SDS [Students for a Democratic Society] organize and recruit for the El Fatah, and have succeeded in destroying synagogues and Jewish institutions by instigating Black radicals mostly concentrated in nine urban centers in the U.S.*[446]

Rabbi Antelman lists three steps Reform Jews plan to use to eliminate all Jewry: "The initial thrust was philosophically Karaitic, an attack on the Talmud. [The Karaites were a Jewish sect founded in Babylonia toward the end of the 8th century, who denied the authority of the Oral Law and the Talmud.] The intermediate stage was complete apostasy, an attack on the Torah. However, the final state is even worse": a complete reversal of all Biblical law. Antelman, writing in 1974, said the Reform "has followers today who are now calling for abolition of capital punishment in our society, who endorse abortion, who seek to justify the tolerance of criminal elements, who approve of adultery and illicit sexual relations and who have even incorporated homosexual congregations into their structure and praise for 'atheistic' rabbis..."[447]

The Reform's planned destruction of traditionally Jewish and Christian society through Masonic revolution was premeditated. Antelman states that "when attempts were

---

[442] Antelman 13, 133.
[443] Antelman 32.
[444] Antelman 133.
[445] Antelman 116.
[446] Antelman 131.
[447] Antelman 32.

made by the Illuminati, Jacobins and Frankists to infiltrate the Masons... their infiltration did not mean that they harbored any particular love for Freemasonry. On the contrary, they hated it with a passion and only wished to utilize the cover of Freemasonry as a means of spreading their revolutionary doctrines and to provide a place where they could covertly meet without arousing suspicion."[448]

Antelman wrote eight years before the authors of *Holy Blood, Holy Grail* exposed Freemasonry as a front for both Sion and the Templars. Now we know that instead of taking over Freemasonry, as many conspiracy researchers have thought, the Illuminati-Frankist Jews were absorbed, then exploited, by the more powerful Masonic Lodges. Freemasonry learned well the Frankist doctrines and usurped their Reform system to destroy the existing order. Jews such as Moses Mendelssohn, and later Karl Marx, Vladimir Lenin, and Leon Trotsky, were used by Freemasonry to replace the old order with their own Gentile Masonic New World Order. Should the conspiracy be exposed, the doctrinally subversive Frankist/Reform Jews would be the scapegoat.

SOCIAL FOMENT

When illuminated Freemasonry first tried to foment women's liberation, women, especially women of low morals, were encouraged to leave their husbands and join the Tugendbunds. Their profession was practiced in the Tugendbund-Grand Orient Masonic Lodges, which gave rise to the licentiousness of the philosophers. The original Tugendbund or Union of Virtue Lodge in Berlin, the one Mendelssohn joined in 1786, met in a whore house where two of Mendelssohn's daughters were employed. After the French Revolution failed, this Order went into rapid decay. A second Tugendbund, more noble than the first, was founded in 1810, and in no way was affiliated with its predecessor of the same name.

Following the Frankist doctrine of reversal, Mendelssohn's writings invert the traditional understanding of the word *virtue,* especially in his perception of the Tugendbund Lodge of Virtue. Nesta Webster quotes Mendelssohn: "'Those who regulate their lives according to the precepts of this religion of nature and of reason are called virtuous men... and are the children of eternal salvation."[449]

According to Edith Miller's *Occult Theocrasy,* this "Union of Virtue" was operated by the "Jewess Henrietta Herz whose husband, Marcus Herz, a Jewish Illuminatus, was the disciple, friend and successor of Moses Mendelssohn. Noted Illuminati were frequenters of this abode of Licentiousness," one of whom was the French revolutionary, Freemason Gabriel Mirabeau. When Mirabeau shuttled between Paris and Berlin on secret diplomatic missions leading up to the French Revolution, he lodged at Henrietta's "Union of Virtue."[450]

The "Honorable" Gabriel Mirabeau, and several of his Grand Orient friends brought the Illuminati into the French Revolution. Miller explains: "The Bishop of Autun [Talleyrand], Mirabeau, and the Duc d'Orleans, Grand Master of the *Grand-Orient* de *France* founded a Lodge in Paris in 1786 which was duly 'illuminated' by Bode and Guillaume Baron de Busche. This was the *Club Breton* which afterwards became known as the Jacobin Club, a name of Templar origin, recalling that of Jacques de Molay."[451]

---

[448] Antelman 116.
[449] Webster 229-230.
[450] Miller 376-377.
[451] Miller 379.

Following the Revolution Mirabeau also fought vigorously in the Constituent Assembly for the emancipation of the Jews, and won. Rabbi Antelman tells the Story:

> *In 1789 there were approximately 40,000 Jews in France, 30,000 of whom lived in ghettos. During the Reign of Terror, all houses of worship were closed in accordance with Jacobin anti-religious policy. The churches and synagogues were reopened after Robespierre was guillotined on July 28, 1794, signifying the end of terror and the Jacobin power base. The Jews could now enjoy the full benefits of a vote taken on September 28, 1791, by the Commune before the National Assembly in which 53 out of 60 districts in France voted in favor of granting all Jews of France complete civil rights on a par with all citizens, which meant that the decision favored the spiritual anti- Semites, for Jews to assimilate.[452]*

Men like Mirabeau, and many hundreds lesser known, either influenced, or came under the hypnotic spell of Weishaupt. Weishaupt, a man who sought a potion to have his sister-in-law's baby aborted after several sexual encounters with her; a man who was a subversive, deceiver and destroyer, as well as a self proclaimed worshipper of Lucifer, was named well by Gerald B. Winrod in *Adam Weishaupt, A Human Devil*. Winrod writes of the degenerate condition of the Masonic Lodges prior to the French Revolution: "Local lodges, thus polluted, became spawns for breeding vice and revolution. It was in these underground centers that the revolutionary activity which produced the French Revolution was hatched. Masonic units, dotted by the thousands all over the map of Europe, were thus transformed into places of anarchy, devoted to creating mob violence."[453]

The effects of the Frankist-Reform on Jews and European society were far-reaching. Shortly after the French Revolution, for instance, the Reform Jews headquartered in Berlin were causing such havoc in society that the Orthodox rabbis prophesied a Jewish holocaust 150 years before the advent of Hitler and Nazi Germany. Rabbi Antelman relates the perspicacity of Jewish rabbis of that time:

> *It is both to the deep prophetic insights and foresight of the rabbis that they already predicted over 150 years before the actual events that a holocaust was going to fall upon the Jewish people. They cited the talmud in Tractate Sotah which asks the question as to why Samson's eyes were blinded in the city of Gaza. "Samson's corruption began in Gaza, therefore, he was punished in Gaza." As it is written (Judges 16:1) "And Samson went to Gaza and saw there a whore." Therefore, he was punished in Gaza, as it is written, "And the Philistines seized him and put out his eyes and brought him down to Gaza." The rabbis compared Mendelssohn and his Berlin circle to the whore [of Samson] and warned that if Israel were to be tempted to Berlin, then the destruction of Israel would come from Berlin, and so it was.[454]*

According to Antelman, "The Frankists today no longer call themselves by that name. The Organization has grown into an international group labelled by outsiders as the Cult of the All- Seeing Eye.[455] A rather interesting custom started to spread like a plague in

---

[452] Antelman 109-110.
[453] Winrod 23.
[454] Antelman 87-88.
[455] Antelman 131-132.

Mendelssohn's time from the Illuminati and Haskala and became a practice among the early Reform. This was the practice of placing a symbol of Illumination [the All-Seeing Eye] into synagogues throughout the world."[456]

Rabbi Antelman's book names many well-known Jews in the Frankist-Reform movement. Almost to the person they were Freemasons although the Rabbi maintains "there was a conspiracy, but it was neither Jewish, nor Catholic nor Masonic."[457]

ROTHSCHILD AND THE OLIGARCHY

Famous and wealthy Jews were also alleged to have been involved in the Illuminati plot. Thus some revisionist authors suspect that the conspiracy was the creation of Jewish world bankers. The most conspicuous allegation involves the German Jew, Meyer Amschel of the Rot Schild, who according to the historians Will and Ariel Durant, took the territorial name as his last name. Rot Schild is German for *red shield*. Anglicized it became Rothschild.[458]

The history of the Rothschild family was recounted by Count Egon Caesar Corti in *The Rise Of The House Of Rothschild.*[459] The Count's evidence, well-documented and authenticated, comes from government archives throughout Europe. It includes letters of communication, business records, and financial transactions.

Meyer Rothschild (1743-1812) was the founder of the greatest banking house in history, originally headquartered in Frankfurt, Germany. From 1770 to 1776, Weishaupt was allegedly financed by the newly organized House of Rothschild.[460] Allegations abound that Meyer Rothschild, along with several prominent Jews, met with Weishaupt in 1773 to plan world revolution.[461] Count Corti, throughout his book, denies these allegations, claiming they have no foundation.

Rothschild is not mentioned in the Priory documents nor is he linked by association to Sion. However, after the French Revolution, he subsidized the challenged kings in their struggle against Napoleon Bonaparte. Yet, "it was Napoleon who in 1810 insisted on applying to the Jews of Frankfurt the full freedom guaranteed by the Code Napoleon."[462]

Napoleon's good will toward Jews was due to their financial support. History reveals that Rothschild loaned money to both sides, which fact has prompted revisionist authors to suspect that he was pitting one side against the other to amass great wealth. The truth is Napoleon himself made the first advance, courting wealthy Jews for their money. Like the kings he was warring against, Napoleon was in desperate need of funds. Rothschild responded, but only to save Jewish lives at Frankfurt, and the loans were in small amounts. As a result, Napoleon awarded all Jews full freedom. Most of Rothschild's loans, however, went to the monarchies.

During the Napoleonic Wars, Rothschild and his five sons became uncommonly wealthy - so much so that their banking house amassed the financial resources with which they make loans to nations to this day. The strength of the Rothschild fortune and the international reach of its interests have fueled the accusations of anti-Semites, who charge

---

[456] Antelman 88-89.

[457] Antelman 15.

[458] Durants, vol. X, 634.

[459] Count Egon Caesar Corti, *The Rise of the House of Rothschild* (1928; Boston: Western Islands, 1972) entire.

[460] Commander William Guy Carr, RCN, *The Conspiracy to Destroy all Existing Governments and Religions* (Canada: published privately, 1959) 1.

[461] Wilgus 154.

[462] Will Durant and Ariel Durant, *The Story of Civilization: The Age of Napoleon,* vol. XI (New York: Simon and Schuster, 1975)603.

Jews of being at the head of a world banking conspiracy. Count Corti reports that Rothschild actually gained his business not through conspiracy but through ingenious business deals. Rothschild was totally honest with all his commerce. His interest rates were consistently lower than his so called "Christian" competitors. In fact, "Christian" bankers could not be trusted at all, for they took advantage of every crisis to charge usurious rates. Rothschild never exploited situations in that way. Moreover, unlike his competitors, his service was prompt. The allegations that he and his sons were funding world revolution by lending equally to both sides were only imaginations of his disgruntled "Christian" competitors, says Count Corti.

Fellow Jewish bankers were also disgruntled with the Rothschilds, a bitterness that was carried into the twentieth century by the Houses of Warburg and Schiff, also headquartered in Frankfurt. Both Max Warburg and Jacob Schiff were Reform Jews, as well as Grand Orient Masons. At the turn of the 20th century, they merged their banking houses through marriage.[463] According to Rabbi Antelman, the Warburgs were deeply involved in the Grand Orient Illuminati plot. In fact, Eric Warburg, the only surviving son of Max Warburg, possesses Illuminati papers that were handed down to him by his father - Illuminati papers he personally photocopied and sent to Antelman.[464]

Meyer Rothschild, patriarch of the Rothschild house, was aware of the Illuminati conspiracy. He even infiltrated it briefly with his own operative. Rabbi Antelman states:

> The Rothschilds utilized the services of Sigmund Geisenheimer, their head clerk, who in turn was aided by Itrig of Berlin, the Illuminati of the Toleranz Lodge and the Parisian Grand Orient Lodge. Geisenheimer was a member of the Mayence Masonic Illuminati Lodge, and was the founder of the Frankfurt Judenloge; for which attempt he was excommunicated by the Chief Rabbi of Frankfurt, Tzvi Hirsch Horowitz. At a later date the Rothschilds joined the Lodge. Solomon Mayer (or Meir) Rothschild (1774-1855) was a member for a short while before moving to Vienna.[465]

Other than this brief membership in the Judenloge, the Rothschilds were not involved in the Illuminati plot, but in fact were heavily embroiled in its opposition. Although Meyer Rothschild himself was not a member of English Freemasonry, as were the kings he served, his sons were. *Mackey's Encyclopedia of Freemasonry* reports: "The Rothschild family of France contributed members to the Craft, but did not take any position of leadership. Baron Nathan Mayer Rothschild was initiated in Emulation Lodge, No.12, October24, 1802, in London."[466]

Evidence reveals that the Rothschilds bankrolled English Freemasonry, while the Warburgs financed French Freemasonry. Therefore, the Rothschild sons not only were banking competitors of the Warburgs, but competitors in conspiracy as well.[467]

As evidenced, Rothschild did figure in the conspiracy, but not on the side of the Illuminati. While helping kings control their finances, and in some cases, hide their wealth

---

[463] Antelman 33.

[464] Antelman 82-83.

[465] Antelman 126.

[466] "Anti-Semitism," *Mackey's Encyclopedia*, vol. III. Mackey was spreading Masonic disinformation when he wrote "The Rothschild family of France contributed members to the Craft, but did not take any position of leadership." William R. Denslow's *10,000 Famous Freemasons* reports that James Rothschild (1792-1868) was raised to the 33rd degree in the French Scottish Rite and listed as attending six Supreme Council conventions between 1841 and 1845 (vol. IV p.74).

[467] Antelman 114. This Masonic banking competition between two Jewish financiers would play a significant role in the Russian Revolution of 1917.

from Napoleon, not only was he increasing his own net worth, he was helping the entire oligarchic Masonic system. His scheme, however, was more noble than the acquisition of wealth. According to Corti Rothschild's primary goal was to win the hearts of kings, hoping to gain freedom not only for his family, but all Jewry.

Consider the facts. Raised in the ghettos at Frankfurt, Rothschild was well aware of the despicable plight of the Jews. Restrictive laws against Jews would not permit him, even as a wealthy man, to break out of these horrid conditions. He died in those same ghettos without realizing his dream. His sole purpose in life was to free the Jews from this contemptible state, while at the same time building a future for his family - an honorable Jewish tradition. No thought of conspiracy ever entered Rothschild's mind, nor corruption taint his practice. To the contrary, he labored to never make so much as an accounting error. Furthermore, his honor was upheld with praise from his royal patrons. When the Revolution did come, royalty, fearing for their lives and their riches, turned to Rothschild for help. He did not let them down.

Although Rothschild never betrayed his royal customers, he really had no concern as to who would rule Europe, so long as his own interests, and that of the Jews, were protected. He was betting that the kings as a whole had a better chance than did Napoleon, especially with England on their side. Therefore, when the French Revolution failed, and Napoleon started making his military advances, Rothschild hid his royal patrons' movable wealth so they could survive in exile should the inevitable come. Although Napoleon pressed Rothschild for greater financial involvement, Rothschild cast his lot with the kings, and won.

THE SECOND TUGENDBUND

Rothschild's first record of funding the Oligarchy against Napoleon came in 1810 when he financed what appeared to be a revival of the first Tugendbund (Union of Virtue). Conspiracy researchers have mistakenly considered the second Tugendbund a continuation of the Illuminati, and Rothschild's membership as proof of his complicity with the original Illuminati plot. The second Tugendbund, however, was quite different from the first. Only the names were identical.

The "identical name" syndrome is a chronic problem for conspiracy researchers. Bear in mind that Satan, the great divider, conceals his strategy with this form of deception. That there are two warring Freemasonries is a prime example of this strategy: both use the same symbols, passwords and grips. Likewise, the existence of two Tugendbunds has confused investigators. We must, therefore, look beyond their identical names to understand their differences. The first Tugendbund was anarchic, revolutionary and licentious. Miller states that the revived "Union of Virtue [was] a purely political league [numbering] in its ranks most of the Councillors of State, many officers of the army, and a considerable number of the professors of literature and science. What was so significant about the second Tugendbund was that it "was obeyed as implicitly as the decrees of Emperor or King."[468]

Herein lies the difference: their leadership. The first Tugendbund was founded by Grand Orient operatives and directed by Illuminati sub-leadership. The second Tugendbund was governed by the Masonic Oligarchy in opposition to Napoleon Bonaparte. By using the name of the first Tugendbund, the Oligarchy was able to acquire

---

[468] Miller 377.

the suppressed membership of the original to help oust the dreaded Corsican - a deceptive, yet brilliant maneuver. We can document this with fact.

> Count Egon Caesar Corti, writing about the second Tugendbund states that Royalty took an active interest in current affairs, and closely followed the powerful movement which was developing in Germany, particularly in Prussia, its aim being to shake off the foreign yoke [Napoleon]. This movement could not as yet come into the open, but in Konigsberg, where the king and the government of Prussia were residing, the "Tugendbund" was formed, a league which ostensibly pursued moral-scientific aims, but the ultimate object of which was deliverance of Germany.
> The principal protector of the league was the minister Baron von Stein; and William of Hesse held an important position in it. Its membership was so broad that it also included Jews, and the Rothschilds appear to have become members. At any rate they acted as go-betweens for the elector's correspondence on this matter, and made payments in favor of the Thgendbund.[469]

Miller, quoting Heckethorn on the function of the second Tugendbund, notes that one of its first acts "was to send auxiliary corps to assist the Russians in the campaign of 1813. Prussia having, by the course of events, been compelled to abandon its temporizing policy, Gneisenau, Scharnhorst and Grollmann embraced the military plan of the Thgendbund."[470]

Thus, we are able to separate the goals of the two Tugendbunds. Although both organizations were German, the first was used by the grass roots Illuminati to dethrone the Bourbon dynasty.

Its purpose was to spread anarchy, licentious living and revolution in an effort to undermine, from a distance, the French Crown, the Roman Church, and orthodox Judaism. When Napoleon spread the Revolution across Europe, the second Tugendbund was then organized as an underground resistance movement controlled by the Masonic royalty to protect their thrones from the advances of Napoleon's army. Both were Masonic Tugendbunds, but not branches of the same conspiracy.

When Napoleon learned of the Tugendbund opposition against him, he suppressed it. This only deepened the intrigue. The second Tugendbund, according to Miller, concealed itself in continental Masonic lodges under English obedience.[471]

THE PRIORY OF SION OPPOSED NAPOLEON

Not only did Rothschild oppose Napoleon; so did the Priory of Sion. The Grand Master at that time was Charles Nodier (GM 1801-1844), who took the helm of Sion following the death of Maximilian of Lorraine. The authors of Holy Blood comment that "After the French Revolution the Prieure de Sion - or at least its purported grand masters - would appear to have been divorced both from the old aristocracy and from the corridors of political power."[472]

With more research, however, they discovered this not to be the case. At first Charles Nodier seemed sympathetic to the French Revolution, as was the case with the previous

---

[469] Corti 63-64.
[470] Miller 378.
[471] Miller.
[472] Baigent 434.

Grand Master. But sympathy only continued so long as there was confidence the Lorraine-Habsburg dynasty would ascend the French throne. The exposure of the Illuminati plot dashed those hopes. When Napoleon, and not the House of LorraineHabsburg, took over France the Corsican naturally became an enemy of the Priory of Sion. By 1804 Charles Nodier "was vociferous in his opposition to the emperor... becoming involved in two separate plots against Napoleon, in 1804 and again in 1812."[473]

That Sion and the Rothschilds were both against Napoleon does not prove a connection, at least not at this time. Count Corti confirms that Meyer Rothschild's primary goal was freedom, and he was willing to buy it, even if it meant financing both sides. He gambled and won, to the chagrin of those who hated Jews. Yet his rapid acquisition of wealth by subsidizing wars only fueled the fires of anti-Semites, who offered this fact as evidence that Jews were the Hidden Hand.

THE SCOTTISH RITE OF FREEMASONRY:
THE SYNAGOGUE OF SATAN

Perhaps the strongest evidence used by those who blame the conspiracy on the Jews is that the most powerful rite in Freemasonry, the Scottish Rite, is known to all Masons as the Jewish Rite. Even today, any Gentile who travels the degrees in the Scottish Rite is considered a Jewish workman. His king is Solomon, and he bows down to a replica of the Ark of the Covenant within the walls of the Symbolic Jewish Temple called Freemasonry. (See Appendix 2, Fig. 2.)

Although English Freemason Cromwell promised the Jews that he would "rebuild Solomon's Temple in Freemasonry," the Scottish Rite was not of English origin, nor was it created by Jews. As we have seen, it was developed on the continent of Europe by Templar Freemasons who were of Scottish descent. Yet, the Scottish Rite is still called the Jewish Rite.

It is an interesting fact that when cults are founded, they take on a Judaic character, or claim to be God's substitute for the Hebrew religion. Most recent examples are the two modern cults of Mormonism and the Jehovah's Witnesses, both founded by Gentile Masons. Careful study reveals that these two institutions believe they are God's elect and claim to be God's reformation of the Jewish religion.

The same was true during medieval days. At the turn of the first millennium A.D., the Knights Templar took on a Judaic character, taking their name from Solomon's Temple. A millennium earlier, during the Apostolic missionary journeys, the Eleusinian mysteries of Greece and Asia Minor claimed to be Jewish. *Mackey's Symbolism of Freemasonry* states: "Of all the Mysteries of the ancients these [Eleusinian mysteries] were the most popular."[474] Miller, in *Occult Theocrasy*, informs us that the Eleusinian mysteries contained twelve degrees, that when completed turned the Gentile initiate into a Jew.[475]

These cults claimed, and still claim to be Jewish, but obviously are not. All were, and are, anti-Christian, making war with the Church, which activities confirm that they are under the control of the Adversary. In keeping with Satan's deceptive "identical name" syndrome, their religious temples can be termed "synagogues," indeed - "synagogues of Satan."

---

[473] Baigent 435.
[474] Albert G. Mackey, Symbolism of Freemasonry 334.
[475] Miller 88-89.

SCRIPTURE AND THE SYNAGOGUE OF SATAN

An interesting Scripture in Revelation 2:9 identifies this conspiracy for what it really is. Jesus was exhorting the Church at Smyrna, when He said "I know the blasphemy of them which say they are Jews, and are not, but are the synagogue of Satan." Again in Revelation 3:9, when Christ was commending the Philadelphia Church, He said, "Behold, I will make them of the synagogue of Satan, which say they are Jews, and are not, but do lie; behold, I will make them to come and worship before thy feet, and to know that I have loved thee."

The churches of Smyrna and Philadelphia were located in Asia Minor, today's Turkey, where the Eleusinian mysteries were immensely popular. These mysteries could be termed "the synagogue of Satan" since, upon completion of the 12th degree. the initiate was pronounced a Jew. Certainly, Revelation 3:9 testifies to the Eleusinian mysteries during the first 100 years or so of Church history, while at the same time it prophesies the Mormons, the Jehovah's Witnesses and similar anti-Christian cults in our day. More specifically, this Scripture refers to Scottish Rite Freemasonry during the last 250 years, considering that the period prophesied for the Philadelphia Church age began around 1750.

Many theologians agree that the seven Churches in the book of Revelation are prophecies of the various ages of Church history. For example, Clarence Larkin believes the Philadelphia Church age began with the great missionary movement in the 1750s. This was also taught by Dr. English and Marian Bower at the Philadelphia School (now College) of Bible.[476] Not surprisingly, Stuart royalty founded the Scottish Rite of Freemasonry in 1747-1748, at precisely the same time the Philadelphia Church period began.

God's timing is always exact. Just when the Philadelphia Church age began to emerge, the Scottish Rite of Freemasonry had advanced its degrees to thirty-two. It was called the Jewish Rite because its system was based upon the Jewish *Cabala*. Yet, it was founded by Gentiles. When Christ admonished the Philadelphia Church, He referred to an entity that He called "the synagogue of Satan, which say they are Jews, and are not, but do lie." The Masonic Lodge portrays itself as the "synagogue of Satan" in the blasphemous scene pictured in Appendix 2, Fig. 2.

The most convincing evidence that Freemasonry is Christ's prophesied "synagogue of Satan" comes from its own rituals. *Father* of *Lies,* written in the 1930s by British author Warren Weston, reveals how the Jewish *Cabala* was used to develop the 33 degrees of the Scottish Rite. Weston maintains that there are ten separate interpretations for each degree. He further states that these interpretations are Cabalistic in nature - originating from the ten Sephiroth, or ten emanations of the Cabalistic god. Weston lists five interpretations:

> the philosophic, political, religious, Judaic, and Luciferian. The Luciferian
> interpretation is listed in Appendix 7 and states that when a Mason reaches the
> 33rd degree, 'The Ego becomes Sovereign Pontiff of the Synagogue of Satan.
> Identified with Satan, the Ego exercises complete Caesaro-papal authority: Man
> is his own King."[477]

---

[476] Bible, Pilgrims Edition, footnotes to Revelation 2 & 3.
[477] Weston 245.

Dr. J. Blanchard, a former 33rd degree Mason and past president of Wheaton College[478], confirms Weston's discovery. After Blanchard became a Christian, he wrote his two-volume *Scottish Rite Masonry Illustrated*. Below is an excerpt which sets forth Blanchard's opinion of Freemasonry:

> *Let the authoritative teaching of Dr. Mackey be continually borne in mind, that:*
> *- "the mission and object of Masonry is the worship of the Great Architect of the Universe." It follows that the lodges must have something for their dupes to do, called worship. And what could wicked men and devils invent craftier or better suited to deceive the simple, than this very scheme of "the Ancient Scottish Rite," which now rules the rites of the world. It seizes and appropriates all of religion but its holiness and justice; and all of Christ but his truth and his atonement. It mixes things sacred with things profane, till the whole compound is profanity; and quoting the Bible as if it believed it true, which notoriously it does not, it has furnished a dark system which angels flee from and which devils inhabit. Every Lodge is a Synagogue of Satan and its ritual is Sorcery.[479]*

The Catholic Church also confirms Dr. Blanchard's estimation. In 1961, prior to Vatican II, the Roman Curia, the supreme government of the Vatican, authored *The Plot Against the Church* as a warning to Catholics that their church had been infiltrated by Freemasonry. The Curia lists five popes who identified Freemasonry as the Synagogue of Satan.[480] *The Plot* was distributed in August 1962 to the 2,200 bishops and cardinals who were attending the Second Vatican Council. The Introduction contained a specific warning about Masonic penetration into the Catholic Church: "A most dastardly conspiracy is in being against the Church. Its enemies are about to destroy its most sacred traditions and to propose such daring and malevolent reforms... In the middle of last year [1961] we discovered that the enemy is again attempting to start a conspiracy to open the doors to Communism, to bring about the collapse of the free world and to deliver the Holy Church into the claws of the Synagogue of Satan."[481]

Secular authors, Masonic authors, Popes, and the Roman Curia - all identify Freemasonry as the Synagogue of Satan. Most significant is the fact that Freemasonry itself claims its Gentile initiates become Jews when joining the Scottish Rite. Since the Scottish Rite was founded in the mid-18th century, which Bible commentators date as the beginning of the Philadelphia Church age, by inference the Scottish Rite affirms Revelation 3:9- "them of the synagogue of Satan, which say they are Jews, and are not, but do lie."

FREEMASONRY'S 33 DEGREES

The Stuarts created what is called Scottish Rite "High Masonry." The Scottish Rite "promised initiation into greater and more profound mysteries - mysteries supposedly preserved and handed down in Scotland. It established more direct connections between Freemasonry and the various activities - alchemy, Cabalism, and Hermetic thought, for

---

[478] Miller 332.
[479] J. Blanchard, *Scottish Rite Masonry Illustrated*, vol.1, 462.
[480] Maurice Pinay, *The Plot Against The Church* (1967; Los Angeles: St. Anthony Press, 1982) 18.
[481] Pinay, Introduction.

instance - that were regarded as Rosicrucian. And it elaborated not only on the antiquity but also on the illustrious pedigree of the 'craft'."[482]

The primary source for the creation of the Scottish Rite degrees came from volumes of convoluted rabbinical opinions known as the *Rabbinical Books of Concealed Mystery*, or the *Cabala*. *Mackey's Encyclopedia of Freemasonry* informs us that the Jews developed the *Cabala* while in the Babylonian captivity.[483]

The *Cabala* was the post-Babylonian tradition of how the rabbis were to understand God. Not hearing from Almighty God during captivity had led the rabbis into the Babylonian apostasy. They had assumed God must be like the pagans' god - unable to communicate directly to man, and thus incomprehensible. To make himself known, the Babylonian god had to reveal himself in creation through thirty-three emanations. Dr. Mackey explains that the emanations took place in three worlds - heaven, earth, and hell. According to the *Cabala*, each world experienced ten emanations called "Sephiroh" - for a total of thirty. Hovering above each world was an occult god. Three gods plus thirty emanations equals thirty-three steps in creation.[484]

Eastern religions are noted for building their theology around triads of numbers. The captive Jews incorporated the numbering system in the *Cabala* ostensibly for interpreting Moses. Mystic numerology begins with "0," represented by the Cabalistic En Soph, the occult god, who in its origin was said to have been nonexistent. From "Nothing," the big Zero in the vast void of space, emanated the "Existent One," represented by the number 1. The "Existent One" was considered a hermaphrodite, having both male and female organs. Over time the "Existent One" was able to divide into separate gods - both male and female, represented by the numbers 1 and 2. The male and female gods cohabited and bore the occult son of god, represented by the number 3. This pagan trinity continued their phallic creative activity through further procreative acts until ten emanations completed the evolutionary cycle, represented by the number 10. Ten (1 plus 0) symbolically takes creation back to the occult god, which, by pagan reasoning, means mankind can become gods through reincarnation.

This cycle of creation is represented by the "Circle" encompassing all ten emanations. Hence, anything disk-shaped or round became the pagan symbol of god. The sun, moon and stars were thus worshipped as gods.

This process is duplicated in each of the three worlds. The numbers in each total eleven (0 through 10), for a grand total of 33. The large circle is known as the "En Soph" to Cabalistic Jews, the "Third Eye" in Hinduism, the "Eye of Osiris" to the Egyptians, and the "All-Seeing Eye" in Freemasonry. The serpent biting its own tail is another symbol of the circle, or eye.

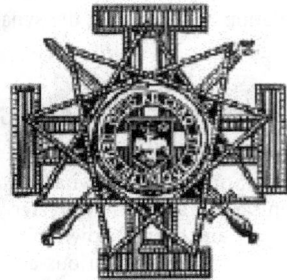

JEWEL OF THE 33RD DEGREE

Cabalistic mystics claim we are a part of the occult god, since we emanated from him. This process, according to all Eastern religions, can be reversed through reincarnation.[485] Moderns call it "the science of evolution," defined by *Webster's Ninth New Collegiate Dictionary~* as "a process of continuous change from a lower, simpler, or worse [state] to a higher, more complex, or better state." These mystics claim that a mental state of godhood can be achieved here on earth

---

[482] Baigent 145-146.

[483] "Cabala," *Mackey's Encyclopedia*, vol.1.

[484] "Cabala."

[485] Herbert Weiner, 9 *1/2 Mystics: The Kabbala Today* (New York: Collier Books, 1969) entire; and Gershom Scholem, *Kabbalah and Its Symbolism* (1960; New York: Schocken Books, 1965) entire.

through meditation. One can arrive at this state more rapidly, the mystics say, by ingesting mind- altering drugs. Therefore, wherever eastern religions are practiced, there will be a substantial increase in drug addiction.

Jewish rabbis came out of Babylon with this doctrine in their *Cabala*. Titus 1:13-14 refers to it as "Jewish fables." *Thayer's Greek English Lexicon* defines "fables" as "a speech, word, saying, a fiction, a fable; an invention, falsehood: the fictions of the Jewish theosophists and Gnostics, especially concerning the emanations and orders of the aeons."[486] "Fables" comes from a Greek word which requires initiation into a secret order to learn of the fable.[487] Scottish Rite Freemasonry acquired this system from the *Cabala* in the 18th century. Today, a Mason who climbs the thirty-three degrees is symbolically practicing the doctrine of reincarnation, the so- called "science" of evolution - the Serpent's religion. Once the Mason reaches the 33rd degree, he is identified with Satan and "becomes Sovereign Pontiff of the Synagogue of Satan."[488]

The "Jewel" of the 33rd degree Mason symbolically tells the same story. It is composed of three interlaced triangles representing the three occult worlds. In the center is the serpent biting its own tail. Here, in symbolic form, we see the truth that Freemasonry is the serpent religion, the religion which claims men can become gods by working their way up the Masonic degrees. The Scottish Rite of Freemasonry, the so-called Jewish Rite, betrays itself as the Synagogue of Satan.

SUBVERSION BY SUPERIMPOSITION:
THE SCOTTISH RITE DEGREES

Fifty years before creating the 33rd degree, Gentile occultists delved deeper into the mysteries. They quickly discovered that some Masons would not accept their teachings. With each new pagan discovery, therefore, a higher degree was added to keep their occult secrets from the lower degree would-be dissidents. The number of initiates in each ascending degree became fewer and fewer, creating a pyramid with a small number of men at the top.

Between 1747 and 1762 the Scottish Rite had increased from the original three degrees of English Freemasonry to thirty-two degrees, superimposing itself on the Blue L'Odge. In other words, by "super-imposition" or the creation of additional, higher degrees, one secret society, the Scottish Rite, took over another, the Blue Lodge. The lower body had no say in the matter. Of course, this left thirty-two degree Templar Scottish Rite Freemasonry ripe for a third secret society takeover.

When Weishaupt came along, his goal was to take over French Grand Lodge Masonry, which practiced the three degree Masonry of the English obedience. First, he superimposed the Illuminati on the clandestine Grand Orient Lodge, not by creating extra degrees but by replacing the Grand Orient's three degrees with illuminated rituals. He then used the Grand Orient to penetrate the Grand Lodge with illuminism. Through this system of superimposition, the low degree initiates in Europe were kept ignorant of the subtle revolutionary developments engineered by the Illuminati in the Grand Orient. By 1789, when the French Revolution began, the majority of Masons were unaware of why they were in rebellion, or who put them there.

Herein lies the danger of Freemasonry. Any individual can subvert any secret society. A Weishaupt, a Lenin, a Hitler, or the Beast of the Apocalypse can take over by

---

[486] James L. Holly, *The Southern Baptist Convention and Freemasonry* (Beaumont, TX: Mission and Ministry to Men, Inc., 1992) 3-4; quoting Thayer's Greek-English Lexicon.
[487] Strong, *Greek* 3454 from 3453.
[488] Weston 245.

superimposition, leaving the lower degrees completely ignorant. Any group (such as the Priory of Sion, the Templars, the Bolsheviks, the Nazis, or Scarlet of the Apocalypse) can do the same. Through this pyramid system naive initiates can be controlled by Satanists, Luciferians, New Agers, atheists, pantheists, communists, fascists, or terrorists. Because their bloody oaths demand unquestioned obedience to the unseen rulers above, the lower degrees blindly follow all dictates handed down to them.

In 1801 the Grand Orient, which had been under the influence of the Illuminati, merged with the Scottish Rite, and imported the doctrine of the Illuminati into this Templar order. The French Grand Lodge joined them the same year, placing all bodies of Freemasonry in Europe under the control of the illuminated thirty-two degree Scottish Rite at Paris.

That same year some Masons in Charleston, South Carolina decided to rule the Masonic world. Again, superimposition was forced on the body of Universal Freemasonry. The *Encyclopedia of Freemasonry* tells us how it happened. Nine American Masons created the 33rd degree, and on their own, without authority from the large body of American Masons, on May 31, 1801, constituted themselves the Mother Supreme Council of the World. The French Grand Lodge, Grand Orient and the Scottish Rite immediately accepted the superimposition of the Charleston Supreme Council because, as Mackey says, "The Supreme Council at Charleston derived its authority and its information from what are called the French [Masonic] Constitutions."[489]

Suddenly, and without a vote from the world body of Masons, the illuminated Templar Scottish Rite Masonic obedience shifted from Europe to the United States - all because of nine men! What if the superimposition had been delayed a century and had been made by Communist Russia instead of Democratic America. What if the top Masons had been Trotsky, Lenin and Stalin instead of nine Americans? Would that have made a difference? If that had happened, would America be throwing off democracy today, as Russia has dismantled Communism?

The hazard for Christians in Freemasonry is that low-degree Masons must always unquestionably obey the unseen authorities above them. When there is a new superimposition, which has always proven to be more sinister than the previous, Masons below must obey the new order. One day the Beast of the Apocalypse may take over in the same manner and become the highest Mason in the world. Orders will descend to worship him as God. Masons will be required to bow down in unquestioned obedience, since their oath demands it.

A one-man superimposition on Universal Freemasonry is not a new thought, for it was successfully accomplished over a century ago by a 33rd degree Gentile Mason from Little Rock, Arkansas. He had been studying the unfinished pyramid of Weishaupt and had discovered the ultimate secret - that the Masonic Great Architect of the Universe was Lucifer. In 1859 he became Grand Commander of the Supreme Council at Charleston. This Mason tried to superimpose his discovery on the hierarchy, but the vast majority opposed him. The few who did agree helped found a Super Rite called the Palladium. The Palladium stayed within the 33rd degree Supreme Council with no additional degrees created. One man, the most revered Mason then and since, became Sovereign Pontiff of Universal Freemasonry. Thirty years later, on July 14, 1889, this man-god of Freemasonry informed the twenty-three Supreme Councils of the world meeting in Paris that Lucifer was the god of Freemasonry - permitting them, at their own discretion, to inform the 30th, 31st and 32nd degree Masons. The lower degree Masons, however, were

---

[489] "Supreme Council," *Mackey's Encyclopedia,* vol. II.

to remain ignorant. In chapter 14 we will learn of Albert Pike's one-man rise to Masonic preeminence.

GENTILE RULE OF FREEMASONRY

A Gentile, not a Jew, has always been at the head of Freemasonry. Although Adam Weishaupt, a Jew, attempted to take over Freemasonry a century before Albert Pike, he was only a babe when the Scottish Rite was born. Therefore, this young Jewish boy could not have had part in its development. In 1761, when Weishaupt was age 13, Frederick H (Frederick the Great of Prussia), a Templar Gentile king, "was by general consent acknowledged and recognized as Sovereign and Supreme Head of the Scotch Rite."[490]

A Gentile, not a Jew, ruled the Scottish Rite prior to the French Revolution. At that time the French Grand Lodge was still loyal to the English obedience. In 1776, when Weishaupt created the illuminati, there were three powerful secret societies in France: the Templar Scottish Rite, the Sionist Grand Lodge and the Sionist-Templar Grand Orient. All were positioning themselves to take France by revolution. None were controlled by Jews.

One final Scripture refutes the Jewish conspiracy theory, placing control of the intrigue squarely in the hands of the Gentiles. In Luke 21:24, Christ is speaking to His disciples about the Jewish question in the last days: "And they [the Jews] shall fall by the edge of the sword, and shall be led away captive into all nations: and Jerusalem shall be trodden down of the Gentiles, *until the times of the Gentiles be fulfilled.*"

Christ's prophecy was partially fulfilled in 70 A.D., when Rome scattered the Jews into all nations. From then until now we have been living in the "times of the Gentiles," which will not end until Christ returns. According to Christ Himself, there is no Jewish conspiracy, only a Masonic conspiracy - and it is Gentile.

---

[490] Miller 189.

8. THE JESUIT CONNECTION (THE SOCIETY OF JESUS)

> In the eighteenth century the Jesuits were charged with having an intimate connection with Freemasonry, and the invention of the Degree of Kadosh was even attributed to those members of the Society who constituted the College of Clermont. This theory of a Jesuitical Freemasonry seems to have originated with the Illuminati.
>
> Mackey's Encyclopedia of Freemasonry[491]

JESUIT CONSPIRACY?

Some revisionist authors have suggested that the Catholic Church is the controller of the Masonic conspiracy through the Jesuit Order. There are several reasons for this viewpoint: (1) the Jesuits preceded organized Freemasonry by almost two centuries; (2) like Masons the Jesuits have several degrees of initiation; (3) like Masons the Jesuits take an oath; (4) like Masons the Jesuits have in the past subverted governments; (5) Jesuits have surfaced in Freemasonry; (6) Jesuits were encouraged and protected by Freemason Frederick the Great during their suppression in 1773; and (7) Weishaupt was at one time a Jesuit.[492]

Charles W. Heckethorn, in *Secret Societies of All Ages and Countries*, believed Jesuits were at the head of the Masonic conspiracy because their ceremonies were similar to those of Freemasonry. "There is considerable analogy," he surmised, "between Masonic and Jesuitic degrees; and the Jesuits also tread down the shoe and bare the knee, because Ignatius Loyola thus presented himself at Rome and asked for the confirmation of the order."[493]

Dr. Mackey scorns the comparison: "Like oil and water the tolerance of Freemasonry and the intolerance of the 'Society of Jesus' cannot commingle."[494]

What are the merits of the charge, quoted at the beginning of this chapter, that "Jesuitical Freemasonry seems to have originated with the Illuminati"?

Nesta Webster addresses the matter by asking whether or not the Jesuits were the conduit of Illuminist-oriental ideas to Weishaupt, the "Bavarian Professor": "How did these Oriental methods penetrate to the Bavarian professor? According to certain writers, through the Jesuits. The fact that Weishaupt had been brought up by this Order has provided the enemies of the Jesuits with the argument that they were the secret inspirers of the Illuminati."[495] Webster concludes: "That in the seventeenth century certain Jesuits played the part of political intriguers I suppose their warmest friends will hardly deny, but that they employed any secret of masonic [sic] system seems to me perfectly incapable of proof... The fact is that the accusation of Jesuit intrigue behind secret societies has

---

[491] "Jesuits," *Mackey's Encyclopedia of Freemasonry*, vol.1.

[492] Miller 308-319.

[493] Charles William Heckethorn, *Secret societies of all Ages and Countries*, vol.11 (London, 1875) 296.

[494] "Jesuits."

[495] Webster, *Secret Societies and Subversive Movements* 197.

emanated principally from the secret societies themselves and would appear to have been a device adopted by them to cover their own tracks."[496]

The debate and speculation has spilt much ink. As Mackey notes, "Almost a library of books has been written on both sides of this subject in Germany and in France."[497] Some of those books happen to be Masonic. Maurice Pinay, quoting the *Abbreviated Encyclopedic Dictionary of Freemasonry* in his book *The Plot Against The Church* (1967), reports that the Strict Observance, which we have learned was indirectly founded by Charles Radcliffe, "was the third freemasonic [sic] innovation of the Jesuits, who stirred up the hope among their supporters to come into the possession of the riches of the old Templars. The chronological history of the Grand masters corresponds to that of the generals of the Society of Jesus."[498]

The Jesuits did indeed follow the Templar Stuarts to the Continent to back the Stuart cause - not because the Stuarts were Templars, but because they were Catholics. Charles Radcliffe, therefore, may well have developed a Jesuit Rite to conceal Templar activity. If so, the Rite seemed to be temporary, since the Stuarts were defeated in 1745.

We must also consider that the claim from the *Masonic Dictionary* that a Jesuit Rite existed, may be disinformation. Such a rite within the Sionist-Templar Strict Observance was never mentioned by the authors of *Holy Blood, Holy Grail,* and their research was extensive.

The *Masonic Dictionary* also mentions the Martinist Order as another Jesuit-inspired organization. Pinay says that the *Masonic Dictionary* defines the Chosen Cohen rite as "a philosophic spiritual, ultra-Jesuitical rite, which was founded in 1754."[499] But we have shown already that the Martinists are Sionist, protecting certain Priory documents.

The *Masonic Dictionary* seems to be publishing disinformation. This may be a ploy by Masonry to implicate and involve the Jesuits in Freemasonry. The Vatican's Roman Curia thinks so. It states the end to which Masonry would use the Jesuits: "The infiltrations of... Freemasonry into the Society of Jesus followed visibly the same aims, for this Freemasonic-Templar rite of the Jesuits wishes apparently to make the Society of Jesus into a new Templar Order with retention of its outer official structure... [The Jesuits then could be] secretly ruled by the enemies of the Church and then [be] used in order to destroy its defenders and with the purpose of making easier the victory of... Freemasonry..."[500]

THE SUPPRESSION AND THE JESUITS

There was a time when Jesuits did flock to the Masonic Lodge. On June 14, 1773, Pope Clement XIV dissolved the Jesuit Order, after which the kings of Europe confiscated their property. The suppression continued under the administration of Pope Pius VI. In 1814 the Jesuits were reinstated by Pope Pius VII.

Oddly enough, at the time of the dissolution (1773), founder of the banking dynasty Meyer Rothschild allegedly met with Weishaupt to plan world revolution. Some believe these two events were connected, since Weishaupt, a Jesuit, was not hindered by the Jesuit suppression. Further analysis, however, reveals that although many Jesuits joined illuminated Freemasonry at that time, they did so not because they were heading a

---

[496] Webster 126, 198.
[497] "Jesuits."
[498] Pinay 621.
[499] Pinay.
[500] Pinay 622.

conspiracy, but because they were seeking protection from both papal and state persecution.

To achieve revolution in France, it was imperative that the Masonic conspirators get rid of the powerful Jesuits. Masonry, and not the Church, was actually behind the Jesuit suppression. Pope Clement XIV succumbed to Masonic pressure. Monsignor Dr. Dillon in his brief account holds that the Jesuit suppression was more Masonic than Catholic: "The Duke de Choiseul, a Freemason, with the aid of the abominable de Pompadour, the harlot of the still more abominable Louis XV, succeeded in driving the Jesuits from France. He then set about influencing his brother Masons, the Count De Aranda, Prime Minister of Charles III of Spain, and the infamous Carvalho-Pombal... to do the same work in the Catholic States of their respective sovereigns."[501]

Although the Jesuits were reinstated in 1814 by Pope Pius VII, the damage had already been done. Some Jesuits had joined illuminated Freemasonry. This has erroneously led a few researchers to conclude that the conspiracy to annihilate the Church and State was of Jesuit origin in retaliation for their suppression.

According to Jack Chick (the most rabid anti-Catholic in the country) in his comic book "Alberto," the higher order of Jesuits are today still members of the Masonic Lodge, including the current Father General.[502] Jesuit involvement in Freemasonry is also confirmed in *The Jesuits* (1987), by former Jesuit, Dr. Malachi Martin.

In *The Jesuits*, Martin traces the history of the Society of Jesus. He says that the Jesuits' original mission was to back the Pope in all his directives. These priests were known as the "Pope's Men." Martin notes the suffering the Jesuits endured as a result of the 1773 suppression. When the Pope, he says, "put their Father General and his advisers into papal dungeons, even as he imposed exile and slow death on thousands of Jesuits who were stranded without help or support in dangerous parts of the world, [when they were reinstated in 1814], [t]he revivified Jesuits started off again, with renewed zeal for the papal will..."[503]

Although some Jesuits joined the Illuminati and Freemasonry during their suppression, Martin believes as a whole they stayed true to the Pope. He places their shift of loyalty after the Second Vatican Council in 1965. He writes:

> Never, it can be said, did the Society of Jesus as a body veer from that mission [of being the "popes men"] until 1965. In that year, the Second Vatican Council ended the last of its four sessions; and Pedro de Arrupe y Gondra was elected to be the 27th Father General of the Jesuits. Under Arrupe's leadership, and in the heady expectation of change sparked by the Council itself, the new outlook - antipapal and sociopolitical in nature - that had been flourishing in a covert fashion for over a century was espoused by the Society as a corporate body.[504]

The Roman Curia was correct. Instead of the Jesuits penetrating the Masonic Order, Freemasonry penetrated the Jesuits. Malachi Martin suggests that Freemasonry infiltrated the Jesuit Order throughout the last century, the effects of which were finally manifest during Father General Arrupe's administration. He confirms that many of the Jesuits are now Masons. The late Father Arrupe was also a Mason. Martin documents that the

---

[501] Dillon 20.

[502] Jack Chick, *Alberto* (Chino, CA: Chick Publications, n.d.) 28.

[503] Malachi Martin, *The Jesuits* (New York: The Linden Press,1987) 31-32.

[504] Martin 35.

Marxist "Liberation Theology," backed by the Jesuits in South America, is Masonic in origin.[505]

THE MASONIC MURDER OF A MODERN POPE

The current involvement of Catholic priests, other than Jesuits, in Freemasonry is documented by David Yallop in his contemporary book, *In God's Name*. His book is subtitled *An Investigation into the Assassination of Pope John Paul I*. Yallop reveals startling information that incriminates Freemasonry in the death of the first John Paul. He notes the mysterious correlation between the 33 degrees of Masonry and the time of the new pope's death: "Sometime during the late evening of September 28, 1978, and the early morning of September 29, 1978, *thirty-three days* after his election, Albino Luciani [Pope John Paul I] died."[506]

Yallop confirms that all the Cardinals and Bishops in the Vatican who were physically proximate to the Pope that night were Grand Orient Masons. He lists some of the Lodges in which they were initiated and gives their Masonic code names. He also notes that Italian Grand Orient Freemasonry founded a lodge called Propaganda Two (P-2), the membership of which was, and still is, primarily Mafia.

What would bring the violent hand of Masonry upon such a popular and untested pontiff? According to Yallop, Pope John Paul I's transgression was that he discovered some priests in the Vatican had joined the Masonic Lodge and were at that moment laundering illegal drug money and conducting illegal banking practices through the Vatican Bank in behalf of the P-2 Masonic Lodge. Word leaked that on September 29 the new pope would replace some 20 of the Bishops and Cardinals he knew were involved. During the night of September 28, however, he mysteriously died. Yallop offers convincing evidence that the Pope was poisoned. He also suggests that killing the Pope on his thirty-third day in office was a Masonic signature.

INFILTRATING THE CATHOLIC CHURCH

How was Masonry able to penetrate the Catholic Church? When did its plan to infiltrate begin? Edith Starr Miller sheds light on these two questions in *Occult Theocrasy*. Miller explains that after the 1789-1793 destruction of old France, and prior to the reign of Napoleon, Grand Orient Freemasonry's aim was to destroy Christianity at its source. From the minutes of the Italian Masonic Lodge, entitled *Permanent Instructions, or Practical Code of Rules: Guide for the Heads of the Highest Grades of Masonry*, Miller quotes:

> *Now that we are constituted in an active body, and that our Order begins to reign as well in places most remote as in those that are nearest our centre, one great thought arises, a thought that has always greatly pre-occupied the men who aspire to the universal regeneration of the world, that thought is, the Liberation of Italy, for from Italy shall one day issue the freedom of the entire world - a Republic of Fraternity, Harmony, and Humanity.*
>
> *Our final aim is that of Voltaire and of the French Revolution, - the complete annihilation of Catholicism, and ultimately of Christianity.*

---

[505] Martin 59, 76, 114.
[506] David A. Yallop, *In God's Name* (New York: Bantam Books, 1984) 6.

> *Under this cloak [of Freemasonry], we may conspire at our convenience, and arrive, little by little, at our ultimate aim.*
>
> *The Pope, whoever he may be, will never enter into a secret society. It then becomes the duty of the Secret Society to make the first advance to the Church and to the Pope, with the object of conquering both. The work for which we gird ourselves up, is not the work of a day, nor a month, nor a year.*
>
> *It may last for many years, perhaps for a century; in our ranks the soldier dies, but the war is continued. We do not at present intend to gain the Pope to our cause, nor to make him a neophyte to our principles, or a propagator of our ideas. Such would be a dream.*
>
> *That which we should seek, that which we should await, as the Jews await a Messiah, is a Pope according to our wants.*[507]

What the Grand Orient desired was either a weak Pope, or one who could be directly manipulated. That Pope arose in 1958. He was not a weak man, but one cunningly groomed by the Grand Master of the Priory of Sion. According to the authors of *Holy Blood, Holy Grail*, while acting as papal nuncio to Turkey in 1935 this prelate had secretly joined a Rose-Croix order, possibly the Priory of Sion.[508]

Grand Master (GM) of the Priory of Sion at that time was artist Jean Cocteau (GM 1918-1963). As helmsman of Sion, his apparent assignment was to steer the Catholic Church away from its centuries-old, anti-Masonic attitude to one that would favor the Brotherhood. A pope groomed in his younger years in a Rosicrucian order would do the job for Sion. Cardinal Angelo Roncalli of Venice was the priest selected by Cocteau. To make sure this prelate met the right people, Cocteau introduced him to those with whom he had spent a good portion of his life - members of royalist and aristocratic Catholic circles. When it came time to appoint the papal nuncio to Turkey, the nod went to Cardinal Roncalli. When it was time for the Catholic aristocracy to lobby for a Pope, a suggestion from Jean Cocteau was sufficient.

An interesting point in this intrigue is that two years before Roncalli ascended the Papal throne, the Priory documents of 1956 list Jean Cocteau as Jean (John) XXIII. The authors of *Holy Blood, Holy Grail* report that two years later, "In 1958, while Coctean still presumably held the grand mastership... the assembled cardinals elected as their new Pontiff Cardinal Angelo Roncalli of Venice."[509] The new pope took the name John XXIII, the same name listed in the Priory documents for his Rosicrucian mentor.

A newly elected Pope traditionally chooses his own papal name, which name signifies in what direction the Vicar of Christ will lead the Church. If he takes the name of a previous Pope, adding one Roman numeral to it, he will follow in that Pope's footsteps. *Holy Blood* authors report that "Cardinal Roncalli caused considerable consternation when he chose the name of John XXIII. Such consternation was not unjustified. In the first place, the name John had been implicitly anathematized since it was last used in the early fifteenth century - by an Antipope."[510]

Who was this Antipope? The *Encyclopaedia Britannica* states that Baldassare Cossa was the Antipope John XXIII, a schismatic Pope from 1410 to 1415. Cossa lived during the days of strongest Protestant Reformation, a time also when Rosicrucianism was on the rise. Since he was ecumenical in philosophy he sided with the schismatics. And as a

---

[507] Miller 427-432.
[508] Baigent et al, *Holy Blood, Holy Grail* 159.
[509] Baigent.
[510] Baigent.

schismatic, Cossa's claim to the name John XXIII is generally considered by the Roman Catholic Church to be illegal.[511]

Because of the Cossa stigma, the name "John" had not been used by Popes until Roncalli in 1958. What is so significant about Cardinal Roncalli's revival of the line of Johns is that he took the precise Roman numeral of the schismatic Antipope, signaling to the Catholic world he not only would follow in this schismatic prelate's footsteps, but would duplicate them. Cardinal Roncalli was known as the "ecumenical Pope."

The authors of *Holy Blood* see another layer of meaning in the name:

"If Pope John was affiliated with a Rose-Croix organization, and if that organization was the Prieure de Sion, the implications would be extremely intriguing. Among other things they would suggest that Cardinal Roncalli, on becoming Pope, chose the name of his own secret grand master - so that, for some symbolic reason, there would be a John XXIII presiding over Sion and the papacy simultaneously."[512]

We believe the significance of the name is otherwise. The Grand Master of Sion certainly knew of this fifteenth century schismatic ecumenical Antipope. The "symbolic reason" for the choice of name was not in the fact that two John XXIII's reigned simultaneously in the mid-twentieth century. It was more likely a confirmation of identity. Grand Master Jean Cocteau, when publishing his own name as Jean (John) XXIII in the Priory documents in 1956, was sending a message to the Priory of Sion's Lost King: "The Pope who names himself John XXIII, as I have named myself in this document, is the one I have been grooming in the doctrine of the Antipope by the same name!" The name would signal the "Lost King" of Sion that Cocteau had succeeded in his mission.

In 1963 both Johns died. The authors of *Holy Blood* summarize the profound effects of John XXIII's pontificate upon the Catholic Church:

> *Whatever the truth underlying these strange coincidences, there is no question that more than any other man Pope John XXIII was responsible for reorienting the Roman Catholic Church - and bringing it, as commentators have frequently said, into the twentieth century. Much of this was accomplished by the reforms of the Second Vatican Council, which John inaugurated. At the same time, however, John was responsible for other changes as well. He revised the Church's position on Freemasonry, for example - breaking with at least two centuries of entrenched tradition and pronouncing that a Catholic might be a Freemason.[513]*

GRAND MASTER COCTEAU SENT ANOTHER SYMBOLIC MESSAGE TO SION

Cocteau, as an artist, helped redecorate many Catholic churches destroyed by World War II. His symbolic messages in art offer more confirmation that the Priory of Sion had turned the Roman Church pro-Masonic. One example can be seen in the church of Notre Dame de France, around the corner from Leicester Square in London. During the war the church was seriously damaged. After the war it was restored and redecorated by artists from all over France. The authors of *Holy Blood, Holy Grail* state that Cocteau was one of them, who, in 1960, three years before his death, executed a mural depicting the Crucifixion. It is an extremely singular Crucifixion. There is a black sun and a sinister, green tinged and unidentified figure in the lower right-hand corner. There is a Roman

---

[511] "John XXII," *Encyclopaedia Britannica: Micropaedia.*
[512] Baigent 160.
[513] Baigent 160-161.

soldier holding a shield with a bird emblazoned on it - a highly stylized bird suggesting an Egyptian rendering of Horus. Among the mourning women and dice-throwing centurions there are two incongruously modern figures - one of whom is Cocteau himself, presented as a self-portrait, with his back significantly turned on the cross. Most striking of all is the fact that the mural depicts only the lower portion of the cross. Whoever hangs upon it is visible only as far up as the knees - so that one cannot see the face or determine the identity of who is being crucified. And fixed to the cross, immediately below the anonymous victim's feet, is a gigantic rose. The design, in short, is a flagrant Rose-Croix device.[514]

The symbology is both striking and blasphemous. The rose affixed to the base of the cross on which a faceless person hangs is representative of the Rosicrucian doctrine of opposites. We know that in Rosicrucian symbolism the rose entwined around the upright portion of the cross represents the Serpent (Satan). Therefore, the anonymous person on the cross would be the Adversary, the Rosicrucian antithesis of Christ. The hierarchy of the Priory of Sion would readily understand the symbolic message: "At the head of the Catholic Church is our pope who represents, not Christ, but the Adversary." The Grand Master of Sion, given the task to steer the Catholic Church toward a pro-Masonic stance, painted his triumph in this mural!

Malachi Martin documents Cocteau's groundwork, upon which the Masonic takeover of the Catholic Church actually followed after the deaths of Jean Cocteau and Pope John in 1963. Martin notes the violence and swiftness of what followed in the Catholic Church:

"Nothing that happened foretold the violent change that awaited the Church, the papacy, and the Jesuits in the 1960s... [I]t is the first time that the Society of Jesus has turned on the papacy... Never, it can be said, did the Society of Jesus as a body veer from that mission until 1965."[515]

The Pope who followed Roncalli in 1963 was Giovanni Battista Montini. Montini took the name Paul VI in a break from John. Yallop notes, however, that Pope Paul was sickly and weak, and documents time and again how he, because of physical and emotional weakness, was manipulated. Paul VI's weak performance caused his thirty-three day-long successor Pope John Paul I, in 1978 to wonder, "Did Pope Paul envisage a change in the Church's position on Freemasonry?"[516] John Paul I was soon assassinated by the Masons.

THE ATTEMPT ON JOHN PAUL II

Karol Woityla from Poland was elected the new Vicar of Christ. Woityla took John Paul's name, adding one Roman numeral, which signified that he would take up his predecessor's anti- Masonic crusade. Martin confirms that Freemasonry once again went to work to oppose the new pope:

> There were revelations that certain circles of the international section of the Masonic Lodge in Europe and Latin America were actively organizing opposition to the Pontiff in Poland; that Vatican prelates - some twenty in all - were formal members of the Italian Lodge; and that once again Arrupe's Jesuits seemed involved with the Lodge circles opposed to the Pontiff. Pope Paul VI had already in 1965 warned Arrupe and the Delegates to the 31st Jesuit General

---

[514] Baigent 158.
[515] Martin 35.
[516] Yallop 178.

Congregation of the dangers in belonging to the [Masonic] Compact; it began to appear to John Paul that the warning had not been too wide of the mark.[517]

In May 1981 there was an attempt on John Paul II's life. Several investigators suspect Freemasonry. France, dominated by Grand Orient Freemasonry, tried to shift blame for the attempted assassination to communist Bulgaria. The leading Paris daily, *Le Monde*, reported on December 3, 1982 that, "Soviet factional opponents of former KGB head Yuri Andropov were suspected to be behind revelations of a Bulgarian connection to the May 13, 1981 attempt to assassinate Pope John Paul II."[518]

Based upon subsequent evidence, however, the *Le Monde* article was apparently Masonic disinformation. The Bulgarian government launched its own investigation to clear its name and discovered that the controllers of Mehmet Ali Agca, the would-be assassin, were Turkish Mafia figure Bekir Celenk and two Italian spies held in Bulgaria. In direct response to the international spotlight on the Celenk case, the Bulgarian government announced on December 22, 1982, that it was placing the two accused Italian spies, Paolo Farsetti and his girlfriend Gabriella Trevisini, on trial. The charge, according to the report issued, was that the pair were agents of a Grand Orient Scottish Rite Free Masonic Lodge called Propaganda Two, the same Lodge accused of assassinating Pope John Paul I![519]

Oddly enough, the attempt on the Pope's life caused John Paul II to change direction and modify~ his opposition to Freemasonry. On January 12, 1983, the Pope issued a revised code of canon law. George W. Cornell, the Associated Press religion writer, claimed that the revised code "moves ahead in legislating reforms and principles approved by the Second Vatican Council of 1962-1965... The code implements other changes in church rules, such as permitting Catholics to become Masons."

As is standard practice with the Masonically controlled press, journalist Cornell is stretching the truth. On August 17, 1985, he clarified what the 1983 revised code of canon law actually provided. It "omitted a provision of the old 1917 code excommunicating Catholics who join Masonic orders." Although the result is essentially the same, that Catholics may join Freemasonry without fear of reprisal, the Vatican still is opposed to Freemasonry. However, Pope John Paul II opened the door for many Catholics to join the Masonic Order.

Jack Chick and Malachi Martin both claim that many Jesuits are Masons. Thus Chick proposes that the Catholic Church, through the order of the Masonic Jesuits, are the conspirators. In support of that theory is the fact that Adam Weishaupt, founder of the Illuminati, was once a Jesuit.

Membership of a few Catholic priests in Masonry, however, is not sufficient evidence to establish the Catholic Church as head of the conspiracy. When considering the eight parts of the Octopus Theory, no evidence emerges that the Jesuits penetrated the hierarchy of Freemasonry. To the contrary. Freemasonry, using a traitor Rosicrucian Pope and apostate Masonic Jesuits, infiltrated the Church. Remember, Freemasonry is the one factor common to all eight legs of the Octopus Theory, not Catholicism (See Preface.) Therefore, in the same manner in which Masonry aims to use renegade Reform Jews to execute their planned destruction of Judaism, so have the Masons used the Jesuits to help annihilate their own Church.

The schism between the Church and the Jesuits began in 1773 when the papacy defrocked the Jesuits. The Vatican's action at that time, right or wrong, is of no

---

[517] Yallop 76.
[518] Investigative Leads 25 Feb.1983, 1.
[519] Investigative Leads 1-2.

consequence. Of significance is the fact that it set in motion a chain of events which resulted in Masonry penetrating the Vatican.

Weishaupt emerged the winner. In that crucial year when Jesuits rushed to join his Order of Illuminati, they did so not because they loved Weishaupt, for they abhorred him as much as he despised them, nor because Illuminism was a Jesuit conspiracy. They joined his Order for one reason - to protect themselves against persecution from Church and State. Little did they realize they were uniting with the Order bent on the destruction of their beloved Church.

We can vividly see the primary weapon of the conspirators as it comes into focus. By involving the Jews and the Jesuits through deception and disinformation in Freemasonry, Masonry could promote its agenda and let its plans grow and mature by diverting the conspiracy hounds to false prey. The "elusive game" in all conspiracy theories, when finally cornered, is Freemasonry. Jews and Jesuits are only decoys. Weishaupt used them both.

VOLTAIRE'S MASONIC ANTI-CATHOLICISM

Former Jesuit Weishaupt was the figurehead of a conspiracy, but not a Jesuit conspiracy. His involvement with Voltaire, a vociferous hater of the Jesuits, is proof of his profound hatred not only of Jesuits, but of all things Christian. The lives of Weishaupt and Voltaire [one of the most prolific illuminated Masonic authors] overlapped by thirty years. Long an illuminist before Weishaupt created the Order of that name, Voltaire gloated over the suffering of the Jesuits. In 1773, upon receiving the news of their plight, he exclaimed, "See, one head of the hydra has fallen. I lift my eyes to heaven and cry 'crush the wretch.'"[520]

Voltaire was not quiet about his intense opposition to Christianity. Dillon quotes him as saying, "I am tired of hearing it said that twelve men sufficed to establish Christianity, and I desire to show that it requires but one man to pull it down."[521]

Born Francis Mary Arouet, Voltaire first joined English Freemasonry while residing in London in 1726-1728. Our own Benjamin Franklin inducted him into French Freemasonry in 1778.

Voltaire did not write under his own name, but used a code name to protect himself.[522] (Earlier we discussed the reason for secret names and name changes.)

According to Dillon, "Voltaire found that the Masonry to which he had been affiliated in London, was a capital means of diffusing his doctrines among the courtiers, the men of letters, and the public of France... In the recesses of its lodges, the political conspirator found the men and the means to arrive at his ends in security."[523]

Voltaire defended lying as a virtue when practiced for the "good" he advocated. Dillon quotes Voltaire as saying, "Lying is a vice when it does evil. It is a great virtue when it does good. Be therefore more virtuous than ever. It is necessary to lie like a devil, not timidly and for a time, but boldly and always."[524] Commander Carr, in *The Conspiracy*, likewise shows Voltaire justifying all kinds of falsehood, telling his fellow enlightened, "'We must make them [the populace] lavish promises and use extravagant

[520] Dillon 6.
[521] Dillon.
[522] Dillon 8.
[523] Dillon 6, 18.
[524] Dillon 8.

phrases... The opposite of what we promise may be done afterwards... that is of no consequence."[525]

Voltaire was a man who scorned all traditional moral restraints. Says Dillon, "He lived without shame and even ostentatiously in open adultery. He laughed at every moral restraint. He preached libertinage and practised it."[526]

During his zenith Voltaire was the hero of the irreligionists. According to the historians Durant, under the influence of Voltaire and his fellows, the whole tone of French society had changed. Nearly every writer in France followed the line and sought the approval of the *philosophes; philosophie* was in a hundred tides and a thousand mouths; "a word of praise from [Freemasons] Voltaire, Diderot, or d'Alembert was more valued than the favor of a prince."

Foreign visitors angled for admission to salons where they might meet and hear the famous *philosophes;* returning to their own lands, they spread the new ideas. [Freemason] Hume, though in many of his views he preceded Voltaire, looked up to him as a master... [Freemason Benjamin] Franklin, and others joined in preparing an English translation and edition of Voltaire's works in thirty-seven volumes (1762). In America the founders of the new republic were deeply stirred by the writings of the *philosophes*. As to Germany, hear [Freemason] Goethe's remarks to Brother Eckermann in 1820 and 1831: "You have no idea of the influence which Voltaire and his great contemporaries had in my youth, and how they governed the [mind of the] whole civilized world... It seems to me quite extraordinary to see what men the French had in their literature in the last century. I am astonished when I merely look at it. It was the metamorphosis of a hundred-year-old literature, which had been growing ever since Louis XIV; and now stood in full power."[527]

Voltaire himself, overcoming the natural pessimism of old age, sounded a note of Masonic victory in 1771, as he evaluated the success of his "philosophy":

> *Well-constituted minds are now very numerous, they are at the head of nations; they influence public manners; and year by year the fanaticism that overspread the earth is receding in its detestable usurpation... If religion no longer gives birth to civil wars, it is to philosophy alone that we are indebted... A usurpation [by Christianity] odious and injurious, founded upon fraud on one side and stupidity on the other, is being at every instant undermined by reason, which is establishing its reign.[528]*

Voltaire equated "fanaticism" with Christianity and "philosophy" with Illuminated Masonry. In Prussia, twenty years earlier, Voltaire had laid out for the Templar king, Frederick II, the Masonic plan to undermine Christianity by "reason." Frederick II had been initiated into Freemasonry in 1738. In 1761 he had been the acknowledged head of the Scottish Rite, himself of the 32nd degree. From 1750-1755, Voltaire had been a guest at Frederick's.[529] Monsignor Dillon outlines the scope of Voltaire's aims and work during that visit:

> *He sketched out for them the whole mode of procedure against the Church. His policy as revealed by the correspondence of Frederick II, and others with him, was not to commence an immediate persecution, but first to suppress the Jesuits*

---

[525] Carr 8.
[526] Dillon 8.
[527] Durants, vol. IX, 784-785.
[528] Durants.
[529] Webster 156.

and all Religious orders, and to secularize their goods; then to deprive the Pope of temporal authority, and the Church of property and state recognition. Primary and higher-class education of a lay and Infidel [sic] character was to be established, the principle of divorce affirmed, and respect for ecclesiastics lessened and destroyed. Lastly, when the whole body of the Church should be sufficiently weakened and Infidelity [sic] strong enough, the final blow was to be dealt by the sword of open, relentless persecution. A reign of terror was to spread over the whole earth, and to continue while a Christian should be found obstinate enough to adhere to Christianity. This, of course, was to be followed by a Universal Brotherhood without marriage, family, property, God, or law...[530]

Of course the French Revolution put the Church to the sword. Dr. Dillon, writing in 1885, thirty- two years before the Russian Revolution, foresaw another tumult, which in the 20th century broke forth again with all the fury of Voltaire's suggestions.

Dillon illustrates Voltaire's intense hatred for the Church by quoting the author's blasphemous comments: "I finish all my letters by saying, "Let us crush the wretch, crush the wretch!""[531] Again, Dillon quotes him writing to Damilaville: "The Christian religion is an infamous religion, an abominable hydra which must be destroyed by a hundred invisible hands. It is necessary that the philosophers should course through the streets to destroy it as missionaries course over earth and sea to propagate it. They ought to dare all things, risk all things, even to be burned, in order to destroy it. Let us crush the wretch! Crush the wretch!"[532]

Depraved men will boldly shake their fist in the face of Almighty God when riding the crest of youth, health and popularity. But when faced with death they cower. So it was with Voltaire. On his deathbed he was in extreme loneliness and fear. He thought of the inventions his corrupt mind had devised against Jesus Christ and His Church. When he lay dying, horror filled his eyes as he cried out "Oh, God! Oh, Christ! I wish that I had paid attention to your words more. Now that I am dying I feel the fires of hell! Oh, God! Oh, Christ!"[533]

By the time of his death, Voltaire had been a member of English Freemasonry for fifty years. Fifty-one days before his death he joined French Freemasonry. Yet the Masonic Great Architect of the Universe was not there to comfort him. Plunging headlong into a Christiess eternity, Voltaire shrieked his last words in the fury of despair and agony, "I am abandoned by God and man."[534]

Dillon quotes a Dr. Fruchen, who witnessed the awful spectacle of Voltaire's death: "Would that all who have been seduced by the writings of Voltaire had been witnesses of his death, it would be impossible to hold out [from becoming a Christian] in the face of such an awful spectacle."[535]

In contrast, *Mackey's Encyclopedia of Freemasonry* reports only the fact of Voltaire's death and the sorrow it caused fellow Masons:

Voltaire was easily misunderstood. He was initiated in the Lodge of the Nine Sisters [an illuminated lodge] at Paris, April 7, 1778. Benjamin Franklin and others distinguished in Freemasonry were members of this famous Lodge. Franklin at the time of Voltaire's initiation was a visitor only but subsequently became Worshipful Master of the Lodge.

---

[530] Dillon 7-8.
[531] Dillon 6.
[532] Dillon 8-9.
[533] Pastors in the National Council of Churches. Jim Shaw, TapeMinistry of Rev. Jim Shaw (audio cassette).
[534] Dillon 10.
[535] Dillon.

Voltaire's death, on May 30, 1778, gave rise to a memorable Lodge of Sorrow, which was held on the succeeding November 28.[536]

One sad note in Christendom is sounded by Dr. Dillon when he confirms that Protestants were glad to see Voltaire's followers triumph over the Catholic Church. In a warning to Protestants, this Catholic priest wrote to "our separated Christian brethren [that] it has been a cardinal point of policy with [Voltaire's] followers to take advantage of the unfortunate differences between the various sects of Christians in the world and the Church, in order to ruin both; for the destruction of every form of Christianity, as well as Catholicity, was the aim of Voltaire, and remains as certainly the aim of his disciples."[537]

Looking at Voltaire's life, and his ceaseless effort to destroy the Catholic Church through illuminated Masonic intrigue, Jesuits were not likely to have used illuminated Freemasonry to further a popish world conspiracy. Instead, Freemasonry deceptively promotes the idea that a few Jesuits and Popes were Masons.

MASONIC DISINFORMATION: CHRISTIAN DIVISION

Disinformation is the primary tool used by Freemasonry to destroy all Christianity. It was used in Weishaupt's day and is still used today to achieve four goals: (1) to entice Christians to join the Masonic Lodge; (2) to pit Protestants against Catholics; (3) to destroy the credibility of any anti- Masonic publication; and (4) to discredit clergy in the eyes of the populace. We will examine a few examples in this order.

CHRISTIANS IN FREEMASONRY

Freemasonry has fabricated stories that some Popes joined the Masonic Order. Although the Popes have condemned Freemasonry almost without interruption and, until recently, have forbidden Catholics to join the Order, Masons have used this lie to entice Catholics into membership. For example, the story circulated about 1884 of Pope Pius IX (1846-1878) seems to comply with the Masonic blueprint of spreading lies for the express purpose of enticing Catholics to reconsider the "virtues" of Freemasonry. The Masons on the continent of Europe believed that by placing the supposed initiation of a pope in America, their lies might escape investigation. The Most Reverend Cardinal Caro y Rodriguez, Archbishop of Santiago, Chile tells the story:

> *The statement that there have been Popes who were Masons has been one of the most despicable inventions which has occurred in Masonry to mislead and deceive ignorant and simple Catholics... They declared positively that Pius IX had been received into a certain Masonic lodge in Philadelphia, they quoted their discourses and declared that several of his autographs were kept in this lodge... The claim was investigated and it was found that in that city, there is no Masonic lodge of the name given... Masons themselves testified that the entire matter was merely an invention. The calumny thus refuted has been revived from time to time, and in the last version care was taken not to specify the lodge or the city. To make it more credible they have placed on the photograph of a Mason with insignias,*

---

[536] "Voltaire," *Mackey's Encyclopedia of Freemasonry*, vol.11.
[537] Dillon 9.

the head of the Pope, cut from his portrait and substituted in place of the Mason
~538

PROTESTANTS AGAINST CATHOLICS

A decade later in 1894, in order to agitate Protestants, Masonic disinformation was directed once again against the Catholic Church in the United States. The organization used to spread the disinformation was the American Protective Association (APA), founded on March 13, 1887, at Clinton, Iowa, by Henry Francis Bowers, an enthusiastic 32nd degree Mason. Bowers insisted that America was founded by Masons against the wishes of Rome. He considered the APA an offspring of Masonry, "'protecting the republican institutions the Masons had established ~ In 1894 *Century Magazine* exposed Bowers as a fraud. Paul Fisher, in *Behind The Lodge Door*, outlines the origin and spread of the calumny:

> *Century Magazine told how the APA circulated a false encyclical of Pope Leo XIII, which purported to assert that the United States belongs to him, and that U.S. citizens are absolved from their oath of allegiance to their country.*
>
> *The false document also said the Pope was to take "forcible possession" of the United States, and "it will be the duty of the faithful to exterminate all heretics found within the jurisdiction of the United States." [Emphasis in original.]*
>
> *That document and similar false statements relating to the Church, including a variety of alleged "oaths of papal leaders and garbled extracts of Catholic writings," were "used as campaign literature all over the land, in all manner of publications, and... their genuineness has been editorially asserted and defended in the organs of the [Masonic] order."*
>
> *Additionally there were tales of consignments of arms being sent to rectories all over the country, as Catholics drilled for war preparations in the basements of their churches. Yet, not a single instance of such wild imaginings, presented as facts, were ever corroborated.*539

Although long since proven to be a fabrication of Masonry, this anti-Catholic propaganda lasted for half a century. Those of voting age during the presidential campaign of John F. Kennedy can remember widespread anti-Catholic sentiment. Even to this day a good part of Protestant Christendom assails Catholics.

Another Masonic sect that spreads disinformation to further divide Protestants and Catholics was the reorganized Ku Klux Klan founded in 1915 by Royal Arch Mason, Colonel William Simmons.[540] Simmons was an ardent admirer of the Ku Klux Klan of post Civil War days (1866- 1869). Again, according to Paul Fisher, the reorganized Klan's viewpoint was strikingly similar to the philosophy of the APA of previous periods.[541] He notes, for example, that "most of the Klan's major leaders were Freemasons." Fisher then documents his claim by naming them on the next two pages.[542]

---

[538] Rodriguez 49-50.
[539] Fisher.
[540] Miller 607.
[541] Fisher 87.
[542] Fisher 95-97.

By 1924 - 1,125,000 Masons were members of the KKK. One of the most prominent Klansman was 33rd degree Mason, Justice Hugo Black of the Supreme Court.[543]

Since so many Masons in the South were Klansmen, Masonic bigotry was transferred to the Klan. In those days the requirement to join the Southern Jurisdiction of Freemasonry was that you must be born free (which excluded blacks), born white, (which excluded blacks), be Protestant (which excluded Catholics), and be 21 years of age.

Like Freemasonry, the Klan not only hated blacks, it hated Catholics. Therefore, to incite the Protestants against the Catholics, a Masonic member of the Klan wrote and published the so- called oath taken by 4th degree members of the Catholic Knights of Columbus. The bogus oath stated that "'the Pope... hath power to depose heretical kings, princes, States, Commonwealths and Governments, and they may be safely destroyed...'" The oath further stated that the Knights would also "wage war 'secretly' using 'the poisonous cup, the strangulation cord, the steel of the poniard, or the leaden bullet...'" Should the Knight prove false, the fake oath says he agrees to "have his brethern [sic] 'cut off my hands and feet and my throat from ear to ear, my belly opened and sulphur burned therein...'"[544]

Although a *New York World* three-month investigation proved the oath false (see September 6, 1921 issue)[545], this Masonic disinformation accomplished what it had set out to achieve. United States Protestants, who were already possessed of an anti-Catholic bias in the first colonial settlements, had been agitated by Freemasonry to oppose Catholicism at every level. This extended even to the 1960 presidential candidacy of John R Kennedy. His assassination, as we shall learn in Volume m of *Scarlet and the Beast,* was plotted by Freemasons.

After the 1960s Freemasonry ceased its war against Catholics and turned against fundamentalist and evangelical Protestants. What happened to cause this shift? - the Second Vatican Council, which permitted Catholics to join Freemasonry. Then, and only then, did the Brotherhood cease its war against the Roman Church, turning instead its efforts toward evangelical and fundamentalist Protestant Christianity.

Coincidence? Not at all. The strategy was calculated, for such a plan has been in Masonic writings for over a century. Italian Freemasonry wrote over 150 years ago: "Our final aim is that of Voltaire and of the French Revolution, - the complete annihilation of Catholicism, and ultimately of (all) Christianity."(See footnote 17.)

ANTI-MASONIC PUBLICATIONS

Masonry also uses disinformation against itself. For what reason? To create outside sensational reports that can later be proven wrong. The motive is to create doubt in the mind of the populace about anything negative said in print about Freemasonry. The late British journalist Stephen Knight discovered this in the 1980s while researching for his book, *The Brotherhood:*

> [T]he investigator has to face the problem of organized secrecy and "disinformation".
> This latter can be crass and easily spotted, like the information passed to me covertly by a high-ranking Freemason posing as a nark, which said that at a certain degree a Candidate was required to defecate on a crucifix. This absurd

---

[543] Fisher 108.

[544] Fisher 92-93. Read the Masonic oaths in Appendix 4 to see the similarity, which suggests a Masonic creation.

[545] Fisher 92.

sort of tactic is aimed at the gullible anti- Mason who is on the lookout for scandal and sensation, and who will believe anything that shows the Brotherhood in an unfavorable light. Such writers do exist, and in some number as I have had to prepare the report. These are the people who repeat what they are told without checking on facts and sources, and who ignore all evidence which runs counter to their own argument. And it is they who fall for the kind of disinformation tactic which several Freemasons attempted to practice on me.[546]

DISCREDITING THE CLERGY

Finally, the most effective disinformation is meant to discredit the clergy in the eyes of the populace. Italian Grand Orient Freemasonry explained the tactic in the early 1800s:

Little can be done with old Cardinals and with prelates of decided character. Such incorrigibles must be left to the school of Gonsalve, and in our magazines of popularity and unpopularity, we must find the means to utilize, or ridicule power in their hands. A well invented report must be spread with tact amongst good Christian families: such a Cardinal for instance, is a miser; such a prelate is licentious; such an official is a freethinker, an infidel, a Freemason, and so on in the same strain. These things will spread quickly to the cafes, thence to the squares, and one report is sometimes enough to ruin a man.

The foreign newspapers will learn and copy these facts which they will know how to embellish and colour according to their usual style.

For respect due to truth show, or better still, quote from some respectable fool as having quoted the number of the journal which has given the names, acts and doings of these personages. As in England and in France, so also in Italy there will be no lack of writers who well know how to tell lies for the good cause, and have no difficulty in doing so. One newspaper publishing the name of a Monsignor Delegate, His Excellency, or Eminence, or Lord Justice, will be quite sufficient proof for the people; they will require no other.[547]

If spreading lies about the morality of notable Christians was Masonic practice 150 years ago, it is unfortunate that today so-called Christians, including television evangelists, often create their own scandals.

In reference to one of the evangelists, the author asked a private investigator to find out if Freemasonry was involved. The investigator is a York Rite Mason and a Shriner on the security staff of this unfortunate world-renowned minister. The author has greeted this investigator several times with a Masonic handshake and has received Masonic information in return. The investigator said that when he personally polygraphed the woman involved, she failed the polygraph. The investigator believes that she was a plant. He said, "What the news reported and what actually took place are poles apart." On the question of the involvement of Freemasonry, he would not say.

A more recent story, widely spread, is that Billy Graham is a 33rd degree Mason.[548] As absurd as this might sound, we must look at the circumstances surrounding this accusation to determine if the rumor is Masonic disinformation. The accusation was made by Rev. Jim Shaw. Shaw, giving his Christian testimony on cassette tape, claims that Billy

---

[546] Knight, *The Brotherhood* 5-6.
[547] Miller 432-433.
[548] *HRT Newsletter,* Spring and Summer 1990.

Graham was present at his 33rd degree initiation ceremony.[549] If true, Graham is in fact a 33rd degree Mason, since by Masonic law no profane person (meaning non-Mason), nor any Mason below the rank of the initiated, can be present during initiation ceremonies.

Shaw offers the names of a few more who were present at his 33rd degree initiation, among them J. Edgar Hoover, Prince Bernhardt of the Netherlands and a President of the United States (which was probably Gerald Ford). Shaw is an honorable man, a man who would not lie, a man who would tell exactly what he *thought* he saw.

If we consider what happened to Jim Shaw two weeks before he was initiated into the 33rd degree, Billy Graham's appearance at his initiation might well have been a disguise - intended for the effect. Shaw says he was led to a saving knowledge of Jesus Christ just two weeks before his initiation. But since he had worked nineteen years for this prestigious position, he felt he had to go through with his initiation. Beforehand, however, the Masonic community had learned that Shaw had become a Christian. At his initiation the Supreme Council asked him if the rumor were true. Shaw affirmed that it was, and proceeded to witness Jesus Christ to the leading men of the world. Then "Billy Graham" entered the room.

If we consider that a hundred years ago, in order to deceive Catholics into joining Freemasonry, a picture of the Pope's head was superimposed on the portrait of a Mason dressed in his Masonic regalia - and if two hundred years ago Charles Radcliffe, the Grand Master of the Priory of Sion, disguised himself as Prince Charles Edward Stuart during a Masonic initiation to make the initiate believe the Pretender King presided over his initiation, we can readily understand why Free-masonry would disguise a Mason to look like Billy Graham to deceive Jim Shaw. By doing so they hoped that Shaw would stay in Freemasonry.

Masonic initiations are conducted in dimly-lit rooms. Consider the advanced technology of makeup artistry today, the deceptive mirrors used by magicians, and impersonators and impressionists who can look and sound identical to the real celebrity or dignitary. With all these possibilities, Rev. Shaw could well have seen and heard a "Billy Graham" impersonator. We should not be surprised at such a stunt pulled by Freemasonry. It is designed to throw the Christian community into turmoil. A hundred years ago Italian Grand Orient Freemasonry planned such a program for the destruction of the church.

THE HALF-TRUTH

Another example of disinformation is Masonic half-truth. Recently the author received a Masonic brochure listing some of the prominent Masons in the United States. Astronaut Jim Irwin was on the list. This declaration puzzled the author, since he had heard Irwin's Christian testimony. During the summer of 1989, the author had the privilege of shuttling Irwin to and from an airport. For three days he was Irwin's escort, getting to know how much this moon-walker loved the Lord Jesus Christ. En route back to the airport the author asked Irwin his opinion of Freemasonry. The conversation went something like this:

Irwin: "I think it is a deceptive tool of Satan."
Author: "Then you have renounced Freemasonry?"
Irwin: "How did you know I was ever a Mason?"

---

[549] Testimony of Jim Shaw, narr. Jim Shaw, Tape Ministry of Rev. Jim Shaw (audio cassette).

When the author told Irwin about the Masonic brochure Irwin said, "I was unaware they were still using my name. I renounced Freemasonry years ago."[550]

WEISHAUPT AND DISINFORMATION

Disinformation to divide Christianity is not a Johnny-come-lately policy of Freemasonry. In 1776 it was the primary tool employed by Weishaupt in his war against the Church. Taking advantage of the preexisting animosity between Protestants and Catholics, and the recent suppression of the Jesuits in 1773, Weishaupt was able to pit Christians against one another. He used Jesuits to write liberal sentiments for the purpose of inciting the Protestants and fed the Protestants lies about the Jesuits on the assumption that Protestants would believe him since he was once a Jesuit himself.

In his disinformation campaign against Catholics, Weishaupt learned of one Leuchtsenring, a hot-headed, Protestant fanatic, who spied Jesuits in every corner. During the Jesuit suppression, Weishaupt introduced Leuchtsenring to Freemason Christoph Friedrich Nikolai (1733-1811), a German bookseller who delighted in bringing Christianity still lower in the opinion of the people by publishing anti-Christian literature. When the union between the two men was made, Weishaupt stood back and watched Leuchtsenring send Nikolai throughout Germany to hunt down Jesuits for exposure in his publications. When Nikolai discovered that Jesuits were equally hated by the Illuminati, Weishaupt gained a most zealous and unwearied champion.[551]

Before Nikolai joined the Illuminati he was an intimate of the Frankist Jew, Moses Mendelssohn, who lived in Nikolai's house from 1762 till the day he died. Nikolai had encouraged Mendelssohn to translate into German Plato's *Republic*.[552] Republican ideals were then brought into the Illuminati. Weishaupt planned to adopt this form of government following the French Revolution.

Later Nikolai helped Weishaupt design the symbols taught in Illuminism after the fashion of Rosicrucian Masonry. Nikolai then set out to preach that the Illuminati was a Christian Order and he won many Protestants to its ranks.[553] Salem Kirban quotes Weishaupt gloating over his successes in a letter to Illuminatus Cato:

> *The most admirable thing of all is that great Protestant and reformed theologians [Lutherans and Calvinists] who belong to our Order really believe they see in it the true and genuine mind of the Christian religion. Oh man, what can not you be brought to believe?*
>
> *These people swell our numbers and fill our treasury; get busy and make these people nibble at our bait... but do not tell them our secrets. They must be made to believe that the low degree that they have reached is the highest.*[554]

---

[550] The late Jim Irwin gave the author permission to tell this story.

[551] Robison 88.

[552] Antelman 80-82.

[553] Robison 88.

[554] Kirban 149. All the quotes between Weishaupt and Knigge were from Robison or Barruel, who in turn received them from the Bavarian government following the confiscation of the Illuminati documents.

Weishaupt employed two opposition Masonic Lodges to help him win Protestant clergy as Illuminati converts. The first was the Strict Observance of Templar rites. The second was Sion's Rosicrucian Martinists. Nesta Webster tells the story:

> The first Masonic body with which the Illuminati formed an alliance was the Stricte Observance, to which the Illuminati Knigge and Bode both belonged. Cagliostro had also been initiated into the Stricte Observance near Frankfurt and was now employed as agent of the combined order. According to his own confession his mission "was to work so as to turn Freemasonry in the direction of Weishaupt's projects"; and the funds he drew upon were those of the Illuminati. Cagliostro also formed a link with the Martinistes, whose doctrines, though derided by Weishaupt, were useful to his plan in attracting by their mystical character those who would have been repelled by the cynicism of the Illuminati. According to Barruel, it was the Martinistes who - following in the footsteps of the Rosicrucians - had suggested to Weishaupt the device of presenting Christ as an "Illuminatus" which had led to such triumphant results amongst the Protestant clergy.[555]

The Protestant theologians' hatred toward Catholicism was so intense that once they were deceived by the lies of the Illuminati, they were deceived forever.

The undertow of Satan is visible as he manipulates events in order to complete the wicked design he has implanted in the minds of degenerate men. Prior to the French Revolution, Weishaupt was Satan's primary tool to destroy both the Church and the Jesuit power. The vacillating decisions of Popes, one suppressing the Jesuits, the other reinstating them, as irrational as they may seem to us, were brilliant maneuvers by Satan. It gave illuminated Freemasonry the opportunity to penetrate the Vatican. It also allowed Masonic entry into secular education, for all Jesuit Academies had been shut down. Moreover, the political positions held by the Jesuits as "King's Confessors" (advisors to royalty) were replaced after 1773 by Illuminated Masons. They remain in these governmental positions in all free nations to this day.

---

[555] Webster 135, 154, 232.

9. SECULAR EDUCATION: A MASONIC BLUEPRINT

Through the activities of our state organizations, the New Age Magazine, our clip service and News Bureau, we are stimulating the public interest and furnishing much valuable material to speakers and writers, and thereby can reasonably claim much credit for the growing interest in favor of compulsory education by the state.

Supreme Council of Scottish Rite Freemasonry,
Charleston, S.C., September 24, 1924

SECULARISM VS. RELIGION

After the Jesuit suppression in 1773, Grand Orient Freemasonry replaced Jesuit academies in Germany with schools called *Philanthropine,* or academies of general education, very similar to our state-controlled primary and secondary schools of today. The Philanthropine were the first schools of Reform Judaism. Their founder was Grand Orient Freemason Sigmund Geisenheimer, head clerk in Meyer Rothschild's Frankfurt bank. According to Rabbi Marvin Antelman, the House of Rothschild financed these schools.[556]

Although the Philanthropine were private (no state funded schools existed in Europe at that time), they were authorized by the illuminated Masonic rulers in the German principalities. The schools offered no religious instruction whatever - God and prayer were intentionally left out. Professor John Robison documents that when the graduates became professionals, morals declined rapidly on a national scale.[557]

In France, meanwhile, laws were passed forbidding Church schools. "laicism" or the secularization of the schools was the new order of the day. With public schools came a new breed of teachers called " atheist."[558]

Msgr. Dr. George Dillon says that the decision to secularize public schools came out of the French Masonic Lodges, one of which was a Lodge named Rose of Perfect Silence. In one of their meetings, he reports, it was asked: "Ought religious education to be suppressed?"

The answer was predictable: "Without any doubt the principal of supernatural authority, that is faith in God, takes from a man his dignity; is useless for the discipline of children; and there is also in it, the danger of the abandonment of all morality... The respect, specially due to the child, prohibits the teaching to him of doctrines, which disturb his reason."[559]

Does this suppression of religion sound familiar? In 1885, Msgr. Dillon already saw the consequences of the secularization of education in society and he rightly asked, "How can we be surprised if the Universities of the Continent have become the hot-beds of vice, revolution, and Atheism?"[560]

---

[556] Antelman 126.
[557] Robison 48-53.
[558] Dillon 80.
[559] Dillon.
[560] Dillon 83.

What Freemasonry initiated before and during the French Revolution has spread throughout the world via Masonic Lodges. The secularization of our educational institutions today with the elimination of Bible and prayer in our schools, is a result of two centuries of secularized education and the creation of modern Biblical criticism, which began in Grand Orient Masonic Lodges on the Continent of Europe. According to Orthodox Rabbi Antelman, at the forefront of this Biblical criticism were Grand Orient, Frankist Jews in their Philanthropine schools.

THE BUND AND ANTI-SEMITISM

As we have seen, the aim of secular education was to destroy both Christianity and Judaism. After 1848 Karl Marx, a 32nd degree Grand Orient Mason[561], carried on the Frankist Reform's subversive work. Marx:

> *was profoundly anti-religious and, in fact, he was against all religions. He is famous for having said, "Religion is the opiate of the people."[562] And in 1844 he remarked, "The criticism of religion is the beginning of all criticism."[563] "It was Karl Marx," comments Antelman, "who was born Jewish and whose family converted to Christianity when he was six, who wrote a book, A World Without Jews. Karl Marx helped promote anti-Semitism?"[564]*

According to Antelman, Marx, the so-called father *of Communism,* "was paid for his services by the League of the Just which was known in its country of origin, Germany, as the Bund per Gerechten."[565] Antelman claims that the League of the Just is an extension of the Illuminati. Members in the League were all illuminated Grand Orient Masons. Actually those who joined the League were the remnants of the old Jacobin Clubs who had fled to Germany after the Reign of Terror ending the French Revolution. The League of the Just, or "Bund" for short, he notes, "was later to become known as the International Communist Party."[566]

"It may be difficult to conceive of how a professed Jew or Catholic would seek to destroy his own religion," writes Rabbi Antelman. "However, one should consider that the Bund's inner circle consisted of unusually gifted intellectuals who were members of a specific religion by birth only, and super wealthy individuals whose boundless ambitions for power had caused them to become unscrupulous."[567]

One such reformer was Abraham Geiger (1810-1874), a rabbi who had joined the Bund per Gerechten, which operated within the illuminated Grand Orient Masonic Lodges.[568] Rabbi Antelman credits the Bund with "conceiving of the ultimate plans for the secularization and destruction of Judaism... Abraham Geiger," he reports, "was the man the Bund chose to be their primary personality to implement the Reform Movement... Due largely to Geiger, the Reform Movement became by 1850 the dominant Jewish schism in Germany."[569]

---

[561] Miller 270, 726.
[562] Antelman 17.
[563] Fisher 284.
[564] Antelman 21.
[565] Antelman 17.
[566] Antelman.
[567] Antelman 25.
[568] Antelman 42.
[569] Antelman 27-28.

Reform Judaism began to open Jewish schools in which the professors could implant the seeds of destruction against their own religion. "They conceived the idea of developing their own network of rabbinical seminaries to ordain their own fraudulent rabbis," says Rabbi Antelman.[570] Antelman further confirms that the Bund in Grand Orient Freemasonry "had planned to build a seminary to be in Geiger's name which would educate and train more phony rabbis for the Reform movement."[571] These same men also laid the groundwork for government sponsored secular schools.[572]

After 1870, when the anti-Semitic Jewish Reform was in its glory, Rabbi Antelman notes that the non-Reform religious Jews became known as the Orthodoxy: "The term Orthodox was to be used as a bigoted derogatory term in the same manner that a white bigot would employ the term nigger. This was in the best tradition of Marx and his Bund sponsors. It should be noted that Marx used the term nigger to indeed degrade all Jews when he published another one of his anti-Semitic diatribes entitled, *The Jewish Nigger*."[573]

In his final condemnation of Karl Marx, Antelman remarks: "Marx's anti-Semitic outlook bore a relationship to... Reform or Conservative movement leaders, [whose] profound hatred for Torah, true Judaism, the Talmud and the rabbis... unfortunately, manifests itself to this very day among large segments of the leadership of the Conservative and Reform movements throughout the Diaspora."[574]

FREDERICK ENGELS, FOUNDER OF "MARXISM"

The life of Karl Marx serves as another example of how anti-Semitic Gentile Freemasonry uses and abuses Jews to front its revolutions.

Every activity of Marx was controlled by a Gentile Freemason, Frederick Engels (1820-1895). Engels, an unlikely subject to become involved in the so-called "revolution of the proletariat," was born to a wealthy Gentile textile mill owner in the Rhineland of Germany. At a young age Engels joined *Young Germany*, which had been established in Switzerland in 1835 at the behest of Freemason Giuseppe Mazzini, an Italian revolutionary, and Freemason Henry Palmerston, at that time Great Britain's foreign minister. Switzerland became the Grand Orient training ground for young Engels.[575] Later in life he joined the Scottish Rite, working his way up to the 32nd degree.

Engels loved journalism, having studied it before graduating from Elberfeld Gymnasium in 1837. Anton Chaitkin, the Jewish author of *Treason in America*, notes that Engels' first major piece of journalism, *Letters from Wuppertal*, appeared early in 1839 in the Hamburg organ of Young Germany, *Telegraph fur Deutschland*. In this sarcastic attack on his home town, Engels blamed poverty, sickness, illiteracy, superstition, drunkenness, and general ugliness, not on the low level of industrial and scientific development, but on "factory work" itself. He also called for atheism as a means of freeing popular consciousness.

Engels spent a year in the Prussian military service, simultaneously immersing himself in the Young Hegelian movement. In 1842 he met the radical democrat Karl

---

[570] Antelman 27.
[571] Antelman 41.
[572] Antelman 23.
[573] Antelman 30.
[574] Antelman 111.
[575] Anton Chaitkin, *Treason in America* (New York: New Benjamin Franklin House, 1985) 290, 291, 293.

Marx, who was then editing the *Rheinische Zeitung* and looking for some new doctrine out of the orbit of Hegel and Young Germany.[576]

In 1842 Engels came of age and was sent to England by his father to train for the position of overall manager of the family's Manchester textile mill. In 1843 he published in Germany his first work on economics, "Outlines of a Critique of Political Economy." In this article Engels attacked Christianity, and "like oppressors."[577]

Engels did not become famous until 1844 when the Deutsche*Franzosische Jarbucher* printed his homage to Thomas Carlyle, the Scottish essayist and historian. Quoting from Carlyle's *Past and Present* on the ultimate solution to man's oppression, Engels wrote that work would make men free: "Who art thou that complainest of thy life of toil? Complain not."[578]

His review of Carlyle is not what won Engels fame - rather, it was the influence of the communist Freemasons who read it. Lord Palmerston became Engels' Masonic promoter and saw that Engels' fame spread throughout Germany via the Masonic-controlled *Jarbucher*, the newspaper co-edited by Karl Marx and Palmerston agent Arnold Ruge.[579] Engels was to develop a doctrine for the communist movement. The Masonic media would promote it.

In Engels' opinion the articles he had written on economics were far superior to his review of Carlyle. He resented the fact that his reputation had been made on what he considered an inferior work. He wrote to Marx, "It is ridiculous that my article about Carlyle should have won me a terrific fame with the 'mass.'"[580]

Obviously, Engels did not realize at that time to whom or what he owed his fame. Freemasonry was promoting him for the greater communist cause. The Continental Brotherhood knew that only a few radicals would read Engels' economics in Young Germany literature. To make a name for Engels, a broader reader base was needed. Carlyle was already famous. Engels would be made famous through Carlyle's work. Anton Chaitkin explains:

> It was now to be Frederick Engels' job to "translate" Carlyle's viewpoint, dressing up feudalism in Hegelian clothes for the edification of German revolutionaries. Thus armed, equipped with a reputation, he now returned to the Continent for a time, meeting Marx in Paris and fastening upon his [sic] as a useful instrument for the propagation of a new doctrine. Marx, the young revolutionary in exile from Germany, was overwhelmed by the economic erudition of Engels' Critique. When Engels then published The Condition of the Working Class in England in 1844, Marx was wholly won over to what should rightfully be called "Engelsism."[581]

Engels, not Marx, was the father of Marxism. Gentile Templar Freemasonry did not intend for its own, especially its wealthy, to be seen as promoters of communism. The left-wing Grand Orient Masons were not developing a system for personal gain, but rather for the future Templar global government. To protect themselves from exposure, Karl Marx "the Jew" was a fit comrade to shoulder Engels' philosophy of communism. At Engels' urging then, and under his tutelage, Karl Marx began to publish the former's

---

[576] Chaitkin 295-296.
[577] Chaitkin 298.
[578] Chaitkin 300.
[579] Chaitkin 299.
[580] Chaitkin.
[581] Chaitkin 300.

communist philosophy. Should there be a backlash, the Jews would be blamed - not Gentile Freemasonry. (See Appendix 2, Fig. 33.)

Marx was more than willing to put his fellow Jews at risk, for he hated his heritage. According to Rabbi Antelman, two of Marx's anti-Semitic works were *A World Without Jews* and *The Jewish Nigger*.[582] When Marx produced this screed for Illuminist Freemason Horace Greeley's *New York Tribune*, Antelman quotes Marx as saying, "Thus we find every tyrant backed by a Jew." In 1856, when he wrote for Greeley on supposed Jewish control of banking, Marx remarked, "'Thus do these loans which are a curse to the people, a ruin to the government become a blessing to the house of Judah. This Jewish organization of loan mongers is as dangerous to the people as the aristocratic organization of landowners."[583]

Marx never held a regular job. When he submitted articles to the *New York Tribune*, articles actually written by Engels, he received a pound or two for each. Marx was paid pennies for another series of Engels' rewrites submitted to the Masonic-trained Foreign Office official David Urguhart.[584]

Realizing in destitute Marx a potential martyr for the communist cause, Engels brought him to England where his subservience was further enforced by a slave-like existence. Left-wing Grand Orient Freemasonry planned to exploit this Jew, using Marx as their mouthpiece to blame the sad state of affairs of the poor on the British Masonic system of capitalism.

It may come as a surprise to many to learn that Engels did not hate capitalism. After all, he was a product of it. What he loathed was the British Masonic oligarchy. From its inception, left-wing French Freemasonry was bent on destroying right-wing English Freemasonry. Since capitalism was synonymous with the British Brotherhood, one must destroy capitalism to destroy the Masonic oligarchy. Communism would be the tool of that destruction.

Marx was only one Jew in a long line of Jews who would be exploited to help accomplish this task. He was intentionally kept poor. Other than a few pennies for some articles he himself did not write, Marx's only other source of income came by way of philanthropic "contributions" from Engels, which amounted to a measly sum of 70 pounds sterling per year, with a low one year of 10 pounds. In comparison, Engels himself drew an annual salary from his family firm of 4,000 pounds sterling. If Engels was so fond of Marx, he certainly would have paid him enough to survive, for Marx's family was starving. Two of his children died of malnutrition and another committed suicide.

The most famous work attributed to Karl Marx is the *Communist Manifesto*. Supposedly written in 1848, it was actually a rewrite of an earlier Engels' piece entitled *Confessions of a Communist*. Of the Marx Engels relationship, Chaitkin writes: "This was to be the pattern. The Cotton Prince [Engels] would write a draft, or simply make a suggestion for the appropriate theme of a work, and pass it along to Marx to put it in 'good revolutionary form.'"[585]

The Templar scheme was working. Karl Marx, the Jew, would be called the "Father of Communism," not Gentile Engels, and definitely not Grand Orient Freemasonry. The so-called "evils" of capitalism would be the whipping boy of communism. Jews would be blamed if the communist conspiracy were ever exposed. In 1848 France experienced the world's first Communist Revolution.

---

[582] Antelman 21, 30.
[583] Antelman 21-22.
[584] Chaitkin 303.
[585] Chaitkin 303.

THE EDUCATIONAL LEGACY OF KARL MARX

As we have seen, from 1842 to 1848 the real voice behind Marx was Frederick Engels. Engels, like Marx, sought to exclude religion from public life and education: "All religious bodies without exception are to be treated by the state as private associations. They are not to receive support from public funds or exercise any influence over public education."[586]

After creating so much havoc in Germany, Karl Marx was forced to leave, finding refuge in France where his doctrines were introduced in the Grand Orient lodges there. While Engels was in England managing his father's expanding textile business, Marx traveled between Paris and London to visit him, finally residing in London until his death in 1883.

Marx, however, left his mark in France. On May 1, *1865*, the 89th anniversary of the founding of the Illuminati, a French Masonic publication, *Monde Maconnique*, proclaimed that "An immense field is open to our activity. Ignorance and superstition [buzz-words for Christianity weigh upon the world. Let us seek to create schools, professorial chairs, libraries."[587]

Just five years later, in 1870, the French Masonic Convention came to the following unanimous decision: "The Masonry of France associates itself to the forces at work in the country to render education gratuitous, obligatory, and laic."[588] And during a Belgian Masonic festival, a certain brother Boulard exclaimed in a speech, "When ministers shall come to announce to the country that they intend to regulate the education of the people I will cry aloud, 'to me a Mason, to me alone the question of education must be left; to me the teaching; to me the examination; to me the solution.'"[589]

Marx also left his mark in England. Dr. Dillon confirms that during the administration of British Prime Minister Henry Palmerston, a 33rd degree Mason, an attempt was made in the 1860s to introduce secularism "into higher education in Ireland by Queen's Colleges, and into primary education by certain acts of the Board of National Education."[590] Both were defeated by the predominantly Catholic body.

The introduction of secularism into higher education, was, however, successful in England. Dr. Dillon wrote in 1885: "There, by degrees, board schools with almost unlimited assistance from taxes have been first made legal, and then encouraged most adroitly. The Church schools have been systematically discouraged, and have now reached the point of danger. This has been directed, first, by the Masonry of Palmerston in the higher places, and secondly by the Masonry of England generally..."[591]

Marx's legacy extended to Italy. During a Masonic congress held at Milan in 1881, the following resolution was adopted: "The suppression of all religious instruction in the schools: The creation of schools for young girls where the pupils can be protected from any kind of clerical influence."[592]

After Benito Mussolini took power in Italy in 1922, and outlawed Freemasonry in 1923, he returned some rights to the Vatican. And in 1924 there was a revival in France of relations with the Vatican. Alarmed, the French Grand Lodge wrote, "if this renewal,

---

[586] Fisher 284.
[587] Dillon 80.
[588] "Laic" comes from the Greek "laikos," meaning "of the people." Laicism means "a political system characterized by the exclusion of ecclesiastical control and influence." Laicization means "to put under the direction of or open to laymen."
[589] Dillon.
[590] Dillon 81.
[591] Dillon.
[592] Miller 282, 285.

as we fear, takes place, it will begin a movement of regression against the laws of laicisation which we have had so much trouble to get passed by the Chamber... It is in the defense of the school and of the spirit of laicism that we will find the programme which can and should bind together the whole Republican party."[593]

In 1928 the Sixth World Congress of the Communist International echoed the anti-religious credo of Marx and Engels when it said: "One of the most important tasks of the cultural revolution affecting the wide masses is the task of systematically and unswervingly combatting religion - the opium [opiate] of the people. The proletarian government must withdraw all state support from the church, which is the agency of the former ruling class; it must prevent all church interference in state-organized educational affairs, and ruthlessly suppress the counter- revolutionary activity of the ecclesiastical organisations."[594]

MASONIC PUBLIC SCHOOLS IN AMERICA

American Freemasonry was involved in free secular education from the beginning of our Republic. *Mackey's Encyclopedia of Freemasonry* provides a complete history of masonic involvement in the creation of the American system of public education.

In "Freemasonry and Public Schools" Mackey reports on all the Masonic educational activity during the 1800s, including the founding of Masonic colleges and fraternities. In 1809 in New York state, "Brother Dewitt Clinton founded the New York Free School Society, which later became the Public School Society of New York... He was Chairman of the Board of Trustees and very active until his death in 1828.[595] Clinton was also a member of the American branch of the Illuminati. He served as Grand Master of the New York Lodge from 1806 to 1820 and was for eight years Governor of New York State.

Mackey tells how state funding of schools evolved: "The Free School was from the start supported by voluntary donations, but as the legislature began to recognize the value of the work that was accomplished, sums of money were granted. About the end of 1817 the Free School was formally established under the supervision of the State and further support from the Masonic Fraternity was no longer required."[596]

By the mid-1850s Freemasonry began a drive to control school teachers by the establishment of a professional association for the same. The Scottish Rite was the primary force behind the founding of the National Education Association (NEA) in 1857, which today is a powerful professional union and political lobby.[597]

After World War I, American Freemasonry began lobbying the Federal government for federally-funded public schools. *Mackey's Encyclopedia of Freemasonry* outlines the story: "The Supreme Council Southern Jurisdiction, United States of America, Ancient and Accepted Scottish Rite in 1920 openly declared itself in favor of the creation of a Department of Education with a Secretary in the President's Cabinet..." Mackey further informs us that the Scottish Rite was responsible for "the passage of what was then known as the Smith-Tower Educational Bill embodying the principle of Federal Aid to the Public Schools in order to provide funds for the equalization of educational opportunities to the children of the nation. The Brethren declared their belief in the compulsory attendance of all children upon the Public Schools..."[598]

---

[593] Léon de Poncins, *Freemasonry and the Vatican* 60-61.
[594] Fisher 284.
[595] "Public Schools," *Mackey's Encyclopedia of Freemasonry*, vol. II.
[596] "Public Schools."
[597] Fisher 144.
[598] "Public Schools."

In this article, Mackey reminds the Brotherhood that when compulsory education becomes a reality, Masons are to encourage parents to make the schools so efficient "that their superiority over all other schools [meaning Church schools I shall be so obvious that every parent will have to send his children to them..."[599]

In the 1920s, 33rd degree Mason Earl Warren was Grand Master of the Grand Lodge of California, and had not yet received his appointment as Chief Justice to the Supreme Court. In his 1936 annual message to the Brethren in California, he said, the education of our youth... can best be done, indeed it can only be done, by a system of free public education. It is for this reason that the Grand Lodge of California, ever striving as it does to replace darkness with light, is so vitally interested in the public schools of our state...

By destroying prejudice [christianity] and planting reason in its place it prepares the foundation of a liberty-loving people for free government...

THE MASONIC WAR AGAINST CHURCH, PARENTS, AND CHILDREN

Investigative journalist Paul Fisher has summarized the goals of Freemasonry in America in creating and promoting a system of compulsory public education: "(1) The destruction of all social influence by the Church and religion generally, either by open persecution or by so-called separation of Church and State; (2) To laicize or secularize all public and private life and, above all, popular education; and (3) To systematically develop freedom of thought and conscience in school children, and protect them, so far as possible, against all disturbing influences of the Church, and even their own parents - by compulsion if necessary."[600]

According to Fisher, this plan was launched on a grand scale when on September 24, 1924, the Scottish Rite Supreme Council met at Charleston, S.C. The Masonic monthly magazine, *New Age*, published the Grand Commander's "Allocution" in the October issue that year:

"Through the activities of our state organizations, the *New Age* magazine, our clip service and News Bureau, we are stimulating the public interest and furnishing much valuable material to speakers and writers, and thereby can reasonably claim much credit for the growing interest in favor of compulsory education by the state."[601]

The same Scottish Rite publication in April 1934 "advocated the public school as the 'only agency' capable of fusing various peoples, tongues and customs; and where it is noted that Masonry was the pioneer in advocating a federal Department of Education."[602]

When World War II began, there was a renewed interest on public school campuses in praying and studying the Bible. In Illinois "release time" was granted by state law. A Mason fought the law all the way to the Supreme Court where *McCollum vs. Board of Education* was heard. The Scottish Rite Supreme Council went to work on McCollum's behalf. Twenty-four articles opposing release time for religious education appeared in the Scottish Rite *New Age* magazine between February 1941, and January 1948. Masons around the nation began attacking the notion of and movement for release time. Justice Black, a 33rd degree Mason, spoke for the majority of the Supreme Court and in 1963 the Illinois State law was struck down.[603]

---

[599] "Public Schools."
[600] Fisher 40.
[601] Fisher 242.
[602] Fisher 293.
[603] Fisher 172, 310, 318.

In 1944 Freemasonry lost a major educational battle when the Servicemen's Readjustment Act, better known as "The G.I. Bill Of Rights," was passed. Paul Fisher says, "The new law provided a wide range of benefits for returning veterans, including virtually free education in the school of the returning serviceman's choice - even in religious seminaries. It was a devastating blow to Masonry's efforts to deny government assistance to 'sectarian' institutions."[604] Fisher lends four pages of documentation to Freemasonry's fight against the Bill.

Upon losing this battle, Freemasonry retaliated. Fisher notes that "Soon thereafter, on January 9, 10, 1945, legislation sponsored by the National Education Association (NEA) - an organization that historically has been closely tied to Scottish Rite Freemasonry - was introduced in the House and Senate. It provided substantial funds for public education, but made no provision for assisting non-public schools."[605] Fisher further documents that the Supreme Council of the Scottish Rite funded the propaganda for passage of this bill.

Freemasonry had its agents everywhere. At this time the National Education Association's Executive Secretary of almost twenty years (from 1935) was 33rd degree Mason, Willard E. Givens. His mission was to consolidate the control of education by the NEA. In *Freemasonry, Antichrist Upon Us*, published in 1957 by an organization called Fragments of Truth at Elon College, North Carolina, we read:

> When the program of Education For A New America was firmly established in the public schools and the NEA-control of education an undisputed fact, 33rd degree Mason, Willard E. Givens resigned as Executive Secretary of the NEA to take over the Educational Program of the prestigious Supreme Council 33 degrees of the Scottish Rite of Freemasonry.[606]

Freemasonry mounted another attack. The mind control tactics required to teach atheism and globalism, which is necessary to successfully inaugurate the future godless one-world government, could not be taught in rural schools where curriculum was controlled by parents. Consolidation was the Scottish Rite's next order of attack against parental influence. Freemasonry sent former Harvard University President James B. Conant (33rd degree Mason, member of NEA's Educational Policies Commission, and member of the Council on Foreign Relations) on a speaking tour. Fragments of Truth tells the story:

> When the massive school building program was being launched early in the 1950's, Dr. James B. Conant was commissioned to tour the country in behalf of school consolidation.
> A summary of Dr. Conant's recommendations was published in booklet form and sent out by the Supreme Council of Scottish Rite to top leaders in 35 southern and western states.[607]

With Masonic propaganda preceding Dr. Conant's tour he was assured large audiences wherever he spoke. In every meeting the audience was peppered with Masons from that particular jurisdiction - Masons awaiting orders from their Grand Master. Following Conant's tour, each of the 35 Grand Lodge jurisdictions ordered its Masonic

---

[604] Fisher 141.
[605] Fisher 144.
[606] *Freemasonry: Antichrist Upon Us* (Elon College, NC:Fragments of Truth, late 1950s) 77-78.
[607] *Antichrist Upon Us*.

constituency in all walks of life to talk positively of consolidation in their work, churches and bars. As a result parents everywhere marched to the polls and voted to surrender their control. Consolidation of 259,000 school districts into 1,600 became a reality.[608]

After consolidation parents were no longer intimate with teachers. As planned, both became alienated by the larger body, the NEA. Gradually but surely the Masonic-controlled NEA became adversarial towards parents. Although the PTA was formed to bridge the gap, it pales in strength to Freemasonry's revolutionary teachers' union.

In the March, 1959 issue of the Scottish Rite's *New Age* magazine, Freemasonry praised the efforts of Masons who were responsible for this educational coup d'etat:

> *[E]very Mason becomes a teacher of "Masonic philosophy to the community," and the Craft is "the missionary of the new order - a Liberal order... in which Masons become high priests."*
>
> *[We proclaim] that this "Masonic philosophy" which has brought forth a "New Order" [has] become a reality by "the establishment of the public school system, financed by the State, for the combined purpose of technological and sociological education of the mass of humanity, beginning at an early age in childhood."[609]*

With parents no longer in control of schools and curriculum, the Masonic-created and -funded NEA went to work on the minds of our children. Former NEA president, Katherine Barrett articulated the new revolutionary role of teachers: "the teacher will be the conveyor of values, a philosopher. Teachers no longer will be victims of change [meaning controlled by parents]; we will be agents of change."[610]

In the same decade as consolidation, Freemasonry began selecting the textbooks that were to be used in the new public school system.

The February 1959 issue of the *New Age* magazine announced an "Evolution of American Education" to Masons throughout the nation and "mandated that members of the Fraternity disseminate Masonic materials in public schools." They were instructed to "take that role seriously."[611] And indeed they did. Fisher gives a few examples of their diligence:

> *In 1959...Franklin W. Patterson, 33rd Degree, secretary of the Scottish Rite Lodge at Baker, Oregon, succeeded in persuading the principal of the local high school to use Masonic- oriented texts in the local public schools. Also, the Scottish Rite bodies of Alexandria, Virginia "placed the New Age magazine in all public school libraries within their jurisdiction."*
>
> *In 1964, Grand Commander Luther A. Smith reported that Masonic booklets had been "distributed by sets to every room in every school" in the Charlotte County, North Carolina public school system. The Superintendent of Schools for that jurisdiction made the Masonic propaganda "required reading."*
>
> *In 1965, Major General Herman Nickerson, 33rd Degree, Commander of the U.S. Marine Corps facility at Camp Lejune, N.C., was commended by the Supreme Council for introducing the Supreme Council's books on "Americanism"*

---

[608] *Word of Life* quarterly (Winter 1990) 24.

[609] Fisher 56-57.

[610] Ralph A. Epperson, *The Unseen Hand* (Tucson, AZ: Publius Press, 1985) 490.

[611] Fisher 57.

into the schools under his command attended by children of Marine Corps personnel.[612]

Freemasonry implemented three of four steps required before our schools could be regarded as atheistic. They (1) preached consolidation; (2) wrested control of education from parents, placing it in the hands of its militant minion, the NEA; and (3) placed its own textbooks in the schools. The fourth and final Masonic blow against Christianity being taught in the classroom, says Fisher, was the 1962/1963 Supreme Court decision outlawing Bible reading and prayers in public schools.[613] Six of the nine Supreme Court Justices were Masons.

Five years later 33rd degree Mason Leonard A. Wenz gloated over Masonry's success in an article, "Masonry And The Bible," written for the *New Age* magazine, February, 1968. Following is an excerpt:

> *The keynote of Masonic religious thinking is naturalism which sees all life and thought as ever developing and evolutionary... The Bible is not today what it once was. Current higher criticism has made obsolete the idea that the Bible is a unique revelation of supernatural truth.[614]*

A few Christian parents, recognizing the atheistic propaganda taught their children, encouraged their fundamentalist and evangelical churches to start private schools. Alarmed that Christian education might persevere and even flourish, 33rd degree Mason Dr. James B. Conant stated:

> *I do believe... there is some reason to fear lest a dual system of secondary education may in some states, at least, come to threaten the democratic unity provided by our public schools.*
>
> *I refer to the desire of some people to increase the scope and number of private schools...*
>
> *To my mind, our schools serve all creeds. The greater the portion of our youth who attend independent schools, the greater the threat to our democratic unity.[615]*

Conant is clearly setting the atheistic education of the Masonic agenda against the education inspired and formed by Christianity and its doctrine. He obviously fears that Christians ("some people") will found enough "independent" schools to constitute a "threat" to Masonic designs, both religious and political.

Dr. Conant further spreads Masonic disinformation by claiming American public schools "serve all creeds." As parents and other concerned citizens so ruefully see today, Freemasonry has effectively banished the creed of Christians from public schools. The Masonic Lodge has replaced Christianity with the evolutionary and atheistic creed of Mystery Babylon.

---

[612] Fisher.
[613] Fisher 56.
[614] Fisher 57.
[615] Epperson 387-388.

MASONS IN THE CHURCHES

As Christians became lukewarm in old France prior to the disastrous French Revolution, so they are in America today. Our "Laodicean" churches are no longer able to mount, much less sustain a fight for righteousness. A survey published in August 1988 by the Association of North American Missions indicts the church. It revealed that most Christians care little about the needs of the Church. "People are placing a higher value on their life-styles than on their church."[616]

This attitude of selfishness and indifference to God's work through the church flourishes because our churches have been penetrated by materialistic Masons. Tom C. McKenney, coauthor of *The Deadly Deception*, reveals a shocking statistic. In July 1989 the author attended a lecture in which McKenney named the two largest Protestant denominations in the United States, and said, 'Through our best estimates, 90 percent of one and 70 percent of the other have pastors who are members of the Masonic Lodge."[617]

Masonic penetration of our churches began at the turn of the 20th century. Myron Fagan, in *The Illuminati*, tells how this effectual take-over was accomplished.

According to Fagan, at the end of the 19th century, Grand Orient Freemasonry deliberately sent Jacob Schiff (son of a Reform Rabbi born in Frankfurt, Germany) to the United States to carry out four specific assignments. The first was to acquire control of America's money system. This was accomplished by founding the Federal Reserve System. The second was to find desirable men who, for a price, would willingly serve as stooges for the great conspiracy. Once found they would be promoted to federal positions in the Congress, on the U.S. Supreme Court, and at all Federal agencies. The agency founded for grooming these men is the Council on Foreign Relations (CFR). The third was to create minority group strife throughout the nation, particularly between whites and blacks. The National Association for the Advancement of Colored People (NAACP) was founded for that purpose. The fourth was to create a movement to destroy religion in the United States, with Christianity as the chief target. This became the task of the National Council of Churches (NCC).[618]

Jacob Schiffs background suited him ideally to his assignment in America. As Rabbi Antelman remarks, "It was Jacob Schiff and his family who played a prominent role in developing the Reform and Conservative apostate Jewish movements and who aided them at critical stages of their development in putting into action the demonic master plan [sic] to undermine all world religions. Fragmentation and divide and conquer tactics were the order of the day."[619]

According to Myron Fagan, Schiff was helped in his first three assignments by several anti- Semitic and anti-Christian Grand Orient Freemasons. Fagan details how Masonic money and power backed Jacob Schiff and established for the German House of Warburg a banking system in America, with J.P. Morgan and John D. Rockefeller as front men.

---

[616] Association of North American Missions' 1985 annual report.

[617] Tom McKenney, author of *The Deadly Deception*, did not say how he arrived at these estimates. Most recent figures for the Southern Baptists were reported at their June 1992 annual convention. Spokesmen at the convention stated that there are 1.3 million Masons who are members of the Southern Baptist Churches and an estimated 14 percent of the Southern Baptist pastors are Masons. (See Appendix 9 for Protestant churches that have denounced Freemasonry.)

[618] The Illuminati, narr. Myron Fagan, two audio cassettes, rec.1967.

[619] Antelman 26-27.

Dr. Carroll Quigley, in *Tragedy And Hope,* concurs with Fagan.[620] As well does Rabbi Antelman.[621]

THE NATIONAL COUNCIL OF CHURCHES

Jacob Schiff, nearing death, did not have enough time to accomplish the destruction of the church in America, his fourth and final assignment He selected Rockefeller to finance and direct an institution to that end. Fagan tells how young men were selected for the ministry and then taught how to dilute the Christian message:

> *The destruction of Christianity could be accomplished only by those who are entrusted to preserve it, by the pastors, the men of the cloth. As a starter, John D. Rockefeller picked up a young, so-called Christian minister by the name of Dr. Harry F. Ward. At the time he was teaching religion at the Union Theological Seminary. Thereupon, in 1907, he financed him to set up the Methodist Foundation of Social Service, and Ward's job was to teach bright, young men to become so-called ministers of Christ and to place them as pastors of churches. While teaching them to become ministers, the Reverend Ward also taught them how to very subtly and craftily preach to their congregations that the entire story of Christ is a myth, to cast doubts on the divinity of Christ, to cast doubts about the Virgin Mary. In short, to cast doubts on Christianity as a whole. It was not to be a direct attack, but much of it by crafty insinuation that was to be applied, in particular, to the youth in the Sunday schools.*
>
> *Then, in 1908, the Methodist foundation of Social Service changed its name to the Federal Council of Churches. By 1950, the Federal Council of Churches was becoming very suspect as being a Communist front, so they changed the name to the National Council of Churches. From this was created the World Council of Churches.[622]*

The communist activity of this Masonic front did not cease with its many name changes. *Reader's Digest,* January 1983, documents that both the National Council of Churches and World Council of Churches have funded communists and terrorists. The title of the six-page article asks the question, "Do You Know Where Your Church Offerings Go?" Without naming Freemasonry, the article depicts how well-meaning Christians have been duped into funding Masonry's anti-Christ revolution:

> *Over a two-year period $442,000 in Methodist churchgoer's money alone had been sent to a number of political organizations, among them... "groups supporting the Palestine Liberation Organization, the governments of Cuba and Vietnam, the pro-Soviet totalitarian movements of Latin America, Asia and Africa, and several violence prone fringe groups in the United States."[623]*

---

[620] Carroll Quigley, *Tragedy and Hope: A History of the world in our time* (1966; Los Angeles: Angriff Press, 1974) 5.

[621] Antelman 26.

[622] Fagan 28.

[623] Rael Jean Isaac, "Do You Know Where Your Church Offerings Go?" *Reader's Digest* (January 1983) 120.

In 1980 churchgoers, responding to hunger appeals, raised over $650,000. The fund-raising project typically showed a photograph of needy children. But, a significant portion of the money went to political activists.[624]

In 1983, according to the *Reader's Digest* article: "The NCC consist[ed] of 32 Protestant and Orthodox communions representing 40 million Christians (Southern Baptists and Catholics are the largest churches that do not belong to the NCC). The Methodist Church, with nine million members, is the largest denomination in the NCC and its chief contributor. After the Methodists, with their 1980 contribution of close to $8 million, come the United Presbyterians with nearly $3 million, followed by the United Church of Christ, with close to $2 million, and the Disciples of Christ and the Episcopal Church, each of which contributes over $1 million."[625]

Church World Service, an arm of the National Council of Churches, engages in political advocacy and contributes churchgoer funds to programs designed to further strategic goals of governments with which CWS leaders sympathize. For example, CWS contributed nearly half a million dollars to Vietnam's concentration camps for "political undesirables." In 1973, at a time when Masonic Jesuits in South America began their "Liberation Theology," the CWS, likewise, embarked on a new direction committing funds to "liberation and justice."[626] If member pastors challenged where these funds were going, they were "punished, some actually forced out of the church."[627]

As might be expected, the article reports that the president of the NCC from 1979 to 1981 embarked on a series of visits to those he described as U.S. "political prisoners."[628] The organization that helped him in selecting which prisoners to visit was listed by the CIA as an international Soviet front organization. *Reader's Digest* points out that many of the executives in the NCC believe that a just society is possible only under communism. Yet, most of the great communist human-rights outrages of our time have never been condemned by the NCC's governing board.

Conversely, the NCC governing board has censured El Salvador, Turkey, Nicaragua (under Somoza), Chile, South Korea and Guatemala, whose violations cannot be compared to those of communist countries the NCC governing board has ignored. Worse yet, the NCC identified several of the communist countries with the worst record on human rights as models for Christians. Cuba, for example, was considered by the NCC as a nation "we believe can inform Christians around the world with a new intensity and depth of insight about the meaning of faith."[629]

The NCC claims that Cuba allows full freedom of worship. Yet, according to the article, no mention was made that "Cuban children are indoctrinated in atheism in schools, and that no one who professes belief in God can be a member of the Communist Party or advance in his career."[630]

GOD: ANDROGYNOUS/NEUTERED

Not only has the National Council of Churches funded Communist revolutions with offerings from churchgoers, it has rewritten the Bible to conform to the Whore of Babylon's male/female- god religion. The first step is to neuter God. James Kilpatrick, in

---

[624] "Church Offerings" 124.
[625] "Church Offerings" 121.
[626] "Church Offerings."
[627] "Church Offerings" 125.
[628] "Church Offerings" 121.
[629] "Church Offerings" 122.
[630] "Church Offerings" 123.

his October 23,1983, Universal Press Syndicate article, "Scriptures Change in Overhaul Job," wrote that "The National Council of Churches was out to take the sex out of Scripture." He added that the NCC is rewriting certain passages of Scripture in the Old and New Testaments "so as to eliminate references to gender, or as an alternative, to spread the gender around. Thus, Jesus no longer would be identified as the 'son' of God, but rather as the 'child' of God. In this egalitarian version, it is 'God the Father (and Mother)."

Member churches were not long in following the National Council of Churches. The largest contributor to NCC, as noted above, is the United Methodist Church. The Associated Press reported on December 10, 1983, that the governing body of the United Methodist Church in Nashville, Tennessee, had "approved guidelines on biblical and theological language that suggest that fewer male nouns and pronouns be used in referring to Jesus." By 1986 the blasphemy had become greater when in Denver, Colorado, the Rocky Mountain Region of the United Methodist Church "adopted a new policy prohibiting ministry' candidates from referring to God as exclusively male in church paperwork and interviews. The policy allows the 'historical' Jesus to be called He, but prohibits any exclusively male reference to a divine or messianic Jesus. The policy also calls for phrases such as Divine Light [a Masonic term] to be used in place of Father, King, or Lord. Candidates are allowed to refer to God as Mother and Father, or as He and She."[631]

"At the root of the problem," says Methodist evangelist Edmund Robb, "is the secularization of the church. The NCC has substituted revolution for religion.[632]

WHAT NEXT?

Not satisfied with their coup of main line churches, the Masonic dominated National Council of Churches is now forbidding Christian instruction of our youth in church child-care centers. An article in the May 9, 1989, *USA Today*, entitled "Church Issue Threatens Child-Care Bill," informs us that the National Council of Churches "supports a provision in the bill that says parents who receive federal subsidies may send their children to programs in churches that avoid religious instruction."

From the beginning the plan of Masonry was to syncretize all religions. Dr. John Coleman, a retired British intelligence officer, confirms that the World Council of Churches (WCC), which is an extension of the National Council of Churches, is dominated by Freemasons. In fact, the first president of the WCC, 1948-1954, was 33rd degree Freemason G. Bromley Oxnam, a Methodist Bishop. Coleman says that the WCC now practices witchcraft. In *Witchcraft in Politics*, Coleman states that the WCC's 6th Supreme Legislative Assembly met in Vancouver, B.C. on July 24 through August 12, 1983. There it was decided to donate funds to the study of the occult.[633]

Once the occult is studied - what next? The "Religion" section of *Time* magazine, May 22, 1989, presents the horrifying prospects. Dr. Richard Mouw, of California's Fuller Theological Seminary, is quoted in that article as saying that the mainline Churches

---

[631] *Omega-Letter* (Dec.1986) 3.

[632] "Church Offerings" 125.

[633] Witchcraft in Politics Today, narr. Dr. John Coleman, audio cassette, rec. 1984 and Denslow, *10,000 Famous Freemasons,* vol. III, 299.Coleman says that the WCC promotes the Masonic one-world doctrine in its magazine, *One World.* Denslow not only lists 33rd degree Freemason G. Bromley Oxnam as the first American president of the World Council of Churches, but adds that he was also president of the Federal Council of Churches (forerunner of the National Council of Churches) from 1944 to 1946 and was one of the presiding officers at the organization of the National Council of Churches at Cleveland, OH in 1950.

that are members of the NCC are now teaching "magic and the occult and the New Age. There's a return to a premodern world view."

Former 33rd degree Mason, Rev. Jim Shaw, exposes the link between Freemasonry and the National Council of Churches. Rev. Shaw stated in a sermon that the pastors in the National Council of Churches and the World Council of Churches are promoting Freemasonry. "I have served in the Lodge with them," said Shaw. "I have a list of many NCC pastors who are working for the Masonic monster with all the strength they have. They are not interested in the Lord Jesus Christ, though they pretend to be."[634] In another sermon Shaw adds, "A preacher in the National Council of Churches is really not 'in' until he is a Mason."[635]

LAICISM AND THE LAODICEAN CHURCH: THE REASON THERE IS NO REVIVAL

The word "secularism" is a synonym for "laicism," which comes from the word "Laodicea," the "lukewarm" church of Revelation 3:14-22. Freemasonry betrays itself as the organization responsible for the laodicean church age. The previous church age, referred to by Scripture as the church at Philadelphia, was commended by Christ for repulsing Masonic advances. For example, in Revelation 3:9, Christ says to the Philadelphia church: "I will make them of the synagogue of Satan, which say they are Jews, and are not, but do lie; behold, I will make them to come and worship before thy feet, and to know that I have loved thee."

Masonic penetration of the Philadelphia church, which transformed it into the secular church of the Laodicean age began over a half century ago and is recorded in the January 1926 issue of the Masonic *New Age* magazine. This Scottish Rite publication urged every member of the Craft to "cast his lot with the Church - to help vitalize it, liberalize it, modernize it and render it aggressive and efficient - to do less is treason to your country, to your Creator, and to the obligation you have promised to obey."[636]

These Masonic infiltrators then went to work on their pastors many of whom joined Freemasonry. *The Craft and the Clergy*, by 33rd degree Freemason, Rev. Dr. Forrest Haggard, interviews Protestant pastors and Jewish rabbis who have joined fellowship in the Lodge. All of them praise the Babylonian religion of Freemasonry. Also mentioned in Haggard's book is the fact that Bishop James A. Armstrong of the United Methodist Church, a former president of the National Council of Churches, is a Mason.[637]

The quotes below, taken from Dr. Haggard's book, are from a rabbi and two Protestant Pastors:

> *Religion and Masonry go hand in hand. The world cannot live without either. Where there is no peace and brotherliness, the study of the Bible diminishes. Where there is discord the spirit of Freemasonry cannot abide. Both seek a role where all men will recognize the fatherhood of God and the brotherhood of man. [Rabbi E.J. Block - Brotherhood Synagogue of New York City.]*[638]

---

[634] Pastors in the NCC who are in Freemasonry, narr. Rev. Jim Shaw, audio cassette.

[635] Kissing Jesus good-bye at the ALTAR OF BAAL, narr. Rev. Jim Shaw, audio cassette.

[636] Fisher 187, 324.

[637] Pastors in the NCC who are in Freemasonry, narr. Rev. Jim Shaw, audio cassette; quoting Forrest Haggard in *The Craft and the Clergy*.

[638] Pastors in the NCC.

I believe that the sense of universal brotherhood in Free-masonry is a very wholesome and meaningful fellowship for this day and age. Where there is so much divisiveness and suspicion in our world, we need the intermingling of men of many creeds and faiths, and Masonry provides this." [Roger L. Fredrickson - First Baptist Church, Sioux Falls, SD.]

I am in a mighty army of men who have committed themselves to minimize the importance of moral and ethical teachings. [Frank M. Bush - First Congregational Church, Salt Lake City, UT.]

PASTORS WITHOUT FAITH

What degenerative results have sixty-six years of conscientious and active Masonic penetration brought to our churches in America? The frightening statistics were gathered by the Jeffrey Hadden survey and published in the December 1987 *Pulpit Helps*, which reaches thousands of ministers. Questions were sent to some 10,000 Protestant clergymen, 7,441 replied. The questions, together with the percentages in the replies are as follows:

"Do you accept Jesus' physical resurrection as a fact? 51 percent of Methodists, 35 percent of United Presbyterians, 30 percent of Episcopalians, 33 percent of American Baptists, 13 percent of American Lutherans, and 7 percent of Missouri Synod Lutherans said 'No.'

"Do you believe in the virgin birth of Jesus? 60 percent of Methodists, 44 percent of Episcopalians, 49 percent of Presbyterians, 34 percent of Baptists, 19 percent of American Lutherans, and 5 percent of Missouri Synod Lutherans said 'No.'

"Do you believe in evil demon power in the world today? 62 percent of Methodists, 37 percent of Episcopalians, 47 percent of Presbyterians, 33 percent of Baptists, 14 percent of American Lutherans, and 9 percent of Missouri Synod Lutherans said 'No.'

"Do you believe that the Scriptures are the inspired and inerrant Word of God in faith, history and secular matters? 87 percent of Methodists, 95 percent of Episcopalians, 82 percent of Presbyterians, 67 percent of American Baptists, 77 percent of American Lutherans, and 24 percent of Missouri Synod Lutherans said 'No."[639]

Many of these so-called Pastors are Masons, trained to liberalize Christianity. This is the fruit of the strategy initiated at the turn of the 20th century when Freemason Jacob Schiff, as we have seen, was for that purpose sent to the United States by atheistic Grand Orient Freemasonry and supported from 1926 by the Southern Jurisdiction of Scottish Rite Freemasonry.

MASONS IN MY CHURCH?

Freemasonry has been so successful through its surrogates, the National Council of Churches and the World Council of Churches, in converting pastors to Masonry that no Christian dare ignore the possibility that his or her pastor may be a Mason.

Examine your Pastor. If he preaches "the fatherhood of God and the brotherhood of man," he is preaching Masonic doctrine - not the doctrine of Christ.

Examine the lay leaders in your church. When their prayers, or the prayers of the pastor, do not end "in Jesus' Name," but end in some alternate, such as "in Thy Name," or an abrupt "Amen," check them out. They may be Masons who do not believe in the Deity of our Lord and Savior, Jesus Christ. By not praying in Christ's name they are

---

[639] "A Falling Away First," *Omega-Letter* (March 1988) 5.

obeying Masonic Law. Most blasphemous are those who pray in the name of "The Great Architect of the Universe!" They are praying to our adversary, the Devil!

Examine your church. Is your pastor, or any of the lay leaders a Mason? You do not have to sit under their Laodicean blasphemy. They have pushed Christ outside the church door. Jesus is knocking for reentry (Revelation 3:20). Attend your annual congregational meeting, and after voting the rascals out, vote Christ back in. Before you call for a new pastor, make sure you investigate to see if he is affiliated with Freemasonry.

Examine your denomination. If there is a struggle between liberal and conservative leadership in the hierarchy, just count those liberal troublemakers and see how many of them are Masons! Become a delegate to your annual church convention and vote the rascals outs!

Finally, if your church is a member of the National Council of Churches, whose funds are channelled to the World Council of Churches, Myron Fagan says, "Your contributions are helping illuminated Freemasonry's plot to destroy religion and your faith in God and Jesus Christ. Thus, you are deliberately delivering your children to be indoctrinated with disbelief in God and church, and which can easily transform them into atheists. Find out immediately if your church is a member of the National Council of Churches and, for the love of God and your children, if it is, withdraw from it at once."[640]

CHRIST'S JUDGEMENT

Most abominable are pastors who become Masons. Former 33rd degree Mason, Rev. Jim Shaw calls them "priests of Baal." Christ condemns them even more strongly. When He walked the earth, the Jewish priesthood had fallen into the same mystic trap. Jesus gave an eternal warning to those apostate leaders in Matthew 23: 14b, 33:

> *"therefore ye shall receive the greater damnation... Ye serpents, ye generation of vipers, how can ye escape the damnation of hell?"*

On the day of judgement so-called ministers of God's Word will stand before our Lord and Savior. They will be required to give an accounting to the Messiah they denied. Jesus will respond to their pleading: "I never knew you: depart from me, ye that work iniquity" (Matthew 7:23).

Freemasonry has taken over some of the mainline churches of America. And our time is the time of the lukewarm Laodicean church age - the last period of the church before Christ returns. We have pushed our Savior outside the door (Revelation 3:20). Without His help we cannot defend against the Masonic scourge. Consequently, we not only find Masonic controlled secular education in our public school Systems, but in our churches as well.

PLANNING THE DESTRUCTION OF CHRISTIANITY

The blueprint to destroy the Church through this means was drawn up over two hundred years ago by Adam Weishaupt, who has been called "The Human Devil." Whether Weishaupt received it from Voltaire or Frederick the Great is not known. Nesta Webster suggests some connection when she notes that "The resemblances between

---

[640] Fagan.

Weishaupt's correspondence and that of Voltaire and of Frederick the Great are certainly very striking."[641]

You recall that from 1750-1755 Voltaire was a guest at Frederick's court.[642] Monsignor Dillon wrote of that visit:

> [Voltaire] sketched out for them the whole mode of procedure against the Church. His policy as revealed by the correspondence of Frederick II, and others with him, was not to commence an immediate persecution, but first to suppress the Jesuits and all Religious orders, and to secularize their goods; then to deprive the Pope of temporal authority, and the Church of property and state recognition. Primary and higher-class education of a lay and Infidel [sic] character was to be established, the principle of divorce affirmed, and respect for ecclesiastics lessened and destroyed. Lastly, when the whole body of the Church should be sufficiently weakened and Infidelity [sic] strong enough, the final blow was to be dealt by the sword of open, relentless persecution. A reign of terror was to spread over the whole earth, and to continue while a Christian should be found obstinate enough to adhere to Christianity. This, of course, was to be followed by a Universal Brotherhood without marriage, family property, God, or law...[643]

Weishaupt took up the cause of Voltaire, providing the vehicle by which the plan would be carried to future generations. When Weishaupt penetrated Freemasonry with illuminism, the Lodge took up the cause, citing Voltaire as a patron. Miller explains in Occult Theocrasy that after the 1789-1793 destruction of old France, and subsequent to the reign of Napoleon, Grand Orient Freemasonry's aim was the same as Voltaire's. From the minutes of the Italian Masonic Lodge, *Permanent Instructions, or Practical Code of Rules: Guide for the Heads of the Highest Grades of Masonry,* Miller quotes: "Our final aim is that of Voltaire and of the French Revolution - the complete annihilation of Catholicism, and ultimately of Christianity... Under this cloak [of Freemasonry], we may conspire at our convenience, and arrive, little by little, at our ultimate aim."[644]

The Masonic Lodge ever since has been bent on the destruction of our families, our churches, our nation, our world, and our God. Freemasonry's ultimate aim is a one-world humanistic government without Christ and His Church. Obviously, the Masonic Lodge is still carrying out Voltaire's plan.

Freemason Voltaire, born fifty-four years before Weishaupt, had laid the groundwork for insurrection. Weishaupt advanced it. Perceiving an eminent revolution in France, which had long been agitating French Masons, Weishaupt saw and took his chance to impose the doctrines of the Illuminati on the existing French Grand Lodge. This gave him a platform from which to operate. Realizing the Grand Lodge had to be separated from English Masonic obedience before it would initiate and fully support a revolution against the monarchy, Weishaupt used the illuminated Grand Orient Masons to subvert the Grand Lodge.[645]

Author and 18th century English Freemason John Robison in *Proofs of a Conspiracy* (1798) quotes a letter from Weishaupt to his illuminatus brother Cato, wherein he states his use of Masonry to another end:

---

[641] Webster, *Secret* Societies 213.
[642] Webster 156.
[643] Dillon 7-8.
[644] Miller 430.
[645] Wilgus 153.

"'The great strength of our Order lies in its concealment; let it never appear in any place in its own name, but always covered by another name, and another occupation. None is fitter than the three lower degrees of Free Masonry; the public is accustomed to it, expects little from it, and therefore takes little notice of ~[646]

Having achieved this goal, Weishaupt's next step was twofold: (1) through revolution win freedom for the subjects of what he regarded as despotic kings and Church; and (2) after revolution inaugurate an ostensibly atheistic government under the guise of democracy. Com- mander Guy Carr in *The Conspiracy*, writes that "Weishaupt never intended that any except specially selected Masons, from the Higher Degrees, should learn 'The Full Secret' of Lucifer. Only those known to have defected completely from Almighty God were initiated into the Higher Degrees of the Grand Orient Lodges and told that the Illuminati were a secret organization with the order dedicated to the cause of forming a One World Government... Weishaupt stated this action would ensure permanent peace and prosperity. Only initiates into the final degree were permitted to know...

It should come as no surprise that the anti-religious Weishaupt opposed the tolerance given Catholicism and the protection granted Protestantism in the English Glorious Revolution. Robison quotes Weishaupt that the revolution he was planning would be."[647] The means to regain Reason her rights - to raise liberty from its ashes - to restore to man his original rights - to produce the previous revolution in the mind of man - to obtain an eternal victory over oppressors - to work the redemption of mankind...

Each of these phrases in order reveals Weishaupt's intent. "Reason" would take the place of Faith. "Liberty" means self-rule, apart from God's dictates. Man's "original rights" according to Weishaupt had begun in the "previous revolution" - the Luciferian rebellion, followed by Adam's rebellion at Eden. The "eternal victory over oppressors" means the overthrow of kings and Church. And finally, man would not need the saving grace of Jesus Christ. Weishaupt's illuminated system would allow "the redemption of mankind,"[648] first politically and second spiritually, without any intervention from God.

Unlike the English, whose Masonic revolution initially protected free enterprise, as well as Crown and Church, Weishaupt's plan was to eliminate thrones and religions altogether. Commerce, he concluded, would be controlled by government. His system foreshadowed communism This is revealed by what Weishaupt's initiates had learned, as they reached the second of three degrees, called Minerval, about the ultimate alms of the Illuminati: "(1) Abolition of all ordered government; (2) Abolition of private property; (3) Abolition of inheritance; (4) Abolition of patriotism; (5) Abolition of all religion; (6) Abolition of the family [via abolition of marriage]; and (7) Creation of a World Government."[649] Current political regimes were hardly indifferent to the revolutionary goals of Weishaupt and his Illuminati. In early 1785 the Illuminati was exposed by the Bavarian government and suppressed. *Mackey's Encyclopedia of Freemasonry* reports that "The Edicts of the Elector of Bavaria were repeated in March and August, 1785, and the Order began to decline, so that by the end of the eighteenth century it had ceased to exist." Mackey of course denies any profound or long-term co-option of Masonry by llluminism. He continues, "Adopting Freemasonry only as a means for its own more successful propagation, and using it only as incidental to its own organization, it exercised while in prosperity no favorable influence on the Masonic Institution, nor any unfavorable effect on it by its dissolution."[650]

---

[646] Robison 112.
[647] Carr 2.
[648] Robison 107.
[649] Kirban 149.
[650] "Illuminati of Bavaria," *Mackey's Encyclopedia*, vol. I.

Mackey would have us believe that the covert penetration of Luciferian globalism into the ranks of Freemasonry disappeared upon the exposure and subsequent suppression of the Illuminati. Such is not the case, however, for the Illuminati infection remains, and its goal of globalism is ongoing in Masonic lodges today. One example is provided by the August 16, 1928, issue of the *Patriot*, a British periodical, which quotes the Orator of the 1922 French Grand Lodge convention: "'My brother Masons, my hope is that Freemasonry, which has done so much for the emancipation of men, and to which history owes the national revolutions, will also know how to make that greatest revolution, which will be the International Revolution.'"[651]

This statement lauding the forthcoming "International Revolution" followed the founding the League of Nations. The Orator's speech confirms in our century not just the survival but the flourishing of the poison of Weishaupt's globalism, with which the Illuminati injected Freemasonry 140 years earlier.

TEMPLARS AND THE FRENCH REVOLUTION

Weishaupt desired that the revolution of 1789 produce pure democracy, much as it was in Israel during the time of the Judges when each Israelite did "that which was right in his own eyes" (Judges 17:6; 21:25). The consequence of this kind of rule, however, leads to anarchy. Such was the case after the French Revolution. History records it as the "Reign of Terror" perpetrated by the Jacobin Clubs. As we shall learn, however, the Jacobins were all Templar Masons. The name "Jacobin," as we know, recalls Jacques de Molay, the Grand Master of the Knights Templar, who was avenged by the French Revolution.[652]

If the Knights Templar, and not the Priory of Sion, was the Order that perfected the French Revolution, then somehow, sometime between Weishaupt's plan and the commencement of the French Revolution, control of the conspiracy transferred from the Priory of Sion to the Knights Templar. This conclusion was confirmed by Abbe' Augustin Barruel in 1799, one year following the publication of Robison's exposure of the Illuminati. During the 1773 suppression of the Jesuits, Barruel, a French patriot and a Jesuit, had joined Freemasonry, rising to the rank of Master Mason (3rd degree). After seeing the devastation caused by the French Revolution, knowing it to be Masonic, he renounced Freemasonry and wrote his *Memoirs Illustrating the History of Jacobinism*. In them he documented that the Jacobin Clubs were Templar Masonic fronts.[653]

Abbe' Barruel, a French clergyman, and John Robison, a professor in Scotland, were two men unknown to each other. They were members of opposing Masonic Orders and wrote in different countries and languages. They both covered the same subject matter and came to the same conclusions - that a conspiracy lay behind the French Revolution. Robison claimed that the Illuminati controlled the conspiracy, while Barruel maintained the Templars were in command.

---

[651] Stoddard, Light-bearers of Darkness 15.

[652] Fisher 27.

[653] I do not have Barruel's books. I have looked in libraries, but have been unable to find a set anywhere. Because it is a rare work Mackey cites this as proof it is full of lies. However, Barruel's work is almost always discussed in every revisionist author's publications, along with Robison's in his Introduction. I have read many sources quoting Barruel.

WEISHAUPT AND KNIGGE

Robison wrote that Weishaupt's strategy was to "unite, by way of one common higher interest and by a lasting bond, men from all parts of the globe, from all social classes and from all religions, despite the diversity of their opinions and passions, to make them love this common interest and bond to the point where, together or alone, they act as one individual."[654]

Nesta Webster has suggested that until Weishaupt came on the scene, Freemasonry on the Continent was at "sea with regard to the whole subject of Masonry and needed someone to give a point [purpose] to their deliberations."[655] In other words, the philosophers in French Masonic Lodges knew how to incite revolution in the minds of the populace but could not bring it to political reality. In their search for a purpose for deliberation, three universal Masonic Congresses were held.

They first met at Wilhelmsbad in 1782. Dr. Dillon writes that "deputies from every country where Freemasonry existed were summoned to meet at Wilhelmsbad in council. They came from every portion of the British Empire; from the newly formed United States of America; from all the nations of Continental Europe, every one of which, at that period, had lodges; from the territories of the Grand Turk; and from the Indian and Colonial possessions of France, Spain, Portugal, and Holland. The principal and most numerous representatives were, however, from Germany and France."[656]

Although Weishaupt was not present at Wilhelmsbad, he sent his assistant, Baron Adolph von Knigge. Knigge, a staunch member of the Knights Templar, was a first-class organizer who had been travelling about Germany proclaiming himself the reformer of Freemasonry. Webster reports that he "presented himself at Wilhelmsbad, armed with full authority from Weishaupt, and succeeded in enrolling a number of magistrates, savants, ecclesiastics, and ministers of state as Illuminati and in allying himself with the deputies of Saint-Martin and Willermoz."[657]

Weishaupt, not yet willing to introduce his plan on how to initiate political revolution, waited patiently. Although the first conference met with failure, Weishaupt met with success, for Knigge had increased the membership in the Illuminati. With these initiates Weishaupt continued his subversion of Freemasonry, while Knigge remained his spokesman.

Two years later the French Grand Lodge Masons were still in the dark as to their institutional mission. Turning to London for the answer, since Masonry originated in England, they wrote a letter to General Rainsford, one of the British Masons who had attended the Congress of Wilhelmsbad. Webster recounts the letter, which in part reads:

> *Since you say that Masonry has never experienced any variation in its aim, do you then know with certainty what this unique object is? Is it useful for the happiness of mankind? Tell us if it is of an historical, political, hermetical, or scientific nature? Moral, social, or religious? Are the traditions oral or written?[658]*

---

[654] Robison, Introduction.
[655] Webster 233.
[656] Dillon 2.
[657] Webster 234. Initiated members included Ben Franklin and other American representatives who took the Illuminati back to the United States and formed fifteen Illuminati Lodges in America.
[658] Webster.

London knew, but remained silent. Weishaupt knew, but was not ready to tell. Unknown to the Priory of Sion, Weishaupt was planning a coup. Nesta Webster notes that he had a very definite object in view - to gain personal control of all Freemasonry.[659] Weishaupt would need Knigge for a while longer, but the Baron soon became an obstacle.

The second Masonic congress convened on February 15, 1785, this time in Paris. Webster reports that many of the Illuminati membership were there: "Bode (alias Amlius) and the Baron de Busche (alias Bayard) were present, also... the 'magician' Cagliostro, the magnetiser Mesmer, the Cabalist Duchanteau, and of course the leaders of the Philalethes, Savalette de Langes, who was elected President, the Marquis de Chefdebien, and a number of German members of the same Order.'[660] This congress failed due to a rift which had developed between Weishaupt and Knigge.

KNIGGE'S TREACHERY

According to *Mackey's Encyclopedia of Freemasonry*, nine years before Baron Knigge met Weishaupt, he had been initiated in the Templar Lodge of Strict Observance at Cassel on January 20, 1772, the same Lodge Sionist Cagliostro joined. In 1780 Knigge was initiated an Illuminatus by Marquis de Costanzo, one of Weishaupt's many disciples. Knigge began a correspondence with Weishaupt under the code name *Philo*, eventually receiving orders to recruit the best of the Strict Observance for the Illuminati.

Realizing Knigge's superior talent, Weishaupt asked him to join him in Bavaria to assist in constructing the advanced degrees for the Illuminati Rite, which had only at that time three degrees. Weishaupt intended for the advanced degrees to penetrate Scottish Rite Masonry in France, turning the French Templars into revolutionaries. Mackey informs us that "Knigge accordingly repaired to Bavaria in 1781, and when he met Weishaupt, the latter consented that Knigge should elaborate the whole system up to the highest mysteries. This task Knigge accomplished, and entered into correspondence with the Lodges, exerting all his talents, which were of no mean order, for the advancement of the Rite. He brought to its aid the invaluable labors of Bode, whom he prevailed upon to receive the Degrees."[661]

Mackey states that when Knigge discovered the Illuminati was not of ancient origin he was at first disillusioned with Weishaupt. Yet, considering Weishaupt a brilliant man, the Baron willingly took the challenge to advance the Illuminati degrees. When reading the account on Knigge in *Mackey's Encyclopedia of Freemasonry* one is left with the distinct impression that the Baron had personal objectives - that he was using Weishaupt for his own advancement, or maybe the advancement of the Templars.

A confrontation between Knigge and Weishaupt did develop at the second Masonic congress at Paris on February 15, 1785. It began when Weishaupt decided to make his move against Knigge.

According to *Mackey's Encyclopedia of Freemasonry*, Weishaupt began to interfere with Knigge's work and "made many alterations and additions, which he imperiously ordered the Provincial Directors to insert in the ritual. Knigge, becoming disgusted with this proceeding, withdrew from the Order and became a savage Anti-Mason."[662] Consequently, the Congress failed and Weishaupt gained an enemy.

Based upon subsequent events, Knigge's "savage anti-Masonry" may have been only a smoke screen. Two weeks after Knigge resigned from the Illuminati, the Elector of

---

[659] Webster.
[660] Webster.
[661] "Knigge, Adolph Franz Friederich Ludwig, Baron Von," *Mackey's Encyclopedia,* vol.1.
[662] "Knigge, Baron Von," *Mackey's Encyclopedia,* vol. III.

Bavaria had in his possession incriminating information about the Illuminati and set out to suppress the Order. Mackey suggests that the Jesuits informed the Elector, but that could not have been possible for two reasons: (1) the Jesuits had been put out of commission twelve years earlier; and (2) they were not privy to Illuminati documents, since Weishaupt had made certain of that. The informant had to be someone high in the Illuminati command, someone close to Weishaupt, someone who had access to all the Illuminati documents. It could only have been Baron Adolph von Knigge, the man who had been thwarted by Weishaupt.

On March 2, 1785, the Elector suppressed the Illuminati. Not until July 10, 1785, did the most damaging evidence reach the Elector.

Supposedly, a low-grade Illuminati initiate, a travelling evangelist named Jacob Lang (or Lanze), had been sent as an emissary of the Illuminati to Silesia. He allegedly was struck and killed by lightning at Ratisbon. Edith Miller states that Weishaupt was with him.[663] Nesta Webster says Lang had been sent by Weishaupt and travelled alone.[664] Myron Fagan says the lightning strike was an act of God.[665]

Evidence suggests that Lang was not killed by lightning at all, but murdered, and his body positioned for discovery. For example, Lang was loaded down with incriminating Illuminati papers, papers which no Illuminatus should have been carrying. The circumstances seem strangely suspicious - almost as if the documents had been planted for discovery. Sewn in Lang's clothes were instructions of the Order and an extensive list of the Illuminati membership. Searches followed in the houses of the named individuals. More incriminating evidence revealed their entire plan, heretofore mentioned, including Weishaupt's coded communications. All was confiscated, the Illuminati banned, and the documents published in their entirety.

Weishaupt, wily and thoroughly sagacious, had years before prepared for the day of governmental suppression. He had written to his Illuminatus brother, Cato, "I have considered every thing and so prepared it, that if the Order should this day go to ruin, I shall in a year reestablish it more brilliant than ever."[666] Weishaupt, however, would not head the reincarnation of Illuminism.

Baron von Knigge, the third man in command of the Illuminati, was aware of Weishaupt's communication. Within two and a half years of the Bavarian suppression the Illuminati did reappear, not under its original name, and not under the guidance of Sionist Weishaupt, but under Templar Baron von Knigge. Edith Miller writes that "In 1788, after the suppression of Illuminism in Bavaria... Knigge attempted to revive it in the German Union," a book publishing company founded by illuminated Freemason Karl Freiderich Bahrdt to enlighten mankind.[667]

Weishaupt, the Jew, was used, then discarded by the Gentile Masonic conspiracy, and finally exiled to Gotha, Germany. Baron Adolph von Knigge went unscathed and was found to be the new leader of the Illuminati - the Illuminati under another name, of course.[668]

---

[663] Miller 373.
[664] Webster 235.
[665] Fagan.
[666] Robison 84.
[667] Miller 374 and Denslow, *10,000 Famous Freemasons,* vol.1, 45.
[668] Webster 235.

THE THIRD CONGRESS

In 1786 the third and final congress was scheduled in secret at Frankfurt, where a Continental Grand Lodge had been established in 1783. By then Grand Orient Illuminism had saturated the French Grand Lodge. In control were the Templar Jacobins. Weishaupt had no part in this final congress. Yet, his Machiavellian proposals suggested in Paris a year earlier were adopted, that in sum embodied the dictum that "In politics the end justifies the means." Msgr. Dillon reports that Illuminated Freemasonry received from the delegates the approval that the ultimate end of Freemasonry and all secret plotting would be: "(1) pantheism for the higher degrees, atheism for the lower degrees and the populace; (2) communism of goods, women, and general concerns; (3) the destruction of the Church, and all forms of Christianity, and the removal of all existing human governments to make way for a universal republic in which the utopian ideas of complete liberty from existing social, moral, and religious restraint, absolute equality, and social fraternity, should reign. When these ends should be attained, but not till then, the secret work of the atheistic Freemasons should cease."[669]

From that time forward the direction of French Freemasonry has been subversion, insurrection, and assassination to accomplish political ends. Nesta Webster states that at the third congress "the deaths of Louis XVI and Gustavus III of Sweden are said to have been decreed."[670] And Msgr. Dillon reports that one of the representatives to this secret conclave was Count de Virene, who was so overcome with horror at the depravity of the body, that he abandoned Illuminism and became a fervent Catholic. This repentant Illuminist wrote to a friend, "'I will not tell you the secrets which I bring, but I can say that a conspiracy is laid so secret and so deep that it will be very difficult for monarchy and religion not to succumb to it."[671]

The French Revolution went off as scheduled, precipitated by the first event staged in 1785 which was the famous "Affair of the Necklace." This Masonic ruse was an attempt to discredit both the Church and the Monarchy by fraudulently exposing the licentiousness of a Catholic priest with Queen Marie-Antoinette.[672] Years later Napoleon would say that in his opinion this plot contributed more than any other to cause the explosion of 1789. In Nesta Webster's opinion, "In its double attack on Church and Monarchy the Affair of the Necklace fulfilled the purpose of both Frederick the Great and of the Illuminati."[673]

---

[669] Dillon 46.

[670] Webster 234. Various authors reported different dates and activities for these three Masonic Congresses. Some only reported one date. However, all dates were within the decade of the 1780s leading up to the Revolution of 1789. From my own studies I have accepted as most plausible these dates for my book.

[671] Dillon 28.

[672] Marie-Antoinette, wife of King Louis XVI, was much hated by the French. Never popular because she was by birth a member of the House of Habsburg, which in France was traditionally disliked, she reached in 1785 a nadir of unpopularity during the prosecution of the Affair of the Diamond Necklace. This case revolved around a cardinal, the Prince de Rohan, who had been tricked into the purchase of a necklace for queen Marie-Antoinette, without her authority and without funds of his own, giving the diamond necklace to a woman whom he thought to be the Queen. Rohan was tried for fraud and acquitted but was nevertheless exiled in disgrace from the French court, thus becoming a martyr in the eyes of the Queen's enemies and of the critics of royal absolutism. In this instance Marie Antoinette was blameless, but what was remembered by public opinion was that a cardinal had thought it possible to seduceand bribe the Queen. The discredit that befell the monarchy in consequence was immense, and Napoleon dated the beginning of the French Revolution from this very episode.

[673] Webster 234-235.

Nesta Webster states that Cagliostro received both money and instruction from a secret society to carry out the plot, after which, in November 1785, he sailed to England. As his activities in London reveal, he reported his success to the British Rosicrucians. Webster notes the use of the Rosicrucian cipher attached to a mysterious notice, appearing in a London newspaper on November 2, 1786: "According to a generally received opinion, Cagliostro was the author of a mysterious proclamation which appeared at this moment in the *Morning Herald* in the cypher of the Rose-Croix."[674]

No conspiracy author has been able to decipher this "mysterious proclamation" made in Rose- Croix hieroglyphics. We know, however, that Cagliostro was a member of a Rosicrucian Order. We know that he received funds from wealthy Englishmen (possibly Rosicrucians) to finance the overthrow of the French throne. And we know that he was the acting Grand Master of the Priory of Sion.[675] Therefore, the "mysterious proclamation" was most likely directed to the Hierarchy of the Priory of Sion, informing them that Cagliostro's mission had been accomplished.

Cagliostro, not Weishaupt, was the real power behind the Illuminati. When Weishaupt's desire for power became insatiable, Cagliostro replaced him with Baron Adolph von Knigge. Knigge then hid the activity of the Illuminati in the German Union.

---

[674] Webster.
[675] Baigent, *Holy Blood* 206.

10. MASONIC CONTROL OF THE MEDIA

> *When we by degrees bring the whole trade of book selling into our hands (as the good writers will bring all their performances into the market through our means) we shall bring it about, that at last the writers who labour in the cause of superstition [Christianity] and restraint [morality], will have neither a publisher nor readers.*[676]
>
> The German Union, 1788

When the Illuminati was suppressed in 1785, Mackey says that there were over 2,000 Freemasons upon its rosters, "among whom were some of the most distinguished men [with Lodges] to be found in France, Belgium, Holland, Denmark, Sweden, Poland, Hungary, and Italy."[677] Following the suppression the name of the Illuminati disappeared, giving Freemasonry in years to come the face-saving opportunity to disassociate itself from the stigma it had appropriated. At first the Craft denied Illuminism had any lasting effect on the Lodge. Thus argues *Mackey's Encyclopedia of Freemasonry:*

> *[T]he Order began to decline, so that by the end of the eighteenth century it had ceased to exist. Adopting Freemasonry only as a means for its own more successful propagation, and using it only as incidental to its own organization, it exercised while in prosperity no favorable influence on the Masonic Institution, nor any unfavorable effect on it by its dissolution.*[678]

Mackey was spreading Masonic disinformation, for other researchers have found that the doctrine of the Illuminati has stayed with Freemasonry to this day. One doubts that its influence, which was so profound and widespread, would disappear without a trace. Edith Miller quotes Thomas Frost from his *Secret* Societies *of the European Revolution,* on the depth of absorption of Illuminism by Masonry: "'The whole of the Masonic lodges comprised in the Grand Orient, 266 in number, were illuminated by the end of March 1789 and there is no doubt that, with the ground so well prepared... the system spread with rapidity.'"[679]

Mackey's denial was for Masonic consumption. Mackey was writing three decades prior to World War I, when a rash of conspiracy books were causing a sensation in Europe. Again, in the 1920s another deluge of revisionist history flooded the old world, accusing the Illuminati of being the force behind The Great War. Ten years later conspiracy researchers had gathered enough evidence to expose the Bolshevik Revolution as being backed by the illuminated Grand Orient. With so much exposure, the Beast began to weaken. When World War II arrived, the Brotherhood was in shambles. According to

---

[676] Robison 171.William R. Denslow's *10,000 Famous Freemasons* informs us that the German Union was founded by several Masons and headed by Freemason Karl F. Bahrdt (1741-1792). Bahrdt was a German doctor of theology who had joined the Illuminati. The object of the German Union "was the enlightenment of mankind." It was dissolved in 1790 by the imprisonment of Bahrdt for libel of Prussian Minister Woellner. Bahrdt was described by one of his biographers as being "notorious... for his bold infidelity and for his evil life." (vol.1, p.45).

[677] "Illuminati of Bavaria," *Mackey's Encyclopedia of Freemasonry,* vol.1.

[678] "Illuminati of Bavaria."

[679] Miller 374.

Mackey's Encyclopedia of *Freemasonry*, by the end of World War II, Continental Freemasonry had been obliterated by the Nazis.[680]

After World War II the Brotherhood decided to take another look at the Illuminati. In 1946, 33rd degree Mason H.L. Haywood, with help from Research Lodges around the world, completed a Supplement to Mackey's two-volume *Encyclopedia of Freemasonry*. Volume III reversed Mackey's earlier denial of Illuminist influence stating that The Order of Illuminati was the greatest single misfortune ever to befall European Freemasonry because it became at once the pattern and the point of departure for a succession of secret, underground, political conspiracies which... divided Masonry and brought disgrace upon its name.[681]

While Haywood admits Weishaupt changed the direction of the Continental Brotherhood, he dates the division between English and French Freemasonry from the entrance of the Illuminati. Yet we have already discovered that the conflict between Scarlet and the Beast began long before Weishaupt's arrival. The French Revolution, with its republican ideals, widened the rift with English Masonry and the suppression of the Illuminati only buried the intrigue deeper. The conspiracy of the Illuminati did, in fact, continue. The name, however, as we have seen, changed.

Did Mackey not know this? Mackey called Professor Robison, the highly respected English Mason who first exposed the Illuminati worldwide, a liar.[682] Mackey also failed in his *Encyclopedia* to reference three significant Illuminati symbols adopted by Freemasonry: (1) the rectangle - representing the Lodge: (2) the All-Seeing Eye - representing the Great Architect of the Universe; and (3) the point within a circle, another form of the eye. Every initiate learns early in his Masonic training that mystical symbolism is the primary agent by which Masonic truth is taught. These three symbols were adopted by Freemasonry from the Illuminati after the French Revolution.[683]

Dr. Mackey was correct in one respect. The "Illuminati" by name did cease. So did Weishaupt's personal involvement. Most conspiracy researchers, however, believe Weishaupt advanced the intrigue until his death in 1830, a date disputed by Mackey, who says Weishaupt died in 1811.[684] Yet, Mackey's contemporary, 33rd degree Mason Robert Ingham Clegg, in his seven volume *History of Freemasonry*, agrees with the 1830 date.[685] It seems reasonable to believe Mackey was involved in a cover-up.

MEDIA CONTROL

Long before Weishaupt was exiled from Bavaria, he communicated his plan to Cato should suppression of the Illuminati occur:

> *[T]he form of a learned or literary society is best suited to our purpose, and had Freemasonry not existed, this cover would have been employed [first]; and it may be much more than a cover, it may be a powerful engine in our hands. By establishing reading societies, and subscription libraries, and taking these under our direction, and supplying them through our labours, we may turn the public mind which way we will.*

---

[680] "World War II and Freemasonry in Europe," *Mackey's Encyclopedia*, vol.111.

[681] Knigge, Baron Von," *Mackey's Encyclopedia*, vol. III.

[682] "Illuminati of Bavaria," *Mackey's Encyclopedia*, vol.1.

[683] "Illuminati of Bavaria."

[684] "Weishaupt, Adam," *Mackey's Encyclopedia*, vol.11.

[685] Robert Ingham Clegg, *Mackey's Revised history of Freemasonry*, vol.1(1898; New York: The Masonic History Company, 1921) 305.

A Literary Society is the most proper form for the introduction of our Order into any state where we are yet Strangers.[686]

Baron Adolph von Knigge, and not Weishaupt, concealed the Illuminati in a network of pre- existing reading societies throughout Germany and France.[687]

Illuminism, perpetuated by Knigge in the German Union (a book publishing company founded by Freemasonry to enlighten mankind, see note 1), controlled the reading societies, some of which were portable, and through which the conspirators turned the minds of the populace toward revolution. In short, 2,000 distinguished Freemasons, once following orders from Sionist Weishaupt, were ostensibly following the same program under the leadership of Templar Knigge. Knigge, with a legion of Masons at his command, monopolized the writing, reviewing, publication, and distribution of most literature in both countries.

The German Union enjoyed only one year of success under Knigge's administration before exposure. Goschen (no first name given), a bookseller from Leipzig, unmasked the Union as Illuminati. This exposure occurred too late, however, for there was no reversing the mind-set that promoted the French Revolution. Professor Robison, in *Proofs of a Conspiracy*, gives no further information about the bookseller Goschen except that he published with "all speed" the information he found on the German Union "on account of the many mischiefs which this Society might do to the world, and to the trade, if allowed to go on working in secret."[688]

Goschen's publication was sarcastically entitled *More Notes than Text*, on *the German Union of X~U, a new Secret Society for the Good of Mankind* (Leipzig, 1789). He wrote the following foreboding statement before reprinting a portion of the notes. (Be aware that the German Union is equating superstition, restraint and fanaticism with Christianity and morality; instruction and enlightenment with revolutionary reason and progress.)

And now, every eye can perceive the progressive moral influence which the Union will acquire on the nation. Let us only conceive what superstition will lose, and what instruction must gain by this; when,

1.   In every Reading Society the books are selected by our Fraternity.

2.   We have confidential persons [2,000 distinguished Masons] in every quarter, who will make it their serious concern to spread such performances as promote the enlightening of mankind, and to introduce them even into every cottage.

3.   We have the loud voice of the public on our side, and since we are able, either to scout into the shade all the fanatical writings which appear in the reviews that are commonly read, or to warn the public against them; and, on the other hand, to bring into notice and recommend those performances alone which give light to the human mind.

4.   We by degrees bring the whole trade of book selling into our hands (as the good writers will bring all their performances into the market through our means) we shall bring it about, that at last the writers who labour in the cause of superstition and restraint, will have neither a publisher nor readers.

5.   Lastly, by the spreading of our Fraternity, all good hearts and sensible men will adhere to us, and by our means will be put in a condition that enables them to work in silence upon all courts, families, and individuals in every quarter, and acquire an influence in the appointment of court-officers, stewards, secretaries, parish-priests, public teachers, and private tutors.[689]

---

[686] Robison 112.
[687] Miller 374.
[688] Robison 166.
[689] Robison 170-171.

Weishaupt had once told Knigge, "'If a writer publishes any thing that attracts notice, and is in itself just, but does not accord with our plan, we must endeavour to win him over, or *decry him.*"[690]

A century later the Conspirators were still in control of the press, evidenced by a statement made in the Supreme Council of Cagliostro's illuminated Rosicrucian Masonic Lodge of Mizraim in Paris, France. The Pronouncement sounded as if Weishaupt himself had penned the words:

> *We shall have a sure triumph over our opponents since they will not have at their disposition organs of the press in which they can give full and final expression to their views... We shall not even need to refute them except very superficially if there should be any found who are desirous of writing against us, they will not find any person eager to print their productions.*[691]

This control of the media has persisted into our times. Vicomte Leon de Poncins gives an example of media control in the 20th century. His book *The Secret Powers Behind Revolution* contains an address by journalist John Swinton to a 1920 press banquet in New York. A portion follows:

> *An independent Press does not exist in America except perhaps in small country towns; journalists know it and I know it; not one of them dares to express a sincere opinion; if they do so, they know beforehand that it will never be printed. I am paid 150 dollars in order that I should not put my ideas in the newspaper for which I write and that I should keep them to myself. Others are paid similar salaries for a similar service. If I succeeded in having my opinions published in a single issue of my newspaper, I should lose my post in twenty-four hours.*
>
> *The man who would be insane enough to give frank expression to his thoughts would soon find himself in the streets on the look-out for another occupation. It is the duty of New York journalists to lie, to threaten, to bow down to the feet of Mammon, and to sell their country... for their salary...*
>
> *We are the tools and the vassals of the rich who keep in the background; we are puppets; they pull the strings and we dance. Our time, our talent, our life, our abilities, all are the property of these men. We are intellectual prostitutes.*[692]

By the turn of the 20th century, Freemasonry had gained influence over, if not control of, a major portion of the world press. Fifty years before Swinton's speech, the Masonic Supreme Council of Mizraim confirmed: "Not a single announcement will reach the public without our control. Even now this is already attained by us inasmuch as all news items are received by a few agencies, in whose offices they are focused from all parts of the world. These agencies will then be already entirely ours and will give publicity only to what we dictate to them."[693]

Many examples of Masonic media control are presented by Miller in *Occult Theocrasy*. In one instance at the turn of the 20th century, Miller reports that the hierarchy in English and French Masonry attempted to unite under a sub-secret Lodge called the

---

[690] Robison 111.

[691] Sergius Nilus, *The Protocols of the Learned Elders of Sion*, trans. Victor E. Marsden (London: n.p., 1934) 184, 186.

[692] Leon de Poncins, *Secret Powers Behind Revolution* (1929; Hawthorne, CA: Christian Book Club of America, n.d.)172-173.

[693] Nilus 182-183.

"Ordo Templi Orientis" (O.T.O.), which Miller calls the Illuminati's "interlocking directorate." In the 1890s illuminated Freemasonry had correspondent Theodore Reuss on the scene in Germany to report on the political events which ultimately led up to World War I. Reuss was both a 33rd degree Rosicrucian English Mason, as well as a 33rd degree Templar Grand Orient Mason. Miller states that in 1902 Reuss co founded (with Karl Kellner) the O.T.O. and appointed 33rd degree English Freemason William Wynn Westcott "as Regent of the Illuminati in England, thus establishing the interlocking directorate" between English and French Masonry.[694]

In reality, Reuss was a double agent for British intelligence, contracting with *Central News,* London; *Daily Chronicle,* London; *Central Press,* London; and United *Press,* New York. He wrote for many non-English publications as well. Reuss was held in high esteem by members of his profession and government and military officials. The following quotes which praise Theodore Reuss are from letters hand written, photocopied and reproduced in Miller's book.[695]

The Central Press, January 16, 1892, wrote, "I must confess that you exercise marvellous ingenuity in collecting a great variety of interesting facts which few others seem to give."

The United Press, February 27, 1894, noted, "he has done in my opinion some very excellent work for us. On several occasions he has beaten the world with his news, and has sent us matter which the German dailies copied three weeks later from our report. If we should lose him I doubt that he could be replaced."

On November 1, 1896, the Captain and Military attaché' in the Berlin embassy of the United States, sent Reuss a letter of thanks. "I have learned several things from you which escaped my notice in the field. Your remarks on the Cavalry, the Bicycle Detachment and the Commissariat Department I have made use of in my report."

How was Reuss able to beat all other news gatherers by three weeks? Miller gives the answer by reproducing 28 pages of correspondence between Reuss and another English Freemason, 33rd degree member John Yarker. Like Reuss, Yarker was in British intelligence and was also a close associate of William Wynn Westcott, a Mason whom Reuss appointed head of the English chapter of the Illuminati. Yarker provided Reuss with advance information.

Masonic operatives disguised as newsmen were everywhere preparing 33rd degree Supreme Council-influenced news stories, which in turn were edited and distributed to other Masonic correspondents for publication in newspapers around the world. In 1922 the Templar Grand Orient Lodge at Paris confirms this tactic carried out by Masonic correspondents. De Poncins quotes the Grand Orient's Supreme Council minutes: "'Written propaganda, coupled with the personal influence of Brethren belonging to the Press, should be increased by oral propaganda in the form of white [reactionary] meetings and conferences...so that the [Supreme Council] may send them whatever communication they think fit."[696]

Paul Fisher, in *Behind the Lodge Door,* quotes historian Mildred Headings on Masonic influence of the media in those days: "Masons influenced at least 47 periodicals throughout France, off and on, during the late 19th and early 20th Centuries."[697] During the Second Empire and reign of Napoleon III, the Sionist Masonic Supreme Council of Mizraim at Paris reported in its convention minutes that All our newspapers will be of all possible complexions - aristocratic, republican, revolutionary, even anarchical - for so long, of course, as the constitution exists... Like the Indian idol Vishnu they will have a

---

[694] Miller 571.
[695] Miller 298, 571 and Appendix IV.
[696] Léon de Poncins, *Freemasonry and the Vatican* 59.
[697] Fisher 242.

hundred hands, and every one of them will have a finger on any one of the public opinions as required. When a pulse quickens these hands will lead opinion in the direction of our aims, for an excited patient loses all power of judgement and easily yields to suggestion. Those fools who will think they are repeating the opinion of a newspaper of their own camp will be repeating our opinion or any opinion that seems desirable for us. In the vain belief that they are following the organ of their party they will in fact follow the flag which we hang out for them.[698]

An interesting phrase at the beginning of this passage is in the statement that Masonry would control the press *"for so long, of course, as the constitution exists."*

History, of course, reveals the French as notoriously lacking confidence in their governments. In its first revolution, French Masonry killed most of its men capable of governing.

After World War I, when Europe's kings were cast down, Sionist Free-masonry had once again lost control in France. In 1922, some 50 years into the Third Republic, the Templar Grand Orient Lodge was encouraging its control of the press once again. De Poncins quotes the Supreme Council minutes of that year:

> *"The Convent [convention] asks the Council to draw the attention of the lodges to the experiment of the lodges in Lower Normandy, which have set up a weekly paper entirely edited by Masons, and to call upon the lodges to follow this example, following different local circumstances, and set up papers throughout the whole of France produced entirely under our control."[699]*

Meanwhile, the Grand Orient intended to propagandize the public by using the existing press. De Poncins quotes from the 1922 Grand Orient Supreme Council minutes:

> *"Circular No.5 concerns propaganda through the Press, and asks lodges to bring to our attention the names of papers likely to publish reports of the Grand Orient, and information on their regularity, their clientele, the quantity of their circulation, and their political sympathies... so that the Council may send them whatever communication they think fit... and to enquire among the republican Press upon whose support Freemasonry could rely if necessary... Our largest financial support must be reserved for the Press which is republican in outlook."[700]*

From the Second Empire until after World War II, the on-going French Masonic revolution has been a roller coaster, changing from Sionist administrations to Templar, and back again. French citizens were carried through two Empires and five Republics, totalling seven constitutions. With each change the secret society in power would start anew, which meant initiating again the long process of monopolizing the press.

PROPAGANDA AND AMERICAN FREEMASONRY

The same propaganda tactics have been used by American Freemasonry. Paul Fisher confirms in *Behind the Lodge Door* that "In the United States, in 1920, the Scottish Rite

---

[698] Nilus 185.
[699] Léon de Poncins, *Freemasonry and the Vatican* 59-60.
[700] Léon de Poncins.

established a news service for 'furnishing accurate and gratuitous information to newspapers."[701]

That a Masonic news service manipulates public opinion in the direction desired by Freemasonry is confirmed in the Scottish Rite's *New Age* magazine, October, 1924, in the same article that documented Free-masonry's involvement in compulsory education. We now quote from the article the same paragraph used in the previous chapter - this time to document Freemasonry's use of the press to form public opinion:

> *"Through the activities of our state organizations, the New Age magazine, our clip service and News Bureau, we are stimulating the public interest and furnishing much valuable material to speakers and writers, and thereby can reasonably claim much credit for the growing interest in favor of compulsory education by the state."[702]*

Fisher says that the July 1928 issue of the *New Age* claimed "'many members of the National Press Club are Masons, not a few of them very prominent Masons."' Fisher lists these "prominent Masons" in *Behind The Lodge Door*.[703] This catalogue reads like a Who's Who of the publishing and broadcasting industry.

Fisher reports that Masonic success in controlling the press was also published in the January 1926 issue of *New Age:* "it is safe to claim that the majority of daily publications seem very friendly in their attitude toward the Craft."[704]

One publisher friendly to the Craft is New Ager and Protestant pastor Dr. Norman Vincent Peale, a 33rd degree Mason. Masonry is so proud of Peale that his name is listed in Masonic brochures throughout America as one of the prominent high Masons who disseminates Masonic thought in his periodical, *Guidepost.* In fact, Peale was on the cover of *The Scottish Rite Journal* (formerly the *New Age* magazine) in March, 1991. "Masonry," said Peale, "became an early and essential part of my success."[705] The three-point outline of his article in the *Journal*, "Enthusiasm Makes the Difference," is "Confidence, Understanding, Enthusiasm (CUE)." These three words, according to Peale, are the CUE to success and happiness. "Take your CUE from Freemasonry as I have," wrote Dr. Peale.[706]

The article never mentions Christ as being the "CUE" to Rev. Peale's success. Nor is Christ the guiding light behind Peale's *Guidepost,* which is one of the New Age movement's most powerful magazines penetrating the Christian community today.

The official, publicly stated anti-Christian policy of *Guidepost* magazine was revealed in May 1982, when Dina Donahue contributing editor of *Guidepost,* held a seminar at Dallas, Texas for Christian authors aspiring to write for Christian magazines, which the author and his wife attended. Donahue informed those present that articles submitted to *Guidepost* must never mention Jesus Christ as Mediator between God and man. Nor can Christ be portrayed as the only Truth, as God incarnate, the only means for salvation, or the only way to God the Father. An article can mention Jesus in His historical position as a prophet and philosopher. The editor gave the following reason for these

---

[701] Fisher 242.
[702] Fisher.
[703] Fisher.
[704] Fisher.
[705] Norman Vincent Peale, "Enthusiasm Makes the Difference," *The Scottish Rite Journal* (March 1991) 6.*The Scottish Rite Journal* was formerly the *New Age* magazine. Freemasonry changed the name after Paul Fisher exposed its massive conspiratorial contents in *Behind The Lodge Door.*
[706] "Enthusiasm Makes the Difference."

restrictions: "*Guidepost* is an interfaith magazine, and Dr. Peale does not want to offend those who are not Christians."[707]

As recently as February 24, 1991, Dr. Peale spoke to the congregation at Robert Schuller's Crystal Cathedral in California. At that Sunday morning service Peale said, "Jesus Christ, Buddha and Krishna are examples of great philosophers who taught how to use mind power."[708]

Finally, Dr. Peale has endorsed *The Jesus Letters*. Its authors are two Connecticut women, Jane Palzere and Anna Brown, who claim that a spirit named "Master Jesus" came to them during meditation and gave them this book. This "Jesus" told Jane and Anna that there is no God outside of us, that God does not heal - only the mind of the person himself can heal; that heaven is for all, not just believers in Jesus, and that every person - including the heathen - has Christ within. This book also promotes spirit mediums and spirit channelers and confides that the real Bible - God's Word - is "limited." There are many "Christs," not just Jesus, the authors insist. On the back cover of *The Jesus Letters* is this enthusiastic endorsement by Norman Vincent Peale: "What a wonderful gift to all of us from you in your book, *The Jesus Letters*... You will bless many by this truly inspired book."[709]

Another "friendly to Freemasonry" publication is the *Christian Science Monitor*, promoted as the favorite newspaper of politicians. Fisher quotes *New Age*, July 1938, as confirming that a number of Christian Science officials have been Masons, and the magazine notes that the *Christian Science Monitor* "devotes considerable space to Masonic activities throughout the world."[710]

From its inception, Christian Science has been influenced by Masons and the art of Freemasonry.

Its founder was Mary Baker Eddy (1821. 1910), who, from a young age was chronically sick. Her first of three husbands, George Washington Glover, was a Freemason, as well as a member of the Oddfellows. Early in their marriage (1843), Glover moved Mary to the Masonic headquarters at Charleston. Six months later he died. In 1853 Mary married Daniel Patterson, a medical practitioner, from whom she was later separated. In October 1862 she applied for medical assistance from Phineas Parkhurst Quimby, a healer who used the occult art of Animal Magnetism discovered by Freemason Mesmer. When Quimby cured Mary of her chronic sickness, she spent the next two years

---

[707] Dina Donahue, Contributing Editor for *Guidepost,* was one of several editors holding seminars for the Seventh annual Brite School of Christian Writing, Dallas, Texas, May 5-8, 1982.

[708] "Hour of Power," Robert Schuller, CBS, KDFW, Dallas 24 February 1991.

[709] Jane Palzere and Anna Brown, *The Jesus Letters,* entire.

[710] Fisher 242. William R. Denslow's *10,000 Famous Freemasons* lists the Masons who were journalists for *Christian Science Monitor* during the time the *New Age* magazine praised the *Monitor* for devoting "considerable space to Masonic activities throughout the world." - Archibald McLellan (Mason), editor of the *Christian Science Journal* and *Christian Science Sentinel* from 1902; editor-in-Chief of *Christian Science Monitor* (1908-1914 (vol. ffi, p.181). Paul S. Deland (32nd degree), joined the *Christian Science Monitor* 1908 (vol.1, p.302). R.H. Markham (Mason), from 1926 was the *Christian Science Monitor* European correspondent (vol. m, p.133). Roland R. Harrison (Masons), joined the *Christian Science Monitor* 1922; executive editor 1924-1929; administrative editor 1939-1940; manager of the Christian Science Publishing Society 1929-1939 (vol. H, p. 192). Albert F. Gilmore (Mason), editor of *Christian Science* weekly and monthly magazines 1922-1929 and president of The Mother Church 1922-1923 (vol.11, p.114). Erwin D. Canham (Mason) began with *Christian Science Monitor* in 1925; head of the Washington Bureau from 1932-1939; general news editor 1939-1941; managing editor 1941-1944; and editor in 1945 (vol.I, p.177). George charming (32nd degree), editor of *Christian Science Journal, Sentinel and Herald* since 1949 (vol.1, p.198). Frederic E. Morgan (32nd degree), president (1938-1954) of Principia, Elsah, Illinois, a school from kindergarten through four years of liberal arts college for sons and daughters of Christian Scientists (vol.111, p.229).

lecturing and trying to "Christianize" Quimby's theories. When Mary Baker practiced Quimby's art of healing, she described the demonic horrors that manifested themselves as "Malicious Animal Magnetism," familiarly referred to by her students as M.A.M. It is claimed that Mary Baker derived her system of healing from Quimby, although she denied it in later years.

In 1866 Mary Baker founded Christian Science. Its belief can be summed up in one sentence: God is spirit - spirit is the opposite of matter - therefore God never created matter. This is the same gnostic belief of the Cathars, which doctrine entered into the religious beliefs of both the Knights Templar and the Rosicrucians.

In 1877 Mary Baker married Asa Gilbert Eddy, who left her a widow in 1882. In 1881 Mary Baker Eddy founded the Massachusetts Metaphysical College in Boston and two years later, when the movement was well established, started publishing the *Christian Science Journal*, now known as the Christian *Science Monitor*.

In 1884 Mrs. Eddy returned to Charleston where she met a woman who had the most influence in her life, Mrs. August Stetson, whose husband was an English Freemason. Mrs. Stetson, who had travelled with her husband to Bombay, India, there learned eastern mysticism, and taught it to Eddy.

On June 13, 1888, the National Christian Science Association held its second annual meeting at Central Music Hall, Chicago. Eddy was the main speaker. From then on Mrs. Eddy's religious future was assured.[711]

The real strength of Christian Science, however, is its "Reading Rooms," where the inquirer can read the movement's literature, which elucidates a gnostic form of Christianity. A Christian Scientist is strongly encouraged to "log" thousands of reading hours. We can recall here what Weishaupt said: "A Literary Society is the most proper form for the introduction of our Order into any state where we are yet strangers."[712] Christian Science reading rooms appear to be what Weishaupt had in mind.

FREEMASONRY AND OTHER MEDIA

Hollywood playwright, Myron C. Fagan, who spent most of his professional life researching the Illuminati, was founder in the 1940s of the Cinema Educational Guild, Inc. The Guild published *The Point*, a monthly exposure of Illuminati influence in America. In 1967-1968 Fagan produced "The Illuminati" on two audio cassette tapes, in which he traces the conspirators' takeover of the U.S. media after Freemasonry founded the Council on Foreign Relations, which in turn, directly or indirectly founded and shaped the primary media of 20th century America. Fagan outlines their genesis:

> *The CFR set up special committees in every state in the Union to whom they assigned the various local state operations... The control of the press was assigned to Rockefeller. [Through him], Henry Luce was financed to set up a number of national magazines, among them Life, Fortune, and others... The Rockefellers also directly or indirectly financed the Cowles brothers, Look magazine and a chain of newspapers. They also financed the man named Sam Newhouse to buy and to build a chain of newspapers all over the country. And Eugene Meyer, one of the founders of the CFR, bought the Washington Post, Newsweek, and other publications. At the same time, the CFR began to develop*

---

[711] Miller 553-556, 738.
[712] Robison 112.

and nurture a new breed of scurrilous columnists and editorial writers and broadcasters.[713]

Myron Fagan also claims that the three major news networks are today dominated by left-wing illuminated Freemasonry. William Sutton confirms the same in *The New Age Movement and The Illuminati 666.* Moreover, Sutton maintains that the logos for each of the three television networks are Masonic symbols. For example, NBC displays the peacock with its tail feathers full of All-Seeing Eyes. In Hinduism, says Sutton, "when the god Indra transforms himself into an animal, he becomes a peacock. In India the peacock was believed to have a thousand eyes in its feathers." He also notes that the Greek goddess Hera "set the hundred-eyed Argus to guard her husband's mistress, Io, after Zeus sent Hermes to charm and kill Argus. Hera used the giant's eyes to ornament the peacock's tail. In Java, the peacock was associated with the Devil. In Mosul in northern Iraq, there is a sect of Yezidis who hold that the Devil is not evil, and call him the Peacock Angel."[714]

NBC could not have chosen a better symbol to represent its antichristian world-view than the All-Seeing Eye peacock. ABC is more subtle by symbolizing itself in the sun-disk, which is just another form of the All-Seeing Eye. CBS is more blatant. Its logo is the Masonic All Seeing Eye, and it daily features on its evening newscast a segment titled "Eye on America," using its logo for the word "eye." Recently, CBS has included a subliminal triangle rotating around the eye. The triangle and eye come on the screen at program breaks just before commercials, with the following voice-over, "This...[pause]...is CBS." The triangle rotates quickly, then shatters into a rainbow of sun rays. It looks identical to the sun-rayed Illuminati capstone and eye hovering over the unfinished pyramid, featured on the back of our $1 bill.

MEDIA AND THE FRENCH REVOLUTION

As we have seen above, the world press, if not under Masonic direction, is heavily influenced by Freemasonry. Revisionist authors typically deal with Masonic control of the press. Leon de Poncins, in *The Secret Powers Behind Revolution* does the same, taking the reader from the French Revolution of 1789 through the Masonic-controlled revolutions in Portugal, Spain, Italy, Turkey, Austria, and Hungary. His book exposes French Masonry's involvement in starting World War I for the purpose of dethroning all the kings of Europe. And, finally, he documents both English and French Masonry's total involvement in the Bolshevik Revolution, the most vicious insurrection in the history of our century. Before each of these catastrophes, Freemasonry manipulated public opinion through the press.[715]

According to de Poncins, the Masons by 1904 were ready to admit their Fraternity's involvement in the French Revolution. "In the [French] chamber of Deputies," writes de Poncins, "during the sitting of 1 July 1904 the Marquis de Rosanbo pronounced the

---

[713] Myron Fagan does not document any of his information in this cassette on "The Illuminati." Like most revisionist historians he is an adherent to one conspiracy theory. His tapes are a way to get a quick and easy overview of Illuminati influence in world affairs. To order these two tapes, see order form in back of book.

[714] William Josiah Sutton, *The New Age Movement and The illuminati 666* (USA: The Institute of Religious Knowledge, 1983) 72.

[715] de Poncins, *Secret Powers*, entire.

following words: 'Freemasonry has worked in a hidden but constant manner to prepare the revolution."'[716]

Rosanbo sat on the right side of the chamber, his Masonic opponents on the left, a system unconsciously established at the first Constituent Assembly in 1789. (Then the Royalists, not wanting to be near the radical Masons on the left, sat as far to the right of the chamber as possible. The moderates sat in the middle. From the French Revolution onward, anti-business communists, socialists, radicals and liberals have been designated "left wing," while pro-business aristocrats and conservatives are called "right wing." Those who want a little of both are "moderates.")

At the time of Rosanbo's speech, when he declared to his Masonic opponents that Freemasonry was revolutionary, the seating arrangement had not changed in the chamber of Deputies. Three Deputies on the Left, each in turn, responded to his accusation:

> *"That is indeed what we boast of."*
> *"That is the greatest praise you can give it."*
> *"That is the reason why you and your friends hate it."*[717]

Rosanbo countered: "We are then in complete agreement on the point that freemasonry [sic] was the only author of the revolution, and the applause which I receive from the Left, and to which I am little accustomed proves, gentlemen, that you acknowledge with me that it was masonry [sic] which made the French Revolution."

> *"We do more than acknowledge it, we proclaim it."*[718]

Rosanbo sat in the Assembly in 1904, during the Third Republic. In 1976, Fred Zeller, former Grand Master of the Grand Orient of France, in his book *Trots Points, C'est Tout* (Three Points, That's All), revealed that between 1912 and 1971, "all of the Third and much of the Fourth Republic of France was dominated by Freemasons, who fought two major anti-clerical reforms in a battle against Church influence."[719] These battles were fought in the Masonic dominated press.

Leon de Poncins has published two more pieces of evidence in which Masons admit their role in fomenting the French Revolution, and implicitly and explicitly credit themselves with the on- going revolution in public opinion. The first is a circular, sent to all Lodges by the Masonic Supreme Council to prepare the centenary of 1789, which proclaimed: "'Masonry which prepared the revolution of 1789 is in duty bound to continue its work; the present state of opinion invites it to do so."[720]

The second is a report read at the Grand Orient Lodge of Nantes, April 23, 1883: "'It was from 1772 to 1789 that Masonry elaborated the great revolution which was to change the face of the world. It was then that the Masons gave to the people the ideas which they had adopted in their lodges."[721]

This latter report refers to the activity of the Grand Orient, which was founded in 1772. By 1782 there were 266 Grand Orient lodges in France. Illuminism was spreading rapidly, but its greatest success and influence was really achieved by Illuminist control of the media of the day - the Reading Societies expanded by Baron Adolph von Knigge.

---

[716] de Poncins 29-30.
[717] de Poncins.
[718] de Poncins.
[719] Fisher 21.
[720] de Poncins, *Secret Powers* 29-30.
[721] de Poncins.

John Robison and Abbe Barruel, both writing in 1798 and 1799 respectively, confirm the Illuminati's use of media. Robison writes that

> the Illuminati hired an army of writers; they industriously pushed their writings into every house and every cottage. Those writing were equally calculated for inflaming the sensual appetites of men and for perverting their judgments. They endeavored to get the command of the schools, particularly those for the lower classes; and they erected and managed a prodigious number of Circulating Libraries and Reading Societies.
>
> They employed writers to compose corrupting and impious books - these were revised by the Society and corrected until they suited their purpose. A number were printed in a handsome manner, to defray the expense; and then a greater number were printed in the cheapest form possible and given for nothing, or at very low prices to hawkers and peddlers with the injunction to distribute them secretly through the cities and villages.[722]

The British *Patriot,* March 7, 1929, comments on the Masons' deliberate corruption and perversion of the old order by the systematic creation of anti-Christian Reading Societies and academic associations:

> For more than half a century the Freemasons had, in fact, been secretly preparing the mind, whose explosion in 1789 wrecked... old France... From 1750 onwards Reading Societies were started in most of the towns in France. Like the Free Thought Societies of the present day, they were under the control of Freemasons... Members of these societies who had been the most easily caught by the Masonic bait, and who, in addition, possessed literary talent, were admitted into groups of a higher degree, the societies called "Academic." Like the Reading Societies, the Academic Societies were secretly directed by Freemasons... who provided the money spent either on prizes given for anti-Christian pamphlets or on the printing and publishing of them.[723]

The Academic Societies consisted of three schools, each having subdivisions. The first school was divided into two degrees, Novice and Minerval. Msgr. Dillon writes that the teachers of the Minervals were instructed "to propose each year to their scholars some interesting questions, to cause them to write themes calculated to spread impiety amongst the people, such as burlesques on the Psalms, pasquinades on the Prophets, and caricatures of personages of the Old Testament after the manner of Voltaire and his school."[724]

FREEMASONRY AND PORNOGRAPHY

These corruptions paved the way for the acceptance of pornographic literature. As we saw in chapter 5, Masonic rituals themselves are pornographic, as are the esoteric meanings of Masonic symbols. Masons say these emblems are ancient representations of god. And Masonry teaches, as do all mystery religions, that creation evolved by uniting

---

[722] Winrod 21-22.
[723] Stoddard, Light-bearers of Darkness 13-14.
[724] Dillon 24.

the male and female principles of nature. Therefore, each of these geometric characters is representative of man and woman in the continual act of creation through intercourse.

It is also historical fact that ancient mystery religions furnished prostitutes in their temples to reenact these "mysteries." In *Haley's Bible Handbook* we learn that the mother goddess was the deification of erotic love. Halley writes that

> Her worship required licentiousness: sacred prostitution in connection with her sanctuaries was a universal custom among the women of Babylonia. In connection with her temples were charming retreats or chambers where her priestesses entertained male worshippers in disgraceful ceremonies. In addition to these prostitute priestesses, every maid, wife or widow had to officiate at least once in her lifetime in these rites.[725]

The American Mason Albert Pike, Sovereign Pontiff of Universal Freemasonry from 1859 to 1891, tried to introduce ritual prostitution in Masonic Lodges, first practicing on his own. For example, he was known in Arkansas to have taken wagon loads of food, whiskey, and women into the Ozark mountains for days of orgies. His attempt to incorporate prostitution in Masonic Temples worldwide occurred on July 14, 1889 in Paris, France, at the greatest Masonic convention since the Congress of Vienna in 1815. Edith Miller quotes a portion of Pike's speech, which was read to the Supreme Councils of the world at that meeting:

> We earnestly recommend the creation of Lodges of Adoption. They are indispensable to the formation of Masons who are indeed Masters of themselves. The priest tries to subdue his flesh by enforced celibacy... The real Mason, on the contrary, reaches perfection, that is to say achieves self mastery, by using his zeal in the Lodges of Adoption in submitting to all natural ordeals. Commerce with women, belonging to all brethren, forms for him an armour against those passions which lead hearts astray. He alone can really possess voluptuousness. To be able, at will, to use or to abstain, is a twofold power. "Woman fetters thee by thy desires," we say to the adept; "Well, use women often and without passion; thou wilt thus become master of thy desires, and thou wilt enchain woman." From which it must perforce result that the real Mason will succeed in easily solving the problem of the flesh.[726]

Pike's idea of controlling one's sensual appetite was to open Masonic whore houses where Masons could balance their sexual drive. Pike claimed such exercises were "taught you by the BALANCE, the symbol of all Equilibrium..."[727]

Pike's method to "balance" a Mason's "sensual appetite" was identical to the licentious pagan temples of ancient Babylon. He wanted Masonic Lodges to be erected for prostitutes. "Lodges of Adoption," he called them, identical to the Illuminati Tugendbunds of Germany prior to the French Revolution.[728]

We reviewed a number of Masonic symbols representing sexual intercourse in chapter five. For example, we learned that the Compass is in the dominant position, with its two legs pointing downward; the Square is in the passive position, with its two legs pointing upward. Interlocked they symbolize the legs of man and woman having continual

---

[725] Halley 97.
[726] Miller 233-234.
[727] Pike, *Morals and Dogma* 854.
[728] Miller 376.

sexual intercourse. Pike confirms that this most prominent Masonic sex force symbol approves of the Mason's never-ending drive for seeking sexual pleasure. In *Morals and Dogma*, he asks, 'What does the symbolism of the Compass and Square profit him [the Mason], if his sensual appetites and baser passions are not governed by... both points of the Compass *remaining* below the Square?"[729]

More perverted than the Square and Compass is the meaning of the letter "G" positioned where the Phallus (male sex organ) and the Cteis (female sex organ) are suggested to unite. American Masons are told "G" represents God. We can reasonably conclude that Masonic ritual is the worship of the male and female sex organs as God. Antiquity knew this as "phallic worship." *Mackey's Encyclopedia of Freemasonry* defines "Phallic Worship" as the worship "of the membrum virile, or male organ of generation," and acknowledges Masonry's adoption of its symbols: "Here we undoubtedly find the remote origin of the *point within a circle,* an ancient symbol which was first adopted by the old sun-worshipers... and incorporated as part of the symbolism of Freemasonry."[730]

PORNOGRAPHY, ABORTION AND HUMAN SACRIFICE

Initiates into Masonry are of course meant to create their own interpretation of Masonic symbols, accepting them at first as representations of "divine power." As they pass through the "chairs" in each degree they are guided by the Masonic hierarchy, who offer more "noble interpretations." Those who accept the nobler meaning, signify their approval of all forms of sex as a natural course of creation. Should they be Judges, Legislators, or Supreme Court Justices, they must, and will defend an individual "right" in a "free society" to practice any form of sex without retribution. In Freemasonry these acts are not sinful, but rather expressions of divine oneness with the creator.

Many problems develop from such a lifestyle, including broken homes, venereal disease, and the use of abortion as birth control. From ancient times the disposal of unwanted children was solved through child sacrifice. Today this crime is committed against the unborn by abortion.

The social ills of modern society - broken families, abortion, pornography, etc., can be found in microcosm in Adam Weishaupt's life. For instance, abortion upon his sister-in-law was Adam Weishaupt's solution to his fathering her illegitimate child. He sought a chemical that would terminate her pregnancy.[731] Weishaupt's promiscuity began with pornography, when, prior to the French Revolution he employed writers of low morals to incite the populace toward licentious living. After the Revolution, pornography was still the medium by which sexual emancipation was achieved. The result was a rapid increase in the birthrate. Reay Tannahill, in *Sex In History*, explains how the higher birthrate was dealt with: "Throughout much of the eighteenth century, infanticide and the abandonment of unwanted children to foundling homes [increased]."[732]

By the end of the 19th century the excuse of "overpopulation" had been manufactured for making birth control acceptable. Overpopulation is not a modern phenomenon. Ancient nations, and to some extent, modern societies, were, and are, faced with famine. Although 19th century mortality rates were already high, some areas of the world still could not sustain their populations. The problem was solved through "oral and anal intercourse, homosexuality, special postures, gestures merely suggestive of coitus, and a host of other techniques. . resorted to in order to achieve satisfaction but avoid

---

[729] Pike 808.

[730] "Phallic Worship," *Mackey's Encyclopedia,* vol.

[731] Wilgus 158.

[732] Reay Tannahill, *Sex In History* (New York: Stein and Day, 1980) 407-408.

conception."[733] Most odious, however, was infanticide, or child sacrifice, sometimes performed as a religious rite to a demon god who wanted blood in exchange for crops.[734] Tannahill gives some examples:

> The simplest and most obvious method of keeping the population down was infanticide, which was to remain as commonplace in Europe, India, and China until the nineteenth century as abortion has become in the West today. Often it may not have been as positive as murder - a matter of leaving a newborn infant exposed to the elements or allowing an ailing one simply to drift away. Often, it may have been more positive. In comparatively recent times some Polynesian tribes are reported to have put two-thirds of their children to death, while the Jagas, warrior nomads of Angola, are said to have killed them all so that the women should not be encumbered on the march; when necessary, they adopted adolescents by force from other tribes. In nineteenth-century Western Australia, there was even a tribe that ate every tenth baby born so as to keep the population down to what the territory would stand.[735]

MASONIC MYTH OF OVERPOPULATION

John Robison explains how the Illuminati hid its pornographic activity in Continental Masonic Lodges:

> I have found that the cover of a Masonic Lodge had been employed in every country venting and propagating sentiments in religion and politics, that could not have circulated in public without exposing the author to great danger. I found that this impunity had gradually encouraged men of licentious principles to become more bold, and to teach doctrines subversive of all our notions of morality... I have been able to trace these attempts made through a course of fifty years... I have observed these doctrines gradually diffusing and mixing with all the different systems of Free Masonry; till, at last, an Association [the Illuminati] has been formed for the express purpose of rooting out all the religious establishments, and overturning all the existing governments of Europe.[736]

The "licentious principles" of the Illuminati gradually found their market on the street. Robison continues, "writers of loose moral principles and of wicked hearts were encouraged by the impunity which the sceptical writers experienced, and ventured to publish things of the vilest tendency, inflaming the passions and justifying licentious manners... and the books found a quick market."[737]

Robison further documents that these writers were educated in illuminated schools called Philanthropine, academies of general education operated by Grand Orient Masons.[738] When the graduates became professionals, morals declined rapidly on a national scale.[739]

---

[733] "Birth Control (Types of) *Encyclopaedia Britannica: Macropaedia.*
[734] "Birth Control (Infanticide)," *Encyclopaedia Britannica: Macropaedia.*
[735] Tannahill 31.
[736] Robison 6-7.
[737] Robison 50.
[738] Antelman 126.
[739] Robison 48-53.

Following the French Revolution the idea of controlling population growth in a promiscuous society found its home in English Freemasonry. The father of our modern theory of population control was an Anglican priest, Thomas Maithus (1766-1834). Dr. John Coleman, in *Freemasonry and the One-World Conspiracy,* states that Malthus was a leading Freemason who published a gloomy document on population control after he was tutored by Freemason Lord Shelburn. In his *Essay on the Principle of Population,* Malthus claimed that population would always outstrip available resources. He could see no way of changing this prospect, only of controlling its development by means of a system of checks and balances. These would necessarily operate against the poor, who formed the numerical majority of the population.[740]

In the 1860s another English Freemason, George Drysdale, spread the population theories of Thomas Malthus by founding the Malthusian League. By 1874 the League was under Masonic control in the person of Annie Besant, a female Mason, drug-pusher, and promoter of free sex. Albert Pike, the Mason who took wagon loads of prostitutes into the Ozark Mountains for days of orgies, was one of Annie's lovers. Annie's brother was Sir Walter Besant, the Mason who first conceived the idea of forming the Quatuor Coronati Lodge of Masonic Research to investigate the origins of Freemasonry.[741]

In reality, birth control was promoted to offset the obvious results of Annie Besant's promotion of women's sexual liberation. The excuse of overpopulation was only a scare tactic to force legislation authorizing contraceptives. Although the Masonic-controlled media promoted Malthus's research, the Malthusian League, and not Malthus himself, was the Masonic front employed to create an acceptable reason behind the "necessity" of birth control.

Freemasonry itself began to promote various methods of birth control, such as contraceptives and abortions. For example, in 1876 a Bristol, England, book distributor was imprisoned for selling *The Fruits of Philosophy: The Private Companion Of Young Married People,* written in 1832 by an American, Dr. Charles Knowlton. The book, a fairly full account of contraceptive practices, was called a pornographic pamphlet The British Solicitor-General prosecuting the case described it in court as "'a dirty, filthy book."' The case resulted in the passing of an obscenity law.[742] Freemason Charles Bradlaugh, leader of Britain's National Secular Society, and Annie Besant challenged the obscenity law by reissuing the pamphlet themselves. Action was brought against them for corruption of youth, but they won the case on grounds of faulty indictment.

Their victory opened the door for more and daring pornography. When the birthrate of both the poor and unwed women skyrocketed, the Maithusian League increased its effort "to agitate for the abolition of all penalties for the public discussion of the population question [and] to spread among the people by all practicable means a knowledge of the law of population, of its consequences, and of its bearing upon human conduct and morals."[743]

Malthusian Leagues began to spread, not only in England, but throughout Europe. Doctors joining the leagues started "medical branches" to assist in manufacturing contraceptives and performing abortions. America was introduced to the concept of birth control by Margaret Sanger (1883-1966), who published a periodical entitled *Woman Rebel.* In 1915 the feminist Mary Ware Dennett formed the first U.S. birth control society, which became known in 1942 as "Planned Parenthood." Margaret Sanger travelled widely to promote the society. Her work resulted in the formation of the International Committee on Planned Parenthood in 1948 at a conference in Cheltenham, England. In 1964 Planned

---

[740] Tannahill 31.

[741] "Famous Men and Masons," *Mackey's Encyclopedia* vol. III.

[742] Tannahill 412.

[743] "Birth Control (History of)," *Encyclopaedia Britannica:Macropaedia.*

Parenthood gained consultative status with the Economic and Social Council of the United Nations and set up headquarters in the United Nations Plaza.[744] Its neighbor at 866 United Nations Plaza, Suite 56617, is the Masonic founded Lucis Trust, formerly Lucifer Publishing Company (see chapter 16). A member of the Lucis Trust, Barbara Marx Hubbard, a female Mason and New Ager, also calls for the elimination of one-fourth of humanity to avoid starvation.[745]

In 1969 Grand Orient Freemasons founded the Club of Rome to expressly study the future overpopulation of the earth. The report, "Limits to Growth," was completed in 1973 to inaugurate the founding of the Trilateral Commission. During the presidential administration of Trilateralist Jimmy Carter, the Club of Rome's report was expanded by a high bureaucratic task force in Washington. On July 24, 1980, the task force released the finished report, called *The Global 2000 Report to the President.* This two-volume study was hailed as the most compre- hensive effort to project global economic trends for the next twenty years. The prospects for the year 2000 were gloomy, claimed the report, because the "carrying capacity" of the globe was not adequate for the predicted population explosion.

Six months later, the Council on Environmental Quality published a second document, *Global Future: A Time to Act.* This document made policy recommendations on the problems *Global 2000* purported only to define. *Global Future* lauded "population control" as the cornerstone of a policy to counter the problems outlined in *Global 2000,* arguing, in effect, that humanity will only be prevented from multiplying too fast by an aggressive program of sterilization, contraception and abortion. If not, *Global Future* prognosticates that millions of people will die by means of famine and violence.

An analysis of *Global 2000* and *Global Future* was published by *Executive Intelligence Review* in August 1982. Their special report, entitled *Global 2000: Blueprint for Genocide,* states that the two Presidential reports "are correctly understood as *political statements of intent* - the intent on the part of such policy-centers as the Council on Foreign Relations, the Trilateral Commission, and the International Monetary Fund, to pursue policies that will result not only in the death of the 170 million cited in the reports, but in the *death of upwards of 2 billion people by the year 2000."*[746] According to the *Blueprint for Genocide,* the two Presidential reports suggested several methods of depopulation, among which were increased abortions, created famines in countries where there were "useless eaters," and if all else fails, a limited and strategically located nuclear war.

As the ancient licentious pagans sacrificed their children to control population, and as eighteenth century Europe practiced infanticide for the same reason, Freemasonry has likewise put the entire human race at risk by its *Global 2000* suggestions.

THE FRENCH PARADIGM

The corruption of pre-revolutionary France provided the pattern for the corruption of Christian America, of which the abominable sin of child sacrifice through abortion is its most horrible and perverted atrocity.

Were there none righteous in France to resist the corruption? Not many! Freemasonry destroyed morality. What few Christians were left were lukewarm. Society was fraught with crime, with every thinkable and unthinkable vice performed, including human

---

[744] "Birth Control (Reformers and reformist groups)," *Encyclopaedia Britannica: Macropaedia.*
[745] NRI *Trumpet.* July 1989, 8.
[746] *Global* 2000: *Blueprint for Genocide,* Special report by the publishers of *Executive Intelligence Review,* August 1982, 1.

sacrifice. There was no love for each other, nor for Christ our Lord. So, God allowed the ravages of hell to destroy them. Those were dark days for the Church. The horror was unspeakable. Malachi Martin gives the accounting:

"France... abolished all religion, beheaded its king, enthroned Reason officially as supreme deity, massacred over 17,000 priests and over 30,000 nuns as well as forty-seven bishops, abolished all seminaries, schools, religious orders, burned all churches and libraries, then sent the Corsican Bonaparte to liberate Italy and Rome."[747]

Before the slaughter, one of the first actions of the revolutionaries was the storming of the Bastille on July 14, 1789. The Bastille was a medieval fortress on the east side of Paris which had been turned into a political prison. Although only seven prisoners were confined there on the morning of its capture (two of whom were madmen), this action became an important symbol in all future Masonic revolutions. Thereafter, the first action taken in a nation where Grand Orient revolutions were in operation has been to open all prisons. The purpose? - to unleash the criminal element to wreak havoc on society. In France, after storming the Bastille, the next action taken by the Masons was to form a new government. Count de Poncins tells how this was accomplished by quoting Freemason Bonnet (no first name given), the orator at the 1904 Grand Orient Assembly:

> During the 18th century the glorious line of the "Encyclopedistes" found in our temples a fervent audience, which, alone at that period, invoked the radiant motto, still unknown to the people, of "Liberty, Equality, Fraternity." The revolutionary seed germinated rapidly in that select company. Our illustrious brother masons [sic] d'Alembert, Diderot, Helvetius, Voltaire and Condorcet, completed the evolution of people's minds and prepared the way for a new age. And when the Bastille fell, freemasonry [sic] had the supreme honour to present to humanity the charter which it had friendly elaborated. It was our Brother, de la Fayette, who first presented the project of a declaration of the natural rights of the man and of the Constitution. On August 25, 1789, the Constituent Assembly, of which more than 300 members were Masons, definitely adopted, almost word for word, in the form determined upon in the Lodges, the text of the immortal Declaration of the Rights of Man.[748]

Abbe' Joseph Lemann, who is quoted in the Preface of Msgr. Dillon's book, *Grand Orient Freemasonry Unmasked*, tells us of another action taken by the Masonic Constituent Assembly:

> "When the question of Jewish emancipation came to be examined by the Constituent Assembly (1789-1791) the deputies who took upon themselves the task of getting it voted were all Freemasons. Mirabeau gave it the persevering help of his eloquence, and Mirabeau was a Freemason of the higher degrees, intimate with Weishaupt and his associates, and closely linked up with the Reform Jews of Berlin. When, after having hesitated for two years, the Constituent Assembly in its second-last meeting, was still hesitating, it was a Freemason and Jacobin, A. Duport, who demanded the vote with threats."[749]

[747] Martin, *The Decline and fall of the Roman Church* 196.

[748] de Poncins, *Secret Powers* 33-34.

[749] Dillon W.

Rabbi Marvin Antelman gives a more concise rendering of the Assembly's vote on civil rights for the Jewish population:

> In 1789 there were approximately 40,000 Jews in France, 30,000 of whom lived in ghettos... The Jews could now enjoy the benefits of a vote taken on September28, 1791, by the Com- mune before the National Assembly in which 53 out of 60 districts in France voted in favor of granting all Jews of France complete civil rights on a par with all citizens.[750]

The Revolution, however, began to falter. Too many Royalists in the Constituent Assembly opposed its radical proposals. The only recourse for the ruthless Templars was to maintain control through fear and terror. *Light-bearers of Darkness* quotes an article, "Revolution, Terror, and Freemasonry," published in the *Revue Intemotionale des Societes Secretes*, on the decision to institute the infamous Reign of Terror:

> In 1789 the revolutionary crimes were prepared by the Committee of Propaganda of the Lodge Les Amis reunis, and the plan of "The Terror" is due to one of its most influential members, the Jacobin Freemason, Adrien Duport [who when questioned as to his plan said], "Now, it is only by means of terror that one can place oneself at the head of a revolution in a way to govern it... It is therefore necessary, whatever repugnance you may have, to resign oneself to the sacrifice of some marked persons.
>
> Instructions in conformity with the plan were given to the principal agents of the department of insurrections which was already organised, and to which Adrien Duport was no stranger; execution followed quickly. The massacre of de Launay, de Flesselles, Foulon, and Berthier, and their heads paraded on pikes, were the first effects of this philanthropic conspiracy.[751]

The riotous rabble, brainwashed by decades of atheistic Masonic literature, were filled with contempt for God and King. In defiance they mobbed the streets of Paris shrieking, "We will have no God, no master." The mob looted churches throughout France and in them blasphem ously held the "Feast of Reason."[752] One author writes, "Then they picked up a woman from the streets of Paris, dressed her in costly robes and profaned the Cathedral of Notre Dame by worshipping her as the Goddess of Reason."[753]

The Revolutionary Tribunal determined that one-third to one-half the population had to be eliminated to establish security for the French Republic. The massacres were carefully organized by the Revolutionary Committees, whose members were selectively chosen by the Jacobin Clubs. The Jacobins were one and all Templar Freemasons. Those who were not Masons had no idea of how to conduct themselves, or even how to survive. Only Masons profited by and directed every aspect of the Revolution. Dressed in the most ragged clothes, with long dirty hair bound by filthy bandannas around their foreheads, parading about in haughty fashion, Masons were the only ones safe from the terror. Then there were the "listeners" everywhere. These spies increased the climate of terror when they returned to the Masonic Lodges and informed the Revolutionary Committees of those whose only crime was decency. Everywhere the demented Masons, clad in rags, sat in front of the guillotine, shrieking with joy at every head that rolled into the gutter, and

---

[750] Antelman 109-110.
[751] Stoddard, *Light-bearers* 14-15.
[752] Webster, *Secret Societies and Subversive Movements* 250.
[753] Winrod 35.

constantly screaming for more and more blood. Paris bragged of the most efficient executioners, despatching twelve heads per guillotine every thirteen minutes. Executioners from other parts of France were sent to Paris to learn their technique.[754]

Many of the acts committed during the Terror defy belief. Typical was the fate of the Princess de Lamballe, a pleasant, middle-aged aristocrat who had escaped from the city. Driven by loyalty to her mistress Marie Antoinette, Princess Lamballe returned to Paris to minister to her. The Princess was promptly seized by the mob, publicly disemboweled, and her private parts paraded through the city as trophies of the triumph of the Revolution! After the storming of the Guilerriers, a young apprentice fell victim to the mob. A great plan was fetched, and a fire built under it. After frying him in butter, the mob ripped apart his flesh and enjoyed a feast.

In western France Keltic peasants and farmers, called calves and dogs by the revolutionists, "were herded into churches and burned to death. Other Kelts were piled into cargo ships, the holds nailed down and the ships sunk. Grand Orient forces went through towns killing everyone in sight, even pulling portable guillotines which worked around the clock."[755]

Between 1789 and 1795, 3.5 million Kelts met their death at the hands of benevolent Grand Orient Freemasonry. To this day, Grand Orient Lodges throughout France re-enact the genocide of Kelts by ritually guillotining calves and dogs during an annual celebration.

The most grandiose celebration in all French Grand Orient Lodges today is the mimed murder of King Louis XVI and his wife, Marie Antoinette. Attending this annual event are the Establishment notables dressed up in elaborate regalia. At the banquet "special stewards herd a number of calves to waiting guillotines. The terrified animals are then beheaded to the cries of 'Death to Louis; death to the king; death to the lilies (the French royal emblem).' The calf heads are then thrown into boiling water and are subsequently consumed by the revelers."[756]

The significance of the ritual is that Louis XVI, a kind and gentle man, was called "the Calf" by the Grand Orient before they beheaded him.

When Louis XVI was executed in 1793, an elderly Mason dipped his hands in the royal blood, and said, "I baptise [sic] thee in the name of Liberty and Jacques." Templar revenge was complete. Albert Pike gloated that "The secret movers of the French Revolution had sworn to overturn the Throne and the Altar upon the Tomb of Jacques de Molay. When Louis XVI was executed, half the work was done; and thence forward the Army of the Temple was to direct all its efforts against the Pope."[757]

Meanwhile, Sionist Weishaupt, author of the French Revolution was in exile far from the dangers he had set in motion. During the Reign of Terror, when the Templars gained control through the Jacobin Clubs, the Grand Orient Lodges founded by the duke of Orleans and illuminated by Weishaupt, ceased activity. In 1793 the Jacobins seized the Merovingian traitor, Philippe, duke of Orleans, and beheaded him. With the Duke dead, Weishaupt had no chance for further contact with the Revolution.

By 1794 there were 6,800 Jacobin Clubs, totaling half a million members.[758] All were former Grand Orient Masons, first taught revolution by Sion's Illuminati, then indoctrinated by the Knights Templar to avenge the death of their medieval Grand Master,

---

[754] Nesta H. Webster, *The French Revolution*, (1919; Hawthorne, CA: Christian Book Club of America, 1969) 419-429.

[755] Walter Wright, "Annual French Festival Has Sinister Backdrop," *Spotlight* 17 June 1991: 10.

[756] Wright.

[757] Pike 823-824.

[758] Durant and Durant, *The Story of Civilization: The Age of Napoleon*, vol. XI, 33.

Jacques de Molay. In so doing they avenged themselves of the injustices brought by their adversaries, the Merovingian kings.

Even with as dominant and organized a force as the Jacobins propelling it, the revolution began to falter. In seeking to bolster their power, the Templars turned on the Royalists, beginning to slay them. The bloodbath was so intense that the Beast began to slay its own. The three Masonic architects of the Reign of Terror, Marat, Danton, and Robespierre, were themselves assassinated or beheaded, and Paris slowly began to return to normal.

The anti-religious fervor of the Revolution was truly demonic. Orthodox Rabbi Antelman notes that "During the Reign of Terror, all houses of worship were closed in accordance with Jacobin anti-religious policy. The churches and synagogues were reopened after Robespierre was guillotined on July 28, 1794, signifying the end of terror and the Jacobin power base."[759] To protect its bloodthirsty terrorists from further legal action, the Constituent Assembly quickly passed a resolution that France would harbor political terrorists. The law remains on the books to this day.

Albert Pike mourned what he saw as the failure of the Revolution: Jacques de Molay and his companions were perhaps martyrs, but their avengers dishonored their memory. Royalty was regenerated on the scaffold of Louis XVI., the Church triumphed in the captivity of Pius VI., carried a prisoner to Valence, and dying of fatigue and sorrow, but the successors of the Ancient Knights of the Temple perished, overwhelmed in their fatal victory."[760]

Pike is referring to Napoleon Bonaparte's failure to conquer Europe for the Templars. The Masonic Templars had selected Napoleon for that purpose after he shored up their Revolution following the Reign of Terror disaster. Msgr. Dillon writes that in 1804 when the Jacobin Napoleon intended to proclaim himself Emperor, he wished to give the Masons a pledge of his principles, and... he did this by killing the Duke d'Enghien, after which he said, 'They wish to destroy the Revolution in attacking it in my person. I will defend it, for I am the Revolution. I, myself-I, myself. They will so consider it from this day forward, for they will know of what we are capable."[761]

In 1799, when Napoleon seized power, Grand Orient Lodges were opened in every place and taken over by the Knights Templar. By 1801 the Grand Orients and Scottish Rite merged. In 1804 Napoleon declared himself Emperor. Nesta Webster writes that within a short time "Nearly 1,200 lodges existed in France under the Empire; generals, magistrates, artists, savants, and notabilities in every line were initiated into the Order. The most eminent of these was Prince Cambaceres, pro Grand Master of the Grand Orient."[762]

There is no record that Napoleon was ever an Illuminatus. There is ample record, however, that he was a staunch Templar. He was a Jacobin, and according to *Mackey's Encyclopedia of Freemasonry*, also a member of Grand Orient Freemasonry, as were his brothers, but only after the Grand Orient merged with the Scottish Rite Templars.[763]

Napoleon, however, failed the Templars. His military adventures became too extended geographically. English Freemasonry, suspicious of his intent, finally sent Freemason General Wellington to defeat him at Waterloo.[764] Meanwhile, in 1815, the

---

[759] Antelman 109.

[760] Pike 824.

[761] Dillon 37.

[762] Webster, *Secret Societies* 255.

[763] "Bonaparte, Jerome; Joseph; Louis; and Lucien" and "Napoleon I," *Mackey's Encyclopedia*, vols. I & II.

[764] "Wellington, Duke of," *Mackey's Encyclopedia*, vol.11.

British Brotherhood, with her Oligarchic aristocracy, was represented at the Congress of Vienna to help reestablish Merovingian rule.

Adam Weishaupt lived to the age of eighty-two and died in 1830 a lonely man. Before he passed into eternity, he called for a Catholic priest and asked to be reinstated in the Church. Some revisionist authors believe this was a ploy by a hardened revolutionist who wanted to make it look as if the Illuminati was buried with him. There may be some merit to this speculation, since he allegedly appointed a successor - an Italian Grand Orient Freemason named Giuseppe (Joseph) Mazzini.

Italy fell shorty after France. Edith Starr Miller tells of an incident in 1824 in which one of the ruling chiefs of the Supreme Council of France, code named Nubio, was sent to Italy to destroy Christian morality there. To instruct him upon his arrival, he was given a *Guide for the Heads of the Highest Grades of Masonry*. This high Mason wrote to Signor Volpi, head of Freemasonry in Italy, "I was appointed to demoralise [sic] the education of the youth of the Church."[765]

Forty-five years later such demoralization remained the mind-set of French Freemasonry. In 1869 the minutes to the Supreme Council of Mizralm Freemasonry (Cagliostro's Sionist creation) read, "Let us foster the idea of free love, that we may destroy among Christian women attachment to the principles and practices of their religion."[766]

Two decades later "free sex" was recommended to Universal Freemasonry as a Masonic lifestyle. In the summer of 1889, as we have seen, Albert Pike suggested to the twenty-three Supreme Councils meeting in Paris that they should erect houses of prostitution, which he called "Lodges of Adoption" for "Commerce with women, belonging to all brethren..."[767]

Clearly, licentiousness is at the heart of the Masonic hierarchy. It is a Masonic rite, since the Masonic Lodge is the modern headquarters of Babylon's sensual religion. This lifestyle was promoted in the Grand Orient Tugendbunds prior to the French Revolution. Using anti-Semitic Reform Jews as fronts, the Tugendbunds taught as virtuous everything contrary to Mosaic Law. Masonic Lodges became dens of corruption and prostitution.

THE MASONIC CORRUPTION OF AMERICA

The history of events in our country leading to the secularization of our culture and the concomitant evil of widespread abortion began during World War II. In retrospect, this sequence is so obviously Masonic that it could not have been an accident, but must have been a calculated plan. Using the Masonic French Revolution as our pattern and gauge, we shall discover that eight of ten steps to destroy Christian America have been accomplished. They are in order: (1) the majority of Supreme Court appointees have been Masons; (2) the same Masonic dominated Supreme Court has reinterpreted our Constitution to imply "Separation of Church and State": (3) the Masonic media has falsely promoted the Constitution as embodying and protecting the "Separation of Church and State"; (4) the Supreme Court has ruled Bible reading and prayer in public schools unconstitutional, because of separation of Church and State; (5) the Masonic- controlled

---

[765] Miller 427.*Permanent Instructions, or Practical Code of Rules; Guide for the Heads of the Highest Grades of Masonry*, was originally given to Nubio. This secret document, published in Italy by the highest authority of the order, was for the guidance of the active heads of Freemasonry in 1818. It was this instruction to which Nubio referred when he wrote to Signor Volpi, "I am appointed to demoralise [sic] the education of the youth of the Church."

[766] Nilus 296.

[767] Miller 233-234.

NEA immediately replaced Biblical morality in public schools with a licentious *new morality;* (6) the Supreme Court promptly legalized pornography to extend the new morality of free sex to public life; (7) the same Court then took action against parental authority over children; and (8) it legalized the distribution of contraceptives and the killing of the unborn by abortion.

We will now document that Freemasonry is the force behind each of the ten steps to destroy Christianity in America. Paul Fisher details this sequence of Masonic successes in *Behind The Lodge Door.* First, he says our Supreme Court was stacked with Freemasons during the three Presidential terms of 32nd degree Freemason, President Franklin Roosevelt. Five of the nine Justices were his Scottish Rite Brothers. The others shared Masonic views. From 1941 to 1971, five to eight Masons sat on the Supreme Court in any given year.[768]

Second, the First Amendment to our Constitution had to be Masonically interpreted to mean "Separation of Church and State." The actual words to the Amendment read: "Congress shall *make no law* respecting an establishment of religion, or prohibiting the free exercise thereof; or abridging the freedom of speech, or of the press; or the right of the people peaceably to assemble, and to petition the Government for a redress of grievances."

Our forefathers wrote the First Amendment so that freedom of religion and freedom of speech would go together. Therefore, it was all Christians' constitutional right to pray and read our Bibles aloud wherever we desired, even in public schools. The amendment states no law shall be made to prohibit this freedom. Therefore, to suppress this constitutional right, Masonry had to nullify the First Amendment with another - its own interpretation. A statement made in 1941 by 32nd degree Freemason, Supreme Court Justice Robert H. Jackson confirms this fact. He said that the Constitution and its amendments "are what the judges say they are."[769] Once a ruling is made, it sets a precedent and becomes law.

"Separation of Church and State" are words that originated in the minds of French Masonic revolutionists, not in the minds of our forefathers. For example, the Masonically-inspired French constitution of 1791 provided for the creation of a system of free, public, secular education, with the result that religion is no longer taught in the public schools in France to this day.[770]

These same restrictions of religion have extended to most communist countries. For example, in the former Soviet Union the phrase, "separation of Church and State" was written into its constitution. But not into ours. After World War II, American Freemasonry determined to follow the pattern of the Soviet Union. To circumvent a blatant act of treason, our Masonic dominated Supreme Court said separation of church and state was "implied" in the First Amendment.

The third step in the Masonic plot to destroy Christianity in America was to activate the Masonic controlled press. The media has repeated over and over the Supreme Court's interpretation of the First Amendment as if it were the actual words of the Constitution. "Separation of Church and State is part of our Constitution," the press reports. "Therefore, religious activity in our state- funded schools is in violation of our Constitution."[771] To this day most Americans believe this Masonic disinformation, because they have not read the Constitution since high school days.

---

[768] Fisher, Appendix A.

[769] Fisher 134.

[770] "Education, Systems of (Religious and other factors - Types of educational systems and their characteristics)," *Encyclopaedia Britannica: Macropaedia.*

[771] "Education, Systems of."

Following the media propaganda blitz, the fourth step to destroy Christian America was to outlaw religious activity (meaning Christianity, of course) in our classrooms. Fourteen years before the 1962-1963 Schempp decision struck down prayer and Bible reading in our public schools[772], Freemasonry began to program its membership to accept the change. The Masonic propaganda was first published in the *New Age* magazine, November 1948. In an article entitled "Religion In The Public Schools," the Southern Jurisdiction of Scottish Rite Freemasonry promoted "natural religion" to replace Christianity in our public schools:

> *The dramatic presentation of the 32nd degree of the Scottish Rite expresses a code of ethics which is essentially natural religion... In this support of natural religion, Scottish Rite masonry presents an excellent example of what might be followed in our public schools... There can be no well-founded objection to the presentation of natural religion.*[773]

The definition of Freemasonry's "natural religion" was explained as the religion of the "knowledge of good and evil" in the *New Age* of January, 1949 and September, 1958. The articles published in this Masonic organ recommended that public school children be taught the "balance between good and evil" and "the knowledge of good and evil."[774] As we know, this is the religion of the Serpent in Genesis 2:16-17; 3:1-5.

Less than three years before the Bible and prayer in public schools were outlawed, the *New Age* (March 1959) bragged of Freemasonry's New Order brought forth by "the establishment of the public school system, financed by the State, for the combined purpose of technological and sociological education of the mass of humanity, beginning at an early age in children."[775] The article confirmed that "sociological education" would be a "Liberal" education.

After the fourth step of outlawing the Bible and prayer in the public schools became a reality, the fifth step came quickly. With Christian morality no longer allowed expression after 1963, the Masonic-created National Education Association (NEA) had free reign as "agents of change" to teach and graduate a generation of "natural religionists" with a "new morality" - or rather, with "no morality." This technique was comparable to the procedure employed by the Illuminati's Philanthropine schools.

As rapidly came the sixth step. Realizing that young minds emptied of Biblical morality in public schools were easy prey for continued seduction after graduation, our Masonic-dominated Supreme Court authorized and in fact protected incitements to indecent living with its ruling on pornography. This time Justice Brennan, not a Mason himself, but whose thinking paralleled Masonic thought, was in the forefront. Fisher explains:

> *In Roth vs. United States, 354 U.S. 476 (1957), Justice Brennan in the majority opinion, while denying that obscenity is protected by the Constitution, posited the unique definition of obscenity as "material which deals with sex in a manner appealing to prurient interests." He then said the test for obscenity is "whether to the average person, applying contemporary community standards, the dominant theme of the material, taken as a whole, appeals to prurient interests." That*

---

[772] Fisher 56, 280. The Supreme Court "stacking" continued until President Nixon reversed the trend in 1973- an unforgivable crime.
[773] Fisher.
[774] Fisher.
[775] Fisher 56-57, 294.

*permitted such publications as Playboy and Penthouse to display pornographic
nudity in their magazines along with articles on politics, the arts, economics, etc.
by recognized experts in their respective fields.*[776]

On the heels of legalized pornography came "human and civil rights" legislation,
which then gave rise to the much publicized "right to privacy," not a legislated right, but
an interpretation of "civil rights." Meanwhile, the "new morality" taught in public schools
began to take hold. Free and open sex, now so much flaunted in both the heterosexual and
homosexual community, became the order of the day. The number of unwed mothers
began to climb.

The seventh and eighth steps to destroy Christian America were taken when the
Masonic- dominated Supreme Court took action against parents' authority over their own
children. Fisher informs us that the Supreme Court's approval of distributing
contraceptives to children without parental consent, and authorizing them to have
abortions without the same consent, parallels Masonic thought.[777] Again, Justice Brennen
was one of the chief architects of the *Roe vs. Wade* abortion decision in **1973**.[778]

Following this legislation came the oft repeated Masonic phrases "women's rights"
and "pro- choice." Again these are not legislated rights, but rights relentlessly publicized
and promoted by the media elite of our country. A quote from *Citizen*, October 15, 1990,
a magazine published by James Dobson's "Focus on the Family," addresses the media
promotion of the Masonic anti- family agenda:

> *Most major newspapers support abortion rights on their editorial pages, and
> reporters are decidedly pro-abortion. A 1985 Los Angeles Times poll found that
> 82 percent of journalists on newspapers of all sizes say they favor abortion rights.
> Some reporters participated in a big abortion rights march in Washington in
> 1989...*
>
> *The nation's largest newspaper chains give money to pro-abortion groups...
> Journalists tend to regard opponents of abortion as "religious fanatics" and "bug-
> eyed zealots..."*[779]

Is there a connection between the anti-family, anti-religious views of the media and
Freemasonry? For an answer recall the statement made in the July 1928 issue of the
Masonic *New Age* magazine: "many members of the National Press Club are Masons, and
not a few of them very prominent Masons."[780]

The Washington Post, one of the newspapers listed by Myron Fagan as pro-Masonic,
provides a classic case study of institutionalizing "pro-choice" bias. The following
statement comes directly from the *Washington Post Deskbook on Style*:

> *The terms right-to-Life and pro-Life are used by advocates in the abortion
> controversy to buttress their arguments. They should generally be used as part of*

---

[776] Fisher.

[777] Fisher 40.

[778] Fisher 280. By this date President Nixon had appointed four non-Masons to the High Court, three
of whom replaced Masons. Brennen, however, still had enough of the old guard to sway the new
Justices for passage of the abortion rights decision. Two of the Justices who played a major role in
the 1973 Roe v. Wade decision had conceded, in private memos, that they knew they were
"legislating policy and exceeding [the court's] authority as the interpreter, not the maker of law."

[779] Citizen, *a periodical of James Dobson's Focus on the Family*, 15 Oct.1990: 10-12.

[780] Fisher 242.

> *an organization's title and in quotations, but not as descriptive adjectives in the*
> *text. Use abortion-rights advocates for those who support freedom of choice in*
> *the matter, and anti-abortion for those who oppose it.*[781]

The *Post's* guidelines for combating the "pro-lifers" apparently insist that they be called "anti- abortionists," and by strong implication, suppressors of women's rights. Conversely, the "pro- abortionist" movement was to be titled "abortion-rights advocates" or promoters of women's rights. These terms, the one negative for those who oppose murder, the other positive for those who relish the slaughter of unborn children, are sanitary words which conceal reality - selective child sacrifice for selfishness and population control. In reality, abortion becomes a "scientific" culling of the human herd.

The priesthood in ancient mystery religions used the same "scientific" excuse, making child sacrifice a religious rite. Ancient practices parallel Masonic thought today, which is deliberately designed to sooth the consciences of those who officiate in the ceremony of the now-legal child sacrifices. Most revealing is the fact that many who work in abortion clinics are Satan worshippers themselves, who, by the act of killing the unborn, are knowingly and willingly performing human sacrifice to their demon god. This fact is confirmed by Carol Everett, a former owner of several Dallas, Texas, abortion clinics. Wendell Amstutz, in *Exposing and Confronting Satan & Associates*, quotes her as saying, "'A tremendous number of occultists work at the clinics. There is a definite link between abortion mills and the occult. People involved in abortion are involved in demonic activity."[782]

Today, moral corruption pervades American society, including the Christian community. Eight of the ten steps taken by Freemasonry to destroy Christian America have been successful. The ninth will be an "anti-proselyting law," first beginning at public schools, but eventually extending to public life, forbidding even the invitation of the unsaved to attend church. The precedent has already been set by French law. A Christian witness, or any religious witness for that matter, is prohibited in French public schools.[783] When (and not if) this law is enacted in America, we can be assured it will be backed by the treacherous Masonic dominated National Council of Churches.

Masonry's tenth step will come quickly if Christians resist the ninth. The "Reign of Terror" in the French Revolution and the "Red Terror" in the Russian Revolution are examples of the "final solution" planned for professing Christians in America. Masonic "New Agers" are preparing the way. Ken Eyers, a New Age spokesman, wrote in *Parade Magazine,* August 9, 1987, "Those who cannot be enlightened [meaning Christians] will not be permitted to dwell in this world. They will be sent [meaning killed] to some equally appropriate place to work their way to understanding."

Apparently, Freemasonry in America is following the blueprint drawn by Freemason Voltaire, who in a letter to King Frederick the Great, head of the Templar Scottish Rite, shared his "final solution": "Lastly, when the whole body of the Church should be sufficiently weakened and infidelity strong enough, the final blow [is] to be dealt by the sword of open, relentless persecution. A reign of terror [is] to spread over the whole earth, and... continue while a Christian should be found obstinate enough to adhere to Christianity."[784]

America today is reaping the fruits of the seeds sown by Weishaupt and his obscene illuminated Freemasonry. One hundred years ago Grand Orient agents were sent to

---

[781] Citizen 10-12 (quoting Washington Post Deskbook on Style185-186).
[782] Wendell Amstutz, *Exposing and Confronting Satan & Associates* (Rochester, MN: National Counseling Resource Center, 1990) 188.
[783] "Muslim Schoolgirl Scarves Banned," *Los Angeles Times* (7 November 1989): n.p.
[784] Dillon 7.

America to undermine Christianity in our nation. In one century Freemasonry accomplished its goal. We just happen to be the last major nation to fall.

REPENTANCE

If apathetic Christians do not resist now, it may be too late later. Jesus Christ, while condemning the Laodicean Church for her apathy, gives us the solution to lift our nation out of its moral decay. In Revelation 3:18-19, He says, "I counsel thee to buy of me gold tried in the fire, that thou mayest be rich; and white raiment, that thou mayest be clothed, and that the shame of thy nakedness do not appear; and anoint thine eyes with eye salve, that thou mayest see. As many as I love, I rebuke and chasten: be zealous therefore, and repent."

Repentance is an act of separation from the world - a turning away from worldly lusts. The Apostle Paul wrote in II Corinthians 6: 14-17:

> *Be ye not unequally yoked together with unbelievers: for what fellowship hath righteousness with unrighteousness? and what communion hath light with darkness? And what concord hath Christ with Belial? or what part hath he that believeth with an infidel?" And what agreement hath the temple of God with idols? for ye are the temple of the living God; as God hath said, I will dwell in them, and walk in them; and I will be their God, and they shall be my people. Wherefore come out from among them, and be ye separate, saith the Lord, and touch not the unclean thing; and I will receive you...*

Our Lord wants us to separate from all that is unclean, unholy and evil. This Scripture specifically implies separation from an eastern religion, as inferred by the words *unbehevers, unrighteousness, dark-ness, Belial,* and *infidel.* It demands we not bring this *idolatry* into our lives.

All these words are linked by the one word *yoked.* In its Greek sense, this word *yoked* is used only once in the New Testament - here, in this verse. It means "to associate discordandy."[785] God warns us against discordant (conflicting, contrary, and incompatible) associations.

The Greek primitive root word for yoked literally means "the beam of the balance as connecting a pair of balances." This definition is descriptive of Freemasonry's "equilibrium" in all things. The Lodge attempts to equalize, or balance all relationships, all actions, and all religions in Freemasonry. Figuratively, this root word means to be "joined by obligation, or servitude by law or obligation."[786]

All eastern religions demand servitude by obligation, binding their priesthood to this course of action by irrevocable oaths. Freemasonry requires the same of its initiates.

Christians are to be separate from this religion. Some, however, have "yoked" with Masons and Freemasonry. As Paul warned, "come out from among them," Jesus Christ warns in Revelation 18:4: "Come out of her, my people, that ye be not partakers of her sins, and that ye receive not of her plagues."

The Greek word translated "plagues" is used only in the book of Revelation. It literally means "a stroke" and figuratively means calamities.[787] Today our nation is experiencing

---

[785] strong, Greek #2086.
[786] Strong, Greek prim. root #2218.
[787] Strong, Greek #4127 from 4141 and 5180.

repeated and escalating calamities brought on by earthquakes, bad weather, AIDS, poor economy, and dishonest businessmen, bankers and politicians.

In ancient Israel the Lord gave King Solomon four steps to check moral decay in his nation. Recall Almighty God's counsel in II Chronicles 7: 14: "If my people, which are called by my name, shall humble themselves, and pray, and seek my face, and turn from their wicked ways; then will I hear from heaven, and will forgive their sin, and will heal their land."

God's invitation is so simple. Yet, in a land of freedom, Christians do not respond to it. Freedom has caused the Church to become lukewarm. Persecution, not freedom, has always purified the Church. Christ did warn of persecution for the Laodicean Church age. He said, "As many as I love, I rebuke and chasten: be zealous therefore, and repent" (Revelation 3:19).

We must humble ourselves, pray, seek God's face and repent. If we want to survive as a Christian nation, we must act on these words from Almighty God, as well as teach them as a way of life to our children. Pastors who are separated from the world need to preach this message of purity to their congregation. In this alone lies our national security. Nothing more! Nothing less! Are we willing? It will take a concerted effort. It is up to us! A healed land will be the result.

IN CONCLUSION

Four of the eight legs of the "octopus theory" are actually part of the conspiracy of French Templarism. Two of the legs were also tentacles of English Sionism - the Jews and Freemasonry. The Jews, nevertheless, participated in the French Revolution for the same reason they participated in the English Glorious Revolution - to gain freedom, as any downtrodden race would do. Concerning the Jesuits, although many joined Masonry, there is no concrete evidence they are the hidden hand. The Illuminati, which was created by the even more secret Priory of Sion, appeared to have been the hidden hand. When the Illuminati was exposed and suppressed by the Templars, the Knights took over the revolution.

Of the seven conspiracy theories discussed, Freemasonry is the shelter in which all lodge – not the Catholic Church, not Judaism. One conspiracy theory has yet to be brought to light. Communism. Is it Templar or Sionist? We will learn of its Masonic creation, Masonic development, and Masonic protection in future chapters.

11. FIRST WAR BETWEEN ENGLISH AND FRENCH FREEMASONRY

> *Many minor German Princes continued to be Freemasons. The Duke of Brunswick was the central figure in the first Masonic conspiracy... The Court of Vienna was more or less Masonic since the reign of the wretched Joseph II. Alexander of Russia was educated by La Harpe, a [Grand Orient] Freemason...*[788]
>
> *The Elector of Hesse, Prince William of Hanau, held broad views in religious matters, associated much with Freemasons and practiced complete religious tolerance.*[789]

Royalty in Europe had long been involved in Freemasonry before Weishaupt came on the scene - not that they were revolutionary, although some of course were - but because they were curious. Freemasonry was considered the custodian of science, something into which an intelligent man should look. It was also anti-Catholic, which suited many of the German Protestant princes. Even Catholic monarchs, nominal in their Christianity, disregarded the Vatican's ban on membership and attached themselves to the Order. After the French Revolution plunged Europe into political chaos, both Protestant and Catholic monarchs changed their attitudes toward the Craft.

As we know, the original intent of the French Revolution was to dethrone the Bourbon dynasty in favor of Sion's Lorraine-Habsburg "King of Jerusalem" cult. Yet, when the Revolution began, the strongest players appeared to be the Templars, who had outsmarted Sion's Illuminati with exposure. Strong evidence of Templar involvement is seen in the appearance of the Jacobin Clubs when the doors of the Illuminati's Grand Orient lodges closed. It is true that most conspiracy researchers view this as nothing more than the Illuminati changing their name. The Jacobin Clubs were illuminated, and, as we have noted before, the name Jacobin recalls Jacques de Molay, strongly suggesting Templar influence, if not control.

At the time of the French Revolution, there were actually three major conspiracies working - all under the Masonic banner. They allegedly united in 1782 at Wilhelmsbad to cooperate in revolution. All three were illuminated at that conference. As subsequent events reveal, however, each had secretly planned its own outcome via the Revolution. For example, the French Grand Lodge, an English Masonic front, was Royalist, wanting a constitutional monarchy. The French Grand Orient, an Illuminati front of the Priory of Sion, fought to replace the Bourbon dynasty with another. The Scottish Rite, a Templar front, planned to avenge a four-centuries-old murder, destroying the monarchy and replacing it with a republic. Thus divided, the revolution was doomed to failure.

Freemasonry's desire to alter the despotic politics of Europe might have been an admirable undertaking, but the outcome could not have been foreseen, nor given the anti-social passions that had been aroused, restraint possible. The French Revolution ended in the Terror. According to *Mackey's Encyclopedia of Freemasonry*, not until December 27, 1801 did two of the warring factions of Masonry, the Templar Scottish Rite and the

---

[788] Dillon 41.
[789] Corti 10.

Grand Orient bodies merge.[790] Soon afterwards, the third Masonic party, the Grand Lodge came into line and all three upheld Napoleon.

De Poncins, in *The Secret Powers Behind Revolution*, explains that

> By wishing to go too fast, freemasonry [sic] miscarried. The excesses of the Terror brought about a violent reaction of the country. Being unable to do better, freemasonry [sic] resumed its philanthropic guise and respectful attitude to social order. It upheld Napoleon, who, moreover, served it by spreading the revolutionary spirit all over Europe... In a word he was for Europe what the revolution had been for France.[791]

NAPOLEON BONAPARTE AND THE TEMPLARS

Napoleon Bonaparte was not a self-made man. He was selected by Templar Freemasonry to salvage the revolution - to solidify the revolution in *his* name, since rumors persisted that the exiled Bourbons would return. Msgr. Dillon writes that "As a lesser evil therefore, and as a means of forwarding the unification of Europe which they had planned by his conquests, the Freemasons placed supreme power in the hands of Bonaparte, and urged him on in his career..."[792]

Although general history presents Napoleon as a fervent Catholic, Msgr. Dillon contradicts that judgment:

> [Napoleon's] letters breathe everywhere the spirit of advanced Freemasonry, gloating over the wounds it had been able to inflict upon the Spouse of Christ. Yet this adventurer has, with great adroitness, been able to pass with many... as a good Catholic...but he was in all his acts what Freemasonry made him. He was mean, selfish, tyrannical, cruel. He was reckless of blood. He could tolerate or use the Church while that suited his policy. But he had from the beginning to the very end of his career that thorough indifference to her welfare, and want of belief in her doctrines, which an early and life-long connection with the Illuminati inspired.[793]

Dillon informs us that Napoleon indeed had connections with Illuminism. He had been a member of a Templar Lodge, the extreme Illuminated Lodge of Lyons, and had given proof of his fidelity to Italian Masonry by kidnapping the Pope.[794] Dillon also quotes Father Deschamps that "Napoleon Bonaparte was in effect an advanced Freemason, and his reign has been the most flourishing epoch of Freemasonry."[795]

While there is no record of Napoleon meeting Weishaupt, ample evidence exists that Napoleon was a Templar Jacobin. When the Illuminati was exposed, Napoleon plunged into Templarism, absorbing all its history he could, fascinated by its past wealth. One of his personal goals as Emperor was to capture the Roman Church and confiscate all Templar documents, which he did in 1810. That year the entire archives of the Vatican, more than three thousand cases of material - including all the documents pertaining to the

---

[790] "Arras, Primordial Chapter Of," *Mackey's Encyclopedia of Freemasonry*, Vol. I.
[791] de Poncins, *The Secret Powers behind Revolution* 49.
[792] Dillon 39.
[793] Dillon 34-35.
[794] Dillon 35.
[795] Dillon 35.

Templars - were brought back to Paris. Although some of these papers were subsequently returned to Rome, a great many remained in France.[796] Freemasonry, in *Mackey's Encyclopedia*, certainly claims Bonaparte as one of its own:

> It has been claimed, and with much just reason, as shown in his course of life, that Napoleon the Great was a member of the Brotherhood... The Strassburg Lodge is said to have toasted Napoleon as a Freemason. The wording of the toast shows that this was before Napoleon became Emperor... In March, 1807, at Milan, [Italy], Napoleon is toasted as "Brother, Emperor and King, Protector."[797]

Clearly Napoleon Bonaparte was brought to power because of Masonry's failure to solidify the Revolution. The Templars especially viewed him as the man who could unite the continent under a Masonic republic. The hated Merovingian Grail kings would once and for all be exterminated. In Napoleon's name the revolution would continue.

TALLEYRAND AND NAPOLEON

The Templars brought Napoleon to power through the assistance of Charles-Maurice de Talleyrand-Perigord (1754-1838), a renegade Catholic priest who had joined Freemasonry. The story of Talleyrand is bewildering, to say the least. In 1779, the year he aligned himself with the Illuminati, he also began his career as a court cleric in the House of Bourbon. In 1780 he was appointed agent general of the French clergy. In 1786, in an attempt to continue the activity of the suppressed Illuminati, Talleyrand, together with Mirabeau and Philippe, Duke of Orleans, founded the Club Breton. Club Breton was taken over by the Templars and renamed the Jacobin Club.[798]

Without a blink, Talleyrand made the transition from the Sionist Club Breton to the Templar Jacobin Club. There he first met Napoleon. In 1788 Talleyrand was appointed Bishop of Autun. He was excommunicated by the Pope when, during the Revolution, he cooperated in the radical reorganization of the church. By the time the revolution had failed, the adroit Talleyrand had proved his worth to the Templars. At his recommendation, the Templars found in Napoleon their strong man, whom they would back to save the gains of the Revolution. "Put Napoleon on the throne and open the Grand Orients," Talleyrand advised.

Talleyrand had no problem switching from the Sionists to the Templars. In fact, throughout his career this wily politician continually changed sides. No one has ever suggested that he might have been a double agent for the Priory of Sion. Yet, his activity suggests that conclusion. For example, while hobnobbing with the Templars in the Jacobin Club, Talleyrand was also a member of a more illusive club called the Philadelphians, a Rosicrucian secret society founded in 1790 that was adversarial to both the Templars and Napoleon.[799]

Conspiracy researchers have said Talleyrand was playing both sides of the conspiracy for his own elevation to power. History records that he was certainly adept at ingratiating himself with any administration. *The Encyclopaedia Britannica* gives a brief account of his political agility:

---

[796] Baigent et al, *Holy Blood* 150-151.
[797] "Napoleon I," *Mackey's Encyclopedia*, vol.11.
[798] Miller 379.
[799] Miller 395 and Baigent, *Holy Blood* 152.

> *A deputy to the National Assembly during the last years of the Revolution and foreign minister [1797-17991 under the Directory, Talleyrand achieved great power and influence under Napoleon I as foreign minister and chamberlain of the empire prior to his resignation [1807]. He then served as a consultant to Napoleon.*[800]

By 1810 Talleyrand began to distance himself from the Emperor. In 1812 he sided with General Malet (a brother Philadelphian) in a conspiracy to overthrow the Empire.[801] In 1815 he was at the Congress of Vienna mingling with Sion's Grail blue bloods.

While historians describe Talleyrand as crafty, underhanded, wily, and adroit, they do not record those with whom he associated in the Rosicrucian Order of the Philadelphians, a Sionist front group. One associate was Charles Nodier, the new Grand Master of the Priory of Sion (G.M.1801-1844).

When Tallleyrand advised the Templars to put Napoleon on the throne, he planned to surround the Emperor with the remnant of Sion's illumined. Talleyrand met with some success, for the moment Napoleon seized power (1799), the Grand Orient lodges, where the remnant of Illuminism sought a home, were opened in every place.[802] That success was shattered, however, when in 1801 the Grand Orients merged with Sion's rivals, the Templar Scottish Rite, which embraced radical republicanism.

The Templars, seeing in Napoleon their chance to unify Europe, permitted the Corsican to declare himself Emperor in 1804. Masonry then conspired during the Empire, assisting Napoleon in 1805 by undermining Austrian and Russian military might at the Battle of Austerlitz, giving Napoleon his greatest victory. Msgr. Dillon explains how the conspiracy worked: "The designs of the Austrian and other generals opposed to him were thwarted, treason was rife in their camps, and information fatal to their designs was conveyed to the French commander."[803]

Masonry was then on Napoleon's side. For the next four years its power of hidden influence and espionage were placed at the Emperor's disposal. Napoleon, however, had no idea his rapid success was due to the Masonic intelligence service. Haughty and arrogant, blinded by power, he believed he was the source of all his brilliant victories. Msgr. Dillon writes that Napoleon's greatest mistake was the encouragement he gave to Freemasonry. It served his "purpose admirably for awhile, that is so long as he served the present and ultimate views of the conspiracy..."[804]

Trouble, however, began brewing between Napoleon and the Templar powers when they watched his brothers, all steeped in the secrets of Freemasonry, placed on the conquered thrones of Europe. When Napoleon desired a wife with Habsburg blood to make his reign in France more legitimate, Freemasonry became nervous.

Napoleon no longer wanted to be Emperor. He wanted to be King. In 1809 he divorced Josephine of the House of Bourbon. Prince Metternich, Austrian minister of foreign affairs, responded in an effort to bring peace to Europe, and arranged for Napoleon to marry a Merovingian princess, Archduchess Marie Louise of the House of Habsburg.[805] Freemasonry feared that the Emperor's power might be perpetuated with this alliance. The consequence of which would be an heir to his throne. A second

---

[800] "Talleyrand," *Encyclopaedia Britannica: Micropaedia.*
[801] Miller 395.
[802] Dillon 35, 38.
[803] Dillon 40.
[804] Dillon 39.
[805] Will Durant and Ariel Durant, *The Story of Civilization: The Age of Napoleon* (New York: Simon and Schuster, 1975) 562.

Napoleon would cause danger to the universal republic Freemasonry could otherwise inaugurate at the death of the first Napoleon.

Msgr. Dillon writes that Freemasonry observed as the Emperor "began to show a coldness for the sect, and sought means to prevent it from the propagandism of its diabolical alms. Then Freemasonry became his enemy, and his end was not far off."[806]

In 1810 Napoleon became the first excommunicate of Freemasonry. Msgr. Dillon writes that in 1812, "Members of the sect urged on his mad expedition to Moscow. His resources were paralyzed; and he was, in one word, sold by secret, invisible foes into the hands of his enemies."[807]

SION AND CHARLES NODIER

While the French Lodges on the Continent were distancing themselves from Napoleon, Masonic intrigue across the channel began to develop in 1811. Freemason and German prince William of Hesse was negotiating with England for landing on the coast for combined action against the French.[808] To assist the Germans, Freemason General Malet, a Philadelphian, made an attempt in 1812 to overthrow the Empire, using England as his base of operation. Commander of the troops was General Massena, Grand Master of the Grand Orient, who at that time was in disgrace with Napoleon. Implicated in the plot were Charles Nodier, Talleyrand and Generals Moreau and Trochot, all Freemasons.[809]

Before embarking on their venture, one of the plotters addressed the assembly of Philadelphians. The speech hints of Sion when the speaker said the fall of the Emperor would be "the last of the oppressors of Jerusalem."[810] - an obvious reference to the Merovingian "King of Jerusalem" cult.

This daring conspiracy almost succeeded. General Malet, however, carried the secret of the Philadelphians to his grave. After Malet's defeat the Priory of Sion appeared to have laid down its arms and picked up the pen. Learning well from the Illuminati that control of the press was a more effective weapon, Grand Masters of Sion from that time forward used the press to manipulate public opinion.

The Priory of Sion had been plotting Napoleon's overthrow since 1804, when he declared himself Emperor. The individual assigned the task was Charles Nodier, the new Grand Master of Sion.

Nodier was an excellent choice. Like Charles Radcliffe, he was born in the enemy's camp. Nodier's father, a Jacobin and an esteemed Master Mason in a Templar Lodge, was Mayor of Besancon and president of the town's revolutionary tribunal. The senior Nodier, in the forefront of Masonic activity and politics at the time, was apparently too busy to know, or even care about the subversive activities of his young and brilliant son.[811]

Nodier the younger is what we would call today an "advanced learner" or prodigy. When he was taken in by the Philadelphians at age ten to be groomed to pilot the ship of Sion, he displayed an extraordinary ability in cultural and political affairs. "By the age of eighteen," write the authors of *Holy Blood, Holy Grail*, "he had established a literary reputation and continued to publish prolifically for the rest of his life, averaging a book a

---

[806] Dillon 39-40.
[807] Dillon 40.
[808] Corti 56.
[809] Miller 395 and Baigent 152.
[810] Baigent 153.
[811] Baigent 152 and Miller 395.

year."[812] In his own time "Nodier was regarded as a major cultural figure and his influence was enormous."[813]

All other qualifications aside, Nodier's literary talent alone would have made him an excellent choice as Grand Master of Sion, for that is what prepared him for his final assignment - an assignment more important to illuminated Freemasonry than that which he had accomplished up to that time. In the 1830s Nodier and his associates were given the task of cataloging the Templar occult books and manuscripts that Napoleon had plundered from the Vatican in 1810.

One of Nodier's colleagues assisting in this task was Rosicrucian Louis Constant (alias Eliphas Levi 1810-1875).[814] In 1870 Levi would play a significant role in the Sionist plot against Napoleon III. According to *Mackey's Encyclopedia of Freemasonry*, Eliphas Levi became a prolific writer about magical Freemasonry[815], which esoterica he obviously had learned while methodically sifting through the Templar manuscripts. Charles Nodier was the first to experiment with deliberate and widely circulated disinformation, a task to which his great literary talents well suited him. In 1816 he wrote *A History of Secret Societies in the Army under Napoleon*. Nodier credits these secret societies with the downfall of Napoleon. Although the Grand Master does mention in his book that the Philadelphians are the main conspirators, he reputedly pledged not to reveal the real identity of their controllers. Nodier writes that "the oath which binds me to the Philadelphes...forbids me to make them known under their social ~[816]

Nodier here admits that the Philadelphians were a "front" for a much larger conspiratorial secret society. *Holy Blood, Holy Grail* suggests that Nodier was concealing the Priory of Sion in the phrase "under their social name." But Sion was not a "social name." In fact, the existence of Sion was so secret that it did not become known to conspiracy researchers until our day, specifically in 1982 when *Holy Blood, Holy Grail* was published. What, then, is the "social name" to which Nodier refers?

The answer can be found by analyzing the Philadelphian plot. Since the Philadelphians used England as their base of operation. and considering the fact that most of the plotters were Rosicrucians, the "social name" to which Nodier was referring would seem more likely to have been the Rosicrucians, or their offspring, English Freemasonry. Possibly Nodier was suggesting that English Freemasonry engineered the plot to depose Napoleon.

At any rate, the Priory of Sion was never revealed. And in any case, Nodier's book suggested other conspirators and plots. The authors of *Holy Blood* describe the effect Nodier's book had on the European community:

> *Nodier's book burst on the scene when fear of secret societies had assumed virtually pathological proportions... People saw, or imagined they saw, conspiracies everywhere... This mentality engendered measures of extreme repression.*
>
> *And the repression. often directed at a fictitious threat, in turn engendered real opponents, real groups of subversive conspirators - who would form themselves in accordance with the fictitious blueprints.*[817]

---

[812] Baigent 434.Nodier used the press to accomplish his assignment. Grand Masters of the Priory of Sion, from his time to the present, use the literary art in their assignments.

[813] Baigent 150.

[814] Baigent 151.

[815] "Levi, Eliphas," *Mackey's Encyclopedia*, vol.1.

[816] Baigent 153.

[817] Baigent.

Nodier left conspiracy hounds chasing phantoms. and Sion's Rosicrucian English Freemasons were free to continue their conspiracy. Whether this was the Grand Master's intended effect, or just an experiment. all future Grand Masters of Sion would manipulate public opinion through the press. This technique was perfected and practiced through "press leaks," which were oft times blatant lies. Other times partial truths, or actual facts were leaked. Leaks of this nature became known as misinformation, or disinformation. Such libels enabled Freemasonry to destroy anyone who did not adhere to the Masonic liberal line: clergyman, politician, king. president. or presidential appointee to the Supreme Court were all at risk.

THE FALL OF NAPOLEON

When Napoleon rose to power, French Freemasonry "became neither afraid nor revolted," writes Msgr. Dillon. "What did it desire in effect? To extend its empire - 'It permitted itself to become subject to despotism in order to become sovereign.' This gives us the whole reason why Masonry first permitted Napoleon to rule, then to reign, then to conquer, and finally to fall."[818]

When Talleyrand discovered that Freemasonry no longer approved of Napoleon's autocracy, he managed to distance himself from the Emperor and prepare for the coming change. In fact, all High Masons were ready to betray the Emperor. They had already determined his replacement should be one far removed from the Catholic Church. And, if at all possible, the new ruler should not be a member of the House of Bourbon. When Napoleon was sent into permanent exile, the French Masons demanded the Protestant and Masonic King of Holland for King of France. "This failing," says Dillon, "they contrived by Masonic arts to obtain the first places in the Provisional Government which succeeded Napoleon. They endeavoured to make the most of the inevitable, and to rule the incoming [Bourbon] Louis XVIII, in the interest of their sect, and to the detriment of the Church and of Christianity."[819]

ENGLISH MASONRY AND THE HOUSE OF ROTHSCHILD

When Continental Freemasonry began supporting Napoleon, the Brotherhood did not foresee that this would weaken its powerful hold on the European monarchs, who were either themselves Masons, or had ministers who were members of the Craft. According to Count Corti, when the Holy Grail kings finally realized that Illuminated Freemasonry was a conspiracy against their thrones, they shifted their allegiance to the resurrected German Tugendbund under the protection of the English Masonic Lodge at Hanover. From there they fought to regain, or to protect their thrones, aided by financing from the Rothschilds and the military might of Great Britain.[820]

British Freemasonry was more than willing to defend the Merovingian kings of Europe. Her own aristocracy feared for their privileges with every victory of Napoleon. De Poncins quotes 33rd degree Grand Orient Freemason J.C. Corneloup, former Grand commander of the Grand College of Rites, who in 1963 in his *Universalism of French Freemasonry* said: "'It is from this era in England that the unwritten but real triple alliance

[818] Dillon 40.
[819] Dillon 43.
[820] Corti 65-66.

dates, between the Monarchy, the Church of England and Freemasonry - an alliance which to this day has been very effective."[821]

Assisting the Masonic oligarchy was the world's most famous banking firm, the House of Rothschild. Its founder, Meyer Amschel Rothschild, had strategically located his sons in Europe to better service the monarchs' war against Napoleon. A well-circulated conspiracy legend was that in 1812, "Meyer Amschel gathered his five sons about his deathbed and divided Europe amongst them."[822] French police records, however, and the records of issued visas, prove this deathbed division a farce, revealing instead that the elder Rothschild's sons had been stationed throughout Europe a decade before Napoleon came to power. "Moreover," says Corti, Rothschild's "illness had come on quite suddenly and developed so rapidly that the idea of recalling the sons who were abroad could never have been considered."[823]

When death did come to the old patriarch in 1812, his eldest son Amschel, and his youngest Carl, had already been managing the bank in his home town of Frankfurt. Nathan, his most aggressive son, had been running their London branch since at least 1801. Solomon was living in Paris, and James (a 33rd degree Mason), who was maintaining communication between Solomon and Nathan in England, was living at Gravelines on the Channel coast in the Department Pas-de- Calais.[824]

Shortly after Nathan Rothschild had arrived in London he had joined English Freemasonry.[825] When the Napoleonic Wars threatened his royal patrons on the Continent, Nathan began seeking support for the European kings in the halls of the London lodges. Consequently, in 1807 the powerful English Navy blockaded all French ports. In 1812, however, Great Britain was at war with the upstart United States of America (War of 1812), and could not be stretched to land troops on the Continent. Finally, on December 24, 1814, London signed a treaty with America, freeing England's military resources. At the Congress of Vienna, when London was assured of the backing of the repentant monarchs who had renounced their Grand Orient affiliation, England's military might went into action for the European oligarchy.

Taking advantage of the weakness of the French Republicans, England sent Freemason Duke of Wellington from his campaign in Portugal to meet Napoleon at Waterloo. The battle could have gone either way, and indeed at one point Napoleon appeared to be winning. When the first military envoy carried to London the report of Napoleon's success over Wellington, the British stock market crashed. Nathan Rothschild cashed in on the low stocks and overnight became the wealthiest man in England, ultimately controlling its central bank. From that day to the end of his life, Nathan was known as "England's banker."[826]

Some conspiracy authors have blamed Nathan for creating the stock market crash, accusing him of falsifying the earlier reports carried from the battle at Waterloo. According to Corti, however, that could not have happened, since the first report was secretly transported by a government envoy. Corti confirms that when Nathan, through his own channels, first heard of Wellington's victory over Napoleon, the stock market had already plunged, and Nathan bought up the stock. Moreover, when Nathan did receive his report of Wellington's victory, he did not withhold it, but rather, immediately gave it to the British government. The British government chose not to credit Nathan's report,

---

[821] de Poncins, Freemasonry and the Vatican 109.
[822] Corti 105.
[823] Corti.
[824] Corti and Denslow, vol. IV, 74.
[825] "Anti-Semitism and Freemasonry," *Mackey's Encyclopedia*, vol.111. Baron Nathan Mayer Rothschild was initiated in Emulation Lodge, No.12, London, October 24, 1802.
[826] Corti 202.

believing instead the earlier report of its own military envoy. The British government delayed one full day until its second courier arrived to confirm Nathan's information. Corti narrates the details of these events:

> On the resumption of hostilities in France, Herries [Commissary-in-chief for financing the British and Allied forces on the Continent] and Nathan [Rothschild] had returned to London, and were anxiously awaiting news of the result of the conflict. Nathan and his brothers had always made a particular point of letting one another have news as speedily as possible, either directly or through their business friends, of any important event that might influence their business, or be a determining factor in new undertakings. Nathan had promised prizes for the most speedy supply of news to boats sailing between England and the Continent. He also instructed his agents throughout the world to give him the earliest possible report regarding the outcome of the expected conflict. Such measures were of particular importance at that time, because none of the modern methods of conveying news had been invented - the stage post, that is, a series of messengers, being the usual way of obtaining it quickly.
>
> Nathan's arrangements worked perfectly for the battle of Waterloo. One of his agents, whose name was Rothworth, waited at Ostend for news of the result. He succeeded in obtaining the first newspaper issue of the successful account of the battle, and with a copy of the Dutch Gazette fresh from the printers, he caught a boat just sailing for London.
>
> He entered the British capital very early in the morning of June 20 [1815], and immediately reported to Nathan, who conveyed the news of victory to Herries, and through him to the British government.
>
> The government [was] at first skeptical as [it] had not received any direct information, and Wellington's envoy, Major Henry Percy, did not arrive with the fieldmarshal's report until the 21st of June. The members of the British government were tremendously impressed by Nathan's advance knowledge of such an important event; and when this became generally known, the public, who were just beginning to learn of the extent to which Nathan was employed by the English Treasury, began to invent all manner of legends regarding the method by which Nathan had acquired this knowledge and the manner in which he had exploited it.
>
> Some said that he had a private service of carrier-pigeons; others that he had been personally present at the battle of Waterloo and had ridden to the coast at top speed. In order to make the story more romantic, he was said to have found heavy storms raging when he reached the Channel and to have crossed at the risk of his life. Nathan was also alleged to have exploited the news on the stock exchange, thus at one stroke creating the enormous fortunes of the Rothschilds.[827]

In defense of the Rothschilds, Corti writes: "Nathan naturally applied the early information that he had obtained to his own profit in his business dealings. He was particularly skilful at exploiting the abnormal conditions of the period, conditions such as always give those with a gift for speculation an opportunity of enriching themselves, while those who stand by passively are reduced to poverty."[828]

Events of this nature occurred throughout the Napoleonic Wars. With the help of the Rothschilds and English Freemasonry, coupled with French Freemasonry's withdrawal

---

[827] Corti 157.
[828] Corti 111.

from Napoleon, the Corsican fell. In fact the Grand Orient was so weakened by this time that it could not oppose the wish of the whole nation of France and was obliged to submit to the return of the Bourbons.

THE WEALTH OF BRITISH FREEMASONS

Through the course of this Continental struggle, England, with its extensive coastline, was untouched by the wars. British merchants of the sea, better known as the British East India Company, transported desperately needed war materials, medicines (mostly opium), and supplies to the Continent. These merchants were all "born and bred" in English Freemasonry. As "Masonic Brothers" they were heir to trade monopolies with Great Britain's European allies. Although Napoleon attempted a blockade, the underground network of Masons on the Continent obedient to the English Grand Lodge helped smuggle war materials to their destinations. The British government encouraged these smugglers with prizes for breaking through the Napoleonic blockade.[829] In this manner Nathan Rothschild was able to fund Wellington's army.

The oligarchy in British Freemasonry, including the House of Rothschild, became extremely wealthy and powerful. In contrast, the European kings, borrowing funds to fight a war of survival, were suffering near bankruptcy. Although the House of Rothschild came to their financial rescue, the loans were endless, building interest upon interest, gradually sapping the kings' wealth. Yet, they had no recourse. They needed the assistance for survival.

Napoleon, in an attempt to break the trade channels between Great Britain and Russia, went to war with Russia. Commerce originating from the shores of sea-girt England, however, could not be stopped, and the British oligarchy exerted an even more powerful political and financial influence upon the Continental sovereigns. At home London was able to devote her principal attention, practically undisturbed, to the development of her commerce and the prosperity of her citizens.

Corti writes that "Towards the close of the eighteenth century England was indisputably the most important commercial power in Europe, and the House of Rothschild had made an exceedingly clever move in arranging that one of its sons, and the most talented one at that, should take up his residence in that Kingdom."[830]

The myth that the Rothschilds alone became wealthy during the Napoleonic Wars is unfounded. The entire British oligarchy benefited - indeed, the whole of Great Britain shared in the wealth. Subsequently, the Napoleonic Wars solidified the marriage between the Rothschilds and English Freemasonry. As a result the Rothschilds moved their banking headquarters to London, where it remains to this day. Moreover, at this point, we witness an awakening of English Freemasonry, which over the next century, gradually transferred the conspiracy headquarters for world dominion from Paris to London. The House of Rothschild was, of course, in a unique position to help; its involvement with English Freemasonry has caused some conspiracy researchers to declare this Jewish clan the Hidden Hand that planned these events.[831]

As Corti however confirms throughout his book, this identification of the Rothschilds as the Hidden Hand is quite impossible. Although the Rothschilds had aligned themselves with the more powerful English Grand Lodge, they did not control the Sionist Masonic

---

[829] Corti.
[830] Corti 107.
[831] Corti 125.

conspiracy. They were probably ignorant of it; the "Priory documents" significantly made no mention of their clan.

TEMPLARS AND THE MISSIONARY GRAND ORIENT

Following the Napoleonic Wars, the French Grand Orient reigned supreme in numbers on the Continent. Msgr. Dillon confirms that upon the defeat of Napoleon Bonaparte, the withdrawing French revolutionary armies left behind a deadly scourge that could not be removed. That "deadly scourge" was the system of atheistic French Grand Orient Freemasonry.[832]

From these European nations, Grand Orient Masonry was then transported to their colonies. For example, Italy took it to Sicily and Africa. Spain and Portugal shipped it to Central and South America, and to the Philippines. Russian soldiers, chasing the retreating Napoleon through Europe, stopped from time to time to investigate the function of Grand Orient Lodges. Many Russian officers fell under the influence of the Grand Orient's revolutionary ideas, carrying them back to their homeland. Russian historian Dmitri Merejkovsky informs us that when these officers returned to Russia, they founded in 1816 a lodge called *alliance de Salut*, "'having for its aim the violent abolition of autocracy."[833]

Mackey's Encyclopedia of Freemasonry writes of the failed revolutionary effort undertaken by this Russian lodge:

> At the end of the Napoleonic Wars and with the return of the army to Russia this Masonic body grew to the extent of having forty lodges under [its] jurisdiction. These lodges under French influence turned their attention to politics, and ended their career in the turmoil of the attempted Revolution in December, 1825.[834]

But the lodges did not end their "turmoil" after their 1825 failure, as Mackey would have us believe. Paul Fisher, using the February 1945 issue of the Scottish Rite *New Age* magazine as his source, tells how the Russian revolutionists fled to France, where they were protected and rejuvenated by the Grand Orient lodges and returned to Russia to continue their "turmoil":

> "[A]fter 1825, many Russian Masons exiled themselves to France where lodges operating in the Russian language were sponsored by the Grand Orient. Some of the exiles later returned to Russia, and organized lodges in St. Petersburg and Moscow. Later, additional lodges were organized in the early 20th Century and had an avowedly political aim and view: namely, that of the overthrow of the autocracy."[835]

---

[832] Dillon 47.

[833] Stoddard, *Light-bearers of Darkness* 172; quoting Dmitri Merejkovsky in *The Mystery of Alexander I.*

[834] "Russia," Mackey's Encyclopedia, vol.11.

[835] Fisher 218.

The reign of Napoleon Bonaparte has been the most flourishing epoch of Freemasonry.[836] This, in spite of the fact that Napoleon was defeated, exiled to Elba, and the House of Bourbon returned to the French throne.

PLANS TO THWART TEMPLAR REPUBLICANISM

During the seventy-five years leading up to the French Revolution, the European kings had cooperated with the tide of Illuminism, either by ignoring it, tolerating it, or joining it through initiation into Continental Freemasonry. They remained, however, absolute monarchs. As such, few had aligned themselves with English Freemasonry. They detested the constitutional monarchy at London, well aware why English Free-masonry favored that system of government. As absolute sovereigns, they wanted no part of it. The Napoleonic Wars, however, forced them to reconsider. Hence, two oligarchic congresses, Vienna in 1815 and Verona in 1822, were held to solidify the unity of European royalty under the British Masonic banner. English Freemasonry represented royalty's only hope against the Templar Republicans.

The Congress of Vienna (September 1814 to June 1815) was the most distinguished political assemblage in European history. The "Big Four" - Russia, Prussia, Austria, and Great Britain - were the major victors over Napoleon. The alliance of their forces, which ousted the Corsican, was the brilliant plan of Metternich, Austrian minister of foreign affairs. Together they had defeated and exiled Napoleon to Elba. The House of Bourbon reclaimed the throne of France. During the Congress, however, Napoleon did break out and create some mischief for a short time before he was defeated at Waterloo, then banished to St. Helena. At Vienna, however, the name of Metternich was on everyone's lips, for he had designed the brilliant defeat of Napoleon.

Also present at the Congress were delegates from Sweden, Denmark, Spain, Portugal, the Papacy, Bavaria, Saxony, Wurttemberg, and defeated France - the latter represented by none other than the Illuminatus and wily double agent of Sion, Talleyrand.[837] Through this mole, the Grand Master of the Priory of Sion was undoubtedly kept abreast of the proceedings.[838]

The Merovingian sovereigns represented at the Congress understood well their royal heritage. The never-ending conflict between the Knights Templar and the Priory of Sion, then raging between French and English Freemasonries, had in the past dashed Sion's dreams of world conquest. The Merovingians were aware that the Napoleonic Wars were just another attempt by the Templars to usurp their thrones. They feared that this recent conflict would not be the last, yet hoped the Congress would establish their millennium-old goal of placing their "King of Jerusalem" on the throne of a United Europe - ultimately to rule a united world.

Four major strategies were developed at the Congress of Vienna to keep Templar Republicanism in check: (1) return the Catholic Church to its original unifying status, a status from which the monarchs had so foolishly departed; (2) establish a powerful monarchical Federation of Europe to prevent the spread of Templar Grand Orient republicanism; (3) reconsider the plight of the Jews, whose previous persecution by the monarchies resulted in their emancipation by their Templar adversary; and (4) establish Switzerland as a neutral State to store their movable wealth should another Templar eruption occur.

---

[836] Dillon 35.

[837] Durants, *Napoleon* 731.

[838] Pre-World War II conspiracy researchers, not knowledgeable of the Priory of Sion, believed Talleyrand represented the Illuminati, and thus kept Weishaupt abreast of the proceedings.

The first topic was not difficult. Before the French Revolution the sovereigns had been deceived into uniting with their Templar adversary, hoping that within French Freemasonry there would be the opportunity to cast off the yoke of Roman Catholicism. At the Congress they realized their error and felt they had to return Catholicism to its original status. Their only obstacle was Czar Alexander I. He was not of Grail blood, and the Christianity of his kingdom was not Roman. Beginning in the 15th century, his nation was Christianized and religiously governed from Constantinople, the Eastern Orthodox Church. Besides, Alexander was solidly anchored in the enemy's camp. He had been steeped in Grand Orient Freemasonry, trained and guided by the depraved in that degenerate society. The Western European kings could progress no further with him, other than agreeing in their mutual desire to rid the world of Napoleon.

THE OLIGARCHY AND CATHOLICISM

Before Napoleon's defeat, the European monarchs had watched in horror as this little Emperor- General progressively destroyed one throne after another through the aid of Republican Grand Orient Freemasonry. As a result many sovereigns who had joined Continental Freemasonry renounced their affiliation, paying dearly to embrace English Freemasonry.

At the two royal Congresses, these nobles began confessing their error one to another, some privately, some in broad speeches. One blue blood was the Comte de Virieu. Virieu had been a delegate at Wilhelmsbad representing the Masonic Lodge of Lyon, *Les chevaliers* bienfaisants. Upon his return to Paris from Wilhelmsbad, he said to a friend, "I shall not tell you the secrets which I have brought back, but what I believe, I may tell you, is that a plot is being hatched, so well contrived and so deep that it will be difficult for religion and for the government not to succumb."[839] At that he renounced Freemasonry and returned to the Catholic Church. He made this confession again at the Congress of Vienna.

At the Congress of Verona seven years later, Count von Haugwitz, who had accompanied his master the King of Prussia, confessed the part he had played in Grand Orient Freemasonry. His speech is recorded by both de Poncins and Dillon. Dillon quotes Haugwitz as saying:

> [When I] arrived at the end of my career, I believe it to be my duty to cast a glance upon the secret societies whose power menaces humanity to-day more than ever. Their history is so bound up with that of my life that I cannot refrain from publishing it once more and from giving some details regarding it.
>
> My natural disposition, and my education, having excited in me so great a desire for information, that I could not content myself with ordinary knowledge, I wished to penetrate into the very essence of things. But shadow follows light, thus an insatiable curiosity develops itself in proportion to the efforts which one makes to penetrate further into the sanctuary of science. These two sentiments impelled me to enter into the society of Freemasons.
>
> It is well known that the first step which one makes in the order is little calculated to satisfy the mind. That is precisely the danger to be dreaded for the inflammable imagination of youth. Scarcely had I attained my majority, when, not only did I find myself at the head of Masonry, but what is more, I occupied a distinguished place in the chapter of high grades. Before I had the power of

---

[839] de Poncins, *Secret Powers* 35.

> *knowing myself, before I could comprehend the situation in which I had rashly engaged myself, I found myself charged with the superior direction of the Masonic reunions of a part of Prussia, of Poland, and of Russia.*[840]

Count Haugwitz continued his long confession describing how Free-masonry is divided into two camps, Deism versus Atheism, obviously referring to deistic English Freemasonry and atheistic French Freemasonry. Haugwitz confessed he was a member of both. Then he warned the Congress against French Freemasonry:

> *It was in the year 1777, that I became charged with the direction of one part of the Prussian lodges, three or four years before the Convent of Wilhelmsbad and the invasion of the lodges by illuminism. My action extended even over the brothers dispersed throughout Poland and Russia. If I did not myself see it, I could not give myself even a plausible explanation of the carelessness with which Governments have been able to shut their eyes to such a disorder, a veritable state within a State. Not only were the chiefs in constant correspondence, and employed particular cyphers, but even they reciprocally sent emissaries one to another. To exercise a dominating influence over thrones, such was our aim, as it had been of the Knight Templars.*[841]

Haugwitz concluded by informing the Congress how the illuminated Templar Grand Orient Lodges commenced the drama of 1789, known as the French Revolution. He lamented, "Of all my contemporaries of that epoch there is not one left - all have been killed... [This] caused me to take the firm resolution of renouncing Masonry."[842]

What deplorable excesses these sovereigns enjoyed for centuries, both tolerating and warring against the temporal dominions of the Catholic Church, they now feared at the hands of the Templars. The discussions at the Congress of Vienna were focused on the protection of their thrones from Templar Republicanism. Their first decision was to restore the Catholic Church to its previous Position. Dillon writes that

> *The temporal power [of the Church] was their stronghold, the rallying point of every legitimate authority in Europe. With a sure instinct of self-preservation, the schismatical Lord of Russia, the evangelical King of Prussia, the Protestant governments of England, Denmark, and Sweden, as well as the ancient legitimate Catholic dynasties of Portugal, Austria, Bavaria, and Spain had determined at the Congress of Vienna on the restoration of the temporal dominions of the Pope. The conservatives of Europe, whether Catholic, Protestant, or schismatic [Eastern Orthodox], felt that while the States of the Church were preserved intact to the head of the Catholic religion, their own rights would remain unquestioned - that to reach themselves his rights should be first assailed.*[843]

This led the world to believe that the kings of Europe were ardent Catholics, when in fact they used Catholicism only as a control mechanism. First, they were Sionist-Merovingians. Second, they were sovereigns. Third, they were Catholics, or if Protestants - tolerating Catholicism.

---

[840] Dillon 42-43.
[841] Dillon 43.
[842] Dillon.
[843] Dillon 48.

The Congress of Vienna was successful in restoring most of the ancient Italian states as well as the states of the Church to their legitimate (meaning hereditary) rulers.[844] It was unsuccessful, however, in its bid to counter the Grand Orient's proposed universal republic with its own monarchical federation, which was the second topic considered at the Congress.

ONE-WORLD GOVERNMENT PROPOSED

Under Napoleon, Templar Grand Orient Freemasonry failed to establish the United Republic of Europe. Now it was Sion's turn, protected by Rosicrucian English Masonry. At the Congress of Vienna, Prince Clemens Lothar von Metternich, Austrian minister of foreign affairs, introduced the concept of a United Federation of Europe. His plan was to form a confederation of kingdoms, each of which was to remain independent, yet having a common governing body at Vienna. The United Federation would combine its military under a powerful federal army for maintaining the peace. Weak states were to be occupied by the Army to halt the spread of republicanism.[845]

Czar Alexander I refused to lend the support of his awesome 500,000-man army and thus the plan failed. He allegedly suspected Illuminati influence in the Congress and blocked its becoming an early League of Nations.[846] He wanted instead to divide the spoils of victory - with Russia, of course, receiving the greater part. The Durants write that in response to Alexander's desires,

> Metternich sought allies against [Czar Alexander] among the delegates of the minor powers. He argued that the principle of legitimacy forbade such spoliation of a king as Russia and Prussia proposed in Saxony. They agreed, but how could they talk principle to a Russia that had 500,000 troops quartered on her western front? Metternich appealed to Lord Castlereagh, who spoke for England: Would not England be uneasy with Russia reaching through Poland and allied with a Prussia swollen with Saxony? What would this do to the balance of power east and west? Castlereagh excused himself; Britain was at war with the United States, and could not risk a confrontation with Russia.[847]

During these discussions, Napoleon had not yet escaped Elba to suffer his final defeat at Waterloo. Metternich, as a last resort, turned to the Priory of Sion's mole, Talleyrand. Metternich detested this crafty man, yet needed his help against Russia. Tallleyrand promised Metternich a well-seasoned French army of 300,000 men. The Durants describe Talleyrand's negotiations and resolution of the situation:

> Tallleyrand secured [the new Bourbon King] Louis XVIII's consent; the two diplomats won over Castlereagh now that peace had been made with America. On January 3, 1815, France, Austria, and Great Britain formed a Triple Alliance for mutual aid in maintaining the balance of power. Russia withdrew her claim to all Poland; and Prussia, having regained Thorn and Posen, agreed to take only

---

[844] Dillon 49.
[845] Corti 151.
[846] Wilgus 172.
[847] Durants, *Napoleon* 732.

two-fifths of Saxony. Talleyrand received most of the credit, and boasted that his diplomacy had changed France from a beaten beggar to again a major power.[848]

Although the Czar of Russia did not obtain all that he had asked for, he sank the Venetian plan for a European federation of monarchs. His action would not be forgotten by Sion, nor would it be forgiven.[849] The next time the Grail bloodline was in a position to dominate the world, Russia would not be able to interfere, for there would be no Czar on its throne.

The Triple Alliance was all that Metternich could muster for his proposed federation of Europe. Although the Merovingians failed in their first attempt at creating a massive state, the concept never died. It did, however, tie the Venetian "King of Jerusalem" cult to British Freemasonry. Sion's plan for a United Europe was only delayed. It would surface again, but not for two centuries.[850]

THE ILLUMINATI AND THE CONGRESS OF VIENNA

Talleyrand's involvement at the Congress of Vienna has convinced many conspiracy researchers that Weishaupt was secretly manipulating the proceedings. Revisionists have furthermore written Nathan Rothschild into the story, presenting him as the financial strong man behind Weishaupt. If true, Weishaupt would have attended the Congress, which was not possible, since he was in exile. Nor was Nathan Rothschild present at the Congress. As confirmed earlier, he was in London awaiting the outcome of Napoleon's new military ventures, which overlapped the Viennese Congress some six months.

In addition, as we have already discussed, there is no positive connection between Weishaupt and the Rothschilds. If Weishaupt had a representative at the Congress, the only logical person would have been Illuminatus Talleyrand. Talleyrand, however, was more intimate with Charles Nodier, the Grand Master of the Priory of Sion, than he was with Weishaupt. Both Talleyrand and Nodier, with the help of Sion's Philadelphians, had, on behalf of the Merovingians and English Freemasonry, conspired against Napoleon. If any leading conspirator influenced the Congress, it would have been Charles Nodier, not Weishaupt, and definitely not Nathan Rothschild. Rothschild's only concern in the outcome of the Congress was freedom for the Jews. For this reason alone the banking family sent representatives to the Congress, not to manipulate world events, but to lobby for Jewish emancipation. This was their only involvement, indeed their only concern at the time, which was the third consideration at the Congress. Corti clarifies the Rothschilds' concerns and interest in the Congress:

> [T]he decision regarding the future status of the Jews was one of the questions to be settled by the Vienna Congress... The choice of Vienna was not very acceptable to the Rothschilds, for Austria was the state which had hitherto so obstinately refused to enter into close business relations with them, and her statesmen, such as Ugarte, still did not really trust the upstart Jewish firm at Frankfort. Moreover, the Rothschilds well knew the strict police control to which foreign Jews were subjected at Vienna, and how greatly all Jews were restricted in their freedom to do business in Austria. As they were determined, however, to

---

[848] Durants 733.

[849] Wilgus 172.

[850] The Priory of Sion inaugurated the United States of Europe, December 31, 1992. See final chapters of this volume.

secure the desired business connections with the Austrian state, they were not tempted to make the realization of their plan more difficult through possible conflicts with the police at Vienna.

Such considerations caused the House of Rothschild to refrain from sending a member of the family there. The Frankfort Israelites sent old Bornes, Jacob Baruch, and J.J. Gumprecht, as their representatives. They were closely watched by the Viennese police; indeed their expulsion was ordered and sanctioned by the emperor himself; but Metternich intervened, and prevented this from being carried out. Metternich's intervention was probably due to the fact that he had known Baruch when he was ambassador at Frankfort. There is no proof that Rothschild had any particular influence with the minister at that time.[851]

SWITZERLAND - THE OLIGARCHY STRONGBOX

During the course of nine months, from September 1814 to June 1815, the crowned heads and their renowned diplomats had redrawn the map of Europe. They were not, however, secure in what they had accomplished. Although they scorned the theories of democratic government and opposed the doctrines of national self-determination, they feared the principles of the French Revolution. Not only had the Revolution endangered their sovereignty, it had compromised their wealth as well. The final agenda at the Congress was to remedy that problem.

The House of Rothschild had in the past played a significant role in the transport and protection of royalty's wealth, but in 1815 their banks were not in neutral nations. A nonpartisan location was needed to satisfy all parties. Austria was not acceptable. Moreover, the Merovingians were insecure in their remote headquarters in Vienna. Should the Templar Republicans revive, territory closer to the French border was more desirable for intelligence gathering. Switzerland had proven its strategic worth earlier. When the Big Four were closing in on Napoleon, Metternich had shifted Austrian imperial headquarters from Vienna to Freiburg, Switzerland, to better organize at close range his defense against the Corsican.[852] Hence, the decision was made at the Congress of Vienna to create Switzerland as a bank with an army attached.[853] Should the revolutions ever again regain momentum, and royalty be exiled from their respective lands, neutral Switzerland would protect them, as well as supply them with ample funds to live several lifetimes in luxury.

England, not hampered by the fears of the Venetian oligarchy and determined to safeguard her commercial and colonial interests, was fully agreed to ratify the neutrality of Switzerland. Before any financial moves were made, however, London required Swiss Grand Orients closed and replaced with Swiss Grand Lodges with English obedience. Only then would England cooperate.

In Paris on November 20, 1815, Switzerland's neutrality was guaranteed by France, Austria, Great Britain, Portugal, Prussia, Sweden, and Russia. A century later, in 1919, at the Treaty of Versailles, neutrality was again confirmed. In 1920 the League of Nations acknowledged Switzerland as "conditioned by a centuries-old tradition explicitly incorporated in international law."[854] The tradition of Swiss neutrality was again upheld from 1935 to 1945 - even while war raged around its borders.

---

[851] Corti 149-150.
[852] Corti 131.
[853] *New Solidarity* 17 May 1985: Supplement A and B.
[854] "Switzerland," *Encyclopaedia Britannica: Macropaedia*.

The Congress of Vienna adjourned on June 18, 1815. Two days earlier Napoleon had been defeated at Waterloo. Over the next few decades the oligarchy's Grail bloodline moved their financial headquarters from Vienna to Zurich, Switzerland. Immediately they went to work absorbing the French Grand Orient Lodges, placing them under English Masonic obedience. Thirty-second degree Mason A.E. Waite, in *A New Encyclopaedia of Freemasonry,* gives us a century of history concerning the Masonic maneuvers in Switzerland. He reports that Swiss Freemasonry was founded by the British as early as 1736. In 1775 the Swiss lodges transferred their allegiance from English Masonry to the German Strict Observance. Under Napoleon the French Grand Orient invaded Switzerland, and a certain number of existing lodges came under its obedience. Geneva was ceded to France during the wars of Napoleon, and Swiss Masonry then became an appendage of the French Grand Orient. In 1818, as demanded by London, English Masonic obedience began to replace the Grand Orients, except in Geneva where the aristocracy permitted one Grand Orient Lodge to function.[855]

By 1844 fourteen lodges in Switzerland had united under English obedience, agreed to a Grand Lodge Constitution, and organized the Grand Lodge Alpina in Zurich.[856] Within a few decades Alpina headquarters moved to Geneva, next to its Grand Orient rival. From these two lodges, both within a neutral nation, both headquartered in the same city, Scarlet and the Beast would continue to plot their separate intrigues to dominate the world. From Geneva both the right wing and the left wing revolutions would spread over the face of the earth. In Geneva both would unite a century later.

---

[855] Arthur Edward Waite, "Switzerland," *A New Encyclopaedia of Freemasonry* (New York: Weathervane Books, MCMLXX) Vol.11. Why would English Freemasonry grant permission to the Grand Orient to continue one lodge in Geneva? It seems to be an unwise decision. A logical answer would be that while brothers fight each other, they also protect one another against a greater enemy. The combined strength of both Freemasonries is needed to destroy Christianity. Thus, throughout this intrigue we find a cooperation and conflict. Neither one wants to destroy the other. Yet, both want to dominate the other.

A spiritual answer offers more understanding. Satan is the grand master of division. Divide and conquer is his strategy. The division, however, is not between God and Satan. What is so strange about Satan's kingdom is that division is within his own ranks, between two forces of evil. Satan rules both Freemasonries, yet both are adversaries. Matthew 12:25-26 confirms that a divided kingdom will fall, suggesting that Satan is divided within himself. This borders on schizophrenia. Only a schizophrenic personality would attempt to govern two opposing kingdoms. Is Satan schizophrenic, condemned to a split personality by God Himself? Chapter 1, volume II of *Scarlet and the Beast* will answer this question.

[856] "Alpina," *Mackey's Encyclopedia,* vol. I.

12. FRENCH FREEMASONRY TRIES, AND TRIES AGAIN

> *Freemasonry in its momentary command of power, failed in its supreme endeavour. Taught by these experiences, its progress has become slower and surer.*[857]

Count Leon de Poncins

In 1796, the survivors of the House of Bourbon escaped to the island of Sicily where they lived protected by the British Navy until after the Battle of Waterloo.[858] When Napoleon was banished to the island of St. Helena, and Europe reorganized under oligarchic rule, the Bourbons offered to return, but the French Freemasons sought a king neither Bourbon nor Catholic. They approached the Protestant and Masonic king of Holland to be king of France. Dillon explains what followed this unsuccessful bid:

> *This failing, they contrived by Masonic arts to obtain the first places in the Provisional Government which succeeded Napoleon. They endeavoured to make the most of the inevitable, and to rule the incoming [Bourbon King] Louis XVIII, in the interests of their sect, and to the detriment of the Church and of Christianity.*[859]

In the first revolution French Freemasonry had shown open hostility to the House of Bourbon. Bizarre as it may seem, when Louis XVIII ascended the throne, he favored the Republican Templar Grand Orient. Stranger yet, Talleyrand became minister. Moreover, other advanced Masons of the Napoleonic empire, such as Emmanuel Sieyes, Regis de Cambaceres, and Joseph Fouche, obtained positions as well. Louis's court was filled with Masonic Templars and Sionists, who were once again plotting against the throne. Dillon outlines the disastrous events that flowed from their schemes:

> *These men at once applied themselves to subvert the sentiment of reaction in favour of the monarchy and of religion. Soon, Louis XVIII gave the world the sad spectacle of a man prepared at their bidding to cut his own throat. He dissolved a Parliament of ultra loyalists because they were too loyal to him. The Freemasons took care that his next Parliament should be full of its own creatures. They also wrung from the King, under the plea of freedom of the press, permission to deluge the country anew with the infidel and immoral publications of Voltaire and his confederates, and with newspapers and periodicals, which proved disastrous to his house, and to Christianity, in France. These led before long to the attempt upon the life of the Duke of Berry, to the revolution against Charles X, to the elevation of the son of the Grand Master, the traitor Duke of Orleans,*

---

[857] de Poncins, *Secret Powers* 95.
[858] Special Report, "Italian General: Dope Mafia a British Protectorate," *New Solidarity* 20 September 1982: 1.
[859] Dillon 44.

Philip the Egalite, as Constitutional King, and to all the revolutionary results that have since distracted and disgraced unfortunate France.[860]

THE FRENCH REVOLUTION OF 1830

Unable to dethrone the Bourbons, the Priory of Sion settled for a constitutional monarchy. This adjustment to political reality in fact was not as strange a departure from the character of Sion as might first appear. The authors of *The Messianic Legacy* explain Sion's reason for accepting a constitutional monarchy:

> *The essence of such a monarchy is that it rests on the basis espoused by the Prieure de Sion and ascribed to the old Merovingian dynasty of France. For the Merovingians, the king ruled but did not govern. In other words, he was ultimately a symbolic figure. To the extent that he remained unsoiled by the tawdry business of politics and government, his symbolic status remained pristine. As one of the Prieure de Sion '5 writers declares in an article, "The king is." In other words, his currency resides in what he embodies as a symbol, rather than in anything he does, or in any real power he might or might not exercise. The most potent symbols always exert an intangible authority, which can only be compromised by the more tangible forms of power.*[861]

The "more tangible forms of power" were of course the plotters in the French parliament, comprised of representatives from both Sion and the Temple. The constant assignment of the Grand Masters of Sion was to steer the ship of Sion toward a course favorable to the interests of the "Lost King." This goal proved more difficult in France than it had been in England. In England, Sion had no adversary. In France, however, a constitutional monarchy was just as easily subverted by the Templars. Such was the case when in the three-day revolution of 1830 the Templars once again took power when royalty was deposed in favor of a republic.

In a speech full of Masonic terminology, de Poncins quotes Freemason M. Dupin, who credits the coup to long-term planning:

> *Do not believe that three days have done everything. If the revolution has been so prompt and sudden, if we have made it in a few days, it is because we had a keystone ready to place, and because we have been able to substitute immediately a new and complete order of things for that which had just been destroyed.*[862]

FREEMASONRY AND ITALIAN REVOLUTION

Meanwhile, Grand Orient Freemasonry was developing a revolution in Italy. Once again evidence from the Masons themselves confirms the Masonic hand behind revolution. De Poncins quotes Chiossone (no first name given), an Italian Mason speaking at the Parisian Lodge Solidarity in 1907, who proclaimed, "The revolutionary attempts

---

[860] Dillon 44.
[861] Baigent et al, *The Messianic Legacy* 198.
[862] de Poncins 50.

which have occurred since 1821 in Italy were the work of Freemasonry."[863] De Poncins continues:

> It was about that period that Giuseppe [Joseph] Mazzini (1805-1872) began his revolutionary activity of which the principal aims were the liberation, the unity and the republicanization of Italy, the suppression of the temporal power of the Pope, the destruction of Austria, and the establishment of republics everywhere.[864]

Mazzini's operation was similar to that of the Illuminati. So similar, in fact, that some conspiracy researchers have suggested that Adam Weishaupt appointed Mazzini as Director of the Illuminati.[865] Mazzini had only been a Mason for three years when Weishaupt died in 1830, but his ruthless character, the researchers claim, had come to the attention of Weishaupt. The only difference between the two was that while Weishaupt was a Luciferian, Mazzini was initially a pure atheist - so successful had the Illuminati propagandists been in denying the existence of God.

THE CARBONARI

Mazzini was initiated into Freemasonry at age twenty-two. At that time the early form of Italian Masonry was called Carbonari. Miller notes the similarity between the ordinances and rituals of the Carbonari and Freemasonry:

> Modern Carbonarism was founded in 1815 by Maghella, a native of Genoa, who, at the time when Joachim Murat became King of the two Sicilies, was a subordinate of Saliceti, the Neapolitan Minister of Police. He [Maghella] was a Freemason, who exempted from initiation and probation all Freemasons who desired to become Carbonari. Any one who has read the statutes and ritual of Carbonarism will see that it is one and the same as that of Masonry.[866]

The plans of the Carbonari were recorded in 1818 in its secret official document under the title *Permanent Instructions, or Practical Code of Rules; Guide for the Heads of the Highest Grades of Masonry*. This document, according to Miller, listed several goals, the last of which stated, "Our final aim is that of Voltaire and of the French Revolution - the complete annihilation of Catholicism, and ultimately of all Christianity."[867]

During Mazzini's early years as a Mason, the Grand Orient had penetrated the Carbonari. Eventually, the latter faded and the former became the dominant Masonry in Italy.

YOUNG EUROPE

Giuseppe Mazzini, after three years of intense revolutionary training (1827-1830), concentrated on recruiting rebellious youth to further his conspiracy of revolution. In

---

[863] de Poncins 64.
[864] de Poncins 64-65.
[865] Kirban 157.
[866] Miller 433-434.
[867] Miller 427,430.

1831 he was exiled from Italy to France. In 1832 he founded for his young revolutionaries their own form of Freemasonry prefixed by the word *Young*.[868] By 1833 *Young Italy* had grown to 60,000 members and was suppressed that year by the Italian government.

In 1835, with the help of Freemason Henry Palmerston, Mazzini founded *Young Europe* in Switzerland.[869] In the same manner in which Weishaupt's conspiratorial ideas continued to spread after the Illuminati was suppressed, Mazzini's *Young* societies continued to organize in new territories long after his death. In the new world they were called *Young America;* in England - *Young England,* in Italy - *Young Italy,* in Turkey - *Young Turks.* On the Continent they were, of course, *Young Europe.*

The *Young* societies consisted of radical and riotous youth, many of whom were later initiated into the Templar Grand Orient lodges in their respective countries. The hierarchy in the Scottish Rite directed their activity, while the Masonic press described them as laborers and students expressing their grievances. This practice still continues today.[870]

All *Young* society members throughout Europe were taught the art of subversion by Grand Orient Freemasonry. They were ready when called upon to agitate, demonstrate, instigate worker strikes, hold rallies, or to spy, bomb, and assassinate. Also known as Anarchists and Nihilists, they were reckless of every consequence, using dynamite, the knife, or the revolver for the benevolent cause of Grand Orient Freemasonry. Msgr. Dillon specifically mentions that these hoodlums (whose protection had been written into the French Constitution), would go to Paris where they were taught the use and manufacture of dynamite.[871]

Although *Young* society members in Mazzini's day were described as loose-knit with no direction, they were in fact highly organized. A few were wealthy. Some were laborers and students, others, paid rioters. The majority had no jobs at all, yet spent money freely - an enigma to those who had no knowledge of their Masonic backers. After their grievances were aired by the Masonic press, public opinion turned in the direction favorable to Grand Orient Freemasonry.

In short, the *Young* society members were hoodlums trained to do the bidding of the Templar Scottish Rite Hierarchy. Their duty was to spread the Templar revolution throughout Europe. Mazzini was their leader.

With this rabble, Mazzini brought Italy her Masonic Revolution. Throughout these insurrections, *Young Italy* hoodlums, with no skills or aims other than causing havoc, supported themselves by robbing banks, looting or burning businesses if protection money was not paid, and kidnapping for ransom. Throughout Italy the word spread that "Mazzini autorizza furti, incendi, e attentati," meaning, "Mazzini authorizes theft, arson,

---

[868] Miller 434.

[869] Wilgus 175.

[870] After the Communist Revolutions in China in 1949-1950 and Cuba in 1959, Freemasonry was outlawed in both nations. Today these two nations are the only two on earth with no Masonic Lodges. It becomes almost impossible to topple these governments without Freemasonry to subvert them. In Russia Freemasonry was outlawed by Stalin in 1922. For that reason he could not be ousted. However, during the 1960s Kim Philby, an English Freemason, and double agent high in British Intelligence, defected to Russia for the express purpose of initiating a young communist leader into Freemasonry, after which he was to turn him to Western views. His name was Mikhail Gorbechev. In 1989 Gorbechev called for Grand Orient Lodges to be reestablished throughout the U.S.S.R., the result of which was the breakup of the Soviet Union. Gorbechev is, in reality, a traitor to Communism. In future chapters we shall learn how English Freemasonry engineered the greatest coup in history through its triple-agent Kim Philby.

[871] Dillon 94.

and kidnapping." This phrase was shortened to the acronym, M.A.F.I.A.[872] Organized crime was born.

A WEISHAUPT-MAZZINI CONNECTION

Many conspiracy researchers, as we have noted, postulate a formal association between Adam Weishaupt, father of Illuminism, and Guiseppe Mazzini. If in fact Weishaupt appointed Mazzini, as some have alleged, no source of documentation has been offered that can be verified. Yet, a comparison of the revolutionary systems of Mazzini and Weishaupt, show both are identical in many areas. For example:

(1) both hierarchies were Masonic; (2) both Masonries offered the same degrees; (3) both used identical symbols, passwords, and grips; (4) both wanted to destroy the Church; (5) both used assassination as a means to an end; (6) both maintained the Luciferian doctrine, although Mazzini adopted it later in life; and (7) both had the goal of establishing a world government. Therefore it is easy to suggest that Weishaupt appointed Mazzini.

Similarities make good circumstantial evidence, and many cases have been won on that alone - that is, if differences are overlooked. Although there are similarities between Weishaupt and Mazzini's purposes and their execution, when examining the two men's differences, it is highly improbable that the activities of the latter are a continuation of the former's program. Weishaupt was a Sionist-Rosicrucian. Mazzini was a staunch Templar.

Secondary differences drive them even further apart. For example, the Priory of Sion was royalist, the Templars republican - a strong political division. The royalists were right wing, the republicans left wing; the right wing was capitalist, the left wing socialist-communist. The capitalists were non-union, the socialists union - this making a strong economic division. The capitalists were rich, the unionized working man poor - which makes for deep social division. Finally, the Sionist conspiracy maintained control through money, while the Templar conspiracy controlled by brute force.

Wars have been fought over any one, or all of these divisive issues. Yet, the defined purpose of the conspirators was, and still is, to unite the world, not divide it. Therefore, a single conspiracy that plans division as a means to unite is illogical. Our forefathers understood this concept when Patrick Henry said, "United we stand, divided we fall!"

Nevertheless, researchers have alleged that the conspirators intentionally designed a program to divide as a means of control. True, people become polarized when divided. As such, a divided nation is so weakened that it can be taken captive. However, divided nations cannot be united, nor can a divided world. The only logical answer to division in conspiracy is that there are two conspiratorial orders vying for control of the one New World Order. We recognize them as Scarlet and the Beast in the book of Revelation. Scripture confirms that Satan controls both.

Satan is the father of division. We see his kingdom divided here on earth, manifested in the struggle between the Knights Templar (French Freemasonry) and the Priory of Sion (English Freemasonry). Masons on both sides of the conspiracy may want to unite, but when Satan is their god, division is certain. The Adversary may think division is a brilliant

---

[872] Konstandinos Kalimtgis, David Goldman, and Jeffrey Steinberg, *Dope, Inc.: Britain's Opium War Against the U.S.* (New York: New Benjamin Franklin House, 1978) 34.

The "Mafia" is defined in *Mackey's Encyclopedia of Freemasonry*, as "persons impatient and contemptuous of constitutional processes of law who reserve vengeance for execution by themselves." Mackey defines the Mafia as a secret society, comparing it to the Italian Carbonari. He denies the Mafia or the Carbonari are Masonic, yet mentions Mazzini as being involved in both. He claims that their members were more radical republicans, and at the same time admits their goals were identical to that of Freemasonry.

maneuver, but Jesus says in Matthew 12:25-26 that it will bring him destruction. This is our hope.

The fact remains, when Weishaupt died, Mazzini did emerge a leader in what appeared to be the same conspiracy. And like Weishaupt, Mazzini and his cohorts did attempt to unite both Freemasonries. In fact, Mazzini met with greater success.

MAZZINI AND INTERNATIONAL FREEMASONRY

Mazzini was in contact with Masonic revolutionaries throughout the world: Giuseppe Garibaldi, leader of the revolutionary army in Italy; Louis Kossuth of Hungary; Stanislas Vorcell of Poland; Alexander Herzen of Russia; Henry Palmerston of England; Otto von Bismarck of Germany; and Albert Pike of the United States. De Poncins notes that twenty-two years after Mazzini's death the *Rivista della Massoneria Italiana* said of him and his assistants: "'Mazzini, Garibaldi and Kossuth shine with unsurpassed glory which make crowned heads turn pale.'"[873]

In fact, before his death, Mazzini, with American Freemason Albert Pike (1809-1891), English Freemason Henry Palmerston (1784-1865), and German Freemason Otto von Bismarck (1815 - 1898), had cooperated in uniting the hierarchies in French, British, and American Masonry in a super rite founded by Albert Pike. All four men, as 33rd degree Masons, were destined to rule Universal Freemasonry through this rite. Miller states that "Albert Pike, in honour of his Templar Baphomet[874], which was in keeping of his first and historic Supreme Council, named the order the *New and Reformed Palladian Rite* or *New and Reformed Palladium*.

The word "Palladian" is the key here to the Templar orientation of the Supreme Council. The word "Palladium" comes from the Hindu "pala," for the male sex organ. "Pala" in Latin means "phallus" and is the universal emblem of kings. Thus, the Palladium ruled like a king.[875] Pike's symbol of Baphomet also represents the generative forces within man, which, according to Masonic doctrine, are the means of man's deification.[876] The Palladium, as the Baphomet, takes its origins from the Templars, not the Sionists-Illuminati. Yet, as we shall see in another chapter, its religious dogma is identical to the Luciferian doctrine established by Weishaupt.

Under the administration of these four High Masons, the doctrines of the Palladium were spread rapidly within the Templar Scottish Rite Lodges. High Masons, with whom Palladians came in contact, were candidates for initiation. They in turn, took the doctrine back to their respective lodges.

LORD PALMERSTON

Pike, Mazzini, Bismarck, and Palmerston were the leaders of Freemasonry in their respective countries. So important to English Masonry was Prime Minister Palmerston that the authors of *Dope, Inc.* state that "nearly every... inhabitant of Britain's political

---

[873] de Poncins 65.
[874] See Appendix 2, Fig. 30.
[875] Miller 712.
[876] Stoddard, *Trail of the Serpent* 41.

nether world followed a chain of command that led through the Scottish Rite of Freemasonry directly to Lord Palmerston and his Successors."[877]

This chain of command enabled Palmerston to assist Masonic revolutions with British pounds. When Mazzini called for financial aid to fund his Grand Orient insurrection in Italy (1848-1865), he turned to Palmerston, who encouraged Parliament to back Mazzini's effort. The duped politicians allocated funds to their Templar adversary.

Following Palmerston's death the Earl of Beaconsfield, Benjamin Disraeli (1804-1881), a Jewish Freemason, was elected Prime Minister, taking up Mazzini's cause. Disraeli had more decency than did Palmerston. Instead of using the taxpayer's pounds, he went to the two leading Jewish bankers, Freemasons Lionel Rothschild and Montefiore, and Mazzini's funding continued.[878] Disraeli later discovered his error and published *Lothair*, a novel about secret societies in European politics. The novel stated, "The world is governed by very different personages to what is imagined by those who are not behind the scenes..."[879]

THE BRITISH EAST INDIA COMPANY

English Freemasonry became interested in Mazzini's Grand Orient MAFIA for a specific reason. To understand why, we must first take a look at a brief history of the British East India Company (BEIC) as told by the authors of *Dope, Inc.*

From the late 1600s the BEIC, whose stockholders were English Freemasons, was heavily involved in opium and slave trading. Slave trading, however, was drastically curtailed when in 1772 Great Britain made it illegal.[880] To make up the slack in revenues, opium sales increased in Europe, where the drug was sold as a treatment for pain. The BEIC became extremely wealthy during the Napoleonic Wars when governments bought the drug by the ton for their wounded soldiers. After Waterloo, however, drug sales dropped substantially. Consequently, the BEIC stockholders began developing a new drug market in China. Assisting them were the vicious Triads, the Oriental secret societies similar to Western Freemasonry. The attempt to develop a China market entangled Great Britain in her First Opium War with China in 1840. After winning that war, merchant Masons throughout the next two decades established many Masonic Lodges in China for the purpose of controlling their drug operation.[881]

Financial catastrophe struck the BEIC once again when the American Civil War (1860-1865) eliminated their largest slave market. To compound their financial woes, after the Civil War, the bottom dropped out of the American opium market when the drug was no longer needed for our wounded soldiers. Moreover, by 1870 the world was at peace, reducing still more the necessity for the legitimate sale of opium.

The BEIC was in serious financial trouble. For two centuries the shipping industry had been the largest industry of England, the industry most responsible for carrying the British flag around the world, the industry that supplied all of Great Britain's colonies. If the BEIC did not generate a new market for its opium, the British economy would collapse.

---

[877] Kalimtgis et al 26.Although English Masonry did not recognize the Scottish Rite, it did, however, include its 33 degrees in 1860. Any Englishman of Masonic note went to the Continent and was initiated in the Grand Orient Scottish Rites. Lord Palmerston was a member of both obediences.

[878] Kalimtgis 33.

[879] de Poncins 120.

[880] Kalimtgis 12-24.

[881] Kalimtgis 12-24.

In the late 1850s, as we shall learn in volume three of *Scarlet and the Beast*, the BEIC had already determined to open Western Europe and the Americas to illegal drugs. This expansion required banking headquarters in the Orient for financing the expansion. Hence, Great Britain entered her Second Opium War with China in 1859-1860, and gained sovereignty over Hong Kong as her prize. By 1873 the BEIC was dissolved and its stockholders well established in banking.[882] Hong Kong became Great Britain's far-eastern banking center, financing both poppy farmers and drug manufacturers.[883]

While Great Britain was entangled in her Second Opium War, English Freemasonry searched for a channel to traffic her drugs in Western Europe. The ruthless character of the Masonic Mafia, similar to that of the Triads, would serve England's passive drug lords well. Great Britain, as protector of Sicily during the Napoleonic Wars, was able to offer Mazzini's displaced Mafia a home on the island of Sicily. In 1860, the year Great Britain ended her Second Opium War, Garibaldi's army, aided by the British navy, invaded Sicily. The Mafia immediately established its headquarters on this island nation, using it as a hub for heroin distribution worldwide. From then until now, attempts to suppress its control of the heroin trade have failed.[884]

THE FRENCH COMMUNIST REVOLUTION OF 1848

While Mazzini was building his Masonic Mafia empire in Italy, the Templar Grand Orients of France were still unsettled as to which political format best suited them. In 1793 pure democracy had ended in anarchy. In 1830, when the three-day revolution dethroned Charles X, the word *socialism* was coined in both the French Grand Lodge and the Grand Orient Lodge to define the type of government with which they would experiment. In 1835 the League of the Just (consisting of the remnant of Masons who had belonged to the ruthless Jacobin Clubs) was founded at Paris to lead the socialist movement.[885]

Pacifist socialism, however, was too slow a process for the impatient former Jacobins and League of the Just. To augment a more rapid solidification of power, the Grand Orient Jacobins once again formed communes, renaming the League of the Just the Communist League.[886] French Freemasonry once again divided in 1840 with the more radical communists on the one side, and pacifist socialists on the other. By 1848 the spokesman for the communists was Levi Mordechai (1818-1883), a German Jew who changed his name to Karl Marx. Marx, a 32nd degree Grand Orient Mason, as well as a Frankist-Reform Jew, had fled Germany to Paris, then moved to London where he resided until his death.

Throughout the year of 1848, Grand Orient Freemasonry coordinated communist uprisings all over Europe. Again, Freemasonry used Jews as fronts. Rabbi Antelman notes that the wealthy Reform Jew, Heinrich Bernard Oppenheim, a member of the Grand Orient's League of the Just, "was one of the masterminds of the 1848 Communist revolution in Germany."[887]

Neal Wilgus, in *The Illuminoids*, expounds on these communist uprisings:

---

[882] Kalimtgis 63-77.
[883] "Drugs and Banking," *Executive Intelligence Review*, 7 September 1982: 35.
[884] Wilgus 194.This drug network is discussed in more detail in volume III of *Scarlet and the Beast*.
[885] Wilgus 175.
[886] Wilgus.
[887] Antelman 27.

> *1848. Another year of disturbance. In a trance-like state occultist Sobrier touches off demonstrations which lead to the fall of the Orleans monarchy in France; Louis Philippe dethroned and Second Republic begins; Louis Napoleon elected president of the assembly. Republic established in Rome. Abdication of Ferdinand I of Austria. Freedom briefly declared in Hungary under Louis Kossuth. Revolts in Denmark, Ireland, Lombardy, Schleswig-Holstein and Venice. Germany briefly united in a parliament at Frankfort; unity destroyed by the King of Prussia.*[888]

Each of the revolutionary leaders operating throughout Europe were known Masons - Masons who had communicated in their lodge meetings the timing of each eruption. France was in the forefront. When the Orleans monarchy was toppled on March 6, 1848, the new provisional government was made up of eleven members, nine of whom were Grand Orient Masons. The first order of business was to receive an official delegation from the lodges - a Masonic parade with all the finery of their regalia.[889]

According to Miller, this delegation consisted of 300 Freemasons: "with their banners flying over the brethren of every rite representing French Freemasonry [they] marched to the Hotel de Ville, and there offered their banners to the Provisional Government of the Republic, proclaiming aloud the part they had just taken in the glorious Revolution."[890]

On March 7, 1848, the Paris newspaper, *Le Moniteur*, reported on this so-called "worker's communist revolution." De Poncins quotes:

> *They saluted the triumph of their principles and congratulated themselves for being able to say that the whole country has received masonic [sic] consecration through the members of the government. Forty thousands masons [sic], distributed in more than five hundred workshops, forming between them but a single heart and mind, were promising their support to achieve the work already begun.*[891]

Two weeks later a new delegation from the Grand Orient, arrayed in their Masonic scarfs and jewels, marched to the Hotel de Ville. Waiting to receive them was Adolphe Cremietix and Gamier Pages, both attended by their political staffs, who also wore their Masonic emblems. Miller quotes a portion of the speech given by the representative of the Grand Master:

> *French Freemasonry cannot contain her universal burst of sympathy with the great social and national movement which has just been effected. The Freemasons hail with joy the triumph of their principles, and boast of being able to say that the whole country has received through you a Masonic consecration. Forty thousand Freemasons in 500 lodges, forming but one heart and one soul, assure you here of their support happily to lead to the end the work of regeneration so gloriously begun.*[892]

---

[888] Wilgus 193.
[889] de Poncins 51.
[890] Miller 185.
[891] de Poncins 51.
[892] Miller 186.

Adolphe Isaac Cremietix (1796-1880), a Jewish Mason, and member of the Provisional Government, replied:

> Citizens and brothers of the Grand Orient, the Provisional Government accepts with pleasure your useful and complete adhesion. The Republic exists in Freemasonry. If the Republic does as the Freemasons have done, it will become the glowing pledge of union with all men, in all parts of the globe, and on all sides of our triangle.[893]

When the National Assembly was formed, Freemasonry was back in control of France and the Second Republic began. Elected as a deputy for Paris was Victor Hugo, Grand Master of the Priory of Sion (GM 1844-1885). Freemason Louis Napoleon, nephew of Napoleon Bonaparte, was elected president of the Assembly. At first Hugo backed Napoleon, but the more the President embraced an authoritarianism of the right, the more Hugo moved toward the Assembly's left.[894]

Since Freemasonry held a majority in the Assembly, the lodge suggested the Assembly follow its dictates. To guarantee Masonic control of the new Republic, Freemasonry proposed to outlaw all competing secret societies, which Communist dictatorships are prone to do. Consequently, a debate arose in the Assembly concerning this question. Non-Masons wanted all secret societies, including Freemasonry, outlawed. A few Masons agreed, stating that Freemasonry was no longer needed, now that the Republic was a reality. Other Masons, however, feared a return of royalty, who might use a competing lodge to subvert the Republic. *Mackey's Encyclopedia of Freemasonry* records a small portion of the debate:

> *Bolette: I should like to have some one define what is meant by a secret society.*
> *Coquerel: Those are secret societies which have made none of the declarations prescribed by law.*
> *Paulin Gillon: I would ask if Freemasonry is also to be suppressed?*
> *Flocon: I begin by declaring that, under a republican government, every secret society having for its object a change of the form of such government ought to be severely dealt with. Secret societies may be directed against the sovereignty of the people; and this is the reason why I ask for their suppression; but, from the want of a precise definition, I would not desire to strike, as secret societies, assemblies that are perfectly innocent. All my life, until the 24th of February, have I lived in secret societies. Now I desire them no more. Yes, we have spent our life in conspiracies, and we had the right to do so; for we lived under a government which did not derive its sanctions from the people. To-day [sic] I declare that under a republican government, and with universal suffrage, it is a crime to belong to such an association.*
> *Coquerel (somewhat confused): As to Freemasonry, your Committee has decided that it is not a secret society. A society may have a secret, and yet not be a secret society? I have not the honor of being a Freemason.*
> *The President: The thirteenth article has been amended, and decided that a secret society is one which seeks to conceal its existence and its objects.[895]*

---

[893] Miller.
[894] "Hugo, Victor" (Political life), *Encyclopaedia Britannica:Macropaedia*.
[895] "Secret Societies," *Mackey's Encyclopedia of Freemasonry*, vol.11.

Freemason Flocon was in favor of outlawing all secret societies, including Freemasonry. The majority of Masons, however, redefined Freemasonry as no longer a secret society, since its subversive objectives of obtaining power were no longer needed. In other words, Freemasonry is a secret society only when not in power. When in power it no longer needs to be subversive; therefore, it is no longer a secret society. Yet, it demands all competitors, such as the Priory of Sion's Rosicrucians, whose king had just been dethroned, be outlawed.

With its success, the now benevolent Grand Orient ceased its communist agitation, became pacifist and was ready to make an attempt to unite Europe. The Masonic Peace Congress was held in Paris in 1849. The Priory of Sion was represented by Victor Hugo, who made the opening speech suggesting Europe unite under the name "The United States of Europe," the first time that slogan was used in those exact words. The effort fizzled for lack of support. Miller notes that "it was not until some years later that it [the United States of Europe] was formally adopted as the slogan of International Socialism."[896]

Concerning the French government, de Poncins informs us that despite the fact that the government was essentially Masonic, the elected National Assembly was patriotic, refusing to obey the guidelines set down by Freemasonry. The Grand Orient, without hesitation, then turned to a man whom it knew to be its own, and in December 1851 assisted Louis Napoleon in a coup d'etat.[897] Victor Hugo made one attempt to resist and then fled to Brussels.[898]

In 1852 Napoleon defied the Grand Orient and proclaimed himself Emperor Napoleon III. After a new constitution was decreed, he instituted a dictatorial regime sanctioned by periodic plebiscites. Napoleon became an enemy of the same Grand Orient that raised him to power.

He ruled as emperor from 1852-1871, when finally he was deposed by schemes authored in the Grand Orient Masonic Lodge, which schemes will be discussed in the next chapter.

Meanwhile, the Grand Orient revolutionary army in Italy, headed by 33rd degree Mason General Garibaldi, was having difficulty defeating the Austrian occupation forces. Mazzini, the political head of the Italian revolution, turned to France for military assistance. Although Mazzini hated Napoleon Ill, and several times attempted to have the emperor assassinated, he asked for Napoleon's help. Together with Piedmont Sardinia, a region northwest of Italy bordering on France and Switzerland, Napoleon III declared war on Austria. The Emperor successfully expelled the occupation army and received Nice and Savoy as a reward.[899]

With Napoleon victorious, the Templars saw another chance to preempt Sion's long-desired United States of Europe. The Templar's version of the same would be called the Federation of Republics. Miller gives a brief accounting of the origins of the movement:

The impulse came again from the masonic [sic] lodges. In 1866, a Freemason named Santallier composed a work on Pacifism for his brother masons [sic] which led to the founding of the Union de la Paix, under the presidency of another Freemason... named Bielefeld. The movement spread to Switzerland and on September 5, 1867, a further Congress was held. The proceedings were enlivened by a duel between the Constitutionalists and the Socialists, who declared that kings, soldiers - and some added priests - must be swept away in order to make room for the new Federation of Republics.

[896] Miller 636.
[897] de Poncins 51.
[898] "Hugo, Victor" (Political life), *Encyclopaedia Britannica:Macropaedia.*
[899] "Napoleon III," *Encyclopaedia Britannica: Micropaedia.*

The Socialists, led by Emile Acollas, won the day. Dupont, Karl Marx's right hand, was invited to represent the First Communist International, of which he was secretary.[900]

Having no unity, the Templar's attempt at uniting Europe under a Federation of Republics failed. The only outcome was the founding of the "League of Peace and Liberty," which published a periodical entitled *Les Etats-Unis de l'Europe.*[901]

Meanwhile, Napoleon III became more belligerent toward Freemasonry. The Grand Orient tolerated him so long as it believed that it could count on his obedience. But, when the Emperor became contentious, says de Poncins, "Then the support was withdrawn in proportion as Napoleon tried to lean on France itself in order to regain his independence."[902]

THE FRENCH REVOLUTION OF 1871

In 1870 Napoleon declared war on Germany and was miserably defeated. He was deposed by Freemasonry in 1871 and the Third Republic began. De Poncins outlines the events:

> The disaster of 1870 hastened events and masonry [sic] was obliged to intervene sooner than it would have desired. Renewing the attempt of 1789 it sustained the commune. On the 26th April 1871, fifty-five lodges, more than ten thousands masons [sic], led by their dignitaries, wearing their insignias, went in procession to the ramparts to place banners there to the number of sixty-two. At the Hotel de Ville, the Mason Tiriforque in saluting the revolutionary power said to the rioters: "Communism is the greatest revolution which the world has been given to behold."
>
> When the Commune was over, the secret societies which had not been able to prevent the election of an assembly with a monarchist majority planned together all over Europe in order to oppose the accession to the throne of the comte de Chambord who represented stable power in legitimacy, heredity and authority.
>
> Freemasonry after having gained as much as it could from the different governments which succeeded each other from 1789 finally reached the form of government which suited it best: that is the Republic under which it is easy for it to seize control.
>
> From that time on France has been rolling downwards. The third republic has mostly applied the laws elaborated by freemasonry [sic] destroying little by little what remained of the elements of social conservation. Taught by the events of 1789, 1830, 1848 and 1871 it goes slowly but surely. The monarchy having definitively been brought down, it is a question of overthrowing the other base of the old society, namely Catholicism [sic]. All the policy of the third republic has been concentrated on this point for fifty years.[903]

In its attempt to overthrow the Church, Freemasonry promoted the doctrine of humanism. De Poncins confirms this by quoting from a speech given by Freemason M. Viviani on January 15, 1901: "'Do not fear the battle offered to you; accept it, and if you find in front of you this divine religion which idealizes suffering by promises of future

---

[900] Miller 636-637.
[901] Miller 637.
[902] de Poncins 51.
[903] de Poncins 52-53.

recompense, oppose it with the religion of humanity which also idealizes suffering by offering it, as recompense, the happiness of human generations."[904]

THE FRENCH MASONIC STATE AND ITS AIMS

At the Masonic convention of 1902, at a time when the Catholic Church was again fighting this godless system in France, de Poncins quotes the Mason who made the closing speech: "This is the last phase of the struggle of the church and its congregation against our republican and laical society. This effort must be the last."[905]

By this time Freemasonry was bold enough to take off its mask and everywhere proclaim its victory. De Poncins quotes the Masonic public newspaper *Matin*, as early as 1893, openly stating in one of its articles:

> We may affirm, without being overbold, that the majority of the laws which the French submit to - we speak of important political laws - have been examined by freemasonry [sic] before appearing in the official gazette. The laws on primary education, on divorce, the military laws and among others the law obliging seminarists to do military service, went from the rue Cadet [headquarters of Grand Orient Freemasonry] to the Palais Bourbon; and they came back inviolate and definitive. In conclusion comes this shout of triumph: "We are still all powerful, but on condition that we compose our aspirations in a simple formula. For ten years we have marched forward repeating: 'Clericalism is the enemy!' We have everywhere schools without religious teaching, priests are reduced to silence and seminarists have to carry the soldier's pack. That is no ordinary result in a nation which calls itself the eldest daughter of the Church."[906]

Following World War One, with the creation of the League of Nations, French Freemasonry made another bid to form a united Europe, this time actually calling it the United States of Europe. Stoddard reveals the story by quoting from the 1922 Convention minutes of the Grand Lodge of France:

> The principal tasks of the League of Nations consist in the organisation of peace, the abolition of secret diplomacy, the application of the right of peoples to self-determination. the establishment of commercial relations inspired by the principle of Free Trade, the repartition of basic matters, the regulation of transport, restoration of normal relations between national devices, and the creation of an international note; the development of international legislation of labour, and especially the participation of an organized working-class in international councils; the spread of a general pacifist education based notably on the extension of an international language; the creation of a European spirit, of a League of Nations patriotism - in brief, the formation of the United States of Europe, or rather World Federation.[907]

In 1923, at its annual convention, Grand Orient Freemasonry sounded its note of praise to the forerunner of the United States of Europe. De Poncins quotes: "'It is the duty

---

[904] de Poncins 54.
[905] de Poncins.
[906] de Poncins 55.
[907] Stoddard, *Light-bearers* 15-16.

of universal Freemasonry to give its absolute support to the League of Nations, so that it [Freemasonry] no longer has to be subject to the partisan influences of Governments."[908]

A toast was then given by the President of the Grand Orient. De Poncins quotes: "'To the French Republic, daughter of French masonry [sic]. To the universal Republic of tomorrow [sic], daughter of universal masonry [sic].'"[909]

Templar French Freemasonry had resigned itself to the fact that its one-world government would have to wait. At first it was to be loose-knit in the League of Nations. Later a more binding European unity could be inaugurated under the name "United States of Europe." A Universal Republic, however, was still a future consideration. For now French Masons concentrated on the election at hand.

The election of 1924 was a triumph for the Grand Orient socialists. At the head of the government was socialist Edouard Herriot. De Poncins quotes R. Mennevee, who wrote in 1928:

> The 11th May 1924, the adversaries of freemasonry [sic] marked the most complete defeat which they have perhaps ever suffered. This republican victory was characterized, from the masonic [sic I point of view, by the fact that there was elected to the chamber of deputies a considerable number of masons [sic] whose quality as such was notorious, while the heads of the anti-masonic [sic] organizations were ignominiously beaten.[910]
>
> The Herriot socialist cabinet of 1924 was dominated by Freemasons. That year A.G. Michel published La dictature de La Franc-maçonnerie sur La France, in which he documented that the policies installed by Herriot's government were first discussed, then drawn up in Grand Orient Conventions during the previous four years." When Herriot won the election, the Grand Orient sent him a loyal address. De Poncins quotes that address: "Before we begin, allow me to send greetings from all Freemasons to our great citizen Herriot, who, although not himself a Freemason, is so successful in putting into practice our Masonic ideas."[911]

The influence of Freemasonry in French politics was thus summarized in 1926 by a well-known Italian author of that era, 33rd degree Freemason, Albert Lantoine. De Poncins quotes Lantoine's praise: "The advent of the Republic permitted Freemasonry to act outwardly and to take such a place in the State that its adversaries could say that France was not a republic but a freemasonic [sic] State."[912]

FASCISM AND NAZISM

France was only one example of a Masonic state. After dethroning the monarchies throughout Europe with World War I, Freemasonry placed its own in governments across the Continent. These men had no prior political or financial experience. In their attempt to socialize government (a system unproven politically and economically), the world was plunged into depression. This gave rise to Fascism. The Fascists and Nazis, however, did not go after Freemasonry as the cause of world unrest. They went after the Jews, so well

---

[908] de Poncins, *Freemasonry and the Vatican* 63.
[909] de Poncins.
[910] de Poncins, *Secret Powers* 56.
[911] de Poncins, *Freemasonry and the Vatican* 57.
[912] de Poncins, *Secret Powers* 55-56.

had Gentile Grand Orient Freemasonry made them the scapegoats in carrying out its diabolical communist conspiracy.

Fascism was nationalistic in nature, opposed to Freemasonry's universalism. Fascists and Nazis were haters of Jews first, then haters of Masons. Their success was due largely to the powerless League of Nations, as well as to the inexperience of Masonic politicians, many of whom were Jews. For example, the French Communist Party leader in the 1930s was Grand Orient Freemason Leon Blum, a Reform Jew. Blum was an intimate friend of the Russian Communist and Grand Orient Freemason Leon Trotsky (Bronstein), also a Reform Jew. Trotsky, residing in Paris at the time, had fled the wrath of Joseph Stalin, who was married to a Jewess.

The Fascists and Nazis were well aware that both Blum and Trotsky were Jews and accused Stalin of being controlled by Jews, who, they claimed, brought Russia the Bolshevik Revolution. (See Appendix 2, Fig. 33.) As designed by Gentile Freemasonry, when Blum rooted out the Fascists from France in the mid-1930s, his Masonic affiliation was not remembered. Jewry and not Freemasonry was accused of controlling the conspiracy behind French communism.

To successfully defeat the extreme right-wing Fascists, Blum formed a collectivist party to maintain control of the tottering government and named it the *Popular Front*. The coalition was among the three warring left-wing factions in Grand Orient Freemasonry, consisting of the Communists, Pacifist Socialists and Radical Socialists. In 1936 Blum was elected Prime Minister. His cabinet, his ministers and his under secretaries were all communist Grand Orient Freemasons.[913]

De Poncins confirms that "This alliance was made under the aegis of Freemasonry. The League for the Rights of Man, under the leadership of Victor Basch and Emile Kahn, played a preponderant part in this union of Left Wing parties."[914]

When Mussolini and Hitler rose to power, they almost silenced the Continental Masonic conspiracy during World War II. For example, both dictators outlawed Freemasonry in their respective countries in 1925 and 1933, perceiving it to be of Jewish origin. Then they set out to obliterate it from the face of Europe. Although the Jews received the brunt of Hitler's wrath, Freemasonry had no idea that in the process it too would be decimated. With European economies in shambles, and the war raging all around, the Lodge could do no better than succumb to persecution.

Throughout the Second World War, English Freemasonry secretly funded Hitler to war against her Templar adversary. The Fuhrer's funding was distributed through the oligarchy Bank for International Settlements (BIS), founded in 1930 and safely headquartered in Basel, Switzerland. Hitler would have succeeded in destroying the Templar conspiracy on the Continent and in Bolshevik Russia had he not turned against England.[915]

Meanwhile, French lodges went underground during the war, forming the resistance movement headed by General Charles de Gaulle. When the war ended in 1945, Grand Orient Freemason Leon Blum was back in power as the provisional president. That year the Grand Orient-directed Gaullists and communist thugs arrested Frenchmen who had collaborated with the Nazis and shot them like dogs. Even their children were tied to execution posts and shot. Their women were paraded naked in the streets, their heads shaven, before being tortured to death. The year the war ended the French Grand Orient

---

[913] de Poncins, *Freemasonry and the Vatican* 190-191.

[914] de Poncins.

[915] English Masonic involvement in creating World War II will be documented in the final chapters of this book.

murdered 1.25 million of its own people. The Masons then appropriated to themselves the property of their victims.[916]

Today, France continues to march under the flag of the Grand Orient, led at this writing by 33rd degree Freemason, Francois Mitterrand, president since 1981. On December 31, 1992, Mitterrand helped inaugurate Masonry's long-awaited United States of Europe. Working hard for its success is Otto von Habsburg, holder of the Sionist title, "King of Jerusalem."[917]

---

[916] Francois Franco, "Nationalism on the Rise in France," *Spotlight* 22 July 1991: 3.
[917] Church 215-231 and Baigent et al, *Holy Blood* 409.

13. THE PROTOCOLS OF
THE LEARNED ELDERS OF SION

> *At first these "Protocols," printed in broad sheets by the millions, were used to stir up fear and hatred of Jews in Germany. They were then re-issued, somewhat revised, and directed at England to stir up hatred of the English. In Russia the "Protocols" were used to back up charges against the Jews for "ritual murders."*
> Mackey's Encyclopedia of Freemasonry[918]

The Jewish Holocaust of World War II fulfilled a prophecy made 150 years earlier by the orthodox rabbis in Germany, who warned the Frankist-Reform Jews that persecution would start at Berlin if they persisted in their amoral destruction of society. To help fulfill this prophecy, anti-Semitic Gentile Freemasonry engineered the exposure of the Jews through the fraudulent creation of *The Protocols of the Learned Elders of Sion*. These *Protocols*, a compilation of twenty-four documents, developed the required anti-Semitism that ended in the death of six million Jews in the midst of World War II.

The Protocols of the Learned Elders of Sion were first said to have been the minutes of the first Zionist Congress at Basel, Switzerland, August 29-31, 1897. According to Robert John, author of *Behind the Balfour Declaration*, the 197 Jewish delegates were a mixture of the orthodoxy, nationalists, liberals, atheists, culturalists, anarchists, socialists and capitalists.[919] In three days these Jews are said to have discussed, debated, then agreed upon a detailed conspiracy for world dominion. The alleged outcome of that Congress was a document containing the minutes to twenty-four lengthy meetings detailing how the Jewish intrigue was to unfold.

It defies imagination, how Jews of such mixed convictions, who find it difficult to agree on any issue within their own persuasion, completed twenty-four *Protocols* in just three days.

Those who read the documents were apparently convinced that Zionist Jews were planning to take over all governments through a well-orchestrated plan of subversion, using the press, secular schools, and Gentile Masonry as a cover. The Jews allegedly were planning to enslave the world through this conspiracy. Their first insurrection was to take place in Russia, which in retrospect many believed to have climaxed in the Bolshevik Revolution of 1917. So well had Gentile Freemasonry placed the Jews in the forefront of that insurrection that the West began hearing rumors of Jews taking over Russia. Appendix 2, Fig. 33 presents the caricatures of these allegations that were printed in newspapers throughout the world.

HISTORY OF THE PROTOCOLS

We have learned that *Sion* is the French spelling for the English *Zion*. The original *Protocols* were written in French, stolen from a Masonic lodge in Paris in 1884 (as we shall see), then taken to Russia where they were translated and first published in that language in 1903.

---

[918] "Anti-Semitism and Masonry," *Mackey's Encyclopedia of Freemasonry*, vol. III.
[919] Robert John, *Behind the Balfour Declaration* (Costa Mesa, CA: Institute for Historical Review, 1988) 30.

After the first publication of the *Protocols* in Russia, they were banned in 1905 by the ill-fated Czar Nicholas II following an attempt to topple his government. In 1917, following the February Revolution, the new Kerensky government confiscated and burned the second edition before it reached the streets and immediately outlawed anti-Semitism.[920] On April 5, 1917, the Russian Jews won emancipation.[921] By October Kerensky's government had lost to the Bolsheviks, who, in the "Red Terror" that followed, appeared to fulfill the slaughter written of in the *Protocols.*

After the Bolshevik Revolution, the *Protocols* made their way back to the West, where, from 1921 to 1935, the newspaper-reading-public of the world was made aware of their contents.

Publishing the *Protocols of the Learned Elders* of Sion was a most malicious crime committed against the House of Israel. At the same time as the *Protocols* began to circulate throughout Europe, conspiracy researchers were attempting to connect the Bolsheviks with the Illuminati. In many ways the two movements were the same. We see this, for instance, in their colors. Weishaupt had selected the color red to represent his bloody revolution. Likewise, the Communists. Since then Communists have been nicknamed "Reds."

Those who opposed the Reds formed their own republic called Belorussia, or White Russia, bordering on Poland, Lithuania, and Latvia. The Whites waged a short-lived counterrevolution against the Reds but lost in 1919 for lack of funds. When the Whites fled to the West, most settled in Germany. With them came copies of the *Protocols.* Soon these documents were in the hands of Hitler, who set out to rid the world of this so-called Judeo-Masonic conspiracy. Hitler's *Mein Kampf* makes mention of the *Protocols* as proof of a Jewish conspiracy.[922]

The *Protocols of the Learned Elders of Sion* have been suppressed so successfully since the Jewish Holocaust that today most people have not heard of them. During the 1920s and 1930s, however, their contents were on the lips of every political official in Europe, Asia and America. Appendix 2, Fig. 10 shows reproductions of two book covers of the French and Spanish editions of the *Protocols.* The Jewish caricatures on the covers reveal the vicious anti-Semitism of the time.

THE BIRTH OF ZIONISM IN RUSSIA

The Zionist movement was the result of anti-Semitic seeds sown in Russia by Grand Orient Freemasonry. In 1840 the German Grand Orient sent Reform Jews to that vast empire where Jewish Orthodoxy was the strongest. Their assignment was to destroy the Russian Jews through assimilation into Russian society. The Reform, however, had not anticipated the power of the leading Russian Rabbi, Tzemach Tzedek, who victoriously opposed them. In retaliation the Reform began to spread lies about the Orthodoxy. Czarist Russia believed these lies and became violently anti-Semitic. Pogroms, which are organized massacres of helpless people, broke out everywhere against the Jews.[923]

Rabbi Antelman informs us that the Reform was headquartered in the Grand Orient "League of the Just," known in Germany as the "Bund." While the Bund financed Karl Marx's communist activity in France and England, it also sought virgin territory to export its communist doctrine to the East. Antelman gives us the details:

---

[920] "Israel," *World Economic Review,* November 1986: 13.
[921] John 64.
[922] Adolf Hitler, *Mein Kampf,* trans. James Murphy (1939; Los Angeles: Angriff Press, 1981)
[923] Antelman, entire.

Reform was now ready for expansion into other areas. The Bund decided to export its heresies to Russia and selected Dr. Max Lillienthal (1814-1882) for the job. Lillienthal was partially successful. In 1840 he succeeded in opening a Jewish school where he could implant the seeds of destruction against Judaism. In December 1841, he laid the groundwork for government sponsored Jewish secular schools in Russia. However, Lillienthal was not totally successful because he had never reckoned with the power of the great Lubavitcher Chasidic rabbi who lived at that time in Russia called the Tzentach Tzedek. It was he who completely dissipated these efforts and taught the Communists a lesson that they never forgot, so much so, that generations later after the revolution they imprisoned this man's descendant known as the Lubavitcher Rebbe of Russia, threatened to kill him and threw him down a flight of stairs.[924]

According to Rabbi Antelman, Max Lillienthal became so enraged with his defeat, that before he left Russia he guaranteed the destruction of his own race there. Antelman writes:

Dr. Lillienthal and his cohorts in Russia made concerted attacks against the Torah and Judaism. Agents of the society were dispatched to spy on the Tzemach Tzedek. They also instigated the writing of scores of denunciatory letters which arrived daily to the Ministry of Interior, Culture and the Secret Police, which spoke against Jewish religious leaders and key merchants, villagers or innkeepers whose morals or integrity they could not compromise. These letters charged rebellion, contempt for Christianity, misappropriation of taxes, violation of the restricted areas which only Jews may inhabit, smuggling, bribery and usury.

On one occasion Lillienthal attempted to impress Count Uvarov, the Minister of Culture. He stated that the rabbis condone all sorts of unethical iniquities with Gentiles including usury and misrepresentation. In addition he accused the rabbis of preaching a policy of separatism from the good Gentile neighborhoods and he claimed that the most notorious offender was the saintly Tzemach Tzedek.

All the years that Lillienthal was in Russia, pressure from above the government, and pressure from below through his educators and enlightenment societies [Grand Orient Freemasonry] continued to be applied to the Jewish communities to assimilate... All during this period the Czar was applying further pressure of assimilating Jews with his forced conscription law so that during 1842-1843, 22,000 Jews had been converted to Christianity and between 1846-1854, 7,000 were baptized. However, things got worse and finally came to a head.

On May 6, 1843, the first meeting of a government commission aimed at finalizing Jewish assimilation was convened. The Tzemach Tzedek stood strongly in opposition to what the conspirators wanted to do. The gauntlet was thrown on the table when he stated that if it was the government intention and that of the Maskilim (seekers of enlightenment) to carry out their plan that he and his colleagues were prepared to suffer death rather than to transgress.[925]

Death is what they received. Pogroms broke out everywhere. Against this terror the Orthodox Jews began to dream of a Jewish homeland, specifically a return to Palestine. During these trying times, the word "Zionism" was coined for their movement. Although Zionism was not officially recognized until 1896-1897, Theodore Herzl (1860-1904), a

---

[924] Antelman 33.
[925] Antelman 35-38.

Viennese Jewish journalist, "offered a focus for a Zionist movement founded in Odessa in 1881, which spread rapidly through the Jewish communities of Russia, and small branches which had sprung up in Germany, England and elsewhere."[926]

Zionism was an escapist reaction that grew from the anti-Semitic seeds sown by the Reform.[927] Within four decades Zionism became a nationalistic movement of Jews around the world. Herzl created the first Zionist Congress held in Basel, Switzerland, in 1897. Twenty years later Russia experienced "the vengeance of the Jews" in the Bolshevik Revolution, so stated those who had read and believed the "evidence" of the *Protocols of the Learned Elders of Sion.*

Rabbi Antelman states that Reform Judaism financed the Bolshevik Revolution through a bewhiskered anti-Zionist Jew named Jacob Schiff, a New York City banker. Speaking to the cause of the Russian pogroms, Antelman carries the reader back to the Reform's failure to assimilate Jews into Russian society. He states, "It was... this stunning defeat that heightened extreme disdain for Russian Jews which was manifested in many ways by Jacob Schiff."[928]

JEWS AND THE TWO 1917 RUSSIAN REVOLUTIONS

Jacob Schiff was a puppet of Max Warburg, the Jewish banker from Frankfurt, Germany. You may recall that the Rothschild and Warburg families were in competition in Frankfurt during the Napoleonic Wars, after which the House of Rothschild moved its banking headquarters to London. Years later competition between the two Jewish clans was manifested in two areas other than banking. First in religion, the Warburg clan were Reform Jews, whereas the Rothschilds were Zionists; second, in Masonic affiliation, the Rothschilds were English Masons, whereas the Warburgs were Grand Orient Masons.

These divisions, and not their banking rivalry, brought the Rothschilds and Warburgs into conflict in the two Russian revolutions of 1917. Although both insurrections were planned by Gentile Freemasonry (see chapter 19), the Rothschilds and the Warburgs took opposite sides in funding the competing factions.

Lord Rothschild, in February 1917, backed the Russian Socialist and Scottish Rite Mason, Alexander Kerensky, who attempted to install a government in Russia similar to that of the United States. At Kerensky's side were Zionist Orthodox Jews. On April 5th all Jews won emancipation.

The other Jewish party, the Reform Jews, did not want socialism, but communism. Their counterrevolution in October was led by Russian Grand Orient Mason, Vladimir Lenin. His uprising was funded by the German Grand Orient Mason Max Warburg. At Lenin's side were anti-Zionist Reform Jews. After the Bolsheviks toppled the Kerensky government, Rothschild funded the White Russians against the Bolsheviks.

Most conspiracy researchers know of the Jewish involvement in both revolutions. Yet, they have been unable to differentiate between the anti-Zionist Reform Jews and the Zionist Orthodox Jews. Not until Rabbi Antelman explained this division in his 1974 book was the Gentile world to know. Lacking this knowledge, investigators in the 1920s blamed the authorship of the *Protocols of the Learned Elders* of Sion on the Zionist Congress of 1897.

---

[926] John 29.
[927] Antelman 33.
[928] Antelman.

ORIGINS OF THE PROTOCOLS

Dating the authorship of the *Protocols* at 1897 has since been established as too late. The *Protocols* date much earlier. Yet Jewry had already been damaged with the world-wide publication of their falsely incriminating contents. For example, the *Protocols* were distributed to the White Russian Army soon after the House of Rothschild began financing the Whites against the Reds. The Whites, thinking they now understood the cause behind the destruction of Russia, indiscriminately slaughtered 60,000 Jews, blaming them for the Bolshevik Revolution. Rothschild grieved over this unwarranted carnage and withdrew his funding, upon which the Whites fell to the Reds. [929] Escaping to the West, many Whites settled in Germany and joined the Nazis. Soon Hitler set out to rid the world of this so-called Jewish conspiracy.[930] The result was six million Jews slaughtered during World War II.

Masons began to promote the Jews as the author of the *Protocols*. From 1920 through 1922 the *Protocols* were serialized in America in *The Dearborn Independent*, a Dearborn, Michigan, newspaper distributed by 33rd degree Freemason Henry Ford. Later, Ford's serialization was bound in a book entitled *The International Jew* and distributed throughout Nazi Germany.

Even young Winston Churchill, a Master Mason at the time, promoted the *Protocols* as Jewish. The London *Jewish Chronicle* of February 13,1920, accused him as follows: "The Secretary of War, Winston Churchill, charges the Jews with engineering a world wide conspiracy for the overthrow of civilization."[931]

Authentic or forged, its contents true or false, to withhold from mention in general history the existence of documents that caused World War II, and with it the ritual murder of six million Jews and five million Gentiles, is a travesty of justice to world history. On the other hand, to speak of them - worse yet, to allow them to be published and read would once again bring certain death to the Jews, so deceptively incriminating is the "evidence" against them. Certainly, the Jews must, and did fight to prove those documents not of Jewish origin. They received vindication from the Court of Berne on May 14, 1935, when the Court ruled the *Protocols* not of Jewish origin.[932]

If not of Jewish origin, from whence came the *Protocols of Sion?* The Court of Berne discovered that the original documents were in French. We have learned that the birthplace and home of the Priory of Sion was, and still is, France.[933] We have also discovered that the Priory of Sion is not Jewish, but a Jewish counterfeit. Moreover, we have suggested that the Priory of Sion may be those individuals, written of by the Apostle John, who "say they are Jews, and are not, but do lie..." Revelation 3:9).

Therefore, if the *Protocols of Sion* is the product of the Priory of Sion, and not of the Zionist Jews, it is understandable why the Jews would denounce it everywhere as a

---

[929] Conspiracy researchers have accused Rothschild of siding with the Communists when he withdrew his financial support from the anti-Communist White Army.

[930] Hitler 174.

[931] John Coleman, *King Makers: King Breakers = The Cecils,* audio cassette 1984, Christian Defense League.

[932] Karl Bergmeister, *The Protocols of the Elders of Zion before the Court in Berne* (1938; Mettairie, LA: Sons of Liberty, n.d.) entire. The author and his wife were in Basel, Switzerland, August 1987. The author offered to pay a Swiss history professor his required fee to obtain copies of the Berne court proceedings on the *Protocols*. The professor became very interested and began to ask questions. When the author mentioned the Masonic connection the historian coldly said, "I don't think I want to work for you."

[933] Since the exiling of the Templars from Great Britain, all Grand Masters of Sion have been from the Continent.

forgery. Finally, in 1921 the London Times "made the sensational discovery through its correspondents in Constantinople... of a French book which they called the *Dialogues of Geneva*, published anonymously at Brussels in 1865. This book, the *Times* affirmed, had been plagiarized by the author[s] of the *Protocols.*"[934]

After the *Dialogues of Geneva* were published, the *Times* is quoted as saying: "'It was soon discovered by the police of Napoleon III that the author of the book was a certain lawyer, Maurice Joly, who was arrested, tried, and sentenced to two years imprisonment [from April 1865], as it was averred that he had written his book as an attack against the government of Napoleon III to which he had lent all the Machiavellian plans revealed in the *Dialogues.*"[935]

Maurice Joly (1831-1878) was a Gentile French lawyer, a writer, Freemason, and member of a Rose-Croix order. Most significant, he was intimate with Victor Hugo (1802-1885), the famous French poet, who was also a member of the same Rose-Croix order.[936] This is the same Victor Hugo, who, following the communist uprisings of 1848, coined the phrase, the "United States of Europe" at the Masonic Peace Conference in 1849.

From 1844 until his death in 1885, Victor Hugo was Grand Master of the Priory of Sion.[937] The authors of *Holy Blood, Holy Grail,* suggest that the Rosicrucian order to which both Joly and Hugo belonged was the Priory of Sion.

Maurice Joly was also a close friend of the Jewish Freemason, Adolphe Isaac Cremieux (1796- 1880). Cremieux was mentioned in the previous chapter as being involved with Victor Hugo in the 1848 communist uprisings in France and was one of the orators applauding its success. Most significant was Cremietix's Masonic rank. He was a 33rd degree Mason sitting on the Supreme Council of the Ancient and Primitive Rite of Mizraim at Paris, the same Rosicrucian Masonic Lodge founded by Sionist-Illuminatus Cagliostro. The rituals practiced in the Mizraim Lodge were the same Isis cult mysteries of Egypt observed by the Priory of Sion. Sion's English Masons also act out the same Isis legend in the Master Mason ceremony.[938]

The facts of Maurice Joly's life make him an interesting man indeed. First, he was a Gentile Frenchman, a lawyer, a Freemason, and a writer. Second, he was the man who wrote the *Dialogues of Geneva* (in French), from which the original version of the *Protocols of the Learned Elders of Sion* allegedly were plagiarized (in French). Third, he was closely associated with Victor Hugo, the Grand Master of the Priory of Sion. Fourth, Joly was involved with Aldolphe Cremietix, a ruler in a Rosicrucian Masonic Lodge, a lodge founded by Sionist Cagliostro. Fifth, both Hugo and Cremieux were heavily involved in the French Masonic Revolution of 1848. This circumstantial evidence points to these three men as having been involved in creating the *Protocols of the Learned Elders of Sion.*

ZIONISM VERSUS SIONISM

Circumstantial evidence? Of course. The activities of Cremieux, however, make the intrigue even more fascinating. For six years (1864- 1870) Cremieux was president of the *Alliance Israelite Universelle,* a genuine Jewish political order founded in 1860, and headquartered in the same Sionist Masonic Lodge where Cremieux sat as a ruler on the

---

[934] Miller 410-411.
[935] Miller 411.
[936] Baigent et al, *Holy Blood* 192, 435-436.
[937] Church 90.
[938] Miller 407.

Supreme Council. The Alliance, an arm of the Priory of Sion, was created to counter the *Zionist* movement that was budding in Russia during the 1850s.

Zionism was nationalistic, desiring a Jewish homeland, whereas the Alliance Israelite Universelle was exactly what its name implies, an Alliance of Universalist Jews. As Universalists, the Alliance encouraged all Jews to keep their identity in Gentile nations. Naturally, they opposed those Jews who longed for a homeland. The Alliance also opposed Reform Judaism, which desired that Jews lose their identity in Gentile nations through assimilation. In subsequent years the Universalist Jews spread throughout Europe, but never crossed the English Channel, where English Freemasonry reluctantly backed Zionism at the bidding of the Rothschilds.

Not only was Zionism a bewilderment to the Universalist Jews, it took Reform Judaism by total surprise. A homeland for the Jews would, in effect destroy the Reform's planned destruction of the Jewish race through assimilation. As a matter of course, then, Reform Judaism, already anti- Semitic, became anti-Zionist.

The Universalist Jews, on the other hand, were not anti-Semitic, but were anti-Zionist - yet, for a different reason than that pursued by the Reform Jews. For example, nationalistic Zionism posed a threat to the counterfeit "King of Jerusalem" cult of Merovingians, who desired someday to reinstate their universal throne at Jerusalem where it had been established during the Crusades. It was the Priory of Sion's ultimate task to crown the "Lost King" on a Jerusalem throne. Therefore, Zionism was on a collision course with Sionism. Should the Zionists succeed in establishing a Jewish homeland, a genuine Jewish king ascending the throne of a bonafide Israelite nation would destroy the millennium-old Merovingian dream. As a matter of course, then, the Priory of Sion became anti-Zionist, founding the Alliance Israelite Universelle to counter the Zionist movement.

The Alliance, although founded by the Priory of Sion, was an exclusively Jewish Order headquartered in a Gentile Rosicrucian Masonic Lodge. Reform Judaism, on the other hand, was Templar, headquartered in Gentile Grand Orient Freemasonry, and hence, an adversary of the Priory of Sion. Yet, Zionism gave cause for the Alliance to ally 'with the Reform in an effort to destroy this nationalist movement.

Adversaries with common enemies make strange bedfellows. These two adversaries would cooperate, if necessary, in a revolution in Russia, either to destroy Zionism at its source, or contain it within Russian borders. Hence, we find many Jews of both persuasions involved in Kerensky's Socialist Revolution and Lenin's Communist Revolution. Kerensky's technique for containing the Zionists was to emancipate the Jews, hoping to quiet their drive for a Jewish homeland. The Bolshevik technique was to forcibly keep the Zionists within Russian borders, disallowing them emigration to the Holy Land.[939]

For sixty years (1860-1920) the information connecting these Jewish movements remained obscure. Not until the 1920s, when many professional and amateur revisionist historians began searching for the source of the *Protocols,* did the documentation about Joly, Cremieux, Mizraim Freemasonry and the Alliance surface. Although a mixture of Jews and Gentiles were found on Mizraim membership rolls, it appeared to tile investigators that the Alliance and the Mizraim Lodge were both Jewish-run institutions.

SION CONFUSED WITH ZION

---

[939] James A. Malcolm, *Origins of the Balfour Declaration, Dr. Weizmann's Contribution* (1944; Torrance, CA: Institute for Historical Review, 1983) 6-7. A copy of this document, only 12 pages long, is in the British Museum, and in 1964 was placed in the Harvard University Library.

Because their symbols were identical, Zionists were also mistakenly implicated with the intrigues at Mizraim. Mizraim's herald was the "interlaced triangle," or six-pointed star of the Priory of Sion. In 1917, when the world first saw the Zionists hoist the so-called "Star of David" on their flag at Palestine, conspiracy investigators assumed Mizraim Freemasonry and the Alliance were connected to Zionism.

The "identical syndrome" of Masonic symbols once again confused investigators. Zionists, however, had more right to the six-pointed star than did the Priory of Sion. Long before the Priory and its Masonic lodges adopted it as their coat-of-arms, it was a Jewish symbol of scattered Israel. Before that it was a pagan symbol. For clarification, we will trace its origin.

The interlaced triangle was originally a decorative motif or magical emblem, symbolic of the pagan star-god in Hinduism. Later it migrated to the Assyrians and there was adopted by the ten northern tribes of Israel before they were taken into captivity in 721 B.C.[940] (II Kings 17:1- 23). This is confirmed by the prophet Alnos, whom God sent to the ten tribes to warn them of impending bondage if they did not repent of their idolatry with Assyrian gods. Alnos, speaking for God, warns Israel in 5:26-27:

> But ye have borne the tabernacle of... Chiun. . the star... god, which ye made to yourselves. Therefore, will I cause you to go into captivity beyond Damascus, saith the Lord, whose name is The God of hosts.

Chiun is the planet Saturn, the star-god, symbolized by the two interlaced triangles, or six- pointed star called the hexagram.[941] The hexagram is also known as the Lucifer Star.[942] Idolatrous Israel had "borne," or carried, "the star...god" by wearing the hexagram as an amulet. It was also carved in the door frames of every Israelite house. ostensibly to ward off the "fire god." Since that time the six-pointed star has been a Jewish symbol found in synagogues from the very beginning of the Diaspora. This was 1,700 years before the Priory of Sion appropriated it in the first millennium A.D.[943] After that it appeared on the heraldic flag of the Jews in Prague in 1527, a full two centuries before Gentile Freemasonry adopted it from the Jewish *Cabala*.[944] Therefore, it would be natural for both the Alliance in 1860 and the Zionists in 1897 to select it as their herald.

To make the symbol even more Jewish, the Zionists in 1904 renamed the six-pointed star "Magen David," or "Shield of David."[945] At their first meeting at Basel in 1897, Robert John reports that "On either side of the main doorway of the hall hung white banners with two blue stripes, and over the doorway was placed a six-pointed 'Shield of David.'"[946]

Since this knowledge was unavailable during the 1920s, it was popular to connect Mizraim Freemasonry, the Alliance and Zionism by this symbol. Also, the word "Sion" in the *Protocols* was suspect. Therefore, these documents were thrown in with the hodgepodge of circumstantial evidence implicating Jews. Throughout the 1920s and 1930s, accusations against the Jews were broadcast everywhere. Naturally, Jews of every persuasion were concerned. For their own survival they must discredit the *Protocols*. And with all their resources they did.

---

[940] John 30.

[941] Bible, Pilgrim Edition, footnote #6 on Amos 5:26.

[942] Spaulding 91.

[943] Geoffrey Wigoder, The *Story of the Synagogue, A Diaspora Museum Book* (Jerusalem: Domino Press, 1986) 20, 49, 79, 90, 103, 152, 165, 174, 186, 194.

[944] John 30.

[945] Webster's Ninth New Collegiate Dictionary (Springfield, MA:Merriam-Webster, 1987).

[946] John 30.

Another enigma confronting researchers was the fact that while Cremieux sat on the 33rd degree Supreme Council of Mizraim Freemasonry (a Rosicrucian Order), he was also Supreme Master of its adversary, the Templar Grand Orient at Paris." Jews were controlling both sides of the conspiracy," investigators would write. Therefore, it was a simple matter to accuse them of writing the *Protocols of Sion.*

In retrospect, there are obvious reasons why Cremieux joined an adversarial Lodge. In those days Masonry was continually receiving advanced occult knowledge from research done on the Templar documents looted from the Vatican archives during the reign of Napoleon Bonaparte. working on this project was the Priory of Sion's Eliphas Levi (Louis Constant 1810-1875). Each advanced enlightenment was cause for the invention of more advanced degrees of Masonry. For example, Mizraim had jumped from 33 to 90 degrees by 1868. In 1871 the Mizraim Rite was carried to London where it was absorbed by Memphis Freemasonry. By 1875 it merged with Memphis worldwide and grew to 97 degrees. In France the Grand Orient remained at 33 degrees.[947]

Stiff esoteric competition between lodges was commonplace. Each had highly specialized agents to penetrate the other's lodges to learn of its new occult secrets. It would be natural, then, for Cremietix to seek knowledge from an adversarial lodge. Hence, he joined the Grand Orient, working his way up the chairs to Supreme Commander. Moreover, Cremietix had a strong dislike for Napoleon m (1808-1873), who was also a member of the Grand Orient. The Grand Orient was known as the Lodge for French politicians. As its Grand Commander, Cremietix had access to state secrets, which would benefit Rosicrucian Great Britain.

Although many conspiracy researchers have tried to connect the two, there was no cooperation between the Rosicrucian Mizraim lodges and the Templar Grand Orients. This fact is confirmed in *Mackey's Encyclopedia of Freemasonry:* "an attempt was unsuccessfully made to obtain the recognition of the Grand Orient of France. [Their non-recognition] had the effect of making them illegal."[948]

Dr. Mackey does admit, however, that Mizraim Freemasonry borrowed from the Grand Orient Scottish Rite degrees. Who borrowed but Cremietix? This was common practice among competing lodges.

Non-recognition meant that Mizraim Freemasonry was considered clandestine by the Grand Orient. How, then, did a Rosicrucian, such as Cremieux, obtain membership in a Templar Lodge, much less become its Supreme Master, if he was known to be a ruler in an adversarial lodge. No conspiracy researcher has given a satisfactory answer, outside of tying the two lodges together. It may be that the Grand Orient was ignorant of Cremietix's affiliation with Mizraim. In this secret war of intelligence gathering from competing lodges, membership lists are suppressed by issuing secret code names to the hierarchy. Cremieux may have been a double agent, as was Cagliostro, founder of Mizraim.

MIZRAIM FREEMASONRY AND INTELLIGENCE GATHERING

Intelligence gathering was established as a Masonic activity at the Congress of Vienna in 1815. When European Grail royalty united within British Freemasonry to protect the Priory of Sion secret, they built for themselves a spy network operating out of the Grand Lodge Alpina in Switzerland. From there they kept an eye on Masonic developments in France by penetrating the Grand Orient with their agents. Alpina's agents were none other than Sionists Cremietix, Joly, and Victor Hugo, the Grand Master of the Priory of Sion.

---

[947] Miller 407-408, 443.
[948] "Mizraim, Rite of," *Mackey's Encyclopedia,* vol.11.

All three were intimate with Rosicrucian Mizraim Freemasonry. It seems likely that Cremietix was a Rosicrucian spy who penetrated the Templar Grand Orient, the lodge for French politicians, working his way through the chairs to the top position.

Edith Miller, in *Occult Theocrasy*, documents that English Free-masonry was in communication with Mizraim during Cremieux's day. Its counterpart in London was Memphis Freemasonry, known in England as "The Ancient and Primitive Rite." The Rite of Mizraim was amalgamated with that of Memphis in 1775.[949] At the head of Memphis in London was 33rd degree Mason John Yarker (1833-1913). A member of its ruling hierarchy in France was Cremieux (1836- 1871). It would have been common practice for Cremieux to transfer state secrets to Yarker through Masonic channels.

BRIEF HISTORY OF MASONIC INTELLIGENCE OPERATIONS

The Templars and Sion have been spying on each other since 1188. Such spying continues to the present day. We will briefly examine the history of Masonic intelligence operations below.

John J. Robinson, author of the recent pro-Masonic book, *Born in* Blood: *The Lost Secrets of Freemasonry*, informs us that in the 12th and 13th centuries the Knights Templar were the precursors of our modern intelligence services. He says they "were known to maintain intelligence agents in the principal cities of the Middle East and the Mediterranean coast, and they would necessarily have employed covert means of communication. International financial dealings required total secrecy, naval operations required it to hide shipping information from Moslem or pirate forces, and military administration over two continents would certainly require it."

When the Templars founded their form of Freemasonry, intelligence operations naturally travelled through a chain of their lodges. Likewise, Sion's Rosicrucians penetrated the masonic working man's guilds a century before Cromwell's revolution. Moreover, Cromwell himself used the secret halls of an aristocratic Masonic lodge called the "Crown" to organize his insurrection.

A century later Adam Weishaupt turned Continental Freemasonry into an intelligence gathering machine. He founded the Illuminati to penetrate Templar French Masonry. His assignment was to ignite the French Revolution and depose the Bourbons on behalf of the Priory of Sion. Instead, the Illuminati itself was penetrated by the Templars. The Revolution occurred as scheduled, but not under the command of Weishaupt.[950]

Adversarial lodges penetrating each other's ranks is not as difficult as one may imagine. The irony is that both Freemasonries employ the same identifying grips and passwords. Entry is granted readily by a spy using these secret codes. Once inside the lodge brother Masons fraternize freely with each other. The unsuspecting brothers tell every- thing they know to an enemy who shakes hands correctly.[951]

An example of how British Masons used intelligence networks in Cremieux's day is given by Msgr. George Dillon. During that time the Prime Minister of Great Britain was 33rd degree Freemason, Lord Palmerston, who was, in a sense, a double agent. Palmerston, a Templar Scottish Rite Mason, was in command of Rosicrucian English Freemasonry. Dillon states that Palmerston, after he failed to acquire financial aid from

---

[949] Miller 407-408, 443.

[950] Robinson 77.

[951] Some of the information the author has been able to gather for this book has come directly from Masons, who readily answered his questions after he had given them the Masonic handshake.

Parliament for Mazzini's Templar Grand Orient revolution in Italy, successfully tapped the British secret service for funding the Italian Masons.[952]

During World War I, we find another example of Masonry's intelligence gathering. This war was the first global conflict between British and French Freemasonry to determine which political system would rule the world - monarchies or republics. In future chapters we shall discuss the Masonic intrigue of that conflict, with one Order penetrating the other to obtain the enemy's battle plans. A hint of the level of intelligence activity is provided by a German author, Friedrich Hasselbacher, whose book, *High Treason of the Military Lodges,* is an unanswerable and damning document. It reproduces in facsimile a mass of letters and "Field Post Cards" from Masons to their lodges in Germany. In one letter, a Brother Mason writes to his Grand Master suggesting that he get in touch with English Masons via the Grand Lodge of Norway, in order to find out their "war aims.[953]

Masonic intelligence services were employed again in World War II. For example, Freemasonry in France was used as a secret service to help the resistance. The story is revealed by Frenchman Henri Coston in *La Republique du Grand Orient,* which de Poncins quotes in *Freemasonry and the Vatican.* Coston confirms that during the Nazi occupation of northern France, Pierre Laval, a French politician, assisted the resistance when he "'attached the services of the secret societies to the Surete Nationale, the state intelligence service.'"[954]

In our day the Masonic Lodge is tied directly to state intelligence services. Agents are placed according to certain requirements and abilities, one of which is the ability to keep a secret. Therefore, agents who are Masons are given preference for top positions. For example, in the U.S.A. the heads of both the FBI and the CIA have always been either 33rd degree Masons, or high initiates in affiliated secret societies. In fact, J. Edgar Hoover (33rd degree) obtained a charter for the FBI's own Masonic lodge, the Fidelity Lodge. Curt Gentry, in his book J. *Edgar Hoover,* informs us that "Membership and attendance at the Monday-night meetings were 'voluntary,' but those who aspired to higher positions soon realized that associating with the director on this one semi-social occasion was almost a prerequisite to advancement."[955]

The weakness in this system of selection is readily apparent, since Masons freely talk to, and advance brother Masons. If an enemy agent joins a Masonic Lodge frequented by an intelligence agent whom he wishes to compromise, his task is simple. Many examples of this are presented by the late Stephen Knight in *The Brotherhood.* Knight, a British investigative journalist, documented time and again how the KGB, prior to and after World War II, successfully penetrated British intelligence by joining Western Freemasonry.

Knight informs us, for example, how after the Bolshevik Revolution, Russian intelligence used Freemasonry to its own ends. The Soviet intelligence service learned of the art of Freemasonry while investigating Russian Grand Orient Lodges. When Stalin outlawed the Brotherhood in 1925, he ordered his intelligence service to establish religious centers for training appropriate agents to be sent to Western and Third World countries. A school for agents bound for Britain and other English-speaking countries was in Lithuania prior to the collapse of the U.S.S.R. These agents were trained in the

---

[952] Dillon 83.This is still practiced today. For example, when the United States Congress failed to back the Contras financially, President Reagan went to the CIA for funding. Hence, the famed "Iran/Contra Affair" involving Oliver North.

[953] *The Growing Menace of Freemasonry in Britain,* 6th ed. (London: n.p., 1936) 17.

[954] de Poncins, *Freemasonry and the Vatican* 196.

[955] Curt Gentry, J *Edgar Hoover: The Man and the Secrets,* (New York: Plume, 1991) 148-149.

exploitation of English Freemasonry.[956] Knight quotes a British Intelligence officer as saying:

> If the KGB had a target in England - somebody they wanted to "turn" or from whom they wanted to obtain information by one of a number of means - and this person was a Freemason, I have no doubt that it would instruct an agent to join the same lodge. That would be an obvious move. If being a Freemason makes a man more likely to bare his soul to another Freemason than to an outsider, any intelligence service worth its salt would exploit that.[957]

One of the most damaging episodes described by Knight was that of a KGB agent turning master spies Kim Philby, Donald Maclean, and Guy Burgess into double agents for Russia. Knight suggests this transformation was accomplished through Freemasonry. The intelligence world was shocked when these three men defected to Russia in 1952 and 1962. It was discovered 30 years too late that Philby, while head of a division in MIS (initials for Mission Impossible, division No. 5), was also a high-ranking KGB agent. The irony in this story is that Philby remained on the British intelligence payroll after defection.[958] He died in Moscow, November 5, 1988- taking to the grave his reason for defecting.[959]

Stephen Knight revealed that the penetration of Western Free- masonry was a standard KGB practice:

> I can reveal that senior officers of British Intelligence are concerned that the KGB has been using Freemasonry in England for decades to help place its agents in positions of responsibility and influence... According to the evidence now available the undoubted "jobs for the brethren" aspect of British Freemasonry has been used extensively by the KGB to penetrate the most sensitive areas of authority, most spectacularly illustrated in the years since 1945 by its placing of spies at the highest levels of both M15 and M16. Even today, members of the security services privately admit that they have no idea of the extent of this penetration.[960]

The "old boy network," the favoritism and the use of Masonry for professional and social advancement - all proscribed by the [Masonic] Constitutions but all nevertheless widespread, as this book has shown - are of obvious value to Englishmen recruited to spy for a foreign power.[961]

---

[956] Stephen Knight, *The Brotherhood* 284.

[957] Knight 290.

[958] John Coleman, "Spy Scandals and Secret Societies," *World Economic Review*, October 1984: 1.

[959] Phillip Knightley, *The Master Spy* (New York: Alfred A. Knopf, 1989) picture facing page 117.

[960] A book entitled *Henry Kissinger, Soviet Agent* was published in1974 by Frank A. Capell, and reprinted by Sons of Liberty in 1987. The author documents that Kissinger was born and raised in Germany during the Nazi regime. According to Capell, as a member of the German Communist Party, Kissinger was easily recruited by the KGB after the war and sent to America to be tutored by Nelson Rockefeller. Henry Kissinger is a man of many colors. He is a Freemason, and member of all three Masonic obediences - English, American and French.

[961] Knight, *The Brotherhood* 284, 286.

CREMIEUX - DOUBLE AGENT

Intelligence gathering, spying, and the use of double agents are commonplace in this war between Scarlet and the Beast. If Great Britain had wanted to penetrate the French government in Cremieux's day, it would have done so through a French Rosicrucian Freemason. Who would be more likely than Cremieux? If he were to become involved in French politics, which he was, he would join the Grand Orient Lodge, to which most French politicians belonged. From there he could learn state secrets and pass them to London.

English Freemasonry had need of spies in French politics for two specific reasons. First, the two movements of socialism and communism, which had developed in Grand Orient Freemasonry were of grave concern to Great Britain's capitalists. Second, Emperor Napoleon III had cooperated with the Grand Orient Revolution in Italy by ousting the oligarchy's Austrian army. Spy master Cremieux and British Freemasonry had something in common. Both hated Napoleon III. If Cremieux was assigned the task of deposing the Emperor, his success would be better realized if he could attain the top position within the Emperor's lodge.

Shades of *Mission Impossible*, you say? Perhaps. Nonetheless, everything Cremieux accomplished was of benefit to English Freemasonry, as well as profit to the oligarchy of the Priory of Sion, which it protected. It is most likely that Freemason Cremieux was a master spy, a double agent, a Rosicrucian mole for British Intelligence in the French Templar Grand Orient administration of Napoleon III. Such a scenario certainly fits the Masonic *modus operandi*.

MAURICE JOLY

Gentile Maurice Joly, whose father was a staunch Italian Mason, was also a Mason. Joly was tied to the Alliance Israelite Universelle through his association with Freemason Cremietix and the Mizraim Masonic Lodge. He was also linked to the Priory of Sion through mutual membership in a Rose Croix order with Victor Hugo. This Masonic influence secured Joly a post in the Ministry of the Interior under Freemason M. Chevreau, just before the coup d'etat in 1851 by Louis Napoleon.

Joly was not included in the new government, nor did he want to be. He had an inveterate hatred of the Bonapartes. Moreover, he disagreed with Grand Orient politics, which politics demanded a strong man to solidify its failing revolution of 1848.[962]

For nine years following Napoleon's 1851 coup, Joly withdrew from politics and satisfied himself by returning to his law practice. Suddenly, in 1860, he began writing articles attacking the government and the Emperor.

What, or who rekindled Joly's anger? The answer is Adolphe Cremieux, who also hated the Emperor. Cremieux's animosity grew from a rebuff he received from Louis Napoleon. At the time of Napoleon's coup, Cremieux was legal adviser to the Bonaparte family and an intimate of Louis Napoleon. When Louis became Emperor, he offended Cremieux by not appointing him to the most desired political post - that of Chief Executive - a position vital in dealing with Great Britain.[963] The Emperor's first mistake was his refusal to appoint his Masonic superior. Cremieux became his enemy.

Napoleon's second error was his refusal to take orders from Grand Orient Masonry, which had placed him in power. Afar his 1851 coup and after declaring himself as

---

[962] de Poncins, *Secret Powers* 51.
[963] Miller 417-418.

Emperor in 1852, he immediately began exerting authority, emulating his great uncle, Napoleon Bonaparte.[964] Now the entire Grand Orient was his enemy.

Napoleon's third mistake was exiling Victor Hugo. We shall soon see that Hugo's exile was a consequence of his disagreements with Napoleon following the coup. The Priory of Sion soon became the Emperor's enemy.

Napoleon's fourth and fatal mistake was military action against Austria's occupation army in Italy. Napoleon's military success in removing this arm of the British Masonic oligarchy from Italy allowed Mazzini's Grand Orient revolution to succeed. With English Freemasonry now his enemy, the Emperor did not have a prayer.

SOURCE OF THE PROTOCOLS

It was unnecessary for British Freemasonry to intrigue against Napoleon, for the Emperor had created enough hostility and enemies on his own. With an angry Cremieux encouraging the pen of an acrimonious Joly, the Grand Orient planned to depose the Emperor. Joly wrote *Dialogues between Machiavelli and Montesquieu*, which was a compilation of articles in which Joly depicted Napoleon III as Machiavelli. As Victor Hugo's poetry had done in the 1850s (discussed later in this chapter), 50 too Joly's articles turned public opinion against the Emperor in the 1860s. And as we learned earlier, the London *Times* (1920) reported that the *Protocols of the Learned Elders of Sion* were plagiarized from Joly's *Dialogues*, which the *Times* called *Dialogues of Geneva*.

Another factor we must consider in discovering the source of the *Protocols* is that in Joly's day communism was the political fad of Grand Orient Freemasonry. Its spokesman was 32nd degree German Grand Orient Mason and Reform Jew, Levi Mordechai (alias Karl Marx).[965] Joly, however, was a Socialist, and hated both communism and Karl Marx. Aware that communists were the remnant of the Jacobins, who had carried out the 1793 Reign of Terror, Joly wrote: "Socialism seems to me one of the forms of a new life for the peoples emancipated from the traditions of the Old World. I accept a great many of the solutions offered by Socialism but I reject Communism either as a social factor or as a political institution. Communism is but a school of Socialism. In politics I understand extreme means to gain one's ends - in that, at least, I am a Jacobin."[966]

Although Joly hated communism, he agreed with its Jacobin principles; yet he accused Napoleon III of that same ruthlessness. What he actually hated was the Emperor's absolutism. Absolutism is what Freemasonry can not tolerate. Jacobinism is fine, but not outside the auspices of the Masonic hierarchy. When Napoleon Ill ignored the orders of his Masonic superiors, Joly's hatred toward him was rekindled by Cremieux. The Grand Orient contracted with Joly to expose the Emperor as Machiavellian. To protect himself, Joly signed the dialogues "Mr. X"

Why did the London *Times* in 1920 call Joly's book the *Dialogues of Geneva?* The answer can be found in the Masonic-Marxist events which took place in Geneva prior to an international communist meeting in London in 1864, the year before Joly published his work. In an earlier chapter we saw that following the Congress of Vienna in 1815, both English and French Masonic lodges were established at Geneva for the express purpose of plotting intrigue on neutral ground. According to Nesta Webster, Geneva, Switzerland, was the meeting-place for all the revolutionaries of Europe.[967] Edith Miller

---

[964] de Poncins, *Secret Powers* 51.

[965] Miller 270, 733.

[966] Miller 412.

[967] Webster, Secret Societies 441.

reports that the Geneva meetings took place in the Grand Orient Masonic lodge, Temple Unique. Those in attendance put the name of the Temple on their cards and bills.

Following the Geneva gatherings, the Communist revolutionists met in London during the summer of 1862. There they attended the London International Exhibition. The Exhibition was a Marxist front used by French Communists to penetrate Great Britain's labor force. This Exhibition marked the beginning of anti-capitalist labor unions. On August 5, 1862, all the delegates met at a dinner given for them by their English colleagues at Freemason's Hall. An address was read which formed the platform for the First Communist International.[968]

On September 28, 1864, the French Communists met again in London at another Masonic lodge called St. Martin's Hall.[969] At this meeting Grand Orient Freemason Karl Marx obtained control of the two-year old International Working Men's Association. A number of secret societies, such as the Anarchists, Nihilists, and Young Europe, were immediately absorbed by this communist body. That same year anarchist Mikhail Bakunin (1814-1876), a Russian Grand Orient Mason, founded his Alliance Sociale Democratique on the exact lines of Weishaupt's Illuminism.[970]

In 1866, one year after Joly's book was published, the inaugural congress of Karl Marx's First Communist International met in Geneva, again at the Masonic lodge, Temple Unique.[971] Miller reports that what was decided at that Masonic meeting was "the abolition of standing armies, the destruction of the monopolies of great companies, and the transfer of railways and other means of locomotion to the people."[972]

Also confirmed at that meeting was the declaration that revolution would be transported to foreign soil - perhaps in reference to Russia, since in Russia, Zionism was to be contained, if not destroyed.

When the First International met again in 1869 at Basel, Switzerland, Russian Freemason Mikhail Bakunin fought for control of the organization. He spoke thus without reserve: "By social liquidation I mean expropriation of all existing proprietors, by the abolition of the political and legal state, which is the sanction and only guarantee of all property as now existing, and of all that is called legal right; and the expropriation, in fact, everywhere, and as much and as quickly as possible by the force of events and circumstances."[973] Thirteen years later, in 1882, on the orders of Bakunin, Czar Alexander II of Russia was assassinated.[974]

TARGET: NAPOLEON III

In finding the answer to why the London *Times* called Joly's book the *Dialogues of Geneva,* we must investigate the Masonic intrigues in Italy, which occurred a decade before the Geneva meetings. In late 1856 the Italian Grand Orient Masons, already known as the Mafia, were contracted by Lord Palmerston of England to assassinate Napoleon III. In early 1857 several Masons met in London to plan the murder. Four were from Russia, one of whom was Mikhail Bakunin.[975] Chairman of the meeting was the Mafia leader himself, Giuseppe Mazzini. At his side were Francesco Crispi (1819-1901), the Sicilian

---

[968] Miller 490.
[969] Miller 491.
[970] Webster, *Secret Societies* 410.
[971] Webster 411.
[972] Miller 492.
[973] Miller 492-493.
[974] Miller 526.
[975] Miller 267, 722.

Mason selected to do the job, and his comrade-in-arms, Freemason Adriano Lemmi (1822-1896).[976]

In January 1858 Crispi and Lemmi met in Paris with Freemason Felice Orsini. Orsini, a lodge brother of Napoleon III, taught the two assassins how to manufacture a bomb, then kept them abreast of the Emperor's movements. During the next few weeks several attempts were made on Napoleon's life, each failing. Crispi and Lemmi escaped, but Orsini was captured, tried and condemned to death. Before his execution on March 13, 1858, Napoleon visited him in prison. Orsini warned the Emperor that if he did not assist the Italian Freemasons in their struggle for democracy, other bombs were reserved for him. Napoleon acquiesced, meeting at Piedmont in July with Count Camillo Benso di Cavour. Mazzini was not at this meeting. Cavour was Grand Master of an English warranted lodge in Italy, a revolutionary lodge competing with Grand Master Mazzini's Grand Orient.[977] Miller tells what united these two rival Grand Masters:

> The policies of the Grand Master Cavour and the Grand Master Mazzini, each representing two different Masonic currents [English and French] emanating from different sources, met on the issue of the destruction of the Papacy which it was hoping to submerge through the unification of Italy.
>
> Cavour aimed at unity in the form of a constitutional monarchy under the house of Savoy, and Mazzini, aiming at a republic, found himself forced into a compromise which obliged him to accept, temporarily at least, a Piedmontese monarchy for United Italy.[978]

Together they agreed to accept assistance from Napoleon. France, with Piedmont-Sardinia, declared war on Austria in order to expel Austria's troops from Italy. Miller quotes the French deputy Monsieur Keller's remark before the legislative body on March 13, 1861 on the cause of these events: "The Italian war was the execution of the will of Orsini."[979]

Meanwhile, Victor Hugo, Grand Master of the Priory of Sion, was in exile writing satirical poetry against Napoleon. Hugo's poetry was intended to manipulate public opinion to drive the Emperor from office. Three of these works were: (1) *Napoleon le Petit*, an indictment of the "little" Napoleon III as opposed to the "great" Napoleon I; (2) *Histoire d'un crime*, a day-by-day account of Louis Bonaparte's coup as seen by a dissentient witness; and (3) *Les Chatiments*, ranking among his most powerful satirical poems, a presentation of Napoleon as a thief and a killer.[980]

As a result, the Emperor's popularity began to decline during the latter half of the 1850s. To perpetuate the decline, Joly was chosen in 1860 to take up the cause, which culminated in the *Dialogues of Geneva* in 1865.

Hugo planted the seed of dissension; Joly cultivated it and Napoleon reaped a harvest of discontent from his subjects. During the latter half of the 1860s, the anti-imperial opposition strengthened. In 1871 Napoleon III was deposed.

JOLY'S SOURCE

---

[976] Miller 244.
[977] Miller 244, 264, 274.
[978] Miller 273-274.
[979] Miller 268.
[980] "Hugo, Victor - Political Life," *Encyclopaedia Britannica: Macropaedia.*

How could Joly, a Rosicrucian Freemason, know of the Communist goings-on in Geneva, which caused the London *Times* to call his book the *Dialogues of Geneva?* Joly was neither a member of the Templar Scottish Rite of Grand Orient Freemasonry, nor its left-wing Communist Party. He hated Communism and would not have attended their meetings if invited.

Here is where Cremieux comes in. As Supreme Commander of the Scottish Rite of Grand Orient Freemasonry, Cremieux was well aware of the agenda of the communist meetings at the Masonic lodge at Geneva and may have attended himself. He is known to have induced Joly to write the *Dialogues.* Whether Cremieux actually handed Joly minutes of those Machiavellian meetings or verbally informed him of their contents is not known. In any case, Cremietix, a fellow Rosicrucian and intimate of Joly, most certainly guided him in the contents of his writings.

This is a Masonic *modus operandi* - as we have seen previously in the relationship between Frederick Engels and Karl Marx. Marx followed Engel's suggestions, putting them in revolutionary form. Likewise, two decades later Cremieux suggested what Joly should write. Joly, a government lawyer prior to the Emperor's rise to power, would be credible. Joly's articles implied that the Machiavellian decisions of the several Geneva Communist congresses were the Emperor's plans for the destruction of France. When bound in a book, the articles were titled *Dialogues of Geneva*. As planned, this Masonic disinformation aroused public opinion against Napoleon III.

Joly wrote only under the guarantee of anonymity; hence the pseudonym, Mr. X. Yet, in order to arouse public opinion, the author had to be revealed as someone with authority - someone acquainted with the political climate of the day. Joly, therefore, was betrayed two months after publication. As a result of this unusual and swift exposure, he was tried, convicted, and sentenced to two years in prison.

Joly's exposure, trial, conviction and punishment are another example of the Masonic *modus operandi*. In this world of Masonic intrigue, where the end justifies the means, there are those expendables who are used as scapegoats to protect the conspiracy. Joly, only a Blue Lodge Mason, was sacrificed for the greater cause. Whether Cremietix exposed Joly is not known, but it is a distinct possibility. Albeit, the scheme worked, and Napoleon III was out of government within six years of the publication of Joly's book.

Who were the winners? First, Rosicrucian English Freemasonry now rid of the man who ousted the oligarchy's occupation forces from Italy. Second, French Templar Grand Orient.

Freemasonry, which deposed an Emperor for refusing to take orders from his Masonic hierarchy. Third, Cremieux, whose vengeance was the deposition of Napoleon III for denying him high political office.

Cremieux's revenge, however, had far-reaching consequences. For example, Joly's book contributed to the release of documents called *The Protocols of the Learned Elders* of Sion, which in turn fueled post-World War I Europe against the Jews, giving rise to Fascism. In this climate, Hitler went unchallenged when he engineered the slaughter of six million Jews and five million Gentiles in concentration camps.

Nesta Webster makes a strong case for Joly as the source of the Protocols. In *Secret Societies and Subversive Movements*, she states:

"The *Protocols* were largely copied from the book of Maurice Joly, *Dialogues aux Enfers entre Machiavel et Montesquieu*, published in 1864. Let it be said at once that the resemblance between the two works could not be accidental. Not only are whole paragraphs almost identical, but the various points in the programme follow each other in precisely the same order."[981]

---

[981] Webster, *Secret Societies* 409.

On the other hand, it is plausible to suggest that the *Protocols* were not a plagiarism of Joly's book at all, but were the actual minutes to the Marxist revolutionary meetings held in the Masonic lodge at Geneva. As earlier suggested, these notes may have been given to Joly by Cremieux. This author's hypothesis is that Joly plagiarized the Geneva minutes, which he reshaped into the *Dialogues of Geneva*.

Whether the *Protocols* were a plagiarism of Joly's book, or the Dialogues a plagiarism of the *Protocols*, the result was the same. Most significant to our investigation is that Joly, a Freemason, was a close associate of Cremieux. Cremieux, in turn, was on the Supreme Council of the Mizraim Masonic Lodge at Paris. *It was from this lodge that the "Protocols" were stolen in 1884.*

If, in fact, Joly did plagiarize the minutes to the Geneva meetings in 1865, apparently they were carelessly stored and forgotten in the archives of the Mizraim Lodge. Two decades later they were "found" by a casual peruser, who, not knowing their original purpose, stole them.

An interesting story concerning the 1884 discovery of the *Protocols* was told in 1934 by Victor E. Marsden in his English translation of the Russian *Protocols*. Marsden had been the Russian correspondent for *The Morning Post* of London when the Bolshevik Revolution broke out. He reports that

> [I]n 1884 [two years after the assassination of Tsar Alexander II by Masonic Nihilists] the daughter of a Russian general, Mlle. Justine Glinka, was endeavoring to serve her country in Paris by obtaining political information, which she communicated to General Orgevskii in St. Petersburg. For this purpose she employed a Jew, Joseph Schorst, member of the Mizraim Lodge in Paris. One day Schorst offered to obtain for her a document of great importance to Russia, on payment of 2,500 francs. This sum being received from St. Petersburg was paid over and the document handed to Mlle. Glinka.
>
> She forwarded the French original, accompanied by a Russian translation, to Orgevskii, who in turn handed it to his chief, General Cherevin, for transmission to the Tsar."[982]

The document was the French original of *The Protocols* of the *Meetings of the Learned Elders of Sion*. General Cherevin did not give them to the Royal Court as Glinka had requested. Instead, he filed them, and they lay dormant for the next two decades.

What lends credence to this story is that Mlle. Justine Glinka was arrested shortly after on trumped up charges, not at all related to the Protocols, and banished to her estate in Orel, Russia. Some believe this was engineered by Freemasonry in an attempt to keep Mlle. Glinka from further investigation.[983] As for the Masonic traitor Joseph Schorst - In payment for his part played in the intrigue, he was hunted down and murdered in Egypt possibly by Masonic agents.[984]

The strongest case for linking the *Protocols of Sion* to Gentile Freemasonry is the *Protocols* itself. Read in the light of Masonic hegemony, the fourth *Protocol*, for instance, seems to confirm that the 33rd degree Supreme Council of Universal Freemasonry, and not Zionist Jews, is the manipulator of world revolution:

> Who or what can dethrone an invisible power? Now, this is just what our Government is. The Masonic Lodge throughout the world unconsciously acts as

---

[982] Nilus 100.
[983] Nilus.
[984] Miller 408.

a mask for our purpose. But the use we are going to make of this power in our plan of action, and even our headquarters, remain perpetually unknown to the world at large.[985]

The "Government" referred to in this *Protocol* could well be the Supreme Council of Freemasonry. And the *Dialogues,* upon which we believe the *Protocols* is based, could have been of much earlier origin than the 1860s, for it echoes Weishaupt's correspondence with his co- conspirators in the Illuminati. The *Dialogues* could as well have been the correspondence between members of the Templar hierarchy, such as Mazzini in Italy, Pike in America, Palmerston in England, and Bismarck in Germany.

It is also just as likely that Karl Marx, or Mikhail Bakunin, both of whom were at the Geneva Masonic Congress, spouted the fourth *Protocol* from that forum. It certainly would have befitted their Communist program. In fact, a segment of *Protocol* twelve could have been spoken at Geneva against Russia by this remnant of Communist Jacobins. It reads:

> *Briefly, in order to demonstrate our enslavement of the Gentile governments in Europe, we will show our power to one of them by means of crimes of violence, that is to say by a reign of terror.*[986]

By using the word "Gentile," the anonymous authors of the *Protocols* suggested to general readers and investigators that the authors and planners of the "crimes of violence" were Jews. When the barbarous Bolshevik Revolution destroyed old Russia, conspiracy researchers pointed to this *Protocol,* because of the word "Gentile," and blamed the Revolution on the Jews, who they believed were retaliating against the Russian czars for their persecution of the Russian Jewish populations.

THE PROTOCOLS, JACK THE RIPPER AND GENTILE "NON-MASONS"

Gentile Freemasonry refers to its initiates as Jews, refers to its lodges as Solomon's Temple, and calls non-Masons Gentiles. Likewise, a republic founded by Freemasonry and governed by Masons is by inference a Jewish nation. Conversely, a kingdom not ruled by Freemasonry, such as Russia, would be considered a Gentile nation. Christian Russia, then, would certainly be called a "Gentile government" by "them that say they are Jews, and are not, but do lie."

Stephen Knight documents the Masonic use of the word "Gentile" in *The Brotherhood.* When a meeting is called at the Masonic Temple, he says Masons converge on the lodge from all directions. "Once inside the Hall, each turned his steps towards the Crypt, which was cordoned off so that no intruder could make his way down the stair and report the goings-on to any 'Gentile'."[987]

Knight connects the *Protocols* to Gentile Freemasonry by examining a seemingly unrelated subject: the notorious murders of Jack the Ripper, committed in 1888 between August and November. "The Jack the Ripper murders in the East End of London in 1888," asserts Knight, "were perpetrated according to masonic [sic] ritual and a subsequent

---

[985] Nilus 158.
[986] Nilus 181.
[987] Knight, *The Brotherhood* 216.

police cover-up was led by the Commissioner and Assistant Commissioner of the Metropolitan Police, both Freemasons."[988]

To comprehend what is meant by "murders...according to Masonic ritual," we must understand the Masonic ceremony of the 3rd degree - the Master Mason degree. Stephen Knight explains the Masonic ritual focus on murder:

> *Much of Masonic ritual centres on murder. At the 3rd degree, the victim is Hiram Abif, mythical architect in charge of the building of Solomon's temple. The ceremony involves the mimed murder of Hiram by three Apprentice Masons, and his subsequent resurrection. The three Apprentices are named Jubela, Jubelo and Jubelum - known collectively as the Juwes [Masonic spelling for Jews]. In masonic [sic] lore, the Juwes are hunted down and executed, "by the breast being torn open and the heart and vitals taken out and thrown over the left shoulder," which closely parallels the details of Jack the Ripper's modus operandi.[989]*

In 1888, Sir Charles Warren was Commissioner of the Metropolitan Police and one of the country's most eminent Freemasons. Two years earlier Warren also helped found the most secret of Masonic Lodges, the Quatuor Coronati Lodge of Masonic Research. Knight reports that Warren impeded the investigation of the murders at every turn, caused endless confusion and delays, and personally destroyed the only clue the Ripper ever left. This was a scrawled chalk message on a wall inside a tenement block near the site of the fourth murder. Beneath the message was a blood-soaked piece of cloth which Jack the Ripper had recently cut from the apron of his latest victim. The message itself, according to a careful copy made by a conscientious PC who was at the scene early - which had been concealed in the Scotland Yard files on the case for nearly ninety years before I gained access to them - read:

> "The Juwes are
> The Men
> That will not be blamed
> for nothing"

> *The moment he was told of this, Warren, who had not previously ventured near the East End, rushed to the place before the message could be photographed and washed it away. This has never been explained. The truth was that Warren, who had been exalted to the Royal Arch in 1861, had realized that the writing on the wall was a masonic [sic] message.*
>
> *Warren, a founder of the Quatuor Coronati Lodge of Masonic Research and by the time of the Ripper murders a Past Grand Sojourner of the Supreme Grand Chapter, knew only too well that the writing on the wall was telling the world, "The Free-masons are the men that will not be blamed for nothing."[990]*

The significance of the word "Juwes" in the Ripper's message will not escape anyone versed in Masonic lore. As Knight pointed out in a previous book, *Jack the Ripper: The Final Solution* (1976), Masons refer to themselves as Jews, and use the word "Gentile," "borrowed from Hebrew and used to mean non-Masonic."[991]

---

[988] Knight 49.
[989] Knight 54.
[990] Knight 54-55.
[991] Stephen Knight, *Jack the Ripper: The Final Solution* (1976; London: Granada, 1977) 158- 159.

How does the message at the scene of the fourth "Ripper" murder shed light by analogy on who may have authored the *Protocols?* First, it confirms that Freemasonry establishes decoys, then calls those decoys Jews. Second, the scrawled chalk message on the wall above the scene of the fourth Ripper murder can be extrapolated and applied to all Masonic intrigues and their authors, including authors of the *Protocols:* "The *Freemasons* are the men that will not be blamed for the *Protocols."* Third, by making the *Protocols* read like a Jewish manuscript, the Gentile Masonic conspiracy continues unimpeded by sending researchers chasing the Jewish scapegoat.

In 1935, after studying the *Protocols* and hearing months of testimony, the court at Berne, Switzerland, declared that they were not of Jewish origin. If we accept the court's declaration, the only logical explanation for the *Protocols* authorship is Gentile Freemasonry: "those that say they are Jews, and are not, but do lie." The creation of the *Protocols* is another facet of the age- old plot of Satan to destroy both Jews and Christians alike.

Stephen Knight's intent in exposing the reason behind the Masonic use of the word "Juwes" was not to reveal Freemasonry's anti-Semitic symbolism, but to tie the *Protocols* to Gentile Freemasonry. He offers even more convincing evidence of the *Protocols* Masonic authorship:" The translator of the *Protocols* claimed they were in the form of minutes which were removed from a large book of notes for lectures. They were signed, he said, by Freemasons of the highest rank, the thirty-third degree."[992]

Thirty-third degree Masons, of course, meet separately from their Masonic brethren of the lower degrees. Significantly, Edith Miller informs us that the name of the meeting hall in Paris where the 33rd degree Supreme Council of Mizraim Masons gathered was the *Sanctuary of Levites,* corroborating Knight's discovery that Gentile Masons refer to themselves as Jews.[993] *Mackey's Encyclopedia of Freemasonry* sheds more light on French Freemasonry's fixation on becoming Jews, when documenting that in the French lodges, "Levite" is the "highest of the Masonic Degrees..."[994] How could a person, or persons, who supposedly forged the *Protocols,* have known to connect Jewish terminology used by a Gentile Masonic Lodge in Paris, unless he, or they, were 33rd degree Masons from that same lodge? We know that Adolphe Cremieux was that Mason who sat on the Supreme Council of Mizraim Freemasonry. We also know that the *Protocols* were stolen from that same Lodge. Stephen Knight concludes:

> It must be stated that the Protocols have been the subject of debate since they first appeared in print. Hitler twisted their meaning and alleged that they proved the existence of a worldwide conspiracy by the Jews, and used them in a hopeless attempt to justify his extermination programme. Chiefly because of the Nazi atrocities many writers have attacked the Protocols as forgeries. The argument continues to rage, and there are strong points both for and against.
>
> An important point to bear in mind is that they had been in existence a long time before they were finally published... Forgeries or not, the product of fanatical minds or not, the fact is they have been taken in deadly seriousness by thousands of people.
>
> Of course, even accepting for a moment that there were no questions of the documents' authenticity, it would still be ludicrous to believe that they form the code by which all Free- masons live. Most Masons do not progress beyond the third degree, so the vast majority of Freemasons before the Protocols were published would never have heard of them.

---

[992] Knight, *Jack the Ripper* 161.
[993] Miller 407.
[994] "Levite of the External Guard," *Mackey's Encyclopedia,* vol.1.

But what they [the Protocols] would have conveyed to those high initiates, who not only read them, but took them seriously, is fascinating and disturbing.[995]

THE MASONIC "PROTOCOL" CONSPIRACY IN RUSSIA

The Reform Jews left Germany for Russia in 1840 to destroy Judaism there. Their tactics were reprehensible, resulting in violence and bloodletting. In anger the Reformers spread vicious lies about their Jewish brothers, inciting Christian Russia to anti-Semitism. The most horrendous were accusations of blood libels. One such incident took place in the small town of Villovich where the Reform Jews took revenge on the local rabbi. They dressed up one of their women as the rabbi's wife. "The impersonation was perfect," wrote Rabbi Antelman. "She appeared before the local priest and said that she saw the rabbi kill a Christian child for Passover. Because of this incident, the rabbi and all the members of his congregation were killed after a brief trial. The rabbi's wife and his five remaining children were tortured into accepting Christianity."[996]

Mackey's Encyclopedia of Freemasonry confirms that "[I]n Russia the *Protocols* were used to back up charges against the Jews for 'ritual murder.'"[997] Is Mackey's statement Freemasonry's subtle way of suggesting that the authors of the *Protocols* were Reform Jews?

PROTOCOLS OF SION AND THE PRIORY OF SION

The authors of Ho*ly Blood, Holy Grail* suggest that the *Priory of* Sion, and not the Reform Jews, was connected to the *Protocols of Sion* in Russia. The authors build their case around Rosicrucian French Masons who had worked their way into the good graces of Czar Nicholas II. Here is their story:

> *The role of Rasputin at the court of Nicholas and Alexandra of Russia is more or less generally known. It is not generally known, however, that there were influential, even powerful esoteric enclaves at the Russian court long before Rasputin. During the 1890s and 1900s one such enclave formed itself around an individual known as Monsieur Philippe and around his mentor, who made periodic visits to the imperial court at Petersburg. And Monsieur Philippe's mentor was none other than the man called Papus.[998]*

Papus (1865-1916), a Gentile, was the Masonic code name for Dr. Gerard Encausse, a 33rd degree Mason from Paris, who became the occult adviser of the ill-fated Czar Nicholas U.[999] Papus was Grand Master of both Memphis and Mizraim Freemasonries, the two Rosicrucian lodges that had merged in 1875. One of Papus's acquaintances was Claude Debussy (1862-1918), a famous composer who set a number of Victor Hugo's poems to music. Debussy was the next Grand Master of the Priory of Sion following Hugo's death in 1885, and reigned in that position until 1918.[1000]

---

[995] Knight, *Jack the Ripper* 161-162.
[996] Antelman 101.
[997] "Anti-Semitism and Masonry," *Mackey's Encyclopedia*, vol. III.
[998] Baigent 190.
[999] Miller 353, 735.
[1000] Baigent 131, 154.

Freemason A.E. Waite tells us that in 1894 Papus was also the Grand Master of the Martinist Masonic Supreme Council in Paris. Martinism admitted both male and female members on equal terms. This Order had a number of lodges throughout Europe and Russia. Chapters were also established in Great Britain, the United States, Argentina and Guatemala, as well as throughout the Orient.[1001]

Martinism was originally founded in 1754 by a Rosicrucian Spanish Jew named Martines de Pasqually, or Martinez Paschalis. The emblem for this branch of Freemasonry consists of six dots, which we have learned in a previous chapter is a subtle form of the Masonic six-pointed star. The six-pointed star is the same herald of the Priory of Sion, the Mizraim Masonic Lodge and Zionism.[1002]

Pasqually's Lodges were first organized at Marseilles, Toulouse, and Bordeaux, then in Paris. Before long Rosicrucian Martinist lodges spread all over France, with the center at Lyons. Martinism was thought to have been a Jewish secret society. It was operated, however, in the same manner as was the Mizraim Lodge, in that Jews and Gentiles alike were members. Behind the scenes, however, was the Priory of Sion, distinguished by the Rose-Croix capstone in Martinist Lodges.

Nesta Webster explains: "After the first three Craft degrees came the Cohen degrees of the same - Apprentice Cohen, Fellow Craft Cohen, and Master Cohen - then those of Grand Architect, Grand Elect of Zerubbabel of Knight of the East; but above these were concealed degrees leading up to the Rose-Croix, which formed the capstone of the edifice."[1003]

Webster also claims that Martinist "disciples inherited from Pasqually a large number of Jewish manuscripts."[1004] She leaves the reader with the impression that these manuscripts are none other than the *Protocols of the Learned Elders of Sion* - in existence a full century before they were stolen from its sister Mizraim lodge in 1884.[1005] If so, these documents may only have suggested Judaic origins because of the Davidic claims expressed within them by the Priory of Sion.

A century later the stamp of "Priory of Sion" is even more evident on Martinism when a Freemason named Alphonse Louis Constant (1810-1875) joined the Martinist Order. Constant was a Gentile Mason who assumed the Jewish name - Eliphas Levi. This is the same Eliphas Levi who assisted the Grand Master of Sion, Charles Nodier, in methodically sifting and cataloging thousands of Templar documents looted from the Vatican by Napoleon Bonaparte. Levi was also acquainted with Nodier's successor, Victor Hugo. After Levi joined the Martinist Masonic lodge, the lodge merged with both the Memphis and Mizraim Lodges.

Levi apparently had access to the forgotten *Protocol* documents in the Mizraim Lodge a decade before they were discovered in 1884. Webster informs us that "[b]efore his death in 1875 Eliphas Levi announced that in 1879 a new political and religious 'universal Kingdom' would be established, and that it would be possessed by 'him who would have the keys of the East.'"[1006]

[1001] Waite, "Martinist Rose-Croix," *A New Encyclopaedia of Freemasonry,* Vol.11, 161-163. Arthur Edward Waite, born in Brooklyn, New York, in 1857, was taken to England by his English mother at the age of two following the death of his father. Waite never returned to America, although he had been given honorary degrees and positions in American lodges. Waite joined English Freemasonry when he came of age.

[1002] Miller 354. (see Appendix 2, Fig. 4 and 5 in *Scarlet and the Beast,* vol.1).

[1003] Webster, *Secret Societies* 166.

[1004] Webster 165-166.

[1005] Webster 310.

[1006] Webster.

Three *Protocols* have significant relationship to this prophecy:

> *Protocol 15: When the King of Israel sets upon his sacred head the crown offered him by Europe he will become patriarch of the world.*
> *Protocol 17: The King of the Jews will be the real Pope of the Universe, the patriarch of an international Church*
> *Protocol 24: I pass now to the method of confirming the dynastic roots of King David to the last strata of the earth.*

The prop of humanity in the person of the supreme lord of all the world of the holy seed of David must sacrifice to his people all Personal inclinations.

These *Protocols* are highly suggestive of the Priory of Sion, those who claim to be of the seed of David. Eliphas Levi most likely was referring to Sion's King of Jerusalem cult when he prophesied, "A new political and religious 'universal Kingdom' will be established, and it will be possessed by 'him who would have the keys of the East."

The authors of *Holy Blood* inform us that Victor Hugo and Eliphas Levi were both members of the same Martinist Lodge.[1007] As we have seen, Victor Hugo was associated with Maurice Joly and Adolphe Cremieux in the sister Lodge of Mizraim Freemasonry. Papus, who was Grand Master of both the Mizraim and Memphis lodges, was also a Martinist, and acquainted himself with Hugo's successor Claude Debussy. All these men, except Cremieux, were Gentiles.

This circumstantial evidence points to the Priory of Sion as the author of the *Protocols*. In the Old Testament, King Solomon himself, who is revered by all Masons, says in Proverbs 14:9, "The common bond of rebels is their guilt."[1008] In other words, these Masonic rebels are guilty by association.

FRENCH MARTINISM AND ENGLISH FREEMASONRY

English Freemason A.E. Waite states that French Martinism had shut its doors to Masons belonging to English Freemasonry.[1009] Yet Edith Miller, in Appendix IV of *Occult Theocrasy*, reproduced a private letter dated March 26, 1906, from one "Dorec" to 33rd degree Grand Orient Mason Theodore Reuss, informing him that 33rd degree English Mason John Yarker was the Martinist delegate in London.[1010]

Miller claims the existence of another private letter, in which Papus refers to himself as the delegate of John Yarker for the Swedenborg Rite in France. Correspondence of this nature between the most note-worthy Masons of that day contradicts Mr. Waite and reveals that Mr. Waite is spreading disinformation by alleging a feud between English Masonry and French Martinism where none exists.[1011]

It is true that Rosicrucian English Freemasonry severed fellowship in 1877 with Templar French Grand Orient Freemasonry. However Martinism is not Grand Orient Templarism, but rather, Rosicrucianism.

Naturally there would be a tie to English Freemasonry. Obviously the French Martinists would want to keep this familial tie secret in order to keep abreast of the developments in Templar French Masonry. Martinism apparently functioned as an

---

[1007] Baigent 436.
[1008] Bible, Living Bible (LB).
[1009] Waite 161.
[1010] Miller 354.
[1011] Miller.

intelligence lodge for English Freemasonry, as did Mizraim. Later the two merged with Memphis, their English counterpart.

A. E. Waite could not have been ignorant of this fact. If cognizant, he would have published an opposing view in an attempt to hide the facts. His motive would be to protect Rosicrucian Orders on the Continent, which were subversive to the Templar Grand Orient. No other interpretation makes sense of why the hierarchy of the Templar Grand Orient - Dorec and Reuss - would expose the connection.

Apparently, Rosicrucian Martinism was a front for the Priory of Sion. English Freemasonry used it as an intelligence gathering lodge in the same manner as it did the Mizraim Lodge. Both having similar doctrine, they merged in 1875. As the Mizraim Masonic Lodge provided for Great Britain moles in the French Templar Scottish Rite Lodge, through double agents such as Cremieux and Levi, so Papus served in that same capacity when Mizraim merged with Martinism following the deaths of Levi and Cremieux in 1875 and 1880.

There are other Martinist ties to British Freemasonry. In 1887 Martinist Freemason Papus joined the Theosophist Society, a Rosicrucian order headquartered in New York, with a branch in Paris. The Theosophist Society was founded in 1775 by female Freemason Helena Blavatsky, who moved her headquarters from New York to London in 1887. In 1891 Papus helped found the Gnostic Catholic Church. In 1895 he became a member of the Order of the Golden Dawn, an English Masonic Rosicrucian order founded in 1887 in London, with a branch in the Paris Lodge Ahathoor. In 1902 Papus became Grand Master of the newly formed homicidal Ordo Templi Orientis (O.T.O.) at Paris, a spin-off of the Golden Dawn.[1012]

In 1899 Philippe de Lyon, protege' of Papus, went to Russia and established the Priory of Sion's Martinist lodge at the imperial court, possibly initiating Grigoni Rasputin, since it is known that Grigorii was a Martinist. Philippe was introduced to the Imperial Court first, oddly enough, by the same man who was Rasp tin's sinister adviser, the anti-Zionist and Reform Jew, Manoussevitch Manouilof (see chapter 19). In 1900 Papus followed Philippe to St. Petersburg, where Papus became a confidant of the Czar and Czarina. Papus visited Russia on at least three occasions, the last in 1906. When he became Grand Master in France of London's O.T.O., Papus then carried the rituals of this homicidal Masonic lodge to Russia, initiating many Russians in St. Petersburg in preparation for the Russian Revolution. Papus died on October 25, 1916, one year before he could taste the rotten fruits of his labor in the bloody Bolshevik Substantial evidence suggests that high Masons in France, England and Russia were involved in the Russian Revolution. In fact communications were shuttled back and forth between Europe and Russia prior to the Bolshevik Revolution by high Masons. Among them were 33rd degree John Yarker, who represented the Martinist Order at London; 33rd degree Papus, who, according to Miller's documents, was under the control of Yarker; Freemason Philippe, who was the mentor of Papus, and Rasputin, who in turn was the Martinist mole in the Royal Court at St. Petersburg following Philippe. All these High Masons were Gentiles not Jews.

As evidenced by the Masonic activities between Russia and France at the turn of the 20th century, both English and French Freemasonry were cooperating in fomenting the Russian Revolution. These activities, with the arrival of the stolen *Protocols* taken from a French lodge and carried to Russia, were significant in stopping Zionism at the Russian border. In 1903 the *Protocols of the Learned Elders of Sion* were first translated into Russian and published. Whether engineered by this coalition of subversives or not, the events which led up to their circulation could not have been by accident.

[1012] Baigent 462.

The authors of Holy *Blood, Holy Grail* outline the sequence of events. The *Protocols* were stolen from the Mizraim Lodge in 1884 and taken to Russia by Mlle. Justine Glinka. She gave a copy to Alexis Sukhotin, the marshal of the district of Orel who in turn showed them to two friends Stepanov and a contemptible old man named Sergei Nilus. In 1903 Nilus presented the *Protocols* to the Czar. The Czar, who had placed himself under the occult council of the two subversive Freemasons, Philippe and Rasputin, declared the document to be an outrageous fabrication and ordered all copies of it destroyed. Nilus was banished from the court in disgrace.[1013]

The document, or a copy of it, survived. In 1903 it was serialized in a newspaper, but failed to attract interest. In 1905 it was published again as an appendix to a book by a distinguished mystical philosopher, Vladimir Soloviov. This time it began to attract attention. In following years it became one of the single most infamous documents of the twentieth century.[1014]

PROTOCOLS OF THE PRIORY OF SION

The authors of *Holy Blood, Holy Grail* argue strongly that the *Protocols* have a Masonic source - the Priory of Sion:

> *Modern scholars have dismissed them as a total forgery, a wholly spurious document concocted by anti-Semitic interests intent on discrediting Judaism. And yet the Protocols them-selves argue strongly against such a conclusion. They contain, for example, a number of enigmatic references - references that are clearly not Judaic. But these references are so clearly not Judaic that they cannot plausibly have been fabricated by a forger, either. No anti-Semitic forger with even a modicum of intelligence would possibly have concocted such references in order to discredit Judaism. For no one would have believed these references to be of Judaic origin.*
>
> *Thus, for instance, the text of the Protocols ends with a single statement, "Signed by the representatives of Sion of the 33rd Degree.*
>
> *Why would an anti-Semitic forger have made up such a statement? Why would he not have attempted to incriminate all Jews, rather than just a few - the few who constitute "the representatives of Sion of the 33rd Degree?" Why would he not declare that the document was signed by, say, the representatives of the international Judaic congress? In fact, the "representatives of Sion of the 33rd Degree" would hardly seem to refer to Judaism at all, or to any "international Jewish conspiracy." If anything, it would seem to refer to something specifically Masonic.*
>
> *The Protocols contain other even more flagrant anomalies. The text speaks repeatedly, for example, of the advent of a "Masonic kingdom.*

[1013] There are many theories concerning the origin of the "Protocols." One is that they were published in 1903 under the direction of Czar Nicholas 11, for which he invested the staggering sum of thirteen million rubles, and encouraged Nilus to prepare it. This theory was one of the first to be promoted, before it was discovered that there was an original in French, and that the documents were stolen in 1884 from a French Masonic Lodge. Some still promote this theory, although it has long since been discredited.

[1014] Baigent 190-195.

The authors of *Holy Blood, Holy Grail* concluded: "On the basis of prolonged and systematic research we reached certain conclusions about the *Protocols of the Elders of Sion*. They are:

1. *There was an original text on which the published version of the Protocols was based. This original text was not a forgery. On the contrary, it was authentic. But it had nothing whatever to do with Judaism or an "international Jewish conspiracy." It issued, rather, from some Masonic organization or Masonically oriented secret society that incorporated the word "Sion."*
2. *The original text on which the published version of the Protocols was based need not have been provocative or inflammatory in its language. But it may very well have included a program for gaining power, for infiltrating Freemasonry, for controlling social, political, and economic institutions.*
3. *The original text on which the published version of the Protocols was based fell into the hands of Sergei Nilus. Nilus did not at first intend it to discredit Judaism. On the contrary, he brought it to the czar with the intention of discrediting the esoteric enclave at the imperial court - the enclave of Papus, Monsieur Philippe, and others who were members of the secret society in question. Before doing so he almost certainly doctored the language, rendering it far more venomous and inflammatory than it initially was. When the czar spurned him, Nilus then released the Protocols for publication in their doctored form. They had failed in their primary objective of compromising Papus and Monsieur Philippe. But they might still serve a secondary purpose - that of fostering anti-Semitism. Although Nilus' chief targets had been Papus and Monsieur Philippe, he was hostile to Judaism as well.*
4. *The published version of the Protocols is not, therefore, a totally fabricated text. It is, rather, a radically altered text. But despite the alterations certain vestiges of the original version can be discerned... These vestiges - which referred to a king, a Pope, an international church, and to Sion - probably meant little or nothing to Nilus. He certainly would not have invented them himself. But if they were already there, he would have had no reason, given his ignorance, to excise them. And while such vestiges might have been irrelevant to Judaism, they might have been extremely relevant to a secret society. As we learned subsequently, they were - and still are - of paramount importance to the Prieure de Sion.*[1015]

The authors of *Holy Blood, Holy Grail* conclude that the *Protocols* issued from the 33rd Degree Supreme Council of the Rite of Mizraim, which in turn is controlled by the Priory of Sion! They were "signed by the representatives of Sion of the 33rd Degree." The phrase "representatives of Sion" does not imply that the signatories were part of a group called "Sion," but rather, is indicative of agents, or, shall we say, a front for some organization which incorporates the name "Sion":

namely the Priory of Sion. The Mizraim Lodge was that front.

The mistake made by the Supreme Council of Mizraim is the mistake made by all Freemasonry. It *never* destroys any of its written work. Every word spoken in every Supreme Council throughout the world is recorded and safeguarded for posterity.

[1015] Baigent.

A handful of modern conspiracy researchers link the covert Priory of Sion to the *Protocols of the Learned Elders of Sion*. These investigators do not see the *Protocols* associated in any way with genuine Jewish Zionism that exists overtly. J.R. Church is one of them. He said, "The title itself, which mentions the 'learned elders of Zion,' seems to refer to the mystery religion of the so- called Holy Grail and to the Priory of Sion organized by Godfroi de Bouillon in 1099 for the purpose of establishing a world government and providing a Merovingian king for its throne."[1016]

Finally, according to the *Chicago Daily News*, June 23, 1920 (p.2), Empress Alexandra, wife of Czar Nicholas II, noted in her diary under the date April 7, 1918 (OS): "Nicholas read to us the protocols of the free masons."[1017]

COMMENTARY ON THE PROTOCOLS OF SION

Protocol 1: Our power in the present tottering condition of all forms of power will be more invisible than any other, because it will remain invisible until the moment when it has gained such strength that no cunning can any longer undermine it.

Before us is a plan in which is laid down strategically the line from which we cannot deviate without running the risk of seeing the labour of many centuries brought to naught.

This Protocol describes an organism that houses a hidden "power." We believe the organism is Freemasonry housing the Priory of Sion. It was the Priory of Sion that founded the Rose-Croix, which in turn founded English Freemasonry. This began many centuries ago, as the Protocol indicates.

The statement, "Before us is a plan... the line from which we cannot deviate without running the risk of seeing the labour of many centuries brought to naught," suggests that Sion is in serious trouble. Perhaps this refers to the establishment of the unexpected movement of Zionism in Russia. The "plan" which is "before us" may also refer to a takeover of Russia to stop the Zionist movement.

Protocol 3: To-day [sic] I may tell you that our goal is now only a few steps off. There remains a small space to cross and the whole long path we have trodden is ready now to close its cycle of the Symbolic Snake, by which we symbolize our people.

When this ring closes, all the States of Europe will be locked in its coil as in a powerful vise.

When the hour strikes for our Sovereign Lord of all the World to be crowned it is these same hands which will sweep away everything that might be a hindrance thereto.

"Ours" they will not touch, because the moment of attack will be known to us and we shall take measures to protect our own.

Ever since that time we have been leading the peoples from one disenchantment to another, so that in the end they should turn also from us in favour of that King-Despot of the blood of Sion, whom we are preparing for the world.

The symbols referred to in this Protocol are of course Rosicrucian. The symbol of the Priory of Sion's Rosicrucian Order is a rose, representing the Serpent, wormed around the upright part of the Christian Cross. The second symbol of the Rosicrucians was the circle, or snake biting its own tail, superimposed on the Christian cross. This same symbol of the snake is incorporated in the 33rd degree Masonic Jewel (Appendix 2, Fig. 7).

Dr. John Coleman, a retired British intelligence officer, states in *Black Nobility Unmasked*, that the Monarchs of Europe have always referred to themselves as "Crowned Cobras." The monarchs of Europe carry the Grail blood. All of them, according to Coleman, are Masons of the British obedience.

[1016] Church 169.

[1017] Richard Pipes, *Russia under the Bolshevik Regime* (New York:Alfred A. Knopf, 1993) 257n.

The statement: "'Ours' they will not touch," etc., eliminates the possibility that the Protocol is Jewish. If the *Protocols* outlined a Jewish conspiracy, the "our" would have evaded the holocaust of Hitler, according to this Protocol. Yet, after World War II it was Freemasonry, as we shall learn in chapter 24, that came back stronger than ever, founding the United Nations.

Finally, this Protocol identifies the Priory of Sion with the statement "King-Despot of the blood of Sion, whom we are preparing for the world." This obviously refers to Sion's reigning "King of Jerusalem."

Protocol 4: Who and what is in a position to overthrow an invisible force? And this is precisely what our force is. Gentile masonry [sic] blindly serves as a screen for us and our objects, but the plan of action of our force, even its very abiding-place, remains for the whole people an unknown mystery.

As we have seen, the Priory of Sion's kings believe themselves to be Jews. When the Priory founded Freemasonry, it was mainly Gentiles who joined. Gentiles are its predominant members and leaders. Naturally the Priory would call Freemasonry "Gentile Masonry."

Protocol 5: In place of the rulers of to-day [sic] we shall set up a bogey which will be called the Super-Government Administration. Its hands will reach out in all direction like nippers and its organization will be of such colossal dimensions that it cannot fail to subdue all the nations of the world.

What is the "bogey" that is to be called "the Super-Government Administration?" There are two possibilities here. First, this could refer to Russian Communism, which would be used to conquer the world. The top governing power in the U.S.S.R. was called the *Supreme Soviet*. Soviet in Russian means *Council*. In other words, it was the Supreme Council that ruled former Soviet Russia, the same Supreme Council we find in 33rd degree Freemasonry. Second, this body could be the League of Nations. Following World War I, as we shall see in chapter 21, the League was founded by French Freemasonry. After World War II, English Freemasonry founded the United Nations. The United States of Europe became a reality by 1993. We shall learn that it too is of Masonic origin. From this may come the world kingdom of the Beast - the ultimate "bogey."

Protocol 8: We shall surround our government with a whole world of economists. That is the reason why economic sciences [work]. [They come] from the principal subject of the teaching given to the Jews. Around us again will be a whole constellation of bankers, industrialists, capitalists and - the main thing - millionaires, because in substance everything will be settled by the question of figures.

Notice this Protocol mentions the "Jews," but in a disconnected sense, as if they are used by the conspiracy for their economic prowess alone. This Protocol suggests why English Freemasonry is overloaded with Jewish bankers and economists. The Priory of Sion admits that Jews are superior economically. Incidentally, the word "Jew" is mentioned only twice in the *Protocols*, and both times in a disconnected sense.

Protocol 10: These schemes will not turn existing institutions upside down just yet. They will only affect changes in their economy and consequently in the whole combined movementof their progress, which will thus be directed along the paths laid down in our schemes.

By such measures we shall obtain the power of destroying little by little, step by step, all that at the outset when we enter on our rights, we are compelled to introduce into the constitutions of States to prepare for the transition to an imperceptible abolition of every kind of constitution, and then the time is come to turn every form of government into our despotism.

This Protocol enunciates the format of English Freemasonry, called "gradualism," whereas its adversary, French Masonry, takes over rapidly and viciously.

Protocol 15: When the King of Israel sets upon his sacred head the crown offered him by Europe he will become patriarch of the world.

Twelve royal families in Europe today have Grail blood flowing through their veins. Two of them carry the title of "King of Jerusalem:" Otto von Habsburg, Pretender to the Austrian throne, and Juan Carlos, King of Spain.

Protocol 17: The King of the Jews will be the real Pope of the Universe, the patriarch of an international Church.

But, in the meantime, while we are re-educating youth in new traditional religions and afterwards in ours, we shall not overtly lay a finger on existing churches, but we shall fight them by criticism calculated to produce schism...

Notice that "The King of the Jews" will replace the Pope. Jews would not be concerned with replacing the Pope. They do not even recognize the Church. On the other hand, the Priory of Sion used the Catholic Church to build its empire. It was subject to the Roman Church for centuries, but withdrew during the Reformation, and through Free-masonry became adversarial to the Church. Naturally, the Priory would want to call their king "the real Pope of the Universe."

Also, notice the reference to New Age religion. Before the New Age can be perfected, the Protocol states that "criticism" must first divide the Church. This "criticism" is likely the new "Biblical criticism," the sources of which Orthodox Rabbi Marvin Antelman has revealed to us. In his book, To *Eliminate The Opiate,* he devotes a whole chapter entitled "The Birth of Biblical Criticism" to the subject. He lays Biblical Criticism at the feet of the Frankist-Reform Jews who were protected by illuminated Masonic lodges in Germany. Rabbi Antelman confirms that Biblical criticism did not originate with Orthodox Jews, but rather; was orchestrated by apostate Jews bent on the destruction of Jude~ Christian religion.

Protocol 20: We shall so hedge about our system of accounting that neither the ruler nor the most insignificant public servant will be in a position to divert even the smallest sum from its destination !sic] with-out detection or to direct it in another direction except that which will be once fixed in a definite plan of action.

Is this the Mark of the Beast?

Protocol 24: I pass now to the method of confirming the dynastic roots of King David to the last strata of the earth.

Certain members of the seed of David will prepare the kings and their heirs, selecting not by right of heritage but by eminent capacities, inducting them into the most secret mysteries of the political, into schemes of government, but providing always that none may come to knowledge of the secrets. The object of this mode of action is that all may know that government cannot be entrusted to those who have not been inducted into the secret places of its art.

The king's plans of action for the current moment, and all the more so for the future, will be unknown, even to those who are called his closest counselors.

Only the king and the three who stood sponsor for him will know what is coming.

The prop of humanity in the person of the supreme lord of all the world of the holy seed of David must sacrifice to his people all personal inclinations.

The Priory of Sion is the protector of the so-called seed of King David. Notice in the second paragraph the statement that many kings and their heirs are being prepared, but only one will be selected. There are twelve royal families of Grail blood in Europe today. The entire 24th Protocol seems to describe the "hidden hand" in the Priory of Sion, which we believe is housed in the 33rd degree of English Freemasonry.

14. LUCIFER: GOD OF FREEMASONRY

The Masonic religion should be, by all of us initiates of the high degree, maintained in the purity of the Luciferian doctrine... The doctrine of Satanism is a heresy; and the true and pure philosophic religion is the belief in Lucifer, the equal of Adonay; but Lucifer, God of Light and God of Good, is struggling for humanity against Adonay, the God of Darkness and Evil.[1018]

Albert Pike, 33rd Degree, 1889

Albert Pike (1809-1891) was a General in the Confederate Army during our American Civil War (1860-1865). From 1859 until his death in 1891, he was the most powerful Mason in the world. He occupied simultaneously the positions of Grand Master of the Central Directory at Washington, D.C. Grand Commander of the Supreme Council at Charleston, S.C., and Sovereign Pontiff of Universal Freemasonry.[1019] He was an honorary member of almost every Supreme Council in the world, personally receiving 130 Masonic degrees.[1020]

On October 26, 1919, twenty-eight years after Pike's death, Alva Adams of Colorado addressed the Supreme Council, Southern Jurisdiction of the Scottish Rite at Washington, D.C., with the following commendation of Albert Pike:

As the Laws King Alfred wrote a thousand years ago are still a part of England's glory and liberty, so in another thousand years will the ideals, the poetry, the moral code and philosophy of Albert Pike be shaping the influence and destiny of Masonry. It is a patent of nobility to be a Brother to this god-like leader - Prince in the House of Solomon and Hiram.[1021]

There is a subversive side to Albert Pike, however, about which many remain silent. Before accession to his prestigious Masonic positions, Pike secretly organized the rebellion of the southern states against the United States, using the Southern Jurisdiction of Scottish Rite Freemasonry to conceal his conspiracy. Most of the political and military

---

[1018] Miller 220-221.
[1019] Miller 221.
[1020] "Pike, Albert." *Mackey's Encyclopedia of Free masonry*, vol.11. Albert Pike was born at Boston, Massachusetts, December 29, 1809, and died April 2, 1891. After spending a short time in Mexico as a young man, he moved to Little Rock, Arkansas and built a mansion there in 1840. It was in Little Rock where he became a General in the Confederate Army during the Civil War. Pike was the Sovereign Grand Commander of the Southern Supreme Council, Ancient and Accepted Scottish Rite, having been elected in 1859. He was provincial Grand Master of the Royal Order of Scotland in the United States, and an honorary member of almost every Supreme Council in the world.
From a Masonic point of view, Pike's worth to the Craft is best shown by his writings. Most prominent is *Morals and Dogma* of the Ancient and Accepted Scottish Rite. Mackey defines this work as "splendid." He says Pike's *Morals and Dogma,* Monitor of the Rite, 1871, is not dogmatic in the odious sense of that word, General Pike using it to mean doctrine or teaching, the book being one of methodical instruction in the philosophy of Freemasonry... The three greatest literary works were the Bible, Shakespeare, and the writings of Albert Pike." The January 1990 issue of the *New Age* magazine states that Pike's *Morals and Dogma* is a "Mason's guide for daily living."
[1021] "Pike, Albert."

leadership of the Confederacy were Masons under Pike's secret command. In reality, our Civil War was another battle in the war between English and French Freemasonry.[1022]

Prior to our 1776 War of Independence, 32nd degree French Templarism had not yet reached America. Although a few Templar lodges from Ireland and Scotland were scattered throughout the northeast, most were military lodges and had not progressed beyond nine degrees. Predominant were the three-degree English lodges. By the time George Washington was elected our first President, 32nd degree Templar Scottish Rite Freemasonry had already been established at Charleston, S.C. - on the 33rd degree parallel. The Scottish Rite assisted our new government in developing French republican ideals. In 1801, nine American Masons created the 33rd degree and the Charleston lodge became the Mother Council of the World.

High-degree Scottish Rite lodges soon dotted the southern portion of the United States, and the Rite moved northeast where low degree English Masonry was strongest. Evidence suggests that to counter this intrusion into English Masonic territory, the British sent John James Joseph Gourgas (1777-1865) to New York to organize clandestine Scottish Rite Lodges throughout that region.[1023]

Gourgas was well-suited to this subversive task. The Gourgas family had been French Scottish Rite Masons living in Switzerland prior to the French Revolution. During the Reign of Terror, the family emigrated to England, where John James Joseph became a well-known merchant on the royal exchange. As a matter of course, he joined low-degree English Freemasonry.[1024]

The Gourgas family sailed from England to Boston in 1803, finally settling in Weston, Massachusetts. J.J.J. Gourgas went to New York around 1806. By 1813 he had organized five clandestine Scottish Rite lodges, one of which was called the Cerneau Supreme Council of Sovereign Grand Inspectors General of the Thirty-Third Degree. These subversive lodges had assisted England in her War of 1812-1814 against the young American nation.

In the early summer of 1813 Emanual de la Motta, a Supreme Council member from Charleston, was visiting New York and discovered the five clandestine lodges. An investigation ensued, and none were found to have received sponsorship from Charleston. After conferring with the Charleston hierarchy, Motta was told to rectify~ the situation as quietly as possible. He immediately worked out a territorial arrangement with Gourgas. Thus was born the Northern Jurisdiction of Scottish Rite Freemasonry on August 5, 1813, with confirmation on December 24th by the Mother Supreme Council at Charleston.[1025]

[1022] Chaitkin 234.

[1023] Chaitkin 161.William R. Denslow's *10,000 Famous Freemasons* informs us that Stephen Morin founded the Ancient and Accepted Scottish Rite in America. Denslow says, however, that "[t]here is virtually no personal data on this man who is one of the Masonic pioneers of the Western world. Who he was, what he did, when and where he was born or died, is not known. On Aug.27, 1761, he was empowered by a patent from the Deputies General of the Royal Art, Grand Wardens, and officers of the Grand Sovereign Lodge of Saint John of Jerusalem" at Paris, to multiply the Sublime Degrees of High Perfection and to create Inspectors in all places where the Sublime Degrees are not established. There is even question as to who granted the patent (i.e., the grand lodge, the accepted !Scottish] rite, or a joint authority of both). At any rate he shortly sailed for the Americas and established bodies of the Scottish Rite in Santo Domingo and Jamaica. He appointed M.M. Hayes a deputy inspector general for North America, and Hayes in turn appointed Isaac da Costa a deputy for South Carolina, where in 1801 the Mother Supreme Council, AASR was created, and eventually spread throughout the U.S." (vol. III, p.231).

[1024] Chaitkin 160-162.

[1025] Harold Voorhis, *The Story of the Scottish Rite of Freemasonry* (Richmond: Macoy Publishing & Masonic Supply Co., 1965) 22-23

Permanent headquarters for the Northern Jurisdiction of Freemasonry was later established at Boston, where English Freemasonry first entered America. Boston was given Masonic dominion over all the states north and east of the Ohio and Mississippi Rivers. This legitimacy gave English Freemasonry a permanent foothold in America from which to continue her subversive activity. The agreement also stipulated noninterference by the South in the Northern Jurisdiction. Hence, behind northern lodge doors big business deals were settled without southern participation or knowledge. Gradually the northeastern Masons became the power brokers for all the nation, dominating industry, finance and politics. Thus, the Northern Jurisdiction of Freemasonry acquired the nickname, "The Eastern Establishment."

The non-aggression treaty signed between the U.S. and England in 1814 did not stop Great Britain from attempting to reclaim the Americas. She may have lost the War of 1812, but through her Scottish Rite lodges of the English obedience in the North, she controlled the northeast's wealth. Southern wealth was counted in slaves. In order to exercise economic control over the South, slavery would have to be abolished. London planned to divide America over the slavery issue. A nation divided would be easy to conquer, if not militarily, then economically and financially. By 1860 we were in a civil war, ostensibly over slavery. (Complete story detailed in Vol.III of Scarlet and the Beast.)

Against this British intrusion into American politics, finance, and industry, General Albert Pike initiated the southern rebellion. In 1859 the Southern Jurisdiction of Freemasonry founded the Knights of the Golden Circle as a front to direct the insurrection. When the South lost to the North, and Abraham Lincoln reunited the Union, the Knights of the Golden Circle plotted Lincoln's assassination. John Wilkes Booth, a 33rd degree Mason and member of Mazzini's Carbonari of Italy, was selected by the Knights to kill Lincoln.[1026]

After Lincoln's assassination, the Knights of the Golden Circle attempted to rekindle the Civil War. Riots erupted throughout the South. Even 3rd degree Freemason, Vice President Andrew Johnson, who assumed the Presidency following Lincoln's assassination, believed these riots were an attempt to incite another civil war.[1027] Young Jesse James (1847-1882), a 33rd degree Freemason and member of the Knights of the Golden Circle, was assigned to rob northern banks to fund this new war. Regarding James's success, Ralph Epperson, in The Unseen Hand, wrote: "It has been estimated that Jesse and the other members of the Knights had buried over $7 billion in gold all over the western states."[1028]

Meanwhile, a crisis was brewing which brought heavy Masonic pressure to bear upon the newly appointed president, Andrew Johnson. During the Civil War, General Pike had led a band of Indians who conducted warfare with barbarity by scalping Union soldiers while they were yet alive.[1029] After the war and Lincoln's assassination, Pike was tried and found guilty of treason. Andrew Johnson, himself a 3rd degree Mason, was pressured by high Masons to pardon brother Pike.

Master Mason Johnson was under no Masonic obligation to pardon his treasonous Masonic superior. For clarification we recite part of the Master Mason ceremony. When the 3rd degree initiate is symbolically raised from the dead by the strong grip of the "lion's paw," he is taught the "Five Points of Fellowship," which are foot *to foot, knee* to *knee, breast* to *breast, hand* to *back,* and *cheek* to *cheek.* The second point of fellowship, which is *breast* to *breast,* teaches "that you will ever keep within your breast the secrets of a

---

[1026] Epperson, *The Unseen Hand* 160 and Chaitkin 223-225, 234.
[1027] Epperson 162.
[1028] Epperson 162-163.
[1029] Fisher 49.

worthy brother Master Mason as inviolable as your own when communicated to, and received by you as such, murder and treason excepted."[1030]

Relentless pressure from Masons was too great, and the President succumbed to their bidding. Paul Fisher reports thatBenjamin B. French, a 33rd Degree Mason and member of the board of directors of the Supreme Council of the Scottish Rite, wrote a letter, dated July 1, 1865, to President Andrew Johnson... urging him to pardon Pike. Additional appeals on Pike's behalf were made to the President by Masons from different parts of the United States."[1031]

Johnson bowed to Masonic pressure and pardoned the man who was most responsible for the Civil War, who undoubtedly was in favor of the assassination of President Lincoln, and who may himself have been directly involved in the plot. Nine months later a list of pardoned rebels, including Pike, was released to the press. Fisher informs us that "[in] March, 1867, the House Judiciary Committee began an investigation into charges by some Congressmen that Johnson should be impeached. Later, when the committee finally issued its report, a key charge against the President was that he pardoned large numbers of public and notorious traitors..."[1032]

Three months later, Freemasonry honored Johnson for pardoning the treasonous Albert Pike. "On June 20, 1867," reports Fisher, "the President received a delegation of Scottish Rite officials in his bedroom at the White House where he received the 4th through the 32nd Degrees of the Scottish Rite as an honorarium."[1033]

The trial for Johnson's impeachment proceeded as scheduled. In May 1868, fourteen months after the Congressional investigation of Johnson was initiated, the final vote fell one short of the necessary two thirds for conviction. Freemasonry celebrated by erecting the only monument to a Confederate general in the nation's capital. Between Third and Fourth Streets stand the U.S. Department of Labor Building and the city's Municipal Building. On public property between these two buildings, on D Street, N.W., "is a statue of Albert Pike, the grand philosopher of Scottish Rite Masonry, who was indicted for treason for his activities during the Civil War."[1034]

ALBERT PIKE'S LUCIFERIAN DOCTRINE

Albert Pike was one of the most physically and morally repulsive individuals in American history. Weighing well over 300 pounds, his sexual proclivity was to sit naked astride a phallic throne in the woods, accompanied by a gang of prostitutes. To these orgies he would bring one or more wagon-loads of food and liquor, most of which he would consume over a period of two days, until he passed into a stupor. In his adopted state of Arkansas, Pike was well known as a practitioner of Satanism.[1035] Although he wrote that he did not believe in the reality of Satan, portraits made of Pike in his later

---

[1030] Ronayne, *Handbook of Free masonry* 213. Former 33rd degree Mason, Rev. Jim Shaw, states in his *Questions and Answers on Freemasonry* audio cassette, that the obligation of a 7th degree Royal Arch Mason is sworn "to keep all secrets of a Companion Mason, whether he be right or wrong, murder and treason not excepted. In the Masonic book, *Webbs Monitor*, page 169, we read: "Right or wrong, his very existence as a Mason hangs upon his obedience to the powers immediately set above him." As such, President Andrew Johnson came under severe Masonic pressure to pardon Pike.

[1031] Fisher 209.

[1032] Fisher 210.

[1033] Fisher.

[1034] Fisher 48-49.

[1035] Chaitkin 234-235.

years picture him wearing the Baphomet, a symbol of Satan, around his neck. (See Appendix 2, Fig. 30.)

Pike was an evil genius of the first magnitude, using his many talents to destructive ends. A gifted polyglot, he was able to both read and write in sixteen ancient languages.[1036] In his study of ancient religions, Pike discovered that Lucifer was the god of pagans and that there was no adversary known as Satan except in the Bible. Lucifer, son of the morning, was known to pagans as the friend of mankind who gave them fire, taught them all the crafts, and showed them the rich ore and precious stones buried in the earth. For these countless benefactions conferred on humanity, jealous Adonay, who claimed to be the true God, united His angels against the brightest angel and unjustly cast him out of heaven.[1037]

Pike reasoned that Adonay, the God of the Bible, was evil for robbing man of his scientific achievements - first by Flood, then by the destruction of the Tower of Babel. Lucifer, according to Pike, was the good god, who returned to man his scientific freedom. And Satan? He was only a fabrication of Christians.

WOULD THE GOD OF FREEMASONRY PLEASE STAND?

Albert Pike continued the work of Adam Weishaupt, introducing Lucifer to the Supreme Council as the Masonic god. In 1843, while Pike was developing his Luciferian Doctrine, two other Masons, poet Henry Wadsworth Longfellow (1807-1882) and Moses Holbrook (d.1844), Sovereign Grand Commander of the Supreme Council at Charleston, were attempting to penetrate the inner shrines of the Fraternity with the doctrine of Satanism. Both had studied thoroughly the occult sciences and enjoyed discussing the mysteries of the *Cabala* with Pike, but were unable to convert the general to Satanism.[1038] When Holbrook died a year later, Longfellow turned to the Independent Order of Oddfellows, hoping they would receive his Satanic doctrine.

The Oddfellows had been founded by Masons at London in 1788 and brought to the United States in 1819 by Freemason Thomas Wildey. At first Longfellow was refused by Wildey, but later obtained secret authorization to use the Order for the introduction of Satanism into the second degree. This rite was to be absolutely secret. Miller informs us that "[t]he adepts of the second [degree] Oddfellows practising Satanism...took the name of Re-Theurgist-Optimates... Longfellow became the Grand Priest of the New Evocative Magic."[1039]

Albert Pike was opposed to a Satanic Rite in Freemasonry because he refused to believe Lucifer and Satan were the same personality. In his book, *Morals and Dogma*, published in 1871, he describes the Cabalistic[1040] meaning of Satan:

> *The true name of Satan, the Kabalists say, is that of Yahveh [sic] reversed; for Satan is not a black god, but the negation of God. The Devil is the personification of Atheism or Idolatry.*
>
> *For the Initiates, this is not a Person, but a Force, created for good, but which may serve for evil. It is the instrument of Liberty or Free Will. They represent this Force, which presides over the physical generation, under the mythologic and horned form of the God Pan; thence came the he-goat of the Sabbat, brother of*

[1036] "Is Freemasonry Part Of The New Age Movement?" *Newswatch Magazine* June 1987: 9.
[1037] Weston 29.
[1038] Miller 211.
[1039] Miller 211-213.
[1040] "Cabala," *Mackey's Encyclopedia*, vol.1. See Appendix 5 for more details on the *Cabala*.

the Ancient Serpent, and the Light-bearer or Phosphor, of which the poets have made the false Lucifer of the Legend.[1041]

Pike accused poets of falsifying the nature and role of Lucifer. For example, Longfellow believed Satan was once Lucifer, and John Milton made the Fallen Angel the hero of the tale in *Paradise Lost.* In contrast, Pike believed Lucifer never fell, that the Rebel Angel is the light of the world today, equal in power to Almighty God, yet less transcendent at the present time. In *Morals and Dogma* Pike sarcastically refers to the book of Revelation which denies Lucifer's equality with God: "The Apocalypse is... the Apotheosis of that Sublime Faith which aspires to God alone, and despises all the pomps and works of Lucifer..."

Pike's ridicule is directed toward those who have faith only in the God of the Apocalypse without giving Lucifer due respect. Pike continues his encomium to Lucifer: "Strange and mysterious name to give to the spirit of Darkness! Lucifer, the Son of the Morning! Is it he who bears the Light, and with its splendors intolerable blinds feeble, sensual, or selfish souls? Doubt it not!"[1042]

With one stroke of the pen, this 33rd degree Mason, whom all Masons revere, denied the finished work of Jesus Christ, the true Light of the world, about which Light St. John wrote his entire book.

LUCIFERIAN RITE FOR THE 33RD DEGREE

Throughout a period of about fifty years Pike developed and then gradually introduced his Luciferian Rite to a select few within the 33rd Degree Supreme Council at Charleston. He also converted the Masonic hierarchy in London, Berlin, and Rome. During the latter part of that development, French atheists began to attack spiritism and symbolism within French Lodges, finally declaring in 1877 that there was no god but humanity. Grand Orient Freemason Karl Marx was one of the main movers behind the atheistic stand taken by the French Lodges. English Freemasonry, which demands a belief in deity, immediately broke fellowship with the French Grand Orient.[1043]

Albert Pike, Sovereign Pontiff of Universal Freemasonry at the time, attempted to mend the English and French division by writing a letter to the hierarchy declaring that Lucifer was the god of Freemasonry. This letter was read on July 14, 1889, at the annual congress of the existing twenty-three (23) Grand Lodge Supreme Councils of the world gathered at Paris, France. The letter was recorded by A.C. De La Rive in *La Fern me et l'Enfant dans Ia Franc-Maconnerie Universe lie. The Freemason,* an English Masonic periodical, noted the reading of the letter in its January 19, 1935 issue. Count de Poncins quotes portions of the letter in *Freemasonry and the Vatican.* The most comprehensive quote, however, comes to us from Edith Miller in *Occult Theocrasy.* Here is what Albert Pike wrote to that Masonic Congress, as quoted by Miller:

> *That which we must say to the crowd is - We worship a God, but it is the God that one adores without superstition.*
>
> *To you, Sovereign Grand Inspectors General, [of the 33rd degree] we say this, that you may repeat it to the Brethren of the 32nd, 31st, and 30th degrees - The*

[1041] Pike 102.
[1042] Pike 321.
[1043] Miller 218, 270.

Masonic religion should be, by all of us initiates of the high degrees, maintained in the purity of the Luciferian doctrine.

If Lucifer were not God, would Adonay [the God of the Bible] whose deeds prove his cruelty, perfidy, and hatred of man, barbarism and repulsion for science, would Adonay and his priests, calumniate him?

Yes, Lucifer is God, and unfortunately Adonay is also God. For the eternal law is that there is no light without shade, no beauty without ugliness, no white without black, for the absolute can only exist as two Gods: darkness being necessary to light to serve as its foil as the pedestal is necessary to the statue, and the brake to the locomotive.

In analogical and universal dynamics one can only lean on that which will resist. Thus the universe is balanced by two forces which maintain its equilibrium: the force of attraction and that of repulsion. These two forces exist in physics, philosophy and religion. And the scientific reality of the divine dualism is demonstrated by the phenomena of polarity and by the universal law of sympathies and antipathies. That is why the intelligent disciples of Zoroaster, as well as, after them, the Gnostics, the Manicheans and the Templars have admitted, as the only logical metaphysical conception, the system of the divine principles fighting eternally, and one cannot believe the one inferior in power to the other.

Thus, the doctrine of Satanism is a heresy; and the true and pure philosophic religion is the belief in Lucifer, the equal of Adonay; but Lucifer, God of Light and God of Good, is struggling for humanity against Adonay, the God of Darkness and Evil.[1044]

THE BIBLICAL ACCOUNT OF LUCIFER'S FALL

The Biblical account of Lucifer's fall, his name-change to Satan, and his rank as "the prince of this world" (John 12:31) all refute Albert Pike's theory. Isaiah 14:12 confirms Lucifer's fall from God's presence:

"How art thou fallen from heaven, 0 Lucifer, son of the morning! how art thou cut down to the ground, which didst weaken the nations!"

Before Lucifer became Satan, rebellion began in his heart. The Fallen Angel desired equality with God, but reasoned he could not achieve it in one quantum leap. His ascent would take time, advancing by degrees. Isaiah 14:13-14 gives us insight to Lucifer's five-step evolutionary plan: "For thou has said in thine heart, I will ascend into heaven, I will exalt my throne above the stars of God: I will sit also upon the mount of the congregation, in the sides of the north: I will ascend above the heights of the clouds; I will be like the most High."

Ezekiel 28:12-15a paints a word picture of Lucifer before his rebellion Lucifer, meaning "to shine... in the sense of brightness,"[1045] was the archangel who dwelt "upon the holy mountain of God." He was created with perfect wisdom and beauty, having as his garment every kind of precious stone. Verse 17a refers to the corruption of his intellect. "Thine heart was *lifted* up because of thy beauty, thou hast corrupted thy wisdom by *reason* of thy brightness..."

The Hebrew word for *reason* suggests the notion of evolution. Its use in the verse above means that Lucifer's brightness caused him to "reason" himself equal to God, or possibly "above" God. As a noun it means "the Highest," i.e. God. Its prime root meaning

---

[1044] Miller 220.
[1045] Strong, *Hebrew* #1966 from 1984.

suggests the act of mounting up to become the Most High. A number of words are used in this sense, such as "ascend, arise (up), climb (up), exalt, excel, (make to) go (up), grow [into], increase, leap, lift (self) up, mount up, (begin to) spring (up), and work [toward]."[1046]

Webster's Dictionary defines reason as "an explanation of, or to use the faculty of reason so as to arrive at a conclusion." Lucifer, the most brilliant of creation, "reasoned" his brilliance was due to a process of "growing into" a god, or "working toward" becoming a god. As Lucifer said in Isaiah 14:14b, "I will be like the most High."

The words "will be" also expand on this idea. In Hebrew, "will be" is a prime root word, which literally means a "prognosticator." Other meanings for the same Hebrew word imply having cunning knowledge which is self-taught through observation, perception, or prognostication.[1047] In the same sense that the Hebrew for "reason" suggests evolution, the Hebrew for "will be" implies the same. Through the science of evolution, Lucifer "reasoned" he would eventually grow into equality with God.

Lucifer deceived himself through this so-called science. Hence when he became Satan, he became the Deceiver, teaching the same Luciferian doctrine beneath the fruit trees at Eden. In Genesis 3:5, he offered Adam and Eve a taste of the religion of good and evil, saying, "God doth know that in the day ye eat thereof, then your eyes shall be opened, and ye shall be as gods, *knowing* good and evil."

The Hebrew word for "knowing" is the same word for "will be," that is, "a self-taught prognostication." Lucifer said "I will be like the most High." He told Adam and Eve they could too - by practicing a system of witchcraft called evolution. Babylonian priests have been teaching it ever since. To them it is known as reincarnation.

Apparently, Lucifer taught his theory to other angels. Some Bible scholars suggest that one-third of the angels rebelled. Revelation 12:7-9 records the resultant war in heaven: "And there was war in heaven:

Michael and his angels fought against the dragon; and the dragon fought and his angels, And prevailed not; neither was their place found any more in heaven. And the great dragon was cast out, that old serpent, called the Devil, and Satan, which deceiveth the whole world..." Verse 4 states: "And [the dragon's] tail drew the third part of the stars of heaven, and did cast them to the earth..."

Billy Graham, in *Angels: God's Secret Agents*, points out that Scripture sometimes refers to angels as stars. Lucifer means "star of the morning."[1048] Therefore, "the third part of the stars of heaven" refers to the number of fallen angels.

When God cast Lucifer out of heaven, the Fallen Angel became Satan, meaning Adversary or Accuser.[1049] He was, and is, the great Deceiver, beginning with Eve (I Timothy 2: 14) and has continued so throughout his career, until the day God will cast him into the Lake of Fire (Revelation 20:10). His rebellion has had many names throughout the ages. At Eden it was called "the religion of the knowledge of good and evil." Scripture refers to the last incarnation of Satan's religion as Mystery Babylon.

The ancient Babylonian religion was one of inventions - inventions of evil. In Genesis 11:6, God said, "nothing they *plan* to do will be impossible for them."[1050] The Hebrew word *plan* means "to plan usually in a bad sense: - consider, devise, imagine, plot, purpose, think (evil)."[1051]

[1046] Strong, *Hebrew* #5921 from 5920 from prim. root 5927.

[1047] Strong, *Hebrew* #3045.

[1048] Billy Graham, *Angels: God's Secret Agents* (New York:Doubleday, 1975) 62.

[1049] Strong, *Hebrew* #7854 from prim. root 7853.

[1050] Bible, NIV.

[1051] Strong, Hebrew # 2161.

We know that Babylonian religions practice licentious living and that their ancient priesthood invented a god that would condone this lifestyle. The priesthood taught that it was an individual's right, indeed his freedom to do as he wills, yet with balance between good and evil.

Babylonian religions had two gods of equal position, one good, one evil. The evil god was restrictive, not allowing man to do as he pleased. Such a god was unreasonable. The good god was reasonable. He gave man permission to invent good or evil, so long as it was balanced. If good deeds balanced or outweighed evil, the individual's reward was reincarnation into a better life and eventually into a god.

Freemasonry today promotes this so-called "science" of evolution and reincarnation. For instance, in the Scottish Rite *New Age* magazine, March 1922, we read: "In each system [of religion], the controlling ideal has to do with the ultimate destiny, the final goal, of humanity; and in each system the urge is strong to bring every power and resource to bear in an effort to realize that ideal..." *New Age* continues that Masonry rejects the Kingdom of Heaven as an other-world kingdom, but believes the Kingdom of God "is to be established among men by the evolution and development of man himself."[1052]

Thirty-third degree Freemason Oswald Wirth identifies the "reasoning" which began at Eden and caused man's fall as the "spark" which ignited the evolutionary process. Wirth was the most celebrated Masonic writer in Europe at the beginning of the 20th century. A Mason of eminent position in the French Grand Lodge at Paris, he inspired a revival of the spiritualism and symbolism which had been attacked by atheists within French Masonry since 1877, when they denied the existence of God.[1053] De Poncins quotes Wirth:

> In the book of Genesis, these ideas are expressed by the myth of the Earthly Paradise, a place of happiness in which primitive man had only to live, as do animals, or children who have not yet come to the age of reason.
> The beguiling serpent, who incites us to eat the fruit from the tree of knowledge of good and evil, symbolises one particular instinct. He breaks away from the conservative instinct and represents both a nobler and a subtler impulse, whose purpose is to make man aware of his need to rise in the scale of beings.[1054]

Albert Pike, with whom Oswald Wirth was well acquainted, had sixty years earlier also written on the primacy of reason over faith. In his most famous work, *Morals and Dogma*, he continually speaks of Christianity with sarcasm. He says, for example, "The dunces [meaning apostles] who led primitive Christianity astray...[did so]...by substituting faith for science.

Science in Freemasonry is *Reason*. Pike, after blasphemously stating that, "the root of the Tree of Life...[is]...the science of Good and Evil," defines *reason* as follows:

> The Absolute, is Reason. Reason IS, by means of Itself. It IS because IT IS, and not because we suppose it. IT IS, where nothing exists; but nothing could possibly exist without IT. Reason is Necessity, Law, the Rule of all Liberty, and the direction of every Initiative. If God IS, HE IS by Reason. The conception of an

---

[1052] Fisher 183.
[1053] de Poncins, *Freemasonry and the Vatican* 84-85.
[1054] de Poncins 87.

Absolute Deity, outside of, or independent of, Reason, is the Idol of Black Magic, the Phantom of the Daemon.[1055]

Albert Pike infers that belief in God by faith alone is demonic. Yet, Scripture stipulates that "[t]he just shall live by faith" (Romans 1:17; Habakkuk 2:4; Galatians 3:11; Hebrews 10:38). And the great 15th century Protestant Reformer Martin Luther affirmed this principle, writing in the margin of his Bible, "live by fides sola," the Latin phrase for "faith alone."

FAITH VERSUS REASON

Faith is never contrary to reason when based upon truth. John 14:6 states that Jesus is Truth. And the good of man's intellect, his reason, is to be found in submission to the Truth.

The prophet Isaiah announces in 1:18 God's tender invitation to errant mankind: "Come now, and let us reason together, said the Lord:

> *though your sins be as scarlet, they shall be as white as snow; though they be red like crimson, they shall be as wool."*

This is righteous reasoning - having faith that God will accomplish what He says. This Scripture is a prophecy of God's provision for man's lost state. At Eden, Adam and Eve accepted Satan's lie of balancing good and evil to become like gods. Their punishment for accepting this corrupt doctrine was separation from God by spiritual and physical death. In desperation man has since tried to work his way back into the good grace of God through a "works salvation," but could not, and cannot, regain his previous state of perfection by his own merits. God had to provide a way. God's love for mankind made redemption possible through faith in the perfect and complete work of His Son, Jesus Christ As the apostle John wrote: "For God so loved the world [mankind], that he gave his only begotten Son, that whosoever believeth in him should not perish, but have everlasting life" (John 3: 16). The apostle Peter likewise said: "The Lord is... not willing that any should perish, but that all should come to repentance" (II Peter 3:9).

The deception in Satan's religion of reason can best be demonstrated by the mythical magic mirror of paganism.[1056] You may recall the children's nursery rhyme about an ugly queen who addressed the mirror for an opinion: "Mirror, mirror on the wall. Who's the fairest of them all?" Of course, the mirror lied. The queen saw her ugly face, yet believed the lie. Like the fairy tale, man will stand in front of the magic mirror and see his evil, yet believe the lie that his good will balance his evil and make him as god - the same self-taught doctrine of Lucifer.

Such a philosophy sounds logical to the deistic college professor who teaches that *reason* is the method by which one arrives at truth.

Students of *reason* parrot the same words. Yet, this philosophy is not modern. It began in the heart of Lucifer. The apostle Paul addressed the root of this sin in Romans 1:18-23:

> *For the wrath of God is revealed from heaven against all ungodliness and unrighteousness of men, who hold the truth in unrighteousness; Because that*

[1055] Pike 737.
[1056] For an example of the magic mirror see Appendix 2, Fig. 18.

which may be known of God is manifest in them; for God hath shewed it unto them. For the invisible things of him from the creation of the world are clearly seen, being understood by the things that are made, even his eternal power and Godhead; so that they are without excuse:

Because that, when they knew God, they glorified him not as God, neither were thankful; but became vain in their imaginations, and their foolish heart was darkened. Professing themselves to be wise, they became fools, and changed the glory of the incorruptible God into an image made like to corruptible man...

Sinful men had made their image of god in the image of man. They reasoned that if God made man in His image (Genesis 1:27), and man is both good and evil, then God must be good and evil. Using this corrupt reasoning, pagan men professed themselves to be "wise." In the Scripture quoted above, Paul says they instead became fools.

The "wise" Serpent hissed this same doctrine of good and evil in the Garden of Eden. Before rebellion entered his heart, the mighty arch-angel was good, "full of wisdom, and perfect in beauty" (Ezekiel 28:12). When sin entered in, he became totally evil. As a result, Lucifer was banished from heaven, and allowed dominion on earth, where he became Satan, the Adversary. He did not, however, accept his fallen condition. He continues to deceive by mimicking himself in his original state as the Light-bearer. Scripture confirms that Satan at will is able to present himself as an angel of light (II Corinthians 11:14); yet, because of his inherent evil, he is unable to retain that disguise for long and thus reverts to "a roaring lion looking for someone to devour" (I Peter 5:8).[1057]

Satan, realizing his depraved condition, yet desiring his former state, founded the religion of the knowledge of good and evil, truly believing himself to have both attributes. Since this condition borders on schizophrenia, Albert Pike could not accept the doctrine of Satanism. Although Pike realized there is a battle between good and evil, he refused to accept that the conflict was within Satan himself.[1058] Therefore, Pike wrote that Satan was not a person, but the negation of God, a force that could be used for good or evil. Accordingly Pike cast Satan as Lucifer, who he thought was light, the god of good, struggling with Adonay, the god of evil.

The Luciferian Doctrine, therefore, must be distinguished from Satanism. Luciferianism is the belief that Lucifer is totally good, that he never fell. Only because of his benevolence to man, claims the Luciferian mystics, was Lucifer forced out of heaven by a jealous god, who did not want man to advance in knowledge. Pike calls this jealous god, Adonay, the God of the Bible.[1059]

One of Pike's first Luciferian converts was 33rd degree Freemason Giuseppe Mazzini (1805- 1872), leader, as we have seen, of the Italian Revolution and founder of the Mafia. Originally Mazzini was an ardent atheist. Later in life - almost three decades prior to Albert Pike's 1889 speech in Paris - Mazzini accepted Pike's Luciferian doctrine. Miller comments on Mazzini's "conversion":

When Pike sent him a copy of his Luciferian rituals, Mazzini was full of an enthusiastic praise for his colleague's work which he expressed in his articles in La Roma del Popolo. The public however failed to understand the sentiment that

---

[1057] Bible, NW.

[1058] See *Scarlet and the Beast,* Volume II, chapter 1; "Lucifer/Satan - The Divided God."

[1059] Strong, *Hebrew* #136. Adonay is one of the Hebrew words for God.

inspired him to proclaim the existence of a divinity and denounce materialism and atheism. One was puzzled to find this man a mystic.[1060]

PALLADIANISM: THE SUPER LUCIFERIAN RITE

Thirty-third degree English Mason, Lord Palmerston, was also converted to Pike's Luciferian doctrine. From time to time Mazzini controlled the Italian revolution from London, soliciting the assistance of Palmerston, who helped finance Mazzini through British military intelligence.[1061] Both men agreed with Pike to unite the hierarchies of French, American, and English Freemasonry in a Super Luciferian Rite. The Rite would be called the New and Reformed Palladian Rite, originally founded in Paris in 1737. One of the meanings that *Webster's Dictionary* gives *palladian* is *safeguard*. As the definition suggests, Pike's Palladian Rite was to "safeguard" the ancient doctrine of mystery religions that proclaimed Lucifer god.[1062]

It is near impossible to discover who are the members of the Palladian Rite today. It takes from thirty to fifty years for such information to emerge. The Reformed Palladian Rite, however, was comprised of Pike, Palmerston, Bismarck, Mazzini, Lemmi (a confidant of Mazzini), and other select few.[1063]

The purpose of the Palladian Rite was not only to combine the two opposing bodies of Freemasonry in the hierarchy of the Supreme Council, but to unite all secret societies under the religion of Lucifer - including non-Masonic orders. Miller confirms this in *Occult Theocrasy:*

> *A 33rd [degree Mason] would be well received everywhere, in any country, in any rite the existence of which is acknowledged. Thus it was particularly the initiates of the thirty-third degree Scottish Rites, who, owing to their extensive international ramifications, were privileged to recruit adepts for Palladism... the lowliest of its initiates being brothers long tested in ordinary masonry [sic].[1064]*

The existence of this rite would be kept strictly secret and no mention of it would ever be made in the assemblies of the lodges and inner Shrines of other rites. Albert Pike was given dogmatic authority and the tide of Sovereign Pontiff of Universal Freemasonry with

---

[1060] Miller 219-220.

[1061] Miller 214, 242, 244, 260-261, 264, 268.This is the first example of how Freemasonry is financially able to invest in, and control revolutions around the world. The Masonic Lodge first grooms an initiate for election in a democratic nation. Once elected, that official works into a position of authority and control, as did Lord Palmerston, fully understanding that his primary function is to further the goals of Freemasonry worldwide. Once he has political clout, he is able to use the "purse" of the nation wherein he resides to pay for Masonic clandestine activity around the world. When most of the politicians are themselves Masons, there is unlimited cooperation. Here is how it works: A democratic nation sends financial aid to revolutionaries, stipulating the money is to be used for food and medicine. However, the taxpayers who foot the bill most likely do not agree with the doctrines of the revolutionaries. Meanwhile, Big Business, whose chairmen are normally 33rd degree Masons, sell military equipment and supplies to the revolutionaries in exchange for the billions given for food and medicine. Throughout this conspiracy, Masons get wealthier by selling to both sides.

[1062] Miller 236.

[1063] Miller 215-218, 239, 267.

[1064] Miller 216.

head-quarters at Charleston, South Carolina. Mazzini, operating from Rome, held the executive authority with the title of Sovereign Chief of Political Action. Miller reports:

> The two secret chiefs, Pike and Mazzini, finally completed the organization of high masonry [sic], establishing four Grand Central Directories for the world, functioning thenceforth to gather information for the benefit of their political policy and dogmatic propaganda.[1065]

These four Sovereign Administrative Directories became known as Propaganda Lodges (P-l). During the 1860s they were presided over by the four most powerful 33rd degree Masons in the world at that time:

Berlin was directed by Otto von Bismarck (1815-1898); London by Palmerston; Washington by Pike (after his pardon); and Rome by Mazzini. In imitation of the original P-l lodges, in 1966 the Italian Propaganda Due (P-2) Masonic Lodge was certified by Italian Grand Orient Masonry. Unlike the original P-I Lodges, which were controlled by the Palladian at Washington, D.C., P-2 fell under the control of English Masonry.[1066]

Membership in Mazzini's four Sovereign Administrative Directories (the P-l Lodges) came strictly from the Supreme Council. To keep exposure of secrets to a minimum, membership was on an ingeniously contrived system of three month rotation. Given only 120 days notice of their appointments in order for them to plan what would appear in our day as politicians going on "fact-finding trips," these high Masons were in truth going on business trips for their particular Masonic Directories. Miller explains the relationship of the Palladian Rite to the four P-I lodges, and to the 33rd degree Supreme Council:

> The Palladian Rite has no share in the functioning of the [P-1] Sovereign Administrative Directory. This should again prove that Palladism is superposed to all the other rites. It is the Luciferian religion and only need concern itself with the triangles which have a separate budget. Being the real hidden power, known only to the perfect initiates, it need not unveil itself even to this permanent committee which constitutes the highest expression of the administrative power of the great international association.[1067]

Here Miller reveals that there are three secret societies superimposed on the 29-degree Scottish Rite and the three-degree Blue Lodge. The first, is the general body of the 33rd degree Supreme Council. Above that the four P-1 lodges are superimposed on the Supreme Council. And finally, the Luciferian Palladian is superimposed over all.

To better understand what position the Luciferian Palladian Rite held in Freemasonry, look at the Illuminati pyramid on the back of the American one dollar bill. The All-Seeing Eye of Lucifer in the center of the Capstone represents the Palladian, while the Capstone itself is the 33rd degree Supreme Council. Therefore, not all within the 33rd degree Supreme Council are Luciferian - only the Palladian "hidden power." The original power brokers in the Palladian were Pike, Palmerston, Bismarck and Mazzini. In a future chapter we will reveal the modern Luciferians.

The relationship of the Palladian to the Supreme Council is strikingly similar to that of Weishaupt and the Illuminati. In the latter, the All-Seeing Eye was Weishaupt and the Capstone was the Illuminati. Apparently (or so it has appeared to conspiracy researchers),

---

[1065] Miller 222.
[1066] This will be discussed in detail in *Scarlet and the Beast*, volume III.
[1067] Miller 239.

the Palladian Rite replaced the Illuminati, suggesting to investigators that Weishaupt appointed Mazzini, who continued the conspiracy under the new name.

True, the conspiracy dropped the *Illuminati* title. The new conspiracy, however, was not a continuation of the old. The Palladian was comprised of Templar Scottish Rite Masons, whereas the Illuminati was a Sionist-Rosicrucian organization. However, a more plausible explanation of the shift in the conspiracy has already been suggested - the Templars seized control of Sion's Illuminati conspiracy shortly before the French Revolution. Templar control was maintained by Pike and Mazzini.

Satan cares little which conspiracy is in power. Both are under his command. Division is his method and madness. Pitting one order against the other is his method of control. If one rebels, or becomes weakened, he reinforces the other. As we have seen, after the French Revolution, the Templar Order was active and flourishing once again. Sion's Illuminati had been suppressed.

When the conspiracy changed hands the leadership was up for grabs. After the Revolution Napoleon Bonaparte had his chance, but he was too visible. Mazzini was the next opportunist, some say appointed by Weishaupt. Yet, there is no real evidence to support this claim. Obviously Satan dangled the carrot in front of Mazzini and he followed it to his death.

Mazzini was one of the three most powerful Masons in Europe. When he was near death, he designated 33rd degree Adriano Lemmi his successor. Lemmi, under Mazzini's direction since 1851, had played an important role as a political assassin during the Italian Revolution. When Mazzini died on March 11, 1872, Albert Pike acceded to Mazzini's wish that Lemmi be his successor.[1068] Lemmi immediately began to strengthen the Mafia, organizing it into the universal crime network we see today. So significant was the information about Lemmi and his Masonic- Mafia empire that Miller devoted 43 pages of her book to organized crime.[1069]

Lemmi's rapid success was due to the fact that the Mafia controlled the heroin trade for English Freemasonry. Great Britain concluded her Opium Wars with China in 1860. With Hong Kong as a prize, the Masonic-owned British East India Company, which had previously transported opium to the West, dissolved in 1873. Its wealthy stockholders - all English Masons - went into off-shore, that is unregulated, banking to launder the Mafia's drug money.[1070]

During this time Albert Pike was in constant contact with the Mafia, assisting in its entry into the United States through New Orleans.[1071]

LUCIFERIANISM:
THE UNIVERSAL DOCTRINE OF FREEMASONRY

Among the many converts to Luciferianism was Albert Gallatin Mackey, a confidant of Albert Pike. It was Mackey who then nominated Pike for the post of Grand Master of the Supreme Council of Charleston. His candidacy unopposed, Pike was duly elected on January 6, 1859.

Albert G. Mackey is widely read in Freemasonry. His books consist of *The Lexicon of Freemasonry, The History of Freemasonry in South Carolina, The Manual of the Lodge, The Masonic Ritualist, The Symbolism of Freemasonry, The True Mystic Tie, Text-*

[1068] Miller 223, 257.
[1069] Miller 253-296.
[1070] Daniel, *Scarlet and the Beast,* chapter 4 (this book).
[1071] Daniel, chapter 3 (this book).

Book of Masonic Jurisprudence, Principles of Masonic Law, Cryptic Masonry, and The Encyclopedia ofFreemasonry.[1072]

Many other 33rd degree Masons then and later acknowledged Lucifer as god, including a 20th century figure, Albert Lantoine. De Poncins describes him as a historian and a thinker of great merit. He was a sincere Freemason, of charming personal character, and he kept apart from all contact with politics. He concealed nothing, and openly declared that he was an atheist. He was severely critical of certain aspects of the Catholic Church but he did not spare Masonry either. He had obviously lost the faith he originally held in democracy and rationalism.[1073]

Lantoine wrote a pamphlet in 1937 entitled *Lettre au Souverain Ponttfe*. It was an open epistle to the Pope to declare a truce between the Catholic Church and Freemasonry. De Poncins quotes an excerpt which illustrates Lantoine's Luciferian belief that the universe is divided into a necessary duality of good and evil:

> *[S]hould we remain at odds with one another? Perhaps.*
> *Perhaps we should... in the very depths of our souls. For your God cannot pardon the Rebellious Angel, and that Angel will never submit or renounce his dominion.*
> *But should we remain enemies? No!*
> *There is a higher sphere where knowledge and Faith, though they cannot meet, can at least tolerate one another. To those seeking the one, to those who possess the other, they give the same delights and the same anguish. There is as much purity and grandeur in the words of the philosophers as in the Word of the Redeemer.*
> *So much the better, I say. Possessing critical and inquisitive minds, we are the servants of Satan. You, the guardians of truth, are the servants of God. These two complement one another. Each needs the other.*[1074]

Lantoine here articulates the so-called "scientifically" required dualism of Albert Pike that "Each needs the other." During a conversation with Lantoine, de Poncins questioned him whether Masons were the "servants of Satan." Lantoine replied, "I was wrong, I didn't use quite the correct term. I should have said servants of Lucifer."[1075]

LUCIFERIAN MASONRY TODAY

Earlier, we met 33rd degree Mason Oswald Wirth, who was affiliated with the French Grand Lodge. He, too, was a Luciferian. In his statement below, he characterizes the "work" of Freemasonry as a scientific activity, in other words a demonic activity, directed by a non- Christian transcendent force:

> *Now the strength of Freemasonry lies in the collective will of its members. When they meet it is only to work, and since no energy is wasted, every lodge is a seed-bed of moral and social change.*

[1072] Denslow, Vol. III 116-117.
[1073] de Poncins, *Freemasonry and the Vatican* 7, 11.
[1074] de Poncins 9, 11.
[1075] dePoncins 11.

> *But do not ask the vast majority of Freemasons to give reasons for what they do. They act by instinct, following shadowy traditions which for centuries have exercised their suggestive influence.*
>
> *Nevertheless there does exist a Masonic Doctrine, even if nowhere explicitly formulated in words, which is to Freemasonry what Christianity is to the Christian Churches; we may call it the science of Masonry...*
>
> *Now the Great Architect, no doubt because he is less transcendant [sic] than the God of the theologians, refers to an entity which does undeniably exist, for the constructive work of Freemasonry has, as its origin and inspiration, an ideal which gives birth to an immense energy. A force superior to themselves impels Masons and co-ordinates their efforts with an intelligence far exceeding that possessed by any one individual among them. Such is the hard fact which emerges and before which we bow our heads. Let every man interpret it as he pleases.[1076]*

Oswald Wirth here admits that the Masonic Great Architect of the Universe is not the God of Christianity. Lantoine and Wirth were friends. Both lived a half century following Albert Pike's death. Both understood Lucifer was the god of Freemasonry, although "less transcendant" [sic] than the God of Christians. Like Pike, they were cognizant of the spiritual activity in Freemasonry, calling it "scientific."

We have discovered that the "work" of Masonry, even if not known or understood by the majority of initiates, is controlled through a few men - men under the direct influence of Satan - Lucifer to them - and his demonic forces of darkness. This was true back then, and remains true today. We will cite two current examples.

The first is from 33rd degree Freemason Manly P. Hall, a philosophical source for the contemporary New Age Movement in America. Hall founded the Philosophical Research Society of Los Angeles, which continues to carry on his teachings. Four of his books of particular interest to Masons are *Freemasonry of the Ancient Egyptians; Dionysian Artificers; An Encyclopedic Outline of Masonic, Hermetic, Quabbalistic and Rosicrucian Symbolical Philosophy;* and *Lost Keys of Freemasonry.*

Lost Keys of Freemasonry was originally published in 1923. In 1976 it was reprinted by The Philosophical Research Society. So important is this book to Blue Lodge Masons that it is distributed to all Masonic libraries by the Masonic publishing house of Richmond, Virginia. Not only does *Lost Keys* confirm that the hierarchy in Freemasonry remains true to the Luciferian doctrine today, but most significantly reveals that the Supreme Council is now willing to inform the Blue Lodge Masons of the Luciferian orientation and direction of Freemasonry. We quote from Hall's lecture on the Fellow Craft degree (2nd degree):

> *The day has come when Fellow Craftsmen must know and apply their knowledge. The lost key to their grade is the mastery of emotion, which places the energy of the universe at their disposal. Man can only expect to be entrusted with great power by proving his ability to use it constructively and selflessly. When the Mason learns that the key to the warrior on the block is the proper application of the dynamo of living power, he has learned the mystery of his Craft. The seething energies of Lucifer are in his hands and before he may step onward and upward, he must prove his ability to properly apply [this] energy.[1077]*

[1076] de Poncins 87.
[1077] Manly P. Hall, *The Lost Keys of Freemasonry* (1923; Richmond: Macoy Publishing & Masonic Supply Co., 1976) 47-48.

The second example which corroborates that the hierarchy in Freemasonry is still under the direct influence of Satan is revealed in the Satanic symbol worn by every Sovereign Grand Commander of the Supreme Council at Charleston. It is the symbol of the Baphomet. The traditional drawing of the Baphomet shows a winged demon with female breasts and a horned goat head. Allegedly this was the god Baal.[1078]

There are several symbols that represent the Baphomet. One is the upside-down five-pointed star with the horned goat head of Mendez pictured inside the star. This rendition symbolizes the "god of lust." The upside-down star is universally recognized in witchcraft as a symbol of Satan. It is also the symbol of the Eastern Star, the female auxiliary of American Freemasonry.

Freemason Eliphas Levi, having studied for forty years the Templar documents confiscated from the Vatican, sketched the Baphomet. It, too, is a demon with a horned, goat head. In addition, it has a serpent's tongue, a long, barbed tail and cloven hind's feet - all traditional symbols of Satan.[1079] *Mackey's Encyclopedia of Free masonry* admits that a symbol of Baphomet was indeed worn by the Knights Templar, but denies that it represented Satan.[1080]

This Baphomet is also concealed in a geometric symbol in the form of the Templar splayed cross with two additional crossbars. This rendition was worn by Satanist and Freemason Aleister Crowley and, according to *The Curse of Baphomet*, is listed as a symbol of Baphomet in the Masonic O.T.O. publication *Equinox*, Vol.3, No.1, page 248.[1081] This same symbol is worn by every Sovereign Grand Commander of Scottish Rite Freemasonry, Southern Jurisdiction. Appendix 2, Fig. 30 shows it around the neck of Albert Pike and embroidered in the Fez of the Past Sovereign Grand Commander of the 33rd degree, Henry C. Clausen. It is also on the letterhead of the current Grand Commander, C. Fred Kleinknecht. (See front pages of this book).

TEMPLAR CONTROL WAS SHORT-LIVED

Pike, Mazzini, Palmerston, and Bismarck succeeded in uniting the Masonic hierarchy in the Luciferian religion, but failed in their endeavor to unite the world politically. Instead, the world was plunged into World War I. Meanwhile, English Freemasonry was not to be outdone by the Templar Palladian Rite. English Masonry had plans of her own to unite all Masonry in the darkest depths of occultism. Her banner today is the "New Age Movement." She intends to annihilate the Church through syncretism with this doctrine. Tomorrow she plans to impose on mankind a one-world totalitarian government controlled by her global Babylonian religion.

Although the hierarchy in Masonry believe Lucifer is good and that in him is light, we are about to record the incredible evil that lurks in the dark minds of the more depraved personalities who have taken up the standard of Albert Pike and are plunging Masonry into perdition.

[1078] Jack Chick, *The Curse of Baphomet* (Chino, CA: Chick Publications, n.d.) 8.
[1079] Charles Walker, *Atlas of Secret Europe* (New York: Dorse Press,1990) 18, 25.
[1080] "Baphomet," Mackey's Encyclopedia, vol.1.
[1081] Chick 11-12.

15. FREEMASONRY AND THE NEW AGE MOVEMENT

> There existed... in antiquity the great time clock in the night sky, which we still share with our ancestors. This is the zodiac, a great turning wheel of twelve constellations making a complete circle every 25,920 years but with each of its twelve constellations in order having ascendancy over the skies of earth approximately every 2,160 years.
>
> According to zodiacal tradition the ascendency of each new sign every 2,000-odd years is accompanied by catastrophic or otherwise crucial events on the earth.[1082]

WHAT IS THE NEW AGE?

As the zodiacal wheel turns to the constellation of Aquarius, astrologers are studying the stars, predicting that a major event will soon occur, which will bring in their World Teacher. From the "New Era" of Emmanuel Swedenborg (1757) until today, the Masonic world has been poised for the coming of the "New Age." In fact, the title of the Scottish Rite monthly magazine, *New Age,* has been suggesting this for over a century.[1083]

"Masonry and the Impending New Era," an article in *New Age,* July 1941 (five months before America entered the Second World War), spoke of the "world government" expected to be established at the conclusion of the war to help usher in a "newer phase of evolutionary progress."[1084] In April 1943 the *New Age* reported that "the struggle for the freedom of man began with the American and French Revolutions, and World War II is the climax of a world ideological struggle which started at the end of the 18th Century. It is the struggle of the New Age against the Middle Age."[1085]

The phrase "Middle Age," as used in the text above, is Masonic jargon for Christianity.

Webster's Dictionary defines the Middle Ages as "the period of European history from about A.D. 500 to about 1500," - the same period of time the Catholic Church dominated European politics.

We can readily decode the Masonic lingo above and accurately name the enemy against which Masons struggle: "It is the struggle of the New Age against the age of Christianity."

Although Masonry's "New Age" dates from the end of the 18th century, the motives of the modern New Age Movement were not manifest until the end of the nineteenth century, when in 1889 the Luciferian Doctrine of Palladism was introduced to the twenty-three Supreme Councils of the world. Before this date the general body of English Masons, including most of the Supreme Council, were not Luciferians, but deists.

[1082] Charles Berlitz, *Dooms-Day 1999 AD.* (New York: Pocket Books, 1981) 15.

[1083] See cover of *New Age* magazine in Appendix 2, Fig. 14.

[1084] Fisher 227.

[1085] Fisher 227-228.

ATHEISTS, SPIRITISTS AND LUCIFERIANS

Three significant events prior to the 1889 Masonic Congress prepared English Freemasonry to accept Lucifer as god. First, in 1877, the existence of God was debated between the atheistic French Grand Orient and the deistic French Grand Lodge. The Grand Orient had replaced the Great Architect of the Universe with the slogan "To the Glory of Humanity," declaring "God is dead?"[1086]

The second event followed that same year when the English Grand Lodge, which requires a belief in deity, broke fellowship with all Grand Orient bodies throughout the world.

The third event, that of founding the Quatuor Coronati Lodge of Masonic Research in London, England, actually had its roots in the 1860s, but did not become a reality until three years before the 1889 International Masonic Congress. In 1860, Great Britain had just concluded her Second Opium War against China when English Freemasonry, in search of her roots, decided to launch a massive investigation of Oriental mystery religions. As a result, Masons in various parts of the British Empire wrote numerous occult books, many of which were repetitive. To avoid further duplication, Freemason Sir Walter Besant, brother of socialist and theosophist Annie Besant, began a drive in the early 1870s to organize a Masonic research lodge to catalog the data. In 1886 the Quatuor Coronati Lodge of Masonic Research, No.2076, London, England, was founded. *Mackey's Encyclopedia of Freemasonry* states that the Quatuor Coronati "has long since become the supreme court of learning and authority in Masonic scholarship throughout the World."[1087]

The constitution of this Mother Research Lodge stipulated that forty of the most prestigious Masons in England be members, one of whom must always be high up in the Anglican Church. When any "Member of Forty" died, the thirty-nine remaining voted on his replacement. Sir Walter Besant was one of the original "Members of Forty."

In 1887 a Correspondence Circle was attached to the lodge. Any Mason of literary, archaeological, or investigative talent could join the Circle. Within a decade the Circle had printed the *Ars Quatuor Coronatorum*, a Masonic encyclopedia coordinating all the secrets of mystery religions in no less than fifty volumes, surpassing in size the *Encyclopaedia Britannica*.

The Members of Forty, whose duty was to study these volumes continually, discovered three important facts that would determine the future course of English Freemasonry. First was that ancient pagan religions worshipped Lucifer in various forms. Second was that the Babylonian priesthood used drugs and sex as a means of people control. Third was that the same Babylonian priesthood instituted human sacrifice as a means of population control. The Quatuor Coronati Lodge thereafter offered assistance to any Mason, or group of Masons willing to apply these discoveries to present day Masonic work.[1088]

By 1889 the hierarchy of English Freemasonry needed only a slight push to plunge headlong into Luciferianism. The World Congress of Freemasonry gave the British Brotherhood the required nudge. On July 14,1889, the twenty-three 33rd degree Supreme Councils were hosted by the French Grand Lodge at Paris. The purpose of this gathering was not to unite the Councils politically, but spiritually - under the banner of the Luciferian doctrine. When Albert Pike's letter of exhortation was read, the hierarchy of the English Grand Lodge accepted the Luciferian doctrine, yet remained loyal to the

---

[1086] Stoddard, *Light-bearers of Darkness* 35.
[1087] "Quatuor Coronati Lodge," *Mackey's Encyclopedia*, vol.111.
[1088] Volume II and III of *Scarlet and the Beast* will expand on this.

Monarchy. The French and American Grand Lodge hierarchies followed, but without giving up their republican ideals.

Although a few Grand Orient Masons had accepted Luciferianism years before this convention, the general body of the Grand Orient lodges, which were formally atheistic, boycotted the French Grand Lodge convention, simultaneously hosting their own congress. There-after, the Grand Orients were disallowed admittance to the annual meetings of the Supreme Council of Grand Lodges.[1089]

Two of the most prominent Grand Orient Masons who did convert to the Luciferian doctrine were women - Britisher Annie Besant (1847-1933), and Russian Helena Petrovna Blavatsky (1831-1891). Both were members of English and French obediences. Both were destined to be the founders of our modern New Age Movement.

Madam Blavatsky had turned to Luciferianism in 1856, when she was initiated into the Grand Orient Carbonari by Mazzini. Blavatsky did more than publish her revolutionary ideals. She lived them. In 1866 she joined 33rd degree Grand Orient Freemason General Garibaldi to fight by his side during the Italian revolution at Viterbo and then at Mentana, where she was seriously wounded and left on the field as dead. In 1875 she founded the Theosophical Society in New York, joined English Freemasonry in 1877, and settled in London in 1887. In London she published her Theosophical magazine, *Lucifer the Light-bringer.[1090]*

Annie Besant, sister of Freemason Sir Walter Besant, was converted to Luciferianism by Albert Pike. At the behest of her brother, she was destined to become the president of the Theosophical Society after Blavatsky's death. Annie was in Paris that fateful 1889 summer when Albert Pike introduced his Luciferian Doctrine to the twenty-three Supreme Councils of Grand Lodge Freemasonry. She was not, however, in Paris to attend that convention. Instead, as an accomplished speaker in her own right, she was scheduled to lecture at the Grand Orient convention, which was hosting three other occult congresses. Her lecture, which met with overwhelming success, was intended to turn the atheists toward Spiritism. De Poncins tells the story:

> In July 1889 the International Workers' Congress was held in Paris, Mrs. [Annie] Besant being one of the delegates. Concurrently, the Marrdstes [sic] held their International Congress and Mrs. Besant moved, amid great applause, for amalgamation with them. And yet another International Congress was then being held in Paris, to wit, that of the Spiritists. The delegates of these occultists were the guests of the Grand Orient, whose headquarters they occupied at 16, rue Cadet. The president of the Spiritists was Denis, and he has made it quite clear that the three congresses there came to a mutual understanding, for, in a speech which he afterwards delivered, he said:
> "The occult Powers are at work among men. Spiritism is a powerful germ which will develop and bring about transformation of laws, ideas and of social forces. It will show its powerful influence on social economy and public life."[1091]

As a result of these three conventions of Unionists, Marxists and Spiritists hosted by Grand Orient Freemasonry, an amalgamation of mystical spiritism with atheism was successfully accomplished. Although atheism remained Grand Orient's published dogma,

---

[1089] de Poncins, *Secret Powers* 25. De Poncins made this statement in 1928 when he wrote this book. However, he was too close to the founding of the League of Nations to know that this Grand Orient creation was the third attempt to unify all Masonry. More on this later.
[1090] Miller 529-535.
[1091] de Poncins, *Secret Powers* 112.

these Masonic congresses started a spiritist movement - the New Age Movement - which today has encircled the globe.

THE UNIVERSAL MASONIC LEAGUE

The most significant outcome of these adversarial Masonic congresses meeting on the same date and location is that shortly after they adjourned, revisionist historians began to observe a gradual transfer of conspiracy activities from Paris to London. Subsequent events suggest that there was a secret agreement between the Unionists, Marxists Spiritists and Luciferians. The Grand Orient had no choice but to cooperate. If its Communist experiment was to be successfully launched, it needed the support of wealthy British Masons.

We can document two events following this monumental Masonic pow-wow, which reactivated communication between the two Masonic enemies First, and almost immediately, the English Grand Lodge began communicating with all continental Grand Lodges and Grand Orient bodies of Freemasonry through the Swiss Grand Lodge Alpina, which recognized, not only the Grand Lodge of France, but the Grand Orients of France, Spain, Italy and Greece. Second, on August 30, 1913, the Universal Masonic League was founded at Berne, Switzerland, where both warring bodies of Freemasonry could meet on neutral ground. *Mackey's Encyclopedia of Free masonry* states that the object of this League was "to further the intimacy of relations between members of all regular Lodges, Grand Lodges, and Grand Orients of all Rites and countries of the world."[1092] Hence, de Poncins writes, "between Anglo-Saxon [English] Freemasonry and Latin [Grand Orient] Freemasonry there are indirect but effective relations which are far closer than is admitted."[1093]

The Universal Masonic League was only the beginning of inter-national Masonic cooperation. The Grand Orient's superficial alienation from annual Grand Lodge Supreme Council meetings compelled English Freemasonry to form sub-lodges, wherein both adversarial Freemasonries could meet on common ground without having to travel to Switzerland. The Quatuor Coronati Research Lodge was assigned the task of creating these lodges.

Msgr. Dillon, although writing in 1885, explained how easy this inter-Masonic communication was to accomplish: "by its [the Grand Orient's] hidden friends scattered through British lodges, there have been at all times, at least in London, some lodges affiliated with Continental lodges. and doing the work of Weishaupt. [Thus, the intercourse between the delegates of English and French Lodges] had an immense effect in causing the vanguard cries of the Continental lodges to find a fatal support from British Masons in and out of Parliament."[1094]

SUB-LODGES OF THE NEW AGE

British conspiracy investigators of the 1920s were unable to detect that the two warring Masonic bodies had united and moved head- quarters to London. They knew only that the Grand Orient had crossed the Channel. They assumed its intent was subversive - to penetrate British lodges. Therefore, several British conspiracy authors began warning the English Masons of a French Grand Orient takeover. One of these was Nesta Webster,

---

[1092] "Universala Framasona Ligo," *Mackey's Encyclopedia,* vol.II.

[1093] Leon de Poncins, *The Dictatorship of the Occult Powers* (Paris:N.p., n.d.) 236.

[1094] Dillon 106, 96.

who in 1924 wrote *Secret* Societies and *Subversive Movements*. Her warning, however, was twenty years too late. At that time the Masonic Luciferians and Spiritists had already organized many popular movements in England as fronts, which could not be connected to Freemasonry without years of research. (The investigator is normally from thirty to fifty years behind in documentation.) Those on the inside of these groups, however, who became disillusioned and broke the occult bonds, were able to illuminate current events. Such was the case in 1930 of another and more revealing author, who was one of the "insiders" of the New Age Movement in her day. Writing *Light-bearers of Darkness* under the pseudonym "Inquire Within," Miss Stoddard (no first name) was one of the "Ruling Chiefs" of the Mother Temple of the Stella Matutina and R.R. et A.C."[1095]

Stoddard informs us that the Stella Matutina was a by-product of the research initiated by the Quatuor Coronati Lodge. As the "Members of Forty" in the Mother Research Lodge received enough occult information to organize debased sub-Masonic lodges, they assisted Masons of degenerate character who would carry out the work. Stella Matutina was founded by two Englishmen near the beginning of the 20th century, each respectively members of the formerly opposed lodges, the Grand Orient and English Grand Lodge. The Grand Orient Mason was Aleister Crowley (1875-1947), who had been initiated into the 33rd degree in Mexico. (A photocopy of Crowley's Grand Orient credentials is in Appendix 2, Fig. 28.) The other co- founder was 33rd degree English Grand Lodge Mason, Dr. William Wynn Westcott (1848- 1925), a London coroner.[1096]

These sub-lodges became known as co-Masonry, since women were permitted to join. Soon, via the sub-lodges, witchcraft and drug abuse spread everywhere, even into the highest circles of society. Satanic jewelry became commonplace. Rituals incorporating mind-altering drugs, orgies and blood sacrifice were discreetly carried out in the heart of the London slums and on remote ancestral estates.

Another of the more publicized of these groups was the Hermetic Society of the Golden Dawn. Golden Dawn is a synonym for New Age and this society was actually a predecessor of Aleister Crowley's Stella Matutina. The Golden Dawn was founded in 1887 by three members of a Rosicrucian Society - possibly even of the Priory of Sion itself. Two of the three - an Anglican priest, Rev. A.F.A. Woodford, a "Member of Forty," and Dr. William Wynn Westcott - were 33rd degree Masons and well-known cabalists. The third was Sam Liddell MacGregor Mathers, a Scot Mason who was connected to the Priory of Sion through his acquaintance with its Grand Master, Claude Debussy.[1097]

Rev. Woodford provided Dr. Westcott with the documentation from the library of the Correspondence Circle that was the basis for the drug-using and sex-codifying Golden Dawn. The group was soon joined by three more well-known Luciferians, Spiritists, and Satanists: Grand Orient Freemason Helena Blavatsky, who remained a member until her death in 1891; poet William Butler Yeats, an intimate of Sion's Grand Master, Claude Debussy; and Satanist Aleister Crowley, the man who was to become known worldwide for his practice of black magic.

English Freemasonry's Mother Research Lodge had two specific goals in mind when founding such sub-societies. The first was to create lodges where Grand Lodge and Grand Orient Masons could find commonality. The second was to use these sub-societies (which had no apparent connection with Masonry by name) to penetrate Masonic and non-Masonic British societies with Luciferianism. This strategy of using sub-lodges deliberately concealed English Freemasonry's involvement in building the New Age Movement, yet left her hierarchy in direct command.

[1095] Stoddard, *Light-bearers,* title page.
[1096] Stoddard 162-175 and Miller 569.
[1097] Baigent et al, *Holy Blood* 154.

What took place was the creation of a more debased Freemasonry on both sides of the Channel, as well as the bringing into existence of a degenerate society. Grand Orient Masons, who had long since initiated women for use in their drug and sex orgies and witchcraft rituals, once again used women to carry their doctrine into English Masonry. Stoddard warned the British Masons of the penetration by Grand Orient Spiritists, who were using female Freemasons in these English co Masonic lodges. She also confirmed that "English Freemasonry is not occult, though it has occult Lodges, and most English occultists [who are] not Theosophists are Freemasons, if men."[1098]

According to Stoddard, the Luciferian New Age plan was to penetrate British society from three directions: (1) through members of the Theosophical Society, i.e., Madam Blavatsky's (and later Annie Besant's) followers, apparently headed by the co-Masons; (2) through members of the Hermetic Orders and Freemasons; and (3) by independents, whether in small groups or individuals.[1099]

BUILDING THE NEW AGE MOVEMENT

These three groups, according to Stoddard, were to operate through the following means:

> Group 1 works on the familiar lines of lectures, magazine publications, etc. [It] attracts a large number of idle women who have the leisure to take a little occultism with their afternoon tea. Practically all the members are people with time and money.
>
> Group 2 is small in numbers. It works by Lodges and circulates manuscripts. Its teaching is done by correspondence, by individual officers, etc. It seldom has lectures. It taps a wholly different class, gets at more varied social strata, has a far larger proportion of men... Most of its men are Freemasons... These people are busy, there are singularly few idle, moneyed or leisured women and men among them, they are very proud and independent... These bodies are older than the Theosophical Society and they do not forget it... They must be got at from within, not from without.
>
> The third group... will accept no authority over them. This group is non-Masonic, consisting of men and women of letters, and must be turned through "popular movements."[1100]

THE "DOUBLE AGENT" STRATEGY

Frenchmen did not understand the English mind. The Grand Orient operatives therefore used British Grand Orient Masons as double agents. They began their Luciferian and Spiritist penetration of English Masonry before the turn of the 20th century, at a time when government. controlled secret intelligence services had not yet been established. Grand Orient Masonry had long since perfected political and social intelligence penetration prior to, and during the French Revolution. Masonic double agents were used then and have continued to be used throughout this intrigue. In a real sense these British subversives were traitors to their own country.

[1098] Stoddard, *Light-bearers* 96, 98.
[1099] Stoddard 96.
[1100] Stoddard 96-99.

The most degenerate British turncoat of all time was the Satanist, Edward Aleister Crowley. Crowley, a heroin addict and sexual pervert[1101], was in 1913 Patriarch Grand Administrator General of British Freemasonry's Ancient and Primitive Rite of Memphis, the same Lodge mentioned in chapter 10 with connections to the Priory of Sion's Mizraim Lodge at Paris.[1102] This evil Masonic lodge incorporated into its rituals the immoral fertility worship of the Dionysian Mysteries, which included both homosexual and heterosexual orgies.[1103] In Mexico Crowley was known as the Beast 666. There he was initiated into the 33rd degree in the Grand Orient Scottish Rite of Freemasonry.[1104]

William J. Petersen, in *Those Curious New Cults in the 80's*, gave us Crowley's background:

> *Crowley, who honored himself with the title "the wickedest man in the world," was born in 1875 as the son of a wealthy British brewer. His parents, however, were converted to Christianity through the Plymouth Brethren, who take the Bible a lot more seriously than they take the organized church. A child prodigy, young Aleister got a fiendish delight out of shocking his parents and playmates, until his mother finally was so outraged that she called him the Great Beast prophesied in the Book of Revelation.[1105]*

Later in life, reports Petersen, Crowley "made a pact with Satan, wrote odes to murderers, called Queen Victoria dirty names, seduced a housemaid and played around with homosexuality. He wrote a collection of pornographic poems and dedicated them to his uncle, advocated the free use of drugs and finally established his own villa in Sicily for continual orgies."[1106] There he revived barbaric rites that had not been practiced since the time of the Dionysian cults in ancient Greece. During one ritual in 1921, he induced a he-goat to copulate with his constant female companion, Leah Hirsig, then slit the animal's throat at the moment of orgasm.

Crowley is famed as the most dedicated Satanist of the twentieth century. He indulged in blasphemy, displaying his hatred of Christianity by baptizing a toad and naming it Jesus Christ. Then he slowly crucified it, reveling in its agonies.

Petersen reports that Crowley's life ended in loneliness and despair. "At the age of seventy-two, in a cheap boardinghouse in Hastings, England, Aleister Crowley, injecting eleven grams of heroin into his wasted body each day, begged for morphine to kill the pain. But the pain wasn't assuaged, and Crowley passed on [in 1947] to meet his Maker."[1107]

ALEISTER CROWLEY AND RITUAL HUMAN SACRIFICE

[1101] David A. Noebel, *The Legacy of John Lennon* (Nashville:Thomas Nelson Publishers, 1982) 101.

[1102] Miller 524.

[1103] "Oriental Rite of Memphis," *A New Encyclopaedia of Freemasonry* vol.11, 241 and Reay Tannahill, *Sex in History* (New York: Stein and Day, 1980) 85, 118.

[1104] Grand Orient Freemasonry, also called "Latin" Freemasonry, was carried to South American and Latin American countries following the conquest of Spain by Grand Orient Freemason Napoleon Bonaparte.

[1105] William J. Petersen, *Those Curious New Cults in the 50s* (New Canaan, CT: Keats Publishing, 1973) 87.

[1106] Petersen.

[1107] Petersen 88.

We mentioned earlier that one of the most immoral Masonic lodges in England was the Order of the Golden Dawn founded in 1887.

Freemason A.E. Waite, author of A *New Encyclopaedia of Freemasony*, was also an early member of this Order. In 1903 a split occurred within the Golden Dawn when some of the initiates, including Waite, rejected deeper immersion into the occult. Miller writes:

> *In consequence of the split, the old organization of Golden Dawn changed its name to Stella Matutina with Aleister Crowley and William Wynn Westcott at its head while the schismatic order, under A.E. Waite and S.L. MacGregor Mathers, the latter a friend of [Freemason] Rudolph Steiner, retained the old name of Golden Dawn. In 1912, Golden Dawn merged with Stella Matutina.[1108]*

The Order of the Golden Dawn produced two horrifying and destructive offshoots, the Order of the Temple of the East and the Thule Society. These two societies were the breeding grounds for the inner core of the Nazi movement. Their amoral systems had long before been concealed in the Supreme Council of Grand Orient Freemasonry. In 1902 at Berlin, under the guidance of the Quatuor Coronati Lodge, Grand Orient Freemason Karl Keilner, also a Theosophist, cofounded (with Theodore Reuss) the Ordo Templi Orientis (O.T.O.), which then absorbed the Order of the Temple of the East. Ordo Templi Orientis (O.T.O.) actually means Order of the Temple of Lucifer.

Blavatsky's Theosophical Society became the recruiting organization for the O.T.O. Debased 33rd degree Freemasons and homicidal miscreants from all over Europe, Russia, and England, soon joined the Oriental Templars. Theodore Reuss, a 33rd degree German Grand Orient Mason and free-lance newspaper correspondent for the London *Times*, was sent to check out Crowley, possibly to encourage him in joining the Ordo Templi Orientis. Reuss said to Crowley, "Since you know our hidden sex teachings, you'd better come into our Order. Crowley agreed, and after a journey to Berlin, was initiated into the O.T.O that same year.[1109]

By the end of the decade Aleister Crowley was at the helm of the London chapter of the O.T.O., the only chapter known to exist today. It is the most destructive Masonic lodge in the world.

Crowley encouraged his initiates to perform human sacrifices, using young boys as victims. He himself allegedly took part in 150 ritual murders.[1110]

Crowley called himself "The Master Therion." Miller says that Crowley, in his book Magick (1930), articulates his rationale for practicing human sacrifice. Miller quotes Crowley in part:

> *The blood is the life. This simple statement is explained by the Hindus by saying that the blood is the principal vehicle of vital Prana. There is some ground for the belief that there is a definite substance, not isolated as yet, whose presence makes all the difference between live and dead matter.*
>
> *It would be unwise to condemn as irrational the practice of those savages who tear the heart and liver from an adversary, and devour them while yet warm. In any case it was the theory of the ancient Magicians, that any living being is a*

[1108] Miller 569-570.

[1109] William Josiah Sutton, *The New Age Movement and The illuminati* 666 (USA: Institute of Religious Knowledge, 1983)120-121.

[1110] Miller, Appendix IV, 46-47. See certificate of Crowley's *O.T.O.I* Grand Orient membership in Appendix 2, Fig. 28 of *Scarlet and the Beast*, vol.1.

storehouse of energy varying in quantity according to its mental and moral character. At the death of the animal this energy is liberated suddenly...

For the highest spiritual working one must accordingly choose that victim which contains the greatest and purest force. A male child of perfect innocence and high intelligence is the most satisfactory and suitable victim.

But the bloody sacrifice, though more dangerous, is more efficacious; and for nearly all purposes human sacrifice is the best.[1111]

ALEISTER CROWLEY: HERO OF SATANIC ROCK STARS

Freemason Crowley's murderous influence continues to this day. He is the hero of the modern Satan worshipers. Anton Szandor Lavey, author of *The Satanic Bible*, and head of the First Church of Satan in California, is an admirer of Aleister Crowley. Cofounder of the Church of Satan is Kenneth Anger, who was initiated into the Golden Dawn and the O.T.O. in the 1940s by Crowley himself.

Many rock stars are also followers of Crowley, and their songs glorify the evils of Satan. For instance, Crowley's picture (and that of Karl Marx) is on the cover of the Beatles' album *Sgt. Pepper's Lonely Hearts Club Band.*[1112] About the album cover, Ringo Starr said, "We just thought we would like to put together a lot of people we like and admire."[1113]

Author Brian Key, who has studied the role of the media in the decline of our culture, has commented that "[t]he Beatles popularized and culturally legitimatized hallucinatory drug usage among teenagers throughout the world... The Beatles became the super drug culture prophets and pushers of all times."[1114] The names of their songs witness to this fact. For instance, one meaning of "day tripper" is to take a shot of heroin in the morning and stay high all day; A "Yellow Sub-marine" in drug parlance is a yellow qualude, or downer; "Strawberry Fields Forever" refers to poppy fields. Poppy, the main ingredient of heroin, is red like strawberries; and in "Hey Jude," Jude means marijuana.[1115]

What are the occult and/or Masonic affiliations or association of rock stars themselves? Led Zeppelin's Jimmy Page, for instance, is a Mason and member of the Golden Dawn. He owns the demon-inhabited house of the late Aleister Crowley, a house said to be haunted by a death curse. Led Zeppelin's drummer, John "Bonzo" Bonham, died in Crowley's mansion, "fueling rumors of sinister overtones resulting from Page's fascination with black magic." Page has praised Crowley as "an unrecognized genius of twentieth century thinking."[1116]

Satanist Keith Richards of the Rolling Stones is not only a Freemason but also a member of both Crowley's Golden Dawn and O.T.O. The evil influence on children who listen to his "music" is enormous. After his heroin arrest he admitted, "There are black magicians who think we are acting as unknown agents of Lucifer." The Rolling Stones spread revolutionary propaganda through their song "Street Fighting Man." Their anthems to Satan, "Sympathy for the Devil" or "Dancing with Mr. D" (the Devil), bear out Richards' comment.[1117]

[1111] Miller 576-577.

[1112] Noebel, *John Lennon* 101.

[1113] David A. Noebel, *The Marxist Minstrels* (Tulsa, OK: American Christian College Press, 1974) 105.

[1114] William Brian Key, *Media Sexploitation* (Scarborough, Ont.:Prentice-Hall, 1976) 137.

[1115] Interview with Jon Kregel, ex-drug dealer turned Christian.

[1116] Bob Larson, *Rock* (Wheaton, IL: Tyndale House, 1983) 152-153.

[1117] Sutton 218-219.

The leader of the Rolling Stones is Mick Jagger. Early in his singing career Jagger was initiated into Crowley's Order of the Golden Dawn by Crowley's disciple, Freemason Kenneth Anger.[1118] Anger's dream was to produce a film glorifying the devil. The movie was to be named *Lucifer Rising*. The part of Lucifer was to be played by Bobby Beausoleil, a young guitar player with the California rock band Love. "After filming for some time, Beausoleil went off the deep end and committed a bestial murder, including writing on the wall with his victim's blood."[1119] Beausoleil was a follower of Freemason Charles Manson, who was also a member of Crowley's O.T.O.[1120]

The groups Black Sabbath and Blue Oyster Cult have had great success selling Satan rock. The first album of Black Sabbath was entitled *Sabbath, Bloody Sabbath*. Its cover clearly showed the cross of Christ placed upside down and the number "666," the mark of the beast. After a concert in Tulsa, Oklahoma, the *Tulsa World* music critic confirmed that the subject matter of Black Sabbath's songs are about "the occult, death and drugs."[1121] Not surprisingly, Ozzy Osbourne, former lead singer for Black Sabbath, is devoted to Aleister Crowley, saying Crowley was "a phenomenon of his time."[1122]

In the early months of their act, Jefferson Airplane's Alice Cooper, American born, and now star of his own rock group of the same name, killed a live chicken on stage. Included in their album *Killer* is the song "Dead Babies." One author reports how Cooper walked "on stage with a life- like-looking doll. With a hatchet he chops it into pieces, gleefully throwing the appendages into the audience. Blood capsules fastened to the back squirt what appears to be blood in every direction. Afterwards, Alice stands holding up the head of the doll, like a decapitated enemy. With one final, demoniacal thrust, he impales the head on a microphone stand..."[1123]

SATANIC MURDERS

The young and impressionable rock and roll audience is programmed at rock concerts to emulate what they see and hear on stage. This is confirmed by Jimi Hendricks, the innovator of the heavy, acid, blues-rock sound of the late 1960s and early 1970s. Hendricks said in an interview with *Life* magazine that "music is a spiritual thing of its own. You can hypnotize people with music, and when you get them at their weakest point you can preach into their subconscious whatever you want to say."[1124]

The message of this rock and roll promotes boldly Satanic ritual murder, resulting in human sacrifices throughout our land. A few examples will confirm this horrifying phenomenon.

On the September 12, 1985, "AM Houston" talk show on KHOU with Roger Gray, psychiatrist Dr. Peter Olsson detailed his investigation into a Satanic murder by junior high school students. "Satanism is in," he said. "It's cool to read the Satanic Bible and worship the Beast. Heavy metal causes it."

Los Angeles, California, was terrorized by a series of Satanic murders. Residents were relieved, as well as shocked, when the "Night Stalker" was finally captured on September 2, 1985. The Associated Press news report stated that the "Stalker" was

---

[1118] *Executive Intelligence Review* 31 August 1982,45-46.

[1119] Noebel, *John Lennon* 102.

[1120] Noebel, *John Lennon*. Documentation of Charles Manson's Masonic affiliation is in chapter 16.

[1121] Noebel, *John Lennon* 105.

[1122] Larson 153.

[1123] Tom Allen, *Rock-n-Roll, the Bible and the Mind* (Beaverlodge, Alberta: Horizon Books, 1982) 55.

[1124] *Life* 3 Oct.1969: 74.

responsible for 16 ritual murders. During his trial Richard Ramirez displayed in the palm of his hand the pentagram (an upside down star within a circle), a symbol of Satan. "Hail Satan!" yelled Ramirez as he was led from the courtroom.[1125]

What made Ramirez kill? According to one news report, "Ramirez was obsessed with satanic themes in the rock band AC-DC's 1979 album, 'Highway to Hell.' The album cover depicts a band member dressed as a devil, while another wears a pentagram-shaped pendant."[1126] Ramirez' favorite song was "Night Prowler." The song says in part:

"Was that a noise out your window, or a shadow on your blind? And you lie there naked, like a body in a tomb, suspended animation as I slip into your room."[1127]

Satanic murders are not limited to the western half of our nation. In Newark, New Jersey, January 1988, "Thomas Sullivan was entranced by the occult as he stabbed his mother at least 12 times and tried to kill his father and 10-year-old brother by setting fire to their house.

Then he slit his throat and wrists with a Boy Scout knife, slumping dead on bloody snow in a neighbor's back yard... Thomas Sullivan Sr. told the *New York Daily News* that all last week his son had been singing a heavy metal song about blood and killing your mother... A few weeks before, while doing a research paper on satanism, the all-American neighborhood paperboy became a defiant, hostile teen buried in library books on the occult and listening to heavy metal rock music."[1128]

On May 16, 1985 the *"20/20"* TV show reported on a national phenomenon: "The Devil Worshippers." Correspondent Tom Jarriel said, "America is being affected. Nationwide we found that minor cases of satanic activity light up the map. Not a single state is unaffected. But even more frightening is the number of reported murders and suicides with satanic clues. All of them were investigated by police, but usually without much result."[1129]

Tom Jarriel told of Ricky Kasso from Northport, Long Island. Kasso and another young man repeatedly stabbed Gary Lawers to death as the victim was forced to pray to Satan. Jarriel said, "Despite numerous signs that Kasso was into satanism and rock music associated with devil worship, police steadfastly refused to label this case satanic. The official explanation: a drug- related crime."[1130]

Jarriel also discussed what has caused these young people to turn to Satanism. First are occult movies and horror movies. Second are the many books which are available on Satanic worship. "And finally," said Jarriel, "music, which is found here in the neighborhood record store under the category of heavy metal music. The satanic message is clear, both on the album covers and in the lyrics, which are reaching impressionable young minds."

Jarriel continued: "And the musical message comes across loud and clear, at concerts and now through rock videos. The symbolism is all there: the satanic pentagram, the upside-down cross, the blank eyes of the beast, the rebellion against Christianity, and again and again, the obsession with death. According to most groups, it's all done in fun. But according to police it's having an effect on many children, a growing subculture that mixes heavy metal music with drugs and the occult. In addition to groups that are blatantly

[1125] Judy Smagula Farah (AP), "'Stalker' suspect enters pleas", *Longview Daily News* 25 Oct.1985: 5-B.
[1126] Associated Press, "Satanism linked to killer," *Longview Morning Journal* 2 Sept.1985: 14- B.
[1127] "Satanism linked."
[1128] Associated Press, "Interest in occult transformed teen before slaying mom, self," *Longview Daily News* 13 Jan.1988: 8-A.
[1129] "The Devil Worshippers," hosts Hugh Downs and Barbara Walters, Prod. Av Westin, corres. Tom Jarriel, *20/20,* ABC, transcript show #521, 16 May 1985: 3.
[1130] "Devil Worshippers" 2.

satanic, there are also many recordings which some believe may contain satanic references in the form of backward messages."

Tom Jarriel asked Northport Police Chief Dale Griffis, "How often do you find heavy metal music indicators at the scene of a crime involving satanic worship?" The Officer answered, "Probably about 35 percent, 40 percent of the calls."[1131]

And finally, in a story on the rock concert to feed the starving Ethiopians, ABC News reported on July 13, 1985 that "If humanity decides to get behind a single message, the possibility to communicate that message is unlimited. Rock and Roll has proven to be the great communicator to the world."

In the eyes of the world, what the rock bands did in "Live Aid" and "Band Aid" was honorable. But by using misfortune to communicate their evil, they deceptively amass multitudes of followers and co-opt them to their destructive program. Like benevolent Freemasonry which created them, their inherent evil is evidenced by the fact that many of the rock groups are admitted Satanists, and admirers of Freemason Aleister Crowley.

In the same manner in which Illuminated French Masonry used the music of Mozart to breed revolution in the minds of youth throughout Europe prior to, and during the French Revolution, Luciferian English Freemasonry today is using Masonic rock stars to preach in song Aleister Crowley's Satanic message to our youth, and successfully turning these youths into murderers.

The rise of Satanic music, drugs, shock-horror movies, and ritual Satanic murders is directly linked to the Masonic Golden Dawn's offshoot, the Ordo Templi Orientis (O.T.O.). Its purpose is to groom the young to accept holocaust when it comes, and to participate in it when the Masonic hierarchy gives the command.

[1131] "Devil Worshippers" 4.

16. NEW AGE MOVEMENT UNITES ENGLISH AND FRENCH FREEMASONRY

The government of the O.T.O... combines monarchy with democracy; it includes aristocracy, and conceals even the seeds of revolution, by which alone progress can be effected. Thus we balance the Triads, uniting the Three in One...[1132]

BOOK OF EQUINOX

When the hierarchy of the Templar Palladium failed to unite permanently the three Masonic obediences, it was Sion's turn. Miller confirms the story told in the Book of *Equinox*, of which a portion is cited above. The word "monarchy" refers to English Freemasonry; "democracy" represents both French and American Freemasonry; and "uniting the Three in One" alludes to all three Masonic obediences.

All three must come to agreement both religiously and politically if world government is to be a reality. However, unity among contradictory religious organizations is impossible. Likewise, unity among opposing political viewpoints is unrealistic. The war between English and French Freemasonry turns on differences of opinion on both these issues. The conflict? Which religious and political system will eventually rule the New World Order?

Atheistic Templar Grand Orient Masonry desired a dictatorship of the proletariat - the lower class - with communism guaranteeing equal distribution of wealth. While awaiting the fruition of this dream, the Grand Orient encouraged laborers to form unions and, with the might of worker strikes, gain their share of the wealth. With this ideology, French Freemasonry was thus able to win the lower classes.

In contrast, Pantheistic Zionist English Freemasonry, whose sovereigns shared power with an elected parliament, desired a New World Order dominated by an aristocracy. For two centuries English Freemasons had kept their society aristocratic, capitalistic, and monopolistic. They had dismissed and forgotten the common laborer, losing him politically to their adversary.

To remedy this divisive stalemate, English Freemasonry attacked the problem by creating dual fronts where commonality could be predicated. First they established political-economic fronts, called "think tanks," where the intelligentsia from both sides of the Channel could discuss a coefficient for politics.[1133] Second they created mystic front organizations intended to appeal to and gratify man's baser instincts, and thus reach and destabilize all levels of society.

English Freemasonry assigned the latter task to the Quatuor Coronati Lodge of Masonic Research, which, as we have seen, in turn developed a variety of degenerate sub-Masonic fronts known as co-Masonry.[1134]

To win the confidence of the French atheists who believed that individuals were endowed with equal, inalienable rights founded upon natural law, the English expanded the concept of *natural law* to include *mythological law.*[1135] The Quatuor Coronati Lodge

---

[1132] Miller 705.

[1133] Discussed in detail in chapter 22.

[1134] Although the Ordo Templi Orientis, or Oriental Templars, associate themselves with the Templars in name, this group is the product of Sion's English Freemasonry.

[1135] Helga Zepp-LaRouche, *The Hitler Book* (New York: New Benjamin Franklin House, 1984) 37.

discovered that pagan religions, in harmony with their cyclical world outlook, had long ago interwoven into their political society mythological law, through which they maintained control of the populace. The dominant figure in these prevailing myths was usually a goddess who symbolized "Mother Earth" and who thus provided the basis for an ideology that man and earth were one.[1136]

Pagan religions taught that Mother Earth required the continuation of creation through procreation, with periodic demands for population control. These myths were carefully cultivated and applied by a designated caste of priests, who designed licentious rituals in their worship as a sacrament to Mother Earth. These rituals, of course, appealed to the base nature of man. Therefore, these mythologies, created by man, became mythological law.

In this religion Mother Earth could become "angry." When she did so it meant that man was multiplying too rapidly. To appease the mother goddess, mythological law demanded human sacrifices, usually of the very young. Paul deParrie, in *Unholy Sacrifices of the New Age*, says, "Whether known as Kali (the many-armed Hindu goddess Kali, who wears for a necklace a chain of human skulls), Diana, Isis, or Astarte, Mother Earth or her dark mirror image consistently required blood as an appropriate offering; she who created (or procreated) also destroyed and devoured her own young in bloody ritual."[1137]

The purpose of the sacrifice was to "save the earth." Nigel Davies, in *Human Sacrifice in History and Today*, confirms: "Both sacrificer and victim knew that the act was required, to save the people from calamity and the cosmos from collapse. Their object was, therefore, more to preserve than to destroy life."[1138]

Mythological law required mothers to willingly give up their children to the flame or to the knife. With the Arioio in Tahiti, "status was based entirely on one's devotion to killing one's own children."[1139] The North American and Mexican Indians "both stressed the belief that the victim would profit from his own sacrifice, thus allowing the executioner to feel no guilt and denying the victim the opportunity to protest his own sacrifice."[1140] Thus, legalized murder became a part of Mother Earth's mythological law of population control.

The Quatuor Coronati Lodge of Masonic Research set out to apply *mythological law* to present- day Masonic work. In the same manner *in* which a designated caste of priests had in ancient times designed rituals of human destruction to appease both Mother Earth and degenerate man, the 33rd degree hierarchy of both English and French Freemasonry (Masons who had already delved into witchcraft), duplicated the system for their budding mystic fronts. By catering to the baser instincts of man, the two Freemasonries found it a simple task to unite under a political system that permitted the free exercise of mythological law.

Diametrically opposed to the Judeo-Christian teaching, it should be no surprise that these sub- Masonic societies became anti-Semitic and anti-Christian. Today they are known as white supremacists. Their plan to "save the earth" through a process of earth purification was, and still is, to annihilate the dark-skinned races, which include the Jews. From this ideology was born the Nazi movement. The homicidal O.T.O. and Thule Society played the most significant role in grooming Hitler for power. The Order of the

---

[1136] Zepp-LaRouche 36.
[1137] Paul deParrie, *Unholy Sacifices of the New Age* (Westchester, IL: Crossway Books, 1988) 22.
[1138] Nigel Davies, *Human Sacrifices in History and Today* (New York: William Morrow, 1981) 13.
[1139] De Parrie 6.
[1140] De Parrie.

Golden Dawn became the connecting link between the German branch of the OTO-Thule and English Freemasonry.[1141]

When English Freemasonry agreed to cooperate with French Freemasonry, the paltry Grand Orient was no match for the suave and wealthy Whore of Babylon at London. Hence, the French method of destruction by brute force was set aside for a more acceptable approach. English Freemasonry planned for a gradual and more scientific depopulation of earth.

During the 1920s and 1930s, British conspiracy researchers realized that the destructive doctrines of French Freemasonry had crossed the English Channel. Several revisionists set out to warn English Freemasonry of what they perceived was penetration by the Grand Orient. They had not yet discovered that the hierarchy in both Freemasonries had united in the Ordo Templi Orientis in 1905.

So secret was the O.T.O. that the majority of Masons are still unaware of its existence today. Yet, this Order is documented as the most evil of Freemasonry, executing the destructive bidding of the hierarchy on a grand scale.[1142] Its creed is "Do what thou wilt shall be the whole of the Law." Its rituals include the use of mind-altering drugs and human sacrifice.

THE PRIORY OF SION AND WITCHCRAFT

Claude Debussy, Grand Master of Sion (GM 1885-1918), was intimate with the English Freemasons who founded the Order of the Golden Dawn, which in turn produced the O.T.O. and Thule Society. He was especially close to Dr. Gerard Encausse (Papus), Grand Master of four Rosicrucian orders in France - Martin, Memphis, Mizraim, and the O.T.O.[1143] At the behest of Debussy, Papus took Martinism and the O.T.O. to Russia to prepare for the destruction of that Christian nation.[1144]

Miller lists the following Masons who were involved in the 19th Century revival of witchcraft, which led to founding the O.T.O.: Wolfgang von Goethe (1749-1832), Eliphas Levi (1810- 1875), Richard Wagner (1813-1890), Hargrave Jennings (1817-1890), Friedrich Nietzsche (1844- 1900), Franz Hartmann (1838-1912), Cardinal Rampolla (1843-1913), Papus (Dr. Encausse 1865-1916), and Karl Kellner (-1905), cofounder (with Theodore Reuss) of the O.T.O.[1145]

Goethe, Levi, Wagner, and Papus are listed in *Holy Blood, Holy Grail* as also being connected to the Priory of Sion. The others were Rosicrucian Masons. Kellner was also a Grand Orient Mason, as was Reuss.

In 1895 the Quatuor Coronati Lodge of Masonic Research shared with Karl Kellner its discovery that pagans had controlled population through human sacrifice. When Kellner informed the German Grand Orient and Grand Lodge hierarchy of this, Friedrich Nietzsche commented, "The 20th Century will be the bloodiest on earth."

In 1902 Kellner organized the homicidal Ordo Templi Orientis and began initiating Freemasons on both sides of the Channel. The original members of the O.T.O. were German Grand Orient Theodore Reuss; and English Masons John Yarker (1833-1913),

---

[1141] See chapter 22.
[1142] John Daniel, Scarlet and the Beast: English Freemasonry, Banks, and the illegal Drug Trade vol. III (Tyler, IX: Jon Kregel, Inc., 1995) chapter 5.
[1143] Baigent et al, *Holy Blood* 154.
[1144] See chapters 13 and 19.
[1145] Miller 572.

William Wynn Westcott (1848- 1925), and MacGregor Mathers. All but Mathers held the 33rd degree.[1146]

Theodore Reuss became head of the O.T.O. upon Kellner's death in 1905. In 1902 Reuss had already named Westcott regent of the O.T.O. in England, thus establishing the interlocking directorate between English and Continental Freemasonry.[1147] In 1912 Reuss initiated Aleister Crowley into the O.T.O. By the time World War I had started, Crowley, a member of both English and French Freemasonry, was at the head of the British branch of the O.T.O.

The O.T.O. drew membership from a wide range of occult organizations: the Gnostic Catholic Church; the Order of the Knights of the Holy Ghost; the Order of the Illuminati; the Order of the Knights of St. John; the Order of the Knights of Malta; the Order of the Knights of the Holy Sepulchre; the Hermetic Brotherhood of Light; the Holy Order of Rose Croix of Heredom; the Order of the Holy Royal Arch of Enoch; the Order of the Knights Templar; the Hidden Church of the Holy Grail; the Ancient and Primitive Rite of Masonry; the Rite of Memphis; the Rite of Mizraim; the Ancient and Accepted Scottish Rite of Masonry; the Swedenborgian Rite of Masonry; the Order of the Martinists; the Order of Sat Bhai; and many other orders of equal merit, or of less fame.[1148]

What is most significant about these organizations is that they are recognized as a mixture of Knights Templar and Priory of Sion secret societies.[1149] As suggested in the Book *of Equinox*, Scarlet and the Beast, for a time at least, united in the Ordo Templi Orientis.

The Oriental Templars operated in the same manner as did Albert Pike's Palladian Templars. Although the O.T.O. incorporated the Templar aura by name, it was not a Templar creation; rather it was Sion's link to the international network of secret societies. Unlike the Palladian, which recruited from only the Templar orders, the O.T.O. recruited from all occult bodies throughout the ~[1150] This network was controlled by the Sovereign Grand Inspectors General of the 33rd Degree in both obediences, who were periodically required to tour and inspect the O.T.O. Lodges.[1151]

THE O.T.O. IN AMERICA

The Ordo Templi Orientis was English Freemasonry's most effective psychological warfare unit. Its duties were twofold: (1) to unite all occult bodies under the Luciferian Doctrine; and (2) to destroy the Judeo-Christian culture worldwide with an onslaught of Satanism. The two Christian nations first targeted for destruction were Czarist Russia and the United States.

Maury Terry, an American investigative journalist, tells in *The ultimate Evil* how the O.T.O. got started in our country:

> *After internal dissension, elements of the Golden Dawn more or less merged into the Ordo Templi Orientis. Aleister Crowley won permission to head a British OTO branch, and the teachings of the OTO entered the United States with Crowley in 1916, during World War I in Europe.*

[1146] Miller 679.
[1147] Miller 571.
[1148] Miller 572.
[1149] Miller 572.
[1150] Miller 574-575.
[1151] Miller 690.

> *Later, during World War II, Crowley helped establish an OTO lodge in Pasadena, California, and OTO branches subsequently sprouted in a number of U.S. cities, including New York and Houston. In effect, a loose network was formed and already functioning via occult shops and bookstores, newsletters, ads in the underground press and other methods...*
>
> *In fact, many believe that the entire occult underground in America today can be traced back to the formation of that Crowley OTO operation in Pasadena.[1152]*
>
> *The Law of the Ordo Templi Orientis is "Do what thou wilt shall be the whole of the Law."[1153] For the pleasure of its members, this "Law" was practiced to its fullest in brothels established throughout Europe and the United States. A segment of the Manifesto of the O.T.O. explains the meaning of that "Law":*
>
> *[The O.T.O.] embodies the whole of the secret knowledge of all oriental Orders; and its chiefs are initiates of the highest rank, and recognized as such by all capable of such recognition in every country in the world.*
>
> *The Order is international, and has existing branches in every civilized country of the world.*
>
> *The aims of the O.T.O. can only be understood fully by its highest initiates; but it may be said openly that it teaches Hermetic Science or Occult Knowledge, the Pure and Holy Magick of Light, the Secrets of Mystic attainment, Yoga of all forms; Gnana Yoga, Raja Yoga, Bhakta Yoga and Hatha Yoga, and all other branches of the secret Wisdom of the Ancients.*
>
> *It also possesses in every important centre of population a hidden Retreat (Collegium ad Spiritum Sanctum) where members may conceal themselves in order to pursue the Great Work without hindrance.*
>
> *These houses are secret fortresses of Truth, Light, Power and Love, and their position is only disclosed under an oath of secrecy to those entitled to make use of them.*
>
> *They are also temples of true worship, specially consecrated by Nature to bring out of a man all that is best in him.[1154]*

Prior to, and during World War II, Pasadena, California, was the O.T.O.'s west coast headquarters in America, while Nyack, New York, was the center of its east coast operation.[1155] More information is written about the O.T.O. brothel - one of the houses of "Truth, Light, Power and Love" referred to above - in Nyack than other locations. It was called Clarkstown Country Club (C.C.C.). At its head was Freemason Dr. Pierre Arnold Bernard (1875-1955), initiated into the O.T.O. in 1916 by Aleister Crowley himself, soon after Crowley arrived in the United States.

Bernard's occult library at the C.C.C. was the largest of its kind in America, consisting of an array of pornographic movies and literature, as well as the finest collection of Sanskrit lore. During its prosperous years, the 1930s, talks on the Veda, its writings and philosophy, were regularly given by Dr. Bernard. The C.C.C.'s promotional literature stated that "[t]he core of this subject [Veda] when reduced to practice is the Yoga System of Patanjali, a scientific scheme of mental and physical development evolved and recorded by the early Indo-Aryans.

[1152] Maury Terry, *The Ultimate Evil* (Garden City, NY: Dolphin Books, 1987) 180-181.

[1153] Miller 687.

[1154] Miller 679.

[1155] Miller 571-581. See Appendix 2, Fig. 28, for the certificate of appointment of Aleister "St" Edward Crowley as National Grand Master of the O.T.O. for Great Britain and Ireland. In Appendix 6 read the instructions of the O.T.O. on blood sacrifices, especially human sacrifices of young males.

Nowhere else in the world with the exception of a few places in India is this work to be found carried to such a degree of perfection."[1156]

Dr. Bernard was nicknamed "Oom," short for "Omnipotent." Women called him "Loving Guru." Often the women told him they felt the need to walk around him three times and then reach out and touch his "lotus."

The lotus flower of India is of course a phallic symbol. An Oom disciple once confided to an outsider:

> Sex is discussed as naturally as hypnosis or reincarnation. Dr. Bernard believes that men and women can learn a lot about living by learning a lot about playing and loving. He teaches the Oriental view of love as opposed to the restrained Western idea. Love, in its physical aspects, is akin to music and poetry. It unites men and women with the infinite.[1157]

Both male and female members of the C.C.C. practiced the mystic Hindu art of Tantrik. A true Tantrik is a practitioner of Tantra, a ritualistic system in certain religions of the Orient. The rites are grossly licentious and are most often invoked in veneration of the Sakti, the Hindu goddesses of female energy.[1158]

When the C.C.C. went into decline and finally sold its property, paranormal activity began to manifest itself in several of its buildings. For example, part of the C.C.C. estate was purchased by the Christian and Missionary Alliance, which is now the campus of Nyack College. Students who attended Nyack in the earlier years may recall the demonic activity in one of the buildings before exorcism.[1159] Today, another dwelling, not associated with the College, but on the original C.C.C. estate, is still manifesting demonic activity. (See picture of house and brief story in Appendix 2, Fig. 31.)

The Pasadena and Nyack centers rapidly networked with other O.T.O. Lodges across North America. The O.T.O.'s publication, *Duties of the Brethren,* confirms the purpose of these retreats:

> Special Profess-Houses for the care of women of the Order, or those whose husbands or lovers are members of the Order, will be instituted, so that the frontal duty of womankind may be carried out in all comfort and honour.[1160]

It is also probable that within this licentious Order, homosexual activity was practiced, for *Duties of the Brethren* also states:

> Every Brother shall seek constantly to give pleasure to all Brethren with whom he is acquainted, whether by entertainment or conversation, or in any other manner that may suggest itself. It will frequently and naturally arise that love itself springs up between members of the Order, for that they have so many and

---

[1156] *Clarkstown Country Club,* (New York: Sales Promotion & Advertising Service, 1935) 6, 14.
[1157] Charles Boswell, "The Great Fuss and Fume over the Omnipotent OOM," *True,* Jan.1965: 88.
[1158] Boswell 32.
[1159] Photocopied documentation gathered from the archives of Nyack College is in the author's possession.
[1160] Miller 693.

so sacred interests in common. Such love is peculiarly holy, and is to be encouraged.[1161]

According to the O.T.O. Manifesto, the O.T.O. also provides "safe houses" for its criminal element:

> *Any injury done by any person without the Order to any person within it may be brought before the Grand Tribunal, which will, if it deem right and fit, use all its power to redress or to avenge it.*
>
> *Public enemies of the country of any Brother shall be treated as such while in the field, and slain or captured as the officer of the Brother may command.*
>
> *The perfect freedom and security afforded by the Law ["Do what thou wilt shall be the whole of the Law"] allows the characters of all Brethren to expand to the very limits of their nature.*
>
> *The secrecy of the Order provides its members with an inviolable shroud of concealment.*
>
> *They obtain the right to sojourn in the secret houses of the O.T.O., permanently or for a greater or lesser period of the year according to their rank in the Order...[1162]*
>
> *The O.T.O. did not go into decline after Aleister Crowley's death in 1947. Maury Terry has discovered its network thriving stronger than ever in America, and connects it to the recent surge of Satanic ritual murders. Included in this network are the drug counterculture operatives, motor cycle gangs, common criminals and rock groups.*

In *Occult Theocrasy*, Miller explains that music is an essential tool in this conspiracy, because it renders an otherwise positive mind passive and negative. Miller states that occult music tends to induce confusion. Lyrics in rock music are prime examples. Minds that are confused will obey and bow to the hidden masters! A person who does not listen to this music, replacing it with uplifting activity, remains positive. A positive mind cannot be controlled.[1163]

You may recall that this brainwashing technique was first practiced by French Freemasonry prior to, and during, the French Revolution. Mozart's music, Mesmer's animal magnetism, and Cagliostro's drugs and witchcraft, are all examples of how the O.T.O. operates today.

THE O.T.O. AND THE CHURCH OF SCIENTOLOGY

After Crowley's death, Freemason L. Ron Hubbard acquired the O.T.O. leadership in America. Robert Anton Wilson, co-author with Timothy Leary of *Neuropolitics* in 1977, explains that "Hubbard's system is derived largely from Aleister Crowley... Hubbard was a member of Crowley's Ordo Templi Orientis in the 1940s; and Hubbard later... invented a system which seems, to those of us who know both, *very* similar to the system taught by Crowley in the O.T.O."[1164]

[1161] Miller 689.

[1162] Miller 679, 680, 682, 683, 691, 692, 695, 698.

[1163] Miller 580-581.

[1164] Robert Anton Wilson, letter, *Conspiracy Digest* 3.1 (1978): 8.

Hubbard was initiated into the O.T.O. in 1944 by Aleister Crowley himself. After Crowley's death, the O.T.O. was headquartered for a time in Hubbard's Church of Scientology. In 1992 *The Auditor,* the journal of Scientology, reports that there are 146 Scientology centers worldwide, with 54 of them in the United States and Canada alone.[1165] Ti*me Magazine,* May 6, 1991, reports "700 centers in 65 countries..."[1166]

This greater number includes Scientology affiliates, many of which are front organizations. *Time* lists them, along with their frightening implications. Sterling Management Systems (SMS), formed in 1983, recruits dentists, chiropractors, podiatrists and veterinarians, guaranteeing them increased income if they attend seminars and take courses that typically cost $10,000. SMS's true aim is to hook these professionals for Scientology, who in turn will recruit their patients. Another such group, Citizens Commission on Human Rights, is at war with psychiatry, its primary competitor. The Commission typically issues reports aimed at discrediting particular psychiatrists and the field in general. HealthMed, a chain of clinics run by Scientologists, promotes a grueling and excessive system of saunas, exercise and vitamins designed by Hubbard to purify the body. It solicits unions and public agencies for contracts. **Narconon** is a chain of 33 alcohol and drug rehabilitation centers in twelve countries. Some of these centers operate in prisons under the name "Criminon." Both are classic vehicles for drawing addicts and cons into the cult. Concerned Businessmen's Association of America holds anti-drug contests and awards $5,000 grants to schools as a way to recruit students and curry favor with education officials. Way to Happiness Foundation has distributed more than 3.5 million copies of Hubbard's booklet on morality to children in thousands of the nation's public schools. Applied Scholastics is attempting to install a Hubbard tutorial program in public schools. The group also plans a 1,000- acre campus, where it will train educators to teach various Hubbard methods.[1167]

The title Church of Scientology is a deception. It is neither Christian nor scientific. Speaking to Hubbard's theology, *Time* says, "In the 1960s the guru decreed that humans are made of clusters of spirits [thetans] who were banished to earth some 75 million years ago by a cruel galactic ruler named Xenu."[1168]

In 1967 the Internal Revenue Service stripped the Church of Scientology of its tax-exempt status. The Masonic-dominated American Civil Liberties Union and the Masonic-created National Council of Churches supported Scientology's position that it is being "persecuted" by anti- religionists. *Time* countered by confirming that Scientologist defectors and critics are themselves continually persecuted by this so-called church. For example, L. Ron Hubbard taught his hierarchy how to use the law against its enemies. The law can be used very easily to harass," he said, "and enough harassment on somebody who is simply on the thin edge anyway... will generally be sufficient to cause his professional decrease. If possible, of course, ruin him utterly."[1169] Another time Hubbard warned his followers in writing to "beware of attorneys who tell you not to sue... the purpose of the suit is to harass and discourage rather than to win."[1170] The legal goal of Scientology is to bankrupt the opposition or bury it under paper.

Time says that defectors and critics find themselves "engulfed in litigation, stalked by private eyes, framed for fictional crimes, beaten up or threatened with death." *Time* reports for example, that two defectors, one a common criminal, the other his hypnotist,

---

[1165] L. Ron Hubbard, *Dianetics* (Los Angeles: Bridge Publications,1950) inside back cover, and "Your Scientology Organizations Across the World," *The Auditor* 1992, back page.
[1166] Richard Behar, "The Thriving Cult of Greed and Power," *Time* (6 May 1991): 50.
[1167] Behar 52-55.
[1168] Behar 51.
[1169] Behar 53.
[1170] Behar 56.

were ordered killed by the Church. Oddly enough, the common criminal was to pull the trigger. He was ordered to kill the hypnotist, then do an "EOC," (end of cycle), which is church jargon for suicide.[1171]

SCIENTOLOGY RECRUITS FOR THE O.T.O.

In 1967, the O.T.O. in England founded the Process Church of the Final Judgement soon after the rise of The Beatles rock group. In the late sixties and early seventies, the Process set up cells in a number of U.S. cities. Maury Terry says that the Process Church took over the O.T.O. in the United States. The Church of Scientology reverted to the position of Blavatsky's Theosophical Society a century earlier - that of a recruiting agency for the O.T.O. Terry said of Michael Carr, who, before his violent death was one of the leaders in the Process Church and a ranking Scientologist:

> *If he's counselling lost souls for Scientology, allegedly helping them discover themselves, he could certainly be working both sides of the street and plucking a few out for recruitment in the Satan stuff. That Scientology movement is fertile ground for latching onto confused people. He'd have his pick of candidates.*[1172]

THE O.T.O. AND PSYCHOLOGICAL WARFARE

The counterculture, which today has permeated our whole society, provided and still provides recruits to the Church of Scientology which spots and selects the confused and drug addicted candidates for the homicidal O.T.O.-Process Church. One such candidate was found in Charlie Manson, who was first recruited by Scientology before he joined the Process Church. At that time the Process Church in America was led by Robert Moore (alias Robert DeGrimston), who, like Manson, was first a Scientologist. Process members worship both Satan and Christ, as did the Priory of Sion and the Templars in medieval days.[1173]

Charlie Manson taught his "family" that he was Jesus Christ returned to bring judgement on America through a race war. "Helter Skelter" was his plan. He believed his instructions were concealed in the lyrics of songs sung by The Beatles.[1174] What Manson taught his "family" about hidden messages in rock music may well be true. Aleister Crowley himself taught such a technique to his initiates - that of writing messages backwards as a means of secret communication.

William Sutton, in *The New Age Movement and The Illuminati 666.* states that Manson was also a Freemason. In support of this he writes that "[d]uring the Tate-LaBianca trials - with Susan Atkins testifying to how good it felt when the knife went into Sharon Tate – Manson was flashing Masonic hand signals to the Judge."[1175] Sutton not only links Manson to Freemasonry, but to Scientology, the Process Church, the O.T.O. and the New Age Movement.[1176]

[1171] Behar 55.

[1172] Terry 245.

[1173] Vincent Bugliosi and Curt Gentry, *Helter Skelter* (1974; NewYork: Bantam Books, 1988) 300.

[1174] Bugliosi, entire.

[1175] William Josiah Sutton, *The New Age Movement and The Illuminati* 666 (USA: Institute of Religious Knowledge, 1983)133.

[1176] Sutton 105-146.

Likewise, Maury Terry documents that the Charlie Manson murders in California and the David Berkowitz - Son of Sam - murders in New York, were both ordered by the same organization, the O.T.O.- Process Church.[1177] One of Terry's first clues of this connection was the use of common terms by Berkowitz's "Sam" cult and the O.TO.-Process Church. For example, the term "German shepherds" was used by both as an allusion to their Nazi heritage. Both killers wore the same Nazi symbols - HT and HH for Hitler, the German SS lighting bolts for Satan and 666 for the mark of the beast. Both were white Aryan, anti. Christian, anti-black, and anti-Semitic.[1178]

Berkowitz, whose murders followed some six years after Manson's, often mentioned Manson in his notes. Berkowitz himself admitted to joining the Process Church in New York in 1975, just six years after Manson's arrest. Process members openly mingling with existing O.T.O. factions were seen in New York City as late as 1973. People such as Berkowitz, Man son and members of the Process Church, and its cells around the United States, make up the current O.T.O. network. All are sub-Masonic and linked as part of an underground web of murder. The "Sam" cult, according to Terry, is headquartered near Los Angeles and has branches in Bismarck, Minot, Houston and New York. These branches shuttle killers and "contracts" back and forth.[1179]

From evidence presented by both Terry and Sutton, there is sufficient documentation to convince the reader that the Ordo Templi Orientis was carried to the United States by English Freemason Aleister Crowley for the express purpose of preparing Christian America for destruction through mass and serial murder, drugs, licentious living, witchcraft, and the psychological terror and social chaos caused by the same. The O.T.O. continues its assault on our society to this day. The O.T.O. is English Freemasonry's psychological warfare unit targeted against Christian America.

O.T.O., MOTHER OF THE NEW AGE

The O.T.O. membership was so vast that the Order boasted having knowledge of all the secrets of occultism on both sides of the English Channel. Miller reports that after Karl Kellner founded the O.T.O., the organization produced a manifesto called *Manifesto of the 0.7:0.* Under the heading "Liber III" is proof that all Masonic and non-Masonic occult orders were under its direct control:

> Karl Keliner revived the exoteric[1180] organization of the O.T.O. and initiated the plan now happily complete of bringing all occult bodies again under one governance... The order is international, and has existing branches in every civilized country of the world.
>
> In its bosom repose the Great Mysteries; its brain has resolved all the problems of philosophy and life. Moreover, it possesses a Secret capable of realizing the world-old dream of the Brotherhood of Man.[1181]

[1177] Terry 181, 307.
[1178] Terry 343-344, 386.
[1179] Terry.
[1180] Miller uses the word "exoteric" to explain that Karl Kellner took this esoteric society out of obscurity from within the hierarchy in the Grand Orient, creating a separate Order that was publicly registered. Its rituals, however, remain esoteric.
[1181] Miller 679.

The "Secret" it possessed, and is now manifesting, is the program followed by the New Age Movement. From this point we are able to trace the present New Age Movement to Freemasonry.

FEMALE FREEMASONS AND THE NEW AGE MOVEMENT

All European Masonic Orders, including the French Grand Orient and many of the British Masonic sub-orders, permitted female membership. Two of the most renowned female Masons were Helena Petrovna Blavatsky and her protege' Annie Besant.[1182] Miller has stated that the names of women members of the O.T.O. are never divulged publicly. It is assumed, however, that Besant was an initiate, since she was frequently seen in the company of O.T.O. male membership. Miller did find mention of Blavatsky in *Freemasonry Universal*, Volume V, part 2, "Autumn Equinox," 1929, an O.T.O. publication which states:

"Madame Blavatsky's masonic [sic] certificate in the Ancient and Primitive Rite of Masonry was issued in the year 1877."[1183] This fact is also confirmed in *Mackey's Encyclopedia of Freemasonry.*[1184]

At the end of the nineteenth century, when English Freemasonry established front organizations to act as conduits of Masonic thought, Madame Blavatsky's Theosophical Society had already been flourishing since 1875. We have seen earlier how Blavatsky had come under the influence and teachings of Joseph Mazzini, who encouraged her to put her revolutionary beliefs into practice by fighting alongside Italian Freemason Garibaldi. Many Masons joined her society, including Albert Pike. The Society, however, was open to Lucifer worshiping non-Masons as well.[1185]

In 1887, one year after the Quatuor Coronati Research Lodge was founded, Blavatsky settled in London and started a Theosophical magazine called *Lucifer the Light-bringer*. While in London she also published two books - *Secret Doctrine* and *Isis Unveiled*. Annie Besant was presented to Madame Blavatsky in 1889 by the socialist, Freemason Herbert Burrows. Besant immediately succumbed to Blavatsky's irresistible magnetism and formidable power of suggestion. After Blavatsky died on May 8, 1891, members in the Theosophical Society battled over leadership for the next sixteen years. Finally, in 1907, at the behest of Freemason Sir Walter Besant, the Quatuor Coronati Lodge appointed his sister, Annie Besant, as President.

Miss Besant was affiliated with a number of sub-Masonic societies and fronts, such as the Fabian Society, the O.T.O. and Aleister Crowley's Masonic Stella Matutina. She had joined the Stella Matutina after it splintered from the Golden Dawn. The two orders were again united in 1912 under the original name Golden Dawn. At that time, Aleister Crowley was one of its leaders. That same year Crowley was initiated into the O.T.O. In 1913 a schism in Besant's Theosophical Society occurred, resulting in 33rd degree Freemason Rudolph Steiner founding the Anthroposophical Society, which also was Luciferian.[1186] Steiner's society became the first link between the Bolshevik Revolution and Freemasonry.[1187]

Besant's Masonic assignment in the Theosophical Society was to find a world leader. Not only was she to find him, but prepare him as the Christ Lord Maitreya - and then

---

[1182] Miller 723.
[1183] Miller 588, 457, 525, 532, 679.
[1184] "Blavatsky, Helena Petrovna," *Mackey's Encyclopedia,* vol.1.
[1185] Stoddard, *Light-bearers of Darkness* 26-29.
[1186] Miller 604-605.
[1187] Stoddard, *Light-bearers* 56, 60, 61.

announce his coming. Her first attempt in 1908 met with failure. Her second try was better known. On December28, 1911, a 16-year-old Hindu boy was allegedly found to be possessed by the spirit of Krishna and the Christ. In 1926 the Society presented him as Krishnamurti, the "World Teacher." Thirty-third degree Mason C.W. Leadbeater, a Masonic author at the turn of the century, was selected to train Krishnamurti as Messiah.[1188]

In the 1920s, when Annie Besant was introducing to the world the Christ Lord Maitreya in the body of Krishnamurti, there was heavy drug consumption in her tent meetings. The London *Patriot*, August 29, 1929, reported that "this drug, according to some occultists, [was] one of the most powerful in 'liberating the spirit from the body."[1189]

Besant's second attempt, however, also failed when in 1929 Krishnamurti became bored with the scheme and retired.[1190] By then Hitler's star was on the rise, and the New Agers were looking to him as their redeemer.[1191]

FUNDING THE NEW AGE MOVEMENT: THE LUCIS TRUST

Another follower of Madame Blavatsky and member of the Theosophical Society was Alice Bailey. Bailey, a self-proclaimed witch whose husband was a Freemason, founded in 1922 the Lucifer Publishing Company of New York, which name has since been changed to Lucis mist to disguise its real origins and identity. *(Lucis* is Latin for *Lucifer.)* Lucifer Publishing marketed Bailey's first book, *Initiation Humcm and Solar.[1192]* Later she published *Externalization of the Hierarchy*, in which she claimed the hierarchy in Freemasonry was responsible for the New Age Movement. She said the "work of destruction" [social destabilization] began in the year **1775**.[1193]

Bailey was probably referring to the Illuminati. Seventy years later Albert Pike revived the conspiracy in the Palladian. At the turn of the century the hierarchy became domiciled in the O.T.O. Today the hierarchy resides in Bailey's Lucis Trust. In 1982 Lucis Trust was headquartered at 866 United Nations Plaza, Suite 566/7, New York, NY 10017-1888. It has since moved to another location in New York. At its helm in 1982 was Freemason Robert S. McNamara, Secretary of Defense under Kennedy and past president of the World Bank. Today McNamara meets regularly with the World Federalist Movement to read Blavatsky and Besant. On a clear midnight he is noted for bathing in moonbeams.[1194]

A few other prominent members of Lucis Trust are David **Rockefeller,** major stockholder in Chase Manhattan Bank and Exxon; his brother John D. Rockefeller iv; an avowed Buddhist; Cyrus Vance, Secretary of State under Jimmy Carter; Rabbi Marc Tannebaum, head of the American Jewish Committee; the Marshall Field family: Anglican Bishop Paul Moore, founder of a school of witchcraft in the Anglican Church of St. John the Divine, New York; Walter Cronkite, retired news anchor of CBS News; Ted Turner, owner of Cable News Network, who promotes the Church of Scientology on his network; and Barbara Marx Hubbard, a prominent speaker for the New Age Movement and the once-considered-running-mate of Presidential candidate Walter

---

[1188] Miller 533, 548.

[1189] Stoddard, Light-bearers 49.

[1190] Stoddard 28-48.

[1191] Hitler's link to English Freemasonry's New Age will be documented in Chapters 22 and 23.

[1192] "Is Freemasonry Part Of The New Age Movement?" *Newswatch Magazine* 7.9 (June 1987) 7-8.

[1193] Newswatch.

[1194] "Satanic Worship Reaches New Heights," *World Intelligence Review* 77 (May 1989) 5, 17- 18 and Dr. John Coleman, *Witchcraft in Politics Today,* audio cassette, rec. Jan.1984, Christian Defense League, Box 449, Arabi, LA 70032.

Mondale. Last, but not least, is 33rd degree Freemason Henry Clausen, Past Supreme Grand Commander of the Supreme Council, Southern Jurisdiction of Scottish Rite Freemasonry.[1195]

The Lucis Trust also accepts corporate memberships. Among them are the following prestigious organizations: the Rockefeller Foundation, the Carnegie Endowment Fund, the United Nations Association, the Theosophical Order of Service, the Findhorn Foundation, Greenpeace USA, Greenpeace UK, Amnesty International, and the Southern Jurisdiction of Scottish Rite Freemasonry.[1196]

Under McNamara's administration, Lucis Trust paid for a full-page ad promoting the New Age in *Reader's Digest*, October 1982, page 203. In December 1991 *Reader's Digest* ran the ad again on page 201. Both ads are reproduced in Appendix 2, Fig. 11. Deceptively written to appeal to all religions, the ads contain the New Age prayer to bring in Lord Maitreya, the New Age Christ.

With such corporate and individual wealth at its disposal the New Age Movement can easily buy multi-million dollar advertising across the nation. The Lucis Trust has undoubtedly taken the place of Weishaupt's Illuminati, Pike's Palladian and Kellner's O.T.O. Its dominant position and purpose are identical to the previous three.

The Lucis Trust has sponsored many Masonic programs, such as the now defunct television talk show, "Faith Focus" of Dallas, Texas. During the period that Faith Focus was on the air (1982- 1985), advertising at program breaks was identical to the *Reader's Digest* ad - the prayer to bring in Lord Maitreya.

Host of "Faith Focus" was Freemason Rev. Walker Railey, a Methodist minister. In 1987 the city of Dallas was shocked when Railey was suspected of strangling his wife. Finally, in September 1992 he was arrested and is now awaiting trial.

In 1987, as Railey was preparing his alibi, he admitted in a recording of being attacked by demons, a not unusual occurrence with those who tamper with the occult.[1197] Alice Bailey would be proud of this "earth purifier."

In reference to the Lucis Trust, Bailey states in *Externalization of the Hierarchy*, that Freemasonry "will meet the need of those who can, and should wield power." She further informs us that Masonry is the "seat of initiation" and "under the All-Seeing Eye the work can go forward."[1198]

The various divines and gurus of the New Age continue to announce the arrival of the world teacher and proclaim the movement's Luciferian doctrines. Among them, Benjamin Creme, a New Age guru, writes in *Share International*, that "Freemasonry, as one of the Paths to Initiation, will be open to all those men and women who fit themselves for entry to the New Age." Creme is today the Masonic New Age Movement's torch-bearer for the emergence of "Maitreya the Christ"" Apparently the Movement has found another body for their "World Teacher" to possess.

Another New Age leader, David Spangler, is author of *Reflection on the Christ*. In this book he, too, proclaims the Masonic Luciferian Doctrine:

> *When man entered upon the pathway to self, he entered into a great creative adventure... of learning the meaning of divinity by accepting to himself the responsibility of a microcosmic world unto whom he is the god... The being that*

[1195] "Satanic Worship."

[1196] "Satanic Worship."

[1197] Associated Press, "Bruises found on Railey's son," *Longview Morning Journal* 13 March 1988: 6-A.

[1198] Newswatch 7-8.

helps man to reach this point is Lucifer... the angel of man's evolution... the spirit of light in the microcosmic world.[1199]

Spangler goes on to blasphemously state that "Christ is the same force as Lucifer." Finally he says:

Lucifer prepares man for the experience of Christhood... [he is] the great Initiator... Lucifer works within each of us to bring us to wholeness, and as we move into a New Age... each of us in some way is brought to that point which I term the Luciferic Initiation... that many people now, and in the days ahead, will be facing, for it is an initiation into the new age.[1200]

Finally, 33rd degree Mason Manly P. Hall, one of the first New Age speakers in America, has informed the occult world of the power of the Blue Lodge Mason. In *The Lost Keys of Freemasonry,* Manly wrote, "The seething energies of Lucifer are in his hands..."[1201]

Freemasonry's New Age fronts have expanded to such magnitude that there are now over 10,000 affiliates in the United States alone[1202], all controlled directly or indirectly by Freemasonry. As far back as 1930, Stoddard explained the Masonic purpose behind these New Age fronts:

Secretly here and there individuals are prepared; these again form groups or centres from which influences spread until they form a veritable magnetic network covering the entire world. Like rays from a hidden sun these groups are apparently divergent and detached, but in reality all issue from the same central body. Studying all these different groups and movements the system is seen to be an insidious and secret dissemination of ideas, orienting and creating the required outlook on life, etc., eventually breaking down all barriers of family, religion, morality, nationality, and all self-initiated thought, always under the cloak of a new and more modern religion, new thought, new morality, a new heaven and a new earth; until it evolves a gigantic robot merely answering to the will and commands of a secret Master Mind.[1203]

The secret "Master Mind" controlling Freemasonry today is, of course, Satan through the Lucis mist. In its hierarchy are members of the Supreme Council of the 33rd degree. Rev. Jim Shaw, a former 33rd degree Mason, tells how the Supreme Council controls this network of occult fronts: "Every thirty-third degree Supreme Council member carries a certificate allowing him presiding entry into all occult bodies in the world."[1204] These

---

[1199] Newswatch.

[1200] Newswatch.

[1201] Manley Hall 48.

[1202] Constance Cumbey, "Is the Antichrist in the world today?" interviewer Dr. Emil Gaverluk (Oklahoma City: Southwest Radio Church, 1982) 4.Constance Cumbey, author of *The Hidden Dangers of the Rainbow,* 1983, states that the New Age Movement "is a network of many, many organizations. I have one directory which lists fifteen hundred networks alone. I have another directory which lists 3,700 organizations. Another directory just shows incredible organization charts."

[1203] Stoddard, *Light-bearers* 105.

[1204] Jim Shaw, "The Degrees of the Adepts: Scottish Rite Series," audio cassette, Tape Ministry of Rev. Jim Shaw, Box 884, Silver Springs, Florida 32688.

high Masons are titled "Sovereign Grand Inspectors General." They quietly move in and out of thousands of front societies to "inspect" them, insuring that Masonry's goal of establishing a one-world government, ruled over by its own created false Christ, is on track.

Freemasonry had an Inspector General on hand during the United Nations' New Age University of Peace conference held on the Island of Malta, March 2-7, 1985. The theme of the conference was "Spirit of Peace." The Inspector General was 33rd degree Prince Bernhardt of the Netherlands, one of the most powerful Masons in the world. Bernhardt is known to conspiracy researchers as the founder of the Bildebergers, precursor of the Trilateral Commission.

Also present at this gathering was Marilyn Fergusson, author of The *Aquarian Conspiracy*. The fourteenth Dalai Lama of Tibet, "His Holiness" Tenzin Gyatso, was there. Coretta Scott King, wife of the late Martin Luther King and a leading proponent of world peace was registered as a guest. Robert Muller, assistant Secretary General of the U.N. and member of the Board of Planetary Citizens, was at the conference. It was Muller, in 1982, who said, "The Human person and planetary citizenship must be given absolute priority over national citizen ship." Freemason Desmond Tutu, Nobel Peace Prize winner in 1984, was also hobnobbing with the occult elite on Malta.[1205]

Tutu is the Anglican Bishop of South Africa. He was deliberately elevated to his position by the Anglican Church in London, so that he could be ready and in place to foment revolution while hiding behind his clerical robes. "This should not surprise our readers," writes the editor of *World Economic Review*, "since it is a well known fact that the Anglican Church leadership in England is riddled with 33rd degree Freemasons. Thus we can now tell you that it was NOT the people of the Anglican Church who gave Tutu his position, it was the Mason-riddled hierarchy inside the Anglican Church that did so."[1206]

A branch of the Anglican Church in America is the Episcopal Church. It too is controlled by English Freemasonry. The *World Economic Review* reports that Lucis Trust member, Bishop Paul Moore of the Episcopal Church of St. John The Divine in New York City, "runs several witchcraft schools on Long Island, the most notable being the Foxfire school. Moore is controlled by the ultra-secret Masonic Quatuor Coronati Lodge in London, which always has as a 'Member of Forty' the head of the Anglican Church."[1207]

THE GREAT "FALLING AWAY" IN AMERICA

How successful has Freemasonry been in furthering her New Age philosophy in the United States? The answer is given in the *Omega Letter* which calls the New Age Movement the fastest growing religious belief system in the United States today. The *Omega-Letter* quotes an article on a recent *American Health* magazine survey which revealed that 69 percent of Americans claim to believe some or all of the New Age Movement's central teachings.[1208]

Scripture of course prophesies this apostasy. The apostle Paul wrote in II Thessalonians 2:1 & 3: "Now we beseech you, brethren, by the coming of our Lord Jesus

---

[1205] "A Strong Delusion," *The Prophecy Newsletter* 1.5 (?):6-7.
[1206] John Coleman, "The Beast Marks South Africa," *World Economic Review* (July 1986): 7.
[1207] John Coleman, "Special Report from South Africa," *World Economy Review* 55 (July 1987): 17.
[1208] Peter Lalonde, "American Health Magazine: Metaphysics Belief on Rise," *The Omega- Letter* 1.12 (Dec.1986): 12.

Christ, and by our gathering together unto him *that day shall not come, except there come a falling away first..."*

The Greek word for "falling away" is *apostasia,* from where we receive our English word *apostasy. Strong's Concordance* defines it as a "defection from truth."[1209] Christ will not return until after there is a "defection from truth."

Christian brother in Freemasonry, you are in fellowship with an order that has caused the great "falling away." And according to Scripture, Jesus Christ will return soon afterward. Before His return He is calling you out of Freemasonry. Hear His voice in Revelation 18:4: "Come out of her, my people, that ye be not partakers of her sins, and that ye receive not of her plagues."

[1209] Strong, *Greek* #646.

17. THE FIRST MASONIC WORLD WAR

> *The present conflict [World War I] is the continuation of that which began in 1789, and one of these two principles [monarchism or republicanism] must triumph or die. The very life of the world is at stake. Can humanity live in freedom; is it worthy of it? Or is it fated to live in slavery? That is the vital question in the present catastrophe...* [1210]
>
> Grand Orient Supreme Council Paris, December 9, 1917

A SUSPECT SCHEME

Albert Pike wrote to Giuseppe Mazzini on August 15, 1871, calling for world war to force all governments to submit to a one-world Masonic Republic. Cataloged, and on display in the British Museum Library at London, the letter reads in part:

> *We shall unleash the Nihilists and the Atheists and we shall provoke a formidable social cataclysm which, in all its horror, will show clearly to the nations the effect of absolute atheism, the origin of savagery and of the most bloody turmoil. Then everywhere, the citizens, forced to defend themselves against the world minority of revolutionaries, will exterminate those destroyers of civilization, and the multitude disillusioned with Christianity... anxious for an ideal, but without knowledge where to render its adoration, will receive the pure light... of Lucifer, brought finally out into public view, a manifestation which will result from a general reactionary movement which will follow the destruction of Christianity and atheism, both conquered and exterminated at the same time.* [1211]

An appendage to this letter surfaced in the Museum in 1949, alleging how Pike intended to soften the world, not by one world war, but by three. According to this latter document, the first war would enable Communism to destroy Czarist Russia and establish militant atheism in its place. The second war called for the rise of Fascism to pit Great Britain against Germany, after which Communist Russia would be in a position to destroy other governments and their religions. The third war would begin by exacerbating the conflict between Judaism and the Moslem world. This would be the final world war, and it would bring complete social, political and economic chaos. From the ashes would arise a universal Masonic dictatorship.

According to Salem Kirban, in *Satan's Angels Exposed,* Pike's three- world-war blueprint has mysteriously vanished from display in the British Museum, while his letter remains cataloged. Kirban says: "It is quite possible that these Illuminati schemes for three World Wars are more recent inventions, post-dated to give authenticity to those who seek to blame the sin and suffering of today's world on some secret few."[1212]

Kirban's analysis is most likely correct, given the fact that two bits of information found in the appendage could not have been foreseen by Pike in 1871. First, Pike's alleged

---

[1210] de Poncins, *Freemasonry and the Vatican* 55.

[1211] Myron Fagan, *The illuminati,* audio cassette, rec. 1967 (transcribed from two audio cassettes by Sons of Liberty, 1985) 8.

[1212] Salem Kirban, *Satan's Angels Exposed* (Rossville, GA: Grapevine Book Distributors, 1980) 161-164.

plan called for the exploitation of Fascism, a term not coined until 1921. Second, Pike mentioned capitalizing on the conflict between Jews and Arabs, a controversy that was nonexistent in his day. Not until after the Balfour Declaration of 1917, a Declaration guaranteeing the Jews a British mandated homeland in Palestine, did this modern conflict arise.

Many revisionist historians, not understanding the conflict between the two Masonic powers, have viewed the three-world-war theory as a single conspiracy. They argue that Pike and his successors have masterminded the events which led to two world wars, and that this coterie will see their program through to the third. It is true, as we shall see, that French and English Freemasonry (in that order) did cause two world wars, but the argument that these events were planned in 1871 is incredible. As Salem Kirban suggests, these "schemes for 3 World Wars are more recent inventions, post-dated to give authenticity.

Hence, the alleged 1871 appendage to Pike's letter is suspect, especially since it was placed in the British Museum in 1949, after two world wars had already been fought. A post-World War II forger of a so- called preplanned three-world-war conspiracy could certainly profit from this Arab-Israeli conflict, a conflict nonexistent in Pike's day. And at that late date, the cause of a third world war was easy to predict by anyone who had knowledge of the Biblical Armageddon, which, according to Revelation 16:16-21, will, in fact, be the final battle - an enormous slaughter in the land of Palestine involving every nation in the world.

Pike's letter, however, is not in question. Using terminology of his day Pike did, in fact, forecast one world war, if not a lesser conflict, such as the Bolshevik Revolution.

Contemplating a world war would not be beneath Pike, given his bloodthirsty nature, such as when he encouraged Indians under his command to scalp live Union soldiers during our Civil War. Nor would world war be beneath his Grand Orient comrade, Joseph Mazzini, who founded the Mafia. Both were Scottish Rite Templars. Templarism was born in blood, having proven its barbarous nature during the French Revolution.

Pike arid Mazzini had both reasoned that world war was necessary to overcome the tedious nation-by-nation process of revolution, a process becoming progressively difficult. Ever since the near catastrophe caused by the Napoleonic Wars, European monarchs had become aggressive in their military preparedness. Hence, a global conflict was necessary to break their might. Not only would such a war wear out their military machine, but Masonic intrigue could go unchallenged at home, since armies would be preoccupied outside their borders.

Conspiring with Pike and Mazzini was 33rd degree German Grand Orient Mason, Otto von Bismarck. (Palmerston, a co-conspirator, had died in 1865.) Their scheme was to entangle Europe in a web of "peace treaties," which in reality pitted monarchies against republics. A simple, yet strategically located crisis would activate the treaties resulting in global conflict.

RECASTING A PLOT

Following the Congress of Vienna in 1815, Austria became the most powerful nation on the Continent. Although Vienna was the headquarters of English Freemasonry in Europe, the British Brotherhood had little or no say in the government of Austria. More significant to London was the alliance between Austria and Russia which threatened British interests. Russia envied Great Britain's rich opium production in colonial India. Alliance with Austria gave the Russian Bear a military advantage. English concern turned to animosity, then to fear by the mid-19th century.[1213] Lord Palmerston, Grand Master of the British Brotherhood, was assigned the task of driving a wedge between the alliance. Dillon briefly describes Palmerston's plan:

> The plan of Palmerston - or the plan of the deadly [Supreme] Council which plotted under him - was to separate the two great conservative empires of Russia and Austria, while, at the same time, dealing a deadly blow at both. It was easy for Palmerston to make England see the utility of weakening Russia, which threatened her Indian possessions.
>
> France could be made to join in the fray, by her ruler [Napoleon III], and the powerful Masonic influence at his command: Therefore, the Russian campaign of 1852 [Crimean War]... Palmerston succeeded with Austria, who withdrew from her alliance with Russia.[1214]

Palmerston's success precipitated some unforeseen events. With Austria weakened, Napoleon III was able to liberate Italy from the fragile occupation army of Austria. Withdrawal of Austrian troops in 1852 gave Mazzini the opportunity to move forward with his revolution.

Meanwhile, King Victor Emmanuel II of the House of Savoy, king of the northern Italian region of Sardinia-Piedmont from 1849 to 1861, made the momentous decision in 1852 to turn his government over to the able, determined Count Cavour. Cavour, a Grand Lodge Mason, was opposed to Mazzini's Grand Orient republicanism, yet was able to come to terms with Mazzini to unite Italy under a Savoy constitutional monarchy.[1215] Conforming to the agreement, Mazzini in 1860, instructed Scottish Rite Freemason General Garibaldi to move against Sicily and Naples to expel the Bourbons. Cavour made sure of Garibaldi's success with Piedmontese gold, which bought the chief functionaries of the King of Naples. Southern Italy soon fell to Garibaldi.

In 1861 Cavour died. Immediately Mazzini's rebels, financed by British intelligence through Palmerston's Masonic connections, forced the abdication of King Victor Emmanuel II from his throne in the northern Italian region of Sardinia-Piedmont. Mazzini then established the Republic of Italy at Piedmont.

To counter Mazzini, King Victor Emmanuel II set up the Kingdom of Italy in Turin on March 17, 1861, and began a campaign to recapture Rome, succeeding on September 20, 1870.

With Rome in Savoy hands, Mazzini's revolution crumbled. He began to think of world war. His co-conspirator and comrade-at-arms, Lord Palmerston, had passed away in 1865. Mazzini looked to Germany, where, in 1862, Freemason Otto von Bismarck (1815-1898) had become Prime Minister. In 1870 Bismarck was the hero of Europe, having defeated Napoleon in the Franco- German war. In 1871 he was appointed Imperial Chancellor of a united Germany, with the created tide of Prince. Mazzini, crazed and near death, contacted Pike to help plan a world war which would dethrone all European monarchs at once. Mazzini wanted Bismarck, who was a diplomatic genius, included in the plot.

[1213] Stoddard, *Trail of the Serpent* 140.
[1214] Dillon 84.
[1215] Miller 266, 272-274.

The Chancellor's task would be to divide Europe into two warring camps through a web of so- called "peace" treaties. In 1872 Mazzini died. Adriano Lemmi became head of the Italian Masonic-Mafia.[1216]

PEACEMAKER BISMARCK

Whether Freemasonry in general, or individual Masons in particular planned World War I, is of no consequence. What is clear is that Masonic leadership divided Europe into two warring camps, triggering World War I. Freemason Bismarck was most responsible.

According to Miller and Webster, Bismarck was in constant communication with Mazzini and Lemmi. As Luciferians, all three hated the atheism of the lower degree initiates in the Templar Grand Orient, but continued the conspiracy in these Lodges in their respective countries to their own ends.[1217] Including Pike and Palmerston, who were Scottish Rite Masons, all five men were in the Templar camp.

Nesta Webster states that Bismarck surrounded himself with Freemasons and members of other secret societies, who assisted him in his task as "peacemaker."[1218] Following the death of Palmerston, the new Prime Minister, Freemason Benjamin Disraeli, brought the British House of Rothschild (whose male members were all in the hierarchy of English Freemasonry) into the plot. This move has caused some revisionist historians to erroneously implicate the Rothschilds as the real power behind the scheme.[1219] A different story, however, is told by Dr. Carroll Quigley, an historian who favored the Masonic conspiracy.

Dr. Quigley (1911-1977) was former Professor of History at the Foreign Service School at Georgetown University.[1220] For twenty years Quigley had researched a portion of the Masonic conspiracy housed within the Council on Foreign Relations (CFR), claiming he was "permitted for two years, in the early 1960s, to examine its papers and secret records."[1221] Quigley compiled his discoveries in a tedious 1,348 page book, *Tragedy and Hope*, which was suppressed after its first printing.[1222] According to Cleon Skousen (sixteen years an FBI agent, and author of *The Naked Capitalist, a digest of Tragedy and Hope*), Dr. Quigley was in favor of the conspiracy. "All through his book," wrote Skousen, "Dr. Quigley assures us that we can trust these benevolent, well-meaning men who are secretly operating behind the scenes. THEY are the *hope* of the world. All who resist them represent *tragedy*. Hence, the title for his book."[1223]

Tragedy and Hope, subtitled *A History of THE WORLD in Our Time*, traces Bismarck's diplomacy from 1871 to 1890, which ended in a treaty called The Triple Alliance. The signatories of the treaty were Germany, Austria, and Italy, collectively

[1216] Dillon 83-85.

[1217] Miller 242, 249-250, 275-276, 723.

[1218] Webster, *Secret Societies* 356.

[1219] Former Russian Commissar, *Trotsky and the Jews behind the Russian Revolution* (1937; Metairie, LA: Sons of Liberty, 1980) 31.

[1220] Dr. Carroll Quigley had studied political science at Harvard,persisted in the private study of modern psychological theory for more than thirty years, was a member of the American Anthropological Association, the American Economic Association, and the American Association for the Advancement of Science, as well as the American Historical Association.

[1221] Carroll Quigley, *Tragedy and Hope* (1966; Los Angeles: Angriff Press, 1974) 950.

[1222] On March 3, 1975, the *Washington Post* ran a story about Quigley entitled "The Professor Who Knew Too Much." When he died, January 6, 1977, a lonely and melancholy man, the *Post* published his obituary.

[1223] Cleon W. Skousen, The Naked Capitalist: A review and commentary on Dr. Carroll Quigley's book TRAGEDY AND HOPE (Salt Lake City: privately printed, 1970) 5.

called the Central Powers. According to Quigley, Bismarck then went to work to construct an alliance of the opposing states. Before his death the stage was set for Great Britain, Russia, and France, collectively called the Allied Powers, to sign a treaty of alliance. In 1907 The Triple Entente was ratified and battle lines drawn.[1224] A manufactured crisis, strategically located, would trigger world war.

SOCIALISM, DEMOCRACY AND MONARCHY

Why should Sionist English Freemasonry, a Brotherhood formed to protect British and European nobility, permit Great Britain to wage war on its own Central Powers kings?

To answer this question, we must examine the complex decisions which faced the British Masonic aristocracy during the half century leading up to World War I. Historians have said the sole cause of the War was an economic battle between Great Britain and Germany. Stephen Knight, a British journalist, presents another viewpoint: "For a mass of reasons England was in turmoil, revolution seemed only a step away and the monarchy was already unpopular."[1225]

Queen Victoria, who reigned in England from 1837-1901, was not well-liked. In her earlier years she was hissed at by her subjects, and seven attempts were made on her life. In Ireland uprisings accompanied demands for Home Rule. Catholicism was making strong inroads in society, and socialistic republicanism was knocking at her door. Victoria had political problems.

In addition, her heir apparent, Albert Edward, Prince of Wales, whom she nicknamed Bertie, was despised for his odious reputation. Every intelligent person in the land, yea, in the entire world knew of his debauchery.

It was customary for the Prince of Wales to join English Freemasonry. On April 28, 1875, Albert Edward (Bertie) was installed as Grand Master. He did not, however, uphold the royal virtues demanded of him by society, and this reflected negatively on Freemasonry. He was an embarrassment both to the Brotherhood and the Crown. His sole purpose in life appeared to be pleasure seeking. In *Clarence, a* biography of Eddy (Bertie's son), Michael Harrison writes of Bertie:

> It was the indiscreet practice of the Prince of Wales to pay social calls on young married women, and to spend considerable time with them alone, after the footman had been instructed not to disturb the tête-à-tête. What made the indiscretion even more noticeable was that His Royal Highness neglected to cultivate the acquaintance of the ladies' husbands - or even to express a wish to meet them.[1226]

Not only was Bertie a disgrace to Queen Victoria and a burden to her authority, but the political pressures during her reign were even more immense. The Templar Grand Orient had penetrated British society with socialist and communist doctrines. The infiltration began in 1849 when Grand Orient Freemason Karl Marx settled in London, living and writing there until his death in 1883. Thereafter, his daughter Eleanor and Marx's mentor, Friedrich Engels, expanded and propagated his work. Consequently, during the latter thirty years of Victoria's reign, the tide of socialism began to spread across England.

[1224] Quigley 212-216.Italy broke with the Alliance and sided with the Allies in World War I.

[1225] Knight, *Jack the Ripper* 81-82.

[1226] Knight 88.

In 1885 socialism received a boost with the publication of the second volume of Marx's *Capital*. By 1886 ten percent of the working population in England was unemployed, and on February 8th of that year, after listening to inflammatory speeches from the socialists, angry crowds rioted, waving their communist red banners.[1227]

The press began to seriously discuss the possibility of a working-class uprising. On November 13, 1887, it happened and is known in history as Bloody Sunday. Nearly a hundred thousand unemployed converged on Trafalgar Square from all sides. Among them were Eleanor Marx and members of the socialist Fabian Society, including Freemason and Marxist George Bernard Shaw, the brilliant speaker and female Freemason Annie Besant, and the artist and poet William Morris, who had declared himself a socialist and a revolutionary. The unfortunate clash caused irreparable damage to relations between police and public, feeding the fires, not only of socialism, but of anarchy as well.[1228]

Prince Edward was not ignorant of the political upheaval in his country. He was aware that the greatest threat to the established order, and hence to English Freemasonry, was the working men. Yet, he constantly alienated the laborer by his anti-social behavior. Consequently, the perhaps normal resentment felt by his subjects turned into bitter hatred when Grand Orient Communists whipped up the sentiments of the working class.[1229]

Knight informs us of the stress the political resentments of the working class placed on English Freemasonry: "As the years passed and the political situation in England grew more dangerous to the established order, there is evidence to show that the Masonic brothers were becoming deeply concerned..."[1230]

To preserve their heritage, and to save their beloved Brotherhood from a coup by the working man's Grand Orient Lodges, aristocratic English Freemasonry made plans to re-exert control over the monarchy. In 1881 Prince Edward received an anonymous letter from the British Grand Lodge, chastising him for his debauchery, and warning him of the consequence to Great Britain should he not repent. Following is a portion of that lengthy letter:

> You have joined yourself to the Freemasons at the right moment, for true Freemasonry is about to be more powerful than Royalty... In England, even at this hour, we are - if the organs of blood and culture speak truly - very near forgetting the use of a Queen.[1231]

Knight continues, "The anonymous writers went on to draw the future king's attention to the Royal Families of Europe so recently overthrown, and to warn him against a similar fate. Throughout the letter, cloaked in the transparent guise of gushing *bonhomie*, one feeling comes through clearly: the Prince of Wales must cease his dissipated life or the throne will topple, *and that poses a threat to the Masons which cannot be countenanced"* [emphasis in the original].[1232]

Bertie did not heed the warning of his Masonic brothers. Hence, when he visited Cork with his wife Princess Alexandra in 1885, the crowd hissed and booed the royal couple, pelting them with onions. In 1888 the name of the Prince of Wales had become so reviled that even his own nephew, the German Kaiser, threatened to cancel a visit to Austria unless the Prince, who was staying in Vienna, departed first Then, in 1898, just three

---

[1227] Knight 83.
[1228] Knight 84.
[1229] Knight 164-165.
[1230] Knight 162.
[1231] Knight 165.
[1232] Knight.

years before he ascended the throne as King Edward VII, Bertie was hissed and mercilessly caricatured during a visit to Paris.[1233]

The working class, having no respect for the Throne, was poised to topple the existing order, and replace it with communism. English Freemasonry had no choice but to overrule the Monarchy. In doing so it appeased the working-class with socialism.

English Freemasonry had already accepted socialism as a corn promise at the 1889 Masonic Congress held at Paris and had since established socialist "think tanks" as political outlets for Masonic thought. The dual problem facing the aristocratic Brotherhood was how to control state socialism in a capitalistic society, and at the same time preserve the Protestant monarchy. The "think tanks" went into session and quickly proposed a simple solution to the first problem:

Freemasonry already controlled business and finance, which in a sense could be termed "corporate socialism"; state socialism could do business with corporate socialism, so long as the Brotherhood dominated politics, which it did.[1234]

The second task of preserving the Protestant monarchy was accomplished through a little Masonic arm-twisting. The Protector of the Throne forced the British Crown to submit to a socialistic democracy, but allowed it to maintain its position as royal figurehead. The Monarchy really had no choice.

Thereafter, Great Britain as a nation went the way of the Grand Orient socialistic democracies on the Continent, with one exception - English Masonic aristocrats, while remaining loyal to the Monarchy, controlled the new social politics. Hence, Great Britain was included in the Demo- cratic Allied Powers, and fought against the Monarchic Central Powers of Europe during World War I. As for the monarchy in Russia, also included in the Allied Powers, French Freemasonry had long ago been at work to republicanize that great nation, planning to topple its monarchy before the global conflict was scheduled to begin. (Chapter 19 discusses this Masonic intrigue.)

In this centuries-old struggle between the two Freemasonries, the British Brotherhood had long anticipated a global conflict, preparing itself for dominance in post-war commerce and finance. Win or lose, the Sionist Brotherhood certainly would include the aristocracy of Europe in its future plan. English royalty could only remain sympathetic toward her European cousins, consoling itself with the fact that neutral Switzerland was created for such a time as this. Meanwhile, the Central Powers must fight a war for survival against the Allied Powers.

THE TRIGGER FOR WORLD WAR I

With the Central Powers pitted against the Allied Powers by a network of treaties, Europe was poised for a crisis to trigger world war. Quigley lists eight crises, which occurred in rapid succession following the signing of The Triple Entente, any one of which could have done the job. They were:

1. 1908 - The Bosnian Crisis
2. 1911 - Agadir and the Second Moroccan Crisis
3. 1911 - The Tripolitan War
4. 1912 - The First Balkan War
5. 1913 - The Second Balkan War
6. 1913 - The Albanian Crisis
7. 1913 - The Liman von Sanders Affair

[1233] Knight, 86, 89.
[1234] Gary Allen and Larry Abraham, *None Dare Call It Conspiracy* (Rossmore, CA: Concord Press, 1971) 17-35.

8.   1914 - Sarajevo![1235]

Ample evidence exists to implicate Freemasonry in all the above. For brevity, however, we will deal only with the Masonic intrigues which led up to Sarajevo, for it was this crisis that historians claim triggered World War I. At Sarajevo, Archduke Ferdinand of the House of Habsburg, heir to the Austrian-Hungarian throne, was assassinated on June 28, 1914. Five weeks later World War I began.

THE LODGE AND FERDINAND'S ASSASSINATION

Conspiracy researchers have more than Albert Pike's letter to confirm that world war was Templar Freemasonry's plan, yea, even its expressed desire. The minutes of that famous 1889 International Masonic Congress at Paris record the words of Freemason A. Francolin, orator of the Grand Orient. De Poncins quotes him:

> The day will come when among the peoples who have not had an 18th century [political turmoil], nor a 1789 [French Revolution], monarchies and religions will collapse. That day is not far off, and we are expecting it... That day will bring about the masonic [sic] universal fraternity of peoples, the ideal which we set up for ourselves. It is our business to hasten its coming.[1236]

In September 1902, Brother J. Desmons, representing the Grand Orient of France, proclaimed at a Masonic Congress held in Geneva, Switzerland: "The dream of my life has always been that all democracies should meet and understand one another in such a way as one day soon to form the Universal Republic."[1237]

On September 15, 1912, two years before the Archduke's murder, the following words were spoken in Paris by a high Swiss Grand Orient Mason on the subject of the heir to the throne of Austria: "He is a remarkable man; it is a pity that he is condemned; he will die on the steps of the throne."[1238]

The plotting began sometime in 1910 in Swiss, French, Hungarian, Serbian and Italian Grand Orient Lodges. A traveling peddler, Karl Kothner of the Grand Lodge of Berlin, heard parts of the conspiracy in Lodges he frequented throughout Europe. Greatly disturbed, he returned to Berlin and delivered the information to Count Dohna Schlodien, his Grand Master. Kothner recorded in his diary the words he uttered to the Count on October 28, 1911 at 11:15 A.M.:

> Being, at first, frank and credulous I made some discoveries during the year in the lodges of other towns abroad, which disturbed me greatly. I came by chance upon proofs that Free- masonry was preparing something terrible against Germany. I overheard certain imprudent remarks which gave me a glimpse of a plan to assassinate the Archduke Franz-Ferdinand, of starting a world war to cause the fall of thrones and altars.[1239]

[1235] "World Wars (Sarajevo, the July crisis, and the outbreak of war)," *Encyclopaedia Britannica: Macropaedia.*

[1236] de Poncins, *Secret Powers* 93-94.

[1237] Stoddard, *Light-bearers of Darkness* 99.

[1238] de Poncins, *Secret Powers* 77.

[1239] de Poncins 84-85.

Count Schlodien, the Grand Master, seemed not to hear Kothner's words. Schlodien's thoughts pondered the accusation. Wanting to believe there was no division in the Brotherhood, he slowly replied, "There is only one Freemasonry."

In 1926 Kothner repeated his story, this time in a letter to the same Grand Lodge under the new Grand Master Dr. Mullendorf. Kothner stressed to Mullendorf that he had "made a communication to Count Dolina [Schlodien), which ought to have given him clear proof that the Freemasons of the Grand Hungarian lodge had exercised criminal activity against Germany and against all the peoples."[1240] Mullendorf tried by every means to force Kothner to retract the admission of this conversation, but failed.

FRANZ FERDINAND'S "CRIME"

What did Franz Ferdinand do to prompt Freemasonry to select him for assassination? De Poncins supplies the answer: "Freemasonry urged the assassination of Franz Ferdinand not because he was an Austrian-German, but because he was an obstacle to the international revolutionary aim of Freemasonry."[1241]

The obstacle Ferdinand presented to Continental Freemasonry was three-fold. First, as a Merovingian, he was destined to be the future Priory of Sion "King of Jerusalem." Second, he was a practicing Catholic. Third, he had committed a crime in the eyes of Masonry, a crime punishable only by death. (Neal Wilgus, in *The Illuminoids*, informs us that the assassination of Archduke Francis Ferdinand of Austria was by Masonic agents.)[1242]

What was Ferdinand's terrible crime? The Scottish Rite *New Age* magazine, September 1952, these many years later, revealed that information in an editorial from which we quote:

> [*The First World] War was precipitated by a "secret treaty" between the Vatican and Serbia, which would have annexed Serbia to the Vatican State and imposed canon law on that non- Catholic country. When the treaty became known, Archduke Franz Ferdinand, "Roman Catholic heir to the Austro-Hungarian throne, known to be a secret party to the policy embodied in the treaty," was assassinated by Gavrilo Princep.[1243]*

Archduke Ferdinand had committed - to the Masons - the unpardonable sin of turning a non- Catholic country into a Catholic domain. Not mentioned in the *New Age* editorial is that the eight plotters involved in the assassination were Masons, members of the "Black Hand" Masonic Lodge, also known as the "Union of Death Brother-hood." The Black Hand was the Serbian counterpart of the Masonic Mafia in Italy.

The *Encyclopaedia Britannica* confirms the nefarious means and ends of the Black Hand. It "used terroristic methods to liberate Serbs subjected to Habsburg or Ottoman rule and was instrumental in planning the assassination of Archduke Francis Ferdinand... The society was formed [1911] and led by Col. Dragutin Dimitrijevic [chief of intelligence for the Serbian general staff]; its membership was primarily made up of army

---

[1240] de Poncins 85.
[1241] de Poncins.
[1242] Wilgus 197.
[1243] Fisher 217.

officers with some government officials... Within Serbia it dominated the army and wielded tremendous influence over the government."[1244]

The Black Hand was the terrorist arm of a more powerful Masonic Lodge, Narodna Odbrana, founded earlier in 1911 by Freemason Dr. Karl Kramarsch, organizer of the Pan Slavic movement. This lodge claimed to be a patriotic Serbian organization pledged to free Serbia from Austrian influence and to achieve specifically the independence of Bosnia and Herzegovina. The Narodna Odbrana had set up a group of physical culture clubs as fronts for its wider activities.[1245]

The aim of Narodna Odbrana was to unite all the Slav southern states into one federation, which could only be achieved through the death of Archduke Ferdinand. Assigned the task to mastermind the Arch-duke's assassination was Freemason Radoslav Kazimirovitch (or Casimirovic). Kazimirovitch had travelled abroad extensively, visiting several Continental Lodges and returning with a cache of revolvers and bombs.

The actual murderer of the Archduke was Gavrilo Princep, who received his arms through Freemason Major Tankosich (or Tankosic). Documents concerning the assassination plot were discovered in a diary in the town of Locznka, a diary belonging to Serbian Freemason Major Todorovitch. The Major's diary was made available to the military court that tried the assassins in the fall of 1914.[1246]

In June 1917 the German *Badische Observer* exposed an even larger conspiracy that supported both the Narodna Odbrana and the Black Hand assassins. The *Observer* accused International Scottish Rite Freemasonry, the same international branch founded by Pike and Mazzini, of printing propaganda against Germany and Austria, propaganda that triggered the Masonic uprisings in Serbia.[1247]

The primary leader of the Serbian uprising was Black Hand founder Col. Dimitrijevic. Dimitrijevic was code-named Apis. He was the political opponent of the Serbian premier Nikola Pasic. Pasic, not known to be a member of the Black Hand, was, nonetheless, influenced by the Russian Grand Orient Mason Mikhail Bakunin, a self-proclaimed Satanist. When the Premier heard a rumor that Apis had plotted Ferdinand's assassination, he saw his chance of ridding himself of his political rival. Pasic warned the Austrian government of the plot, but his message was too cautiously worded to be understood.[1248]

Subsequent events, however, suggest it was understood, but ignored. Count de Poncins quotes a personal report from Count Czernin in his book *Im Welt-Knege (In the World War)* that the Archduke was well aware of the Freemason plot against his life:

> The Archduke knew quite well that the risk of an attempt on his life was imminent. A year before the war, he informed me that the Freemasons had resolved his death. He also told me the town where that decision was said to have been taken, and mentioned the names of several Hungarian and Austrian politicians who probably knew something about it.[1249]

SARAJEVO: JUNE 28, 1914

[1244] "Black Hand," Encyclopaedia Britannica: Micropaedia and "Balkans, History of the; (Ill. The Balkans after 1914)" Encyclopaedia Britannica: Macropaedia.

[1245] Miller 601.

[1246] Miller 601-602.

[1247] Miller 602.

[1248] "World Wars (Sarajevo, the July crisis, and the outbreak of war)," *Encyclopaedia Britannica: Macropaedia.*

[1249] de Poncins, *Secret Powers* 86.

On June 28, 1914, Archduke Franz Ferdinand and his pregnant wife, Archduchess Sophie, were coming to Sarajevo for an official tour. The royal couple were riding in the back of a black 1910 Graef und Stift limousine, which had been borrowed for the occasion. The rear half of the roof was folded back exposing the couple. Sophie was wearing a huge hat. The Archduke wore a blue tunic and plumed hat.

An eye-witness to the assassination was Helena Navratilova, a 21-year-old seamstress, who had prepared for the high-spirited holiday from dressmaking chores. As she wandered through the crowds to catch a glimpse of the royal couple, she stopped near the end of the Cumurja Bridge. Next to her was a young man she later learned was of Jewish ancestry, a Serbian nationalist named Gavrilo Princip.

"The car was going this way, coming across the bridge," Helena said. "They had to stop because they were going to turn around. Someone in the crowd almost broke my nose throwing flowers at the royal couple."

When the car slowed down at the end of the bridge (now known as Gavrilo Princip Bridge in honor of the assassin), Helena said, "Suddenly the young man next to me jumped up and started shooting. At first people just stared... It only took a few seconds... He ran away."[1250]

Neither the Archduke nor his wife moved, but an instant after the attack, the Archduchess collapsed quietly on her husband's shoulder. Count Harrach heard the latter say softly: "Sophie, Sophie, do not die. Live for the sake of our children." Franz remained quietly seated supporting the Archduchess. A trickle of blood appeared on his lips. To Count Harrach's questioning Franz repeated several times in a weakening voice, "It is nothing, it is nothing." Then he lost consciousness. When the palace of the governor was reached, the two bodies were quickly carried to a bed on the first floor. The doctors in attendance could only declare that death had already taken place.[1251]

De Poncins provides more detail of the assassination. From his description of Count Harrach's action after the first attempt on the Archduke's life, it appears as if the Count knew from what direction the second attempt would be made:

> On the 28th June 1914 the Archduke, heir to the crown of the Austrian monarchy, and his wife succumbed to the bullets of Serbian freemasons [sic]... Distributed among the crowd were eight assassins armed with bombs and revolvers, of whom the most resolute were Cabrinovic, Princip, and Grabez.
>
> Opposite the Cumurja bridge Cabrinovic threw his bomb. It fell on the car and then rolled to the ground where it exploded, wounding several persons including the occupants of the car immediately following. The Archduke had his car stopped in order to inquire about the wounded, and then the programme arranged upon was continued. When the reception at the town hall was ended, Count Harrach placed himself for the return journey standing on the left hand step of the car, so as to protect their Highnesses from an attempt upon them from that side. But on this occasion it came from the right. At the corner of Francis-Joseph Street, the car stopped just in front of one of the assassins, Princip, who fired at close range several shots from an automatic.[1252]

[1250] Larry Gerber (AP), "Helena Navratilova: The assassination that triggered WWI," *Longview Daily News* 3 July 1984: 9B.

[1251] de Poncins, *Secret Powers* 79.

[1252] de Poncins 78.

On October 12, 1914, the assassins were tried, and Freemason Cabrinovic unconcernedly told the judges of the military court: "In Freemasonry it is allowed to kill."[1253] Excerpts from the Pharos Shorthand Transcript of their trial reads as follows:

> *The President - Did you believe that Slavs of southern Austria-Hungary would gain any advantage from your act?*
> *Princip - We were agreed upon the choice of means for helping the southern Slavs.*
> *The President - What were those means?*
> *Princip - Murder; the disappearance of all those who were opposed to the realization of Pan- Slavia and who are injust [sic] to the people.*

Certain passages of the interrogations during the trial confirm the influence and involvement of international Freemasonry in the plan to kill the Archduke Franz Ferdinand:

> *Cabrinovic - He [Casimirovic] is a Freemason, even in some degree one of their chiefs. He travelled abroad immediately [after the men had offered themselves to carry out the assassination]. He went to Russia, France and Buda-Pesth. Every time when I asked Ciganovic how far our projects had advanced, he replied that I should know when Casimirovic should return. About this time Ciganovic also told me that the Freemasons had already condemned to death the heir to the throne two years ago, but that they had not found men to carry out their judgment.*
> *Premusic - Have you read the books of Rosic?*
> *Cabrinovic - I have read his treatise on Freemasonry.*
> *Premusic - Were these books distributed in Belgrade?*
> *Cabrinovic - I set them in type as a printer.*
> *Premusic - Tell me, do you believe in God or anything?*
> *Cabrinovic - No.*
> *Premusic - Are you a Mason?*
> *Cabrinovic - Why do you ask me that? I cannot answer you on that subject.*
> *Premusic - Is Tankosic a Mason?*
> *Cabrinovic - Yes, and Ciganovic also.*
> *The President - From which it follows that you also are a Mason, for a Freemason never admits to anyone but another Mason that he belongs to that society.*
> *Cabrinovic - Please do not ask me about that subject for I shall not reply.*
> *The President - Tell me something more about the motives. Did you know before deciding to attempt the assassination that Tankosic and Ciganovic were Freemasons? Had the fact of you and they being Freemasons an influence on your resolve?*
> *Cabrinovic - Yes.*
> *The President - Did you receive from them the mission to carry out the assassination?*
> *Cabrinovic - I received from no one the mission to carry out the assassination. Freemasonry had to do with it because it strengthened me in my intention. In Freemasonry it is permitted to kill. Ciganovic told me that the Freemasons had condemned to death the Archduke Franz Ferdinand more than a year before.*
> *The President - Did he tell you that from the very beginning or only after you spoke to him of your wish to carry out the assassination?*

[1253] Miller 602.

Cabrinovic - We had already spoken about Freemasonry but he said nothing to me of the condemnation to death before we had quite decided to carry out the assassination.

The following passage is from the interrogation of Princip, who fired the fatal shots at the Archduke and who also confirms the origin of the assassination plot in the Lodge:

The President - Did you speak about Freemasonry with Ciganovic?
Princip (insolently) - Why ask me that?
The President - I ask because I must know. Did you speak to him about it or not?
Princip - Yes, Ciganovic told me that he was a Freemason.
The President - When did he tell you that?
Princip - He told me when I was asking about the means of carrying out the assassination. He added that he would speak with a certain person and that he would receive the necessary means. On another occasion, he told me that the heir to the throne had been condemned to death in a Masonic Lodge.
The President - And are you also a Freemason?
Princip - Why that question? I shall not reply. (After a short silence): No.
The President - Is Cabrinovic a Mason?
Princip - I do not know. Perhaps he is. He told me once that he was going to join a lodge.[1254]

De Poncins reports that "Twenty accused persons appeared on the 12th October 1914 before the military court at Sarajevo. All were Masons. Eight were directly concerned in the murder. The four most active participants were Princip, Cabrinovic, Grabez and hue. All were young men from 18 to 20 years old, mostly students."[1255]

Illic and two other accused were condemned to death and hanged on February 2, 1915. Princip, Cabrinovic and Grabez were sentenced to 20 years imprisonment, but all died in prison before World War I ended.

WORLD WAR I BEGINS

Five weeks following the assassination of Archduke Ferdinand, World War I began. The signatories of the two international treaties of alliance Freemasonry had spent 50 years constructing took action. On the night of August 3-4, 1914, German forces invaded Belgium. Great Britain, which had no concern with Serbia and no express obligation to fight either for Russia or for France, was committed to defend Belgium. On August 4 England declared war on Germany.

Austria-Hungary declared war on Russia on August 5; Serbia against Germany on August 6; Montenegro against Austria-Hungary on August 7 and against Germany on August 12; France and Great Britain against Austria-Hungary on August 10 and on August 12, respectively; Japan against Germany on August 23; Austria-Hungary against Japan on August 25 and against Belgium on August 28.

Italy had confirmed the Triple Alliance on December 7, 1912, but submitted formal arguments for disregarding it. Its reasons were twofold. First, Italy was not obliged to support its allies in a war of aggression. Second, the original treaty had stated expressly

---

[1254] de Poncins 80-84.
[1255] de Poncins 80.

that the alliance was not against England. Italy, having a constitutional monarchy, eventually sided with England.

On September 5, 1914, Russia, France, and Great Britain concluded the Treaty of London, each promising not to make a separate peace with the Central Powers. This alliance was called the Allied or Entente Powers or simply the Allies.[1256]

When World War I began, American Freemasonry immediately went into action. The May 1917 issue of *The Freemason*, a British Masonic monthly, confirmed American Masonic activity: "Already during the first weeks of the war a great masonic [sic] meeting held in the United States passed a resolution to give to Great Britain and her allies all possible support in the present war."[1257]

That support came by way of favorable propaganda created by journalists who were Masons and from 33rd degree Col. E.M. House, personal advisor to President Woodrow Wilson. While Wilson was crisscrossing the nation campaigning for re-election on the slogan, "He Kept Us Out of War!" Col. House was making behind-the-scenes agreements with England which committed America to entering the war.[1258]

The Freemason stated further: "Freemasonry comprises more than two millions members. Every American mason [sic] knows very well what that means for the safety and duration of the Republic. The world war is the struggle of democracy against autocracy, and the future of the world will be democratic, whether the German Kaiser knows it or not."[1259]

When President Woodrow Wilson (not a Mason, but favorable to the Craft)[1260], stood before Congress in 1917 and declared war on Germany, he solemnly announced that "the war was against the German government only and not against the German people."[1261]

At the International Congress of Freemasonry at Paris in April 1917, one of the subjects of deliberation was how to provoke Germans against the monarchy, since the basis of peace must be the deposition of William II of Germany and Charles I of Austria.[1262] It was determined that Masonic journalists should create propaganda against the monarchies in Germany and Austria to send to newspapers in their respective countries.[1263] Immediately following the Masonic congress, all major newspapers around the world parroted Masonic thought: "Peace cannot be concluded before William II and Charles I are deposed."[1264]

A communication from the Masonic Supreme Council at Paris dated December 9, 1917, and written by Freemason A. Lebey, was entitled *Dans l'atelier maconnique*. Lebey not surprisingly cast the struggle in predictable revolutionary terms: "The question is to know which is right, good faith or falsehood, good or evil, liberty or autocracy. The present struggle is the continuation of that which began in 1789; one of the two principles must triumph or perish. The very life of the world is at stake."[1265]

[1256] "World Wars (Sarajevo, the July crisis, and the outbreak of war)," *Encyclopaedia Britannica: Macropaedia*.

[1257] de Poncins, *Secret Powers* 87.

[1258] Allen 65."Colonel" House was the front man for the international banking fraternity. He manipulated President Woodrow Wilson like a puppet. Wilson called him "my alter ego." House played a major role in creating the Federal Reserve System, introducing the graduated income tax and getting America into World War I. House's influence over Wilson is an example that in the world of super-politics, the real rulers are not always the ones the public sees.

[1259] de Poncins, *Secret Powers* 87.

[1260] Haywood, "Wilson, Woodrow," *Mackey's Encyclopedia*.

[1261] de Poncins, *Secret Powers* 87.

[1262] de Poncins 87.

[1263] Miller 602.

[1264] de Poncins, *Secret Powers* 87.

[1265] de Poncins 88.

In an obvious attempt to direct his message to German Freemasons, Lebey scolded them for defending their motherland. He then offered them the following instruction: "Motherland, republic, the revolutionary spirit and socialism are indissolubly joined."[1266]

In response to overwhelming Masonic support of the Allies throughout the democratic nations, Freemasons in Germany began to prepare the defeat of their own nation. Freemason Vater, the German social democrat, spoke at Magdeburg during a meeting of a workman's and soldier's council in 1919, making clear the manner in which that preparation was effected:

> *Since 25th January 1918 we have methodically prepared the revolution. It was a difficult task and full of danger; we paid for it by many years of prison. The social democratic party had seen that great strikes do not lead to revolution and that it is necessary to use other means to that end. The labour has brought its fruit. We organized desertions at the front; we provided the deserters with false papers, money and propaganda leaflets inciting to desertion. We sent our agents in all directions, principally to the front, in order that they might work upon the soldiers and disintegrate the army. They advised soldiers to desert to the enemy and it is thus that the downfall was brought about, little by little, but with certainty.[1267]*

In summation, the true aim of the first Masonic world war was the overthrow of monarchies, the degradation of the Catholic powers, and the triumph of the world republic. President Coolidge publicly recognized this in a speech reported by Reuter-London on June 14, 1927:

> *"The chief question at stake in this formidable conflict [World War I] was to decide which form of government was to predominate among the great nations of the world: the autocratic form or the republican form. Victory remained finally on the side of the people."[1268]*

Continental Freemasonry was in total control of the events which led to World War I. As such it took advantage of the global conflict to cast down thrones. That which was attempted following the French Revolution of 1789 (i.e., the republicanizing of Europe by the Napoleonic Wars) was perfected by World War I. Following this conflict, Masonic republicanism, whether democratic, socialistic, or communistic, replaced what had previously been monarchies and kingdoms. Pike and Mazzini's plan was fulfilled.

[1266] de Poncins.

[1267] de Poncins 89.

[1268] de Poncins.

18. THE HUNGARIAN MASONIC REVOLUTION

> *All the revolutions which overthrew the monarchist regimes of Central Europe in 1918 were inspired and directed by Masons, and it was Masons who were given posts in the new governments of Hungary, Germany, Austria and Czecho Slovakia. Almost all these revolutions rapidly degenerated into bloody convulsions with distinctly Communist tendencies, under Bela Kun, Liebnecht, Rosa Luxembourg, Kurt Eisner and others.[1269]*
>
> Vicomte Leon de Poncins

The post-World War I Hungarian Revolution offers more evidence of Masonic involvement than do others. With its failure, the Hungarian government dissolved the lodges, confiscated their libraries and published their archives, exposing Freemasonry's flagrant involvement in the upheaval. Distressed, the Hungarian Masons called upon their brethren throughout the world to come to their aid.

Revolution first erupted in Hungary in 1848, the year Grand Orient Freemasonry had scheduled all Europe to revolt. Its leader was the great Magyar, Freemason Louis Kossuth (1802-1894). *Mackey's Encyclopedia of Freemasonry* gives a brief history of Kossuth's career:

> *Appointed, 1848, Minister of Finance and upon a dispute with Austria over the revolt of the Croats, he assumed charge and declared the independence of Hungary. After Gorgei's defeat at Villagos, 1849, he was forced to flee to Turkey. Imprisoned and later released, he then lived in England for several years, in constant touch with Mazzini, Italian Revolutionist. During this period he also visited the United States.[1270]*

The 1848 Hungarian Revolution was suppressed by Austria with aid from Russia. Kossuth, accompanied by Italian Freemason Adriano Lemmi, arrived in the United States in 1851 and settled in Cincinnati, Ohio. Lemmi returned to England that same year to assist Mazzini in his Italian Revolution. On February 28, 1852, Kossuth spoke to the Masonic Brethren at Center Lodge No.23, Indianapolis, Indiana:

> *The Masonic brotherhood is one which tends to better the condition of mankind, and we are delighted to know it enlists the attention of so many Brethren... as we find surrounding us here. Besides the great antiquity of the Order which should endear it to all good Masons, its excellent precepts and high moral teachings must induce all good members of the Order to appreciate its benevolent purposes and useful works. To one like myself, without a country or a home, dependent upon the hospitality of strangers for life and protection, a great substitute for all my privations is, I find, to be surrounded by Brethren of the Masonic Order.[1271]*

[1269] de Poncins, *Freemasonry and the Vatican* 156.
[1270] "Kossuth, Lajos or Louis," *Mackey's Encyclopedia*, vol.1.
[1271] "Kossuth."

On another occasion Brother Kossuth proclaimed his longing for a universal Masonic order: "If all men were Freemasons, oh, what a worldwide and glorious republic we should have."[1272]

Mackey's Encyclopedia of Freemasonry reports that Kossuth's revolutionary career ceased after the Hungarian Revolution: "After the Austro-Hungarian reconciliation, in 1867, under Emperor Francis Joseph, Kossuth ceased any further efforts politically and his death occurred at Turin [Italy] in 1894."[1273]

THE GRAND LODGE:
RECONCILIATION AND APPEASEMENT

Although the Hungarian revolt in 1848 against Habsburg rule failed, Austria compromised in 1867 and formed the Dual Monarchy that made Hungary internally autonomous. The reconciliation, designed to appease the Hungarian Grand Lodge Masons, was fought by the Grand Orient Masons, but to no avail. By the turn of the 20th century, Hungarian Freemasonry was once again at work undermining the existing order. This time, however, it was Grand Lodge Freemasonry, not Grand Orient. Observing London's move to preserve both the Crown and her aristocratic Brotherhood, the Hungarian Grand Lodge realized that if it did not propose and conform to a social democratic agenda, it would lose sway in the country to Grand Orient communism. In a report signed on February 24, 1911, by Paul Szende, the venerable Grand Master of the Rosicrucian Martinovics Masonic Lodge, we find passages such as the following:

> *We readily recognize that charity such as we now practise does not correspond with our ideas. We must concentrate our attention on the necessity of achieving radical changes in the actual society.*[1274]

The "radical changes" started with a concerted effort to gain control of the press. By the time World War I had begun, Grand Lodge Masons owned most of the nation's media and began to propagandize the military. The daily newspaper *Vilag* was specifically responsible for the weakening of discipline in the Hungarian army. Throughout the war copies were distributed by the thousands in the trenches.[1275]

The House of Habsburg realized it was being undermined by its own Grand Lodge Freemasonry. To ease the impending disaster of losing the war, the "King of Jerusalem" cult began making friendly gestures toward the Craft in preparation for the coming political change. Masons returned their good will on April 29, 1918, through their Grand Master, 33rd degree Dr. Arpad Bokay, who traveled to Vienna and delivered an extremely patriotic speech:

> *The enemies of Hungary are also the enemies of Austria; those who are in league to destroy Austria wish to do the same for Hungary; it is the monarchy which, in the tempest of the world war, has protected the peoples of Austria-Hungary in the most efficacious manner...*

[1272] "Kossuth."
[1273] "Kossuth."
[1274] de Poncins, *Secret Powers* 74.
[1275] de Poncins.

By October 1918 the Hungarian Grand Lodge, composed of radical bourgeoisie (the middle class) and members of the Social Democratic parties, were in league with the reigning monarch.[1276]

Together they formed a political coalition called the Hungarian National Council headed by Count Mihaly Karolyi, which unsuccessfully tried to establish a constitutional monarchy. The Council "advocated an end to the union between Austria and Hungary, peace with the Allies, the introduction of civil liberties and broad social and economic reforms, the formation of liberal political institutions [Masonic lodges], and concessions to the non-Magyar nationality groups of Hungary. The council gained widespread support, including that of the Budapest garrison, which forced King Charles IV [r.1916-1918] to appoint Karolyi prime minister [October 31, 1918]. The council became Karolyi's Cabinet."[1277]

Austrian Grand Lodge Freemasonry hailed ascension of the National Council to governmental power. On the first page of its monthly bulletin, which was then able to appear without hindrance, were these words of praise:

> The new state of things came as a surprise. All at once we had become free republicans, masters of ourselves. We were no longer the slaves and martyrs of a bureaucratic government that without critic or resistance served militarism and selfdomination.[1278]

The Grand Lodge Symbolique of Budapest unanimously decided to send to Count Karolyi and his Masonic dominated revolutionary National Council a message of goodwill: "Hungarian Freemasonry will support the new Government with all its power, since it finds the latter very favourable for the accomplishment of its aims."[1279]

On November 2, 1918, Grand Master Dr. Bokay made a significant speech describing the Masonic program desired for Hungary. Following are extracts from that speech:

> The masonic [sic] programme is also the programme of the national Hungarian council and of the popular government which has just been formed.
>
> Our way is thus made clear to us. We are marching shoulder to shoulder with them, we are working with them, we are helping them in their great and heavy, but also thankful task, so that ancient Hungary may with perturbation enter the beloved land of new Hungary which is the most ardent wish of every good patriot.
>
> Our beloved and highly esteemed brothers are working today [sic] in the first rank, and that entirely reassures us, for we know them and we know that they will carry out in a masonic [sic] spirit the work which they have undertaken.[1280]

On that same day the Grand Lodge Symbolique stated its feelings toward the new government: "The government which is in power now seeks the same ideals as ourselves. Many of our brothers are members of the Government, which is a guarantee for us that the Hungarian Revolution will follow the path of radical reforms. Our duty is to help it with all our means."[1281]

[1276] De Poncins, *Freemasonry and the Vatican* 156.
[1277] "Hungarian National Council," *Encyclopaedia Britannica:Micropaedia.*
[1278] De Poncins, *Secret Powers* 69.
[1279] De Poncins 75.
[1280] de Poncins 69.
[1281] de Poncins 75.

On November 13, 1918, King Charles declared he could no longer participate in the government. The National Council immediately proclaimed Hungary a republic, and on November 16, named Count Karolyi its provisional president. Karolyi in turn dissolved the union between their new state and Austria.[1282]

The new government planned to adopt extensive land reform measures and to convene a constituent assembly. The economy, however, was deteriorating, causing much unrest. The non- Magyar nationality groups (Serbs, Rumanians, and Czechs) occupying Hungarian territory refused to remain part of Hungary, wanting, instead, to remain autonomous.[1283]

THE GRAND ORIENT:
THE SOVIET REPUBLIC OF HUNGARY

Furthermore, the Allies were putting strong demands on Karolyi's socialist government - demands he could not resist. Pressure from the extreme left was equally severe. The Grand Orient Communists, rapidly gaining strength, considered the Grand Lodge socialists too bourgeois. The new government contained no members of the proletariat - the lowest social or economic class. The communists threatened a counterrevolution. Hungary, weary of war and bloodshed, wanted to avoid further bloodletting. Karolyi's cabinet resigned, transferring power to the Grand Orient. The Soviet Republic of Hungary was formed March 21, 1919.[1284]

Leading the communists was the bloodthirsty, 33rd degree Jewish Freemason Bela Kun (Cohen). Kun was Grand Master of the Grand Orient Lodge Haladas at Debreczin. Although political and economic conditions made his coup bloodless, it did not remain so. Grand Orient Freemasons began blaming the middle and upper classes for Hungary's problems, suggesting they be eliminated.

Assisting Kun were the following Grand Orient Masons: Comrade Kunzi, Minister of Public Instruction; Comrade Jaszi, National Minister of the Soviets; Comrade Ageston Peter, Comrade Lukazs, Comrade Diener Denes Zoltan; Comrade Alexander Garbai (Joseph Pogany), head of the army; Comrade Ronai, Minister of Justice; Comrade Varga Weichzelbaum for finance; Comrade Vince Weinstein as governor of the capital; Comrade Moritz Erdelyi and Comrade Sezso Biro, for the police; and the bloodthirsty Comrade Tibor Szamuelly, Prime Minister.[1285]

Szamuelly engineered the slaughter of the bourgeoisie while travelling about Hungary in his special train. An eyewitness (of which there were few) gives the following account:

> This train of death rumbled through the Hungarian night, and where it stopped, men hung from trees, and blood flowed in the streets. Along the railway line one often found naked and mutilated corpses. Szamuelly passed sentence of death in the train and those forced to enter it never related what they had seen. Szamuelly lived in it constantly, thirty Chinese terrorists [Triads] watched over his safety; special executioners accompanied him. The train was composed of two saloon cars, two first class cars reserved for the terrorists and two third class cars reserved for the victims. In the latter the executions took place. The floors were

---

[1282] "Hungarian National Council."

[1283] "Hungarian."

[1284] "Hungarian."

[1285] de Poncins, *Secret Powers* 122.

stained with blood. The corpses were thrown from the windows while Szamuelly sat at his dainty little writing table, in the saloon car upholstered in pink silk and ornamented with mirrors. A single gesture of his hand dealt out life or death.[1286]

Within weeks Bela Kun and his Masonic comrades had destroyed the old order. Hungarian refugees carried the news of the bloodshed to America, prompting an investigation. In 1920 a committee of the Legislature of New York, presided over by Senator Lusk, published a report on revolutionary activities in Hungary. Following is a portion:

> *There was no opposition organized against Bela Kun. Like Lenin he surrounded himself with commissaries having absolute authority. Of the 32 principal commissaries 25 were Jews, a proportion nearly similar to that in Russia. The most important of them formed a Directory of Five: Bela Kun (Kohn or Cohen), Bela Vaga (Weiss), Joseph Pogany (Schwartz), Sigismond Kunfi (Kunstatter), and another. Other chiefs were Alpari and Szamuelly who directed the Red Terror, as well as the executions and tortures of the bourgeoisie.[1287]*

The Grand Orient had so cunningly fronted the Jews that the atrocities of the Communist republic caused Hungary to become violently anti-Semitic, as well as anti-Masonic. Three months after forming the Soviet Republic of Hungary, Bela Kun and his comrades fled to Russia, where they continued their slaughter under Lenin and Trotsky. Hungary formed a constitutional monarchy under the regency of Admiral Horthy. Freemasonry was immediately outlawed, Grand Lodges and Grand Orients alike. Secret documents outlining Freemasonry's role in the Hungarian Revolution were seized and published throughout Hungary.[1288]

HUNGARY RESISTS MASONRY

Universal Freemasonry began to exert pressure on Hungary for having outlawed the Craft. Hungary was accused of making an undemocratic move against a benevolent democratic society. During the Peace Conference at Versailles in 1919, Freemason Berthelot, the French Minister, asked Count Apponyi, head of the Hungarian Peace Delegation, to reestablish Freemasonry. The same request came from British representatives at Vienna and Budapest. And the United States government refused a loan to Hungary because the lodges were not reopened.

In March1922, the Masonic newspaper Latomia of Leipzig, Germany, published lamentations over the suppression of benevolent Free-masonry, of which a portion follows:

> *We are able to give the following information concerning the sad fate of Freemasons in Hungary from information supplied by one of our Hungarian brothers resident in Nuremberg.*
>
> *After the catastrophe [World War I], the Freemasons, who had sent another address of welcome to the Emperor Franz Joseph during the war, fervently*

[1286] de Poncins.
[1287] de Poncins 124.
[1288] "Hungarian."

embraced the socialist republican ideology out of the noble conviction that the time had come when the Masonic ideal would be accomplished. In their writings they made active propaganda in its favour and most of the leaders were Freemasons.

But next, when Hungary was overwhelmed by a wave of Bolshevism, the men in power [the Grand Orient Communists] soon began to oppress [Grand Lodge] Masonry as a bourgeois institution.

The reaction which, thanks to foreign assistance, shortly afterwards set in and succeeded in regaining power, inspired by clerical leadership, closed the lodges, occupied their premises, seized their funds and anything else they found there...

In their distress, our Hungarian brothers turned to the North American Grand Lodges. The result was that, as Hungary was then negotiating a loan in America, the reply came back that this loan could not be considered until lawful institutions were reestablished in Hungary, a clear allusion to the prohibition of Freemasonry.

Thereupon the Hungarian government was obliged to open negotiations with the ex-Grand Master. The free resumption of Masonic work was proposed to him, on condition that non- Masons should have the right of access to the sessions. This was naturally refused by the Grand Master and the loan miscarried.[1289]

In September 1922, the Masonic monthly, *Maconnique de Vienne,* announced from Italy that Grand Master Torrigiani (later killed by Mussolini because he was a Mason) promised to intervene at the Geneva Conference. Through the governments of various Masonic powers, he would bring pressure to bear on the Hungarian government. France acted energetically in the same direction. The Hungarian government made it clear, however, that so long as Freemasons carried on their activities in secret, they could not be reestablished with their old privileges. It will remain to the honor of the Hungarian government that it did not yield, courageously facing all these difficulties.

Freemasonry never forgot the nation that so steadfastly rebuked its power. At the Yalta Conference in 1943, a conference negotiated by the world's three leading Masons (Roosevelt, Churchill, and Stalin), Hungary was handed over to the Soviet Union. After the Second World War, Stalin punished Hungary. In 1955-1956 the Hungarian revolt against her Soviet masters was brutally crushed.

Only recently has this nation won freedom, but not without meeting Masonic conditions. In 1984 an unknown Russian, Mikhail Gorbachev, travelled to London and Paris for a secret meeting with Otto von Habsburg, pretender to the Austrian throne. An agreement was made to release four East European nations to the West if the Pretender would help uncouple the United States from Europe.[1290] One year later Gorbachev came to power. In 1989 he made good his promise - handing to the West the nations of Poland, East Germany, Czechoslovakia, and Hungary. Before their release, however, Gorbachev called for Grand Orient Masonic Lodges to be reopened in Budapest. Moreover, he asked French Masonic leaders to assist in efforts to reactivate lodges in Czechoslovakia, East Germany, and Poland.[1291]

When Freemasonry is permitted free reign in a country, there is revolution - either gradually, as in the United States, or rapidly, as in Europe following World War I. The recent revolutionary changes in Poland, East Germany, Czechoslovakia, and Hungary are thus comprehensible. What is perplexing is the revolution in Russia during the latter half of 1991. December of that year the Soviet Union was dissolved. For the first time in

---

[1289] de Poncins, *Secret Powers* 157-158.

[1290] John Coleman, "Black Nobility Unmasked," audio cassette, 1984.

[1291] Texe Marrs, "Gorbachev and Masonry," *Flashpoint,* (September1990): 2.

revolutionary history, we have witnessed a peaceful and bloodless transition from communism to democracy. Have both Freemasonries come to an agreement that the world must be democratic? Or, has English Freemasonry engineered the greatest coup d'état of all time?

The world stands in awe, yet the righteous remain cautious.

19. THE RUSSIAN MASONIC REVOLUTION

The first Revolution in March 1917 is said to have been inspired and operated from [Masonic] Lodges and all the members of Kerenski's Government belonged to them.[1292]

MACKEY'S ENCYCLOPEDIA OF FREEMASONRY

The Romanov dynasty was powerful. Its religious and political traditions were so deeply rooted that both Freemasonries cooperated in the Russian Revolution. The czars were beyond the reach of parliamentary pressure. Russian high officials were independent, and so wealthy that Western capital had no influence on them. Russia was rich with forests, her topsoil fertile, the earth abundant with natural resources.

In an article for the *German Weltkampf*, July 1, 1924, Alfred Rosenberg, the man who brought the *Protocols* to Hitler, stated:

> *Russia possessed wheat in abundance and continually renewed her provision of gold from the mines of the Urals and Siberia. The metal supply of the state comprised four thousand million [four billion] marks without including the accumulated riches of the Imperial family, of the monasteries and of private properties. In spite of her relatively little developed industry, Russia was able to live self-supporting.[1293]*

Such independence posed an obstacle to fomenting a revolution in Russia. Decades, maybe a century, would be needed to weaken the control of the mighty czars. Once the populace, including the intellectual classes, had been propagandized, London penetrated the inner shrines of the Russian aristocracy, while Paris crippled the economy through worker strikes. World War I was the final blow that paralyzed the nation, making it easy prey for a complete revolution.

These facts caused de Poncins to say, "The Russian Revolution of 1917 was fomented at the height of the First World War with the help of international Freemasonry, and the principal leaders of the Kerensky regime were Masons: this movement quickly degenerated into Boishevism."[1294]

The Bolsheviks were backed by Grand Orient Freemasonry, which wanted Russia's wealth communized. English Freemasonry and her Sionist allies wanted revenge on Russia for torpedoing the Metternich Plan at the Congress of Vienna (1815), which "Plan" would have established a Monarchical Federation of Europe. Furthermore, the uncooperative Romanovs, who were not of Grail blood, posed a grievous threat to Sion's "King of Jerusalem" cult.

Grand Orient Freemason G. Vinatrel, in *Communism and French Masonry* (1961), gives another reason why both Freemasonries were able to cooperate in the Russian Revolution:

[1292] "Russia," *Mackey's Encyclopedia*, vol.11.
[1293] De Poncins, *Secret Powers* 139.
[1294] De Poncins, *Freemasonry and the Vatican* 156.

> *[Freemasonry's] diversity... is no obstacle to the profound unity of Masonic thought. All Freemasons throughout the world demand Tolerance for the ideas of others.*
>
> *All Freemasons adopt the celebrated motto which was bequeathed by the Grand Orient to the Great French Revolution:*
>
> *"Liberty, Fraternity, Equality." This slogan has raised up the peoples. In turn it was adopted by Latin America and then by revolutionary China. The Russian Revolution in February 1917 spoke the same Language.[1295]*
>
> *Masonic historian, Gaston Martin, summed up the situation in his Manual of History of the French Masons in France:*
>
> *All Freemasons of the three obediences [French, English, and American] which are on friendly relations with one another belong to what in politics is called "the Left." The shades of doctrine which divide them are not such as to hinder agreement among all their members.[1296]*

De Poncins confirms that the hierarchy in "Freemasonry prepared the ground for the coming and triumph of Communism, very often without the knowledge of its members, many of whom would probably have been terrified if they had seen clearly where the principles which they propagated with such ardour and unawareness were leading."[1297]

When the Masonic hierarchy agreed to cooperate in the Russian Revolution, the politico- economic system installed was to be socialism. Karl Marx had determined that communism was unworkable without the support of state socialism. And state socialism needed the deep pockets of corporate socialism to survive. English Freemasonry, which controlled state and corporate socialism at home, could easily cooperate with state socialism abroad. Socialism, not communism, became the system of politics and economics in Russia following the Revolution. "Communism" was only a bogey word. Thereafter, all Masonic powers cooperated in making the new Union of Soviet Socialist Republics (U.S.S.R.) a success.

London's involvement in, and funding of the Revolution was confirmed by Dr. Carroll Quigley when he observed, "There does exist, and has existed for a generation, an international Anglophile network which operates, to some extent, in the way the radical Right believes the Communists act. In fact, this network... has no aversion to cooperating with the Communists, or any other groups, and frequently does so."[1298]

Count de Poncins noted the same connections in 1930 when he revealed that the revolutionary socialists, who ostensibly were at war with capitalists, always seemed to have plenty of funds.

> *We are told that socialism is the revolt of the workers oppressed by capitalism: that it is the rising of those who have nothing against those who possess.*
>
> *In this connection, let us remark, in passing, that all the money is rather on the side of those who have nothing. The anti-revolutionary organizations are indeed constantly hindered by lack of funds whilst this difficulty does not exist for the revolutionary socialist parties which have obviously at their disposal limitless resources.[1299]*

[1295] de Poncins, *Vatican* 136-137.

[1296] de Poncins, *Vatican* 155.

[1297] de Poncins.

[1298] Quigley, *Tragedy and Hope* 950.

[1299] de Poncins, *Secret Powers* 138.

EXPERIMENT IN COMMUNISM

The hierarchies of both Freemasonries were able to set aside their differences to "experiment" with communism. Freemasonry's goal was, and is, a utopian world government - offering "Liberty, Fraternity, and Equality" to all men and women. Which political system would rule the world had not yet been determined. All possibilities had to be considered. Democracy had already been proven, but did not solve the problem of Equality. Socialism by itself was unworkable. In tandem with democracy, socialism appeared to do better, but hindered Fraternity. The theory behind world communism was certainly utopian, but it too required an intermediate period of state socialism. The question remained of how communism would affect Liberty.

The Romanov dynasty was the last obstacle to Freemasonry's world government, therefore imperial Russia was selected for the communist experiment. If the experiment worked, Universal Freemasonry had hopes of some day merging East and West into a utopian New World Order of communism. If not, communism would be dismantled and social democracy would reign in the New World Order.

Joseph Stalin, a Rosicrucian Mason at the time he took power in Russia in 1924, understood the Masonic scheme and fought hard for the success of socialism. He knew socialism would require outside financing. Citizens in advanced countries, he said, had to be taxed to provide foreign "'aid to the backward nationalities in their cultural and economic development. [Otherwise], it will be impossible to bring the various nations and peoples within a single world economic system that is so essential to the final triumph of socialism."[1300]

RUSSIA: TARGETED IN 1843

In 1843, the celebrated Jewish poet Heinrich Heine organized into a book a selection of articles he had written for the *Augsburg Gazette* between 1840 and 1843. The book, *Lutece*, prophesied the horrors of a future communist revolution in Russia. Listen to Heine's uncanny prophecy:

> *I have not described the storm itself. I have described the great storm-clouds which bore the approaching tempest, advancing dark and menacing across the sky. I have made frequent and exact descriptions of those sinister legions, those titans buried underground, who lay in wait in the lowest ranks of society; I have hinted that they would arise from their obscurity when their hour was come. These shadowy creatures, these nameless monsters, to whom the future belongs, were then usually only looked down on through lorgnettes; from this angle they resembled fleas gone mad. But I have shown them in their greatness, in their true light, and seen thus, they resemble if anything, the most fearsome crocodiles and gigantic dragons that have ever emerged from the foul abyss.*
>
> *Communism is the secret name of this tremendous adversary which the rule of the proletariat, with all that that implies, opposes to the existing bourgeois regime. It will be an appalling duel. How will it end? That is known to the gods and goddesses in whose hands lies the future. For our part, all we know is that, however little talked-of at present, however miserable an existence it drags out in concealed attics on wretched beds of straw, Communism is nonetheless the dark*

[1300] Epperson, *Unseen* 325.

hero, cast for an enormous if fleeting role in the modern tragedy, and awaiting only its cue to enter the stage.

There is an approaching rumble of hard times filled with upheavals. Any prophet wishing to write a new Apocalypse will have to invent new monsters so frightful that the old symbolic beast in St. John would appear in comparison no more than cooing turtle-doves and gracious Cupids. The gods hide their faces out of compassion for the poor insignificant human creatures, their wards for centuries, but perhaps also out of fear for their own fate. The future smells of Russian knouts, of blood, of impiety and of violent blows. I advise our descendants to have good thick skins on them when they are born into this world.[1301]

Was this a prophecy, or had Heine "inside" knowledge that Russia was condemned by Freemasonry to a communist political system? The answer can be found in the Masonic activity which took place during his day.

You recall that in 1844, Frederick Engels' review of Thomas Carlyle's book, *Past and Present*, promoted communism and was published by a German Masonic newspaper founded by Arnold Ruge.[1302] Ruge was a disciple of both Henry Palmerston and Giuseppe Mazzini. In 1848 Karl Marx, with the assistance of Engels, wrote the *Communist Manifesto*. Marx was then introduced to Ruge by Heinrich Heine, after which Marx was made editor of Ruge's Masonic newspaper in Paris.[1303] Engels, Ruge, Mazzini, Marx and Heine were comrades in Grand Orient Freemasonry. Lord Palmerston was Scottish Rite. All six were the initial force behind the communist experiment.

A CENTURY OF MASONIC INTRIGUE

Masonic intrigue had already begun to undermine the power of the Czars when these powerful Masons started planning the communist experiment. As in Europe, Freemasonry in Russia was divided between the English Grand Lodges and the more radical French Grand Orients. The Grand Orients followed the doctrine of Adam Weishaupt:

1. Abolition of all ordered government
2. Abolition of private property
3. Abolition of inheritance
4. Abolition of patriotism
5. Abolition of religion
6. Abolition of marriage
7. Creation of a world government[1304]

Freemasonry arrived in Russia from Scotland about 1772. During the early years of Catherine II'S reign (1762-1796), the Craft reached throughout Russian high society when the Empress declared herself Protector of Masonry. On September 3, 1776, twelve lodges united and formed the National Grand Lodge. In 1779 a Swedish Provincial Grand Lodge was established. In 1784 the Imperial Grand Lodge was formed in St. Petersburg. Meanwhile, Nikolay Ivanovich Novikof, a Russian writer, became Grand Master of the first Grand Orient Lodge in St. Petersburg. Unknown to Catherine, Novikof initiated three princes of the Russian aristocracy (Leopuchin, Troubetskoi, and Turgenjef) into the Order and indoctrinated them in the art of subversion. When a revolution was attempted in 1792,

---

[1301] de Poncins, *Vatican* 99-100.
[1302] Chaitkin 299 and Miller 489. See chapter 12 of this volume.
[1303] Miller 489.
[1304] Kirban 149.

Catherine exiled the three princes to their estates and imprisoned Novikof in the Fortress Schlusselburg.[1305]

Masonry was suppressed by Catherine and reinstated by Emperor Paul I (r.1796-1801). At first Paul favored Freemasonry and in 1796 released Novikof, but at the urging of the Jesuits, he closed the lodges in 1797 and exiled most of the dangerous element.[1306]

Napoleon had been in power two years when the evil Alexander I (r.1801-1825), a dabbler in witchcraft, succeeded Paul. (This is the same Alexander who, at the Congress of Vienna in 1815, thwarted the Metternich Plan for a Monarchical Federation of Europe.) In 1803 Grand Orient Freemason Johann V. Boeber asked Alexander to revoke Paul's ordinance banning Freemasonry. *Mackey's Encyclopedia of Freemasonry* gives the account of what happened:

> *Boeber, counselor of state and director of the military school at St. Petersburg, resolved to remove, if possible, from the mind of the Emperor the prejudices which he had conceived against the Order. Accordingly, in an audience which he had solicited and obtained, he described the object of the Institution and the doctrine of its mysteries in such a way as to lead the Emperor to rescind the obnoxious decrees.[1307]*

Boeber, aware of the Emperor's predilections for witchcraft, described the mysteries of the Grand Orient from that perspective. The Emperor responded, "'What you have told me of the Institution not only induces me to grant it my protection and patronage, but even to ask for initiation into its mysteries."[1308]

[1305] Stoddard, *The Trail of the Serpent* 139.William R. Denslow in *10,000 Famous Masons* informs us that Nicolay Ivanovich Novikof (1744-1818) attempted to found Masonic schools when Catherine the Great ordered him arrested. She then waged war against Freemasonry. (vol.111, p. 276).

[1306] "Paul I," *Mackey's Encyclopedia*, vol.11.

[1307] "Alexander I," *Mackey's Encyclopedia*, vol.1.

[1308] "Alexander I." After Alexander I joined Freemasonry, he surrounded himself with brother Masons. But, in 1922, the European kings convinced him of the danger of Freemasonry, upon which time he banned the Order. A few of the powerful Masons in his court are listed in Denslow's *10,000 Famous Freemasons*.

Alexander A. Gerebzov - Russian Major General was raised in a Paris lodge and opened the Grand Orient Lodge *Les Amis Reunis* at St. Petersburg on June 10, 1802. His lodge, a military lodge, was impregnated with French ideas, and represented the "liberal" branch of Russian Freemasonry, believing in abolishing religion, national and social differences, and forming a true brotherhood of man. (vol.11, p.106)

Count Alexander I. Ostermann Tolstoy (1770-1837) -Russian infantry general who distinguished himself in the wars against Napoleon. Member of *Les Amis Reunis* Grand Orient Lodge at St. Petersburg. (vol.111, p.294)Konstantin Pavlovich (1779-1831) – second son of Paul I and brother of Alexander I. Both he and Alexander were initiated into Freemasonry at the same time. Paviovich became a member of Grand Orient Lodge *Les Amis Reunis*. (vol.111, p.320)

Mikhail M. Speransky (1772-1839) - initiated at a secret meeting of the Grand Lodge of the *Polar Star* (sometimes referred to as *Northern Star*) at the request of Alexander I. He was later a member of a governmental committee to look into the political status of all Masonic lodges. (vol. IV~ p.174)

Count Pavel Andreevich Shuvalov (1773-1823) - aide-decamp to Emperor Alexander I, was elected ruler of the Russian Directorial Grand Lodge in 1814 to replace Boeber. The grand lodge was so split with dissension that Shuvalov declined the post, and Count Mussin- Pushkin-Bruce was elected in his place. (vol. IV, p.137)

Count Mussin-Pushkin-Bruce - Russian secret councillor and chamberlain of Emperor Alexander I, was head of *Directorial* Grand Lodge of Russia in 1814. Also Grand Master of Grand Orient Lodge *Astrea* in 1815. He received the edict onAug. 1, 1822 from Alexander I to close all his Grand Orient lodges. (vol. III, p.250)

Mackey's Encyclopedia of Freemasonry concludes: "Accordingly, Alexander was soon after initiated, and the Grand Orient of all the Russias was in consequence established with Boeber as Grand Master."[1309] (Boeber was also ruler of the directorial Grand Lodge.)

Meanwhile, in 1804 Napoleon had crowned himself emperor of France and immediately started planning war against Europe. His greatest victory the Battle of Austerlitz against Austria and Russia, came a year later. By 1810 Napoleon had consolidated most of Europe into his empire His downfall began with his disastrous invasion of Russia in 1812. The Allied coalition revived, and in 1814 Napoleon was defeated and exiled to the island of Elba.

During the war against France, Russian military officers had attempted to establish travelling lodges under the jurisdiction of the Grand Orient Les Amis Reunis lodge at St. Petersberg. They succeeded in founding five, but found it difficult to consolidate them. When Russian troops occupied Paris in 1814, the Grand Orient assisted the Russian military lodges in uniting in a new lodge called Astrea. With the return of the army to Russia, Astrea grew to have forty lodges under its jurisdiction. Under French influence these lodges turned their attention to politics.[1310]

At this time many Russian aristocrats visited France and became fascinated with the liberal ideas of the French Revolution. They returned to Russia importing two Grand Lodges called Northern Star and Southern Star. Many influential and wealthy Russian nobles were initiated into both lodges. These were the "near powerful" who aspired to democratize Russia with a Constitutional Monarchy and Duma (parliament).[1311]

Meanwhile, an irregular Grand Lodge named Vladimir, which in 1810 became subject to Swedish jurisdiction, was attempting to negotiate reforms with the Emperor.[1312] Proving unsuccessful, it was replaced by the more democratic military lodge Astrea. Astrea influenced Alexander in preparing constitutional reforms, but was not radical enough for Pavel Ivanovich Pestel, then Grand Master of the Grand Orients of all Russia. Hence, Pestel and others, with Novikof, separated from Astrea and founded the Alliance du salut, a Grand Orient military lodge formed in the regiment of the Guards. The Guards, whose duty was to protect the Emperor, were gradually imbued with the more radical revolutionary ideals.[1313]

At the 1815 Congress of Vienna, Alexander was warned against his allegiance to Grand Orient Freemasonry, which was bent on the destruction of both Crown and Church. The Czar, too mesmerized by the intrigues of witchcraft, refused to give up his association, even in the face of losing his empire to the republicans. Upon his return to Russia, rather than suppressing the order, he instead nominally affirmed "The Holy Alliance," which was "to support the Christian Church and to stem the rising tide of

---

Count Adam Rgevussky was Grand Master of the Russian Grand Orient Lodge *Astrea* in 1820, following Count Mussin-Pushkin-Bruce. His deputy grand master was Prince Alexander Lobanov-Rostovsky, who was an honorary member of several Polish lodges in Warsaw and Cracow. (vol. iv; p.29)

Sergei Stepanovich Lanskoy (1787-1862) was deputy grandmaster of the Grand Lodge Provincial of Russia in 1817.Lanskoy also received the edict on Aug. 1, 1822 from Alexander I to close all his Grand Lodges. (vol. III, p.54) Aleksander S. Pushkin (1799- 1837) - Russian poet and Freemason. (vol. III, p.372)

[1309] "Alexander I."

[1310] "Russia."

[1311] Epperson, *Unseen* 100-101.

[1312] "Russia."

[1313] Stoddard, *Trail* 139.

radicalism, revolution and subversion"[1314] - all of the essence of the Masonry which he embraced.

Realizing the danger The Holy Alliance posed to Freemasonry, the Grand Orient sent one of its female Masons to infiltrate the Russian Royal Court. Her name was Madame Bouche, known to the adepts as Sister Salome, a spiritualist. Gradually she worked her way into the good graces of the Czar, who brought her into his court as personal advisor. After eighteen months, during which time she had many secret interviews with the Emperor, she was supplanted by another and more persuasive medium-somnambulist of Grand Orient Freemasonry, the famous Madame de Krudner. This witch acquired such an influence over the Czar that his ministers became alarmed. They plotted against the prophetess, and Madame de Krudner was summarily banished from the Russian Court.[1315]

At the 1822 Congress of Verona, Czar Alexander was still attached to the Grand Orient. Prince Metternich, now Prime Minister of Austria, again warned the Emperor of the danger of this association to his rule, and not only his, but to the governments of all Europe if kings and princes did not ban the Order. Mettenich's exact words were, "If Governments do not take efficacious measures... Europe runs the risk of succumbing to attacks upon it ceaselessly repeated by these associations... Absolute monarchies, constitutional monarchies, and even republics, are all threatened by the Levellers."[1316]

This time the Czar listened. Upon his return to Russia, he dissolved by imperial ukase (decree) all Grand Orients and Grand Lodges, fearing that such democratic organizations would topple the State. Pestel began immediately to plan the Czar's assassination and subsequent overthrow of his empire.

Since 1814, Pestel had been persistent in his attempt to unite all of Russia, Poland, Bohemia, Moravia, Dalmatia, Hungary, Transylvania, Servia (Serbia), Moldavia, and Valachia under a federal republic. Conspiring with him were many princes initiated into Freemasonry and indoctrinated in subversion. When Pestel disclosed his plans to murder the whole Russian imperial family and proclaim a republic, Prince Jablonowski of Poland (a fellow Mason) recoiled in horror, and the Poles were allowed to form their own government.

The revolution was planned for 1829, but the sudden death of Alexander in 1825 hastened the revolt. The uprising occurred on Mon. day, December 14, 1825, failed, and the leaders of the "Decembrists," as the rebels were called, were arrested. They were executed a few months later.[1317]

Under the new Czar, Nicholas I (r.1825-1855), Freemasonry was severely suppressed. The Scottish Rite *New Age* magazine (February 1945) reports:

> *[A]fter 1825, many Russian Masons exiled themselves to France where lodges operating in the Russian language were sponsored by the Grand Orient. Some of the exiles later returned to Russia, and organized lodges in St. Petersburg and Moscow... and had "an avowedly political aim and view; namely, that of the overthrow of the autocracy."[1318]*

[1314] Miller 36.

[1315] Miller 36-37.

[1316] Stoddard, *Trail* 138. Metternich used the word "Levellers" to indicate the destruction of Templar Grand Orient Freemasonry. "Levellers" was the original name in England of the Scottish Stuart Templar Masonry, later carried to France. There it became the Scottish Rite and merged with the Grand Orient in 1801.

[1317] Stoddard, *Trail* 140.

[1318] Fisher 218.

While Russian Masons were in training in France, Freemasonry lay dormant in their motherland until the rise to power of Nicholas I's successor, Alexander II (r.1855-1881). Alexander ascended the throne alter the disastrous Crimean War - a war designed by Freemason Lord Palmerston of Great Britain to dissolve Russia's alliance with Austria. Under great pressure from Masons abroad, particularly Lord Palmerston, Alexander realized the necessity of permitting "political institutions" outside of government - such as Freemasonry - to function. By 1857 lodges had reopened in St. Petersburg, giving English Freemasonry the opportunity to penetrate the Imperial Court with Masonic subversives. When Palmerston died in 1865, the cause was taken up and directed by Albert Pike and Joseph Mazzini.

MIKHAIL BAKUNIN

Mazzini maintained contact with revolutionaries throughout the world. One was a man who was to cast the sinister shadow of terrorism not only over his own age, but over ours as well. He was Grand Orient Freemason Mikhail Bakunin (1814-1876), a Russian disciple of Weishaupt, who, ironically, was a hater of the Jews.[1319] The authors of *The Messianic Legacy* recount Bakunin's Masonic credentials:

> *Having spent more than twenty years working his way up through the ranks of Freemasonry, Bakunin had acquired a metaphysical philosophical framework for his social and political ideas. Bakunin was a self-proclaimed Satanist. According to one commentator, he saw Satan "as the spiritual head of revolutionaries, the true author of human liberation." Satan was not only the supreme rebel, but also the supreme freedom-fighter against the tyrannical God of Judaism and Christianity. The established institutions of church and state were instruments of the oppressive Judeo-Christian God, and according to Bakunin it was a moral and theological obligation to oppose them.[1320]*

Ralph Epperson, in *The New World Order*, quotes Bakunin on the attributes of Satan:

> *"Satan [is] the eternal rebel, the first freethinker and the emancipator of worlds. "He makes man ashamed of his bestial ignorance and obedience; he emancipates him, stamps upon his brow the seal of liberty and humanity, in urging him to disobey and eat of the fruit of knowledge."[1321]*

In 1857 Bakunin was in England with Mazzini to plan the assassination of Napoleon III.[1322] On August 5, 1862, he was one of the delegates at the London International [Worker's] Exhibition. The delegates met in Freemason's Hall at a dinner hosted by their English colleagues. The after- dinner speech formed the foundation of the International Working Men's Association - known later as the Communist Inter-national. September 24-28, 1864, Bakunin was at St. Martin's Hall, London, attending, with Mazzini and Marx, the founding of the International Working Men's Association. Mazzini and Marx were placed on a subcommittee to prepare the constitution.[1323] In 1869 Bakunin fought

---

[1319] Clarence Kelly, *Conspiracy against God and Man* (Boston:Western Islands, 1974) 211.
[1320] Baigent et al, *Messianic Legacy* 146-147.
[1321] Epperson, *The New World Order* 67.
[1322] Miller 267.
[1323] Miller 218-219, 490-491.

for control of the International, which held its convention that year in the Masonic Temple Unique at Geneva. At that meeting Bakunin thus spoke of the strategy for the triumph of Communism:

> By social liquidation I mean expropriation of all existing proprietors, by the abolition of the political and legal state, which is the sanction and only guarantee of all property as now existing, and of all that is called legal right; and the expropriation, in fact, everywhere, and as much and as quickly as possible by the force of events and circumstances.[1324]

On September 29, 1872, when a split occurred in the ranks of the participants in the Hague Congress of the International, some sided with Bakunin, while others rallied around Marx. Marx's followers wanted a non-violent revolution through worker strikes. Bakunin's adherents founded the Anarchist Party, urging terrorism and assassination as the means of overthrowing all forms of existing governments. Bakunin described the revolutionary in his famous *Catechism:*

> The revolutionary is a man dedicated. He must have neither personal interests, business, sentiments, nor property. He must be absolutely absorbed in a single exclusive interest, a single thought, a single passion, revolution. He despises and hates actual morals; for him all is moral which favours the triumph of revolution, and immoral and criminal which impedes it. Between him and society there is a fight to the death, incessant and irreconcilable. He must be prepared to die, to endure torture, to put to death with his own hands all those who are obstacles to revolution.[1325]

On March 1, 1881, a disciple of Bakunin succeeded in assassinating Alexander U with a nitroglycerine hand grenade. The identity of the assassin was never known, because he himself was blown apart when one of the grenades exploded in his pocket.[1326] The imperial police rounded up several anarchists, one of whom was the older brother of Vladimir Lenin, and executed them for having taken part in the assassination.[1327]

After Alexander II's assassination, Alexander III (1881-1894) ascended the throne. Freemasonry was once again suppressed but was by then too powerful to destroy.

LENIN

In 1870 Vladimir Ilich Ulyanov was born to a Jewish mother and Gentile father. Ulyanov, better known as Lenin (1870-1924), was eleven-years-old when his brother was executed for his part in the assassination of Alexander II. During his adolescence, Lenin adopted and absorbed revolutionary ideals which his brother had embraced and took Bakunin as his idol, as had his brother.

Lenin's future revolutionary party structure derived directly from Bakunin, as Lenin himself acknowledges in his notebooks. Almost quoting Bakunin, Lenin stated, "'We do

---

[1324] Miller 492-493.
[1325] Stoddard, *Trail* 107.
[1326] W. Bruce Lincoln, *The Romanous* (New York: Doubleday, 1981) 437-447.
[1327] Epperson, *Unseen* 101.

not believe in eternal morality... Everything is moral which is necessary for the annihilation of the old exploiting social order and for uniting the proletariat."[1328]

In 1889, while a student at the University of Kazan, Lenin joined Grand Orient Freemasonry. There he started reading Marx and soon was expounding Marxist principles. Later he wrote: "Atheism is a natural and inseparable portion of Marxism, of the theory and practice of scientific Socialism. Our propaganda necessarily includes propaganda for atheism."[1329] Lenin revealed his anti-Christian and anti-Semitic nature when he said, "We must combat religion. This is the ABC of all materialism and consequently of Marxism."[1330] Leninism became a mixture of Marx and Bakunin.

In 1894, when the ill-fated Czar Nicholas II (r-1894-1917) ascended the Imperial throne, Russia was still prey to Freemasonry. In 1895, Lenin and nine others, including Leon Trotsky, founded the Social Democratic Labor Party, the forerunner of the Communist Party.[1331] These revolutionists were divided between an extreme terrorist wing led by Lenin, and a broader and looser membership that had merged imperceptibly with radical middle-class liberalism, led by Trotsky. Lenin's group, after it had won a majority vote during its second congress held in Brussels and London in 1903, took the name Bolshevik (derived from the Russian word for "majority"). The loose-knit group, which lost the vote to the Bolsheviks, became known as the Mensheviks (derived from the Russian word for "minority"). From 1900 to 1905 Lenin's group was plotting the violent overthrow of the Russian government.

Unlike Trotsky, who initially was willing to ally with the liberal middle class, "Lenin believed that his Bolsheviks should never ally themselves with the liberal forces of the bourgeoisie under any circumstances."[1332] Yet, Lenin had no aversion to accepting their money from abroad. For example, during the spring of 1905, Lenin was in London negotiating for funds from the socialist Fabian Society, whose membership were mostly liberal middle- and upper-class Masons, such as H. G. Wells, George Bernard Shaw and Annie Besant. After this meeting, several of the wealthy Fabians loaned Lenin large sums of money.[1333]

Much more serious to the Russian government at the time, however, was its disastrous war with Japan, which had begun in 1904. The conflict stemmed from an earlier struggle between Japan and China over Korea, which Japan had won decisively in 1895. Forced to protect his far eastern interests, the Czar sided with China, demanding Japan return to China the Liaotung Peninsula, which it did in 1896. In 1898 the Russian government acquired the peninsula from the Chinese, and built a naval base in the ice-free waters at Port Arthur, thus antagonizing Japan.

In retaliation, Japanese forces made a surprise attack on Russian warships in Port Arthur on the night of February 8-9, 1904.[1334] Grand Orient Freemasonry immediately saw its opportunity to weaken Russia, making it less able to resist revolution. Lenin's revolution, which was scheduled for the spring of 1905, would better realize success if the military were gone. By financing the Japanese against the Russians, the Grand Orient would force the Czar to reinforce his eastern front, leaving the western front stripped of military personnel and resources. A loan of $30,000,000 was issued to the Japanese from

---

[1328] Epperson 378-379.
[1329] Epperson, *New World Order* 123.
[1330] Epperson 220.
[1331] Epperson, *Unseen* 101.
[1332] Lincoln 655.
[1333] Epperson, *Unseen* 101.
[1334] Epperson 101-102.

a Warburg affiliate bank in New York, a bank run by Grand Orient Freemason Jacob Schiff. This fact is confirmed in the official *Jewish Communal Register* of 1917-1918:

> *The firm of Kuhn, Loeb and Company floated the large Japanese war loans of 1904-5, thus making possible the Japanese victory over Russia... Mr. Schiff has always used his wealth and influence in the best interest of his people. He financed the enemies of autocratic Russia and used his influence to keep Russia from the money market of the United States.*[1335]

Lenin returned to St. Petersburg in the spring of 1905 to receive additional funds from a Mason named Joseph Stalin. Stalin, known in Masonic circles as the Jesse James of the Urals, had joined the Bolsheviks in 1903. From 1903 until his reception by Lenin, Stalin had been robbing banks to help fund Lenin's impending revolution.[1336]

Lenin's revolution began on May 1, the anniversary of the founding of the Illuminati.[1337] He and Trotsky were still divided in their efforts, both publishing separate radical newspapers to foment their respective styles of revolution in the labor force.

Trotsky's means to power was worker strikes; thus he formed in St. Petersburg a "Soviet [council] of Workers' Deputies." The president of the "Soviet of Workers" was a Russian lawyer by the name of Khrustalyov, but its silent leader was Trotsky. Although Lenin took no active part in the Soviets, he and Trotsky independently spread anti-government propaganda through their papers. Both men were instrumental in causing sixteen hundred worker strikes, involving a million men and women.

Meanwhile, Nicholas II, with most of his military on the eastern front fighting a war with Japan, found himself with an inadequate number of troops to thwart revolution at home. Needing to end the war with Japan, he sent Count Witte to negotiate peace. By October, when the revolution had reached its climax, peace had been made with Japan. One final strike was called by the Bolsheviks - a nationwide railway strike designed to keep Russian troops from returning home. When Lenin, Stalin and Trotsky were captured, the strike fizzled. Lenin was exiled to Switzerland, Stalin and Trotsky to Siberia. Trotsky escaped to Europe and then to New York.

Faced with the threat of political collapse, Czar Nicholas issued a manifesto promising to convoke a national Duma or Parliament, which would share in the law-making process. The election, held in April 1906 on a rather broad franchise, produced a Duma with a left-wing majority. Count Witte became Russia's first Prime Minister. Reforms demanded by the Duma, such as redistribution of landowners' estates to peasants with or without compensation, amnesty for political prisoners, equal rights for Jews and for religious dissenters, and autonomy for Poland, were unacceptable to the government. After two months of deadlock, Nicholas dissolved the Duma.[1338]

A ruthless suppression of Freemasonry followed. Hundreds of revolutionaries were executed, while massive Jewish pogroms spilt innocent blood. When the discipline of the armed forces was restored, elections were held for a second Duma in February 1907. The elections produced a body even farther to the left than the first. By June it too had been dissolved.

[1335] Commissar 25.

[1336] Fagan, *The Illuminati* 8. The transcript of Fagan's two audio cassettes are in the author's files.

[1337] Epperson, *Unseen* 102.

[1338] "Russia and the Soviet Union, History of (The Dumas)," *Encyclopaedia Britannica: Macropaedia.*

STALIN

Iosif Visarionovich Dzhugashvili (1879-1953) changed his name to Joseph Stalin in 1903 when be began robbing banks. Earlier he had trained for the priesthood in a theological seminary in Tiflis. In 1900 he lived for a year with Georg Ivanovich Gurdjieff (1870s-1949), a "magi" of Tibetan mysteries from the region of Georgia.[1339] Gurdjieff, a Rosicrucian Mason, hobnobbed with English Masons and was a proponent and teacher of racist-gnostic mysticism.[1340] While in Georgia, Stalin was initiated into Martinist Freemasonry by Gurdjieff and became a closet anti- Zionist. Married to a Jewess, Stalin was not an anti-Semite.

TROTSKY

Lev Davidovich Bronstein (1879-1940) was born of Jewish parents. His father, a wealthy grain mill owner in Kherson (South Russia) owned an estate at Yanovka, which lies not far from Kherson. Bronstein's views were identical to that of the Alliance Israelite Universelle (which proposed the involvement of Jews in all walks of Gentile society), but he showed no evidence of being anti-Zionist. To hide his years of revolutionary activity, Bronstein changed his name to Leon D. Trotsky.

Most people first learned of Trotsky's existence and activities in 1917, when he entered the political arena in Russia and presented himself as the intimate "friend" and co-worker of Lenin. Only those more closely acquainted with Marxist movements and revolutionary propaganda in Europe remembered that Trotsky and Lenin were enemies in earlier years.

Trotsky, at age 19, used the secrecy of Grand Orient Lodges to organize a revolutionary society in Nicolayev, a port on the Black Sea near his home. Many poor and deceived Protestants, who had been persecuted by the Orthodox Church of Russia, were easy recruits for his Masonic revolution. The seeds of discontent began to germinate as he succeeded in perverting the meetings of these Russian Protestant Christians.

In 1899 he and a number of his Masonic friends were arrested by the Czar's police and exiled to Siberia. He escaped in 1902 and fled to western Europe. Trotsky was merely one of many Russian political emigrants who were then populating the back alleys of European capitals. Eventually he went to London where he had occasion to visit with Lenin, who was himself travelling abroad in search of funding. Trotsky, not yet willing to yield to the violent overthrow of government as demanded by Lenin's Bolsheviks, avoided Lenin's suggestion that they unite.

From London Trotsky went to Austria and then to Paris. While in Paris he frequented the Grand Orient Lodges, soliciting financial and political support for his own revolution. There he was encouraged by the more radical communists to reconsider violence if the more mild form of workers' strikes did not prove successful. As a Marxist, Trotsky succeeded in winning the confidence of the leaders of Marxism in Paris, and from then on we find him closely associated with the two Masonic headquarters of the Russian revolution.[1341] Thus, it was in London and in Paris that Trotsky got his real start as an international figure.

With blessings from the French Grand Orient, Trotsky was sent back to Russia to foment revolution. He arrived in the spring of 1905 and founded a daily newspaper,

---

[1339] Baigent et al, *Messianic Legacy* 147.
[1340] Helga Zepp-LaRouche, *The Hitler Book* (New York: New Benjamin Franklin House, 1984) 88.
[1341] Commissar 10-11.

Nachalo (The Beginning). Shortly thereafter he formed the "Soviet of Workers" in St. Petersburg. Lenin, who had returned to Russia soon after Trotsky, took no active part in the Soviets, but satisfied himself with editing his own radical revolutionary daily called *Novoya Zhizn* (New Life).

Although these two men would cooperate in the 1917 Bolshevik Revolution, Lenin was Trotsky's rival, not only politically, but journalistically as well. Trotsky's newspaper had a much larger circulation than did Lenin's - up to half a million copies daily. Trotsky was also backed financially by wealthy Jewish publisher Dr. Herzenstein. Lenin's circulation was much smaller and wielded much less influence.

Both papers, however, reached Germany where they were read by the House of Warburg. Max Warburg, a Grand Orient Freemason had already been observing both men, and was presently assisting them by funding the Japanese war against Russia. Trotsky's publication made Warburg aware that this rebel's viewpoint on world revolution was identical to his own. Warburg knew that a man like Trotsky would go far in solidifying a revolution if properly supported and supplied with plenty of money. But to run a revolutionary government was not his strength. Warburg chose the more intellectual Lenin. Trotsky and Lenin's future cooperation undoubtedly was encouraged by the House of Warburg.

The Bolshevik movement did not originate with the poor and downtrodden of Russia, as we have been led to believe, but by wealthy Grand Orient Masons from Berlin and Paris, and affluent left- wing English Masons from London.

In *Trotsky and the Jews behind the Russian Revolution* (1937), written anonymously by one of Trotsky's former Soviet Commissars, we read:

> *The ties between Trotsky and the powers backing him doubtless became closer after the 1905 revolution. As factual head of the St. Petersburg "Workers Soviet," he had demonstrated his disregard for all restraint when offered an opportunity to stir mobs of criminals into a blood- thirsty frenzy.*[1342]

The inability of the worker strikes to topple the government forced Trotsky to rethink his style of revolution. He finally agreed with Lenin and Bakunin that a successful revolution must maintain a constant slaughter of undesirables - a never-ending reign of terror.

With the failure of the revolution, Trotsky again was exiled to Siberia. Hardly had he been brought to his destination when he escaped, hurrying back to St. Petersburg, where he was hidden by his Masonic comrades.[1343] After a short stay, Trotsky left Russia on a mission to tour Europe - speaking in one city, then another, always just ahead of the police. He also played the role of correspondent for influential Russian and European newspapers and periodicals distributed on the Continent.

Meanwhile, in Paris, aristocratic Russians who had been exiled to France after the first Duma was dissolved in the summer of 1906, were preparing their own Masonic revolution. *Mackey's Encyclopedia of Freemasonry* gives the details:

> *A few prominent Russian intellectuals joined French lodges. Professor Bajenoff joined at Paris the Scottish Rite Lodge Les Amis Reunis. Paul Jablochkov, world-famous electrician, founded the Lodge Cosmos under the Ancient Accepted Scottish Rite at Paris where in 1906 about fifteen Russian publicists joined French lodges. These Brethren on their return to Russia organized two lodges,*

[1342] Commissar 14-15.
[1343] Commissar 16.

one in St. Petersburg, the Polar Star, and a lodge at Moscow. These lodges were instituted with great ceremony in May, 1908, by two representatives of the Grand Orient of France and up to 1909 six lodges were organized. There was an interval in their activity over police restrictions and then these lodges were reopened in 1911, working under the Grand Orient of France, with practically no ritual and having an avowedly political aim in view, namely, that of the overthrow of autocracy... In 1913 and 1914 the organization... had about forty-two lodges chiefly composed of members of the cadet-party. The first revolution in March 1917 is said to have been inspired and operated from these lodges and all the members of Kerensky's government belonged to them.[1344]

SION, ANTI-ZIONISM, AND THE RUSSIAN REVOLUTION

Zionism was an unexpected bombshell dropped in the midst of the Russian conspiracy. During the 1840s and 1850s, when Reform Judaism's anti-Semitic doctrine of assimilation failed to destroy the Jewish Orthodoxy in Russia, Czar Nicholas I was encouraged to prosecute pogroms against the Jews. The Orthodoxy responded by dreaming of a homeland and organized their nationalistic dream under the banner of "Zionism." Naturally the Reformers became anti- Zionists.

Zionism also had an enemy in the Priory of Sion, which was head-quartered in the Mizraim Lodge at Paris. Sion's ultimate goal was, and still is, to establish a universal throne in Europe occupied by Sion's counterfeit "King of Jerusalem." This goal was seriously threatened by the rise of Zionism. To counter the nationalistic tendency among Jews, or to at least contain the spread of Zionism, the Priory of Sion in 1860 founded the Alliance Israelite Universelle also headquartered in Mizraim Freemasonry at Paris. Through a series of complex events (explained in chapter 13), Mizralm Freemasonry produced the *Protocols* of *the Learned Elders of Sion.*

Reform Jews by the thousands joined the Alliance Israelite Universelle to fight the spread of Zionism. Conversely, the House of Rothschild assumed the leadership of European Zionism, donating large sums of money to its cause. In doing so, they found themselves confronted with the formidable forces of non-Zionist groups in America and Europe - groups which came to be later controlled by Jacob Schiff and his friends, the Warburgs.[1345]

Meanwhile, in 1875, Mizraim Freemasonry merged with two other Rosicrucian Orders, Memphis and Martin. In 1884 Sion arranged for the "theft" of the *Protocols of the Learned Elders of Sion* from its own Mizraim Lodge at Paris. The *Protocols* were then carried to Russia as propaganda against Zionist Jews, but lay dormant for the next two decades.

The timing of the publication of the *Protocols* in 1905 is indeed suspicious, especially since two men of Jewish ancestry, Lenin and Trotsky, were inciting revolution that year. Jewish pogroms of the most gruesome nature followed. The pogroms, instead of destroying Zionism, as they were intended, compelled the Jews to seek protection by siding with one of the two revolutionary groups, the Bolsheviks or the social democrats. Financing the Bolsheviks were the anti-Zionist Warburgs, while the social democrats were funded by the pro-Zionist Rothschilds.

Meanwhile, the Priory of Sion assigned two charlatans the task of undermining the power of Nicholas II. These men were not Jews, but Gentile Rosicrucian Masons. They were seer Louis Philippe, protege of the French occultist Dr. Gerard Encausse (Papus),

---

[1344] "Russia."
[1345] Commissar 31.

who was Grand Master of the lodge from where the *Protocols* were stolen, and faith healer Grigoni Rasputin, who succeeded Philippe.

Subsequent events suggest that Philippe and Rasputin's Masonic assignment was two-fold. After they successfully penetrated the Russian imperial court as advisors, they were (1) to suggest pogroms be unleashed against the Jews; and (2) give incompetent advice to weaken the empire.

These two charlatans wielded influence at a time when Russia's leadership was at its weakest. In 1894, when Nicholas II ascended the throne, he was not the real power. Rather it was his wife Aleksandra, to whom the Czar was passionately devoted to a fault. Nicholas was timid by nature, though he possessed great personal charm. Aleksandra had the strength of character that he lacked, and he fell completely under her sway. Under her influence he sought the advice of spiritualists and faith healers. Philippe, then Rasputin, offered their services.

Philippe was introduced to the Imperial Court first, oddly enough, by the same man who was Rasputin's sinister adviser, the anti-Zionist and Reform Jew, Manoussevitch Manouilof.[1346] Philippe claimed to be able to see into the future and to change the course of events.[1347] Aleksandra suggested to Nicholas that Philippe be the Imperial Court Advisor. Soon the quack became indispensable to both Emperor and Empress.

Papus, Philippe's mentor from Paris, visited Russia on two separate occasions, conveying instructions to "Dr." Philippe. Together, both men organized Rosicrucian Martinist lodges in Russia to spread their pernicious anti-Zionist doctrine. Philippe and Rasputin were at least acquainted, if not in league, for Rasputin joined one of these lodges. As subsequent events will suggest, Papus also chartered O.T.O. homicidal lodges in Russia in preparation for the impending slaughter. Philippe practiced his witchcraft in the court from the mid-1890s to 1902, with Rasputin taking over in 1905.

Philippe's ascendancy and domination of the imperial court was not by chance. Desperate, without an heir to the throne, Nicholas and Aleksandra consulted the French quack on how to produce a son. He convinced them that he could help. In 1902 Philippe announced the Czarina's pregnancy and predicted the babe would be a male child. After six months the court had to admit that she had not become pregnant. The embarrassing publicity forced Philippe to leave Russia under a cloud, but not before he set the stage for the acceptance of his successor. Philippe said to Aleksandra, "Someday you will have another friend like me who will speak to you of God."[1348] Of course, that friend just happened to be Rasputin, who arrived in St. Petersburg a few months after Philippe's departure.

Late in 1903 Aleksandra did indeed become pregnant and on July 30, 1904, bore a son and named him Aleksei. Aleksei had a disease for which there was no known cure and little effective treatment. The only heir to the throne was a hemophiliac.

The year 1905 was rocked by war abroad and revolution at home. By October Count Witte had completed peace negotiations with Japan. The first Communist revolution had come to an end, and the emperor had just agreed to a political transition to democracy.

In November faith healer Rasputin was introduced to the imperial family. When he demonstrated an ability to ease the suffering of the young Aleksei, he was welcomed into the family circle as a close and trusted friend. Aleksandra came to revere him as the holy man that Philippe had prophesied would come. She believed that Rasputin was sent by God to save her son, the Romanov dynasty, and the Russian autocracy. Rasputin was accepted as the Imperial Court Advisor and his word became law.

[1346] Stoddard, *Trail* 140.
[1347] Lincoln 631.
[1348] Lincoln.

In 1905 the timely release on unsuspecting Russia of the *Protocols of the Learned Elders of Sion* filled the land with renewed anti-Semitism. Rasputin informed the Czar that the uprising that year was a Jewish conspiracy to destroy the Romanov dynasty. He advised Nicholas to slaughter the Jews, which advice led to the pogroms of Kiev, Alexandrovsk, and Odessa.[1349] For protection the Jews flocked to join the two revolutionary groups.

With the success of the pogroms, Rasputin's Masonic assignment was only half complete. His second objective was to further weaken the dynasty by placing incompetent legislators in the Duma. Carroll Quigley wrote: "Rasputin used his power... to interfere in every branch of the government, always in a destructive and unprogressive sense."[1350]

The outbreak of World War I temporarily strengthened the monarchy and resulted in Nicholas' further suppression of Freemasonry and repudiation of the Duma. Rasputin reacted by turning the Czarina against the Czar's grand nephew, who was Commander-in-Chief of the Russian army. Aleksandra immediately suggested to her husband that he assume supreme command himself. Although Nicholas did not interfere in operational decisions, his departure from the political scene had serious consequences. In his absence supreme power was passed to the empress. The *Encyclopaedia Britannica* reports that

> *[a] grotesque situation resulted: in the midst of a desperate struggle for national survival, competent ministers and officials were dismissed and replaced by worthless nominees of Rasputin. The court was widely suspected of treachery, and ant dynastic feeling grew apace. Conservatives plotted Nicholas' deposition in the hope of saving the monarchy.*[1351]

PLANNING THE SECOND BOLSHEVIK REVOLUTION

The outbreak of World War I found Trotsky in Austria editing the revolutionary paper, *Pravda*. Grand Orient Freemasons had already assassinated Archduke Ferdinand. Masons had made inroads into Austrian politics, and many Austrian police were Freemasons. Instead of confining Trotsky, as they had other Russian subjects, the police warned him to leave Austria as quickly as possible. He moved on to Paris, leaving behind a library and many revolutionary manuscripts. These documents were preserved by the Masonic lodge at Vienna and later sent to Russia after the Bolshevik Revolution.

From Paris Trotsky travelled to Switzerland, where Lenin was already in residence. The Third International (commonly known as the Communist International or Comintern) soon began to take more definite form.[1352] The year was 1915.

[1349] Stoddard, *Trail* 140.

[1350] Quigley 101.

[1351] "Nicholas II of Russia," *Encyclopaedia Britannica:Macropaedia*.

[1352] The First International was founded under the name International Working Men's Association at a mass meeting in London on September 28, 1864. Karl Marx was elected one of the 32 members of the provisional General Council and at once assumed its leadership. It disbanded in July 1876 amongst strife. The Second International was founded at the great Masonic congress in Paris in July, 1889. It was a loose federation that did not set up an executive body until eleven years after it was founded. Headquartered in Brussels, its second meeting was held there in 1891. By 1912 it represented the socialist parties throughout the world. Lenin was a member. World War I divided the Second International between right-wing and left-wing factions. The right wing was pacifist, wanting to end the war. The left wing, led by Lenin, wanted to take advantage of the World War to instigate civil wars in all monarchist nations. Two years later Lenin led the Bolshevik Revolution in Russia. In 1919 his Party became known as the Comintern, or Third International, known today as

From Switzerland Trotsky moved to Spain. When the Russian government notified Spanish authorities that Trotsky was there, he was again arrested. Masons in Madrid contacted London to assist, but English Freemasonry, planning its own revolution in Russia, refused to help Trotsky. Strange as it may seem, Trotsky was exiled to New York City.

By this time Trotsky had become quite famous in Russian Jewish revolutionary circles. When he stepped off the ship in New York, a reception committee of Russian Jews with flowers and music greeted him. There he was introduced to Grand Orient Freemason Jacob Schiff, the financial protege' of the German Grand Orient Masons Felix and Max Warburg. Schiff immediately placed Trotsky in the editorial offices of the radical Russian newspaper *Novy Mir* (New World), which was then published in New York. It was 1916.

KERENSKY'S DEMOCRATIC REVOLUTION

Meanwhile, a democratic revolution, headed by Alexander Kerensky and the aristocrats from the Polar Star Lodge, was brewing in Russia. Kerensky, a 32nd degree Scottish Rite Mason, was a member of the Social Revolutionary Party. This Party had acquired a considerable following, which in 1917 was divided into four groups - the Left Wing, the Moderate Internationalists, the People's Social Party, and the Right Wing under Kerensky.[1353]

Kerensky's February revolution was a product of a war-torn Russia, and proclaimed the same democratic ideals as the American Revolution. He planned a coup with help from the corrupt and incompetent Imperial Duma[1354], which had been filled with dupes of Rasputin. Two years earlier, in 1915, during the First World War, Russia had lost about a million men. In 1916 another million were killed in one battle alone - the "Brusilov" counterattack against Austria.[1355] By this time the prestige of the Czar had fallen so low that the nation, the military, and even the Emperor's own royal house was split. For example, Prince Georgi Yevgenievich Lvov, who was a member of the aristocratic Polar Star Lodge, was plotting the coup with Kerensky.[1356]

"It was this turmoil," said the former Russian Commissar, "which provoked the original overthrow of the Czar and brought about the attempt to establish a modern Republican regime under Kerensky. Everybody close to those in command of the armies knew that the ruling powers of Imperial Russia had divided."[1357]

Czar Nicholas was indifferent toward the political division at home. His immediate concern was the heavy toll the world war was inflicting on the Russian population. In spite of the treaty he had signed with England and France, a treaty which specified that there would be no separate peace negotiated with the Central Powers, Nicholas needed to end the war to save his nation. The faction of militarists around the Czar argued for staying in the war, but Nicholas refused. He planned one final offensive to be launched in early spring. The German army was to be thrown back, if possible, as far as Warsaw, and peace negotiations with the Central Powers were to begin.[1358]

---

the Communist Party. Trotsky founded the Fourth International while in exile in Mexico. It is responsible for all South American Communist movements.

[1353] Webster, Socialist *Network* 40-50.

[1354] Commissar 23

[1355] Quigley 243-244.

[1356] Knight, *The Brotherhood* 283.

[1357] Commissar 20.

[1358] Commissar.

Great Britain, desperately needing the Russian war machine to keep the Germans occupied on the eastern front, was provoked into backing the Kerensky revolution. Kerensky had earlier sent word to London that his government would keep Russia in the war if the British would finance his coup. With help from the House of Rothschild, London immediately responded. By the fall of 1916, English Masons were secretly meeting with Kerensky.[1359]

The English Mason most responsible for negotiating terms with Kerensky was 33rd degree Mason Lord Alfred Milner (1854-1925), head of the conspiratorial Round Table Groups. *Macmillan's History of the Times* confirms that

> [o]n January 19, 1917 Milner left London at the head of an Allied mission which, during three weeks in Petrograd, laid down a suitable scheme for keeping the Russian forces supplied with Western munitions... It was widely believed at the time that the February Revolution [installing Kerensky] was hatched at the British embassy.[1360]

COERCING THE UNITED STATES INTO WORLD WAR I

With Russia weakened, the Allies were rapidly losing the war to the Central Powers. Not only did England need Russia to stay in the war, she needed the United States to enter. The British government hoped to capitalize on the power and influence of world Jewry. The *Encyclopedia of Jewish History* also confirms that Zionist leaders in England pinned their movement's future on a British victory. Zionists saw the war as a unique opportunity, especially when it appeared that England was about to lose the support of Russia. The *Encyclopedia* states that

> [t]he British were anxious to have world Jewry on their side believing that this would engender widespread Jewish support for British policies. In particular, Britain wished to persuade the United States to join the war, and Russia to remain a combatant... Many in Britain believed that a British pro-Zionist declaration would lead American and Russian Jewry to put pressure on their respective governments in favor of Great Britain.[1361]

THE BALFOUR DECLARATION

Freemasons were the vehicle through which the British plan was communicated. James A. Malcolm, an Armenian, reveals the extent of the Masonic network in *Origins of the Balfour Declaration*, a white paper written in 1944 and held by the British Museum, as well as Harvard University Library. In *Origins*, Malcolm tells the story of his personal involvement in the events and politics leading to the Balfour Declaration.

In 1916 Malcolm was appointed one of five members of the Armenian National Delegation to take charge of the Armenian interests during and after the war. In this official capacity, he had frequent contacts with the British Cabinet Office, Foreign Office and War Office. He also had contact with the French and other allied embassies in London

---

[1359] Miller 466.

[1360] *History of the Times: 1912-1920*, vol. IV (New York: Macmillan,1952) 244.

[1361] "The British Mandate and the Zionists," *Encyclopedia of Jewish History*, 1986 ed., 139.

and was in touch with French authorities when he travelled to Paris. Malcolm was educated in England and knew influential British Jews:

> When I came to England as a boy for my education, in 1881, I was placed under the guardianship of an old friend, and agent of the family, Sir Albert (Abdalla) Sassoon in London, and cultivated Jewish friends, including Colonel Goldsmid. After leaving Oxford, while dabbling in journalism, I met Mr. Edward Fitzgerald, who was then a roving correspondent for the Daily News on the Continent. He had met Herzl in Vienna and Con- stantinople and told me a good deal about him and his Zionist ideas, which naturally interested me very much. In London, I heard from Colonel Goldsmid and other notable Jews about projected Jewish settlements in Palestine... Of course, I had read Byron, George Eliot and Oliphant about the Jews. Later, during my business travels in Eastern Europe and in Russia, I saw something of the Jewish centres and I always remembered my father had told me that wherever they were, the Jews never failed each Passover to drink to "next year in the Land of Israel."[1362]

In late autumn of 1916, when England first learned that the Czar was weary of war and ready to negotiate his own separate peace, Malcolm visited Sir Mark Sykes in the War Cabinet at Whitehall. Malcolm said that Sykes "spoke of military deadlock in France, the growing menace of submarine warfare, the unsatisfactory situation which was developing in Russia and the general bleak outlook... The Cabinet was looking anxiously for United States intervention."[1363]

Sir Mark said he had tried to enlist substantial Jewish influence in the United States, but was unsuccessful. The German House of Warburg, which controlled American banking, was obviously not interested. Malcolm explained to Sir Mark that he was approaching the wrong Jews - that there were two sets of Jews, Zionists and anti-Zionists. The latter were members of the Alliance Israelite Universelle, thus could not be persuaded. Among them were Felix Warburg and Jacob Schiff in the United States. The British would have to approach the Zionists. "There are tens of thousands, perhaps hundreds of thousands, of such Jews. You can win the sympathy of the Jews everywhere, in one way only, and that way is by offering to try and secure Palestine for them," said Malcolm.[1364]

Sir Mark was interested. Malcolm said he should discuss it with Lord Milner, who was also a member of the War Cabinet. When Sir Mark made this suggestion, Milner became greatly interested, but did not know how England could promise Palestine to the Jews. Malcolm suggested he contact Justice Brandeis, a 33rd degree Jewish Scottish Rite Mason on the United States Supreme Court. Brandeis was intimate with Col. Edward House, a 33rd degree Jewish Grand Lodge Mason, who was constantly at President Woodrow Wilson's side. Both Brandeis and House were Zionists. A few days later Sir Mark informed Malcolm that the Cabinet had agreed to his suggestion and authorized him to open negotiations with the Zionists. Malcolm was then introduced to Dr. Chaim Weizmann, a Jewish English Freemason and ardent Zionist. Weizmann, along with two other Zionists, Sokolow and Greenberg, agreed to solicit the help of American Jewry. Malcolm wrote:

[1362] James A. Malcolm, *Origins of the Balfour Declaration* 1. This document is held by the British Museum and Harvard University Library. A copy is in the author's possession.
[1363] Malcolm 2.
[1364] Malcolm 3-4.

> *The results of the talk were very satisfactory. The first step was to inform Zionist leaders in all parts of the world of the compact and Sir Mark said they would be given immediate facilities for cables to be sent through the Foreign Office and War Office, through the British Embassies and Consulates. A special detailed message was at once sent to Justice Brandeis in cipher through the Foreign Office.[1365]*

The British talks with Zionist Jews resulted in a general understanding that in return for Palestine, the Zionists would work for active Jewish sympathy and support for the Allied cause in the United States.[1366] On February 7th, 1917, during the time Kerensky was deeply involved in his revolution, Anglo-Zionists gathered at the house of Dr. Gaster to hear Sir Mark's plan. Present were James de Rothschild, Dr. Weizmann, Mr. Sokolow, Dr. Tchlenow and Mr. Sacher and others.

Messages were sent to Zionist leaders in Russia to encourage them to aid the Kerensky revolution. When the message was taken to France, the headquarters of the Alliance Israelite Universelle, all the Jews there, with the exception of Baron Edmond de Rothschild, scoffed at the idea that any appreciable number of Jews would ever want to go and settle in Palestine. They retorted, "Zionism was only an idealistic obsession of a few Eastern European Jewish fanatical nationalists who themselves would never go to Palestine, much less settle on the land there."[1367]

Until the last minute, French Jewry, represented by the powerful Alliance Israelite Universelle and its Secretary Freemason M. Bigart, was straining every nerve to sabotage the British-backed Zionist project.[1368] In contrast, when the message reached Rome, the Pope said, "The Vatican and the Jews would be good neighbours in Palestine."[1369]

At first the Arabs were unhappy. But when Freemason T.E. Lawrence (of Arabia) worked with them through the Masonic lodges (founded earlier by Mazzini as *Young Turks* and later to be called the *Muslim Brotherhood)*, they finally reconciled to the bargain.

Each step in this process was with the full knowledge and approval of two powerful Jewish Masons, Justice Brandeis in America and Dr. Weizmann at London, who actively interchanged cables.[1370] With the exception of the German and American Warburgs, Jewish cooperation was solidified. Dr. Weizmann then discussed the plan with Freemason Lord Balfour, who, as Foreign Secretary, would have to sign the declaration for a Jewish homeland.

Freemason Weizmann drafted the declaration. It was cabled to Freemason Brandeis in Washington. From there it was carried to Free-mason Edward House at the White House, who submitted it to President Wilson to secure his concurrence. When Freemason Baron Edmond de Rothschild in France agreed to it, it was then submitted to the British War Cabinet and to Freemason Balfour, who as Foreign Secretary signed it on November 2, 1917. In history this document is known as the *Balfour Declaration*. On April 6, 1917, seven months before the *Balfour Declaration* was signed, the United States had already entered the war on the side of the Allies - one month following Kerensky's revolution.

Throughout this Zionist intrigue, English Freemasonry was backing Kerensky to keep Russia in the war. Since all available armed forces were concentrated on the Austro-German front, Kerensky's revolution was relatively easy and non-violent. Prince Lvov

---

[1365] Malcolm 5.
[1366] Malcolm.
[1367] Malcolm 7.
[1368] Malcolm.
[1369] Malcolm 8.
[1370] Malcolm.

had forced the peaceful abdication of the Czar on March 15, after which Kerensky became Justice Minister in the Provisional Government headed by Lvov. Kerensky immediately established a full system of civil liberties, but he erred in two areas: (1) he postponed much needed social and economic changes until the establishment of a future constituent assembly; and (2) he kept Russia in the war.[1371]

Kerensky's revolution took Trotsky, Lenin and the Warburgs completely by surprise. Trotsky's Russian Commissar remarked, "Had they expected an early outbreak of the revolution, the Warburgs would have had Trotsky and Lenin in readiness somewhere in Russia itself or nearby Scandinavia."[1372]

There are four reasons why the German Warburgs opposed Kerensky's government: (1) Russia, Germany's enemy, was still in the war; (2) Kerensky's revolution, although Masonic, was too bourgeois; (3) Kerensky was backed by Zionists; and (4) Kerensky's government was funded by Rothschild, the Warburgs' financial competitor.

PROTECTING TROTSKY AND LENIN

English Freemasonry and the Rothschilds may have surprised their German-American rivals by the February-March coup by the Duma, but anti-Zionists Jacob Schiff and those allied with him, namely the Warburgs of New York and Hamburg, were not caught unprepared. As head of the Kaiser's secret service, Max Warburg immediately began to plan a counterrevolution. An emergency meeting was called in the Grand Orient Lodge at Hamburg. Coded cables between Hamburg and New York crisscrossed the Atlantic. Schiff was ordered: "Prepare Trotsky!" Lenin, still in Switzerland, was told to meet Trotsky at St. Petersburg, where further instructions would follow. Myron Fagan picks up the story:

> Right from the outset of [Kerensky's revolution], strange and mysterious goings-on were taking place in New York. Night after night, Trotsky darted furtively in and out of Jacob Schiffs palatial mansion. And, in the dead of those same nights, there were gatherings of hoodlums on New York's lower East side, all of them Russian refugees at Trotsky's headquarters, and all were going through some mysterious sort of training process, but it was all shrouded in mystery. Nobody talked, although it did leak out that Schiff was financing all of Trotsky's activities; then, suddenly, Trotsky vanished, so did approximately 300 of his trained hoodlums. Actually, they were on the high seas in a Schiff-chartered ship bound for a rendezvous with Lenin.[1373]

In Switzerland Lenin was feted with a farewell party in his Masonic hideaway. Myron Fagan continues, "Men of the very highest places in the world were guests at that party... [One of them] was Max Warburg of the Warburg banking clan in Germany, whose family financed the Kaiser's war machine, and who the Kaiser had regarded by making Max Chief of the Secret Police of Germany."[1374]

A report issued by the Committee of Public Information, Washington, D.C., reveals that the United States Government was fully aware of the Communist movements led by Lenin and Trotsky. The government further knew that a trust fund of $20 million had

---

[1371] Quigley 385.
[1372] Commissar 22.
[1373] Fagan, *The illuminati* 18-19.
[1374] Fagan 19.

been set up in Trotsky's name in a Warburg bank. The response was inaction. Woodrow Wilson presided in the White House. At his side was his alter ego, 33rd degree Freemason Col. House. Together they squelched the government report entitled *German-Bolshevik Conspiracy*, which in part stated: "the bank of Max Warburg & Company of Hamburg, and the Rhineland Westphalia Syndicate had opened an account for Trotsky's enterprise."[1375] This trust fund was placed in the Nya Banken at Stockholm, Sweden.

English Freemasonry was also aware of Trotsky's movements, in part through their White House mole Col. House, and also by British Intelligence surveillance of Trotsky in New York. When Trotsky, with his band of 300 terrorists, set sail for Russia, his ship was intercepted and taken into custody by a British warship off the coast of Canada. He and his band were detained in Halifax, Nova Scotia, and brought to the nearby Amherst prison camp.

The British-Rothschild-Masonic alliance underestimated Jacob Schiff and his German-American Grand Orient allies. Schiff, through Freemason Col. House, rushed instructions to President Wilson to order the British to release the ship intact with Trotsky's hoodlums. Wilson obeyed, warning the British that if they refused, the United States would not enter the war. The British buckled to U.S. pressure.[1376] The United States entered the war on April 6. The British kept their part of the bargain and Trotsky was set free on April 29, 1917.[1377]

Trotsky proceeded to Russia, stopping at Stockholm to pick up a 20 million dollar Warburg bank draft. Meanwhile Max Warburg prepared Lenin's transport. Lenin and his group of communist terrorists were loaded into a sealed freight car and carried across German territory to Russia at the height of World War I.

On November 5, 1919, Winston Churchill, a 3rd degree Mason, admitted to the House of Commons, in camouflaged terms, that Freemasonry was behind Lenin's revolution:

> *Lenin was sent into Russia... in the same way that you might send a phial containing a culture of typhoid or of cholera to be poured into the water supply of a great city, and it worked with amazing accuracy. No sooner did Lenin arrive than he began beckoning a finger here and a finger there to obscure persons in sheltered retreats in New York, in Glasgow, in Berne, and other countries, and he gathered together the leading spirits of a formidable sect, the most formidable sect in the world.[1378]*

Several years after Trotsky's brutal slaughter of Russians, Londoners began to question why the British released him. In 1924, J.D. Dell, a prominent London publisher, sent a letter to Lloyd George, Prime Minister of Great Britain from 1916 to 1922, asking him for an answer. Part of Dell's letter reads:

> *It is clear enough now, as you are aware, that the revolution in Russia in 1917 was no mere spontaneous rising of the masses, but was deliberately engineered, both from within and without Russia, by her inveterate enemies. Germany has been accused of aiding Russia's enemies in this bloody business by the despatch of Lenin's secret train but so far no accusation has been made against this country [England] in connection with Trotsky's passage from America to Russia.*

[1375] Commissar 26.
[1376] Fagan 19.
[1377] Commissar 27.
[1378] Kelly, Conspiracy 4.

Germany has an excuse, she was at war with Russia. But what excuse have we? To help the torture of a war-time Ally in the way we helped to torture Russia is a crime of such magnitude that it would be impossible to expiate it voluntarily, but we must try.

In order to attain the object mentioned in the beginning of the letter (to acquit the conscience of Britishers and to bring the chief perpetrators to book) kindly let me know whether you accept any responsibility for the release of Trotsky from his arrest in Halifax, N.S., or his passage through to Russia. As head of the British Government at the time you are of course officially responsible. If however you disclaim responsibility it is necessary for you to indicate where this lies.[1379]

Dell never received an answer to his letter. Although silence suggests complicity with Trotsky's communist revolution, that was not the case. Lloyd George could not defend his decision to release Trotsky without implicating English Freemasonry's role in funding Kerensky's socialist revolution to keep Russia in the war. Nor could he reveal London's negotiations with American Jews to lobby for America's entry into the war. Lloyd George hated the communists as much as did Dell. To release Trotsky was a matter of national survival, requiring no explanation.

THE BOLSHEVIKS OVERTHROW KERENSKY'S ELECTED GOVERNMENT

After Trotsky's arrival in Russia, he and Lenin joined hands for the first time at Petrograd in May 1917, one month after America entered the First World War. The bandit Joseph Stalin was at their side. Immediately they set out to solidify control. With $20 million at their disposal, Lenin put on a powerful propaganda campaign to replace Kerensky and his provisional government with a nationwide system of soviets or councils.

A series of attacks were then directed at the financially entrenched Rothschilds and their newly created republican government. The first blow was aimed directly at the Russian army and navy. "Such a move was necessary for two reasons," wrote the Commissar. "First, to deprive rival revolutionary parties of the possibility of preventing anarchy, and second, to defeat the more conservative, moderate aims of the Rothschilds."[1380]

What Lenin and Trotsky needed was an army of the proletariat, and this they had to create. The middle class, who were mostly agreeable to Kerensky's socialistic views, were reluctant to side with the radical proletarians, who fiercely embraced the Grand Orient communist doctrine. Lenin and Trotsky had to build the foundation for their "dictatorship of the proletariat" by using the "down trodden underdogs of civilization," as the Marxist gospel called the criminals and parasites of society.

The Commissar, using the French Revolution and the storming of the Bastille as an example of the Bolshevik's tactic, explained how Lenin and Trotsky recruited this element: "When the slums, alleys, taverns, brothels and inns of the cities and villages were unable to supply the needed majorities for the Soviets, the jails of the country and Siberia's convict colonies had to produce them."[1381]

In July 1917, Trotsky's new army created an uprising at Petrograd. No one suspected a counterrevolution against Kerensky. Indeed, the Russian people had hoped that some

---

[1379] Commissar 28.
[1380] Commissar 30-31.
[1381] Commissar 32-33.

day, perhaps after the end of the war, a bloodless revolution might occur and that such a revolution would result in lasting liberal reforms for the country. They hoped Kerensky would fulfill that dream. They were not prepared for, nor did they want the bloodthirsty Bolshevik Revolution.[1382]

The uprising at Petrograd was ostensibly in protest of Romanov participation in the provisional government. Consequently, the uprising led to the resignation of Prince Lvov. In an effort to gain control of the situation, Knight said that "Kerensky took over as Prime Minister and appointed exclusively Masons to the government."[1383]

Shortly thereafter the first general election for the first Constitutional Assembly took place. Both the Socialists and the Communists campaigned. Lenin's Bolsheviks were clearly in the minority. Soundly defeated, the Bolsheviks retaliated by staging their "October Revolution" in which they killed, jailed or exiled the rightfully elected representatives of the people.[1384]

The Bolsheviks did not grow rapidly, but they did win over two local military contingents in two chief cities. Dr. Quigley gives the details of the situation:

> On November 7, 1917, the Bolshevik group seized the centers of government in St. Petersburg and was able to hold them because of the refusal of the local military contingents to support the Provisional Government. Within twenty-four hours this revolutionary group issued a series of decrees which abolished the Provisional Government, ordered the transfer of all public authority in Russia to soviets of workers, soldiers, and peasants, set up a central executive of the Bolshevik leaders, called the "Council of People's Commissars," and ordered the end of the war with Germany and the distribution of large landholdings to the peasants.
>
> The Bolsheviks had no illusions about their position in Russia at the end of 1917. They knew that they formed an infinitesimal group in that vast country and that they had been able to seize power because they were a decisive and ruthless minority among a great mass of persons who had been neutralized by propaganda.[1385]

Stephen Knight reports that when "the Bolsheviks took over the country, Kerensky and most of the Masons involved in the earlier revolution fled to France, where they established lodges under the aegis of the Grand Orient of France."[1386] *Mackey's Encyclopedia of Freemasonry* gives us detailed information of their activity:

> After the Bolshevik Revolution most members of these lodges emigrated, and after a long inactivity they were successful in forming under the auspices of the Grand Orient of France a new Polar Star Lodge at Paris. Four other lodges working in Russia have been organized under the Grand Lodge of France, and there is also a Lodge of Perfection and a Rose Croix Chapter working in Russian at Paris the rituals of the Ancient and Accepted Scottish Rite under the Supreme Council... The four Craft lodges work with a committee which in fact represents what the Brethren believe to be the future Grand Lodge of Russia. The Supreme

---

[1382] Commissar 20.
[1383] Knight, *The Brotherhood* 283.
[1384] Commissar 34-35.
[1385] Quigley 386.
[1386] Knight, *The Brotherhood* 283.

> Council has sanctioned a temporary committee in the higher degrees which represents the nucleus of the future Supreme Council for Russia.[1387]

GENTILE FREEMASONS, JEWS AND THE BOLSHEVIKS

The deception of all Masonic deceptions was to make world Jewry believe they were the engineers of the Bolshevik Revolution. The deception was reinforced by Masonic symbols that were taken as Jewish symbols. For example, in the first years of the Communist regime, public buildings were occasionally decorated with the six-pointed Magen David, the Star of David. (This was later changed to the five-pointed star, or pentagram, which is a symbol of the Masonic O.T.O.). Consequently, the Jewish monthly publication, *Jewish World* (July 10, 1929), published an article entitled "The Ideals of Bolshevism." It spoke to the revolt of peoples against the social state, against the evil, the iniquities that were crowned by World War I under which the world groaned for four years. The article ended with this statement: "there is much in the fact of Bolshevism itself, in the fact that so many Jews are Bolshevists, in the fact that the ideals of Bolshevism at many points are consonant with the finest ideals of Judaism."

Rabbi J.L. Magnes, speaking in New York in 1919, listed by name the prominent Jews who headed various Communist uprisings. All were documented as having been Grand Orient Freemasons. Below is a portion of that speech:

When the Jew applies his thought, his whole soul to the cause of the workers and the despoiled, of the disinherited of this world, his fundamental quality is that he goes to the root of things. In Germany he becomes a Marx and a Lasalle, a Haas and an Edward Bernstein; in Austria Victor Adler, Friedrich Adler; in Russia, Trotsky. Compare for an instant the present situation in Germany and Russia: the revolution there has liberated creative forces, and admire the quantity of Jews who were there ready for active and immediate service. Revolutionaries, Socialists, Mensheviks, Bolsheviks, Majority or Minority Socialists, whatever name one assigns to them, all are Jews and one finds them as the chiefs or the workers in all revolutionary parties.[1388]

In April 1919, while Trotsky was still in his glory and before Stalin came to power, M. Cohen, Jewish editor of the *Communist*, a Kharkoff, Russia, newspaper, wrote:

> One can say without exaggeration that the great Russian social revolution has been made by the hand of the Jews. Would the sombre, oppressed masses of Russian workmen and pea- sants have been capable by themselves of throwing off the yoke of the bourgeoisie? No, it was especially the Jews who have led the Russian proletariat to the Dawn of the International and who have not only guided but still guide today [1919] the cause of the Soviets which they have preserved in their hands.
>
> We can sleep in peace so long as the commander-in-chief of the Red Army is Comrade Trotsky... Jews bravely lead to victory the masses of the Russian Proletariat.[1389]

The United States government was made aware of the influence of Jews in the new Communist government by its own American Expeditionary Forces headquartered in Siberia. Two letters from Captain Montgomery Schuyler (placed in our National Archives

---

[1387] "Russia."

[1388] de Poncins, *Secret Powers* 128.

[1389] de Poncins, *Secret Powers* 128-129.

in 1934) tell the story. The first, dated March 1, 1919, was written to Lt. Colonel Barrows, Vladivostok. The second, dated June 9, 1919, is addressed to the Chief of Staff, A.E.F., Siberia. Following are excerpts:

> *It is probably unwise to say this loudly in the United States but the Bolshevik movement is and has been since its beginning guided and controlled by Russian Jews of the greasiest type, who have been in the United States [trained by Trotsky] and there absorbed every one of the worst phases of our civilization without having the least understanding of what we really mean by liberty.*
>
> *A table made in April 1918 by Robert Wilton, the correspondent of the London Times in Russia, shows that at that time there were 384 "commissars" including 2 Negroes, 13 Russians, 15 Chinamen, 22 Armenians and more than 300 Jews. Of the latter number 264 had come to Russia [with Trotsky] from the United States since the downfall of the Imperial Government.[1390]*

Victor E. Marsden, the Russian correspondent for the London *Morning Post*, was in Russia during the first two decades of the 20th Century. In December 1919 he wrote a 23-page booklet, *Jews in Russia*, published by the Zionist Judaic Publishing Company of London. The booklet listed by name the Jews who were commissars. Following are their positions and numbers:

Council of the People's Commissars Jews	of 22 members: 17
Commissariat of War Jews	of 43 members: 34
Commissariat of the Interior	of 64 members: 45 Jews
Committee of Foreign Affairs	of 17 members: 13 Jews
Commissariat of the Exchequer Jews	of 30 members: 26
Commissary of Justice Jews	of 19 members: 18
Commission of Hygiene Jews	of 5 members: 4
Commissariat of Public Instruction Jews	of 53 members: 44
Commission of Social Aid	of 6 members: 6 Jews
Commission of Works Jews	of 8 members: 7
Commission for Reconstruction Jews	of 2 members: 2
Delegates of Bolshevist Red Cross Jews	of 8 members: 8
Provincial Commissioners Jews	of 23 members: 21
Journalists for Pravda and Izvestia Jews	of 42 members: 41
Commission of Enquiry on the late Officials of the Empire Jews	of 7 members: 5
Committee of Enquiry upon the Assassination of Nicholas II members: 7 Jews	of 10

[1390] Copies of these two letters are in the author's files.

Supreme Council of General Economy	of 56 members: 45 Jews
Bureau of the First Soviet of Workmen and Soldiers of Moscow	of 23 members: 19 Jews
Central Committee of the IV Red Army	of 34 members: 33 Jews
Central Committee of the V Red Army	of 62 members: 33 Jews
Central Committee of Social Democratic Party	of 12 members: 9 Jews[1391]

Of the 546 members in Lenin and Trotsky's Bolshevik administration, 447 were Jews.

The *Jewish Encyclopedia* however, is quick to explain that "'Since the revolution the Jews have most of all appeared in connection with Freemasonry.'"[1392] In other words, the Bolshevik Revolution consisted of Jews as Masons, and not Jews as Jews.

Herein lies the truth behind world revolution. Freemasonry is the common denominator, not Judaism. Yet, with 82 percent of the new Communist Government staffed by Jews, we can easily understand how the world was convinced that the Bolshevik Revolution was a Jewish uprising. (See Appendix 2, Fig. 33.) Hitler was so convinced, and though he was guilty of murdering six million Jews, just as the Bolsheviks were guilty in Russia of butchering over three million Gentile Russians, Freemasonry itself was never implicated.

This was Freemasonry's plan all along, and Lenin, half Jewish, knew it. His Masonic duty was to solidify control of the Russian Revolution by using the Jews and then destroying them. As a follower of Bakunin, his plan from the beginning was anti-Semitic and anti-Christian: the age-old Satanic plot to destroy both religions.

The full-blooded Jew Leon Trotsky, although ignorant of this plan, was himself manipulated by the Reform Jews that funded Lenin. Anti-Semitic Gentile Freemasonry used Trotsky to destroy both Crown and Church, after which Lenin was to destroy Trotsky and his Jewish followers. Upon the premature death of Lenin, this assignment passed to Stalin.

TROTSKY'S RED TERROR

Shortly after the October Revolution, Trotsky accepted the position of Commissar of War, and took over the military forces of the Soviets, calling them the "Workers' and Soldiers' Soviets." The Soviets consisted primarily of unscrupulous criminals, many of whom, it appeared, had been initiated into the Ordo Templi Orientis (O.T.O.). This barbarous Red Army, as it called itself, joined remnants of the Russian army and navy. (According to historian Richard Pipes in *Russia under the Bolshevik Regime* (1993), the Red Army adopted in 1918 as its emblem the Masonic five-pointed star, or pentagram.)[1393] To strengthen his forces, Trotsky conscripted the entire male population and tried to restore some sort of military discipline.[1394]

Trotsky's former Commissar told how Trotsky took over the Russian army with these ruffians:

> *The Soviets eventually replaced the commanding officers and their staffs, and the first thing the new militarists did was to break up the machinery of the Imperial army and to remove Russia from the ranks of Entente Powers which the Rothschilds had lined up against Germany.*

[1391] Victor E. Marsden, *Jews in Russia* (Metairie, LA: Son's of Liberty, n.d.) 7-23.

[1392] Pinay, *The Plot Against the Church* 112.

[1393] Pipes 102n.

[1394] Commissar 35-36.

> *No one was better prepared for such a task. I have seen Trotsky at the height of his career; have witnessed his activities during the time he was dictator over Russia and director of all the revolutionary forces of the world. I know that no pagan war of the dark ages, no medieval crusade or inquisition has produced a more murderous leader than this beast. His large number of Political Commissars which he had been organizing and instructing for months, together with their spy system within the army units, made every attempt to oppose him impossible. He did not hesitate to exterminate ruthlessly any individual or group which was suspected of disloyalty.*
>
> *The notorious Soviet Secret Service, first known as "CHEKA" and now existing as the GPU [KGB], was started by Trotsky as part of the military machine. It has always been a terror to both the civilian population and the army.*[1395]

BLOODSICKNESS: MASONIC SYMBOLS AND RITUAL SLAUGHTER

Communism was supposedly the dictatorship of the proletariat, the lowest social or economic class of society. The stamp of a Bolshevik was long, unkempt hair. Bolsheviks were those who were unskilled and unable to find work, those who did not want to work, and those who were common criminals. Bolsheviks imitated Trotsky's appearance. Their Colors were red, hence they were nicknamed the "Reds."

In opposition to the Reds were the Whites from Belorussia, or White Russia, a province in the western part of Russia bordering Poland. Beginning early in 1919, the White Russian Army fought the Red Army for four years, but succumbed for lack of funds.

The Bolsheviks were in power one year when the armistice was signed on November 11, 1918, terminating World War I. That same month the Allied Powers sent expeditionary forces into Russia to observe the Bolshevik Revolution. As Masonic powers, the Allies were not to intervene in this Masonic revolution, no matter how bloody it became. They were there only to observe and report.

Captain Montgomery Schuyler, with the American Expeditionary Forces in Siberia, describes the dearth of ruling ability of these longhaired Bolsheviks when he made his General Report on June 9, 1919, to his Chief of Staff:

> *Both the civil and military departments at Omsk, at the present time, suffer from the lack of men trained in leadership, and of executive ability. The only ministers were of the longhaired, loud-mouthed type and spent so much time in fruitless discussion that they were never able to get any action even on the most urgent matters.*[1396]

The duty of the Soviets was to eliminate the middle and upper classes. De Poncins confirms this in a quote from a man by the name of Latsis (no first name available), the director of the Red Terror in the Ukraine:

> *"We are not making war against individuals in particular. We are exterminating the bourgeoisie [middle and upper classes] as a class. Do not look*

[1395] Commissar.

[1396] Captain Montgomery Schuyler's *General Report* on June 9, 1919, to the Chief of Staff, Siberia, is filed in the National Archives of the United States in the War Records Division; a copy is in the author's possession.

in the enquiry for documents and proofs of what the accused person has done in acts or words against the Soviet Authority.

The first question which you must put to him is, to what class does he belong, what are his origin, his education, his instruction, his profession."[1397]

Consequently, those who were educated - those who knew how to run a business and a country - were slaughtered. How Russia was to survive economically and politically after killing the educated and skilled of the country was never considered by the ignorant hate-crazed communists. Like the Grand Orient Jacobins of 1793, the Grand Orient Communists destroyed old Russia economically and politically.

These criminals made up Trotsky's Red Army and conducted the "Red Terror." The best, and most imaginative executioners were placed in the CHEKA, forerunner of the KGB.

Stephen Knight, author of *The Brotherhood*, while researching how the KGB infiltrated Western governments without detection, discovered that Freemasonry was the channel. Knight was told by a Mason that the "records of Freemasonry in Tsarist Russia would have fallen into the hands of the CHEKA, the KGB's predecessor, in 1917. A close study of Freemasonry would certainly have been made by Soviet intelligence officers then."[1398]

A more plausible explanation of the Masonic elements of the CHEKA is that the CHEKA itself was an exclusive Masonic Lodge. The Masonic symbols left on victims slaughtered by the CHEKA suggest that the CHEKA consisted of homicidal O.T.O. Masons. For example after the White Russians recaptured Kiev, the expeditionary forces entered that city in August 1919. The expedition's Rohrberg Commission of Enquiry found the execution hall of the CHEKA in the following state:

All the cement floor of the great garage (the execution hall of the departmental CHEKA of Kief) was flooded with blood. This blood was no longer flowing, it formed a layer of several inches: it was a horrible mixture of blood, brains, of pieces of skull, of tufts of hair and other human remains. All the walls riddled by thousands of bullets were bespattered with blood; pieces of brains and of scalps were sticking to them.

A gutter twenty-five centimeters wide by twenty-five centimeters deep and about ten meters long ran from the centre of the garage towards a subterranean drain. This gutter along its whole length was full to the top with blood... Usually, as soon as the massacre had taken place the bodies were conveyed out of the town in motor lorries and buried beside the grave about which we have spoken; we found in a corner of the garden another grave which was older and contained about eighty bodies. Here we discovered on the bodies traces of cruelty and mutilations the most varied and unimaginable.[1399]

The mutilations described by the Commission were definitive signs that the victims suffered from O.T.O. Masonic ritual murders. For example, some bodies were disemboweled, while others had their tongues cut out - mutilations descriptive of punishment given Masons who reveal secrets and/or who talk. (See the Masonic oaths in Appendix 4.)Some corpses had wedges driven in their hearts, others had limbs chopped off, and had literally been hacked to pieces. Others' eyes had been gouged out while yet

---

[1397] de Poncins, *Secret Powers* 148.

[1398] Knight, *The Brotherhood* 290.

[1399] de Poncins, *Secret Powers* 149-150.

alive, a practice typical of the Masonic ritual mutilations performed during the "Ripper" murders on the east side of London in 1888. The best evidence that the CHEKA was nothing more than an O.T.O. Masonic Lodge performing Satanic ritual murders, were the numerous Masonic symbols carved into the flesh of victims' heads, faces, necks and torsos.[1400]

Published in the *Scotsman,* on November 7, 1923, are the following counts of the slaughtered:

> "28 bishops, 1219 priests, 6000 professors and teachers, 9000 doctors, 54,000 officers, 260,000 soldiers, 70,000 policemen, 12,950 property owners, 535,250 members of the intellectual and liberal professions, 193,290 workmen, 618,000 peasants."[1401]

The Denikin Commission of Enquiry reported 1,700,000 victims slaughtered during 1918-1919. By the winter of 1920 another 1,500,000 were butchered. A total of 3,200,000 innocent Russians went to their graves in this benevolent Grand Orient working man's Paradise. Their only crime was that they belonged to the middle or upper class.[1402]

One of the most renowned leaders of the Red Terror was Batjko Machno (Dad Machno), an ex- convict in South Russia. In the city of Jekaterinoslaw, he and his ritual murderers slaughtered several thou-sand non-combatant citizens within a few days. In the territory of Kherson, where Trotsky's father owned a grain mill, Machno's band came upon a group of more prosperous villages, surrounded one of them - Eichenfeld - sacked it without cause or provocation, and murdered 81 men and four women. Only two men over sixteen years of age were spared out of the entire male population of this little village.

On November 29, 1919, a detachment of these marauders came upon another group of villages located not far from Trotsky's parental estate at Yanovka. This time they murdered 214 people - because they were prosperous.

In thousands of instances, fathers, husbands, brothers, and sons were compelled to watch these beasts as they raped their wives, mothers, young daughters and sisters. The men were held at bay with sabers and guns, and crippled or murdered if they dared to help their loved ones.

When the Red Army had spent its ammunition on defenseless Russians, Trotsky sent instructions to continue the executions by means other than shooting. Hundreds of victims were assembled at a time, their hands and feet securely tied, their bodies weighted down with scrap iron; they were pushed off the pier at Eupotoria, a small insignificant town on the west coast of the Crimea. In a similar way thousands more were drowned in Odessa and other coastal cities.

In 1921, when the White Army was no longer able to resist the Red Army in the Crimea, it abandoned South Russia for good. Bela Kun (Cohen), who had been the architect of the "benevolent" Grand Orient slaughter in Hungary, became Trotsky's commander-in-chief in the unarmed Crimea. The people in this area were driven into the sea in masses.[1403]

The deliberate slaughter did not kill as many as did the created famines that followed. Later called the "reorganization of agriculture," Trotsky's agents had taken for themselves every piece of farm equipment that could be converted into money. When widespread food shortages resulted, the Red Army ruthlessly confiscated every bit of grain they could

---

[1400] de Poncins.
[1401] de Poncins 150.
[1402] de Poncins 151.
[1403] Commissar 38-43.

find. If the Red Army suspected the farmers of hiding small quantities of grain for their own needs, or for seed, mass executions followed.

Cattle were slaughtered and horses taken for the Red cavalry, or used for military transport work. The immediate result of Trotsky's "reorganization of agriculture" was the famine of 1921-1922. To the rescue came American Freemason and Reform Jew, Armand Hammer. Twenty-seven million people in a nation that had previously exported grain to all parts of Europe had to be fed by the American Relief Administration and auxiliary organizations headed by Hammer. Hammer made his first million dollars on this venture. In 1945, Stalin himself told Winston Churchill that during that period "twelve million peasants died in the reorganization of agriculture alone."[1404]

Russian Grand Orient Freemason Nikolay Ivanovich Bukharin (1888-1938), head of the Petrograd Committee of the Russian Communist Party (and later killed by Stalin), gloated over the bloodbath of the Bolshevik Revolution - a revolution financed and sustained by Grand Orient Freemasonry. De Poncins quotes from a letter by Bukharin, reproduced by the French *La Revue universelle*, March 1, 1928:

> *"Here, in our country [Russia], where we [Bolsheviks] are absolute masters, we fear no one at all.*
> *"The country worn out by wars, sickness, death and famine (it is a dangerous but splendid means), no longer dares to make the slightest protest, finding itself under the perpetual menace of the CHEKA and the army.*
> *"Often we are ourselves surprized by its patience which has become so well-known... there is not, one can be certain in the whole of Russia, a single household in which we have not killed in some manner or other the father, the mother, a brother, a daughter, a son, some near relative or friend."[1405]*

The Bolsheviks of course enthroned man as God, and attempted to banish God from all private and public society. Shortly after the success of the revolution, in an act of grotesque irony which revealed the true nature of the Masonic-communist revolution, the Bolsheviks "proposed to erect in Moscow a statue to Judas Iscariot, who they said hanged himself in despair over the thought of what humanity must suffer under Christianity."[1406]

A story published in the *Ost Express*, January 30, 1923, and in the *Berliner Taegeblatt*, May 1, 1923, reveals how widespread and endemic to Bolshevism was the hatred of the revealed God of Jews and Christians. The story reports that Trotsky was presiding over a meeting in Moscow that same year, a meeting organized by the propaganda section of the Communist Party, to judge God. Five thousand men of the Red Army, men who claimed there was no God, were present to see God judged. "The accused was found guilty of various ignominious acts and having had the audacity to fail to appear, [God] was condemned in default."[1407]

The civil war between the "Whites" and "Reds," which lasted from 1919 to 1922, caused the death of 28 million Russians - more than 16 times the men Russia lost during

---

[1404] Commissar 45-46. One of the most powerful Jewish Masons in the world brought famine relief to the Ukraine. He was 33rd degree, Dr. Armand Hammer (d. at age 92, December 10, 1990). Hammer denied ever joining the Communist Party, but his father had. In his autobiography *Hammer*, 1987, page 15, Armand Hammer said: "As a newly qualified young doctor, I went to Russia in 1921 to work in the Urals among the victims of famine and an epidemic of typhus. For supplying much-needed grain to the starving Russians, I was personally thanked by Lenin, who took me under the wing of his patronage."

[1405] de Poncins, *Secret Powers* 149 and Miller 615, 723.

[1406] de Poncins 144.

[1407] de Poncins 144-145.

World War I. The famine that swept the land starved another five million. With so many absurdities and brutal atrocities, the Bolshevik Revolution began to crumble. William T. Still, author of *New World Order* writes that

> *Lenin had to admit that Marxism as an economic system was a failure. He instituted a radical economic reform. He eliminated the Marxist barter system and returned currency and wages to the Russian people. In less than a year, three quarters of all retail distribution was in private hands. Peasant farmers were allowed to sell most of their grain on the open market. In a matter of months, starvation began to disappear.[1408]*

In May 1922, Lenin had a cerebral stroke and, after a series of such attacks, died in January 1924. On his deathbed, Lenin said:

> *I committed a great error. My nightmare is to have the feeling that I'm lost in an ocean of blood from the innumerable victims. It is too late to return. To save our country, Russia, we would have needed men like Francis of Assisi. With ten men like him we would have saved Russia.[1409]*

Joseph Stalin, then a 33rd degree Rosicrucian Freemason, became embroiled in a power struggle with Trotsky. Stalin won, continuing the bloodbath for the Masonic hierarchy. Stalin sent to the grave over 40 million Russians - four times the number slaughtered by Hitler.[1410] Stalin, however, was a Mason, and thus information or news of the magnitude of his slaughter was hidden and suppressed for years.

The letter sent by Albert Pike to Joseph Mazzini in 1871 prophesying the union of atheism and savagery found partial fulfillment in the Bolshevik Revolution. It reads in part:

> *We shall unleash the Nihilists and the Atheists and we shall provoke a formidable social cataclysm which, in all its horror, will show clearly to the nations the effect of absolute atheism, the origin of savagery and of the most bloody turmoil.[1411]*

RULE OF THE SUPREME COUNCIL

When Imperial Russia was swept away by the Grand Orient Bolshevik Revolution, Kerensky fled to France. In 1922 Freemasonry set up several Russian-speaking lodges in Paris under the jurisdiction of the Grand Orient of France and its Supreme Council. The purpose, according to the Masonic periodical *Builder,* June and August 1927, was to house "a temporary committee recognised [sic] by the Supreme Council of France, which will subsequently become the Supreme Council of the Scottish Rite in Russia. The task will consist: 'In restoring to Russia a normal government and in establishing ordinary conditions of economic and political life.'"[1412]

[1408] William T. Still, *New World Order* 142.
[1409] Still 142.
[1410] Still.
[1411] Recorded in chapter 17.
[1412] Stoddard, *Trail* 140-141.

When the task was complete, the highest legislative body of the Soviet Union consisted of two chambers, one of which represented the overall population and the other the constituent republics. Named after the 33rd degree Supreme Council in Freemasonry, it was called the *Su- preme Soviet. (Soviet* in Russian means *Council.)* This name signified to the Masonic world that the Soviet Union was a total Masonic State. Just as the walls surrounding our local Masonic lodges protect the secrets of Masonry, so too did Stalin's "Iron Curtain" keep the truth of his Masonic state secret. But to those who understood the Masonic significance of the Supreme Soviet, it was a portent of Freemasonry's future Universal Republic.

De Poncins sagely observed the real attitude of complicity of western states toward the newly created Masonic state of the Soviet Union: "In consequence, Masonic governments pretend to blame Bolshevism by condemning its unpopular excesses, whilst in fact they are supporting it and making it last until the means are found for it to evolve into a more lasting form."[1413]

What was the status of Masonry within the Soviet Union? When Stalin took power and lowered the Iron Curtain around the world's first Masonic nation, he had no more use for local lodges. Totally sagacious, the bandit became the cat who turned on and swallowed the other cats. Stalin realized that if Masonic Lodges were permitted the freedom to operate, they could pose a serious threat of counterrevolution. To make sure the workers' paradise would never be overthrown, all Freemasonry was vilified and banned as an institution. Stephen Knight, quoting from the English Masonic monthly, *The Freemason,* 1934, tells how this was accomplished:

> *"As soon as the Bolshevik State was declared, Freemasonry was proscribed. This anti- masonic stand was enshrined in a resolution of the fourth Congress of the Communist International: 'It is absolutely necessary that the leading elements of the Party should therefore bring about a definite breach with classes and should therefore bring about a definite breach with Freemasonry. The chasm which divides the proletariat from the middle classes must be clearly brought to the consciousness of the Communist Party. A small fraction of the leading elements of the Party wished to bridge this chasm and to avail themselves of the Masonic Lodges. Freemasonry is a most dishonest and infamous swindle of the proletariat by the radically inclined section of the middle classes. We regard it as our duty to oppose it to the uttermost."[1414]*

Although Freemasonry as an institution was outlawed, Freemasonry as an ideal along with some of its rituals was incorporated into the Soviet Union. And the Soviet Union was run by the Communist Party. Until recently, the Communist Party controlled the Supreme Soviet in the same manner as the hierarchy in Freemasonry controls the Supreme Council.

Anyone initiated into the Communist Party in the 1930s underwent the same ceremony prescribed in the Blue Degrees, with a slight variation of replacing the Masonic apron with the Communist red handkerchief. The authors of *The Massonic Legacy* tell how the initiation was conducted:

> *Admission into the Party was as portentous, as ritualistic, as fraught with the evocative resonance as initiation into... Free-masonry. In children, particularly, the religious impulse was often deliberately activated, then systematically*

[1413] de Poncins, *Secret Powers* 155.
[1414] Knight, *The Brotherhood* 283.

channelled into Party interests... Amid various quasi-liturgical vows and pledges, the new Pioneer was given, as a sacred talisman, a red handkerchief. This piece of cloth was declared to be his most precious possession. He was instructed to guard it, revere it, preserve it from the touch of anyone else's hand.[1415]

Although Stalin outlawed Freemasonry as an institution, he used the Masonic system in many ways, one of which was to infiltrate Western intelligence organizations. Stalin was aware of Freemasonry's importance to Western society. He knew that the British and American intelligence services were rife with Masons, that the chiefs of the secret services were wrapped up in Freemasonry. In 1936 Stalin set up training centers for the exploitation of Western Freemasonry.[1416]

STALIN'S ANTI-ZIONISM

Lenin did not live to see Zionism restrained in Russia. This task passed to Stalin. Stalin, a Martinist Rosicrucian Freemason, was a closet anti-Zionist. He was apparently not only aware of the anti- Zionist motives of the Priory of Sion, but cognizant of his duty to contain Zionism within Russian borders. Stalin's actions betray this program, for he rewarded the Priory of Sion by purging Jews from government, and then closed Soviet borders to keep Zionists from emigrating to Palestine. James Pool tells the story in Who *Financed Hitler:*

> *After the revolution the Jews were gradually pushed aside by the more brutal leaders arising from the non-Jewish masses. The change that occurred in the top Soviet leadership from 1926 to 1937 is an historical example of this process: The Jewish leaders of the revolutionary period, Trotsky, Zinoviev, Kamenev, were shoved aside by Stalin and other non-Jews.*[1417]

Throughout his career as head of the Soviet Union, even until death, Stalin remained violently anti-Zionist. This fact was confirmed by his daughter, who, on June 4, 1990, confessed that Stalin wanted to get rid of all Zionists. She said that in 1952, one year before his death, Stalin began another purge, accusing Zionists of trying to overthrow him.[1418]

In contrast, Trotsky's actions suggest that he was not a participant in the anti-Zionist conspiracy. For example, as an ardent Communist, Trotsky desired to spread Communism worldwide. Dr. Quigley exposed the conflict between Stalin and Trotsky on this matter, which ultimately led to Trotsky's death:

> *The rivalry between Stalin and Trotsky in the mid-1920's was fought with slogans as well as with more violent weapons. Trotsky called for "World revolution," while Stalin wanted "Communism in a single country."*[1419]

[1415] Baigent et al, *Messianic Legacy* 148-149.
[1416] Knight, *The Brotherhood* 284.
[1417] James Pool and Suzanne Pool, *Who Financed Hitler?* (New York: Dial Press, 1978) 103.
[1418] "Stalin - A time for Judgement," WROC (channel 9 cable) Rochester, New York, 4 June 1990.
[1419] Quigley 395.

When Stalin lowered the Iron Curtain, Trotsky went into a rage, screaming, "You have betrayed the Revolution! You have betrayed the Revolution!"[1420] What Trotsky obviously did not realize was that if Zionism was to be contained in Russia, Communism must suffer the same fate.

When Trotsky protested too loudly, Stalin had no time for this unenlightened bewhiskered pest, and he sought to kill him. Trotsky escaped to France where he was protected for a time by his Jewish friend, Grand Orient Freemason and French Premier, Leon Blum.[1421] Blum was also outspoken against Stalin's "iron curtain" policy, stating directly to the Russian dictator, "You have betrayed the spirit of world revolution."[1422]

The long arm of Stalin's secret service reached to France in search of Trotsky. Trotsky was on the run again, this time to Mexico. Mexican Grand Orient Freemasonry, which had solidified its 100-year-old revolution soon after World War[1423] welcomed Comrade Trotsky with open arms, providing him housing and all manner of luxuries.

Within the protective walls of the Mexican Grand Orients, Trotsky founded the Fourth Communist International, with the intent of returning to Russia to assassinate Stalin. But Stalin found him first. In 1940 the NKVD, later to be called the KGB, assassinated Trotsky.[1424]

[1420] de Poncins, *Freemasonry and the Vatican* 102.

[1421] E. Matthews, *What is Communism?* white paper, 9-10.

[1422] de Poncins, *Vatican* 102.

[1423] Most Rev. Francis Clement Kelley, *Blood Drenched Altars* (1935; Rockford, IL: Tan Books, 1987) entire.

[1424] Wilgus 198-208. The CHEKA was renamed GPU in 1922, then changed to NKVD in 1934, changed again to MGB in 1944, and finally to KGB in 1954.
The Fourth Communist International came back to haunt South America. Eighteen years after Trotsky's assassination, Grand Orient Freemasonry was again cooperating with Communism, this time, south of our border. This activity, however, did not go undetected by the Catholic Church. On February 20, 1959, the Plenary Assembly of Cardinals, Archbishops and Bishops of the Argentine, under the presidency of Cardinal Caggiano, published a long collective declaration on Freemasonry, from which de Poncins quotes:
"In 1958 the Fourth Anti-American Conference of Freemasonry, which was held in Santiago, Chile, declared that 'the Order helps all its members to obtain important posts in the public life of the nations.' After this came a dissertation on the theme of' 'The Defense of Laicism,' to be followed by directions as to the new tactics to be adopted by Freemasonry, which coincide with the latest instructions of the Communist International. Freemasons are to work for the triumph of laicism in all walks of life, and Communists are to subvert social order in order to create a favourable terrain in which to achieve their ends. This is how the instruction is worded:
'Intensify the campaign of laicisation through the intermediary influence of the different political parties. Try and appease the alarm of the Catholic Church at Freemasonry by avoiding direct Masonic action. Intensify the action which will unsettle the unity of the working-class movements, so that they may the more easily be stifled afterwards.
Freemasonry and Communism for the moment are pursuing the same objective in Latin America, which is why they must try and work together in the best possible way, without allowing the slightest sign of their alliance to become public.
On March 26-28, 1959, the Second International Congress for Universal Fraternity was held in Montevideo during Holy Week. The purpose of this Congress was to "subordinate the Masonic ideal of universal fraternity to the expansion of the Soviet Communist International" (de Poncins, *Freemasonry and the Vatican*, 153).
Likewise in Africa, Freemasonry and Communism were comrades. In 1961 Monsignor Perraudin, Archbishop of Ruanda in Africa, on his return from Europe, addressed a letter to the priests of his diocese. The letter was quoted in the Catholic review *Verbe*, July-August 1961, from which de Poncins quotes:
"It is impossible to give even a brief account in this letter of all the journeys and approaches that I have made in Europe. My visits and my contacts have shown me how completely they support us in

Stalin eliminated Trotsky not because Trotsky was a Jew. Nor did he systematically persecute Jews, as we have been led to believe. The Jews he killed were a threat to his Sionist assignment of containing Zionism within Russian borders. The record speaks for itself. The few Jews who did leave Russia were not permitted to emigrate to Palestine. Not until Mikhail Gorbachev came to power in 1985, were these restrictions lifted.

THE FINAL COUP

Can anyone doubt that Freemasonry, specifically English Freemasonry, is behind the recent break-up of the Soviet Union? From the moment Kerensky's democratic government was ousted by the Bolsheviks, London backed the White Russian counterrevolution. When the atrocities of the Red Terror were exposed, London was strengthened in her resolve to topple the Soviet Union.

The seriousness of the situation in the Soviet Union was brought to light by Admiral "Blinker" Hall, head of British naval intelligence. Hall informed his colleagues at the end of World War I that the "most durable monster Western intelligence has ever faced had surfaced in Moscow... Therefore, it was not only necessary to discover the other side's secrets but to protect our own from disciples of communism, one of whom could well be the colleague beside you."[1425]

In the early 1920s, the British Special Intelligence Service (SIS) made its first attempt to break up the Soviet Union. They nearly succeeded. The plot called for an uprising of the bodyguards of the communist leaders, who would seize Lenin and Trotsky. (The plot also included the assassination of Lenin if the occasion arose, which it did, but failed.)

British agents would then establish a provisional anti-communist government. However, agents loyal to the communists penetrated the operation, and the whole plot fell apart. Phillip Knightley, author of The Master Spy (1989), said that the CHEKA, realizing a formidable foe in the SIS, from that moment planned "the long-term... Soviet penetration of Western intelligence..."[1426]

When Hitler rose to power, London made a second attempt to destroy the Soviet Union by pushing Nazi Germany east to war with Russia (see chapter 22). Having failed to topple the Soviet Union with Hitler, London continued her objective. "The Final Coup" was well thought out and took 59 years to perfect.

The most brilliant intelligence operation to topple a nation involved English Freemasonry, the KGB and a man named Kim Philby, one of England's senior intelligence officers in MI-6 (Mission Impossible, department 6). As a young man, Philby was groomed for the task by his father, Freemason St.-John Philby. The senior Philby was the British intelligence specialist in the Arabian peninsula for forty years following the Bolshevik Revolution. He assisted in setting up Masonic Lodges throughout Arabic speaking nations.[1427] Although there is no record that young Philby joined Freemasonry (and he stated he had not), his father taught him free-thinking. Moreover, he was educated at Cam-bridge, a college rife with secret societies, including Freemasonry. There he

---

Europe in these difficult times. I have encountered many most praiseworthy and generous gestures of help.

"My dominant impression, however, is that insufficient account is taken in Europe of the amplitude of the struggle for which the whole of Africa is the prize; Communism and Freemasonry are playing a satanic gamble for it, and the older Christian countries do not sufficiently understand that it is the Church of which they are members, their own Church, which is in mortal danger in Africa..." (de Poncins, Vatican, 154).

[1425] Phillip Knighdey, The Master Spy (New York: Alfred A. Knopf, 1988) 90-91.

[1426] Knightley 37, 91-92.

[1427] Robert Dreyfuss, Hostage to Khomeini (New York: New Benjamin Franklin House, 1980) 119.

learned the politics of the intellectual Left and became a communist during the Third International, *but never joined the Party*. When he graduated in June 1933, he went to Vienna under orders from the French Communist Party, which was headquartered in the Grand Orient at Paris.[1428]

When Philby knew all there was to know about the enemy, he was hired by British intelligence as a correspondent and in 1939 sent to Spain to observe the communist revolution in progress there. No one knows for sure when, or if, he was "recruited" by the KGB, but he did give away secrets. The secrets he gave to his controller, however, were miniscule compared to those he never revealed, such as operation "Ultra" during World War II. (Ultra was the code name given to information gathered through deciphering German signal traffic produced by the radio enciphering machine known as "Enigma.")[1429]

After the War, Philby was given permission by British intelligence to try the "full double." He was so instructed: "If an opportunity arises to convince the Russian intelligence service that you are willing to betray your own service and work for the other side, then you have permission to seize it."[1430]

In 1949 Philby was sent to Washington as Great Britain's SIS representative in the United States, working in liaison with the CIA and the FBI. By the time he left Washington to return to London, no other British intelligence officer was as well equipped to perform "The Final Coup" on Soviet Russia.

When he returned to London, Philby began to develop his cover that would make the KGB believe he was a Soviet double agent. In 1952 two British SIS agents, Donald Maclean and Guy Burgess, defected to Russia. Philby was suspected of helping them. In 1955, 33rd degree Freemason J. Edgar Hoover cleared Philby of involvement.[1431] After this reprieve, Philby was sent to the Middle East as a correspondent for the London *Observer* and *The Economist*. The real reason for this transfer was to debrief his father. The senior Philby introduced his son to the entire range of his Middle East contacts. Together, Philby and Philby traveled the Middle East from 1955 until September 1960, when SL John Philby died.[1432] The time had come for Kim Philby's defection.

In January 1963, Philby disappeared while on his way to a diplomatic party in Beirut. In April he surfaced in Moscow. Shortly thereafter, Khrushchev fell from power. After 1963 the West heard nothing of Philby, until 1979. That year Western intelligence discovered that Philby had just been promoted to the rank of General of the KGB. Then in 1980, shocking news came from London that Kim Philby had never had a KGB controller, that Sir Anthony Blunt had all along been Philby's intelligence controller for Britain's Royal Court. Translated, this meant that Philby was a triple-agent, a British intelligence operative disguised as a Soviet double-agent.[1433]

In the next few years Brezhnev died and each of the next two Soviet leaders, Yuri Andropov and Konstantin Chernenko, died suddenly and under mysterious circumstances.

When Mikhail Gorbachev came to power, Kim Philby granted an unprecedented interview to Phillip Knightley, author of *The Master Spy*. Knightley's conclusion was that "the British had let him [Philby] go."[1434] In "The Final Coup," the last chapter of his book,

---

[1428] Knightley 28-30, 38.
[1429] Knightley 99, 116.
[1430] Knightley 147.
[1431] Knightley 192.
[1432] Dreyfuss 229.
[1433] Dreyfuss 217-219.
[1434] Knightley 258.

Knightley records Philby's statement: "In Gorbachev I have a leader who has justified my years of faith."[1435]

What did Philby mean? The policies implemented by Gorbachev dismantled the Soviet Union. Was Philby involved in this process? Was this his assignment? Did he have something to do with bringing Gorbachev to power?

In 1984, one year before Gorbachev took office, he travelled to the two Masonic headquarters in London and Paris, to make a "report." Subsequent events suggest that while on that trip he was initiated into French Freemasonry. The next year, in 1985, Gorbachev was at the helm of the Soviet Union. A major Paris daily newspaper, *Le Figaro*, reported on Gorbachev's intense interest in Freemasonry. By 1989 reports were coming out of France that Gorbachev was planning to reopen Masonic lodges inside the Soviet Union and its satellite states. According to *Floshpoint* (September 1990), a monthly newsletter published by Texe Marrs exposing the most current developments in the conspiracy, "Both of the top masonic [sic] organizations in France, the Grand Orient... and the Grand Lodge... are now working on this high priority project."[1436]

When Freemasonry is permitted to operate within a nation, there will be revolution. The peaceful demise of the Soviet Union in December 1991 can only be attributed to the activity of these new lodges established inside Russian borders since 1989. We may never know what intrigue took place to topple communism, but on December 26, 1991, when Gorbachev voluntarily stepped down from power, he said in true Masonic terminology, "I hereby discontinue my activities at the post of president of the Union of Soviet Socialist Republics. We're now living in a New World!"[1437]

IN CONCLUSION

The Russian Revolution occurred in cooperation with English Masonic Socialists, funded by the House of Rothschild, and in conflict with Grand Orient Communists, funded by the House of Warburg. English Masonry wanted the Zionists out of Russia in order to establish a Jewish homeland in Palestine, while French Grand Orient Masonry desired to keep the Zionists within Russia. Russian Jews, although covertly manipulated by both Gentile Freemasonries, played a significant role in the two Russian Revolutions of 1917. Even the wealthy Rothschilds and Warburgs were pawns in the hands of the Priory of Sion and the Gentile Templars. Jews were used, then abused as scapegoats. Freemasonry went unscathed.

Indeed, the Russian Revolution, the secret conflict it provoked between English and French Freemasonry, and the financial competition it generated between the Rothschilds and the Warburgs, was, and still is, only a manifestation of the thousand-year-old struggle between the Priory of Sion and the Knights Templar.

[1435] Knightley 255.

[1436] Texe Marrs, "Gorbachev and Masonry," *Flashpoint* (Sept.1990) 2.

[1437] Georgia Anne Geyer, "After six years, Mikhail Gorbachev left office and achieved greatness," *Longview News Journal* 1 Jan.1992, 4-A.

20. THE MASONIC RITUAL MURDER OF CZAR NICHOLAS II

> *The murder of the Tsar was committed by men under the command of occult forces: and by an organization which, in its struggle against existing power resorted to the ancient cabbalism in which it was well versed.*[1438]

Kerensky's revolutionary government had successfully negotiated a peaceful abdication of the Czar on March 15, 1917. When the Bolsheviks came into power six months later Leon Trotsky, Lenin's Commissar of War, was not satisfied until the emperor and his entire family were murdered. To leave the Romanovs alive would pose a danger to the Bolshevik Revolution should the Russian people call for their return.[1439]

In much conspiracy literature, those who see a Jewish conspiracy behind the catastrophic revolutions of our century, claim that a Jew ordered the Czar killed:

> *On July 17, 1918 at Ekaterinenburg, and on the order of Trotsky's CHEKA, the commission of execution commanded by a Jew named Yourowsky, assassinated by shooting or by bayoneting the Czar, Czarina, Czarevitch, the four Grand Duchesses, Dr. Botkin, the manservant, the woman servant, the cook and the dog.*[1440]
>
> *The members of the imperial family in closest succession to the throne were assassinated in the following night. The Grand Dukes Mikhailovitch, Constantinovitch, Vladimir Paley and the Grand Duchess Elizabeth Ferodorovna were thrown down a well at Alapaievsk, in Siberia. The Grand Duke Michael Alexandrovitch was assassinated at Perm with his suite.*[1441]

Did a Jew as a Jew, or a Jew as a Mason kill the Czar? This distinction is significant, as subsequent events of modern history show. If a Jew as a Jew were guilty of this crime, as was believed by all anti-Semites, including Hitler, the danger of a Jewish holocaust was real. But, if a Jew as a Mason killed the royal family, his Jewishness had nothing to do with the murders. Any Mason could have performed the act. But then, had any Mason committed this crime, the anti- Semitic Gentile Fraternity would not have been able to make the Jews their scapegoat.

TERRORISTS OR CULT MURDERERS?

Was the murder of Czar Nicolas II and his family carried out by terrorists? Or were the perpetrators members of one of the Masonic-Satanist cults previously discussed in this book? A brief comparison of Masonic terrorists and Satanists will help us consider this question.

[1438] Nilus, *Protocols* 235.
[1439] de Poncins, *Secret Powers* 168.
[1440] de Poncins 153.
[1441] de Poncins 153-154.

First, terrorists, who murder indiscriminately, have a twofold purpose. One, they desire to bring worldwide attention to a specific cause. Two, they hope to polarize a government to gain concessions for their cause or ideology.

Satanists, on the other hand, murder passionately and for a different reason. The murders they commit are part of a ritual, which may or may not be Masonic. The ritual murder requires documentation either by the carving of occult symbols in the flesh of the victim's body or the painting, usually with the blood of the victim, of the symbols on walls surrounding the scene of the murder.

Satanists usually act singly or in discrete, very small groups, accountable to no formal polity. Terrorists, on the other hand, are many, and are controlled by a larger body, such as a state. Some are controlled by Freemasonry itself, such as Bakunin's anarchists and nihilists. That Freemasonry has authorized and contracted such terrorist services is confirmed by a statement found in the minutes of the 33rd degree Supreme Council of Mizraim Freemasonry at Paris in the mid-1800s:

"It is necessary for us to acquire the services of bold and daring agents, who will be able to overcome all obstacles in the way of our progress."[1442]

The Czar and his royal house were not killed by terrorists. That the assassins were more confidential, more discriminating - too passionate and ritualistic in their assignment, indicates they were Satanists. We will discuss at the end of this chapter the symbolic message painted on the wall above the bodies that was not only Satanic, but cabalistic, indicating the assassins could have been Masons on a mission.

SYMBOLS OF MASONIC RITUAL MURDER

Masonic symbols are left at the scene of ritual murders for several reasons: (1) to show the hierarchy in Freemasonry that this was a Masonic murder; (2) to warn all Masons to follow the Masonic code of silence, or suffer a like fate; (3) to document the ritual nature of the murder for completing initiation into a higher Masonic degree; or (4) to prove to the Masonic paymaster that the "hit man" accomplished his task.

One recent murder which bore the signs of Masonic involvement occurred June, 1982 in London, England. The victim was Roberto Calvi, an Italian banker and Grand Orient Mason, who apparently was ritually murdered at the hands of English Freemasonry. A photograph of his body is reproduced in David A. Yallop's book *In God's Name* (pages 212 and 213). The picture, numbered 59, shows the following Masonic symbols:

1. Calvi was hung from London's Blackfriars Bridge. Blackfriar was the name of the lodge to which Calvi belonged in Italy.
2. He was hung next to a sewer outlet to indicate the murderers' opinion of him.
3. A Masonic cable-tow, used to lead the initiate around the room during initiation ceremonies in the Blue Degrees, was around his neck, indicating he was led from Italy to London by higher degree Masons. The cable tow is also "defined in Masonic ritual as representing the cutting of the throat."[1443]
4. Mason bricks were found in his pockets.

Stephen Knight in his book *The Brotherhood* also records the presence of the same Masonic clues or messages on Calvi's body and the significance of the body's location:

> There were many rumours [about Calvi's death]: the Mafia, with whom Calvi had connections, had murdered him; frightened and despairing, he had

---

[1442] Knight, *Jack the Ripper* 160.
[1443] Knight 169.

committed suicide; he had been ritually done to death by Freemasons, a masonic [sic] "cable-tow" around his neck and his pockets filled symbolically with chunks of masonry, the location of the murder being chosen for its name - in Italy, the logo of the Brotherhood is the figure of a Blackfriar.[1444]

What had Calvi done to bring such a gruesome end upon himself? He had committed an unpardonable sin. Calvi stole from several British Masonic bankers and others approximately 1.3 billion dollars, according to bank records.

Calvi's scheme began in 1963 when he created his first of many shell companies. That year he formed a company in Luxembourg called Compendium. The name was later changed to Banco Ambrosiano Holdings and was used to siphon money from a bank he was destined to control. In 1971, Calvi became managing director of Banco Ambrosiano in Milan, Italy. From then and until his death shortly after the Falklands War, the "Knight," as he was affectionately called by his friends, was involved with a cadre of Italian Masons in a maze of dishonest transactions. Yallop gives an overview:

[Calvi's] ability to dream up crooked schemes for laundering Mafia money, exporting lire illegally, evading taxes, concealing the criminal acts of buying shares in his own bank, rigging the Milan Stock Exchange, for bribery, for corruption, for perverting the course of justice, arranging a wrongful arrest here, a murder there - his ability to do all of this and more puts the Knight in a very special criminal class.[1445]

Just before the Falklands War began in the spring of 1982, Calvi opened a branch of Banco Ambrosiano in Argentina. Yallop informs us that "Calvi diverted millions of dollars, some of it from British banks...to purchase Exocets for Argentina."[1446] It is not pleasant for British Masonic bankers to reflect that British soldiers were killed by French Exocet missiles purchased by Argentina with money stolen from their own banks by Grand Orient Freemason Calvi.[1447] One can only conclude from the Masonic symbology on and around the body of Calvi, that Calvi's murder was meant to warn other Masons in his position not to steal from their Masonic brethren.

A second notorious example of Masonic symbols left at the scene of ritual murders is examined by Stephen Knight in *Jack the Ripper: The Final Solution*. Jack the Ripper allegedly was a sexual pervert who raped, then brutally murdered five prostitutes on the East End of London from August through November, 1888. Each woman's mutilated body was photographed by Scotland Yard and the evidence sealed for 100 years. Knight, a British journalist, had connections at Scotland Yard and in 1975 was permitted to study the pictures. He said that the bodies of the victims "bear striking similarities to each other - and extraordinary parallels with the ritual killings of Freemasonry."[1448] For example, the women's stomachs were cut open and their bowels slung over their left shoulder. Their throats were cut from left to right. Two triangles of flesh, one right-side-up, the other up-side-down, were cut out of both sides of their cheeks. "All Jack the Ripper's victims," says Knight, "were dispatched according to an age-old Masonic ritual."[1449] Finally, the

---

[1444] Knight, *The Brotherhood* 305.
[1445] Yallop 141.
[1446] Yallop 287.
[1447] Yallop 141, 287, 298, 316.
[1448] Knight, *Jack the Ripper* 167.
[1449] Knight 166.

last victim was killed at Mitre Square, where only the most important lodges met.[1450] (See "Masonic Oaths" in Appendix 4.)

What had these women done to incite such vicious crimes? Stephen Knight gives us a brief background of the political unrest in England before he answers the question:

> It was a period when England was perilously unstable. Many believed that revolution was just beyond the horizon. The prostitutes had learned first-hand of a secret the most potent forces in the British government had been striving to maintain for nearly four years. The Prime Minister himself believed that if the secret got out, the throne itself would be in peril. In an age of fierce anti-Catholic feeling, Prince Albert Victor Christian Edward, grandson of Queen Victoria and Heir Presumptive to the throne, had illegally married and fathered a child by a Roman Catholic commoner.[1451]

To conceal the shame from potential scandal, the royal physician, Freemason Sir William Gull, committed the wife of the Prince to a lunatic asylum where she died in 1928. Four years after the wife was committed, the five prostitutes learned of the secret and planned to blackmail the most powerful Mason in England - the King. Sir William Gull decided that "the only safe way to silence the women was to eliminate them. And the proper way to execute them was as traitors to the nation... they would be mutilated according to the penalties laid out in masonic [sic] ritual."[1452]

Knight makes a strong case that "Jack the Ripper was not one man but three, two killers and an accomplice."[1453] All three men - the royal physician, the royal coachman, and the royal artist - he says, were Freemasons commanded by a Masonic king to rid himself of blackmailers.

Another notable example of Masonic ritual murder occurred in the mid-1970s, and is discussed by Dr. John Coleman in *Update on Secret* Societies (1984); and *The Future of Latin America* (1985). Coleman was a British intelligence officer in Angola and Rhodesia during the Grand Orient communist revolutions in those two nations in the 1970s. On many occasions he interrogated revolutionists in both countries and discovered that they were professionally trained at the London School of Economics, which teaches Milner, Marx, and Engels.

At the height of the atrocities committed by the rebels, Dr. Coleman visited the Elam Mission Station in Angola. There were no survivors. He viewed the remains of thirteen (a Masonic sacred number) white missionaries who had been hacked to death. One 55-year-old woman had an axe buried in her head. A three-year-old baby girl was pinned to the dirt floor with a bayonet through her temples. "All the victims," says Coleman, "bore the signs of Masonic ritualistic murder - all disemboweled, and cabalistic symbols carved all over their bodies - lips and noses cut off."[1454]

Murderers like those who killed the Angolan missionaries are often members of a degenerate Masonic Lodge such as the Ordo Templi *Orientis* (O.T.O.). In the United States such were Charles Manson and David Berkowitz, who ritually murdered their victims during the 1960s and 1970s. Another such murderer in America was self-proclaimed Satanist Richard Ramirez, nicknamed the "Night Stalker." Like Manson and Berkowitz, Ramirez left Cabalistic-Masonic symbols at the scene of his murders.

[1450] Knight 176.
[1451] Knight, *The Brotherhood* 52.
[1452] Knight 53.
[1453] Knight, *Jack the Ripper* 15.
[1454] John Coleman, Update on Secret Societies, audio cassette, rec.1984, CDL, Box 449, Arabi, LA. and The Future of Latin America, audio cassette, rec. 1985, CDL.

We should remember that one of the requirements of an O.T.O. initiate is to learn the black magic arts of the Jewish *Cabala*.[1455] Albert Pike, in *Morals and Dogma*, says, "all the Masonic associations owe to [the *Cabala*] their Secrets and their Symbols."[1456] *Mackey's Encyclopedia of Freemasonry* informs us that the *Cabala* teaches white and black magic, spells and incantations, performed with symbols and occult numerology.[1457]

At the time Czar Nicholas II was murdered, the Masonic O.T.O. had allegedly been in operation in Russia since 1905. We have documented that Freemason Dr. Gerard Encausse (Papus), Grand Master of Mizraim, Memphis and Martin Freemasonry in France, commissioned Martinist lodges in Russia on two separate occasions when he visited there at the turn of the 19th century. There is every reason to believe that Papus would have established O.T.O. lodges in Russia. The ritual murders and Masonic symbols cut into the bodies of victims during the Bolshevik Red Terror suggest the presence and operation of O.T.O. initiates in the ranks of the Bolsheviks.

Freemason Mikhail Bakunin, a Russian anarchist and Satanist, was a student of the *Cabala*.[1458] Many of the Soviets were filled with disciples of Bakunin. It is not difficult to imagine the hand of the Satanists reaching out to strike down the Czar and his family - Satanists who understood Cabalistic symbology.

SION, THE *CABALA*, AND THE MURDER OF THE CZAR

The assassination of the Czar and his household was a Masonic ritual murder. On the wall where the imperial family was killed was a mysterious inscription written in the blood of the murdered. It consisted of three cabalistic "L" letters with a line drawn beneath them. (See photograph in Appendix 2, Fig. 12.) In the photograph the characters appear as though reversed and written from right to left. This is not the case, however, and is explained by the position assumed by the writer who stood with his back to the wall with his right arm stretched down forming the letters from left to right in true cabalistic style.

When the presence of these occult symbols at the scene of the Czar's murder first became known in the 1920s, many books were published explaining the three "L" letters: Kircher, *Oedpus Aegyptiacus;* Lenain, *La Science Cabbalistique;* Dee, *Monas Hieroglyphcia;* H. Krumrath, *Amphitheatre de l'eternel sapience;* and Franck, *La Cabbale.* These studies concluded that there were two possible meanings to the inscription: First: "Here the King was struck to the heart in punishment of his crimes"; second: "Here the King was sacrificed to bring about the Destruction of his Kingdom."

And what of the line drawn beneath the three "L's"? In magical "science" the horizontal line is the symbol of the passive principle. According to cabalistic interpretation, the line drawn beneath three "L" letters indicates that those who killed the king did so, not of their own will, but in obedience to superior command.[1459] That "superior command" may have come from the Priory of Sion. Sion would want the Romanov family eliminated because they were not of Holy Grail extraction.

"In obedience to superior command," these murderers performed a rite of Black Magic in obedience to a degenerate occult organization. In response to this order, the assassins commemorated their act by a cabalistic inscription in cipher, an inscription which belonged to the rite, perhaps the rite of a cabalistic and degenerate Masonic Lodge, such as the O.T.O. Gentile Freemasons Philippe, Papus, and Rasputin belonged to such

---

[1455] Miller 575.
[1456] Pike, *Morals and Dogma* 744.
[1457] "Cabala," *Mackey's Encyclopedia of Freemasonry*, vol.1.
[1458] Epperson, *The New World Order* 67.
[1459] Nilus, *Protocols* 230-235.

an occult enclave when they were the occult advisers of the ill-fated Czar Nicholas II. Papus was an intimate of Claude Debussy, Grand Master of the Priory of Sion, which Order hated Russian royalty, and wanted to crush the Zionist movement.

The Priory of Sion was well versed in the *Cabala*. Whoever wrote this cabalistic inscription at the scene of the Czar's murder was also educated in the secret symbols of this Jewish book. Is this proof, then, that the assassin was a Jew performing a ritual murder? No, to the contrary. Overwhelming evidence suggests he was a Mason. Of what nationality is irrelevant.

21. COMPETING FOR WORLD GOVERNANCE: THE ROUND TABLE VS. THE LEAGUE OF NATIONS

> *The paramount social purpose of French Masonry was to help establish a permanent peace in Europe. Long before Woodrow Wilson's presidency it held conferences for discussing a League of Nations... It is true that a Masonic Congress held in Paris in 1917 by representatives of the Allied or neutral countries advocated a League of Nations...*
>
> Mackey's Encyclopedia of Freemasonry[1460]

Throughout most of the 19th century, French Freemasonry appeared to be the dominant revolutionary force in the Old World. English Freemasonry, by comparison, seemed dormant. The once powerful British Empire on which the sun never set, was on the wane following the loss of its American colonies. Anything said of World Government emanated from Paris, not London.

The decline of the British Empire during the 1800s was perpetuated by the Little Englanders, an anti-imperialistic liberal movement that believed expanding the colonial empire was expensive and wasteful. They were convinced that trade between colonies - England's primary source of income - was certain, no matter who governed the colonies. Colonies, they believed, "would eventually separate from the mother country, voluntarily if they were given the rights of Englishmen, or by rebellion, as the American colonies had done, if they were deprived of such rights."[1461]

English Freemasonry was also to blame for the decline of the British empire. Since its beginning the English Brotherhood was aristocratic, capitalistic, and monopolistic. Aristocratic incomes came from ground rent, banking and trade. Another source of this wealth was vast sums of drug money from the Orient. The poor working class had no part in such a sophisticated economic system and began to rebel.

French Freemasonry was the force behind their rebellion. As we have seen, during the third quarter of the 19th century, Grand Orient Mason Karl Marx, living in England, spread his communist doctrine among the British. His utopian concepts took root. Before Marx died in 1883 the Grand Orient doctrine had divided British subjects between liberals and conservatives, which division penetrated English Freemasonry as well. During the 1880s, left-wing Freemasonry, represented by the Marxist Fabian Society, began to incite worker strikes and riots. Right-wing Masons, in the privileged ruling class, were in danger of losing their power if something was not radically changed.

Change did come in 1889. At the great Masonic Congress in Paris that year, English Freemasonry accepted socialism as a compromise. After returning to England, British Masons (both right and left) began to organize socialist "think tanks" as political outlets. One of the think tanks founded in 1902 was called the "Coefficients," which in 1909 evolved into the Round Table.

[1460] "League of Nations and Masonry," and "War II, World, and Freemasonry in Europe," *Mackey's Encyclopedia*, vol. III.
[1461] Quigley 129.

The problem facing the right-wing aristocratic Brotherhood was how to control state socialism in a capitalistic society. The "think tanks" proposed a simple solution to the problem: Freemasonry already con-rolled business and finance, which in a sense could be termed "corporate socialism"; state socialism could do business with corporate socialism, so long as the Brotherhood dominated politics, which it did - both left and right.

BRITISH RACE PATRIOTS

The left-wing Masons referred to the right-wing Masons as "British race patriots." The right- wing aristocracy held the exalted opinion that the British race was at a higher evolutionary level than other races. In 1877, Freemason Cecil Rhodes (1853-1902) drafted for the British race patriots a three-step program for world dominion. The first program exposed their racial assumptions. Rhodes wrote:

> *If we had retained America there would at this moment be millions more of English living. I contend that we are the finest race in the world and that the more of the world we inhabit the better it is for the human race. Just fancy those parts that are at present inhabited by the most despicable specimens of human beings. What an alteration there would be if they were brought under Anglo-Saxon influence. Look again at the extra employment a new country added to our dominions gives. I contend that every acre added to our territory means in the future birth to some more of the English race who otherwise would not be brought into existence.[1462]*

The second part of Rhode's program outlined imperial ambitions. Rhodes explained: "It is our duty to seize every opportunity of acquiring more territory. And we should keep this one idea steadily before our eyes - more territory simply means more of the Anglo-Saxon race, more of the best, the most human, most honourable race the world possesses."[1463]

The third part of the program set forth English Freemasonry's political goals for world peace. Rhodes said that "the absorption of the greater portion of the world under our rule simply means the end of all wars."[1464]

British race patriots got their greatest encouragement in the 1870s. During that decade a handful of aristocratic Masons, realizing how ineffective Great Britain had been in dominating politics in the modern world, set out to return England to her days of glory. The scheme began with a speech in 1870 by Freemason John Ruskin at Christ Church, Oxford.

John Ruskin (1819-1900) was born of wealthy but strict parents. A writer, critic, artist, and British race patriot, he had received his formal education at Christ Church College, Oxford University. A course on Plato's *Republic* had been his favorite. Cleon Skousen, in *The Naked Capitalist*, says that Ruskin's inspiration and devotion to the creation of an elite of race patriots derived directly from the *Republic*, which he read almost daily. In the *Republic*, Plato called for "a ruling class with a powerful army to keep

---

[1462] "Rhodes' 'Confession of Faith' of 1877," *Conspiracy Digest* 4.4 (Fall 1979): 8.
[1463] "Rhodes' 'Confession of Faith' of 1877," *Conspiracy Digest* (Winter 1979-80): 8.
[1464] "Rhodes' 'Confession of Faith.'"

it in power and a society completely subordinate to the monolithic authority of the rulers."[1465]

Ruskin's studies of ancient political philosophers taught him that the most effective way to conquer a man is to capture his mind. Realizing that a century earlier French Masons had captured the working man's mind through revolutionary propaganda, Ruskin set out to expand the concept of mind control through educating the working man.

In 1870 Ruskin was asked to return to Oxford to hold a chair in the fine arts. His inaugural lecture, which set forth his views on the ruling class as developed from Plato's *Republic*, sent shock waves through Oxford. The undergraduates to whom Ruskin spoke were the scions of British aristocracy. They listened with awe at Ruskin's message, of which a portion follows:

> *[You, the undergraduates are] the possessors of a magnificent tradition of education, beauty, rule of law, freedom, decency, and self-discipline but... this tradition [can] not be saved, and [does] not deserve to be saved, unless it [can] be extended to the lower classes in England itself and to the non-English masses throughout the world. If this precious tradition [is] not extended to these two great majorities, the minority of upper-class Englishmen [will] ultimately be submerged by these majorities and the tradition lost. To prevent this, the tradition must be extended to the masses and to the empire[1466] [emphasis added].*

Ruskin has been touted by historians as a protector and educator of the downtrodden masses of the working man and the poor. In fact he had another rationale for proclaiming such ideas. He planted in the fertile minds of his Oxford students the theory that if they educated the working man and elevated him to the middle class, he would then labor in behalf of the aristocracy to perpetuate the tradition of the upper-class Englishmen - which tradition was controlling the finances of nations through central banking.

Ruskin taught his students that it was the essential duty of the aristocracy to guarantee the poor were educated - not at the expense of the aristocracy, but so that an expanded middle class could rule for the benefit of the aristocracy. This arrangement would be a type of legal slavery where both classes would benefit. Through the power of finance, the ruling class would maintain control from behind the scenes, while the working class would have opportunity to share in the common wealth made available through loans.[1467]

Ruskin was successful in transferring this vision to his students at Oxford. They in turn became the Masonic movers and shakers in the new politics and economics that today govern the seven industrial powers of the world - the United States, Canada, England, Germany, France, Italy, and Japan.

Six key men in Ruskin's audience of undergraduates were Arnold Toynbee, Arthur Glazebrook, George Parkin, Philip Lyttieton Gell, Henry Birchenough, and Alfred Milner. These men were so moved by Ruskin's speech that they devoted the rest of their lives to carrying out his ideals. Cecil Rhodes joined them in 1873. In honor of Arnold Toynbee, who died in 1883, they built Toynbee Hall in 1884 as a model for government housing projects, and it remains so to this day.[1468]

[1465] W. Cleon Skousen, *The Naked Capitalist* (Salt Lake City: Privately printed, 1970) 54.
[1466] Quigley 130.
[1467] Skousen 25-28.
[1468] Quigley 130-131.

FREEMASON CECIL RHODES

Cecil Rhodes (1853-1902) began his eight-year college career three years after Ruskin's speech. He was so impressed when he read the speech that he copied it in longhand and kept it with him for the rest of his life. Rhodes too believed that the British and their Empire were the blessing of Providence to the earth and its inhabitants - that only the elite could and should rule the world to the benefit and happiness of mankind. To that end Rhodes labored for the rest of his short life.

As a youth, Rhodes was sent by his parents to join his brother in South Africa to mine for diamonds. He was already wealthy by the time he started his education at Oxford in 1873. Because he divided his life between studying at Oxford and mining diamonds at Kimberley, South Africa, it took Rhodes eight years to graduate.

In 1877, seven years after Ruskin's emotional appeal, Rhodes while yet a student at Oxford and only 24 years of age, wrote the first of seven famous wills that spanned his lifetime. Each of the seven wills was discrete and legally binding, not superseding each other. The first will called for the formation of a "secret society" whose primary function would be focused on returning England to her former glory. He viewed English Freemasonry and its conspiracy as impotent and in effect defunct in this regard. When the society was finally organized after his death, membership consisted only of English Freemasons. It soon became the most powerful appendage of the British Brotherhood.

Rhodes' new conspiracy would incorporate most of the developing world, and recapture the United States. Following are excerpts of this first will, in which he compares the ineptitude of English Freemasonry with his own scheme:

> *[The day] I [became] a member in the Masonic order, I [saw] the wealth and power they possess, the influence they hold. I think over their ceremonies and I wonder [how] a large body of men can devote themselves to what at times appear the most ridiculous and absurd rites without an object and without an end.*
>
> *Why should we not form a secret society with but one object - the furtherance of the British Empire and the bringing of the whole uncivilized world under British rule, for the recovery of the United States, [and] for... making the Anglo-Saxon race but one Empire?*[1469]

By the time he graduated from Oxford, Rhodes had built up enough collateral, that with backing from the House of Rothschild, he was able to finance the purchase of DeBeers diamond mining company and Consolidated Gold Fields in South Africa. By 1890 he had become the British administrator and financier of South Africa.

DeBeers and Consolidated produced for Rhodes a present-day equivalent of $10 million annual income. When he died in 1902 at age 48, his third will dictated that a trust of his disciples govern the gigantic fortune he left behind. Of his seven famous wills, the two most remembered are his first, which funded the secret society he had outlined but had not originated in his lifetime, and the last, which established an educational grant to the University of Oxford - the Rhodes Scholarship.

RHODES SCHOLARSHIPS

[1469] "Rhodes' 'Confession of Faith' of 1877," *Conspiracy Digest 4.4* (Fall 1979): 8.

The Trustees of the Rhodes Scholarship at Oxford, who select students for the prestigious scholarships, are members of the secret society of which Rhodes dreamed.

Adhering to the racial beliefs and prejudices of Cecil Rhodes, the Rhodes Scholarship was originally highly selective and racist. Until 1976 the Scholarship was given only to hand-picked white males with at least five years' residency in the British Commonwealth or colonies, the Republic of South Africa, or the United States of America. The first Rhodes Scholar was an American who became an English Mason working hard for the British Masonic conspiracy.[1470]

The recipients of the Rhodes Scholarships have never been required to be Masons, but are, however indirectly controlled by English Freemasonry for the rest of their lives. As you recall, the control mechanism was established by John Ruskin, who realized and taught that the mind of the laborer could be controlled through education - not to elevate the laborer at the expense of the aristocracy, but so that an expanded middle class could rule for the benefit of the aristocracy.

Rhodes Scholars are schooled at Oxford by English Masonic professors, who, for a century have been believers in and promoters of the natural superiority of the British race. Not surprisingly Rhodes Scholars become British race patriots. Upon graduation they return to their respective countries to act out the role for which they have been educated. Masons or not, as Anglophiles favoring England and everything English, they further the English Masonic conspiracy. Some become professors. Others go into finance, politics, or become political advisors. In America, in addition to their chosen vocation, they become "fellows" in one or more of the Anglophile Masonic fronts, such as the Brookings Institute, the Council on Foreign Relations, or the Trilateral Commission.

One example of how an American Rhodes Scholar has furthered the English Masonic conspiracy in America can be seen in the life of Dr. James H. Billington. Billington, not known to be a Mason, is listed in the 1980 membership roster of the Council on Foreign Relations.[1471] After receiving his doctorate in 1954 at Oxford as a Rhodes Scholar, Billington taught history for seventeen years at Harvard and Princeton - making sure his students learned all there was to know about the "benevolent" revolutionary role played by French Freemasonry in world events. Since 1973 he has been the Director of the Woodrow Wilson International Center for Scholars at the Smithsonian Institute in Washington, D.C.

Although Billington did much to impart the tenets of Continental revolutionary Freemasonry to his students at Harvard and Princeton, his greatest contribution to the English Masonic conspiracy is his book *Fire in the Minds of Men: Origins of the Revolutionary Faith* (1980), *an* authoritative book on Continental revolutionary movements. Of Freemasonry Billington says, "So great, indeed, was the general impact of Freemasonry in the revolutionary era that some understanding of the Masonic milieu

---

[1470] "Rhodes Scholarship," *Encyclopaedia Britannica:Micropaedia.*According to William R. Denslow's *10,000 Famous Freemasons,* the first Rhodes Scholar became an English Freemason working hard for the English Masonic conspiracy. His name was Sir Ellis Robins, an American by birth, borne in 1884 in Philadelphia. Graduate of the U. of Pennsylvania, he was chosen as the first Rhodes Scholar for Oxford U., England. He became resident director in Africa of the British South Africa Company in Rhodesia. In 1933 he was made a commander of the Order of St. John of Jerusalem. He became district Grand Master for Rhodesia in 1937, as well as grand inspector of the Royal Arch chapters there. He was appointed Past Grand Deacon of the Grand Lodge of England in 1934. (vol. IV~ p.51)

[1471] Council on Foreign Relations 1980 Annual Report (New York:Harold Pratt House, 1980) 129.I have found no documentation that Billington is a Mason, yet he is well-schooled in the Masonic conspiracy. Accepting the fact that he is not a Mason tends to prove that Rhodes Scholars and members of the CFR are not required to be Masons; yet they are working hard for the English Masonic conspiracy, as Billington's works confirm.

seems an essential starting point for any serious Inquiry into the occult roots of the revolutionary tradition."[1472] Billington notes that the Masonic lodges of Geneva provided the setting for the first apostles of modern communism.[1473] He also confirms the Black Hand's Masonic link.[1474] The Black Hand, you recall, was the name of the Grand Orient Masonic lodge responsible for the assassination of Archduke Ferdinand, which assassination triggered World War I.

Why Billington's book is so important to English Freemasonry is revealed in his statement in the introduction: "This book seeks to trace the origins of a faith, perhaps THE faith of our time. What is new is the belief that a perfect secular order will emerge from the forcible overthrow of traditional authority."[1475]

The "faith of our time" to which Billington refers is that of the title of his book - the "Revolutionary Faith" - and more specifically, the Masonic Faith. The "forcible overthrow of traditional authority" of which he speaks obviously refers to the Judeo-Christian heritage of the West.

What benefit to English Freemasonry was Billington's book if it exposed the three-century-old Masonic conspiracy to destroy our Judeo-Christian heritage?

The answer is partially found in Albert Pike's letter to Giuseppe Mazzini in 1871. Pike, who was anti-Christian as well as anti-communist, wrote that the day would come when "the multitude disillusioned with Christianity...would receive the pure light...of Lucifer, brought finally out into public view, a manifestation which will result from a general reactionary movement which will follow the destruction of Christianity and atheism, both conquered and exterminated at the same time."[1476]

We see the partial fulfillment of Pike's letter in our day. For example, since the beginning of the 1980s we have seen the expansion of Luciferianism in the New Age Movement. The New Age Movement is the brainchild of English Freemasonry. At the dawn of the 1990s we have witnessed disillusionment with atheism with the demise of the Soviet Union. Communism and the Soviet Union are the brainchild of French Freemasonry.

So what does Billington's book have to do with furthering the English Masonic conspiracy? It is simply a scholarly exposure of the other side - the French side of the Masonic conspiracy. Such an exposure has obviously benefited English Freemasonry. Since Billington's book was published, Luciferianism has been on the rise, while atheism and communism are on the wane.

THE FOUNDING OF RHODES' SECRET SOCIETY: THE ROUND TABLE

In his third will Rhodes left his entire estate to Freemason Lord Nathan Mayer Rothschild I (- 1915) as trustee, with the stipulation that his gigantic fortune be used by his disciples to carry out the program he had envisioned. As trustee, Rothschild appointed Freemason Alfred Milner to head up the secret society for which Rhodes' first will made provision. Lord Milner (1843-1925) was the ideal man for the job. He once wrote: "I am a British nationalist. If I am also an Imperialist, it is because the destiny of the English race...has been to strike fresh roots in distant parts... My patriotism knows no geographical

---

[1472] James A. Billington, *Fire in the Minds of Men* (New York: Basic Books, 1980) 92.
[1473] Billington 91.
[1474] Billington 110-111 and his footnotes 159-161.
[1475] Billington 3.
[1476] Fagan 8.

but only racial limits. I am an Imperialist and not a Little Englander, because I am a British Race Patriot."[1477]

From 1897 to 1905, Milner was governor-general and high corn missioner of South Africa. After Rhodes' death and his appointment by Rothschild to chair Rhodes' secret society, Milner recruited a group of young men from Oxford and from Toynbee Hall to assist him in organizing his administration of the new society. All were respected English Freemasons. Among the group were Rudyard Kipling, Arthur Balfour, Lord Rothschild, and some Oxford College graduates known as "Milner's Kindergarten." In 1909, Milner's Kindergarten, and some English Masons from the Coefficients Club, founded the Round Table. The grandfather of all modern British Masonic "think tanks" was born.

Three powerful think tank offshoots of the Round Table are: (1) the Royal Institute of International Affairs (RIIA), organized in 1919 in London; (2) the Council on Foreign Relations (CFR), organized in 1921 in New York City; and (3) the Institute of Pacific Relations (IPR), organized in 1925 in twelve countries holding territory in what today we call the Pacific Rim.[1478]

Subsequent events reveal that the initial assignment of the Round Table was not necessarily to destroy the political experiments of French Freemasonry, such as socialism and communism, but to cooperate with them for the advancement of the English Masonic conspiracy. For this reason the Round Table think tanks opened their membership to men with contrary political and financial opinions, men who were noted Marxists such as H.G. Wells (1866-1946) and John Maynard Keynes (1883-1946). Yet with few exceptions, all were English Free-masons, or members of appendages of English Freemasonry. Dr. Carroll Quigley in *Tragedy and Hope* (1966) says, "Through [Milner's] influence these men were able to win influential posts in government and international finance and became the dominant influence in British imperial and foreign affairs..."[1479]

In 1902, the year Cecil Rhodes died, H.G. Wells anticipated the future existence of these British Masonic think tanks in a work entitled *Anticipations of the Reaction to Mechanical and Scientific Progress upon Human Life and Thought*. In this literary piece, Wells explained the strategy by which aristocratic English Freemasonry would reach its goal of world dominion. He called it an "Open Conspiracy" as opposed to French Freemasonry's closed, or secret conspiracy.

> *The Open Conspiracy will appear first, I believe, as a conscious organization of intelligent and quite possibly in some cases wealthy men, as a movement having distinct social and political aims, confessedly ignoring most of the existing apparatus of political control, or using it only as an incidental implement in the attainment of these aims. It will be very loosely organized in its earlier states, a mere movement of a number of people in a certain direction, who will presently discover with a sort of surprise the common object toward which they are all moving... A confluent system of mist-owned business organizations and of Universities and reorganized military and naval services may presently discover an essential unity of purpose, presently begin thinking a literature, and behaving like a State - a sort of outspoken Secret Society - an informal and open*

[1477] White, *Dark Ages* 26.
[1478] Quigley 132.
[1479] Quigley.

freemasonry [sic]. In all sorts of ways they will be influencing and controlling the apparatus of the ostensible governments.[1480]

Wells is obviously speaking here of the Round Table, of which he was to become a founding member in 1909. The activity of the Round Table, operating as "an informal and open freemasonry," closed the era of British colonialism and opened the new era of a Commonwealth of Nations. Under Lord Milner's direction, from 1909 to 1913, Round Table Groups, as its appendages were referred to outside of Great Britain, were organized in the chief British dependencies and in the United States. The scheme included bringing the United States of America once again under the dominance of London. These Round Table Groups still function in eight countries today, and keep in touch through their quarterly magazine, *The Round Tavie.*[1481]

While the Round Table is an Anglophile secret order, conspiracy researchers in America have described it as left-wing because of its anti-American activity. Dr. Quigley explains:

> *There does exist, and has existed for a generation, an international Anglophile network which operates, to some extent, in the way the radical Right believes the Communists act. In fact, this network, which we may identify as the Round Table Groups, has no aversion to cooperating with the Communists, or any other groups, and frequently does so.*[1482]

INSIDE A BRITISH MASONIC THINK TANK:
THE "COEFFICIENTS"

Great Britain's think tanks met at regular intervals - some annually, others on weekends, or once a month at private clubs. The membership of the think tanks consisted of a mix of right-wing and left-wing Masons. Whenever England faced a crisis, the discussions in their meetings would sometimes become intense. After much debate, however, a consensus would be reached on how London would react to or resolve a crisis.

Before we consider the discussion in one of these think tanks, we must understand the mind-set of the British oligarchy at the beginning of the 20th century. H.G. Wells in *Experiments in Autobiography* gives us this insight:

> *The undeniable contraction of the British outlook in the opening decade of the new century is one that has exercised my mind very greatly... Gradually, the belief in the possible world leadership of England had been deflated, by the economic development of America and the militant boldness of Germany...*
>
> *Our liberalism was no longer a larger enterprise, it had become a generous indolence. But minds were waking up to this. Over our table at St. Ermin's Hotel wrangled Maxse, Bellairs, Hewins, Amery, and Mackinder, all stung by the small but humiliating tale of disasters in the South Africa war [Boer War], all sensitive*

[1480] H.G. Wells, *Anticipations of the Reaction to Mechanical and Scientific Progress Upon Human Life and Thought* (New York:Harper and Brothers, 1902) 285.
[1481] Quigley 144.
[1482] Quigley 950.

to the threat of business recession, and all profoundly alarmed by the naval and military aggressiveness of Germany...[1483]

The "table at St. Ermin's Hotel" was a gathering of British Masons who had been meeting monthly since 1902 at the Coefficients Club. The discussion that follows, as reconstructed by Carol White in *The New Dark Ages Conspiracy*, occurred at the Club in 1903 and reveals the frustration felt by the growing threat of Germany.

Leo Maxse opened the discussion by blurting out rhetorically, "This country needs a great war. We can take no chances; we must destroy the German peril."

After some debate it was suggested that the best way to destroy Germany was to instigate a war between that country and Russia.

Halford Mackinder, coughing slightly, responded: "If we allow war between Germany and Russia, and do not intervene, Germany will crush Russia."

H.G. Wells, looking to Bertrand Russell for agreement, said, "The British Empire must be a world-state or nothing. [It] is like an open hand all over the world. We must have an aristocracy - not of privilege, but of understanding and purpose - or mankind will fail."

Russell responded, "If you people have your way we will be drawn into a war. Conceivably a very humiliating war for England may occur at no very distant date, but I do not think there is any such heroic quality in our governing class as will make that war catastrophic."

"Are you suggesting that we accept defeat?" A number of voices broke out at once.

"Victory, define your terms please," Russell retorted. "If Germany and Russia are bled, that is victory? Anything else is sham? Your war and your victory are chimera."

Milner, his voice cracking with the intensity of his emotion, called out: "Russell, this is treason. I am an imperialist because I am a race patriot. We must maintain our honor, or we are through as a nation. We will lose the respect of the colonies."[1484]

According to White, the consensus of the think tanks that followed after the Coefficients stopped meeting in 1908 was twofold. First, America's industrial-military complex must be captured to fight Great Britain's wars, pay its bills, and force London's policies on the rest of the world. Second, Germany, France, and Russia must be pitted against each other in conflicts that were expected to erupt into war.[1485]

The Coefficients Club was one of the first of many British race patriot think tanks. Carol White names a few powerful ones which followed:

> On the higher level of control, since 1902, the British oligarchy has created numerous interlocking institutions - from the Aspen Institute to the Tavistock Institute to the Brookings Institution to the New York Council on Foreign Relations and its more notorious spin-off the Trilateral Commission [1973] - in a loose association of men whose outlook is that of the British oligarchy. Like the Jesuits, the British have concentrated on the universities as the controlling centers of intellectual thought.[1486]

When the Coefficients disbanded in 1908, most of the English Masons who had attended then founded in 1909 the British Round Table, more informally known as the

---

[1483] H.G. Wells, *Experiments in Autobiography* (New York:Macmillan Co., 1934) 653.
[1484] White 6-7.
[1485] White 9-10.
[1486] White 196-197.

Cliveden Set.[1487] Cliveden was the name of the Freemasonic Astor family estate where the Round Table met.

The Round Table and its "think tank" spin-offs were the first crises managers. They did not conspire to create crises to overthrow governments, as did French Grand Orient Masons. The Round Table's doctrine of "gradualism" meant that these organizations took a "wait and see" attitude. Instead of instigating the political and economic chaos that pervaded society prior to and after World War I, they managed it to the advantage of Great Britain.

Most of these conspirators were 33rd degree Masons. Their motto, emblazoned on their Supreme Council Jewel, is "Order out of Chaos." "Order" was their desire, "Chaos" their dilemma. After studying a problem and agreeing on a solution, they would then make themselves available to the seven industrial powers around the world as advisors. In turn, these governments seemed always to react positively to their suggestions. The Round Table followed this model of crisis management during World War I and through the upheavals of the Russian Revolution. As World War I stale-mated, Round Table discussions were once again launched. The Round Table urged the funding of Kerensky's revolution in order to keep Russia in the war. As you recall, Lord Milner him self negotiated the terms with Kerensky. When Kerensky was defeated by the more ruthless Grand Orient Bolsheviks, it was back to the Round Table for more discussion.

"Gradualism" was their strategy. They were in no hurry.

WOODROW WILSON AND THE LEAGUE OF NATIONS

World War I ended in 1918. In January 1919 the Paris Peace Conference convened. In June the Versailles "Peace" Treaty called for world peace to be supervised by a League of Nations. History records that non-Mason President Woodrow Wilson "succeeded in incorporating in the treaty a provision for the formation of a League of Nations to ensure world peace."[1488]

What history does not record is the fact that constantly at Wilson's side was his personal advisor, "Colonel" E.M. House, a 33rd degree Grand Lodge Mason. House was aware of the Grand Orient's role in discussing a League of Nations before World War I began. *Mackey's Encyclopedia of Freemasonry* confirms that "[l]ong before Woodrow Wilson's presidency [1913] it [French Masonry] held conferences for discussing a League of Nations..."[1489]

The Round Table's program was to cooperate with all political experiments for the purpose of eventually taking them over. House, in effect, was English Masonry's liaison to the American president, and through House the leader of the most powerful nation in the world became a stooge of English Freemasonry. Although the League of Nations was the direct creation of French Freemasonry, House urged Wilson to propose a League of Nations that would insure world peace. History has since credited Wilson with the concept.

FRENCH FREEMASONRY'S LEAGUE OF NATIONS

On November 11, 1918, the date hostilities had been brought formally to an end by a series of armistices, Freemasonry was ready to arbitrate an international settlement

---

[1487] White 11.
[1488] "Wilson, (Thomas) Woodrow," *Encyclopaedia Britannica; Micropaedia.*
[1489] "League of Nations and Masonry."

between the victors and the vanquished. The Paris Peace Conference - which opened on January 18, 1919, and closed a year later on January 16, 1920, with the inauguration of Freemasonry's first World Government - was a Masonic masterpiece. President Wilson led the American delegation (most of whom were Masons) to the opening of the Peace Conference and again at the signing of the 'Treaty of Versailles on June 28, 1919.

History would have us believe that the 'Treaty of Versailles was drawn up during the first five months of the Conference.[1490] Yet two years earlier in June, 1917, while the war was still raging throughout Europe, clauses for the treaty had already been worked out at a great international Masonic congress.

Preliminary planning for this congress had begun January 14-15, 1917, at the Grand Orient in Paris. A summary of that meeting was sent to all Masonic powers throughout the world, with a cover letter inviting them to attend the congress to discuss drafting the constitution of the League of Nations. Colonel House received his invitation by cable. Following are excerpts:

> *In sending you the summary of minutes of the Conference of the Masonic Jurisdictions of the Allied Nations, which was held at Paris on 14th and 15th January, 1917, as well as the resolutions and the manifesto therein adopted, it is our Masonic privilege to inform you that this Congress decided to hold a Masonic Congress at the Grand Orient of France, in Paris, on 28th, 29th and 30th of June next.*
>
> *The object of this Congress will be to investigate the means of elaborating the Constitution of the League of Nations, so as to prevent the recurrence of a catastrophe similar to the one at present raging which has plunged the civilized world in mourning.*
>
> *It was the opinion of this conference that this programme cannot be discussed solely by the Freemasonry of the Allied Nations, and that it is a matter also for the Masonic bodies of the neutral nations to bring what light they can to the discussion of so grave a problem.*
>
> *It is the duty of Freemasonry at the close of the cruel drama [WWI] now being played out, to make its great and humanitarian voice heard, and to guide the nations towards a general organization which will become their safeguard. It would be wanting in its duty, and false to its great principles, were it to remain silent.[1491]*

The Congress took place on June 28-30, 1917, at the headquarters of the Grand Orient of France in the Rue Cadet, Paris. Attending were representatives from the leading lodges of allied and neutral countries - Italy, Switzerland, Belgium, Serbia, Spain, Portugal, Argentina, Brazil, and the United States. The Grand Lodge of England boycotted the conference in honor of her fallen brother monarchs in Europe. English Freemasons, however, were in attendance as representatives of the Round Table.

The complete minutes of the Congress, entitled *Minutes of the International Masonic Congress of Allied and Neutral Nations,* came to light in 1936 when published in their entirety by Count Leon de Poncins.[1492] A photocopy of the cover and title page of the Minutes, which display Masonic symbols, are in Appendix 2, Figs. 32 and 32a.

[1490] "Paris Peace Conference," *Encyclopaedia Britannica:Micropaedia.*

[1491] de Poncins, *Freemasonry and the Vatican* 51-52.

[1492] de Poncins 51.

The Congress opened at 2:30 **P.M.**, with Brother Corneau in the chair. As President of the Grand Orient of France, he began the meeting with a speech, in the course of which he said:

> *This Masonic Congress of the Allied and neutral Nations has come at the right time. We all know the disasters of the past [WWI]; now we must build the happy city of the future. It is to undertake this truly Masonic work that we have invited you here.*
>
> *What are we faced with? This war, which was unleashed by the military autocracies has become a formidable quarrel in which the democracies have organized themselves against the despotic military powers.*
>
> *Thus it is absolutely indispensable to create a supranational authority, whose aim will be not to suppress the causes of conflicts, but peacefully to resolve the differences between nations.*
>
> *Freemasonry, which labours for peace, intends to study this propaganda agent for this conception of universal peace and happiness. That, my Most Illustrious Brethren, is our work. Let us set to it.[1493]*

Brother Corneau then gave the chair to Brother Andre Lebey, Secretary of the Council of the Grand Orient of France. His report which he read on the Constitution of the League of Nations, a lengthy document, subtly suggests the ancient struggle between the warring ideologies of the Templars and the Priory of Sion as they were being played out in the war between the Templars' Scottish Rite Grand Orient and the Priory's Habsburg dynasty. Following is a short portion of his report:

> *The great war of 1914...has gradually and continually brought into definition itself the character of the struggle, which is revealed as one between two opposing principles: Democracy and Imperialism, Liberty and Authority, Truth proving its good faith, and Falsehood plunging deeper and deeper into shady intrigues... [Throughout the war] there is not one event which has failed to bear witness to this gigantic duel between two hostile principles.*
>
> *We are invited to succeed in the work which was compromised by the Holy Alliance [Oligarchic Congress of Vienna, 1815], by reason of its principles, which are contrary to ours, and through the universal but guaranteed reconciliation of men, to make manifest the proof of our principles. We will crown the work of the French Revolution.[1494]*

Brother Lebey continues by stressing the fact that Freemasonry itself cannot dictate peace terms, but certainly can formulate the conditions by which peace must be achieved:

> *The more one studies the present situation, the more one realizes that the abdication of the Hohenzollerns [German royal family] is the means of attaining the League of Nations. It is not for us, my Brethren, to define or demarcate the conditions of peace... but we can at least indicate the... principal points we consider necessary: In principle, the liberation or unification of all the nations which are today oppressed by the political and administrative organization of the*

[1493] de Poncins 52.
[1494] de Poncins 52-53.

Hapsburg Empire into States which the said nations shall select by a referendum.[1495]

This speech was greeted with applause, and Brother Corneau proposed the nomination of a Commission to examine the conclusions of Brother Lebey's report. Brother Nathan of the Grand Orient of Italy opined that the Committee should not deal with the discussion of peace terms, but should deal only with the Charter of the League of Nations, and discuss and vote upon the articles of the Charter, which was the principal object of this Masonic Congress.

The second session opened the following afternoon. Brother Nathan's opinion of the previous day - that the Congress should not discuss peace terms - was ignored. The conclusions presented for vote by Brother Lebey on behalf of the Commission included terms for a peace treaty. The Congress adopted the conclusions, which contained, among others, the following resolutions:

> *The Unity, autonomy and independence of each nation is inviolable. A people which is not free, that is to say, a people which does not possess the liberal and democratic institutions indispensable to its development, cannot constitute a Nation. International legislative power is to reside in a Parliament. Just as the Constituent Assembly in 1789 drew up the Table of the Rights of Man, its first care will be to draw up the Table of the Rights of Nations, the charter guaranteeing their rights and their duties.*[1496]

The Congress adopted the proposal that these resolutions be sent to all the governments of the Allied and Neutral nations. Then, Brother Meoni of the Symbolic Grand Lodge of Italy laid the resolution of the Italian delegation before the delegates. Before reading the resolution, Brother Meoni read the following report:

> *Reality... shows us that there exists one unique and supreme necessity: future humanity must be established on absolutely new foundations, secured by the conclusion of solemn treaties which should include the creation of an international Court of law, effectively supported by an international force. Thus, the reconstitution of Europe and the humanity of the morrow cannot be abandoned to the whim of dynasties, diplomats, and ruling class interests.*
>
> *It is obvious that we are confronted with two diverse and antipathetic conceptions of the nature and functions of the State. On the one hand is the imperialist idea, which despises the rights of peoples and is today represented by the preying empires which unleashed the criminal aggression, and on the other hand, the democratic idea, which asserts these same rights.*
>
> *Hence the necessity, for the peace of the world, that the conception of an aggressive military hegemony be destroyed. How will this result be achieved? Doubtless, through the integral triumph of the principle of nationalities. "National life," wrote Joseph Mazzini, "is the means; international life is the end." The whole destiny of Europe and of the new humanity is involved in the resolution of this problem of nationality. After the failure of the German plan will come the Federation of the United States of Europe, by liberty and by right.*

[1495] de Poncins.
[1496] de Poncins 53-54.

How, then, will this end be achieved?

> *Firstly, by the suppression of all despotism... and secondly, by the regulation of international conflicts by arbitration.*[1497]

Brother Meoni then read the resolution of the Italian delegation which, among other things, affirmed:

> *The unflinching determination of all the Masonic Powers represented at the Congress... to see that nations which had been shattered or even obliterated by long centuries of despotism and militarism... had the right to reconstitute themselves.*[1498]

After discussions, this resolution was adopted, and the Congress then approved the following motions, which among other things, praised President Wilson for suggesting a League of Nations:

> *This Congress sends to Mr. Wilson, President of the United States, the homage of its admiration and the tribute of its recognition of the great services he has rendered Humanity.*
> *Declares that it is happy to collaborate with President Wilson in this work of international justice and democratic fraternity, which is Freemasonry's own ideal,And affirms that the eternal principles of Freemasonry are completely in harmony with those proclaimed by President Wilson for the defense of civilization and the liberty of peoples...*
> *Declares that faithful to their traditions, and like their glorious ancestors, the Freemasons today are still the devoted labourers of the emancipation of the human race...*
> *Warmly appeals to all the Brethren for their support in the task of bringing into being the League of Nations, which alone can guarantee the future and the liberty of peoples, and international justice and law.*[1499]

Weigh these texts carefully word for word, and it will be found that not only did Masons intend to rule the governments of the world through the League of Nations, they actually asserted the incredible theory that, while the rights of each nation are "inviolable," nevertheless, a people which is governed by an autocratic regime does not constitute a nation and therefore cannot join the League. The League denied all rights to nations whose political regimes were not considered sufficiently democratic. Conversely, any nation under the influence of Grand Orient republicanism became an organ for control and coercion at the service of the League of Nations.

Apart from the Masons who were present at this Masonic Congress, few people knew of the secret meeting, or of the function Freemasonry assumed in drawing up the Treaty of Versailles. It was not until 1936 that de Poncins was able to obtain the official report of the Conference, which he immediately published.

[1497] de Poncins 54.
[1498] de Poncins 54-55.
[1499] de Poncins 55.

Concerning the Treaty of Versailles, de Poncins wrote: "It must be observed that all the conclusions adopted in the course of these talks at the Masonic Congress in 1917 became an integral part of the Treaty of Versailles two years later..."[1500]

Count de Poncins concluded, "It is a frightening thought that an occult organization, owing responsibility to no one, can direct the course of European politics without anyone being aware of the fact."[1501]

THE TREATY OF VERSAILLES

The Treaty of Versailles (named for the city of Versailles where it was signed, which city is now within the corporate limits of Paris), demanded that Germany pay war reparations to the victor nations, The final draft was distributed throughout Paris to Allied officials just before sunrise on May 7, 1919. Those who received it knew immediately that it was a disaster. The intense hatred of Grand Orient Freemasonry toward the dethroned kings of Europe as embodied in that document was shocking. The Treaty prescribed that defeated Germany, now cast in the role of the sole culprit of the war, should pay billions of gold marks in war reparations.

Obviously, what the financially deprived Grand Orient nations desired was the wealth of the fallen monarchs. The Treaty, for example, demanded that Germany give up some of her richest provinces, much of her natural resources, and her colonies. In addition, Germany was stripped of all rights, trade concessions, and property in foreign countries. Moreover, the Allies reserved "the right to retain and liquidate all property and interests of German private nationals or companies."[1502] Of course, Great Britain was not so concerned with acquiring a portion of Germany's wealth as she was pleased that this industrial giant and world competitor had been vanquished.

Reparations were even more severe. The Allies obtained a virtual blank check from Germany, claiming that "since Germany was responsible for the war she was liable for the costs and damages incurred by the victors."[1503] The total indemnity was to be set at $32 billion, plus interest. The schedule of payments was fixed annually at $500 million, plus a 26 percent tax on exports. Interest charges were set so high that the debt increased each year, no matter how faithfully Germany made payments.[1504]

So unjust was the Treaty that it was almost universally condemned. English economist and Freemason John Maynard Keynes, representing the left-wing Fabian Society at the Paris Peace Conference, was appalled. After reading the contents of the Treaty he could not sleep. He, with General Smuts of South Africa walked the deserted streets of Paris. Herbert Hoover, who at that time was chief of the Allied Food-Relief Services and a senior American economic advisor, received his copy of the Treaty at 4:00 A.M. He was horrified by its severity. Too upset to go back to sleep, he too walked the streets. Lord Curzon, the British Foreign Secretary, felt the Treaty was setting the stage for a second world war. He correctly predicted, "This is no peace; this is only a truce for twenty years!"[1505] Even President Woodrow Wilson thought the Treaty was too harsh. He said, "If I were a German, I think I should never sign it."[1506]

[1500] de Poncins, *Freemasonry and the Vatican* 57.
[1501] de Poncins 57.
[1502] Pool and Pool, who *Financed Hitler?* 179.
[1503] Pool and Pool.
[1504] Pool and Pool.
[1505] Epperson, *Unseen* 261.
[1506] Pool and Pool 177.

Several German high officials refused to sign the "unjust" treaty and resigned. On June 28, 1919, the remaining German officials, upon threat of invasion, signed.

BENEFICIARY OF THE VERSAILLES TREATY

French Grand Orient Freemasonry was the chief beneficiary of the First World War and the Treaty of Versailles. Grand Orient Freemasonry was the principal behind both and Grand Orient Masons wrote the script.

As for the League of Nations, French Freemasonry was also the force behind its creation, and for the most part, determined its direction. The League, however, was not intended for French Freemasonry alone. The Grand Orient made this clear several years later, when in 1923 at its annual convention, all Freemasonry was invited to participate, as the following minutes confirm:

> It is the duty of universal Freemasonry to co-operate absolutely with the League of Nations in order that it may no longer have to submit to the interested influences of Governments.
>
> The principal task of the League of Nations... [is]...the creation of a European spirit... in brief, the formation of the United States of Europe, or rather World Federation.[1507]

Of course, the British race patriots in English Freemasonry were not at all happy with a United States of Europe that would eventually merge into a World Federation, for it was evident to them that French Freemasonry intended to dictate policy in the League of Nations. The Round Table went into session to determine what could be done. The conclusion, as subsequent events will reveal, was to usurp control of the League. This meant that both the British and American governments would have to participate in the League. England's cooperation was certain, but the United States Congress had read the Versailles Treaty, and wanted nothing to do with the League. Yet it was imperative that the Americans cooperate if English Freemasonry was to be successful in a coup of the League. The consensus of the Round Table, therefore, was to send a delegation to the Peace Conference, and while there, meet with the American Round Tablers to see how best to change the attitudes of the American people, not so much to save the League, but

---

[1507] Stoddard, Light-bearers 15.
With this 1923 speech, the doors were opened for Germany to enter the League of Nations. German Freemason Gustav Stresemann (1878-1929), a member of the Lodge, *Friedrich der Grosse* and an honorary member of the Grand Lodge, *Zu den 3 Weltkugeln,* was Chancellor of Germany in 1923 and Minister of Foreign Affairs, 1923-1929, during the difficult years following WWI. He secured Germany's admission to the League of Nations on an equal status with the great nations. His speech before the League of Nations, seeking German admission, was full of Masonic overtones: "The divine Architect of the earth has created humanity not as a conformed unity,but as people of different blood who express their souls in their own language. But the supreme will of the divine order is not to turn against each other, but to help each other to higher development." At the end of the speech he gave a Masonic sign, assuring Germany's entry into the League. Later the Nazis said that he "misused his membership in Freemasonry for political purposes." (Denslow, *10,000 Famous Freemasons,* vol. IV~, p. 202)

to guarantee that the American people would fully cooperate with the next World Government - a World Government that English Freemasonry intended to control.[1508]

AFTER THE PEACE CONFERENCE: NEW ROUND TABLES

The Round Table thus made its appearance at the Paris Peace Conference to organize a takeover. The Round Table conspiracy involved a few Americans summoned to the Peace Conference - Americans who were willing to betray their own country for prestige and money. They were 33rd degree Grand Lodge Mason "Colonel" Edward Mandell House (1858-1938), personal advisor to President Woodrow Wilson; John Foster Dulles (1888-1959), later to be appointed Secretary of State under U.S. President Eisenhower; 33rd degree Scottish Rite Mason Christian Herter (1895-1966), later to be appointed Secretary of State under Eisenhower after Dulles' death[1509]; Allen Dulles (John's brother), later to be appointed director of the CIA in 1951; and Walter Uppmann (1889-1974), later to become one of the liberal establishment's favorite syndicated columnists and contributing journalist to *The New Republic,* the Anglophile magazine in America named after the Round Table's design for recapturing the United States.

On May 19, 1919, just twelve days after the final draft of the Treaty of Versailles had been distributed and condemned by the world, "Colonel" House led his coterie of Americans to the Majestic Hotel in Paris to meet with members of the Round Table "in order to form an organization whose job it would be to propagandize the citizens of America, England and Western Europe on the glories of World Government."[1510]

The outcome of this secret meeting was to expand the Round Table, not only in England, but in America and the Far East by creating additional front societies to influence foreign policy in Great Britain, the United States and the Orient.

Returning to London, the Round Tablers met at Cliveden, the estate of the Masonic Astor family, who owned two London newspapers, *Pall Mall Gazette* and *The London Times*[1511], to plan their strategy. The front organization in Great Britain was the Royal Institute of International Affairs (RIIA). The chief financial supporter of the RIIA was the Astor family. In the Far East the Masonic front was the Institute of Pacific Relations (IPR). The machinations of the IPR involved America in a ten-year drug war in Vietnam for English Freemasonry - a war not intended to be won militarily, but won "dopefully."[1512] In America the Round Table front society was the Council on Foreign Relations (CFR).

The organizational structures for both the RIIA and the CFR were drawn up at the Paris Majestic Hotel meeting. The 'PR was organized later.[1513] "Colonel" House took the plans for the CFR back to America, where he completed its charter.[1514] On July 29, 1921, the CFR was founded.[1515]

Earlier we had mentioned Dr. Quigley's comment that "this network... the Round Table Groups, has no aversion to cooperating with the Communists, or any other groups,

---

[1508] Gary Allen and Larry Abraham, *None Dare Call It Conspiracy* (Rossmoor, CA: Concord Press, 1971) 78.
[1509] Fisher 248-250.
[1510] Allen 79.
[1511] Quigley 132 and Chaitkin 385.
[1512] John Daniel, *Scarlet and the Beast: English Freemasonry, Banks, and the illegal Drug Trade* (Tyler, TX: Jon Kregel, Inc. 1995) entire.
[1513] Quigley 952.
[1514] Still 157.
[1515] John A. Stormer, *None Dare Call It Treason-25 Years Later* (Florissant, MO: Liberty Bell Press, 1990) 186.

and frequently does so." The purpose of these groups, of course, is to develop a unifying front in the project to create World Government with all three Masonic obediences (American, English and French) cooperating. Hence, membership in the CFR contained a mixture of Masonic persuasions.

At the founding meeting of the CFR were the following Masons: 33rd degree Grand Lodge Mason "Colonel" House: 33rd degree Scottish Rite Mason Christian Herter; Grand Orient Masons Paul Warburg and Jacob Schiff, both American bankers; Scottish Rite Mason Averell Harriman, who in 1972 negotiated America's shameful withdrawal from Vietnam; and 33rd degree Scottish Rite Mason Bernard Baruch, a Jewish banker and investor in silver. Other founding members with no record of being Masons were Walter Lippmann, the Dulles brothers (John and Allen), the bankers J.P. Morgan and John D. Rockefeller. Rockefeller's two sons are today members of Lucis (Lucifer) Trust, which funds the Anglophile New Age Movement.[1516]

The CFR immediately set out to replace pro-American politicians with Anglophile politicians. From the 1920s through World War II, pro-America Masons dominated key positions in our government. For example in 1923,69 percent of congressman and 63 percent of senators were Masons. By 1948 that percentage dropped to fifty-four and fifty-three respectively. By 1984 the percentages had fallen to twelve and fourteen percent respectively.[1517]

What is not normally realized is the fact that these positions, once staffed by pro-America Masons, are now filled by persons who are members of the pro-British Masonic front, the Council on Foreign Relations. For example, in the 1920s and 1930s, many young and aspiring politicians were "appointed" to the CFR where they were educated on the merits of Anglophile internationalism. Likewise, young American intellectuals selected for the Rhodes Scholarship and educated at Oxford, were sent back to the United States to careers in politics.

These students of the CFR came of age in 1939 when they began filling posts in our federal government. By 1945 the State Department had been completely taken over by the Council on Foreign Relations.[1518]

Since its 1921 founding and continuing through the Nixon administration in the 1970s, twelve of eighteen Secretaries of the Treasury have been members of the CFR. Another twelve of sixteen Secretaries of State have been members. Since 1944, all Presidential candidates, both Republican and Democrat, have either been members of the CFR or its 1973 offshoot, the Trilateral Commission. The only exception was Harry Truman, who though a 33rd degree Mason was not voted into office. Six of the seven Superintendents of West Point, every Supreme Allied Commander in Europe, and every U.S. Ambassador to N.A.T.O. has been a member of the CFR.[1519]

BRITISH WORLD GOVERNANCE AND THE UNITED NATIONS

After World War I, French Grand Orient Freemasonry considered itself mistress of the future. Grand Orient Masons were in charge of the new European politics from 1918 to 1930.[1520] They promised the world an era of peace, happiness and prosperity through Grand Orient-created socialism and communism. Instead Europe was plunged into revolution followed by counterrevolution, fought between proponents of English and

---

[1516] Allen 82 and Epperson, *Unseen* 169, 196.
[1517] Still 158.
[1518] Wilgus 203-204.
[1519] Stormer 186 and Skousen 54.
[1520] de Poncins, *Freemasonry and the Vatican* 57.

French Freemasonry. Traditional monarchies, under the aegis of English Freemasonry, were destroyed in favor of French Freemasonry's socialist and communist republics. Left-wing dictators - more despotic than former sovereigns had ever been - ruled the new republics.

Grand Orient republics, whether communist or socialist, became instruments for terror and disruption of order. French Freemasonry showed that when in power it was incapable of governing and maintaining order. General chaos and financial breakdown followed - ending in the Great Depression of the 1930s.

In Germany, Austria, Hungary and Italy, communism was eventually strangled at great cost and much bloodshed. In place of communism, authoritarian regimes sprang up by popular consent.

Such were the dictatorships of Admiral Horthy in Hungary, Mussolini and fascism in Italy, Chancellor Dollfuss in Austria, Hitler and National Socialism in Germany.

By 1939, the French Grand Orient, previously thinking itself mistress of the future, found it had fallen on difficult times. De Poncins wrote:

> *"The results were disastrous. The Treaty of Versailles quickly led to widespread breakdown of order, to revolutionary unrest, to the opposing reactions of the Fascist and Hitler regimes, to the Spanish Civil War, and finally to the Second World War."*[1521]

THE WHORE OF BABYLON MOUNTS THE BEAST

English Freemasonry, which had been patiently implementing its policy of "gradualism" through the Round Table Groups, saw its opportunity to regain dominance, not by reinstating her kings throughout Europe, but by funding the extreme right-wing dictators who had wrested government from the hands of the extreme left-wing despots. (See next three chapters.)

In 1939, when World War II began and the League of Nations ceased operations, London's Round Table Groups in America made their move to take over world governance. That year the Council on Foreign Relations offered its services to the U.S. State Department. By 1940 the State Department had created the Division of Special Research headed by CFR member Leo Pasbolsky. The job of Pasbolsky and his CFR staff was to submit a plan for the replacement of the League of Nations: they named their replacement body the United Nations.[1522] At least forty- seven members of the CFR were in the delegation to the U.N. Conference in San Francisco in 1945. And CFR members occupied nearly every significant decision-making spot at the Conference.[1523]

The stage was now set for America's entrance into this world body. The House and Senate had been made sympathetic and receptive with significant CFR membership, and when it was time to vote, performed as expected. The United States not only joined the United Nations, but the Rockefeller Foundation donated the land on which the United Nations building was built. Not surprisingly, David Rockefeller was chairman of the Council on Foreign Relations.

By founding the United Nations, English Freemasonry had wrested control of world government from French Freemasonry. As for America, what we had gained during our

---

[1521] de Poncins.
[1522] Wilgus 202-204.
[1523] Skousen 52.

War of Independence in 1776, we returned to England with the creation of the Council on Foreign Relations.

22. ENGLISH FREEMASONRY AND THE HITLER PROJECT

> *Hitler's entire personal career was, after all, but one product of the oligarchy's cultish world outlook, and it was the same oligarchy which, on the urging of Hjalmar Schacht [Germany's leading banker], decided to raise onto its shield in 1932. Hitler was their man![1524]*

In Vienna, Austria, it is Friday, January 24, 1913, eighteen months and four days before the fatal bullet will pierce Archduke Ferdinand's jugular vein. Near the aristocratic district of Hietzing in the southwest section of the city, just blocks from Emperor Franz Joseph's summer palace, 34- year-old Freemason Iosif Dzhugashvili is soliciting funds for Lenin's revolution from Alexander Troyanovsky, son of a high Czarist official. Last week in a Russian publication called *The Social Democrat*, Dzhugashvili was debuted as Joseph Stalin.

Downtown at Cafe Central sits 34-year-old Grand Orient Freemason Lev Bronstein awaiting the arrival of Jewish financier and Grand Orient Freemason Doctor Alfred Adler. "A very good morning, Herr Doktor Trotsky," says Adler, as he sits down beside Leon Trotsky. To his bimonthly *Pravda* readers, Bronstein is known as Trotsky. He is in Vienna again to scrounge enough funds for his next issue.

Across town, Josip Broz, a 20-year-old Jewish mechanic, has just arrived to work at the Daimler auto plant at Wiener Neustadt, very close to the capital. Broz is a playboy and spends much of his wages on dancing, fencing and pretty girls. "Thank God its Friday," he chuckles to a fellow worker. The shop is looking forward to the Automobile Mechanics Ball tonight. Unlike Stalin and Trotsky, Broz is not worried by ideologies, nor should he be. Not for three decades will he become Marshal Tito, dictator of communist Yugoslavia.[1525]

In the poorest northeast section of the city, a block from the River Danube in the Mannerheim (slum house) for men, a not quite 24-year-old, gaunt, aspiring artist sits for hours in his personal chair in the common room of the house. He is unemployed. On the floor beside him lies a stack of *Ostara*, an anti-Semitic, white supremacist journal. He stops painting, picks up a copy of *Ostara* and reads again about the revolutions that have plagued Europe. The new issue speaks of the recently failed Russian Revolution of 1905. It mentions Leon Trotsky, editor of *Pravda*, as being a ringleader, and notes he may be a Jew. Behind all the uprisings, so reports *Ostara*, are the Jews, Jesuits and Masons.

The artist drops the journal and picks up his paintbrush. "I'm a man of imperial destiny," he mutters. "Rienzi has given me the mandate to destroy these destroyers of society!"

His thoughts flash to the opera house at Linz and Richard Wagner's *Rienzi*. He has seen the opera more than one hundred times and remembers the methodical and scholarly planning of Rienzi, the Roman Tribune, his remarkable feats of heroism, patriotic oratory and political cunning, the combination of which were responsible for his triumphs. Suddenly, the artist rises from his chair, and to an audience of flop house companions, the unknown Hitler becomes Rienzi, who, in two and a half decades will move a nation to World War II.

[1524] Helga Zepp-LaRouche, *The Hitler Book* (New York: New Benjamin Franklin House, 1984) 16.
[1525] Frederic Morton, *Thunder at Twilight* (New York: Charles Scribner's Sons, 1989) 3-23.

Frederic Morton, author of *Thunder At Twilight* (1989) vividly renders the content and manner of Adolf Hitler's sporadic orations:

> *Hitler would straighten up in his chair. He had been working all along, hunched over. Now the brush would drop from his hand. He would push the palette aside. He would rise to his feet.*
>
> *He began to speak, to shout, to orate. With hissing consonants and hall-filling vowels he launched into a harangue on morality, racial purity, the German mission and Slav treachery, on Jews, Jesuits, and Freemasons. His forelock would toss, his color-stained hands shred the air, his voice rose to an operatic pitch. Then, just as suddenly as he had started, he would stop. He would gather his things together with an imperious clatter, stalk off to his cubicle.*
>
> *And the others would just stare after him. They had come to accept his fits along with his "chair." He was, after all, a good man otherwise. And he did give his Mannerheim audience a good show, producing so dramatically the gesticulations of a clown and the screeching of a demon.*[1526]

As yet Hitler had only impassioned denunciations of the "Judeo-Masonic" conspiracy, as he called it. At that time, at least, he did not intend to jeopardize his own life for his vision as did Rienzi, for when Austria began recruiting men for the impending world war, Hitler fled to Germany to avoid the draft.[1527] Within a year he was arrested, taken for an Army physical, and on February 5, 1914, the Hitler file was closed with the conclusion: "'Unfit for military or auxiliary service; too weak; incapable of bearing arms.'"[1528]

Later, however, when Germany and Austria were losing the war and manpower was limited, Hitler was drafted. And he was a fine soldier.

THE HITLER PROJECT

A number of forces were behind the political creation of Adolf Hitler (1889-1945). Perhaps unknown to many is that a significant portion of Nazi ideology had its origin in Great Britain. We must, therefore, discuss the diverse British influences on the Nazis, which include: (1) a number of English Masons with racist views; (2) the secret societies through which they operated; and (3) Holy Grail mysticism. All three played crucial roles in creating Hitler.

Inventing a Hitler began in the mid-19th century. At that time English Freemasonry had come to the stark realization that French Freemasonry was rapidly becoming more powerful. Karl Marx was living in England, injecting his communist poison into the veins of the labor force. Likewise, Joseph Mazzini, Grand Master of Grand Orient Italy, was using London to launch revolutions across the Continent. Most insulting were the prominent English Masons who assisted both men, further weakening the aristocratic Brotherhood.

If this trend persisted, Grand Lodge London would become subservient to Grand Orient Paris. To remedy the problem, several aristocratic English Masons organized political secret societies as vanguards for revolution. Members of these societies would be placed in strategic positions in various nations around the world to penetrate political,

---

[1526] Morton 13-14.
[1527] Morton 58.
[1528] Morton 151.

financial and educational institutions with policies that would benefit Great Britain. Some fronts, both on the Left and Right, operated strictly on political or socioeconomic lines, such as the Fabian Society and the Round Table Groups. Others reverted to eastern mysticism, or out-right Satanism. All were Masonic and operated by British race-patriots.[1529]

In order to regain ascendancy in the struggle for world power, English Masonry would need to disseminate its notions of racial superiority and the occult (which were closely linked), and create a political engine to combat the spread of communism among the working and lower classes. In short, English Masonry would eventually need a charismatic leader who could embrace all three elements of its design. In retrospect it seems inevitable that English Freemasonry would need to discover or create, if not Adolf Hitler, someone like him. It is this endeavor of the British Brotherhood that we call the "Hitler Project."

THE MYSTIC FRONTS OF ENGLISH FREEMASONS

Edward George Bulwer-Lytton (1803-1873), the First Baron Lytton of Knebworth, was the youngest son of wealthy parents, Gen. William Bulwer and Elizabeth Lytton. After graduating from Cambridge, Bulwer-Lytton traveled in Europe, returned to England, and married in 1827. His political career began in 1831 when he entered Parliament. In 1841 he resigned in protest against repeal of the corn laws. Freemason Benjamin Disraeli converted him into a Tory (Conservative Party), and in 1852 he returned to Parliament.[1530]

Bulwer-Lytton not only was an aristocrat, statesman, historian, orator, and man of letters, he was one of the most prolific and popular English novelists of the 19th century. By 1836 he had achieved the greatest literary reputation of the day. In fact, few men in literary history have enjoyed the reputation and popularity that were Lytton's during his own lifetime. His works were read and admired not only in England, but in Germany, France, Italy, and America as well. He is best known to Americans for his 1838 novel, *The Last Days of Pompeii.*[1531]

Bulwer-Lytton, a British race patriot, expressed his white supremacist doctrine in his 1871 novel *Vril: The Power of the Coming Race,* which concerns a superman race of white Aryans that would take over the world. He was also a well-known practitioner of witchcraft, studying all the medieval writers on divination and magic. He believed a solid basis of truth underlay the black arts. He maintained a lifelong interest in the occult and was heavily involved with it and with the Societas Rosicrucian Anglia, of which he was Grand Patron.[1532] This Rosicrucian Society was founded in London in 1866. Only Master Masons of good standing and repute were admitted to it as members. Among them were the following notable occultists: William W. Westcott, S.L. MacGregor Mathers, John Yarker, A.E. Waite, Eliphas Levi and Theodore Reuss (head of the O.T.O. in 1905). According to a letter from Yarkerto Reuss, dated February 14, 1902, Weishaupt's Illuminati papers, which had been confiscated by the Bavarian government in 1785-1786, had been entrusted to the care of the Societas Rosicruciana Anglia.[1533]

[1529] Zepp 37.
[1530] "Lytton, Edward George Earle Bulwer-Lytton," *Encyclopaedia Britannica: Micropaedia.*
[1531] Richard Oilman, "The mysterious influence of Edward Bulwer-Lytton," *Conspiracy Digest* 3.2 (Spring 1978): 1.
[1532] Oilman, "Bulwer-Lytton" 2-3.
[1533] Miller 499-512.

Lytton, along with this membership, studied and carried out various magical rituals, and on many occasions attempted occult experiments, including the conjuring up of "elemental spirits."[1534]

One such occasion was related by the clairvoyant Douglas Home, who "witnessed the novelist [Lytton], in a seance, make contact with a spirit which claimed to have influenced the author in his writing of the romance *Zanoni.*"[1535]

Mackey's Encyclopedia of Freemasonry lists Bulwer-Lytton as a Mason, and confirms his Rosicrucian affiliation, tying him to the Priory of Sion conspiracy.[1536] In fact, suggests another author, "his epic *King* Arthur and the Provencal knight character, Walter de Montreal, in [another of his novels] *Rienzi* suggest his theology might have included Grail mysticism."[1537]

BULWER-LYTTON: GODFATHER OF THE NAZIS

Bulwer-Lytton is recognized by conspiracy researchers as the Godfather of the Nazi movement. A direct line of Freemasons implemented Lytton's teachings, founding and controlling secret societies based upon them. These societies can be directly linked to Hitler and his Nazi Party. Hitler was also inspired by Lytton's novels *Rienzi: The Last* of *the Roman Tribunes:* and *Vril: The Power of the Coming Race.*[1538]

In 1887, fourteen years after Lytton's death, the first of the mystic societies based on Lytton's teachings was founded. At the behest of the Quatuor Coronati Lodge, the Hermetic Order of the Golden Dawn was founded on the doctrine of Lytton's Rosicrucian Society. Moreover, the Golden Dawn's racist rituals had a double source: they were known to have been heavily derived from Holy Grail mysticism, and incorporated elements of the pagan rituals outlined in Lytton's 1871 novel, *Vril: The Power of the Coming Race. Vril* was the story of a superman race of white Aryans that would take over the world.[1539] The swastika was a key symbol of the Golden Dawn.

The founding of another secret society can be traced to Bulwer-Lytton. Before his death Lytton had been intimate with female Freemason Helena Blavatsky. Blavatsky later became a member of the Golden Dawn. In fact, Lytton had so influenced Blavatsky by the Isis cult that she wrote the book *Isis Unveiled.*[1540] In another book *Secret Doctrine*, Blavatsky warns her readers against Lytton's *Vril* as "the terrible sidereal [astral] Force, known to, and named by the Atlanteans... and by the Aryan[s]... It is the Vril of Bulwer Lytton's *Coming Race...it* is this Satanic Force that our generations were to be allowed to add to their stock of Anarchist's baby-toys... It is this destructive agency, which, once in the hands of some modern Attila... would reduce Europe in a few days to its primitive chaotic state with no man left alive to tell the tale."[1541]

Although Blavatsky realized the danger of Lytton's theories, and warned her readers of the destruction to humanity that the astral Force of Vril would bring should the wrong person appropriate its power, she persistently drew upon Lytton's novels for the Theosophical Society's teachings and rituals.[1542]

[1534] Oilman, "Bulwer-Lytton" 2-4.
[1535] Charles Walker, *Atlas of Secret Europe* (New York: Dorset Press, 1990) 146.
[1536] "Famous Masons," *Mackey's Encyclopedia,* vol. III.
[1537] Oilman, "Bulwer-Lytton" 4.
[1538] Oilman 1.
[1539] Oilman 2, 4.
[1540] Kalimtgis et al 182.
[1541] Walker 146-147.
[1542] Oilman, "Bulwer-Lytton" 3-4.

Bulwer-Lytton's influence extended to India through his son, Edward Robert Bulwer-Lytton (1831-1891), who was Viceroy and Governor-General of India from 1876 to 1880. Under Lytton's governorship, opium production in British India saw its greatest expansion. Lytton junior also opened his home to the cultists who were inspired by his father. One was Freemason Rudyard Kipling (1865-1936), who as we learned in the previous chapter, was a member of Milner's Round Table. Another was Madame Blavatsky. Both Kipling and Blavatsky employed the swastika as their personal coat of arms.[1543]

The influence of Bulwer-Lytton senior extended to Continental Europe as well. Lytton's novels were the favorite reading of German composer and Freemason Richard Wagner (1813-1883). Wagner was so taken by Lytton's *Rienzi: The Last of the Roman Tribunes* that he adapted it for the libretto of his first major opera, also titled *Rienzi*.[1544] Conspiracy writer Edith Miller lists Wagner as an early member of the O.T.O. before it was officially organized in 1902.[1545] Wagner also was an outspoken race ideologue and anti-Semite, who was involved in the 1848 German Grand Orient revolution. He was exiled from Germany in 1849.[1546]

Rienzi would provide an excellent blueprint for a 20th century dictator. The *Conspiracy Digest* informs us that "it would have been better for mankind if this Wagnerian opera had never come into existence. Because the fusion of Bulwer-Lytton's historical novel with the evil genius of Wagner's music was the fateful synthesis which sparked Hitler's Nazi dream."[1547]

As suggested by the flophouse scene at the beginning of this chapter, attending a performance of the opera *Rienzi* proved to be one of the most significant and profound experiences of Hitler's life. His first of what would be over a hundred returns to see *Rienzi* performed occurred with a friend, August Kubizek, in Linz, Austria, in November 1906. Kubizek reports that Hitler's whole personality changed after that performance. Outside the opera house Hitler spoke of a "mandate which, one day, he would receive from the people, to lead them out of servitude to the heights of freedom... He spoke of a special mission which one day would be entrusted to him."[1548]

Soon after the opera, Hitler made one of his many pilgrimages to the grave of Wagner. During the 1930s, when Hitler had made good his mandate, he and Kubizek were guests at the home of Richard Wagner's 86-year-old widow. There Hitler related what he had experienced during and after the 1906 performance of *Rienzi*. Concluding his account to Frau Wagner, Hitler is quoted as solemnly stating: "'In that hour it [National Socialism] began.'"[1549]

Hitler felt that his only predecessor was Richard Wagner. He read all of Wagner's writings and said the composer's political essays were his favorite reading. Hitler never hesitated to acknowledge his debt to Wagner. He is quoted as saying, "'Whoever wants to understand National Socialist Germany must know Wagner.'"[1550]

[1543] "Kipling, Rudyard," *Mackey's Encyclopedia*. vol.1.

[1544] Oilman, "Bulwer-Lytton" 2.

[1545] Miller 679.

[1546] Carol White, *The New Dark Ages Conspiracy* (New York: New Benjamin Franklin House, 1980) 115 and "Wagner, (Wilhelm) Richard," *Encyclopaedia Britannica: Micropaedia*.

[1547] Oilman.

[1548] Oilman.

[1549] Oilman 2-3.

[1550] James Pool and Suzanne Pool, *who Financed Hitler?* (1948; New York: The Dial Press, 1978) 122.

THE GOLDEN DAWN IN BERLIN

After the Golden Dawn was organized in 1887 on the racist doctrine espoused by Bulwer-Lytton, the order had established lodges by the turn of the century in several leading European cities including Berlin, which would soon boast a large ornate Golden Dawn temple.[1551] Before and during World War I, the Berlin Golden Dawn had spawned two other secret societies: (1) in 1902 the Ordo Templi Orientis (O.T.O.), which was later controlled by English Freemason Aleister Crowley; and (2) in 1918 the Thule Society, which discovered and groomed Hitler. The Thule Society's doctrine was identical to that contained in Lytton's *Vril: The Power of the Coming Race*. Blavatsky's doctrines of Theosophy became the Satanic bible of the Thule.[1552]

Wulf Schwarzwaller, in *The Unknown Hitler* (1990), confirms that English Freemasonry indirectly influenced Hitler through its Masonic and sub-Masonic societies. Regarding the Thule Society, he notes the "cross-links to the English Brotherhood of the Golden Dawn, to the theosophists of Madame Blavatsky, and to the notorious magician and adventurer Aleister Crowley,"[1553] who was at the head of the Ordo Templi Orientis (O.T.O.). These three mystic societies - the Golden Dawn, O.T.O., and Thule society - like fly traps, lured, caught, polished, and then elevated, Adolf Hitler. Once in power, the Fuehrer came completely under their spell.

Crowley had much in common with Hitler. First, both drew inspiration from Bulwer-Lytton's occult novels, Crowley claiming they contained secrets for higher initiates of magic.[1554] Second, Crowley's Ordo Templi Orientis (O.T.O.) and Hitler's Thule Society were both creations of English Freemasonry and identical in their homicidal orientation. When Hitler began gaining power, Crowley and the Russian occultist G.I. Gurdjieff (the same Gurdjieff who initiated Joseph Stalin into Martinist Freemasonry) sought contact with Hitler.[1555] Gurdjieff succeeded.

Another 33rd degree English Mason who certainly had indirect (and possibly direct) contact with Hitler was Viscount Horatio Herbert Kitchener (1850-1916). *Mackey's Encyclopedia of Freemasonry* states that Lord Kitchener was accomplished in oriental languages, which enabled him to advance Freemasonry in the Orient. As a famous English soldier serving seven years in India, he was responsible for founding three Lodges there, becoming Grand Master at Punjab. While serving in Egypt he was Grand Master of both Egypt and Sudan. He also visited Japan, Australia and New Zealand.[1556]

During his sojourn in India, Kitchener made many trips to Tibet where he was introduced to the German general Karl Ernst Haushofer. Haushofer, himself a Freemason and member of the Berlin Golden Dawn, had before World War I spent many years as military attaché in Japan and traveled extensively in Asia. Kitchener, and the Russian occultist G.I. Gurdjieff, also an expert on Tibetan mysticism, initiated Haushofer into the secret cult of the Tibetan lamas (who claimed to possess the secret of the "superman") and introduced him to the meaning of the swastika.[1557]

The swastika was originally a symbol of the sun-god in India. In Sanskrit it means "all is all."[1558] In Hinduism the swastika is both right-handed and left-handed. The right-

[1551] Oilman, "Bulwer-Lytton" 3.
[1552] Kalimtgis et al 182.
[1553] Wulf Schwarzwaller, *The Unknown Hitler* (1989; New York:Berkley Books, 1990) 54.
[1554] Oilman,"Bulwer-Lytton" 1.
[1555] Schwarzwaller 100.
[1556] "Kitchener, Viscount Horatio Herbert," *Mackey's Encyclopedia*, vol.1.
[1557] Zepp 88.
[1558] John Toland, *Adolf Hitler* (1976; New York: Galantine Books,1984) 87.

handed swastika, rotating clockwise, "symbolized light, white magic, creative force."[1559] Rotating counterclockwise, it means darkness, black magic and destruction.

In 1919 Haushofer joined the Thule Society and introduced its membership to the meaning of the swastika, which became the Thule Society's coat of arms. Thus, from Haushofer, Kipling, Blavatsky, and others, the swastika found its way into the German cults that would later form the core of Nazism.[1560]

That same year Haushofer became a university professor and director of the Munich Institute of geopolitics. In that position he was destined to school Hitler in geopolitics and assist the Fuehrer in writing *Mein Kampf (My Fight)*. Later, as a prominent figure in the Nazi Party, Haushofer would send the core of the SS back to Tibet for initiation. Before they returned he established for them the *Vril Society*, which in turn would compose the inner core of the Nazi Party. The notion for the Vril, of course, was derived from Bulwer-Lytton's 1871 novel, *Vril: The Power of the Coming Race*.

Haushofer's Vril Society rituals were imported from Rosicrucian English Freemasonry[1561], including the Luciferian doctrine of Blavatsky's Theosophy Society. Only a slight twist was needed to accommodate the notion of a "Superman Race."

Alfred Rosenberg (of whom we will discuss at length later in this chapter) was the member of the Thule Society who introduced *The Protocols of Sion* to the West. He was also the creator of the religious ceremonies for the Vril. Rosenberg had to be cautious in his approach, since the overwhelming majority of the "Aryan" German race adhered to the Christian faith. Christians were already anti-Masonic, especially Catholic Christians, and their cooperation was needed for Hitler's coming destruction of the "Judeo-Masonic" conspiracy. To avoid a direct assault on Christianity, Rosenberg promoted gnostic distortions of Christianity for initiates to the Vril. In this scheme, Lucifer and Christ became the same personality. Lucifer-Christ, then, was a prophet for the master race, which meant, of course, that Christ must belong to the "Aryan race." The earthly parents of Christ, therefore, were not Jewish, but rather Roman legionnaires of Persian descent. This racially northern Christ-hero became the scourge of all racially inferior peoples and rationalist elements of the population. In the myth of the Vril Society, Lucifer-Christ "fought against the Satan of racial inferiority and rationality."[1562] (Racial inferiority was assigned to the Jews and the rationalists were members of Continental Freemasonry).

Membership in Haushofer's Vril Society was limited to the SS and the hierarchy of the Nazi Party - Himmler, Goering, Alfred Rosenberg, and the Fuehrer himself, along with his personal physician, Dr. Morell.[1563] These men were deeply involved in the same Luciferian Doctrine as English Freemasonry, though it was twisted slightly for their own needs. And they practiced witchcraft with a vengeance.

Not surprisingly, Haushofer's Berlin-based Vril Society, through the Golden Dawn of Berlin, had links with Golden Dawn devotees in Great Britain. Until 1941, members of the Vril, Thule and Berlin Golden Dawn were in continual communication with the London Golden Dawn. Communication was broken off in May 1941, when Rudolf Hess (also a member of the Berlin Golden Dawn[1564], and the closest man to Hitler) made his famous abortive peace mission to England. Before Hess's flight, Haushofer and his son Albrecht gave Hess the names and addresses of Golden Dawn contacts in Great Britain,

---

[1559] Schwarzwaller 59.

[1560] Kalimtgis et al 215-216.

[1561] Baigent et al, *Messianic Legacy* 159.

[1562] Zepp 95-96.

[1563] Schwarzwaller 100.

[1564] Kalimtgis et al 182, 215.

as well as names of other prominent English Masons who favored peace between England and Germany.[1565]

Another important intellectual influence on Hitler was the writings of 33rd degree Mason Friedrich Wilhelm Nietzsche (1844-1900). In fact, the name *Nazi* is a derivative of *Nietzsche*. That Hitler's last birthday gift to Mussolini in 1943 was *The Collected Works of Nietzsche* testifies to the enduring influence of this philosopher upon Hitler.[1566]

Edith Miller lists Nietzsche, along with Wagner, as a member of the O.T.O. before it was officially registered in 1902.[1567] Helga Zepp, authoress of *The Hitler Book* confirms the influence Nietzsche had on the Nazi movement:

> *Everything the Nazis later made into reality was already lurking within Nietzsche's tormented brain, darting about with increasing frenzy... the idea of a master race, the mystically inspired hatred of Christianity, and its final and ultimate form, the Ecce Homo, where Nietzsche cries out: "Have I made myself clear? - Dionysus against the Crucified..."*[1568]

Nietzsche was an aggressive spokesmen for English Freemasonry, although he realized that war between England and Germany was inevitable and that when it started it would cause the greatest bloodbath known to history.[1569] In *Will to Power,* he wrote, "Our entire European culture has long been moving with agonizing tension, increasing from decade to decade, and is now tumbling loosely, restlessly, violently into catastrophe: like a river which wants to reach its end, which no longer thinks, which is afraid to think."[1570]

Nietzsche, while under the influence of narcotics, is also quoted as saying, "While millions fall trembling in the dust, we are close to the dionysian." Dionysus was the Greek god of drunkenness and orgiastic revelry. For Nietzsche "the dionysian" meant creativity, powers of imagination versus rationalism. Hitler, also a drug addict, brought about the fulfillment of Nietzsche's prophecy.

THE THULE SOCIETY'S HOLY GRAIL MYTH

While members of the Golden Dawn were organizing the Thule Society, the Quatuor Coronati Lodge of Masonic Research at London concocted the Thule myth from the legend of the mythical Atlantis and based it upon Holy Grail mysticism. According to the authors of the Thule myth, the word "Thule" signifies a prehistoric "golden age" of Aryans in northern Europe which ended in sudden catastrophe. In this myth, the Aryans were in possession of the Holy Grail, but after their demise, the Grail was lost. So seriously did the Nazis embrace this legend of Aryan supremacy that Hitler's SS experts

---

[1565] Gilman, "Bulwer-Lytton" 3.After being tried at Nuremberg, Hess was not executed, apparently because he was a brother Mason. He was instead given life in solitary confinement, this to keep British involvement in creating Hitler silent. In 1988, at age 94, Hess died in prison with his secret intact.
[1566] Morton 196.
[1567] Miller 679.
[1568] Zepp 53.
[1569] Zepp 65.
[1570] Zepp 70-71.

in Aryan esoterica actually conducted a search for the Grail in Southern France, with the support of Heinrich Himmler.[1571] Zepp explains how the Nazis interpreted the legend:

> The Thule Society and the Nazis took up this myth of the Grail and interpreted it so that the Grail was understood as an inscribed stone or tablet. This tablet was a crucial document of Aryan gnosticism, preserved and passed on from Aryan prehistory. According to the myth of the Grail, the tablet was finally hidden in a Grail fortress in southern France; according to the Nazi lore, it originally came from Aryan Persia, then reached Jerusalem, and was brought to Rome after Jerusalem was destroyed. [From Rome] it found its way to southern France...[1572]

THE THULE SOCIETY: ITS FOUNDER AND MEMBERSHIP

Since the Thule Society's doctrine was similar to that of the Merovingian Grail kings, it was not surprising to learn that its constituents were aristocrats. Membership consisted of lawyers, judges, university professors, police officials, aristocratic members of royalty, leading industrialists, surgeons, physicians, scientists, as well as rich businessmen, like the proprietor of the elegant Four Seasons Hotel in Munich in which the society was headquartered.[1573]

These headquarters became the command center for the counterrevolutionary underground of European royalty at a time when Grand Orient communist revolutions were sweeping post- World War I Europe. Thule Society letterheads and literature displayed the swastika, and large swastika flags decorated its plush meeting rooms and offices.[1574]

Although the Thule Society was an offshoot of the Golden Dawn, its official founder and head was Baron Rudolf von Sebottendorif (1875-1945), a Knight of the Masonic Order of Constantine (Turkish Freemasonry). Sebottendorff was the leader of the "Turkish Crescent," which fought in the Balkan War of 1912-1913 against the Grand Orient revolutionists backed by Serbia. In the ranks of the revolutionists were Jews, and consequently during that conflict Sebottendorff became violently anti-Semitic. In 1913 he returned to Germany fortified with a vast knowledge of the occult and substantial funds from an unknown source. During the next four years he made extensive contacts with the leading members of numerous international occult groups that were rapidly proliferating in Germany at that time, focussing his contacts on the Order of the Golden Dawn. Late in 1917 Sebottendorff was in Munich to begin organizing the Thule Society. With assistance from Golden Dawn members, on August 17, 1918, the Thule Society was officially founded.[1575] Sebottendorff elevated himself to Grand Master, then recruited from among the German noble families and aristocracy to use the Society as their counterrevolutionary headquarters. To his later discredit and ultimate downfall, Sebottendorff published a list of the Thule Society's membership.

Sebottendorff claimed he had been sent to Germany by the Ascended Masters of Islam, who "had entrusted him with the mission of illuminating Germany through the revelation of the secrets of advanced magic and initiation into ancient oriental

---

[1571] Zepp 97.
[1572] Zepp 97.
[1573] Pool and Pool 7.
[1574] Pool and Pool 8.
[1575] Zepp 86-87.

mysteries."[1576] One of the mysteries Sebottendorff imparted to the Thule membership was the so-called revelation that the Jews were behind world revolution and therefore must be annihilated.

ANTI-SEMITISM AND THE THULE SOCIETY

Another Thule Society member who added strength to Sebottendorff's anti-Semitic accusations was Alfred Rosenberg (1893-1946). Rosenberg grew up as a Baltic German in Revel, Estonia, and spoke perfect German and Russian. He studied architecture at Moscow University and graduated there in 1917. He witnessed Kerensky's revolution in February and saw it destroyed in October by Lenin, a half-Jew, and Trotsky, a full-blooded Jew. In the spring of 1918, he read the newspaper headlines which announced the assassination of the Czar and his royal household at the hands of a Jew. Then he watched as 82 percent of the new Communist bureaucracy was staffed by Jews.

In October 1918 Rosenberg arrived in Munich. To his dismay he discovered that German Communists were mostly Jews. No matter. In his baggage he carried a copy of the most damning evidence against them. Upon joining the Thule Society, he presented the *Protocols* OJ *the Learned Elders of* Sion to its membership.

The Thule Society's membership was pro-aristocratic, oligarchic and monarchical. Driven by fear of the communists, the Thule's declared, political aim was two-fold: (1) the extirpation of what the membership called the communist Judeo-Masonic conspiracy; and (2) the return of the Hohenzollerns to the German throne. Hence, the membership was willing to embrace a dictator (for a while at least), who would lead Germany out of the clutches of the communist beast and return her to her original dynastic glory.

At the beginning of November 1918, German Grand Orient Communists took over the government in Munich. Shortly thereafter, on November 9, Sebottendorff spoke before a meeting of the entire membership of the Thule Society to issue a call to arms against Judah. He ended his speech with the declaration: "Remember that you are a German! Keep your blood pure!"[1577] This admonition became the motto of the Thule Society, which thereafter publicly espoused German racial superiority, anti-Semitism and anti-Communism.[1578]

Rosenberg, with Dietrich Eckart (another top officer of the Thule), 7 were the first to publish the *Protocols* outside of Russia.[1579] Eckart was both a Freemason and a Rosicrucian, and possibly a member of the Golden Dawn. He broke from Freemasonry because he could not embrace its internationalism.[1580] Finding his spiritual home in the Thule Society, Eckart, a dedicated Satanist, was a master of magic and practiced rituals that were anything but harmless.

Eckart participated in a series of seances with Rosenberg and the infamous Russian occultist G.I. Gurdjieff.[1581] During these seances, Eckart was "told of the imminent appearance of the German messiah, a Lord Maitreya." Eckart was further instructed about

---

[1576] Richard Gilman, "Nazis, Mystics, and Islam: In search of the Nazi-Muslim Connection," *Conspiracy Digest* 2.3 (Summer 1977): 7.

[1577] Pool and Pool 8.

[1578] Pool and Pool 8.

[1579] Zepp 95.

[1580] Schwarzwaller 57.Schwarzwaller claims that Eckart also broke from Rosicrucianism, which may only mean he broke from the Golden Dawn. But when we consider he was a member of the Thule Society, and the Thule Society espoused the same Luciferian doctrine as the Golden Dawn and Blavatsky's Theosophy, Eckart was still a Rosicrucian.

[1581] Gilman, "Nazis" 6 and Epperson, *New World Order* 130-131.

his own destiny. He was "to prepare the vessel of the Anti-Christ, the man inspired by Lucifer to conquer the world and lead the Aryan race to glory.[1582]

Eckart was a heavy drinker who used "drugs, including peyote, the South American hallucinogen, which Aleister Crowley introduced into Europe's artistic and occultist circles. In his younger years in Berlin, Eckart spent some time in a psychiatric clinic because of morphine addiction."[1583] This man was destined to become Hitler's mentor.

THE THULE:
MONARCHISTS IN SEARCH OF A PARTY AND LEADER

As stated above, in early November 1918, the German Grand Orient communists, known as Spartacists (Adam Weishaupt's code name)[1584], took power in Munich. They ruled Bavaria from November to May, during which time there were a series of communist insurrections throughout Germany. Their largest uprising was scheduled for May 1, 1919, the birthday of Weishaupt's Illuminati. Anticipating this event, the voluntary monarchist troops, called Free Corps (which, unbeknownst to the general population, were financed by the Thule Society), surrounded Munich. In retaliation, the Spartacists, who had in their possession the membership list of the Thule Society, which had been irresponsibly published by Sebottendorff, raided the Thule headquarters and took seven members hostage. When the Free Corps units tightened their ring around the city, the hostages were stood up against a wall in the courtyard of the Luitpold High School and shot. Four of the seven were titled aristocrats, including the beautiful young secretary of the society, Countess Heila von Westarp, and Prince Gustave von Thurnund Taxis, who was related to several European royal families.[1585]

Sebottendorff, founder of the Thule Society, was blamed by the membership for his careless, and as it turned out, fatal publication of the Society's membership list, which fell into communist hands. From then on, Sebottendorff's influence in the Thule Society declined and in 1923 he returned to Thrkey.[1586] Meanwhile, Dietrich Eckart, the man destined to discover and groom Hitler, became one of the most powerful members of the Thule Society's hierarchy.

After the Free Corps troops liberated Munich from the communists, the Thule Society felt it was time to come out in the open as an anti-communist movement. In its own newspaper the *Thule Collection*, the Thule announced that it was the financier behind the Free Corps. Publisher of the *Thule Collection* was one Diederichs (no first name available), a leading publisher of Masonic books, and member of an English Grand Lodge. Diederichs also published *Tat*, the most important public newspaper in Weimar, Germany. *Tat's* editor was Hans Zehrer, also a prominent English Mason. Later, when Hitler declared that the "Third Reich" would be established by his Nazi Party, Zehrer wrote that the leadership of the "Third Reich" could be "guaranteed only through elites and oligarchs." Within Zehrer's Masonic circle were many wealthy and influential oligarchs. All favored a return of the Hohenzollern monarchy. Most belonged to the Thule Society.[1587]

After World War I, the monarchists were still a very powerful force in Germany, enjoying tremendous social prestige and popularity among the upper class. The German

---

[1582] Epperson 130.
[1583] Schwarzwaller 56-57.
[1584] Pool and Pool 8.
[1585] Pool and Pool 9.
[1586] Gilman, "Nazis" 6.
[1587] Zepp 252-253.

People's Party and the Nationalist Party (the two largest conservative political parties) were pro-monarchist. Moreover, the monarchists, which included conservative industrialists, controlled tremendous financial resources, including the inherited fortunes of the various royal and princely families.[1588] Although the Kaiser had abdicated in 1918, wealthy Germans were still his loyal subjects.

The first goal of the Thule aristocrats was to form a political party to win back the masses, especially the laborers, whom they said had been ''poisoned with the Jewish ideas of communism and internation-alism.''[1589] Most of the German aristocracy were members of the Thule Society and its hierarchy recognized that the Thule program would be automatically rejected by the masses if its political party was headed by someone of a privileged class. Thule thus recruited Anton Drexler and his German Workers' Party (GWP), financing and promoting it as its own political party. The GWP adopted the anti-Semitic and pro-monarchist Thule agenda.

Meanwhile, Dietrich Eckart composed a bardic verse in which the coming of a national redeemer was prophesied. Obviously, his so-called "prophecy" was prompted by the seances with Gurdjieff where Eckart received his "annunciation" that he was destined to prepare a messiah for the German people. A few weeks after the Free Corps' liberation of Munich, Eckart brought to the Thule supreme council the idea that the hour for a great charismatic leader had come. Below is a portion of the verse, which he read:

> *[We need a leader] familiar and foreign at the same time, a nameless one... We must have a fellow as a leader who won't wince at the rattle of a machine gun. The rabble must be given a damned good fright. An officer wouldn't do; the people don't respect them any more. Best of all would be a worker, a former soldier who could speak. He needn't be very brainy; politics is the most stupid business in the world... I'd rather have a stupid vain Jackanapes who can give the Reds a juicy answer and not run away whenever a chair-leg is aimed at him than a dozen learned professors who sit trembling in wet pants.[1590]*

The final requirement for this charismatic leader was: "He must be a bachelor! Then we'll get the women."[1591] The Thule was well on its way to accepting Adolf Hitler.

GRAIL MYSTICISM AND THE UNKNOWN HITLER

While in Vienna, the still obscure Adolf Hitler read every occult book he could lay hands on. Not only was he familiar with the history of the Masonic revolutions during the past century, he was also aware that the two Freemasonries vied for power. As an imperialist, he hated Grand Orient Freemasonry, not only because it destroyed thrones, but because he mistakenly supposed it to be controlled by Jews. He appeared to favor English Freemasonry. Most of his Masonic heroes were tied to the Grand Lodge or Rosicrucian conspiracy.

Can we link the anti-Semitism of the Priory of Sion to Adolf Hitler, either by direct formation or indirect influence? As we saw in chapter 1, the Priory of Sion founded anti-Semitic Rosicrucianism as a front organization. In chapter 13 we discovered that Sion also created the Alliance Israelite Universelle to counter the Zionist movement In chapter

---

[1588] Pool and Pool 270.

[1589] Pool and Pool 8.

[1590] Pool and Pool 20.

[1591] Pool and Pool.

19 we saw how Sion's agent, G.I. Gurdjieff, persuaded Joseph Stalin to intercept Zionists at the Russian border in an attempt to contain the Zionist movement. We saw further that Stalin's "iron curtain" policy failed to stop the movement. Could it be that Hitler was next in line to take up where Stalin failed? Did agents of the Priory of Sion also educate and groom the future Fuehrer to carry out the "Final Solution" in hopes it would once and for all crush the Zionist movement?

Every indication suggests that Hitler was a product of the Priory of Sion, if not directly, at least through its Grail mysticism. For example, in 1906, before the world had ever heard of him, Hitler made his first visit to the Linz opera house to see *Rienzi*, an opera based upon Grail mysticism. In 1907, he joined an anti-Semitic Rosicrucian order in Vienna called the "Order of the New Temple." The New Temple blamed Jews and Freemasons for the European revolutions of the previous century. Long before he arrived in Germany, Hitler had set his mind to crush the Judeo- Masonic conspiracy. As Hitler would testify at his trial in Germany in 1924: "I left Vienna an absolute anti-Semite, a deadly enemy of the collective Marxist world-view, and as a pan-German in my orientation."[1592]

During his sojourn in Vienna, Hitler also learned of the "King of Jerusalem" cult, its Grail mysteries and its Spear of Longinus.[1593] Hitler became an avid adherent to the doctrine of Sionism, so much so that the authors of *The Messianic Legacy,* when comparing the messianic orientation of the Third Reich to that of the Priory of Sion, found them to be identical.[1594]

In 1909, when Hitler was a 21-year-old, he became intrigued by the legend of the Spear of Longinus and believed, as the legend purported, that the destiny of the world lay in its magical powers. The Spear of Longinus (also known as the Spear of Destiny) was supposedly the one that pierced the side of Jesus. It was said to have passed through the hands of forty-five Merovingian emperors from 752 to 1806. According to the legend, whoever possesses the Spear will rule the world. The Spear of Destiny was in the possession of the Habsburgs while Hitler was in Vienna.[1595]

Hitler frequently went to the Habsburg Treasure House Museum where he stood for hours at a time gazing at the Spear. At that time, Hitler was on the hallucinogenic drug mescaline, in an attempt to learn the secret path to the lost Grail.[1596] We can only imagine Hitler's thoughts as he stood before the Spear: "If only I could possess the Spear, I could rid the world of the Judeo- Masonic conspiracy." Hitler became obsessed with the idea of his crusade. Rev. Church takes us deeper into Hitler's fevered trance before the mystical Spear:

> *One day Hitler went to the Treasure House to study the Spear of Longinus. Hour after hour he gazed upon the relic, as if in Transcendental Meditation. According to his own testimony he went into a trance: "The air became stifling so that I could barely breathe. The noisy scene of the Treasure House seemed to melt away before my eyes. I stood alone and trembling before the hovering form*

[1592] Zepp 105.

[1593] Baigent et al, *Holy Blood, Holy Grail* 164, 450.aigent says, "Early in 1944, when Gisors was occupied by German personnel, a special military mission was sent from Berlin with instructions to plan a series of excavations beneath the fortress." (Gisors, as you recall from chapter 1, was the home of the first Grand Master of the Priory of Sion.) Hitler also sent an expedition to Rennes-le-Chatean in southern France in search of the Templar treasury.

[1594] Baigent et al, *Messianic Legacy* 161.

[1595] Church 57.

[1596] Church 64.

of the Superman - a Spirit sublime and fearful, a countenance intrepid and cruel. In holy awe, I offered my soul as a vessel of his Will."[1597]

Was the mighty spirit, before whom Hitler stood, the same Satanic Force of Vril spoken of by Madame Blavatsky? Was it this awesome Power that gave Hitler his mandate outside the opera house at Linz where he first viewed Richard Wagner's *Rienzi?* Possibly, for that day at the Habsburg Museum, Hitler gave himself to the spiritual hierarchies of darkness to become the vessel of the spirit of Antichrist.

After his encounter with this "fearful Spirit," Hitler became intrigued with the legend of the Holy Grail, believing himself to be the reincarnation of the Grail's Landulph of Capua and ninth- century Lord of Terra di Labur. Hitler also believed that the legend of Percival in search of the Holy Grail was "a prophecy to be replayed on the stage of world history a thousand years later in the twentieth century."[1598]

After Hitler became the Fuehrer of the German people, says Rev. Church, he "and the other members of his satanic group chose the 'advantages' of the drug shortcut to attain higher consciousness in their quest for the Grail."[1599] As noted earlier, author Helga Zepp reports that according to Thule lore, the Holy Grail had been changed from a golden cup to a golden tablet, and that SS experts searched for and apparently found what they thought was the Grail tablet. As Zepp concludes, "The Nazis in the inner mystic circle thought they were now able to understand the contents of the tablet, which had never been deciphered, and to penetrate further secrets of Aryan gnosticism."[1600]

At Vienna on October 13, 1938, five years after Hitler came to power, the messiah of the Aryan race finally took possession of the *Spear of Longinus* and placed it in the Hall of St. Katherine's Church at Nuremberg. Five and a half years later, when the Allies began bombing Nuremberg, the Nazis removed the Spear from the Church and with other treasures, placed it in a protected vault. On March 30, 1945, when the Americans were expected to invade the city, the treasures were once again removed, but the Spear was inadvertently left behind. One month later at 2:00 **P.M.** an American soldier retrieved the Spear of Destiny. That same hour Hitler took his own life in a bunker fifty feet below Berlin. General Dwight Eisenhower, commander of the Allied Armies in Europe, bluntly said, "Return the Habsburg Regalia to Austria."[1601]

On January 6, 1946, the imperial treasures, including the Spear of Longinus, were back in the Habsburg Treasure House, where they remain to this day. Rev. Church says, "According to legend, whoever owns the Spear can rule the world... And members of the royal family of the Habsburg dynasty are today among the prime movers and shakers behind the unification of Europe."[1602]

FREEMASONRY, VRIL MYSTICISM AND THE SS

Like Hitler, the 55 had deep roots in occult mysticism. But its organizational success owed much to Hitler's study of Freemasonry.

Duplicating the pyramid structure in the lodge, the SS was a secret society within another secret society, called the Vril. Moreover, the cold-blooded 55 were Satan worshippers. Their insignia (SS), shaped like two lightning bolts, is an ancient symbol of

---

[1597] Church 65.
[1598] Church 43.
[1599] Church 65.
[1600] Zepp 98.
[1601] Church 68.
[1602] Church 69.

Satan. In Eastern mysticism the lightning bolts signify the speed and power by which the Adversary of God was cast out of heaven.[1603] Jesus Christ Himself said in Luke 10:18, "I beheld Satan as lightning fall from heaven."

"The Nazi hierarchy established the 55 as a secret society, developing its character from a mixture of Tibetan, Masonic, and Jesuit mysticism. 55 Reichsfuehrer Heinrich Himmler was a necromancer, frequently conducting seances for the 55 hierarchy at his castle in Wewelsburg."[1604]

Each 55 officer took a secret blood oath to obey Hitler without question. Collectively, they were the ears and eyes of the Fuehrer - present at every meeting of political or social significance, yet never taking part in discussions. Instead, they just sat or stood in the background, observing and taking notes.[1605]

THE HITLER PROJECT AND ANTI-ZIONISM

We have discovered that the first two decades of the 20th century saw several mysterious rendezvous among a number of Rosicrucians and with the future Fuehrer of the Third Reich. These Rosicrucians played significant roles in the Hitler Project. We will review these meetings and discuss the possibility that these rendezvous were not happenstance, but prearranged appointments made by agents of the Priory of Sion.

In Vienna in 1900, Peter Adolf Lanz, a Benedictine monk who had become obsessed with his study of Freemasonry, changed his name to Jorg von Liebenfels and founded a Rosicrucian order called the Order of the New Temple. The name "New Temple" was a play on words, meant to replace the "Old Temple" or the old Templar order. The "old Templar order," which was embodied in Continental Freemasonry, was believed by Liebenfels to be controlled by the Jews. Wulf Schwarzwaller, author of *The Unknown Hitler*, informs us that esoteric and Masonic elements were important in Liebenfels' secret society, in which the blond, blue-eyed Germanic Master Race struggled against the "inferior" dark races. Liebenfels planned to replace the class struggle with the racial struggle, which would go "all the way to the castration knife.[1606]

Under his given name, Lanz, Liebenfels had taught in a Benedictine cloister school from 1890 to 1900. He must have known Adolf Hitler, for the future Fuehrer had attended the school during the latter half of that decade. Before that the school had been directed by Abbe' Peter Hagen who was an expert in oriental mysticism. The Abbe's personal coat of arms was the swastika, a wooden carving which stood above the abbey door. Hagen left behind an extensive library of mystical works, which was completely absorbed by Liebenfels. In 1900, when Liebenfels founded the Order of the New Temple, he selected the swastika as the Order's coat of arm.[1607]

In 1901 Liebenfels began to publish an anti-Semitic journal called *Ostara*. In 1905 he published his "major work," *Theo-zoology or the Knowledge of Sodom's Monkeys and the Electron of the Gods*. In this book Liebenfels demanded the total extermination of the darker-skinned races, offering in support the doctrine of English Freemason, Rev. Thomas Maithus, who suggested that the earth would soon be overpopulated, requiring the extermination of useless eaters.[1608]

[1603] Daniel, *Scarlet and the Beast,* vol. II, chapter 1.
[1604] Infield 19-22.
[1605] Infield 20.
[1606] Schwarzwaller 26.
[1607] Zepp 102.
[1608] Zepp 102-105.

According to Liebenfels, the Jews as "the most intelligent of the ape-races" as he put it, were also the most dangerous. As useless eaters, he said Jews must be exterminated first. Liebenfels also pointed to the British colonial regime and its "race-patriots" as an example to follow in making the white race supreme.[1609]

The New Templar Order saw itself as a human breeding society. Its aim was to produce new Aryan heroes. It was no small surprise that Hitler, while living in Vienna, passed by the building which displayed the swastika symbol - the symbol so familiar to him during his Benedictine school days. Nor was it surprising that he entered to visit his old schoolmaster. Hitler admitted that in 1907 he joined an anti-Semitic order in Vienna, which could only have been the New Templar Order. Hitler, for instance, was an avid reader of Liebenfels' *Ostara*. In 1909, when in one of his three moves he missed several issues, Hitler went to New Templar headquarters to pick up the missing copies, leaving his new address with Liebenfels. Moreover, Liebenfels claimed Hitler as one of his disciples, writing to an occultist in 1932: "Hitler is one of our pupils. You will one day experience that he, and through him we, will one day be victorious and develop a movement that makes the world tremble."[1610]

In 1910 another significant rendezvous took place in Vienna. That year Rosicrucian and English Freemason Lord Kitchener stopped off at Vienna on his way to London. Kitchener had been in the Orient where he and G.I. Gurdjieff had completed initiating the future Nazi Karl Ernst Haushofer into the Tibetan mysteries. Within eight years Haushofer would be training Hitler in geopolitics. In fourteen years he would be assisting the Fuehrer in writing a portion of *Mein Kampf* And in twenty years, he would be training Hitler's SS in Tibetan mysticism and founding the Vril Society for them.[1611]

Why did Kitchener go by way of Vienna on his return from the Orient? Liebenfels may have the answer, for he claimed that Kitchener joined his order." It seems the mysterious rendezvous at Tibet and later in Vienna were only the beginning of a series of secret assignations that occurred in connection with the "Hitler Project."[1612]

A pivotal figure in these communications was the mysterious G.I. Gurdjieff, the Russian mystic who held extraordinary power over the so many and varied followers of Rosicrucianism connected with the Hitler Project.[1613] Gurdjieff was himself a Martinist Rosicrucian. He also was an agent of the Czarist secret police.[1614]

It seems very likely that Lord Kitchener and Liebenfels, as Rosicrucians, were agents of the Priory of Sion. Their use by Sion was not necessarily dependent on their cognizance. No evidence exists that Liebenfels had prior communication with the Kitchener-Gurdjieff. Haushofer trio. Nevertheless, the precise timing of the meetings among these powerful Rosicrucians is definitely suspicious. Kitchener, Liebenfels and Hitler belonged to the same Rosicrucian order. All three were in the same city at the same time. Is it not plausible to suggest that Liebenfels arranged a meeting between Hitler and Lord Kitchener?

Gurdjieff's importance emerges when we consider that he trained the key players in the "Hitler Project." In 1900, for example, Gurdjieff initiated Joseph Stalin into Rosicrucian Martinism.[1615] (It was the Hitler-Stalin Pact of 1939 that started World War II.) And as we have noted, after his encounter with Stalin, Gurdjieff rendezvoused with Kitchener in Tibet to initiate Rosicrucian Haushofer into the Tibetan mysteries. Then in

---

[1609] Zepp.

[1610] Dusty Sklar, *The Nazis and the Occult* (New York: Dorset Press,1977) 21.

[1611] Schwarzwaller 26.

[1612] Zepp 104.

[1613] Walker 242 and Stoddard, *Trail* 242.

[1614] Gilman, "Nazis" 8.

[1615] Baigent et al, *Messianic Legacy* 147.

1910, Kitchener was in Vienna visiting the Rosicrucian Liebenfels, who was Hitler's first mentor. After the Russian Revolution, Gurdjieff and the Russian Rosenberg (the one who brought the *Protocols* to Germany), appeared in Germany[1616], participating in a series of seances with Thule's Dietrich Eckart. It was during these seances, as we have mentioned, that Eckart received his annunciation that he was destined to prepare the man who would lead the Aryan race to glory.[1617] Was Eckart Hitler's final mentor? Or was it G.I. Gurdjieff?

If Gurdjieff, an agent of the Priory *of Sion*, was the common link among the key players of the Hitler Project, what would these mysterious rendezvous mean for the Zionist movement? As a Martinist, Gurdjieff would have been anti-Zionist. He was. As an agent in the Czarist secret police, he would have been anti-Semitic. He was. When initiating Stalin into the various Martinist degrees (which process, as we learned in chapter 19, took one year), Gurdjieff would have had plenty of time to indoctrinate Stalin in an anti-Zionist program, which as we saw resulted in the raising of an "iron curtain" around the borders of the Soviet Union to keep the Zionist Jews in Russia.

The rest of the players with whom Gurdjieff came into intimate contact would have had less conspicuous functions in the Hitler Project, such as finding, indoctrinating and raising the Fuehrer to power. To complete the preparation of the future Fuehrer, Gurdjieff would have sought contact with Hitler to give him his final instructions. And in fact Gurdjieff did meet with Hitler one evening until dawn during the height of Nazi power.[1618] What transpired on that all- night vigil is a matter for speculation, but certainly that meeting did not consist of nebulous conversation. That was not Gurdjieff's way. If Gurdjieff was true to form, he would have taken Hitler through several occult seances to "discover" his mission. The terrible final result was the Jewish holocaust, which was an attempt to destroy once and for all the Zionist movement.

HITLER, ECKART AND THE NAZI PARTY

On November 7, 1918, the communists took over the Bavarian government, forcing the abdication of Kaiser Wilhelm II. The monarchy was replaced by a Social Democrat government under the aegis of Grand Orient Freemasonry. At its head was the communist and Grand Orient Freemason Kurt Eisner, a Jew. The German people responded with mixed emotions. Corporal Adolf Hitler lay in a military hospital, cursing the Social Democrats as traitors to the Fatherland.[1619] On November 9, the head of the Thule Society, Baron Rudolf von Sebottendorff called a meeting of the Thule membership to discuss taking up arms against the Jews. Two days later the Armistice that ended World War I became official, and the Thule Society quietly prepared for counterrevolution. At the beginning of December, Thule members planned to capture Eisner. In January the League of Nations was founded at the Paris Peace Conference. On February 21, 1919, Eisner's hundred-day reign ended with his assassination. The Thule Society was investigated by the police. In May troops of the Thule's Free Corps ousted the remaining communists. That same month Hitler was released from the hospital and moved to Munich.

In June the defeated German generals signed the humiliating Treaty of Versailles, which placed the German people in the ranks of the unemployed and caused rampant inflation. Hitler saw his opportunity in the humiliation of Germany under the unjust treaty. The German people, hungry and threadbare, would be receptive to an Aryan messiah. He

---

[1616] Douglas Hill and Pat Williams, *The Supernatural* (New York:Signet Books, 1965) 105.
[1617] Epperson, New World Order 131.
[1618] Gilman, "Nazis" 8 and Sklar 64.
[1619] Pool and Pool 176.

would be their messiah. He would defy the victors, scrap the treaty, and promise a new life.

Hitler's Kampf (Fight) began in the beer halls around Munich. Members of the Thule Society frequenting these beer halls discovered a little, *frail*, mustachioed man who was exciting crowds with an anti-communist doctrine of white racial superiority similar to their own. The Thule Society did not create Hitler, it discovered him. Hitler had long ago developed his own hate- filled, white supremacist, anti-Semitic outlook. The Thule Society had long wished for such a man. When Hitler surfaced, they recognized him and were ready to claim him as their own.

James Pool, in Who *Financed Hitler*, describes the substance of Hitler's speeches in the beer halls of Munich:

> When Hitler denounced the Versailles Treaty in the dark, cavernous back rooms of Munich's beer halls, his speeches were based on emotional rather than logical appeal. The smoke filled air and the noisy clatter of beer mugs hardly provided the ideal atmosphere for a political meeting, but once Hitler began to speak a hushed silence settled over the room. The men and women in the audience were desperate, their clothes were threadbare, and their faces gaunt from hunger. They knew nothing about economics or industry; they only knew they couldn't face unemployment, hunger, and poverty much longer. Standing on a solid wooden table, Hitler spoke with fiery determination that gave the people faith. He said the Versailles Treaty was responsible for their misery; if they only had the will to resist, the treaty could not be forced upon them... The rise and fall in the volume of Hitler's voice and the increasing tempo of his speech held the audience spellbound. Men sat and listened with their mouths hanging open; women began to sob. The speech thundered to a climax and with a dramatic, sweeping gesture of his right arm Hitler seemed to be, as he said, "pushing the Versailles Diktat in the dustbin of history."[1620]

Dietrich Eckart met Hitler after one of his outbursts against the Versailles Treaty. Here was the one he had prophesied - the one the "Ascended Masters" had commissioned him to prepare as the vessel of the Anti-Christ! In Hitler he saw the messiah of Germany, the savior of the Aryan race for whom he had searched. With a little instruction Hitler would dance to his tune.

Eckart took Hitler to the Thule headquarters at the Four Seasons Hotel. There hung the swastika flag with which Hitler had become so familiar during his days with Liebenfels. It was no small wonder that the future Fuehrer felt at home among his new friends at Thule.[1621]

Eckart put his library at Hitler's disposal. He completely changed Hitler's public persona, molding him into a political demigod. "He made Hitler a master rhetorician, and with the aid of psychedelic drugs, initiated him into various occult mysteries."[1622] Finally, the Fuehrer was ready for his "coming out." In August 1921, Eckart published an article that first announced Hitler as the Fuehrer of the German people. Wulf Schwarzwaller writes in *The Unknown Hitler*:

> With Eckart as his mentor, the gauche and inhibited Hitler... quite suddenly developed astonishing qualities and talents. He became an outstanding organizer

---

[1620] Pool and Pool 193.
[1621] Schwarzwaller 56.
[1622] Gilman, "Nazis" 7.

and propagandist capable of leading people astray and sweeping them along with him... With the help of Eckart, he had mastered the secrets of the art of oratory to such a degree that observers credited him with the force of an "African medicine man or an Asian shaman.[1623]

In the fail of 1919, Hitler joined Drexler's Thule-backed German Workers' Party, which was still meeting in the beer halls. Hitler's charismatic speeches increased membership in the fledgling Party. Within a short time, Hitler dominated the Party, pushing Drexler to the sidelines and putting his new friends from the Thule Society in key positions. Under Hitler's direction an obscure workers' party left the clubs and beer hails to become a mass movement. Hitler's speeches mesmerized vast audiences, converting even his opponents into enthusiastic devotees.[1624]

During the summer of 1920, Hitler renamed the German Workers' Patty the National Socialist German Workers' Party (NSDAP) in an effort to attract conservative nationalists and proletarians to its ranks. In 1923 the name was changed again to the Nazi Party. Hitler began denouncing Jews and Freemasons everywhere.

THE SWASTIKA: OCCULT SYMBOL OF THE NAZI PARTY

Hitler wanted a flag of powerful symbology for his Nazi Party. His abhorrence of Bolshevism demanded a more brilliant red than that of the communist flag. From among many designs, he picked one suggested by Thule member Dr. Krohn: "A red cloth, symbolizing socialism, with a white circle in the middle standing for nationalism, with a black swastika in a white circle expressing the 'victorious struggle of the Aryan.'"[1625] Krohn's swastika was right handed, as was the herald of the Thule Society. Hitler insisted on a left-handed swastika which turned counter clockwise - a symbol of darkness, black magic and destruction.[1626]

Although Hitler himself was devoted to the occult, he had no time or sympathy for Freemasonry. For instance, in 1923 the Nazis needed larger headquarters in Munich, but had no funds. Dr. Kuhlo, the director of the Association of Bavarian Industrialists, came to Hitler's aid and offered him the Hotel Eden for a modest rent. While negotiating terms, Kuhlo casually suggested to Hitler that the Nazi Party might suppress the articles published against Freemasonry. Hitler recalled, "I got up and said good-bye to these kindly philanthropists. I'd fallen unawares into a nest of Freemasons"[1627]

Spurred to fury by this Masonic attempt to manipulate him, Hitler's Kampf began to intensify. He planned to destroy those "Judeo-Masonic" conspirators by using their own ammunition. Like the Masons and the Jesuits he had studied in Vienna, Hitler decided to employ religious techniques to advance his Kampf. After one of his characteristic attacks on Freemasonry, he said:

> *[Freemasonry's] hierarchical organisation and the initiation through symbolic rites, that is to say without bothering the brains but by working on the imagination through magic and the symbols of a cult - all this is the dangerous element and the element I have taken over. Don't you see that our part must be of this*

[1623] Schwarzwaller 58-59.
[1624] 102.Schwarzwaller.
[1625] Schwarzwaller 59.
[1626] Schwarzwaller 59-60.
[1627] Pool and Pool 70.

character? An Order, that is what it has to be - an Order, the hierarchical Order of a secular Priesthood.[1628]

The man who was Hitler's mentor in the occult and creator of his political persona died that year. Shortly before his death, Dietrich Eckart said to those gathered at his bedside: "Follow Hitler! He will dance, but it is I who have called the tune! I have initiated him into the 'Secret Doctrine,' opened his centres in vision and given him the means to communicate with the Powers."[1629]

Eckart's influence on Hitler did indeed extend beyond his death. On April 1, 1924, after their failed November coup, Hitler and his gang were placed in prison. There Hitler wrote *Mein Kampf.* The section on geopolitics was ghost written by Haushofer, the man initiated into the Tibetan mysteries by Gurdjieff and Kitchener. And although Hitler later denounced all affiliation with the Thule Society and dissolved the Society in 1934, he nonetheless dedicated his book to his deceased mentor Dietrich Eckart.[1630]

Hitler remained immersed in the occult until he took power in 1933. So much so that Winifred Wagner, daughter-in-law of the famed Richard Wagner, once warned the Fuehrer: "'Beware of black magic. White and black magic are still accessible to you. But once you have given yourself over to black magic, it will determine your destiny.'"[1631]

CHRISTIANS, NEW AGERS, AND MASONS

The ordinary German was unaware that black magic was at the heart of Haushofer's and Rosenberg's Vril Society. So effectively did the Vril Society present and promote itself as Christian, that it won many Protestants and Catholics over to Hider. For example, a conclave of deceived German Protestants declared, "Hitler's word is God's law, the decrees and laws which represent it possess divine authority." The Catholic Mayor of Hamburg is on record as saying, "We need no priest. We can communicate direct to God through Adolf Hider."[1632]

Conversely, New Agers saw beyond the Christian facade of the Vril Society and recognized Hitler as their messiah, the one who would usher in the Age of Aquarius. In 1932, Dr. Karl Strunkmann, under the pseudonym Kurt von Ensen, wrote *Ado if Hitler and the Age to Come,* in which he described the required destruction of the Christian Age (Age of Pisces) by the Third Reich:

> *Today we are living through the catastrophic transition from the Age of Pisces to the Age of Aquarius. We are at a change of aeons, as at the time of the birth of Christ, when humanity left the Age of Aries and entered the new Christian Aeon of Pisces. An old world collapsed, a new one rose up: the Christian Occident. And now, 2,000 years later, a new, powerful "die and become again" is beginning: destruction of the Occident and rise of the new Atlantic world. The Third Reich's mission is to demolish the dying Occident. The shaping of the new*

[1628] Baigent et al, *Messianic Legacy* 155.
[1629] Epperson, *New World Order* 131.
[1630] Gilman, "Nazis" 7-8.
[1631] Schwarzwaller 100.
[1632] Baigent et al, *Messianic Legacy* 153.

Atlantic cultural empire in the Aeon of Aquarius will be the task of the Fourth Reich.[1633]

The only religious order other than Judaism not finding favor with Hitler was Freemasonry. When the Fuehrer outlawed the Lodge in 1932-1933, Masons found themselves in a quandary. Seeing their religious enemy, Christianity, flourish under the Third Reich, they knew they must ape their adversary if they were to survive. Therefore, German Freemasonry decided to promote itself as Christian. Author Paul Fisher explains:

> *In 1933, various German Masonic lodges changed their names in an effort to avoid being closed down by Hitler... Commenting on the situation, The New York Times noted that German Masonic lodges were adopting Christian names. One called itself the National Christian Order of Frederick the Great.*[1634]

When this attempt at disguise failed to impress Hitler, German Freemasonry, which was Templar in origin, changed its by-laws to give itself a Rosicrucian flavor: "This order professes a German Christianity which has much in common with the primitive sun worship. The order's symbols are the sun and the cross."[1635]

Nothing the Masons invented gained the Fuehrer's approval. The "secret doctrine" that Hitler reserved for himself, even withheld from his closest collaborators, was his intent to destroy the Judeo-Masonic conspiracy throughout Europe. He would start in Germany. In 1934 Hitler demanded that all Masonic Lodges in the Third Reich be closed. As for the rest of Europe, Hitler, and Hitler alone, would announce the date of their demise.

FINANCING HITLER

Aristocrats and the Intelligentsia

Hitler's rise to power would have been impossible without the financial contributions of thousands of common folk. Yet, these givers pale in comparison to the people who filled his coffers with millions of dollars, among them artists and members of the intelligentsia. The musician Karl Klindworth, a former friend of Freemason Richard Wagner, for instance, permitted his wife to finance Hitler.[1636] The son of Richard Wagner also granted his wife Winifred permission to fund the mesmerizing, bachelor Fuehrer.

The Fuehrer received most of his money, however, from the aristocracy and royalty of Germany, Austria, Britain, Czechoslovakia, Finland, France, Italy, Holland, Hungary, Switzerland, and Sweden - many of whom had lost their titled positions during the post-World War I Grand Orient Revolutions. In exchange for their financial backing, Hitler led them to believe that he would restore their thrones. A few examples follow.

Prince August Wilhelm, Kaiser Wilhelm's son, joined the Nazi party. This was the first tentative step toward an alliance between Hitler and the Hohenzollerns. The royal family had hoped that the alliance would assure that Hitler would supply popular support

---

[1633] Zepp 71-72.
[1634] Fisher 222.
[1635] Fisher 223.
[1636] Pool and Pool 122.

for restoring the monarchy in exchange for money and contacts from the Prince and the power elite.[1637]

Prince Ratobor Corvey, one of the wealthiest nobles of Silesia, was an early supporter of Hitler, and rumored to be one of the best-paying members of the Party. Many Silesian aristocrats were pro-Nazis. Count Rex-Gieshubel, told his friends: "Times will improve for the landowners if Hitler comes to power. And besides, Hitler will restore the monarchy."[1638]

Prince Waldeck-Pyrmont, an heir to the throne of one of the small German states, had been a member of the Free Corps after World War I. In the early 1930s he became an 55 officer. The Grand Duke of Hesse was also a regular contributor to the Nazi Party. Another of Hitler's early supporters was the Duke of Coburg. The Duke was English, but gave generously to the Nazi Party, and was proud to wear his brown SA uniform in public. Another regular donor was the son-in-law of the Kaiser, the Duke of Brunswick. His son was a member of the 55.

The Hohenzollerns supported Hitler in the hope his patriotic movement would restore their throne.[1639] Indeed, Hitler was very careful not to irritate them. The Fuehrer stated in two pamphlets published in 1929 and in 1932 respectively that he intended to establish a National Socialist dictatorship for "a transitory period." Hitler claimed he wanted to take over the state with the Nazi Party "only until the German people had been freed from the threat of Marxism and could then reach a decision as to whether the final form of government would be a republic or a monarchy."[1640]

So solid was the aristocracy's support of Hitler that when the Kaiser's son, Prince August Wilhelm, joined the Nazi Party, he openly campaigned for Hitler. In 1930 the Prince was Hermann Goering's travel companion on a speaking tour in East Prussia and the Rhineland. The political marriage of these two forces in German political life occurred on July 9, 1931, when the Nazi Party united with the monarchist Nationalist Party.

Of the powerful businessmen who backed Hitler, the most famous is probably the German industrialist, Gustav Krupp. Carl Duisberg, the founder of I.G. Farben, the great chemical trust that manufactured the poisonous gas to kill the Jews, also financed Hitler. Other contributors included Fritz Thyssen, a multimillionaire industrialist, who was chairman of the board of Germany's largest firm, the United Steel Works; Ernst Tengelmann, the wealthy director of an important Ruhr coal mining company; and Dr. Hjalmar Schacht, the most prominent banker in Germany and generally regarded as the country's financial wizard.

The Versailles Treaty had given cause and hardened these business- men and bankers in their nationalist resolve. The treaty, for example, was responsible for the destruction of the property of the Krupp firm, worth over 104 million gold marks.[1641] Faced with such vicious restrictions that prevented Germany from entering and competing in world markets, it is little wonder most German business and financial leaders backed Hitler.

Standard Oil and Hitler

The Rockefeller's Standard Oil Company of New Jersey, the largest petroleum corporation in the world, invested heavily in rebuilding Germany after World War I.

[1637] Pool and Pool 270-271.
[1638] Pool and Pool 421.
[1639] Pool and Pool 421.
[1640] Pool and Pool 425.
[1641] Pool and Pool 185, 195.

The CEO of Standard Oil was Walter C. Teagle. Charles Higham in *Trading with the Enemy* informs us that "[f]rom the 1920s on Teagle showed a marked admiration for Germany's enterprise in overcoming the destructive terms of the Versailles Treaty."[1642] To assist the Germans, Teagle had imported Standard tanks and tank cars and disbursed them throughout Germany. He also established a friendship with Hermann Schmitz, the CEO of I.G. Farben, the German chemical company founded by Carl Duisberg. By the time the Nazis came to power, Teagle was director of American I.G. Chemical Corp., a subsidiary of I.G. Farben. Teagle made sure that Standard invested heavily in American I.G. and that American I.G. invested heavily in Standard.[1643]

Anxious that Standard protect its interests in Nazi Germany, Teagle made many visits during the 1 930s to Berlin and to the Standard tanks and tank cars throughout Germany. In addition, prior to World War II, Standard sold fuel to the German Air Force, then built a refinery in Hamburg that produced 15,000 tons of aviation gasoline for Goering every week.[1644] The refinery continued operation throughout the war.

Prior to the war Standard Oil tankers, staffed with Nazi crews, fueled German U-boats. From 1939 until Pearl Harbor, Standard Oil also furnished Hitler artificial rubber. Just before Hitler conquered Holland, Rockefeller's Standard Oil agreed with Standard Oil of Holland to stay in business together, even if America entered the war against Germany. Royal Dutch Shell of Holland also cooperated with Standard Oil. After the Nazis invaded Holland, cooperation continued as agreed. The CEOs of these companies felt their motives were "patriotic." Each agreed that Hitler should destroy the Soviet Union and hoped that he would.[1645]

In 1943, the American trade journal for the petroleum industry, *The Petroleum Times*, confirmed that the relationship between Rockefeller's Standard Oil and I.G. Farben was still in force as of that date.[1646] I.G. Farben confirmed the accusation with a report that in part stated: "[T]he innumerable benefits that Germany had obtained from her American friends, including the use of tetraethyl, without which the war effort would have been impossible...had been approved by the U.S. War Department."[1647] As we know, the U.S. War Department was then dominated by the Council on Foreign Relations (CFR). At the head of the CFR was David Rockefeller. The I.G. report also revealed that during the war Rockefeller's Standard Oil Company sold $20 million worth of petroleum products, including airplane benzene, to I.G. Farben.

Prince Bernhardt, Founder of the Bilderbergers

Grand Lodge Freemason Prince Bernhardt of the Netherlands, a major stockholder in Royal Dutch Shell, also backed Hitler. Bernhardt was a German-born Prince. After Hitler conquered Holland, Bernhardt renounced Freemasonry and became an 55 officer. After the war he returned to the Brotherhood, and is today a 33rd degree Mason in The Hague Grand Lodge. In 1954 Prince Bernhardt hosted for the members of the British Round Table a super-secret meeting at the Bilderberg Hotel in Oosterbeek, Holland. When Journalists heard of the gathering, but could not discover the name of the hush-hush group, they labeled the attendees the Bilderbergers.[1648] The Bilderbergers have since met

---

[1642] Charles Higham, *Trading With The Enemy* (New York: Dell Books, 1983) 53.
[1643] Higham 54.
[1644] Higham 57.
[1645] Higham 54.
[1646] Higham 239.
[1647] Higham.
[1648] Wilgus 126.

at least once a year. As we have learned in chapter 16, Bernhardt is today one of the Masonic Supreme Council Inspector Generals who frequents many neo-Nazi New Age Movement gatherings.

The Masonic King of England

Edward VIII was crowned both king and Grand Master of English Freemasonry on January 20, 1936. Edward, however, married a divorced commoner from the United States and was forced to abdicate eleven months later on December 10th. His younger brother ascended the throne the next day and downgraded Edward's title to the Duke of Windsor. In July 1940 the Duke assumed the governorship of the Bahamas.[1649]

Edward VIII not only supported Hitler, he did so loudly. From the time of Hitler's rise to power, the Windsors were fascinated by the Fuehrer and his New Order in Europe. Speaking in Masonic terms, the King expressed the views of the Brotherhood concerning Hitler: "What-ever happens, he said, "whatever the outcome, a New Order is going to come into the world... It will be buttressed with police power... .When peace comes this time, there is going to be a New Order of Social Justice. It cannot be another Versailles."[1650]

During his short reign, King Edward VIII made every effort to promote Nazism. As a result some of the most prominent aristocrats in England joined the Nazi Party.[1651]

Henry Ford

Henry Ford became a Master Mason in Palestine Lodge No.357, Detroit, Michigan on November 28, 1894. He continued a staunch member of this lodge for almost 53 years.[1652]

Everything Ford did for the Nazi movement appears to have furthered the goals of English Freemasonry. For example, in 1920, when the Protocols of *Sion* were being published everywhere, it is said that Ford became frightened by the Russian Revolution and the rapid spread of communism throughout the world. He believed the anti-Semitic claims that Jewish capitalists and Jewish communists were partners conspiring to gain control over the nations of the world through communism. To expose the so-called conspiracy of the Jews, Ford bought a country newspaper in Michigan called the *Dearborn Independent* and turned it into a conspiracy digest against the Jews.

The *Dearborn Independent* seriously charged that several well known Jews in America were the instigators of World War I. One of them was Bernard M. Baruch, a 33rd degree Freemason, known as the "pro-consul of Judah in America," a "Jew of Super-Power." When requested by news reporters to comment on Ford's charges, Baruch replied, tongue-in-cheek, "Now boys, you wouldn't expect me to deny them would you"[1653]

[1649] ."Windsor, Prince Edward, duke of," *Encyclopaedia Britannica:Micropaedia.*

[1650] Higham 201.

[1651] Higham 202.

[1652] William R. Denslow, *10,000 Famous Freemasons*, vol. II, (Trenton, MO: Missouri Lodge of Research, 1958) 62.

[1653] Pool and Pool 87.

Entering the fray was 33rd degree Jewish Mason "Colonel" Edward House, who urged President Woodrow Wilson to act against Ford. When Wilson called upon Ford to stop his "vicious propaganda," Ford refused.[1654]

In 1922 Ford's articles were compiled in a book entitled, *The International Jew.* Translated into German, the book was renamed *The Eternal Jew.* This book led many Germans to become Nazis.[1655]

Finally, Ford struck at the Jews where they would later prove to be most vulnerable. He financed Hitler. His first contribution was $40,000, then $300,000. Ford's funds continued to flow to Hitler until World War II broke out in 1939.[1656] One year later, in September 1940, Ford received the 33rd degree in a New Jersey lodge in the Northern Jurisdiction of Scottish Rite Freemasonry[1657], which is under the English Masonic obedience.

Why should the British-controlled Northern Jurisdiction of Freemasonry honor Ford with the 33rd degree after he financed the Nazis, unless it was to reward him for furthering the Masonic conspiracy against the Jews?

The Bank for International Settlements

A prominent, international bank - the Bank for International Settlements (BIS) also played a murky but definite role in financing Adolf Hitler. Dr. Quigley informs us that the BIS, founded in 1930 in Basel, Switzerland, was "a private bank owned and controlled by the world's central banks which were themselves private corporations. This system was to be controlled in a feudalistic fashion by the central banks of the world acting in concert, by secret agreements arrived at in frequent private meetings and conferences."[1658]

The *Encyclopaedia Britannica* agrees with Quigley, but adds that the BIS was an "international bank established at Basel, Switzerland in 1930 as the agency to handle the payment of reparations by Germany after World War I..."[1659]

As we know, war reparations were demanded from Germany in June 1919 by the Versailles Treaty. We should note the gap of years between the treaty and the founding of BIS. Would it not be ludicrous to establish a collection agency for war reparations ten years after the agreement which set terms, and one year following the world's worse financial crash? In 1929, Germany had no funds with which to pay reparations! Furthermore, in 1931, one year after the BIS was founded, all the European powers, except France, had ended reparations demands. Two years later, Hitler repudiated all reparations.

If not to collect reparations, what actually was the function of the BIS? Recent information uncovered by British historian Charles Higham and published in his book *Trading with the Enemy* (1983), states that the BIS "was to be a money funnel for American and British funds to flow into Hitler's coffers and to help Hitler build up his war machine."[1660]

The BIS was completely under Hitler's control by the outbreak of World War U. Higham says, "Its continuing existence was approved by Great Britain even after that country went to war with Germany..."[1661]

[1654] Pool and Pool 88.
[1655] Pool and Pool 90.
[1656] Pool and Pool 111.
[1657] Denslow 62.
[1658] Quigley 324.
[1659] ."Bank for International Settlements," *Encyclopaedia Britannica: Micropaedia.*
[1660] Higham 24.
[1661] Higham 29.

For example, on the BIS board was the eccentric Montagu Norman, CEO of the Bank of England and "a rabid supporter of Hitler."[1662] The major stockholder in the Bank of England was the House of Rothschild, which controlled finances for the Round Table Groups, such as the Council on Foreign Relations, the Royal Institute of International Affairs and the Institute of Pacific Relations.

Many individuals who were associated with the BIS and named by Higham in his book are known Masons and/or members of the Round Table Groups (although he does not mention that fact). According to Higham, Hjalmar Schacht, Hitler's Minister of Economics and president of the Reichsbank, was a closet English Freemason[1663] who urged English bankers to establish the BIS to fund Hitler's war: "It was written into the Bank's charter, concurred in by the respective governments, that the BIS should be immune from seizure, closure, or censure, whether or not its owners were at war. These owners included the Morgan-affiliated First National Bank of New York...the Bank of England, the Reichsbank, the Bank of Italy, the Bank of France, and other central banks.[1664]

To take the heat off London, it was rumored that the idea for establishing an international bank was the brainchild of an American in America. It was called the *Young Plan*, after the American lawyer Owen D. Young. Young, in reality, was the "front" agent for J.P. Morgan of the CFR.[1665] Moreover, the president of the BIS was Thomas H. McKittrick, also an associate of the Morgans.[1666]

What motivated English Masonic bankers to build up Hitler's military and armaments? Such a project could only endanger the world, for English Freemasonry was well aware of Hitler's hatred of communism. Support of Nazi Germany's war machine would mean war between Germany and Russia. Such a conflict could trigger another world war. Why did these British bankers take such suicidal action?

According to Higham, the BIS financed Hitler as a means to another end: to sweep and garner the gold of Europe for the benefit of what Higham calls "The Fraternity." (The Fraternity, as we have seen, is just another name for Freemasonry.) In the next chapter, we will document the greatest gold heist in history as Hitler conquered nation after nation, shipping their gold reserves to the Bank for International Settlements.

Hitler Becomes Dictator of Germany

In 1932 Germany was paralyzed by political stalemate. The monarchists, although long relegated to political insignificance, saw in the crisis a chance to gain power. The monarchists' newspaper *Sueddeutsche Monatshefte* stated their view that only monarchism could solve the existing political crisis.[1667]

The ex-Kaiser also saw opportunity in the crisis, understanding it as his chance to return. Rear Admiral von Eschenburg promised the Kaiser the cooperation of the Navy. But to avoid civil war, the army would also have to cooperate. It was loyal to Hitler, and Hitler demanded an important concession from the Kaiser. He wanted to be Chancellor.[1668]

[1662] Higham 27.
[1663] Denslow, vol. IV, 105. Hjalmar Shacht belonged to the Lodge Zur Freundschaft under the Grand Lodge of Prussia.
[1664] Higham 23.
[1665] Quigley 310.
[1666] Higham 29.
[1667] Pool and Pool 424.
[1668] Pool and Pool 424-425.

Fritz Thyssen, a loyal monarchist, was convinced that Hitler would take the office as Chancellor merely as "a transitional stage leading to the reintroduction of the German monarchy."[1669] Thyssen invited a number of the aristocracy to his house to put the question to Hitler. Rider answered in distinct and unambiguous tones that he "was merely the pacemaker of the monarchy."[1670] Hitler was finally given the Chancellery in January, 1933, but not without many bribes and blackmail from both sides.

Hitler of course never intended to return the government to the monarchy. He would not abandon his pact with Satan, which he made in 1909 in the Habsburg Museum to possess the Spear of Longinus (Spear of Destiny). Possession of the Spear, he believed, would enable him to crush the Judeo-Masonic conspiracy and to rule the world himself.

In 1934 Hitler merged the offices of Chancellor and President, becoming the Fuehrer and a virtual dictator. He then moved against the "Judeo-Masonic" conspiracy. Hermann Goering, acting on Hitler's orders, dissolved all lodges, including those which purported to be Christian. Goering also dissolved the Thule Society. The Nazi newspaper, *Voelkischer Beobachter* announced on August 8, 1935 the final dissolution of all Masonic lodges in Germany. The paper blamed the Order for the assassination at Sarajevo, which precipitated WWI, saying that Freemasonry believed the time had come for a "bloody war between nations and the erection of a world republic."[1671] Also in 1935, Hitler struck his first blow at the Jewish people with his infamous racial laws, called the Nuremberg Laws.

Hitler and the Cliveden Set

After the Bolshevik Revolution and the rise of Stalin in the Kremlin, English Freemasonry's Round Table Groups had calculated that an eventual war with Russia was inevitable. When Hitler came to power he demanded that England return the colonies taken from Germany after World War I. The "think tanks" of English Freemasonry were convinced that unless Hitler were appeased, he would declare war against Great Britain. London preferred that Hitler turn his eyes to the fertile Ukrainian wheat fields of the Soviet Union and attack Russia. If the U.S.S.R. won, England and her economic royalists would face only communism. If Germany won, the Nazis, having expanded their territories eastward, would be exhausted by war and could make no demands on England. London's role was to strengthen Germany in her preparations for the coming war with Russia (to be funded through the BIS) and at the same time prepare the British psychologically to fight if these geopolitical calculations were askew.[1672] How all this was to be accomplished was left up to the Round Table "think tanks," specifically, the Royal Institute of International Affairs (RIIA).[1673]

The RIIA went into session for nine months, beginning in the fall of 1937. Dr. Quigley says that the RIIA "was sometimes spoken of as the 'Cliveden Set,' named after the Astor country house [in England] where they sometimes assembled."[1674] The Astors were the financial backers of the RIIA and their son, William Astor, its chairman.

The American and British Astors are related, their lineage dating back to our Revolutionary War. John Jacob Astor (1763-1848), a German-born American, was a wealthy fur trader, capitalist and Grand Master of the New York Masonic Lodges. The

---

[1669] Pool and Pool 425.
[1670] Pool and Pool 426.
[1671] Fisher 223 and Denslow, vol.11, 83.
[1672] John L. Spivak, "England's Cliveden Set," *Conspiracy Digest* 5.4 (Fall 1980): 1-3.
[1673] Spivak 1-3.
[1674] Quigley 133.

British clan, also Masons, bought their way into the British aristocracy. During the 1930s they owned five seats in Parliament and controlled two of the most powerful and influential newspapers in the world, the *London Times* and the *London Observer*. In addition, their financial interests stretched into banking, railroads and life insurance.[1675]

The Lady of the Cliveden estate was Nancy Witcher Astor (1879-1964), an American from Virginia. At the turn of the 20th century, she married into the British clan. Viscountess Astor, or Lady Astor, as she was affectionately called, was the first woman member of the British Parliament (1919-1945). Other family members in Parliament included her husband and two relatives in the House of Lords, and her son (chairman of RIIA) in the House of Commons.

In the late spring of 1937, Joachim von Ribbentrop, Nazi Ambassador to Great Britain (later the Nazi Foreign Minister), informed Neville Chamberlain, Prime Minister of England, "Der Fuehrer is displeased with English press attacks upon him, [his] Nazis and [his] Nazi aggressions. Der Fuehrer wants it stopped."[1676]

By early summer 1937, Lady Astor had entertained von Ribbentrop at her town house in London.[1677] Ribbontrop asked Lady Astor to reverse her paper's anti-Nazi bias, encouraging her to join the Fuehrer's anti-Communist crusade. Lady Astor agreed in return for assurances that the Fuehrer would set his sights on conquering Russia. Ribbontrop and Lady Astor made a secret alliance to cooperate toward their mutual goals.[1678] Gradually the Astor-controlled *London Times* assumed a pro-Nazi bias on its very influential editorial page. During October 1937, for example, The *Times* printed letters supporting Hitler's demands for the return of the colonies taken from Germany under the terms of the Versailles Treaty.[1679]

In the fall of 1937, the Astors began inviting "friends" to their country estate on weekends to "play charades." Each friend held a strategic position in the British government. This cadre of aristocrats and intellectuals, all of whom were interchangeable with the Round Table, Freemasonry, the RUA and Parliament, became known as the "Cliveden Set" Their weekend retreats, which, in reality were Round Table discussions, charted a course that the Cliveden Set hoped Hitler would take. *That* course was war with Russia.

The Cliveden Set was known and reported around the world as being the real center of British policy-making during the Chamberlain appeasement period (1937-1939).[1680] Carol White in *The New Dark Ages Conspiracy* quotes the *New York Times* as saying: "The so-called Cliveden Set are widely regarded as the most influential of Germany's sympathizers in England... The apparent strength of Germany's case in this country [England] comes from the fact that Germany's best friends are to be found in the wealthiest 'upper crust' of British life... Joachim von Ribbentrop... knew his England better than some of his critics when he urged Britain to join his anti-Communist crusade."[1681]

Freemason H.G. Wells would attend most of the weekend "charades." A remark in his *Autobiography* (1934) reveals much about the preceding and prevailing climate of pro-Aryan ideas in England and the Continent: "In those days I had ideas about Aryans extraordinarily like Mr. Hitler's. The more I hear of him the more I am convinced that his

---

[1675] Spivak 1.
[1676] Spivak 2.
[1677] Spivak 1.
[1678] White 139.
[1679] Spivak 1.
[1680] White 139.
[1681] White.

mind is almost the twin of my thirteen-year-old mind in 1879; but heard through a megaphone [and] implemented."[1682]

At the first weekend "charades party," the Cliveden Set sought an alliance with Hitler and Mussolini against the Soviet Union. Wells, Bertrand Russell, and the other utopians hoped that Britain would be able to stay neutral. Churchill and Mountbatten correctly predicted that Britain would have to come into the war to make sure that Hitler was contained.[1683] At any rate, the consensus was to send Lord Halifax to visit Germany. Meetings were set for mid-November 1937 at Berlin and Berchtesgaden. The final outcome, according to French intelligence, was that Halifax "pledged England to a hands-off policy on Hitler's ambitions in Central Europe if Germany would not raise the question of the return of the colonies for six years."[1684]

The real reason for delaying discussion for the colonies for six years was to give Hitler time to expand his territory and arm his military for a successful war against the Soviet Union. If the calculations of the Cliveden Set were correct, at the end of six years, Hitler would cease demands for the return of Germany's colonies.[1685]

Late in January 1938, Lord and Lady Astor invited to Cliveden (along with the RIIA usuals) Neville Chamberlain, Lord Halifax, Lord Lothian, and their *London Observer* editor, J.L. Garvin. This meeting initiated the appeasement policy of Chamberlain. On March 11, Hitler invaded Austria unopposed. From Austria, Hitler gained more men for his army, large deposits of magnesite, timber forests and enormous water-power resources for electricity.[1686]

The Cliveden Set went into their final and historic weekend charades party on March 26-27, 1938.[1687] Present were Neville Chamberlain and a cadre of Round Tablers, including H.G. Wells and an associate of Lord Rothschild, Sir Ernest Cassell.[1688] They were already aware that Hitler's eyes were set on Czechoslovakia. With it, the Fuehrer would get the Skoda armament works, one of the largest in the world, and the factories in the Sudeten. Next door were Hungarian wheat and Rumanian oil. He could dominate the Balkans, destroy potential Soviet air and troop bases in Central Europe, and poise Nazi troops within a few miles of the Soviet border. The Cliveden Set decided to continue Chamberlain's Appeasement Policy[1689]: "to turn Germany east rather than west."[1690]

While Chamberlain negotiated with Hitler over the fate of Czechoslovakia, the Astor newspapers published a vicious attack against the country, warning the Czechs that they were failing to make the Germans comfortable. Said the *London Times* editorial of September 8, 1938: "The stinking Czech sausage should be crushed."[1691]

The Cliveden Set easily introduced its plan to the British government since five of the Astors were in Parliament, including William Astor, chairman of the RIIA. William Astor was also parliamentary private secretary to the Home Office.

In sum, it is clear to see that the Round Table, as the policy-forming body of English Freemasonry, supported Hitler in an effort to achieve its own end - the destruction of the Soviet Union. Manipulating Hitler, they thought, was a simple matter.

"The Hitler project," writes Carol White in *The New Dark Ages* Conspiracy, "was a collaboration effort that involved the entire spectrum of the oligarchy and its agents...

[1682] H.G. Wells, *Experiments in Autobiography* (New York:Macmillan Co., 1934) 73-76.
[1683] White 138.
[1684] Spivak 2.
[1685] Spivak 2.
[1686] Spivak 3.
[1687] Spivak 1.
[1688] White 139.
[1689] Spivak 3.
[1690] White 25.
[1691] White 140.

How he [Hitler] was to be contained and directed against the Soviet Union was another matter."[1692]

In Conclusion

Hitler was created by a number of forces. First of these were occult forces, then banking forces, and finally, political forces.

We have learned that the occult influences upon Hitler were manipulated by the sub-Masonic societies of Sionist English Freemasonry. These groups included the Order of the Golden Dawn, the Ordo Templi Orientis (O.T.O.), and the Thule Society. These Rosicrucian, white-supremacist secret societies urged the destruction of the Jewish race, not because they were necessarily anti- Semitic, but because they were anti-Zionist.

Sionist English Freemasonry also funneled money to Hitler through the Masonic banks controlled by members of the Royal Institute of International Affairs (RIIE) and the Council on Foreign Relations (CFR), using the services of the Bank for International Settlements (BIS). The BIS not only funded Hitler's war against Russia, but its officers directed him to loot the gold reserves in every nation he conquered.

Finally, Sionist Freemasonry in England influenced and manipulated British foreign policy toward Hitler through her Round Table Groups, which met over the course of nine months to devise a plan directing Hitler toward Russia.

The Fuehrer, however, had plans of his own. In 1939, he double-crossed the British with the Hitler-Stalin Pact and the world was plunged into its second global conflict. In *The Hitler Book*, author Helga Zepp summarizes the ultimate naiveté' of the machinations of the Cliveden Set: "If we consider that Neville Chamberlain" and others were "supporting Hitler in hopes that Hitler would go to war against the Soviet Union, then the Second World War begins to look like a classic case of miscalculations on the part of all involved."[1693]

[1692] White 18.
[1693] Zepp 75.

23. HITLER'S DESTRUCTION OF FRENCH FREEMASONRY

> *When World War II came, [the Axis Powers] attacked not Judaism nor Freemasonry but a hyphenated monstrosity which they called Judeo-Masonry; so that in spite of itself... English Freemasonry was dragged into the very focus of world-affairs; and European Masonry, which was not clear of political involvement, was obliterated.*[1694]

MACKEY'S ENCYCLOPEDIA OF FREEMASONRY THE AXIS POWERS AND FREEMASONRY

World War II was a Fascist war funded by English Masonic interests against French Freemasonry. In every nation the Nazis conquered, the continental Brotherhood was obliterated. The Axis powers - Germany, Italy and Japan - nearly destroyed the Templar Masonic conspiracy.

Mussolini was the first to rise to power and the first to outlaw Freemasonry. On February 13, 1923 the Grand Fascist Council resolved that since "Freemasons pursue a programme and employ methods contrary to those which inspire the whole activity of Fascism, the Council calls upon those Fascists who are Freemasons to choose between membership of the National Fascist Party and Freemasonry."[1695] *Mackey's Encyclopedia of Freemasonry* records the hostility of Italian Fascism toward Masonry:

> *Late in 1923 young Fascist toughs began to burn, loot, and destroy lodge rooms and their furniture - even in Milan. On January 10, 1925, the Parliament outlawed the Fraternity. In a debate on the Bill, Mussolini thundered: "The Bill will demonstrate that Freemasonry is out of date and no longer has the right to exist in the present century.*[1696]

On January 10, 1925, Masonic activity presumably ceased in Italy. The lodge, however, secretly plotted the assassination of Mussolini.

On November 5, 1926, General Luigi Capello, who refused to renounce Freemasonry, was arrested and accused of being the mastermind behind the plot. *Mackey's Encyclopedia* reports that Capello was brought to trial in the Spring of 1927, and sentenced to an imprisonment of thirty years, the first six to be in solitary confinement. Almost immediately secret police arrested [Grand Orient] Grand Master Torrigiani, tried him in secret court, and banished him to starve to death on one of the Lipari islands, to be followed later by some hundreds of other Masons... By the time Mussolini opened World War II with the rape of Abyssinia, Italian Freemasonry had become completely obliterated - for the time being.[1697]

[1694] "Anti-Semitism and Masonry," *Mackey's Encyclopedia of Freemasonry*, vol. III.
[1695] "War II, World, and Freemasonry in Europe," *Mackey's Encyclopedia*, vol.111.
[1696] "War II."
[1697] "War II."

Hitler's war against the Lodge began four years after Mussolini's. *Mackey's Encyclopedia* reports that "[I]n 1927 Joseph Goebbels set up an exposition in Berlin to display regalia, furniture, books, etc., taken from Masonic Lodge rooms... In 1933, and in almost one of his first utterances as Prime Minister of Prussia, Hermann Goering declared that 'in National Socialist Germany there is no place for Freemasonry."[1698] In the fall of 1935, Wilhelm Frick (1877-1946), Minister of Interior under Hitler from 1933-1943, acting on the decree issued by President von Hindenburg in August, which charged that the Masonic lodges had engaged in "subversive activities," called for the immediate disbandment of all lodges throughout Germany and ordered a confiscation of their property.[1699]

During a Brown Shirt street parade in Berlin, Masons were hauled through the streets in a cage like animals. How many were mobbed, beaten to death, murdered, executed, or sent to concentration camps in Germany may never be known. On August 28, 1939, the Nazi news- paper, *Voelkischer Beobachter,* reported a speech by Rudolph Hess made two days earlier at Graz, which included the statement "Jews and Freemasons want a war against this hated Germany, against the Germany in which they have lost their power." At the outbreak of World War II in 1939 about 700 lodges in Germany had been destroyed and 100,000 German Masons had disappeared.[1700]

In March 1938, a year before World War II began, the storm troops marched into Austria. Upon entering Vienna, Hitler abolished Freemasonry and sent 90 percent of the Masons to the concentration camp at Dachau, or had them shot.[1701] Many were Jews. The troops then looted the gold from Austrian banks and packed it into vaults controlled by the Bank for International Settlements (BIS). From Vienna the gold was shipped to Switzerland.[1702]

After the German occupation of Austria, Hitler made Artur von Seyss-Inquart the Minister of Defense, and later that year Governor of Austrian territory. (In 1918 Seyss-Inquart had formed an anti-Jewish and anti-Masonic secret society which resembled Freemasonry, having several degrees with secret vows.)[1703]

Hitler chose Austria as his first conquest so that he could take possession of the legendary Spear of Destiny. Rev. Church says that with it Hitler believed "he could rule the world. On October 13, the Spear, along with the crown of the Holy Roman Empire, was taken to Nuremberg, the center for the Nazi movement, and placed in the Hall of St Katherine's Church."[1704]

The Nazis then marched on Czechoslovakia. Grand Orient Mason Dr. Edvard Benes, president of that new republic from 1935 to 1938, naively welcomed Hitler as preferable to the Merovingian Habsburgs, the former rulers. On March 15, 1939, Hitler followed his storm troops into Prague, arrested the directors of the Czech National Bank and held them at gunpoint, demanding their $48 million in gold reserves - gold that could not be found in the bank's vaults. Nervous bankers told Hitler that days earlier the BIS had instructed the Czech bank to forward the gold to the Bank of England. Montague Norman, governor of the Bank of England and a rabid supporter of Hitler, had already made a paper transfer of the gold to Berlin "for use in buying essential strategic materials toward a future war," reports Higham.[1705]

[1698] "War II."
[1699] Denslow, vol. II, 83.
[1700] "War II" and Denslow, vol. IV, 398.
[1701] "War II."
[1702] Higham 26.
[1703] Denslow, vol. IV, 123.
[1704] Church 63.
[1705] Higham 26-27.

After learning the Czech gold was secure, Hitler closed all Masonic lodges, confiscated their property, imprisoned their members, and shot their leaders, many of whom were Jews. Benes escaped to France, then to England.

The Fraternity was likewise obliterated in Greece. In April 1940 the Nazis closed the lodges in Holland and confiscated their real estate. The Masonic jewels and leather aprons gathered from the lodges were sent to Berlin and used for making military goods. The Nazis then "arrested hundreds of Masons, among whom a number of Grand [Lodge] Officers committed suicide under torture."[1706]

That same month Freemasons suffered equal punishment in Belgium. Raoul Engel, Past Grand Master of the Belgium Grand Lodge, and Georges Petre, Grand Master of the Belgium Scottish Rite, were among eleven of twelve 33rd degree Masons murdered. A total of 112 Masons were shot during the Nazi occupation. Their properties were confiscated and the rest of their members imprisoned.[1707] The Belgian gold reserve was shipped to the central bank in France, then transferred to the Reichsbank. From the Reichsbank it was shipped to the BIS at Basel.[1708]

Norwegian Vidkun Quisling (1887-1945), who had founded his own political party, the National Union, with a platform calling for the suppression of communism and the freeing of Norwegian labor from unionism, was the chief collaborator in the Nazi conquest of Norway in 1940. The Nazis proclaimed him sole political head of Norway and head of the state council of 13 Nazi-dominated commissioners. In this capacity he took over the beautiful Masonic Temple in Oslo and converted it into an officers quarters, ruining it for Masonic use. He ordered all the library and belongings shipped to Germany. After the war he was tried by the Norwegian courts. Ironically, the trial, in order to seat more spectators, was held in a former Masonic lodge room. He was convicted and shot in 1945.[1709]

In Poland, Romania, Yugoslavia, and Denmark, the Germans carried out the same program of suppression, confiscation, imprisonment, torture, and execution of Masons. And the terrorism often was extended to the families of Masons as well.[1710] Since many Masons were Jews, the world press began accusing Hitler of persecuting Jews alone. The press failed to distinguish them as Masons, and of course, failed to mention the fact that Gentile Masons suffered the same fate. All told, the Nazis deliberately murdered eleven million persons, of whom six million were Jews.[1711]

When the Germans entered France in 1940, they confiscated Masonic property, looted lodge funds, burned Masonic buildings, killed hundreds of Masons, imprisoned thousands more, and sent tens of thousands to labor camps in the Reich. Before the troops left Paris, they confiscated the city's great Masonic library which they carried to Berlin where it was burned.[1712] As for the gold reserve of France, it went untouched, since her central bank was a member of the BIS.

Hitler established a puppet government in occupied France at Vichy. General Philippe Petain, Premier of Vichy France, announced that "no Masonic dignitary could hold office or retain army commissions."[1713] Bernard Fay, French author in 1935 of *Revolution and Freemasonry, 1680-1800* and professor of American civilization at the College de France, published documents and lists of French Freemasons, which resulted in deportation, or

---

[1706] "War II."
[1707] "War II" and Denslow, vol.11, 22.
[1708] Higham 38.
[1709] Denslow, vol. IV, 3.
[1710] "War II."
[1711] Infield 16.
[1712] "War II."
[1713] "War II."

death for thousands of them.[1714] When the Ambassador to England, Joseph P. Kennedy, heard of the activity in Vichy, he asked for a meeting with Goering in that city. Kennedy, a Catholic, was anti-Masonic. After the meeting, the father of the 35th president of the United States donated a considerable amount of money to the German cause.[1715]

In February 1942 Hitler published his official decree against Freemasonry:

> *Freemasons, and the ideological enemies of National Socialism who are allied with them, are the originators of the present war against the Reich. Spiritual struggle according to the plan against these powers is a measure necessitated by war. I have, therefore, ordered Reichsleiter Alfred Rosenberg to accomplish this task in cooperation with the Chief of the High Command of the armed forces. He has the right to explore libraries, archives, lodges, and other ideological and cultural establishments of all kinds for suitable material and to confiscate such material for the ideological tasks of N.S.D.A.P. for scientific research work. The regulations for the execution of this task will be issued by the Chief of the High Command of the armed forces in agreement with Reichsleiter Rosenberg.[1716]*

On March 1, 1942, Hitler ordered Rosenberg to seize all libraries and materials found in Masonic lodges in occupied countries.[1717] Years later the Nazis were accused of burning history and literature books in great bonfires in the streets of Berlin, when in reality they were burning the Masonic libraries and materials confiscated from occupied countries.

As in Italy and Germany, so in Japan. *Mackey's Encyclopedia of Freemasonry* confirms that "in Japan, China, Philippine Islands, Singapore, Malaya, Burma, Thailand, and Indo-China they [the Japanese] destroyed Masons and Masonic buildings with the same ferocity as their Teutonic allies."[1718]

The Japanese government first became alarmed with Freemasonry after an Imperial investigation in 1936. It called Freemasonry a "mysterious world organization." The 65-year-old Kobe Masonic Club was viewed as "a secret society of Judea which has been picturing a phantasm of a mysterious world."[1719] Investigative journalist Paul Fisher describes the organization of the Japanese Masonic lodges:

> *The Kobe Masonic Club came into existence in strict privacy. The Club was made up of several lodges, such as the Rising Sun Lodge, and the Lodge Hyogo and Osake (Scottish). Most of the leading foreign residents from England, America, France, Switzerland, Sweden and Denmark "secretly affiliated themselves with the club,"which had as a principal object, to "bring about a world revolution."[1720]*

Before the United States Congress declared war on Japan on December 7, 1941, ten American Masons were forced to leave Japan.

In October 1942 the Scottish Rite *New Age* magazine ran an article by one of the ten. Fisher says, "The anonymous author of the article told of the thoroughness with which

---

[1714] Denslow, vol. II, 39
[1715] Higham 204.
[1716] Denslow, vol. II, 236.
[1717] Denslow, vol. IV, 70.
[1718] "War II."
[1719] Fisher 228.
[1720] Fisher.

the Japanese Government investigated Freemasonry. 'Nothing has been left undone or unseen by them within the capabilities of those in charge."[1721]

As in Italy, Germany and Japan, so in Spain. The Spanish Civil War of 1937 to 1939 was in retaliation for the bloody Masonic Spanish Revolution of 1930. In 1930 Stalin sent communists to Spain as technicians to assist the faltering revolution. All were Grand Orient Freemasons. Among them was Bela Kun, the bloodthirsty leader of the Hungarian Grand Orient Revolution. These Bolsheviks planned their strategy within the protected walls of the Spanish lodges.[1722] The method used by these communist revolutionists to strengthen the Spanish Revolution was identical to that of the Bolshevik Revolution - the mass slaughter of Spaniards. In addition, they destroyed masterpiece works of art and architecture, which all the gold in the world could not reconstruct, while large numbers of intellectual achievements were also destroyed.[1723] Through these brutal means, the beleaguered Grand Orient Spanish Masons were strengthened.

On December 10, 1931, the *Official Bulletin of the Spanish Grand Orient* announced that, "After a Jesuit Monarchy it is only natural that a Masonic Republic should act as a liberator... Today the Masons are in power, and it was high time that they should be."[1724] By 1932, however, the new Masonic politicians began to splinter into various political factions. The September *Grand Orient Bulletin* attempted to unite them by explaining that political debates "should be carried out in a spirit of absolute respect for the political views of Masonic brothers, without the slightest trace of partisan spirit but solely for the defense of the great principles of our August Order."[1725] Count de Poncins tells why the Grand Orient Spanish Revolution turned into a civil war:

> *Like most of the European revolutions since 1917, this one began under the slogan of liberalism and democracy. It soon brought about disorder, social conflicts, chaos, and finally left all the other left-wing parties in the grip of Communism. Yet under the Popular Front, the alliance of the Freemasons and the left-wing parties, including Communism, held fast throughout the revolution until it was finally obliterated by the Spanish Nationalist uprising.[1726]*

The Spanish Nationalist Front, which broke the back of the revolution, was led by General Francisco Franco. When Franco took power away from the Grand Orient Communists, anti-Masonic laws were passed and "membership in a lodge automatically called for imprisonment for ten years, later changed to twelve years. In one town... 80 men were garroted on six scaffolds for being Masons; in another 50 were made to dig a trench and then were shot and buried in it."[1727]

Franco was a staunch monarchist, planning to return King Alfonso XIII to the throne. But the king died in 1941, just after abdicating his rights to his third son, Don Juan.[1728] As for Franco's participation in the Second World War, he remained neutral after he gained control of Spain, but showed sympathy toward the Nazi cause by opening his borders to Hitler's troops for rest and relaxation.

Franco appeared to be an agent of the Priory of Sion. In 1954, Don Juan and Franco came to an agreement that Don Juan would relinquish to Juan Carlos, his eldest son, the

---

[1721] Fisher 228.

[1722] de Poncins, *Judaism and the Vatican* 107.

[1723] de Poncins.

[1724] de Poncins, *Freemasonry and the Vatican* 164.

[1725] de Poncins 167.

[1726] de Poncins 158-159.

[1727] "War II."

[1728] "Alfonso XIII," *Encyclopaedia Britannica: Micropaedia.*

position of pretender to the Spanish throne. In July 1969 Franco designated Juan Carlos as his legal heir and Spain's future king.[1729] When Franco died in 1975, King Juan Carlos I ascended the throne and on November 22, 1975 founded a constitutional monarchy. Carlos, a Merovingian, claims title to "King of Jerusalem!"

Franco, Hitler and Mussolini took the reigns of government away from Templar Grand Orient Freemasonry in their respective countries and then obliterated the Brotherhood throughout Europe. Only Franco and Mussolini planned to return rule to their Merovingian sovereigns. Franco was successful in his goal of protecting the Grail bloodline of Spain, mainly because he avoided war with Great Britain's Masonic oligarchy.

Mackey's Encyclopedia of Freemasonry concludes: "The Masonic Fraternity has a long memory... but it has nowhere in its memory any martyrdom such as that of those years; and it is hoped it never will have again: but it will carry a long memory into the future also, and a thousand years from now it will not have forgotten Spain, and Greece, and Holland, and France, and Italy of 1940 A.D."[1730]

THE "HITLER PROJECT" FAILED

We can determine how the "Hitler Project" failed by examining certain evidence from the Nuremberg Trials following World War II. The Nazi banker and closet Grand Lodge Freemason Hjalmar Schacht testified that he had attempted to unite the oligarchy bankers "to join with the Greater German Reich in a war against the Soviet Union."[1731] The plan involved a continental anti- Bolshevik crusade, but Hitler would have no part in this conspiracy. He saw it as directed against German supremacy and raged against those who dared to describe his war against the Soviet Union as Europe's war. In an effort to make his Masonic adversaries understand his intent, Hitler used their own terminology when explaining, "We are not fighting for a new European order, but for the defense and security of our vital interests."[1732]

Instead of Germany going to war with Russia, as English Freemasonry's Round Tablers had hoped, on August 23, 1939, von Ribbentrop signed a non-aggression pact with Stalin and Vyacheslav Molotov, Commissar of Foreign Affairs. Stalin's reward was half of Poland. It appeared that the Cliveden Set had been double-crossed. When Hitler and Stalin invaded Poland on September 1, 1939, like it or not, Great Britain was plunged into World War II. A treaty with Poland obligated her, with France, to declare war on Nazi Germany on September 3, 1939.[1733]

In early October Stalin gloated over the fact that Russia had thwarted English Freemasonry's anti-Bolshevik plans with the Hitler-Stalin Pact.[1734] At the end of the month Molotov said of London and France's declaration of war on Germany: "it is not only senseless but also criminal to wage a war to wipe out Hitlerism and disguise this as a fight for democracy."[1735]

On May 10, 1940 Hitler opened seven weeks of Blitzkrieg (lightning war), which encompassed the fall of the Netherlands and Belgium by the end of May and of France by the 22nd of June.

[1729] "Juan, Don and Juan, Carlos I," *Encyclopaedia Britannica:Micropaedia*.
[1730] "War II."
[1731] Zepp 302.
[1732] Zepp 303-304.
[1733] Zepp 76.
[1734] Zepp 77.
[1735] Zepp.

The British were horrified by the collapse of France. Hitler declared publicly, however, that he did not want war with Britain. Desmond Seward in *Napoleon and Hitler* (1989) informs us that Hitler wanted to make peace with England, guaranteeing "the survival of the British Empire which accorded with his own racial and historical philosophy."[1736]

By this time the Hitler-Stalin Pact was in serious trouble. While Hitler was invading western Europe, Stalin saw his chance to expand his territory and seized Bessarabia and the northern Bukovina from Romania, which seriously alarmed the Fuehrer, since it threatened his oil supplies. On December 18, 1940, Hitler began planning Operation Barbarossa, the code-name given the planned attack on Russia. Via the American Embassy at Berlin, closet Grand Lodge Freemason Hjalmar Schacht, president of the Reichsbank and economics minister, kept his English Masonic friends informed of Germany's imminent attack on Russia. When the war started on June 23, 1941, England was forced to ally with Russia for show, but delayed assisting the Soviet Union for three months, anticipating Germany could conquer Russia within six weeks.[1737]

As you recall from the previous chapter, Mason Winston Churchill warned the Cliveden Set that if England was to be successful in pushing Hitler east, she would be forced to enter the war to contain Germany on the western front When Churchill's analysis proved correct, he said, "This time there must be no mistake. Russia must be crushed."[1738] The Russian Bear, however, was too powerful for Hitler, and English Freemasonry had to settle at Yalta.

[1736] Desmond Seward, *Napoleon and Hitler* (New York: Viking,1989) 187.
[1737] Seward 193.
[1738] White 148.

24. YALTA, POST-WAR MASONRY, AND THE UNITED NATIONS

[At Yalta] There were certain... Freemasons who served as intermediaries between Roosevelt and Stalin; this confirms the enormous influence which the... Masonic advisers of his immediate circle exerted over Roosevelt, and their Communist tendencies.[1739]

THE SURPRISE ATTACK ON PEARL HARBOR?

When President Franklin D. Roosevelt realized that Hitler planned to destroy the Masonic conspiracy, he decided, without Congressional approval, to enter America into World War U. The United States had first be provoked, however. So one year before Pearl Harbor, Roosevelt notified the Southern Jurisdiction of Scottish Rite Freemasonry to inculcate a pro-war mind-set among American Masons. The Masonic *New Age* magazine promptly went into action to accomplish this task. Paul Fisher recounts the rationale promoted by the *New Age* for U.S. involvement in the war:

> *Although the New Age had been somewhat ambivalent about the war against the Axis Powers prior to 1939, its militancy on the issue galvanized after the Duke of Kent, brother of the reigning king, George VI, was selected as the Grand Master of the Grand Lodge of England in 1939.*
>
> *By late summer 1940 [sixteen months before Pearl Harbor], the New Age [August issue] became a strong advocate of U.S. involvement in the war, at first urging direct aid to England, but later pressing for direct American entry into the war.*
>
> *An editorial called the Brotherhood to "rally to the support of England, not alone because that country is the last stronghold of Freemasonry in Europe..." The editorial said the "enemies" of the Craft [Nazi Germany] "would have reason to respect the military power influence could marshal in this country," if it chose to do so.[1740]*

While the *New Age* magazine was encouraging Masons to create pro- war public opinion in America, Roosevelt had already begun to prepare for Pearl Harbor. In September 1939, soon after Great Britain declared war on Germany, the White House cancelled the 1911 U.S. commercial treaty with Japan. In addition, our government cut off eleven raw materials which were vital to Japan's war machine. In December 1939, the embargo was extended to cover light metals. If Japan could not get petroleum, bauxite, rubber, and tin by trade, it would be forced to seize areas producing these products. The Japanese would have to attack the Dutch Indies, which the Japanese militarists knew "would inevitably lead to an American war on Japan. Facing this problem, the Japanese militarists reached what seemed to them to be an inescapable decision. They decided to

---

[1739] de Poncins, *Freemasonry and the Vatican* 186.
[1740] Fisher 223.

attack the United States first. From this decision came the Japanese attack on Pearl Harbor on December 7, 1941."[1741]

Intelligence information available to the U.S. government about the movements of the Japanese navy and other military forces, the Japanese government's instructions to staff in its Washington embassy, as well as the cancelled trade agreement and subsequent embargo of raw materials essential to Japan's war economy - all suggest that the U.S. government, or persons in it, had a greater knowledge of the likelihood of war with Japan than most Americans. The pattern of ignored warnings and coincidental lapses of security at Pearl Harbor itself also suggest a treacherous complicity at some level of government (and the military) of the impending disaster at Pearl Harbor.

One year before Pearl Harbor, for instance, American Naval intelligence had cracked the Japanese code. One month before the attack, the White House knew that Japanese armed forces were mobilizing and moving southward. By November 20 the State Department was aware that a task force of the Japanese navy, including four of the largest Japanese aircraft carriers, were steaming toward the Hawaiian Islands. On November 27 a warning to prepare for war was sent from Washington to Pearl Harbor, yet Pearl Harbor neither increased precautions nor moved to a higher level of alertness. At the end of November, messages from Japan to its U.S. Embassy were intercepted by U.S. Army Intelligence showing clearly that the negotiations between Japan and the United States were only proforma. In early December, Army Intelligence knew that the Japanese Embassy in Washington had been ordered to destroy all its codes and to prepare its staff for departure. On the evening of December 6, three aircraft carriers needed for the impending war against Japan - the Lexington, Enterprise, and Saratoga - sailed out of Pearl Harbor to open sea where they would escape attack. In the early morning hours of December 7, the anti-torpedo net entering Pearl Harbor was "carelessly" left open. Five midget submarines, dropped from larger Japanese subs, entered and operated within the harbor. These submarines were detected at 3:42 **A.M.** before they entered the harbor, but no warning was sent until 6:54 **A.M.**, and only after one had been attacked and sunk.[1742]

At the same time that morning an army enlisted man detected on radar a group of unidentified planes coming down from the north 132 miles away, but his report was ignored. At 7:30 **A.M.** an enlisted sailor noticed twenty-four planes about a mile over his ship. His report was ignored. "In the next half-hour these early arrivals from the Japanese carriers were joined by others, and at 7:55 **A.M.** the attack began."[1743] The next day "Brother" Roosevelt asked Congress to declare war on Japan.

POST-WAR MASONRY IN JAPAN

The Constitution of Japan forbade anyone from joining Freemasonry. Thirty-third degree Freemason General Douglas MacArthur was positive that Hitler had poisoned the minds of the Japanese against the Masonic Order. He promised himself "that if and when he got to Japan, he was going to make sure that provision was eliminated from any future Constitution."[1744]

The status of Masons in Japan changed dramatically with the defeat of the Japanese. When MacArthur became Supreme Commander in post-war Japan, he informed 33rd

---

[1741] Quigley 570.
[1742] Quigley 735-745.
[1743] Quigley 740-742.
[1744] Henry C. Clausen and Bruce Lee, *Pearl Harbor: Final Judgement* (New York: Crown Publishers, 1992) 149.

degree George M. Saunders, Imperial Recorder of the Shrine of North America, that his Occupational Government in Japan "was molded on the precepts of Freemasonry."[1745]

The five-star general's first order was to reopen Masonic lodges throughout Japan. Most of MacArthur's hand-picked generals and many of the lesser rank men, who held key positions during the occupation, were Masons. MacArthur's aide, Major Michael Rivisto, was made first Grand Master of the Tokyo lodge by the Masonic Supreme Council at Charleston, S.C. The Sovereign Grand Commander of the Southern Jurisdiction of Scottish Rite Freemasonry confirmed that all except one successor to General MacArthur were active Masons and members of the Scottish Rite. The Japanese have since concluded that Freemasonry had much to do with the success of the occupation. By 1955[1746], Takashi Komatsu, a 32nd degree Freemason and Shriner, was the first native-born Japanese to become master of a Masonic lodge in Japan. That same year Ichiro Hatoyama, the Prime Minister of Japan, was raised a Master Mason.

HITLER'S "FINAL SOLUTION"

According to *Mackey's Encyclopedia of Freemasonry*, Hitler initially meant to eliminate the Masons, not the Jews. Hitler assumed that in killing all Masons he would eliminate the Judeo- Masonic conspiracy. Not until the latter half of the war did he incorporate as a priority his "Final Solution," which was the wholesale killing of Jews.[1747] During this period the better part of six million Jews were sacrificed to Scarlet and her Nazi creation.

In the summer of 1941, as Germany prepared her "surprise" attack on Russia, and Japan her attack on Pearl Harbor, Hitler summoned Himmler and ordered him to be ready to "carry out the Final Solution of the Jewish question." The Wannsee Conference, which was held to plan the "Final Solution," was scheduled for January 20, 1942 - 44 days after Pearl Harbor.[1748]

The timing of the "Final Solution" apparently coincided with America's entry in the war. As Japan's ally, Hitler knew the problem the Japanese were having with the United States' embargo of steel and oil. He was aware of on-going negotiations between Japan and the United States to ease tensions between the two countries. But war seemed inevitable.

HITLER AND THE RUSSIAN FRONT

Meanwhile in the summer of 1940, to the consternation of the world, Hitler overran France. The Fuehrer was convinced that Great Britain would now make peace. England, desiring to push Germany east, refused, Hitler made his first fatal mistake. "Operation Sealion" - the code name for the attack on Great Britain - was fixed for September 21, 1940.[1749]

That same month Hitler and Stalin were negotiating the Tripartite Pact (involving Germany, Italy and Russia) to divide Europe. Stalin's many demands, however, angered Hitler, and in retaliation he decided to attack Russia. The code name for this attack was "Operation Barbarossa." Closet Freemason Hjalmar Schacht, Hitler's leading banker and

---

[1745] Fisher 229.
[1746] Fisher 229-230 and Denslow, vol. III, 38: vol. II, 196.
[1747] Infield 75.
[1748] Infield 75, 97.
[1749] Quigley 688-690, 693-696.

economics minister, made England aware of the Fuehrer's plan. Hitler's battle with Great Britain ended on June 22, 1941, the day "Operation Barbarossa" began.

On July 12, 1941, England made a false show of support to Russia by signing an alliance which obliged military assistance. Stalin immediately demanded that the British invade western Europe to relieve Russia of the German advancement on the eastern front. London stalled, convinced that Hitler would conquer the Soviet Union in six weeks, thus eliminating the communist threat. When the war dragged on for three months, Stalin made more demands. To appease him, the United States signed an agreement with the Soviets at the end of September to send them military arms.[1750] "Operation Barbarossa" dragged on until the Russian winter set in and defeated Hitler. English Freemasonry, realizing her planned destruction of the Soviet Union at the hands of the Nazis was doomed, began to prepare for a settlement at Yalta.

THE MASONS AND YALTA

By 1941 England and the United States were the only major nations with functioning Masonic lodges. Lodges in Europe, Africa and the Orient had been decimated. No lodges had existed in Russia since the mid-1920s, when the Soviet Union in effect was made one colossal Masonic lodge with a type of Masonic initiation transferred to the Communist Party. Russia, England and the United States, therefore, were the only Masonic powers left on earth. Together, the three conspired to destroy Hitler and divide Europe between East and West. De Poncins reads the events at Yalta in the same way, describing the conference as an "example of the secret Masonic origin of a [disastrous] political decision."[1751]

The Yalta Agreement was not the brainchild of Franklin Roosevelt or Winston Churchill. These two powerful Masons were instead secretly discussing the post-war restoration of the Habsburg thrones. Both regarded the collapse of the monarchical system as one of the primary factors which had led to the rise of totalitarianism and, especially, to the phenomenon of Nazism. They agreed that the restoration of thrones was the best means of holding the shattered shell of post- war Europe together. They talked of restoring the Habsburgs to the thrones of Austria and Hungary, with Otto von Habsburg presiding over a form of imperial confederation of the Danube. According to Otto von Habsburg, "they also discussed the possibility of installing Lord Louis Mountbatten as emperor of a new German confederation."[1752]

ROOSEVELT AND DR. BENES

To test Masonic reaction to a monarchical restoration, Roosevelt and Churchill leaked the information to a few powerful Grand Orient Masons in exile. One was Dr. Edvard Benes, the exiled President of Czechoslovakia and undisputed leader of the Little Entente group of States. As a democrat of very advanced ideas - which included a justification for communism - Benes was an important player in international politics. And as a fanatical Freemason, he waged a Masonic war against the Habsburgs his entire life. In fact, in 1938, when faced with the Nazi invasion of his own Czechoslovakia, he said, "Rather Hitler

[1750] Quigley 727.
[1751] de Poncins, *Vatican* 64.
[1752] Baigent et al, *Messianic Legacy* 373.

than the Habsburgs."[1753] His faith in the Fuehrer proved to be an error, for Hitler closed the lodges and killed or imprisoned the Masons.

Benes fled to France where he established a Czechoslovak national committee, which moved to London in 1939. In London he assumed the presidency of a provisional government in exile. In 1943 he cemented Czechoslovakia's former friendly relations with the Soviet Union through an alliance with that country.

It was in 1939 when he arrived in London that he first heard the rumor of the post-war restoration of the Habsburg thrones. He was horrified. A fierce supporter and devoted ally of Stalin, Benes would rather have post-war Czechoslovakia a satellite of the Soviet Union than a kingdom ruled by a Habsburg. This "brilliant" politician put as much confidence in Stalin as he had in Hitler.[1754]

Benes also enjoyed considerable influence over Roosevelt, both being High Masons. In an attempt to checkmate the Churchill-Roosevelt arrangement for a monarchical post-war Europe, Benes asked for a meeting with the President to discuss an alternate plan.[1755] The result was "the preparation and conclusion of the Yalta agreement."[1756]

Dr. Benes urged Roosevelt not to cancel the advances made by Grand Orient Freemasonry by supporting the absurd proposal to restore thrones. He wanted Roosevelt to give communism a chance. Benes argued that communism was better than absolutism, offering the Soviet Union as an example. He had studied Stalin, said Benes, and knew him personally. Stalin could be trusted. Had he not broken with Hider? "Brother" Stalin would also help destroy Nazism if offered half of Europe.[1757]

Benes suggested to Roosevelt that he be permitted to visit with "Brother" Stalin and negotiate the terms of an agreement. Roosevelt agreed, but Churchill strongly objected.

On April 17, 1948, an article by Demaree Bess appeared in *The Saturday Evening Post* entitled "Roosevelt's Secret Deal Doomed Czechoslovakia." Bess had interviewed Dr. Benes during the war, and this excerpt from her account of these events highlights Benes' supreme confidence in Stalin:

> *I had a long talk with [Benes]...during the first Russo-Finnish war... The Hitler-Stalin pact was then still in force, but Doctor Benes told me he had sent word to the President through an American intermediary, urging him not to lose faith in Stalin.*
>
> *When the break between Hitler and Stalin did come, in the summer of 1941, Doctor Benes was naturally pleased, as were all Allied statesmen.*
>
> *President Roosevelt, disregarding Churchill's objections, made it possible for Doctor Benes to visit Moscow. The Czech leader had two long talks with Stalin himself. The result was a treaty of alliance, signed on 12 December [1943]. The two countries agreed to combine against any possible future German aggression. Doctor Benes pledged that he would suppress all organized anti-Russian groups in Czechoslovakia after the liberation of that country. Stalin in turn personally guaranteed that Russia would not interfere in Czechoslovakia's postwar development. When the pact was announced in a joint conference, Doctor Benes faced the Russian leader directly and said, "Mr. Stalin, I have complete*

[1753] de Poncins, *Vatican* 64, 101, 169.

[1754] de Poncins 169.

[1755] de Poncins 64.

[1756] de Poncins 169.

[1757] de Poncins 64.

confidence in you. We have signed an agreement for non-interference in domestic affairs, and I know you will keep it.[1758]

The Saturday Evening Post article tells how Roosevelt sought Benes' guidance in dealing with Stalin:

> *The following account of how President Roosevelt and Doctor Benes worked together in formulating wartime Russian policies was told to me by Doctor Benes himself, in several conversations which I had with him during and since the war.*
>
> *The story begins in the spring of 1939, several months before the outbreak of war. The Czech statesman first sought refuge in London, but after a few months he visited the United States...and a secret meeting was arranged one week-end at the Roosevelt's Hyde Park home.*
>
> *Mr. Roosevelt knew that Dr. Benes was a close student of Russian affairs, and that he was personally acquainted with Stalin.*
>
> *"The chief question in my mind," said Roosevelt, "is how to get an agreement with the Russians which will stick. Some of my advisers say that is impossible. They insist that the Russians cannot be trusted to keep any agreement if they see an advantage to themselves in breaking it. What do you think about this?"*
>
> *The Czech leader replied confidently, "I have given long and careful thought to that matter. I have studied and restudied the actions of the Soviet Government ever since it was founded, and particularly since Stalin rose to power. And it is my considered opinion that if Stalin himself pledges his personal word, then he can be trusted completely."*
>
> *Today, as we piece together the record of the eventful wartime years, it appears that Mr. Roosevelt was wholly convinced by Doctor Benes' conclusion, and that henceforth the President's policy towards Russia was to be based upon his confidence in Stalin's personal word. This explains his intense desire to meet Stalin face to face, first at Teheran and later at Yalta.*[1759]

Life magazine, September, 27, 1948, reported President Roosevelt's almost sublime confidence in Stalin. To William C. Bullitt, a former ambassador of the United States at Paris, the President said, "Bill, I think that if I gave him [Stalin] everything that I possibly can and ask nothing from him in return, *noblesse oblige,* he won't try to annex anything and will work with me for a world of democracy and peace."

Bullitt later reported his response to President Roosevelt as follows: "I reminded the President that when he talked of *noblesse* oblige he was not speaking of the Duke of Norfolk but of a Caucasian bandit whose only thought when he got something for nothing was that the other fellow was an ass, and that Stalin believed in the Communist creed which calls for the conquest of the world for Communism."[1760]

YALTA: THE PAX OF UNIVERSAL FREEMASONRY

Through all these conversations, the participation of France, the headquarters of Grand Orient Freemasonry, was never considered - for at least three important reasons. First, France's activity during World War H was less than Masonic, for the Vichy

---

[1758] de Poncins 180-181.
[1759] de Poncins 178-179.
[1760] de Poncins 175.

Government had sided with the Nazis in outlawing the Brotherhood. Second, by creating a more powerful Bolshevik beast, France had forfeited its Grand Orient prestige to the Soviet Union. The third and perhaps most significant reason for the Allies excluding France from participating at Yalta was self-preservation.

For two centuries Europe had been in conflict because the head. quarters of the two Freemasonries - Paris and London - were too proximate. It would be in the interest of English Masonry if the power. base of the communist Grand Orient were relocated to a remote part of the earth - say to Moscow. That done, world peace would follow and Sion's long-desired United States of Europe could be realized under British capitalism if French communism were subdued.

The Yalta Agreement, then, was ostensibly a plan to maintain peace within Universal Freemasonry. Grand Orient Russia, and not Grand Orient France, was to share the world equally with English and American Freemasonry. Count De Poncins explains why America was the logical arbiter between the two Freemasonries:

> *Freemasonry in the United States, while maintaining its union and friendly relations with the Grand Lodge of England, occupies an intermediary position between English Freema- sonry and the Grand Orients of Europe. Some of its branches are nearer the English conception [Northern Jurisdiction, Boston - commonly known as the Eastern Establishment], and others the European [Southern Jurisdiction, Charleston].[1761]*
>
> *In such an understanding, Freemason President Roosevelt would be the obvious mediator between Churchill and Stalin.*

Yalta would achieve harmony in Universal Freemasonry by dividing the world among the three great Masonic powers. Western Bloc nations, including France, would fall under the influence of English Freemasonry. These nations would be known as the "First World" of capitalistic nations. Eastern Bloc nations, including France's far eastern possessions, would fall under the influence of the Soviet Union. These nations would be known as the "Second World" of communist nations. Developing nations would be known as the "Third World," or non-aligned nations, and would be up for grabs. English Freemasonry and the Communist Grand Orients would have equal opportunity to capture any Third World nation and place it under its Masonic sphere of influence, except for those in Central and South America. The Western Hemisphere was not to be influenced by either Russia or Great Britain, leaving the Grand Orients and Grand Lodges of Latin and South America under the influence of American Freemasonry.[1762]

France was both rewarded and punished at Yalta. Rewarded for her Masonic Resistance Movement during World War II (more details later) and punished for her anti-Masonic Vichy government For instance, some of the African States were placed under French Grand Orient influence, while her far eastern possessions were placed under Soviet influence. The rest of the Third World nations were subject to capture by either Masonic power, which explains the post- war revolutions on the continent of Africa and the past political turmoil in South Africa.

THE YALTA AGENDA

[1761] de Poncins 116.

[1762] The communist revolutions in Cuba and Nicaragua revealed that Soviet Russia could not be trusted to stand by any agreement.

The three main players at Yalta (Roosevelt, Churchill and Stalin) were famous Masons. At their side were only high political Masons and their Masonic advisors. The Yalta agenda included: (1) the destruction of Hitler; (2) the division of Europe between English Freemasonry and Grand Orient Russia; and (3) cooperation in uniting the three Freemasonries in a New World Order to be called the United Nations.

A famous and extremely important letter discovered by the Spanish government in March 1943 confirms the Masonic agenda of Yalta. Written on White House stationary, the letter was dated February 20, 1943, and was signed by President Franklin D. Roosevelt. It was addressed to a Jewish Freemason named Zabrousky, who was then acting as a liaison officer between President Roosevelt and Stalin. The letter reads:

> *Dear Mr. Zabrousky,*
>
> *The United States and Great Britain are ready, without any reservations, to give the U.S.S.R. absolute parity and voting rights in the future reorganization of the post-war world. She will therefore take part (as the English Prime Minister let him know when sending him the first draft from Aden) in the directing group in the heart of Councils of Europe and of Asia; she has a right to this, not only through her vast intercontinental situation, but above all because of her magnificent struggle against Nazism which will win the praise of history and civilization.*
>
> *It is our intention - I speak on behalf of our great country and of the mighty British Empire - that these continental councils be constituted by the whole of the independent states in each case, with equitable proportional representation.*
>
> *And you can, my dear Mr. Zabrousky, assure Stalin that the U.S.S.R. will find herself on a footing of complete equality, having an equal voice with the United States and England in the direction of the said Councils. Equally with England and the United States, she will be a member of the high tribunal which will be created to resolve differences between the nations, and she will take part similarly and identically in the selection, preparation, armament and command of the international forces which, under the orders of the Continental Council will keep watch within each State to see that peace is maintained in the spirit worthy of the League of Nations. Thus these inter-State entities and their associated armies [international police force] will be able to impose their decisions and to make themselves obeyed.*
>
> *This being the case, a position so elevated in the tetrarchy of the universe ought to give Stalin enough satisfaction not to renew claims which are capable of creating insoluble problems for us.*
>
> *In this way, the American continent will remain outside all Soviet influence and within the exclusive concern of the United States, as we have promised the countries of our continent it shall.*
>
> *In Europe, France will gravitate into the British orbit. We have reserved for France a secretariat with a consultative voice but without voting rights, as a reward for her present resistance and as a penalty for her former weakness.*
>
> *Portugal, Spain, Italy and Greece will develop under the protection of England towards a modern civilization which will lift them out of their historical decline.*
>
> *We will grant the U.S.S.R. an access to the Mediterranean; we will accede to her wishes concerning Finland and the Baltic and we shall require Poland to show a judicious attitude of comprehension and compromise; Stalin will still have a wide field for expansion in the little, unenlightened countries of Eastern Europe - always taking into account the rights which are due to the fidelity of Yugoslavia*

and Czecho-Slovakia - and he will completely recover the territories which have been temporarily snatched from great Russia.

Most important of all: after the partition of the Third Reich and the incorporation of its fragments with other territories to form new nationalities which will have no link with the past, the German threat will conclusively disappear in so far as being any danger to the U.S.S.R., to Europe and to the entire world.

Turkey - but it will serve no useful purpose to discuss that question further, it needs full understanding and Churchill has given the necessary assurances to President Inonu, in the name of us both. The access to the Mediterranean contrived for Stalin ought to content him.

Asia - we are in agreement with his demands, except for any complications which may arise later. As for Africa - again what need for discussion? We must give something back to France and even compensate her for her losses in Asia. It will be necessary to give Egypt something, as has already been promised to the Wafdist government. As regards Spain and Portugal, they will have to be recompensed for the renunciations necessary to achieve better universal balance.

The United States will also share in the distribution by right of conquest and they will be obliged to claim some points which are vital for their zone of influence; that is only fair. Brazil, too, must be given the small colonial expansion which has been offered to her.

In view of the rapid annihilation of the Reich, convince Stalin - my dear Mr. Zabrousky - that he ought to give way, for the good of all, in the matter of the colonies in Africa, and to abandon all propaganda and intervention in the industrial centers of America. Assure him also of my complete understanding and of my entire sympathy and desire to facilitate these solutions, which makes more timely than ever the personal discussion which I propose - the above is only a general outline of a plan which is intended for further study.

This is the issue and the whole issue.[1763] (Signed Franklin Roosevelt)

Key words and phrases in this letter reveal its Masonic orientation. Examples: (1) France was placed under "the British orbit," meaning English Masonic influence; (2) France's reward and penalty was for her Masonic resistance (more later) and her anti-Masonic Vichy government; (3) "the little, unenlightened countries of Eastern Europe" are the anti-Masonic Eastern European monarchies; (4) the partitioning of the Third Reich "to form new nationalities which will have no link with the past" refers to replacing the one-time monarchies with communism; and (5) "to abandon all propaganda and intervention in the industrial centers of America" means to stay out of our trade unions.

De Poncins comments: "It is an undeniable fact that the agreements reached at Teheran and Yalta were in conformity with the lines indicated in this famous letter."[1764] From the 5th to the 10th February, 1945, the famous meeting between Stalin, Roosevelt and Churchill took place at Yalta, in the Crimea, where certain agreements were concluded which put in pawn the future of the world. Almost all the discussions took place between Roosevelt and Stalin. It was Roosevelt who personally and in secret took the Yalta decisions. Without any mandate, without consulting anybody outside his two or three intimate counselors who were present, without reference to anyone at all, Roosevelt signed agreements of extreme importance which committed the Western World as a whole."[1765]

[1763] de Poncins, *Vatican* 182-184.

[1764] de Poncins 186.

[1765] de Poncins 171.

When Bliss Lane, American Ambassador to Poland, received the report on Yalta on February 12, 1945, he was utterly astounded. He said, "ASI glanced over it, I could not believe my eyes. To me, almost every line spoke of a surrender to Stalin."[1766]

De Poncins concludes: "It is a frightening thought that an occult organisation, owing responsibility to no one, can thus in secret direct the policies of one country or of a group of countries."[1767]

Following is a summary of what Freemason President Roosevelt handed over to the Russians in the Yalta Agreement:

1. *The Baltic countries - Latvia, Estonia, Lithuania.*
2. *All the eastern part of Poland, which the Russians had occupied in 1939, following the Molotov-Ribbentrop agreement.*
3. *All eastern and central Europe, including Berlin and Prague.*
4. *Access to the Mediterranean through the recognition of Grand Orient Freemason Tito as ruler of Yugoslavia and the abandonment of his rival, the monarchist Mihailovich.*
5. *Manchuria ceded to Russia without the knowledge of Chiang Kai-shek, the Chinese republican leader, and in flat contradiction of the undertakings which had been given to the latter at Cairo.*
6. *Inner Mongolia, North Korea, the Kuril Islands, and the part of Sakhalin (French Indo- China, or Vietnam).*
7. *In addition, at Yalta the Allies engaged themselves to hand over to the Russians all nationals classed as "Soviet citizens," that is, all anti-Communist Russians who had sought refuge in the English, American and French zones, together with all refugees from satellite countries such as Hungary, Rumania, Bulgaria, etc. The "Soviet citizens" clause led to innumerable personal tragedies; for years afterwards, secret police agents of the N.K.V.D. tracked down Soviet or ex-Soviet nationals even in the heart of Paris.*[1768]

De Poncins rightly characterizes the Soviet adherence to the Yalta Agreement as selective and self-serving: "At Yalta, in exchange for definite advantages, Stalin gave only vague and theoretical engagements, which consisted in allowing democratic, free and independent governments to be established in the zone assigned to Russian domination. Once the Yalta agreement was signed, the Russians demanded and obtained the fulfillment of all the clauses which were favourable to them, but did not observe any of those which they had undertaken to respect."[1769]

Yalta was a prime example of a Masonic diplomatic disaster such as seldom has been known in history.

RESTORATION OF THE GERMAN LODGES

In 1934, when Hitler had closed the German lodges, Masons destroyed or otherwise secured most documents that related to membership and went underground to work in

---

[1766] de Poncins 171.

[1767] de Poncins 64.

[1768] de Poncins 172-173.

[1769] de Poncins 173.

small circles against Hitler's suppression. Their movement became known in history as the German Resistance.[1770]

According to tradition, Prince Louis Ferdinand, heir to the Hohenzollern throne, was involved in the Resistance as head of *Grossloge von Deutschland*.[1771] The Hohenzollerns were split between anti-Masons and Masons. Members of the Protestant northern clan, from which the Prince's family came, were Freemasons controlled by British intelligence. Members of the southern clan were nominally Catholic and, by reputation at least, anti-Masonic.[1772]

A year before the war ended, the Masons made a bid to return the Prince to the German throne. Their plot included assassinating Hitler. Dr. Otto John, the official Nazi Party member assigned to the top management of Lufthansa Airline, had, without detection, remained a Mason. He was peripherally involved in the July 20, 1944 attempt on Hitler's life. When the attempt failed, John fled to Brazil where he turned himself over to British intelligence.

From there he moved to England and was assigned to the Psychological Warfare Division.[1773] His task was to recruit to the intelligence service captive Germans who would be useful to the British during post-war reconstruction.

John was put in charge of Camp Number 11 in Bridgend, England, where the British held captured generals, admirals, SS-leaders, and other leading individuals of the Third Reich. John selected those from this Nazi hierarchy who had previous ties with Freemasonry. They would become the leadership in the new post-war German army.[1774]

At war's end German Masons were eager to reactivate their lodges. On October 1, 1945, a Grand Lodge Freemason who reflected the general view and program of Masonry, one Wilfrid Schiek, a resident of Munich, wrote a letter to the Commander of U.S. Forces in Europe urging him to move rapidly in that direction. Schiek requested that the civilian radio network be utilized to help locate other German Masons. He also urged that the leader in the new German Republic be a Mason. In fact, every Freemason, he said, must run for all political posts to assure party lines remain consistent with Masonic thought. He stated that the Craft must take over all institutions for education to propagate the ideas of world Freemasonry. Finally, he said that Christianity must be actively opposed.[1775]

Because of the uncertain security risk secret societies posed to post War Germany, the Occupation Intelligence Division (G-2) had been instructed to prohibit any secret organization from meeting. Schiek's letter only confirmed to military commanders that Freemasonry was a security risk. Consequently, on December 10, 1945, Herr Schiek received a reply from the military commandant, "Request denied!"[1776]

Another pro-Masonic communication, dated April 1, 1946, was sent from the legal division of the Office of Military Government (OMG), Germany, to the Commander of U.S. Forces. It noted "that members of the Hohenzollern family were Freemasons and that the Craft 'flourished' under the Weimar Republic."[1777] The inference was, "If Freemasonry was permitted then, why not now?"

[1770] Fisher 224.
[1771] Zepp 241.
[1772] Zepp 234-235.
[1773] Zepp 235-236.
[1774] Zepp 236.
[1775] Fisher 224-225.
[1776] Fisher 225-226.
[1777] Fisher 226.

The answer is found in the Yalta Agreement, which assigned West Germany to British influence. German lodges, when they did open, were to adhere to English Masonic obedience. Not until London had sufficient control of all German lodges would any be permitted to reopen. The establishment of this control would take time. To assert her influence, English Freemasonry's first priority was to establish its own press. In 1946, London called on Freemason Hans Zehrer, the former editor of *Tat* during the Weimar Republic, to start a newspaper chain under British Masonic control.[1778]

FLAG OF EAST GERMANY

Finally, on July 23, 1947, the Allied Military Government for Germany approved the reactivation of one German Grand Lodge of Freemasonry. This Lodge rapidly organized Social Discussion Clubs throughout West Germany. In a conference of twelve of these Clubs held on September 23-27, 1947, the discussion was on the formation of a United States of Europe.[1779]

Almost everyone in post-war Germany who achieved any significant position or rank belonged to a Masonic Lodge.[1780] When the Federal Republic was formed in 1949, the presidency, a largely ceremonial post, was filled by Freemason Theodor Heuss. (Heuss' Masonic books were among those burned as "un-German" after Hitler's accession to power.)[1781]

From 1946 to 1949, Heuss served on the parliamentary council that wrote West Germany's constitution. In 1949 he invited Freemason Dr. Otto John to return to Germany as president of the Federal Office for Protection of the Constitution (BVS), West Germany's counter-espionage unit. BVS' mission, as an arm of British intelligence, was to deny communist Grand Orient Freemasonry a foothold in West Germany.[1782] The Grand Orient was firmly in control of communist East Germany (the German Democratic Republic), as evidenced by its new national emblem, the communist hammer and the Grand Orient compass emblazoned on its flag.

The real power in West Germany was Konrad Adenauer, first chancellor of the Federal Republic. Not known to be a Mason, he was, however, anti-communist. Adenauer considered Otto John a "British stooge" and sought to put in his own people, an effort which failed because of the intervention of the British high commissioner. Freemasons Otto John and Prince Louis Ferdinand characterized Adenauer as "American property."[1783]

Dr. John's position as head of counterespionage required he make contact with East Germans. Adenauer misunderstood this and instigated an investigation of John and his East German "friends." John was excellent at playing the double, and in 1954 "defected" to East Berlin where he remained for seventeen months. When he returned to West Germany a year and a half later, Adenauer had him arrested and tried in federal court. Freemasons Dehler and Stammberger (no first names available) took up John's defense, but the sleuth was found guilty in 1956 and sentenced to four years hard labor.[1784] Otto John's replacement for West Germany's intelligence chief was Reinhard Gehlen, a hate-

---

[1778] Zepp 252, 254.
[1779] Fisher 227.
[1780] Zepp 199.
[1781] "Heuss, Theodor," *Encyclopaedia Britannica: Micropaedia.*
[1782] Zepp 238-239.
[1783] Zepp.
[1784] Zepp 239-241 and West 238.

crazed anti-communist, who had been Hitler's chief espionage agent on the eastern front.[1785]

PROTECTING MASONS AT NUREMBERG

Nazi Germany was the first and only nation to be tried for "war crimes." Conspiracy researchers have since questioned - not why the Nazis were prosecuted for killing eleven million Jews and Gentiles - but why the Bolsheviks have yet to be condemned for the mass murder of over forty million Russians.

The answer is obvious. In a world controlled by Freemasonry, guilt is determined not by the severity of the crime, but by who is killed. In Bolshevik Russia Masons killed non-Masons, whereas in Nazi Germany non-Masons killed Masons. The Nuremberg Trials presented indict- ments against a regime that dared lift its sword against Freemasonry.

The Chief Prosecutor at Nuremberg was Robert H. Jackson, a 32nd degree Mason and Justice of the United States Supreme Court. Justice Jackson resigned from the high court to accept this most prestigious Masonic assignment.[1786] On August 8, 1945, he chose Nuremberg as the site for the trial because it was the "city where the Nazis had celebrated their greatest triumphs, held their party meetings with mass torchlight processions, and in 1935 announced the infamous racial laws."[1787]

Justice Jackson set out to compile extensive documentary material with which he intended to prove the guilt of the leading Nazis.[1788] In an interview with the Scottish Rite *New Age* magazine (August 1949) Jackson revealed his Masonic interests and bias. He suggested that the real victims of Nazi tyranny were not the Jews but rather the Masons. He commented that "among the earliest and most savage of the many persecutions undertaken by every modern dictatorship are those directed against the Free Masons." Jackson also declared that Masons "have suffered persecution under dictators more uniformly than any other class of victims,"[1789] including the Jews.

One of the first events at the Nuremberg Trials was the presentation of Hitler's official decree against Freemasonry in 1942, which reads in part: "Freemasons and the ideological enemies of National Socialism who are allied with them are the originators of the present war against the Reich. Spiritual struggle according to plan against these powers is a measure necessitated by war.

I have, therefore, ordered Reichsleiter Alfred Rosenberg to accomplish this task in cooperation with the Chief of the High Command of the armed forces."[1790]

Justice Jackson wanted to try the Nazis on conspiracy charges for starting a war of aggression against Freemasonry. The British opposed the conspiracy approach, as naturally they would since their own Freemasons were guilty of conspiring with the Germans to build a Nazi war machine against Russia.[1791]

The French sided with the English, arguing most vehemently against a conspiracy charge. Together the French and English persuaded Jackson that a conspiracy charge was not necessary for most of Hitler's men. But what about Hjalmar Schacht, Hitler's leading banker and economics minister? Schacht, as Jackson said in the pre-trial London meeting

---

[1785] Zepp 241.
[1786] Fisher 23, 282.
[1787] Zepp 276-277.
[1788] Zepp 281.
[1789] Fisher 23, 282.
[1790] Denslow, vol.11, 236.
[1791] Zepp 286-287.

with the French and the English on July 16, "is either a major war criminal or nothing... Only a theory of a common plan or of conspiracy will catch him and his kind..."[1792]

Jackson was unaware that Schacht was a Freemason under the employ of the English Brotherhood. Nor could they inform him without implicating the Masonic Oligarchy in the Hitler project. Much would be at stake for England were Schacht to be tried on conspiracy charges. The following facts about him would come out at the trial: (1) his mingling with the international Freemasons during the Versailles reparations negotiations; (2) his financial assistance in bringing Hitler to power: (3) his maneuvers in making Hitler "socially acceptable" among industrialists and nobility, suggesting to the British Freemasons in 1932 they back Hitler in his attempt to restore the monarchy; (4) his involvement in the Bank for International Settlements (BIS) in financing Hitler's war of aggression; (5) his collaboration with Great Britain in maneuvering the Fuehrer to attack the Soviet Union in 1941; and (6) his communication from Basel (1942-1943) with American bankers, urging them to continue the war in common against Russia.[1793]

A conspiracy trial against Schacht would definitely be too costly for English Freemasonry, especially if the four most crucial years of Schacht's intercourse with London (1932-1936) were to be examined. During that time Schacht had made his most important international financial deals with British Central Bank chief Montagu Norman, who was openly sympathetic toward the Nazis. Both Schacht and Norman were on the board of directors of the BIS. Even before the Nazis seized power, Schacht and Norman had frequent secret conferences in Badenweiler. Moreover, to insure a Nazi takeover, Norman had refused credit to the Weimar government.[1794]

If the British Masonic Oligarchy was to avoid fouling its own nest, this evidence must be suppressed at Nuremberg. It is no surprise the British delegation vehemently opposed bringing Schacht to trial on conspiracy charges. The Americans and Russians argued as passionately for bringing the charges. The French, who had originally sided with the English, finally broke the deadlock, siding with the Americans and Russians.

The British delegation may have lost the battle, but they did manage to limit the charges on which Schacht would be tried from the events of 1937 onward. This maneuver prevented exposure of the crucial years (1932-1936) of Schacht's intercourse with English Freemasonry.[1795]

Since the prosecution had agreed to exclude the years during which Schacht was conspiring with Anglophile CFR bankers in America and Masonic bankers in London to support the Nazis, the Nuremberg plaintiffs could not prove the existence of a long-term Nazi plan and conspiracy for a war of aggression. Higham, in *Trading with the Enemy*, said of Schacht: "Never in those days on the witness stand was he asked about the Bank for International Settlements... The Nuremberg Trials successfully buried the truth of the Fraternity connections... Charged with engineering the war when he had only wanted to serve the neutralist policies of Fraternity associates, he was understandably acquitted... Conveniently for the Fraternity, Goering and Himmler committed suicide, carrying with them the secrets..."[1796]

Zepp writes in *The Hitler Book* "At least with respect to prosecuting Schacht, Justice Jackson [although a Mason] was very much on the outside looking in. The world of international finance was a closed society, and Schacht was emphatically part of it."[1797]

[1792] Zepp 288.
[1793] Zepp 292, 293, 296 and Knightley 35.
[1794] Zepp 293.
[1795] Zepp 290-291.
[1796] Higham 233.
[1797] Zepp 301.

Hjlmar Schacht's own defense at Nuremberg is remarkable. When he revealed that he belonged to the lodge *Zur Freund-schaft* under the Grand Lodge of Prussia, he was acquitted.[1798] Some of the other Nazi defendants did not fair so well.

TO THE ANTI-MASONS - DEATH BY HANGING

Artur von Seyss-Inquart, the anti-Mason who Hitler placed as governor of Austrian territory, was hanged as a war criminal. Alfred Rosenberg, closely questioned at Nuremberg concerning his attacks on Freemasonry and Jews, as well as his confiscation of Masonic libraries and records, was hanged as a war criminal. Joachim von Ribbentrop offered the following in his defense: "I have been a patriot all my life. I have placed myself at the disposal of Adolf Hitler in the desire to help him save our country from ruin in 1933 and to build up a strong and united Germany in Europe... I always was an opponent to the radical party programme. I have always opposed the policy against the Jews, churches, Freemasons, etc., which I considered in principal a fault and which has caused considerable difficulties in foreign politics" He was not believed and was hanged as a war criminal. Wilhelm Frick, who in 1935 called for the immediate disbandment of all lodges throughout Germany and ordered a confiscation of their property, was hanged as a war criminal. Bernard Fay, the French professor in the Vichy government who published documents and lists of French Freemasons, which resulted in deportation or death for thousands of them, was sentenced to life imprisonment at hard labor for his intelligence with the Nazis. Rudolph Hess' anti-Masonic speech of August 28, 1939, was read at the Nuremberg Trials, part of which stated that "Jews and Freemasons want a war against this hated Germany, against the Germany in which they have lost their power." Because of Hess' involvement with the Order of the Golden Dawn, however, he was given life imprisonment with solitary confinement instead of death.[1799]

THE NAZIS AND THE BUILDING OF WESTERN LNTELLIGENCE

One year into World War II, German intelligence had effectively shut down British intelligence. In a 1940 speech, Heinrich Himmler, Reichsfuhrer of the 55, named every British Special Intelligence Service (SIS) agent in Germany.[1800] Furthermore, French Freemasonry, which had been the best intelligence gathering machine the world had ever seen, was vanquished by the Nazis! Great Britain, whose intelligence apparatus was integrated with English Freemasonry[1801], was aghast. London and Washington, therefore, set out to investigate how Nazi intelligence was able to achieve superiority without their knowledge. They discovered that Hitler's success was his own superior secret society called the SS.

As we learned in chapter 22, the Nazi hierarchy established the SS as a secret society, developing its character from a mixture of Tibetan, Masonic, and Jesuit mysticism. Heinrich Himmler was a necromancer, frequently conducting seances for the SS hierarchy at his castle in Wewelsburg.

We also learned that the SS was a secret society within a secret society called the Vril Society. The Vril Society was deeply involved in the same Luciferian Doctrine as English Freemasonry, practicing witchcraft with a vengeance.

[1798] Denslow, vol. IV 105.
[1799] Denslow, vol. II, 39, 83; vol. IV, 70, 123, 282, 398.
[1800] Knightley 98.
[1801] Knight, *The Brotherhood*, entire.

At the head of Vril was Hitler. Each SS officer took a secret blood oath to obey Hitler without question. Collectively, the SS were the ears and eyes of the Fuehrer - present at every meeting of political or social significance, yet never taking part in discussions. Instead, they just sat or stood in the background, observing and taking notes.

The mysterious aura surrounding the arrogant SS struck terror in the heart of every German citizen who came into contact with these silent, sinister members in black uniform. And as Glen B. Infield, in *Secrets of the 55* (1982), writes: "The reputation of the SS... as the brutal killers responsible for millions of deaths during the Third Reich has not diminished in the slightest over the postwar years."[1802]

The SS was a highly effective, intrastate terrorist organization of four divisions: (1) the Gestapo was the civilian secret state police arm. Its chief was Heinrich Mueller; (2) the Waffen-SS was the military arm, supposedly the Nazi army, or at least controlled by the Wehrmacht; (3) the 55- Totenkopiverbande, a branch of the Waffen-SS, furnished the sadistic guards for the concentration camps and death camps; and (4) the Sicherheitsdienst, or SD, was the Security Service, or intelligence branch of the SS, operated by Reinhard Heydrich.

To develop a more ruthless 85, Hitler had Himmler make each division competitive with the other. Consequently, each "tried to gain more power and influence with Hitler by actions approved by the ruthless Fuehrer."[1803] As a result, "Himmler's SS had become the most dreaded police force in history."[1804]

Himmler never wavered in his ambition to make his SS the masters of Germany. Hitler even feared him, bypassing Himmler for Heydrich, grooming the latter as the next Fuehrer. In 1942 Heydrich was assassinated in Czechoslovakia - by a jealous Himmler, some have claimed.[1805] Heydrich was replaced by General Reinhard Gehlen, Hitler's chief espionage agent on the eastern front.

Hitler established the SS to operate apart from government control, emphasizing that it was a completely independent organization within the Nazi movement.[1806] Although a small budget was allotted by the state, it generated its own income through four large corporations it secretly owned.[1807] Its greatest wealth, however, was acquired by looting gold reserves in nations conquered by the Nazi army, and later, from gold arid jewels extracted from concentration camp victims. This loot, along with the profits generated by the four corporations owned by the SS, were deposited in the Bank for International Settlements (BIS) in Switzerland.

[1802] Infield 2.

[1803] Infield 5.

[1804] Infield 24.

[1805] Stanley E. Hilton, Hitler's Secret War in South America, 1939-1945 (New York: Ballantine Books, 1982) 192-193. The British and American Intelligence networks cooperated,beginning in 1940, and operated from the International Building in Rockefeller Center, with over 1,000 agents. It was known as the British Security Coordination (BSC) and was headed by Englishman William Stephenson. "As part of its apparatus for combating the enemy, Stephenson's new organization included a special operations center called Camp X, in Canada on the north shore of Lake Ontario. It was here that British guerrillas trained and other special missions against the enemy were planned. The most famous of such missions was the assassination of the Sicherheitsdienst chief, Reinhard Heydrich, which was planned and practiced at Camp X and executed in 1942 in Czechoslovakia. One part of Camp X was Station M, a laboratory and staff responsible for producing false letters and other documents designed to embarrass or deceive the enemy." Station M may have delivered a letter which suggested that a jealous Himmler had Heydrich killed.

[1806] Infield 20.

[1807] Infield 134.

THE POST-WAR NAZI AND NEO-NAZI NETWORK

By 1942 the Gestapo had accumulated hundreds of chests of gold and jewels consisting of monocles, spectacle frames, watches, cigarette cases, lighters, wedding rings, dentures and teeth fillings taken from murdered concentration camp victims. They melted down the gold into bars weighing 20 kilograms each and deposited them in the Reichsbank.[1808] In 1944, when Hitler realized that it was inevitable Germany would lose the war, he and his Nazi hierarchy began depositing the gold bars with the BIS. Later that year, at their fourth annual meeting in time of war, the American president of the BIS and the polished British board members sat down with their enemies, the German, Japanese and Italian executive staff, to discuss what to do with the $378 million in gold that had been sent to the Bank by the Nazi government for use by its leaders after the war.[1809]

In 1945 the BIS began assisting the Nazis by making "financial transactions that would help the Nazis dispose of their loot."[1810] The majority of the wealth was transferred to Argentina, where it has since been used to build up English Freemasonry's South American network of drug production and distribution. Assisting English Freemasonry was the newly formed post-war Nazi International.

After the war, under great pressure from the U.S. Treasury Department, the BIS was compelled to hand over a mere $4 million in looted gold to the Allies.[1811] *The New York Times* reported that "the [Treasury] experts who came to hunt down the Reich's hidden assets were suddenly relegated to obscure roles."[1812] Chairman of the CFR, David Rockefeller, showed his appreciation to Thomas H. McKittrick for his role as head of the BIS by making him vice president of the Chase National Bank of New York after the War.[1813]

The Nuremberg Trials successfully buried the truth of the Fraternity's connections with the BIS. Hjalmar Schacht, president of the Reichsbank and Nazi economics minister, was never asked about the theft of the Austrian gold, nor about his involvement with the BIS.[1814] Moreover, every attempt to find out what happened to the Czech gold was blocked by the British delegation.[1815] And as stated earlier, conveniently for English Freemasonry, Goering and Himmler committed suicide.

NAZI INTERNATIONAL

Near war's end, the Dulles brothers (John and Allen), both members of the Anglophile Council on Foreign Relations (CFR), advised London and Wall Street to leave the Nazi-Swiss headquarters untouched, along with the funds they had squirreled away there.[1816] The Anglophile banking fraternity had already determined who among the Nazi hierarchy would be permitted to re-emerge with a clean record, who would be spirited off abroad, and who would be quietly incorporated into the Anglo-American secret service.[1817]

[1808] Higham 23, 39.
[1809] Higham 23.
[1810] Higham 241.
[1811] Higham 40.
[1812] Higham 242.
[1813] Higham 40.
[1814] Higham 233.
[1815] Higham 236-237.
[1816] Zepp 24.
[1817] Zepp 21.

By 1944, Nazis, including members of the SS, began to flood into Switzerland where Nazi sympathizers and financiers protected them. In fact, a lodge was founded in Lorrach-Schopfheim as "a refuge for many ex-Nazis."[1818] The most prominent of the Masonic sympathizers was Francois Genoud, a Swiss banker, who after meeting Hitler in 1929, joined the Nazi Party. In 1939 Genoud became a member of the Nazi Swiss National Front. He made frequent trips to Berlin, where in 1943, he and Martin Bormann made preparations for the period following the expected collapse of the Reich. They were planning a secret "Fourth Reich" on a global scale. Genoud would become the key neo-Nazi figure in all future market transactions for Swiss and other foreign bank accounts. Genoud's financial advisor, until his death in 1970, was Grand Lodge Freemason Hjalmar Schacht, Hitler's banker and economics minister, who was acquitted at Nuremberg.[1819]

In 1950, when aware that American intelligence was on his trail, Genoud fled from Switzerland to Belgium and then to Tangiers where he met with high Arab officials. In 1951 he went to Malmo, Sweden, ostensibly to found the "European Social Movement" for a "New European Order." This "movement" became known to conspiracy researchers as *Nazi International*. Present at the founding were former German SS officers Heinz Priester and Fritz Richter, and two members of the Masonic oligarchy, Sir Oswald Mosley of Great Britain and Count Loredan of Italy. Also present was Pierre Clementi, ironically an ardent anti-Mason during his time with the French Volunteer Division of the Vichy regime. According to Helga Zepp in *The Hitler Book*, "This 'movement' has been the spawning ground for every neo-Nazi organization of the past thirty years.

Shortly after the Malmo meeting, Francois Genoud moved Nazi International headquarters to Lausanne, Switzerland, where the neo-Nazi intelligence newsletter *Courier du Continent* is still published today. This newsletter initiated the erroneous contention that "mass murder was never practiced in the concentration camps."[1820]

Genoud attached his Nazi International operation to Swiss Grand Lodge Freemasonry, causing the editors of *World Intelligence Review* to comment that "Lausanne is the home of the satanist core of Freemasonry, and some of the worst crimes against humanity were hatched in that city."[1821]

For example, during the 1970s and 1980s, Genoud's Nazi International was the financial backer of the European right-wing terrorist organizations, such as the Red Brigades. Throughout the 1980s Genoud funded the PLO and other anti-Zionist Arab fronts. Moreover, he provided the finances for the plot to assassinate Pope John Paul H in St. Peter's Square on May 31, 1981. This fact was confirmed by the Bulgarian government after the Masonic Lodge at Paris blamed the Bulgarian KGB for the attempted assassination. In its own defense, the Bulgarian government launched an investigation, the result of which traced the finances provided for the would-be assassin Ali Agca to Francois Genoud.[1822]

Today, Nazi international still has at its command an extensive financial apparatus, which is primarily supported by earnings from the loot amassed by the Third Reich. In addition to the plunder deposited in the Bank for international Settlements, Zepp reports:

> *Between 1943 and 1945, [additional] loot had been invested in not less than 700 private holdings by Hitler's private secretary Martin Bormann, a close friend of Genoud. Of these 700 companies, 214 are in Switzerland, 200 in the Near East*

[1818] Martin Short, Inside The Brotherhood: Further secrets of the Freemasons (New York: Dorset Press, 1989) 14.

[1819] Zepp 327, 329.

[1820] Zepp 331.

[1821] "Satanic Worship Reaches New Heights," *World Intelligence Review*, May 1989: 16.

[1822] Zepp 322-323.

34 in Turkey, and numerous others in Asia and Latin America. In 1973, ninety tons of the gold in global circulation was in the hands of the Nazis, thanks to the machinations of Hitler's former economics minister Hjalmar Schacht, who, after his acquittal at Nuremberg, directed the reorganization of the Nazi International's finances in collaboration with Francois Genoud.[1823]

With help from men like Schacht and Genoud, many Nazis were spirited away to settle in South America. There they established themselves in various Masonic orders, which today are manifested in the extreme right-wing drug cartels. Volume III of *Scarlet and the Beast* will trace the neo-Nazi drug empire of English Freemasonry in South America.

THE NAZIS AND THE HOUSE OF WESTERN INTELLIGENCE

Phillip Knightley, in *The Master Spy*, writes, "The idea of a permanent secret service as part of the bureaucracy of a country is a comparatively recent one. The CIA came into existence only in 1947; Britain's 515, from which the others sprang, dates from 1909. Before that, major powers got by with small military intelligence departments that were expanded during a war and starved for funds the rest of the time."[1824]

Accordingly, European nations shut down their military intelligence departments after World War I. For this reason Hitler was able to build his SS virtually unhampered by Western intelligence competition. When Nazi Germany was defeated, it is evident why the West wanted Hitler's intelligence network at its disposal. The British especially craved it, since British intelligence was an arm of English Freemasonry. The United States needed it, because America lacked any central intelligence system.

Washington did have the FBI, founded in 1924 by Freemason J. Edgar Hoover. The FBI, however, was not intended for international spying. Its initial function was to spy on the newly- formed organized crime networks of the Mafia that had recently invaded the American industrial cities. But with the growing menace of the Soviet Union (created by the greatest Masonic blunder in history at Yalta), America was forced to develop an intelligence operation on a broader scale than that offered by the FBI. The American government authorized its military intelligence to seek out former SS agents to assist in building our international spy network.

America's occupation forces were instructed to protect as many SS officers as possible, especially those experienced on the eastern front. Author Glenn Infield observes: "It is ironic, for instance, that many former SS officers and men either avoided trial or were later released from their war crimes prison sentences because they could be useful to the United States in its containment policy against the Soviet Union."[1825]

President Roosevelt started the process by which the Nazi SS would be protected. Even before America entered the Second World War, Roosevelt wanted to know what Hitler had at his disposal that enabled him to gain power so rapidly, solidify control so completely, and destroy Continental Freemasonry so resolutely. In 1940 he sent General William "Wild Bill" Donovan to Europe on a fact-finding mission.

Freemason Roosevelt could not have picked a more able man than Freemason Donovan, a student of eastern mysticism. In the 1930s Donovan was a featured speaker

---

[1823] Zepp 324-325.
[1824] Knightley 86.
[1825] Infield 188.

at the O.T.O. Masonic camp grounds at Nyack, New York.[1826] He made contacts there that would serve him well when he arrived in Europe.

Donovan discovered that Interpol (International Police), founded at Vienna in 1923, had been taken over by the Nazis after their invasion of Austria in 1938. By 1940 the Nazis had transferred the entire Interpol apparatus to Wannsee near Berlin. Under the direction of Nazi intelligence chief Reinhard Heydrick, Interpol became the world's most advanced international intelligence force.[1827]

Donovan returned to Washington and recommended to the President the founding of a central intelligence agency on the scale of Heydrick's Interpol. In 1941 Donovan was made head of the new Office of Coordinator of Information (OCI).[1828] In 1942 Interpol chief Heydrich was assassinated in Czechoslovakia by a jealous Himmler. General Reinhard Gehlen became the new head of Nazi intelligence. That same year Donovan's OCI evolved into the Office of Strategic Services (OSS).[1829] In 1942-1943 Donovan and his men were sent to Great Britain to be trained by the SIS. SIS officer Kim Philby was working in London at the time as a KGB double.[1830]

In 1943 the Nazi 55 officers, anticipating the inevitable fall of the Reich, planned for their escape to a new homeland in South America via Switzerland. Preceding them to Argentina was Juan Peron and other pro-Nazi leaders, who took power in that South American country in 1946.[1831]

In 1944 the attempted assassination of Hitler solidified the resolve of the SS to escape to South America. The Germans began sending millions of dollars worth of jewels, paintings and cash to Switzerland and Argentina for safekeeping. Donovan meanwhile had prepared a plan outlining for Roosevelt a central intelligence agency similar to Interpol. But with the war winding down, Donovan's plans were pigeonholed.[1832]

In 1945 Roosevelt died. Mussolini was killed. Hitler committed suicide. The war ended and Freemason Harry S. Truman became President.[1833]

That same year, after the Allied governments occupied Italy, the OSS (forerunner of the CIA) pressured Italy's weak and impoverished government "to use Freemasonry... to prop up a sickly democracy threatened by Soviet-inspired destabilization and the prospect of a communist election victory.[1834] The OSS backed the strongest Masonic faction, the Grand Orient, appointing its Grand Master, Guido Laj, as vice mayor of Rome. It was largely through Laj's efforts that the Italian Freemasons were once again able to start work after years of persecution under Mussolini. The OSS then created Italy's three secret services and staffed them with Italian Freemasons, which have remained essentially local

---

[1826] Clarkstown Country Club 128.
[1827] Wilgus 202.
[1828] Wilgus.
[1829] Wilgus.
[1830] Knightley 117.
[1831] Wilgus 202.
[1832] Wilgus 203.
[1833] Epperson, *Unseen Hand* 308-315.
Wisconsin state Senator Joe McCarthy accused 205 people within the State Department of being communists, including President Truman. What McCarthy did not know was that when exposing communists in American politics he was actually exposing the Masonic Council on Foreign Relations (CFR) and Freemasons themselves, many of whom were Jews. Freemasonry viewed this as Hitlerism all over again. Consequently, McCarthy was discredited. Arthur Goldsmith, a Jewish Freemason and member of the American Communist Party, founded the Communist front called the National Committee for an Effective Congress. It was this "Committee" that wrote up the charges against Senator McCarthy. McCarthy's attorney was also a Jewish Freemason, who guided McCarthy to self-destruction. This information can be read in various books on the subject.
[1834] Short 399, 407.

intelligence-gathering operations for the USA ever since. In Italy Freemasonry, politics and spying go hand in hand.[1835]

Meanwhile, General Gehien, Heydrich's replacement, had planned to offer his services to the West after the war. Infield writes that Gehlen's plan was simple. He made copies of all his important documents dealing with intelligence work on the eastern front, put the copies into 50 steel cases, and buried them in the Bavarian mountains. He was aware that the U.S. had no intelligence organization operating behind Russian lines because the Soviet Union was an ally. He was convinced, just as Hitler was, that the United States and the Soviet Union would not remain allies long after the end of World War II, that the two nations would eventually fight each other over the control of Europe.[1836]

Gehlen and his skeleton staff of Foreign Armies East hid out in the Bavarian mountains awaiting the arrival of the Americans. In May 1945 Gehlen peacefully surrendered to American troops and was promptly sent to a prison at Miesbach and ignored. The Russians were also in search of Gehlen, wanting to capture him before the Americans. Little did the American authorities know that he had already surrendered to an American unit. Not until they learned the Russians were looking for him, did Washington discover they already had him.

When Gehlen was interrogated by General Edwin Luther Sibert, he "offered to place himself, his Foreign Armies East staff, and his intelligence files at the disposal of the United States."[1837] He was promptly flown to Washington. FBI director, Freemason J. Edgar Hoover, and CFR member Allen Dulles, former station chief for the OSS in Switzer. land, "decided that it would be in the best interests of the United States to take Gehlen up on his offer. Moral considerations would have to take a back seat, and they so advised the Pentagon."[1838]

In the minds of these two men, this was the only logical move, for after World War II the greatest fear of the West was not the Nazis, but communism. As early as the 1930s the Communists had influence in the American labor unions, prompting President Roosevelt to request of Stalin at Yalta "to abandon all propaganda and intervention in the industrial centers of America." According to J. Edgar Hoover, the West Coast Longshoreman's Union, headed by Harry Bridges, "was practically controlled by Communists;" the Communists "had very definite plans to get control of John L. Lewis's United Mine Workers Union; and the Newspaper Guild had strong Communist leanings." If the Communists gained control of just three unions, Hoover maintained, they "would be able at any time to paralyze the country."[1839]

This crisis compelled the FBI and the OSS/CIA to protect and use ex- Nazi's against Communists, as well as approach the Mafia for its assistance. After all, the Mafia thrives in a free enterprise system, but would not be able to exist under communism. The "Family" should be willing therefore, to protect its own American interests against the Communists. As one Mafia hit-man put it, "Most people don't know that in those times when our country was threatened [with communism], the Family, as we called it after World War II... put aside all their differences with Uncle Sam or even local authorities... And we all were taught that the Families' ways aren't the right way, but even the Families did what was necessary to protect their country. When it comes down to it, we're all still

[1835] Denslow, vol.111, 47 and Short 407.
[1836] Infield 201.
[1837] Infield 201-202.
[1838] Infield 203.
[1839] Curt Gentry, J Edgar Hoover (New York: Plume, 1992) 206-207.

Americans when somebody shoots at us... We operated in our own way but we got the job done at a time when the free world was very vulnerable."[1840]

To acquire assistance from the Mafia, J. Edgar Hoover met with New York mob boss Frank Costello on regular occasions at the Stork Club or at the Waldorf, where both had complimentary suites. In these secret meetings it was apparently agreed on by both men that the Mafia would be permitted to take over the trade unions to keep the Communists out, for Stalin had not heeded President Roosevelt's request. It is reported that Hoover told Costello, "You stay out of my bailiwick and I'll stay out of yours."[1841]

From then on Hoover closed his eyes to organize crime activity in America, prompting him to say, "There is no such thing as organized crime, no such thing as a Mafia."[1842] And his associates knew better than to question his intelligence. To Hoover the denial of a Mafia was patriotic.

After the agreement between the FBI and organized crime, the Mafia furnished Hoover with "hit squads" to eliminate suspected Communists or Communist sympathizers.[1843] Likewise, the Mafia cooperated with the OSS/CIA during and after World War U. For example, "when the time came to send our boys into Sicily and behind the lines in Europe, General Donovan asked the Families to send their soldiers into the war. That was how the OSS worked, and it never stopped working that way even after it became the CIA."[1844]

As was normal practice after war, the OSS disbanded. Its agents were moved to military intelligence agencies and to the State Department. Along with Gehlen, additional Nazi and British agents were received in the U.S. to train America's budding central intelligence force.[1845]

In 1946 Freemason President Truman decided to implement the original plan of Freemason Donovan to establish a permanent U.S. intelligence agency. In 1947, by executive order, the Central Intelligence Agency (CIA) was founded. In addition, the National Security Act of that year established the Department of Defense and the National Security Council.[1846] Infield writes: "After the CIA was formed in 1947, the Gehien group joined it as the Soviet intelligence arm and worked with the CIA until 1956 when the organization transferred to the new West German government as its intelligence section... This was one of the most closely guarded secrets shared by the 55 and the United States government following the war."[1847]

Gehlen salvaged for the CIA many former SS and Gestapo intelligence officers who had superior knowledge of Russia. Less important members of the SS were spirited away to South America by Freemason Licio Gelli, an anti-communist Italian under contract with the CIA. In 1966 Gelli founded the Propaganda Duo (P-2) Masonic Lodge in Italy, patterned after Mazzini's Propaganda Uno Mafia Lodges. P-2 was to control South American drug traffic for English Freemasonry via Nazi International. Gelli's drug runners were former SS officers whom he initiated into P-2 Freemasonry.[1848]

The authors of *The Messianic Legacy* (1986) tie P-2 Freemasonry to an authority even higher than Nazi International: "According to an Italian parliamentary commission, the organisation behind P2 lay 'beyond the frontiers of Italy...' In 1979...a defector from P2

[1840] Michael Milan, *The Squad* (New York: Berkley Books,1992) 3-4.
[1841] Gentry 329.
[1842] Gentry 326.
[1843] Milan, entire.
[1844] Milan 5.
[1845] Wilgus 203-204.
[1846] Wilgus 204.
[1847] Infield 203.
[1848] Yallop 113-114 and Daniel, *Scarlet and the Beast,* vol. III, entire.

- a journalist named Mino Pecorelli - accused the CIA. Two months after this accusation, Pecorelli was murdered."[1849]

Martin Short has suggested, however, that the "authority" above P-2 is English Freemasonry, the ultimate beneficiary of the illegal drug activity of P-2 and Nazi International.[1850] As we shall soon discover, the CIA does the bidding of English Freemasonry.

Meanwhile, in 1949, when the Gehlen organization was transferred to CIA control, Paris-based Interpol was granted consultive status by the newly formed United Nations.[1851] Interpol had been reorganized in Brussels in 1945, after which its headquarters were moved to Paris, home of Grand Orient Freemasonry.[1852] From there it kept English Freemasonry abreast of Grand Orient activity in France, while at the same time, sent espionage agents to spy on countries dominated by the Grand Orient.[1853] That same year the British sent SIS double agent, Kim Philby, to Washington to work in liaison with the CIA and the FBI.[1854] In 1963 triple agent Philby "defected" to Russia with the assignment to dismantle the Soviet Union.

Meanwhile, in 1956, when Reinhard Gehlen replaced Freemason Otto John as the new Bundesnachrichtendienst's chief (West Germany's Federal Intelligence Service), he was given a large estate in Pullach near Munich for his use. There, he and his former SS intelligence officers produced reports on the Soviet occupied zone as well as the Soviet Union and Eastern Europe. Moreover, the Gehien intelligence organization had connections with Nazi International networks throughout the world.[1855] Because of the cooperation established between the CIA and 515, English Freemasonry was privy to all this top secret information.

UNITED NATIONS:
THE BRAIN-CHILD OF ENGLISH FREEMASONRY

As the West's intelligence network was being developed by post-war Nazis, the second Masonic World Government in as many decades was founded in 1945 - this time, however, under the control of English Freemasonry's Anglophile Council on Foreign Relations.[1856] The CFR began its planning in 1939 for what would become the United Nations after World War II. In 1940, on the advice of the CFR, the U.S. State Department set up a "Special Research Division," headed by CFR member Leo Pasbolsky, to create the basic structure of the United Nations. Pasbolsky's committee was totally staffed by members of the CFR. By 1945 the CFR had taken over the State Department, and that same year at least 47 CFR members were in the American delegation to the U.N. Conference at San Francisco.

Masonic influence, if not outright control, dominated the post-war geopolitics of the U.S. and the Administration and membership of the U.N. By the end of World War II, English Freemasonry had taken over the government of the United States through its CFR front. It also controlled the United Nations, as was confirmed by the Vatican's Cardinals of the Roman Curia in *The Plot Against the Church* (1967) by Maurice Pinay. Pinay says

[1849] Baigent et al, *The Messianic Legacy* 352.
[1850] Short 398.
[1851] Wilgus 205.
[1852] Wilgus 204.
[1853] Pinay 611.
[1854] Knightley 149.
[1855] Zepp233-234.
[1856] Wilgus 203-204.

the Roman Curia reported that from its creation, the United Nations has been controlled in fundamental points by Freemasonry. Freemasons have occupied key bureaucratic positions and sat in many national delegations of states. Whether communist, anti-communist or neutralist, according to the Roman Curia, Freemasons still occupy the most important positions in all three camps.[1857]

ENGLISH FREEMASONRY, THE U.N., AND THE IMF

In 1934, the year President Roosevelt appointed Freemason Henry Morgenthau to Secretary of the Treasury[1858], the United States currency was taken off the gold standard and the Masonic seal of the Illuminati (with its All-Seeing Eye atop the unfinished pyramid) was placed on the back of our $1 bill.[1859]

Before America entered the war, Secretary Morgenthau had acquired a mistrust for English Freemasonry's big money power. He was aware that British Masons controlled the Bank for International Settlements (BIS). He also knew that the Nazis were using the BIS as a storehouse for their stolen loot, but said nothing about it.

On March26, 1943, Congressman Jerry Voorhis of California entered a resolution in the House of Representatives calling for an investigation of the BIS. Morganthau was interested, but being a Mason, would have no part in a public investigation of his English Masonic brothers. The resolution died in Congress. Apparently Congress felt the same as Morganthau, for at that time 54 percent of the Congress and 53 percent of the Senate were Masons.[1860] In January 1944, Washington State Congressman John M. Coffee introduced a similar resolution. Again, it was tabled.[1861]

The British Masonic oligarchy, apparently feeling the heat during the summer of 1944, called a meeting at Bretton Woods, New Hampshire, to resolve the problem. The conference was packed with British Masons, including John Maynard Keynes, Anthony Eden, and Bertrand Russell. American Masons were present as well. Among them was Morgenthau.[1862]

Morgenthau felt that the BIS should be quietly disbanded. CFR member Dean Acheson, along with bankers Winthrop Aldrich and Edward E. Brown of the Chase (later Chase-Manhattan) and First National banks of New York, wanted it retained. Aldrich and Brown were supported by the Dutch delegation and by J.W. Beyen of Holland, the former president of the BIS. Leon Fraser of the First National Bank of New York also stood with them. So did the British delegation. English Freemason Keynes felt that the BIS should continue until a new world bank and an international monetary fund were set up in the soon-to-be United Nations.[1863]

Freemason Morgenthau insisted the BIS must go and approved its disposal, but at the close of the Bretton Woods Conference, the Bank for International Settlements was still in business. So it was that in those last months of World War H, gold looted by the Nazis poured into the Swiss National Bank and was laundered, then transferred to the BIS to be used for another day.[1864]

[1857] Pinay 610.
[1858] Higham 25 and Fisher 247.
[1859] E. Raymond Capt, *Our Great Seal* (Thousand Oaks, CA: Artisan Sales, 1979) 39.
[1860] Higham 33.
[1861] Higham.
[1862] Higham 35.
[1863] Higham 36.
[1864] Higham 40.

Before the Bretton Woods Conference adjourned, however, the formation of the International Monetary Fund (IMF) was discussed, and a year later founded under the auspices of the United Nations. The same Anglophile central bank stockholders who owned the BIS also owned the IMF. The reported purpose of the IMF was to loan money to Third World nations for industrial development. It soon became apparent that those developing nations could not stay solvent without producing illegal drugs to pay off their ever increasing national debt.

According to Dr. John Coleman, a former British intelligence officer, London foresaw the day when Hitler first rose to power, when it would need drug revenues fr6m South America. Coleman reports: "In 1933 the British government had invested $7 billion dollars in land in South America that was only capable of growing drugs."[1865] When the South American nations were unable to pay their national debts to the IMF, millions of acres were leased by white-gloved Englishmen to grow "a more salable produce for export."[1866]

THE ASSASSINATION OF JOHN F. KENNEDY

After World War II, the ex-Nazis in South America had established a network of Masonic lodges that extended north to Cuba. Cuba became their hub for distribution of South American "export produce." Cuban dictator Fulgencio Batista and the Mafia controlled this small Caribbean island. Fidel Castro toppled Batista in 1958. On January 1, 1959, Castro took charge of Cuba, kicked out the Mafia and shut down the Western Hemisphere's largest distribution depot for South American drugs.

With the loss of Cuba, South American Nazis contacted Allen Dulles, their CFR friend at the head of the CIA, and pressured him to rid Cuba of Castro. During the latter months of the Eisenhower administration, Dulles put together the strategy for the CIA-backed Bay of Pigs invasion scheduled for April 17, 1961. He also appointed two CIA agents to initiate "the recruitment of underworld figures to perform the murder" of Castro.[1867]

Meanwhile, John F. Kennedy, and not the Eisenhower-groomed Nixon, was elected as the 35th President of the United States. Kennedy's entire political career had been a war against the Mafia. He considered the Mob's exile from Cuba a victory. He saw the Bay of Pigs as a threat to his ultimate goal of destroying the Mob. Kennedy, therefore, pulled the plug on the Bay of Pigs air support promised by the CIA, leaving Castro in power. The CIA, the Mafia and the South American Nazi drug cartels, not to mention English Freemasonry, were angry.

Jim Garrison, the New Orleans attorney who brought the only case of conspiracy charges against a defendant for the murder of John Kennedy, implicated both the CIA and the Nazis in the assassination of Kennedy, but failed to mention the Mafia or English Freemasonry.[1868] The thesis of David E. Scheim's book on the Kennedy assassination is contained in its title: *Contract America: The Mafia Murder of President John F: Kennedy* (1988).[1869] David S. Lifton, in *Best Evidence: Disguise and Deception in the Assassination of John F Kennedy* (1980), shows how deeply involved the CIA was in the

---

[1865] Coleman, audio cassette tapes; The Drug War Against America,1984; The Future of Latin America, 1984; Narcotics Trade From A To Z, 1986; and Dope International, Ltd., 1987.
[1866] *New Solidarity* (17 May 1985): Supplement A and B.
[1867] David E. Scheim, *Contract America: The Mafia Murder of President John F Kennedy* (New York: Zebra Books, 1989) 215.
[1868] Scheim 71.
[1869] Scheim, entire.

plot *to* kill JFK. He leaves no doubt that the CIA covered up both the plot to kill the President and the alteration of the President's body after the assassination.[1870]

The most damning evidence for the CIA's complicity in the murder of JFK is the recent book *First Hand Knowledge; How I Participated in the CIA-Mafia Murder of President Kennedy* (1992) by Robert D. Morrow. Morrow claims that he, on CIA orders, was the one who purchased the three rifles that killed JFK, that J. Edgar Hoover and Richard Nixon both knew of the plot and that the government closed its eyes to the assassination plans. He says that Vice President Lyndon Johnson was told by Hoover why JFK had to be killed - that he had de-escalated the Vietnam War - a CIA war to control the illegal drugs in that part of the world. The war was resumed by Johnson one day after the assassination. Finally, Morrow describes the deliberate and systematic executions of those involved in the conspiracy.[1871]

The FBI was also in on the cover-up. Hoover recruited a band of killers from the "boss of bosses" -Mob chieftain Frank Costello. Michael Milan (pseudonym), author *of The Squad* (1989), was one of them. On Hoover's orders, Milan, and two other hit men, killed "embarrassing" witnesses to the Kennedy assassination.[1872]

The Warren Commission continued the cover-up.[1873] Dr. John Coleman, former British intelligence agent, in *Secrets of the Kennedy Assassination Revealed* (1990), bluntly says that the Warren Commission was a Masonic cover-up. For example, the late Earl Warren was a 33rd degree Mason as is Gerald Ford, who was his fellow Commissioner. Against all expert evidence to the contrary, "[I]t was Ford," says Coleman, "who 'invented' the one-bullet theory. It was Gerald Ford...who insisted that the experts who picked up the rifle had made a mistake in identifying it as a Mauser. It was Ford who said the doctors and nurses at Parkland Hospital in Dallas were 'mistaken' about the wounds to President Kennedy's head."[1874]

CFR member Allen Dulles was also on the Commission. He too was in on the cover-up. Author David Scheim shows that "[t]hroughout the Commission meetings, Dulles concealed his knowledge of relevant CIA Mafia assassination plots against Castro..."[1875]

Dr. Coleman informs us that "[o]ne aspect of the Kennedy murder is never mentioned in any of the foregoing." Coleman does not specifically say, but infers that English Freemasonry was behind the plot to kill Kennedy, because Kennedy "dared to buck the British...control of the White House..."[1876]

With the Bay of Pigs a fiasco, English Freemasonry needed to find another clearing house for its drug trade. Freemason Licio Gelli, the man who had been hired by the CIA after World War II to spirit the SS to South America, once again came to the rescue of English Freemasonry's Nazi drug overlords. In the mid-1960s, Gelli had established a chain of P-2 Masonic Lodges throughout South and Central America through which drugs could be transported to North America.[1877] According to Zepp, those involved in the P-2 operation were "certain oligarchical families (particularly in Italy, Switzerland, and Great Britain); their associated financial institutions... secret conspiratorial societies,

---

[1870] David S. Lifton, *Best Evidence: Disguise and Deception in the Assassination of John F Kennedy* (New York: Carroll & Graf, 1988) entire.

[1871] Robert D. Morrow, *First Hand Knowledge: How I Participated in the CIA-Mafia Murder of President Kennedy* (New York:Shapolsky Publishers, 1992) 162, 181, 195, 199, 205, 207, 242, 249, 263, 285-300.

[1872] Michael Milan, *The Squad* (1989; New York: Berkley Books,1992) 219-229, 276, back cover.

[1873] Scheim 230-240.

[1874] John Coleman, *Secrets of the Kennedy Assassination Revealed*, Parts 1 and 2, cassette tapes, rec. 1983 and 1990. Library of John Daniel.

[1875] Scheim234.

[1876] Coleman, Secrets.

[1877] Yallop, entire.

particularly of Freemasonic and other pseudo- religious stripes; the international organized crime network; and the still-extant 'Nazi International.'"[1878]

PROTECTING THE PRIORY OF SION DOCUMENTS FROM THE NAZIS

Although the *Encyclopedia of Freemasonry* states that Hitler obliterated the Grand Orient on the Continent, pockets of Grand Orient Masonry did survive. According to Freemason Meyer Mendelsohn, a French Jewish refugee who emigrated to the United States after the war, Masons who escaped the carnage continued to operate in secret circles in the private security of locked homes to carry on their Masonic work.[1879] This underground Masonic network, headed by Charles de Gaulle, became known in history as the "French Resistance," and ironically, involved the Priory of Sion and its Grand Master, Jean Cocteau.[1880]

English Freemasons, acting through British intelligence, became embroiled in the Priory's resistance affairs, even to ten years after the war.[1881] Their purpose was to smuggle important Priory documents out of France to be held in safekeeping in England. The authors of *The Messianic Legacy* list eight Englishmen who were involved in this effort, all of whom were directors of insurance companies and probable members of the Priory of Sion. After World War II, these men began obtaining genealogies establishing the legitimacy of a Merovingian claim to the French throne.[1882] In 1956 the Priory of Sion went public for the first time and registered itself in the French *Journal officiel.*[1883]

Since the Yalta Agreement placed France under the influence of English Freemasonry, de Gaulle's 5th French Republic was not only Masonic, but Sionist as well. In 1962 Sion's World War II Masonic resistance fighters were rechristened the Association for the Fifth Republic. This Association organized the smuggling of the Priory documents to England.[1884] To conceal its activity, the Priory of Sion acquired the services of the Knights of Malta to do the actual smuggling. The documents were kept in England for 25 years before being returned to France.[1885]

British journalist Stephen Knight, author of *The Brotherhood* (1984), states that the Order of the Temple of St. John of Jerusalem (located in Palestine and Rhodes), and the Knights of Malta on the island of Malta, are English Masonic Military Orders.[1886] Both were spin-offs from the Knights Hospitaller of St. John, or the Hospitallers as they came to be known. The Hospitallers were the competitors of the Knights Templar during the Crusades. After the 1314 persecution of the Templars, the Hospitallers acquired the Templar holdings.[1887]

[1878] Zepp 320.

[1879] Fisher 224.

[1880] Baigent et al, *The Messianic Legacy*, Resistance movement in France, 258, 349, 366; in Germany, 328-329.

[1881] Baigent et al, *Messianic Legacy* 254.

[1882] Baigent et al, *Messianic Legacy* 254.

[1883] Baigent et al, *Messianic Legacy* 255.

[1884] Baigent et al, *Messianic Legacy* 256.

[1885] Baigent et al, *Messianic Legacy* 260.

[1886] Knight, *The Brotherhood* 44.

[1887] Baigent and Leigh, *The Temple and the Lodge* 95, 99.

One group of Hospitallers landed on Malta, changing its name to the Knights of Malta. Napoleon conquered the island during his wars, and afterwards the British fleet returned it to the Knights.[1888] The authors of *The Messianic Legacy* state:

> In international law, the current status of the Knights of Malta is that of an independent sovereign principality. The Grand Master is recognised as a head of state, with a secular rank equivalent to a prince and an ecclesiastical rank equivalent to a cardinal... The upper grades of the Order are still fastidiously aristocratic. The highest Knights must be able to display a coat of arms dating back at least three hundred years in unbroken succession from father to son.[1889]
>
> The twentieth-century Order of Malta is, needless to say, ideally placed for intelligence work... Today, the Order of Malta is believed to be one of the primary channels of communication between the Vatican and the CIA... It is not uncommon for CIA directors to be Knights of Malta. John McCone, for example, was a Knight. The agency's current Director, William Casey [since deceased], is also a Knight. Former Director William Colby was reportedly offered membership in the Order but is said to have declined with the words "I'm a little lower key."[1890]

The majority of these men were also Masons. Moreover, many members of the Italian P-2 Masonic Lodge are members of the Knights, including Grand Master Licio Gelli. The Knights of Malta are viewed as an ideal conduit for English Masonic intelligence gathering.[1891]

In reference to the connection between the Priory of Sion and the Knights of Malta, the authors of *The Messianic Legacy* make this statement: "Both Orders, though perhaps for different reasons and with differing priorities, were apparently intent on the creation of some sort of United States of Europe."[1892]

The United States of Europe has long been the desire of both Freemasonries. English Freemasonry, however, was in the dominant position after World War II. To maintain control of the political developments on the Continent, English Freemasonry was in need of the Priory documents. Through the Order of the Knights of Malta, the British Brotherhood forged certain signatures to obtain the documents from France. The Knights of Malta actually transported the documents to London.[1893]

The Priory of Sion is clearly the All-Seeing Eye of English Freemasonry, which "seeks to bring about a monarchical or imperial United States of Europe..."[1894] This goal will be achieved, not by revolution but rather, by "hijacking an already established order and gradually transforming that order from within."[1895] The authors of *The Messianic Legacy* suggest that the drug trafficking P-2 Masonic Lodge of Italy is that order.[1896]

[1888] Baigent et al, *Messianic Legacy* 357.

[1889] Baigent et al 358.

[1890] Baigent et al 358-359.

[1891] Baigent et al 360. It is an interesting fact that before President George Bush invaded Panama to get Noriega, and before Gorbachev cracked down on the three Baltic nations Lithuania, Latvia, and Estonia, both leaders met together in a secret meeting during the fall of 1989 on the island of Malta, home of the Knights of Malta. Did each agree at Malta to not interfere in the other's aggressive ventures?

[1892] Baigent et al 362.

[1893] Baigent et al 269.

[1894] Baigent et al 372.

[1895] Baigent et al 372.

[1896] Baigent et al 372.

Turning to Scripture we see that this machination was prophesied in Revelation 18:23, which states of Mystery Babylon: "by thy sorceries were all nations deceived." We have learned that the Greek word for "sorceries" strongly suggest the drug trafficking of Mystery Babylon, which today is housed in English Freemasonry. English Freemasonry conducts this business by loaning money to Third World nations (who cannot repay their loans without growing drugs); by leasing millions of South American acres to the drug growers; and by acquiring the services of P-2 Masonic Lodges to smuggle the drugs northward. When the nations of the world are sufficiency "deceived," that is, impotent and degraded by drug addiction and its accompanying social problems, English Freemasonry's Priory of Sion will place on the throne of the United States of Europe her "King of Jerusalem."

Europe has not lost its desire for monarchy. Several possible avenues are open for the Priory of Sion to install its "King of Jerusalem" on a European throne. As the authors of *The Messianic Legacy* note: "In Spain, King Juan Carlos is entering upon the second (now third) decade of his reign, presiding over the first democracy his country has known for some thirty-five years, and this arrangement has thus far proved successful. In France, royalist movements continue as vigorous as ever, while the president himself assumes an ever more regal air. Whenever she visits Vienna, Otto von Habsburg's mother, the former Empress Zita, a woman now in her nineties, draws adulating crowds of the kind usually associated with the Pope. During 1984 and 1985, certain newspapers again began to speculate about a possible Habsburg restoration in Austria."[1897]

The authors of *The Messianic Legacy* ask: "If monarchy itself continues to exercise such appeal, how might that appeal be augmented if a specific monarch or monarchical candidate could also claim, in strict conformity with the original meaning of the term, to be a Messiah?"[1898]

[1897] Baigent et al 374.
[1898] Baigent et al 374.

25. THE ADDRESS OF SCARLET

> *Then lifted I up mine eyes, and saw, and behold four horns. And I said unto the angel that talked with me, What be these? And he answered me, These are the horns which have scattered Judah, Israel, and Jerusalem. And the Lord shewed me four carpenters. Then said I, What come these to do? And he spake, saying, These... are come to fray them, to cast out the horns of the Gentiles, which lifted up their horn over the land of Judah to scatter it.*
>
> Zechariah 1:18-21

Zechariah describes two mysterious entities at war - the horns of the Gentiles against the four carpenters. The horns are responsible for scattering the twelve tribes of Israel throughout the world. The carpenters retaliate with revolution to cast out the horns and emancipate the Jews.

THE FOUR HORNS

Dr. E. Schuyler English, editor of the journal *Our Hope* during the 1940s and 1950s, and Marian Bishop Bower, professor at Philadelphia School (now College) of Bible, comment on the meaning of the word "horns" in prophecy: "In the Bible, *horns* speak of power, often the power of a Gentile king."[1899]

The first Biblical record of a Gentile king was Nimrod, the "mighty one" who built Babylon. Archaeologists have discovered that this monarch wore a crown of bull horns, which may be the reason Scripture has since identified a world power by this symbol.[1900] Nimrod's system of rule was to unite religion with politics, thus inaugurating what is known as the Babylonian System. Genesis 10:8,10 and 11:2,4 give us a brief history of Mystery Babylon's beginning:

> *And Cush begat Nimrod: he began to be a mighty one in the earth... And the beginning of his kingdom was Babel, and Erech, and Accad, and Calneh, in the land of Shinar [Babylonia]... And it came to pass, as they journeyed from the east, they found a plain in the land of Shinar; and they dwelt there... And they said, Go to, let us build us a city and a tower, whose top may reach unto heaven; and let us make us a name, lest we be scattered abroad upon the face of the whole earth.*

The "city" stands for the political or civil power of the king and the "tower" represents the king's divine or religious power. In ancient pagan religions the king united both powers.

Nimrod's Babylonian system formed the pattern by which all kingdoms afterwards would be governed: that is with religion and state united. Many centuries later a Babylonian king named Nebuchadnezzar would be the first to lift up his "horn" over the

---

[1899] Bible, Pilgrim Edition, footnote to Zechariah 1:18.
[1900] Alexander Hislop, *The Two Babylons* (Neptune, NJ: Loizeaux Brothers, 1916) 32-37.

land of Judah. Nebuchadnezzar is the first of these four historic horned powers mentioned by Zechariah. The other three powers were Medo-Persia, Greece and Rome.[1901]

THE FOUR CARPENTERS

English and Bower suggest that Zechariah's four carpenters "were workmen, perhaps carvers or smiths - workers in iron... God wanted to make clear that He has an instrument to destroy every power that works against Him... The workmen were to crush the world-powers which had scattered both Judah and Israel, and which were determined to wipe them out."[1902]

What in fact these two Bible commentators have just described is a Masonic revolution. "Carpenter" as we know is a synonym for "mason." Masonic symbols display the tools of carpenters such as the square and compass, which is the chief symbol of Freemasonry. The French Masonic Revolution (a working man's uprising) was the first to destroy a modern Gentile kingdom and fully emancipate the Jews. French Freemasonry was also the first to form workers' unions, using the force of strikes to paralyze a nation. The 1848 and 1871 French Masonic revolutions were both organized from 500 workers' unions. Likewise, the 1905 Grand Orient Bolsheviks coordinated over 1,600 strikes involving a million men and women in St. Petersburg.

Almighty God inspired Zechariah to use *carpenters* as the word to represent four Masonic conspiracies against four Gentile world powers. In Hebrew *carpenter* literally means *mason*. Furthermore, the Hebrew primitive root figuratively describes a Masonic conspiracy: "to devise (in a bad sense); hence (from the idea of secrecy) to be silent, to let alone...conceal...practise secretly, keep silence, be silent, speak not a word, be still, hold tongue." A derivative of the prime root defines *carpenter* as a mystery religion: "magical craft; also silence: - cunning, secretly." When the prime root is capitalized, it means "a Levite," which the Masonic Scottish Rite, or so-called Jewish Rite, claims as one of its tides. Another derivative of the primitive root means "spiritually deaf," which deceived Masons certainly are.[1903]

The action taken by the four carpenters in the passage from Zechariah was to "fray" and "cast out" the Gentile powers. *Fray* in Hebrew means "to shudder with terror."[1904]

The four carpenters could represent four modern Masonic revolutions that have actually terrorized and dethroned four Gentile kingdoms that have persecuted the Jews. In fact terrorism, which is suggested by the Hebrew word *for fray,* has been the tool used in all Grand Orient style revolutions. Indeed, the kings of Europe shuddered with terror when the French Revolution began, as did Frenchmen during the "Reign of Terror" and Russians during the "Red Terror."

THE "HORNS": PAST AND FUTURE

English and Bower also state that the four "horns" refer specifically to Babylon, Persia, Greece and Rome. Daniel 2 also prophesies the rise and fall of these four powers. According to Daniel, the fourth declines, but will never cease to exist. Instead, it divides into two legs (Constantine's Eastern and Western empire) and then divides further into ten toes.

[1901] Pilgrim, footnote to Zechariah 1: 19.
[1902] Pilgrim, footnotes to Zechariah 1:20-21.
[1903] Strong, *Hebrew* #2796, 2790, 2791, 2792, 2795.
[1904] Strong, *Hebrew* #2729.

Daniel 7:7 describes the ten toes as a Beast with ten horns. Revelation 13:1 also describes the Beast as having ten horns. Both are the same end-time Beast.[1905] Many Bible commentators refer to the ten toes and ten horns as the "revived Roman empire," which they believe will include ten European nations in the end-days.[1906]

We can possibly understand the fourth horn mentioned by Zechariah as indeed the horn of the Roman Empire, but of Rome as it extended to medieval Europe where the old Roman empire became known as the Holy Roman Empire. Europe's Babylonian system of united Church and State continued to be governed, spiritually at least, by Rome. And the old Rome, the Holy Roman Empire was rabidly anti-Semitic. Not until the violent "carpenter" revolutions began 300 years ago, was the Roman horn" of the Gentile kings "cast out" and Jews emancipated.[1907]

Perhaps Zechariah's four carpenters represent the four major Masonic revolutions documented throughout this book: English (1688), American (1776), French (1789), and Russian (1917). Not only did these four revolutions emancipate the Jews in their wake, they also prepared the ground for Israel's revival as a nation in 1948. We can trace the stages of this movement: France gave full emancipation to the Jews in 1791. Russia gave birth to the Zionist movement in the latter half of the 19th century. England gave Palestine to the Zionists following World War I. And America guarantees Israel's survival today.

These four carpenter revolutions fought against a Babylonian system that united religion with crown. Revelation 17 refers to this system as Mystery Babylon, the Mother of Harlots. At the time the revolutions began, the Harlot was headquartered at Rome. Where is her headquarters today?

BABYLON WEST

The actual location of Mystery Babylon in place, time and religion or church, has fascinated many. The history of Scarlet's travels reveals that as world kingdoms have marched westward, so in tandem have Satan's headquarters advanced. Revelation 18 discloses that Scarlet's religion controls kings, commerce and politics. Satan's seat, therefore, must be established at the center of a dominant world power when Crown and Religion have never been separated.

Following the Great Flood, Satan set up his seat of power at Babylon, When Christ walked the earth, Satan was headquartered at Jerusalem. When the Adversary was unable to crush Christianity at its source, Rev. Clarence Larkin in *The Book of Revelation* (1919) suggests that Satan followed the Church to continue his incessant war against her. Thus Satan's center of operation transferred to Pergamos, Asia Minor, at that time the western edge of the Christian movement. Satan's apparent intent was to block further missionary outreach westward to the continent of Europe.

In Revelation 2:13, Christ speaks of "Satan dwelling" at Pergamos'. "I know thy works, and where thou dwellest, even where Satan's seat is: and thou holdest fast my name, and hast not denied my faith, even in those days wherein Antipas was my faithful martyr, who was slain among you, where Satan dwelleth."[1908]

[1905] Pilgrim, footnote to Daniel 7:7.

[1906] Pilgrim, footnote to Daniel 2:31.

[1907] Although Freemasonry is a tool of Satan, Almighty God permitted the Masonic "carpenters" to: (1) destroy the Gentile "horns" that scattered the Jews; (2) give the Jews their freedom; and (3) return the Jews to Palestine.

[1908] Clarence Larkin sheds more light on Satan's seat in Pergamos.On page 22 he writes: "When Attalus III, the Priest-King of the Chaldean hierarchy, fled before the conquering Persians to Pergamos, and settled there, Satan shifted his capital from Babylon to Pergamos."

Each westward move of the Church has been accompanied by Satan and his harlot religion, Mystery Babylon. Thus, when the Roman Empire was the dominant kingdom, Satan left Pergamos for Rome, and Scarlet (Mystery Babylon) followed. The Apostle Peter's reference to Babylon in I Peter 5:13 indicates that the early Christians were aware that Mystery Babylon had located there: "The church that is at Babylon, elected together with you, saluteth you."[1909]

Rev. Hislop in *The Two Babylons* (1916), subtitled *The Papal Worship proved to be The Worship of Nimrod and His Wife*, lends his entire research to the premise that Mystery Babylon took up permanent residence in the Church at Rome. He states that "it has always been easy to show, that the Church which has its seat and headquarters on the seven hills of Rome might most appropriately be called 'Babylon,' inasmuch as it is the chief seat of idolatry under the New Testament, as the ancient Babylon was the chief seat of idolatry under the Old."[1910]

Rev. Clarence Larkin was of the same opinion. Larkin claims that the descriptions of the Seven Churches of Revelation (chapters 2-3) -Ephesus, Smyrna, Pergamos, Thyatira, Sardis, Philadelphia, and Laodicea - are prophecies of Church history. He suggests that Mystery Babylon traveled Irom Babylon to Pergamos, then from Pergamos to Rome. Larkin asserts that the period of dominance of Roman Catholicism in church history is prophesied in Revelation 2:18-19, which addresses the church in Thyatira.

Bible commentators English and Bower held that same opinion. In their annotations to the Pilgrim Edition of the Holy Bible, they noted that the word "Thyatira" means "continual sacrifice." They linked this meaning of Thyatira with the main act of worship of the Catholic Church, "the sacrifice of the Mass," which is a continual ordinance within the Roman Church.[1911]

In Revelation 2:20-23, Christ, through the Apostle John, issues a severe condemnation of the church at Thyatira:

> *Notwithstanding I have a few things against thee, because thou sufferest that woman Jezebel, which calleth herself a Prophetess, to teach and to seduce my servants to commit fornication, and to eat things sacrificed unto idols. And I gave her space to repent of her fornication: and she repented not. Behold, I will cast her into a bed, and them that commit adultery with her into great tribulation, except they repent of their deeds. And I will kill her children with death; and all the churches shall know that I am He which searcheth the reins and hearts; and I will give unto every one of you according to your works.*

Clarence Larkin identifies "that woman Jezebel" in the church of Thyatira with the Jezebel of Israel. He writes:

> *Jezebel, the wife of Ahab, was not by birth a daughter of Abraham, but a princess of idolatrous lyre, at a time, too, when its royal family was famed for cruel savagery and intense devotion to Baal and Astaate... Ahab, king of Israel, to strengthen his kingdom, married Jezebel, and she, aided and abetted by Ahab,*

[1909] William Steuart McBirnie, in *The Search For The Twelve Apostles*, page 56, believes that Peter was literally at Babylon.Yet, other scholars suggest he was in Rome when he wrote his epistle. Phillips Modern English Bible places the word "Babylon" between quotation marks. The Living Bible footnotes it confirming that "Babylon was the Christian nickname of Rome."

[1910] Alexander Hislop, *The Two Babylons: The Papal Worship* proved to be the Worship of Nimrod and His Wife (1916; Neptune, NJ: Loizeaux Brothers, 1959) 2.

[1911] Bible, Pilgrim Edition, footnote on Thyatira, Revelation 2.

introduced the licentious worship of Baal into Israel, and killed all the prophets of the Lord she could lay her hands on.

There is no question that, whether Jezebel was a real person [in the Church] or not, she typified a "System" and that "System" was the "Papal Church." When the "Papal Church" introduced images and pictures into its churches for the people to bow down to it became idolatrous. And when it set up its claim that the teaching of the Church is superior to the Word of God, it assumed the role of "Prophetess." A careful study of the "Papal System" from A.D. 606 to the Reformation A.D. 1520, with its institution of the "Sacrifice of the Mass" and other Pagan rites, reveals in it the sway of "Jezebelism." It was also a period of "Jezebelistic Persecution," as seen in the wars of the Crusades, and the rise of the Inquisition.[1912]

It seems indisputable that Rome, at that time the mightiest power on earth, was the headquarters of Satan and his Babylonian religion. Rome, however, is not the greatest power today. Yet Alexander Hislop leaves the Mother Harlot in the Roman Church, while his contemporary, Clarence Larkin, terminates "Jezebelism" around 1520 A.D.

SEARCHING FOR MYSTERY BABYLON'S NEW HOME

William R. Goetz, in *Apocalypse Next*, a book listing incredible indications that long-prophesied cataclysmic events are coming upon the earth, attempts to locate Mystery Babylon's present headquarters by looking for the seat of a religion which permits all other religions to join her fellowship. "Quite apparently," says Goetz, "no one religion like Protestantism, or Islam, or Catholicism could get all other religions to join it, though many such attempts have been and are being made. Unquestionably, whatever religion it is, it will have to have a strong appeal - far stronger than the pull of watered-down Christianity today."[1913]

Goetz suggests that this religion will include "the occultic practices - such as black magic, seances, demon contact, miracles, witchcraft, sorcery and astrology."[1914] He then provides yet another criterion to help discover the present-day Mother of Harlots: "Proper biblical interpretation, which demands that the first use of a term in Scripture be followed in every successive use, soon confirms that we are close to solving the mystery of what religion the 'harlot' could possibly represent."[1915]

Applying Goetz's formula to Scripture, we know that ancient Babylon produced the "Mother of Harlots." That the Whore of Babylon was also the Mother of Harlots" indicates that she has many offspring. She is not an offspring or child herself, but the original mother of all false religions.

Applying Goetz's criteria to the Catholic Church, we discover that the Church at Rome could never have been Mystery Babylon, the Mother of Harlots, since her roots were not at Babylon. Nor could she have been an offspring. For example, Thyatira, which Clarence Larkin claims is prophetic of Roman Catholicism, was one of our Lord's seven churches, and not an offspring of the Harlot. Christ Himself recognized Thyatira as His own. He did not call her the "Mother of Harlots," but did condemn her for fornication with Jezebel, which is representative of her idolatry with the Mother Harlot.

[1912] Clarence Larkin, *The Book of Revelation* (1919; Philadelphia:Clarence Larkin Estate, n.d.) 22.

[1913] William R Goetz, *Apocalypse Next* (Beaverlodge, Alberta, CD:Horizon House Publishers, 1980) 184.

[1914] Goetz 186.

[1915] Goetz.

We find a similar case of idolatry in the Old Testament. Jeremiah 3 records that God divorced Israel for whoring after Babylonian deities. The Jews had previously fallen into the same sin as the Christians at Rome. Is Israel Mystery Babylon too? Of course not. Yet Mystery Babylon did pass through her. Likewise, Mystery Babylon has passed through the Roman Church, but the Roman Church is not herself the Mother of Harlots.

MYSTERY BABYLON IDENTIFIED

In our day, the Harlot must be a mystery religion with roots in Babylon, a religion that is known as the "Mother" of all modern harlot religions. Her form of worship, however, is not the only criterion for identification. Revelation 17-18 gives us further clues about her. In the last days, before her destruction by fire, she must be in control of kings, commerce, finance, and big business on an international scale. The Roman Church lost that control during the last three centuries of political revolutions.

A powerful worldwide order does comply with the criteria provided by Goetz and indicated by Scripture. The Mother Harlot, or Scarlet, is a mystery religion, admitting so in her own secret publications. Since 1717 all modern cults, secret societies and false religions organized in the Western world have issued from her womb. All religions older than she can join her ranks without discrimination. Other indications are that her associates (or lovers) are the rulers of governments: her hierarchy controls world banking, commerce and industry; and most significantly, she commands the illicit manufacture and trafficking of drugs to all nations.

This mysterious entity, not tied to any religious system, yet allowing all to join her ranks, operates on her own in the maturity of the Mother Harlot. Presenting herself as a Judeo-Christian organization, she has all the markings of "Mystery, Babylon the Great, the Mother of Harlots," and claims in her own publications to originate at Babel. She is not headquartered at Rome, but has moved farther west.

We can trace her movement by means of Revelation 18:24: "[I]n her was found the blood of prophets [while she passed through Israel], and of saints [while she passed through Rome], and of all that were slain upon the earth [while she resides in her present headquarters following the Reformation]."

Her final goal is a universal brotherhood, governed by a global political system under her idolatrous command. She is the Harlot of Revelation riding upon the political Beast. Her exit from the Catholic Church began with the Protestant Reformation.

THE OLD WORLD ORDER

The Protestant Reformation and carpenter revolutions of our modern era, which had their beginnings three centuries ago, were the only avenues of escape from the progressively despotic Roman Church, which was in union with equally despotic European kings in what is called the Old World Order. Together they had created for their subjects such untenable conditions that a New World Order was soon to throw off the yoke of oppression.

The duration of the Roman Church's entanglement with worldly empires recalls the words of Christ in Revelation 2:21-23 to the (Catholic) Church at Thyatira: "And I gave her space to repent of her fornication; and she repented not. Behold, I will cast her into a bed, and them that commit adultery with her into great tribulation, except they repent of their deeds. And I will kill her children with death; and all the churches shall know that I am he which searcheth the reins and hearts: and I will give unto every one of you according to your works."

MYSTERY BABYLON EXITS THE ROMAN CHURCH AND ENTERS SECRET SOCIETIES

Christ's prophecy of tribulation for the Thyatira church age has been fulfilled. The savagery of the Inquisitions, performed in the name of Christ by vain and pompous Popes, made barbarians look like gentle lambs. As a result, pagans, who had converted to Christianity for convenience, began to form secret societies to protect themselves. Protestants fought in the open. Thus, the Reformation arose from not only Protestant Christians, but protesting pagans as well.

When Mystery Babylon could no longer control the Vatican, she exited the Catholic Church during the Reformation and buried her conspiracy in secret societies with the intent of destroying the Church through political revolution. Freemasonry became the largest and most enduring secret society to house Mystery Babylon. Through Masonic lodges the Whore of Babylon achieved her revolutionary goals. The *Little Masonic Library* readily admits that "in the Reformation Masonry severed its connection with Catholicism..."[1916]

In another place the *Little Masonic Library* acknowledges Freemasonry's birth with the Reformation: "Indeed, we have not duly considered how truly Masonry, in its modern form, was a child of the Reformation, allied, as it was, with the movement, or group of movements, out of which came the freedom of the peoples, the liberty of conscience, and the independence of manhood."[1917]

MYSTERY BABYLON: FROM ROME TO LONDON IN 1717

We know that Clarence Larkin terminates "Jezebelism" (Mystery Babylon in the Catholic Church) around 1520 A.D. It was during this time (1534) that King Henry VIII insisted that Parliament replace the Catholic Church in England with the Church of England. Every British monarch since has usurped the position of the pope as head of the state church. In 1688 the English Masonic "Glorious Revolution" did not alter the king's position. Instead, Freemasonry took control of the Church. British journalist Stephen Knight confirms that "The Church of England has been a stronghold of Freemasonry for more than two hundred years."[1918] In the 1950s the archbishop of Canterbury, sixteen bishops and more than 500 Anglican priests were Masons.[1919] French Freemason Marius Lepage in *Le Symbolisme* (October, 1953) said "It is absolutely useless for a Frenchman to try to understand English Masonry unless he realizes that the crown, the Anglican Church, and the United Grand Lodge of England are one God in three person."[1920]

What Christ condemned in the church at Rome, the Church of England embraced. On June 24, 1717, four London Masonic lodges united in the Grand Lodge, then established the claim that English Freemasonry is rooted at Babylon, with Nimrod its founder.[1921] This is also the date Freemasonry purports that the Catholic Church began to lose its hold on kingdoms. Speaking to the Grand Orient Convention at Paris in 1902, Grand Master

---

[1916] Joseph Fort Newton, "The Great Light in Masonry," *Little Masonic Library*, vol.111(1924; Richmond, VA: Macoy Publishing & Masonic Supply Co., 1977) 190.
[1917] Newton 188.
[1918] Knight, *The Brotherhood* 240.
[1919] Short 74.
[1920] Short 55; quoting Marius Lepage.
[1921] "Nimrod," *Mackey's Encyclopedia of Freemasonry*, vol.11.

Delpech said, "The Church of Rome, based on the Galilean myth, began to decline rapidly from the very day on which the Masonic association was established."[1922]

In 1737 English Freemasonry established the tradition of making her kings honorary heads of the Grand Lodge. This move, in effect, made British monarchs priest-kings of modern Mystery Babylon. To this day, England has never wavered from her Babylonian system. Even when French Freemasonry forced the separation of church and state in all its revolutions, English Freemasonry remains in control of church and state to this day.

In summary, Zechariah's fourth horn, the Roman empire, represents the Babylonian monarchical system of rule extended to medieval Europe, under which Jews suffered. When the European "horns" were "cast out" by the "carpenter" revolutions, Jews were emancipated, church was separated from state, and the Babylonian system shifted from Rome to London.

REVELATION SHEDS LIGHT ON ENGLISH FREEMASONRY AS MYSTERY BABYLON

The greatest book of prophecy in the Bible promises a special blessing to those who read it, understand it, and do those things written therein (Revelation 1:3). In this book the account of the two Masonic conspiracies in the text referred to as "Mystery Babylon" and the "Beast" is prophesied. The history and end-time destruction of Mystery Babylon is recorded in Revelation 17 and 18. In 17:1-9 the apostle John describes Scarlet as shown to him by Jesus Christ.

> *I will shew unto thee the judgement of the great whore that sitteth upon many waters: With whom the kings of the earth have committed fornication, and the inhabitants of the earth have been made drunk with the wine of her fornication. So he carried me away in the spirit into the wilderness; and I saw a woman sit upon a scarlet coloured beast, full of names of blasphemy, having seven heads and ten horns. And the woman was arrayed in purple and scarlet colour, and decked with gold and precious stones and pearls, having a golden cup in her hand full of abomination and filthiness of her fornication: And upon her forehead was a name written, MYSTERY, BABYLON THE GREAT, THE MOTHER OF HARLOTS AND ABOMINATIONS OF THE EARTH. And I saw the woman drunken with the blood of the saints, and with the blood of the martyrs of Jesus: and when I saw her, I wondered with great admiration. And the angel said unto me. Wherefore didst thou marvel? I will tell thee the mystery of the woman, and the beast that carrieth her, which hath seven heads and ten horns... And here is the mind which hath wisdom. The seven heads are seven mountains on which the woman sitteth.*

MASONIC OATHS IDENTIFY MYSTERY BABYLON

That Scarlet's worship is hidden in "mystery," or eastern mysticism, is agreed to by William Goetz in *Apocalypse Next.* Goetz states that modern Mystery Babylon will not be a church of watered-down Christianity, but rather must be a secret organization which practices witchcraft.[1923]

[1922] de Poncins, *Freemasonry and the Vatican* 73.
[1923] Goetz 177-186.

A close look at the Greek of the Scripture text above confirms this interpretation of Mystery Babylon. The Greek word for *mystery* means "to shut the mouth; a secret through the idea of silence imposed by initiation into religious rites."[1924] This definition concurs with the meaning of the Hebrew word for "carpenters" in Zechariah's vision at the beginning of the chapter: "to devise (in a bad sense); hence (from the idea of secrecy) to be silent, to let alone... conceal... practise secretly, keep silence, be silent, speak not a word, be still, hold tongue."

The "initiation into religious rites" in all Babylonian mystery religions includes taking blood oaths of silence. For those who take the oaths (if one is to believe their veracity), a cruel death is administered if silence is not maintained.

For illustration, we shall consider the consequences of taking the Masonic oaths in each of the first three degrees of Freemasonry. At the end of the initiation, the candidate swears to keep all Masonic secrets, "binding myself under no less penalty than that of having my throat cut across... tongue torn out by its roots... breast torn open... heart plucked out... body severed in twain... bowels taken from thence...should I ever knowingly violate this my solemn obligation..." After the oath is taken, the Worshipful Master of the lodge says to the Senior Deacon, "he is bound to us by an obligation, a tie stronger than human hands can impose."[1925]

Who imposes this inhuman tie but Satan, the Master Deceiver? James 5:12 warns Christians against taking such secret oaths, because they are deception: "But above all things, my brethren, swear not, neither by heaven, neither by the earth, neither by any other oath: but let your yea be yea; and your nay, nay; lest ye fall into condemnation."

The Greek word for the type of condemnation of which James speaks means "deceit" and is used in this sense only once in all the New Testament.[1926]

Deceit is at the heart of Freemasonry, according to the greatest Mason of all time, Albert Pike. In fact, in *Morals and Dogma*, Pike writes that in the Blue Degrees "the initiate... is intentionally misled..."[1927]

Something more than deception binds the initiate when he takes the blood oaths. Oswald Wirth, a well-known 33rd degree French Grand Lodge Mason, confirms in his book *The Ideal Initiate* (1927) that the act of taking the Masonic oath is, in fact, selling one's soul to the Devil:

> It is a serious matter to ask for Initiation, for one has to sign a pact... [which]... demands that the man's soul be truly committed in the act. It is not, then, like driving a bargain with the Devil, in which the Evil One allows himself to be tricked; it is an agreement entered into seriously on both [the Devil and the Initiate's] sides, and there is no escape from its clauses... [T]he Initiate himself is by that very fact indissolubly bound to his masters... It would all be nothing... if you could ask to be initiated free of all obligation, without paying with your very soul.[1928]

Revelation 18:11 and 13 confirms that Mystery Babylon "buyeth" the "souls of men." This purchase is made by Satan through the initiate's own blood when he takes the Masonic oath.

[1924] Strong, Greek #3466.
[1925] Ronayne, *Handbook of Freemasonry* 70-71, 123, 173.
[1926] Strong, Greek #5272.
[1927] Pike, *Morals and Dogma* 819.
[1928] de Poncins, *Freemasonry and the Vatican* 48; quoting Oswald Wirth.

Dear Christians in Freemasonry, the apostle Paul says in I Corinthians 6:20 that already your souls "are bought with a price," and that price the precious blood of our Lord Jesus Christ (I Peter 1:18-19). You have committed a grievous sin when you took the Masonic oath. God is merciful. He will forgive you if you ask Him, and He will renew you to the joy of your salvation if you repent - that is, if you turn away from Freemasonry.

MODERN MYSTERY BABYLON, DECEPTION AND DRUG TRAFFICKING

We know from Masonic sources that Freemasonry deceives its own initiates. There is, however, a broader deception announced in Revelation 18:23b: "by thy sorceries were all nations deceived."

This verse unveils Mystery Babylon's control of the manufacturing and trafficking of illegal drugs worldwide. Four Greek words are employed to define sorceries as used in the above Scripture. They are: (1) *phar*makeja, meaning magic medication in the practice of witchcraft; (2) *pharmakeus* and *pharmakon*, meaning a magician or sorcerer who manufactures and sells spell- giving potions; and (3) *pharmakos*, having the same meaning as *pharmakon*.[1929]

In no other place in Scripture, except in reference to Mystery Babylon, are these Greek words for *sorcery* used in the sense they are here to indicate the manufacture, sale, and consumption of drugs. From them come our English form of pharmacist, pharmacy, and pharmaceutical.

We have already outlined the tradition and history of sorcery and drug use in both Freemasonries. In the previous chapter, we suggested the extent of English Freemasonry's post- World War II drug empire. Volume III of *Scarlet and the Beast* is devoted entirely to tracing the Whore of Babylon's universal control of growing, manufacturing, distributing, and financing illegal drugs for the express purpose of deceiving the world into accepting her New Age Antichrist. English Freemasonry's involvement with illicit drugs may be the strongest evidence that today London is home for Mystery Babylon.

MOTHER OF HARLOTS

Revelation 17:4-5 exposes the perfidy of Scarlet's character: She is not only a harlot religion, but the "MOTHER" - the first born of Babylon - and the progenitor of all false religions. Therefore, she is called MYSTERY BABYLON THE MOTHER OF HRRLOTS.

As we have seen, English Freemasonry, the mother of all Freemasonry, claims her roots in ancient Babylon. With over 9,000 temple-lodges scattered throughout most nations of the world, (and with over 7,000 in Great Britain alone, including 1,700 in London) English Freemasonry is the largest harlot religion on earth today. Moreover, this modern Whore of Babylon has given birth to hundreds of modern secret societies, cults, think tanks, and a variety of political orders.

Edith Miller, in *Occult Theocrasy* (1933), names many of the offspring of English Freemasonry. We will list the major ones by nation, including some that appeared after the publication of Miller's book

---

[1929] Strong, Greek #5331, 5332, 5333.

- England: Societas Rosicruciana in Anglia, Ancient and Primitive Rite of Memphis, Theosophical Society, Order of the Golden Dawn, Stella Matutina, Fabian Society, the Round Table Groups, rock and roll stars, and illegal drugs.
- Germany: Illuminati, Strict Observance, Martinist Order, Tugendbunds, Anthroposophical Society, O.T.O. and the Thule Society.
- France: Scottish Rite, French Grand Lodge, Grand Orients, Jacobins, Communism, Socialism, Alliance Israelite Universelle, League of Nations, European Economic Community, and the United States of Europe.
- Italy: Carbonari, Young Societies, Propaganda Duo (P-2) drug running lodges, and the Mafia.
- Russia: Nihilists, Anarchists, and the Soviet Union.
- Moslem countries: Moslem Brotherhood.
- America: Scottish Rite, York Rite, Eastern Star, Shriners, Odd fellows, Mormons, Jehovah's Witnesses, Christian Science, B'nai B'rith, Ku Klux Klan, Lucis mist, O.T.O., Process Church, Church of Scientology, National Council of Churches, Council on Foreign Relations, the Trilateral Commission, the United Nations, and the New Age Movement.

Grand Orient Freemason, Brother J.C. Corneloup, Grand commander of Honor of the Grand College of Rites, confirms in *Universalism of French Freemasonry* (1963) that English Freemasonry claims mother-hood to all Freemasonry:

> *The bitterness [between the two Freemasonries] clearly reveals that London considered that it was the Mother Grand Lodge, and that all the others were subsidiaries whom it wanted to keep in its dependence, the sign of a strong desire to set up universality to its exclusive profit.*
>
> *Two hundred years after this struggle broke out, we still find as lively a spirit of hostility, though couched in less truculent terms, on the part of the Grand Lodge of England with regard to French Masonry, apparently concentrated against the Grand Orient of France, but equally apparent against the Grand Lodge of France.*
>
> *The fact is that we are confronted with two organisations sprung from the same stock [operative Masonry], and palpably born at the same time [mid-1600s] and in the same country [England], but which have evolved differently because one developed in powerful middle-class, intellectual and aristocratic surroundings [English Freemasonry], and the other in a much more democratic climate [French Freemasonry].*
>
> *[Therefore], the United Grand Lodge of England could go on and celebrate the universality of Freemasonry; it could even, priding itself on being the Mother Lodge from which all others have sprung, claim to put this universality into practice to its own profit, with the right to dominate the whole of Masonry.*

In 1929, the United Grand Lodge of England took a step of capital importance by publishing its *Fundamental Principles for the Recognition of Grand Lodges...* London claims the right to lay down Masonic law; the United Grand Lodge of England claims to dominate the Masonic world, to be the sovereign judge of the authenticity of the different Masonic powers, and to impose its law upon them. Confident in its powers of intimidation, which it has skillfully cultivated, and owing to the pusillanimous ignorance of the leaders of the different obediences, who are afraid of the least suggestion of a rupture, it arbitrarily fixes the criterion for regularity in such a way that it can always, in the last resort, make a decision according to its sole good pleasure. But what is their aim, or rather, their dream?

> *They want to make the Mother Grand Lodge the unique sovereign authority over the whole of Masonry throughout the world, in order to condemn every group suspected of being able to overshadow it, to qualify every independent obedience as irregular and schismatic, and above all, to destroy, or at the very least to isolate enemy number one: the Grand Orient of France, which for 190 years has been regarded as a dangerous rival.[1930]*

The remainder of this chapter will examine the various attributes of this Mother Grand Lodge - Mystery Babylon, the Mother of Harlots, as enumerated in Scripture - and relate them to what we know of modern-day English Freemasonry, its heresies, machinations, wealth, and centers of operation.

> *"The inhabitants of the earth have been made drunk with the wine of her fornication."*
> *Revelation 17:2*

As we have learned, the modern New Age Movement began in English Freemasonry's most secret Masonic Lodge, the Quatuor Coronati Lodge of Masonic Research. By investigating eastern mysticism, the Quatuor Coronati discovered that the religion of English Freemasonry is identical to that of Nimrod's Babylon, including the use of drugs, the practice of free sex, and the performing of pagan ritual human sacrifice. Today English Grand Lodge is intoxicating the earth with this idolatry.

> *"The kings of the earth have committed fornication [with her]." "A golden cup [is] in her hand."*
> *Revelation 17:2,4*

The protector of the Priory of Sion's Merovingian kings is aristocratic English Freemasonry, who may be in possession of the golden Grail cup. Rev. J. R. Church relates the legend which places the Grail cup in England:

> *According to the [Priory of Sion] legend, Joseph of Arimathaea took the cup from which Christ drank at the Last Supper and brought it to the cross at Calvary. When Gaius Cassius, a Roman centurion, took his Spear and pierced the side of Christ, Joseph of Arimathaea caught His blood in the golden Cup. The Cup has now come to be known as the Holy Grail... In the years that followed, Joseph of Arimathaea was said to have taken the Holy Cup to England, where he and his offspring became the Guardians of the Grail.[1931]*
> *"A golden cup... full of abominations and filthiness..."*
> *Revelation 17:4*

[1930] de Poncins, *Freemasonry and the Vatican* 106-111.
[1931] Church 53.Rev. Church elaborates more on the Cup on p.76 of his book: "Mary Magdalene reportedly fled Jerusalem in A.D. 70, with her 'sacred' children. She sailed across the Mediterranean to France, bringing the cup from which Christ drank the Last Supper and in which her alleged uncle, Joseph of Arimathaea, had caught the blood of Christ. Some accounts say that Joseph took the Grail on to England, while other accounts hold that Mary Magdalene kept the Grail in France."

Rev. Church elaborates on something even more blasphemous than the Holy Grail legend:

> Now, take a deep breath and consider what I believe to be the greatest heresy of history. These so-called guardians of the Grail have made the cup to become symbolic of another "vessel" which supposedly contained and preserved the bloodline of Christ, namely the body (or perhaps I should say the womb) of Mary Magdalene! This age-old worship of the Magdalene appears to be the result of an esoteric mystery religion, which I believe is described in Revelation 17 as Mystery, Babylon the Great.[1932]

If the Harlot's cup resides in England and is protected there, as Rev. Church suggests in his previous comment, he connects Mystery Babylon to English Freemasonry, albeit indirectly. Rev. Church is of course referring to the Priory of Sion in his statement "an esoteric mystery religion." We know, however, that Sion founded English Freemasonry.

We also know that Mystery Babylon is the union of church and state. British journalist Stephen Knight connects Mystery Babylon to the Anglican Church when he confirms that the Church of England "has been a stronghold of Freemasonry for more than two hundred years."[1933] The Church of England is a state church, in fact, the only remaining state church in the West. And, as we have seen, the British monarch is head of both the Church and Freemasonry.

The American equivalent of the Anglican Church is the Episcopal Church. The influence of the Harlot in the Episcopal Church is revealed by a telling event reported by Rev. Church: "In May, 1984, a four foot bronze statue of the Crucifixion was unveiled at the Episcopal Cathedral of St John the Divine in Manhattan. The figure on the cross was that of a naked woman - complete with undraped breasts and rounded hips."[1934] This work of art which blasphemes the figure of our crucified Savior was created by sculptress Edwina Sandys, granddaughter of the most famous English Freemason of our day, Winston Churchill. It was sculpted in honor of the Masonic- created United Nations' Decade for Women.

The bishop who presides over the Cathedral of St. John the Divine is English Freemason Bishop Moore. In chapter 16 we learned that Moore, who has turned the Cathedral into a Babylonian temple, is a member of Lucis mist, formerly known as the Lucifer Publishing Company. Rev. Church reports how deeply these former Christians have drunk from the cup of Babylonian religion:

> The Cathedral of St. John the Divine is a center for New Age Movement activity. It appears to be yet another symbol in what I call the myth of Mary Magdalene. James Parks Morton, who is the Cathedral Dean, organized the display [of the woman on the cross] and said that it sends a positive message to women. He and his followers thought it reflected a "mystic Christian view that sees Christ as our mother." It is the same pagan concept that promotes Mary Magdalene as the wife of Jesus - and vessel bearing the bloodline of Christ.
>
> In an esoteric sense, the womb of Mary Magdalene becomes the Grail - preserving the bloodline or lineage of Jesus. Her offspring supposedly married into the royal family of the Franks, eventually producing a king to sit upon the

---

[1932] Church 76-77.
[1933] Knight, *The Brotherhood* 240.
[1934] Church 77.

throne - Merovee, from whom has come the so-called sacred Merovingian bloodline.[1935]

All Christians today are under assault. We will soon be a persecuted minority, and the Temples of Babylon, like the Cathedral of St. John the Divine, will lead the charge.

> *"[She is] decked with gold, precious stones and pearls..."*
> *Revelation 17:4*

The wealth of modern Mystery Babylon is surpassed only by the previous wealth of King Solomon. Is it possible that Scarlet's wealth came from the ancient treasury of Solomon?

The value of Solomon's wealth is recorded in I Kings 10 and II Chron. ides 9. Using today's value of gold. Solomon's treasury would be worth approximately $14 billion. History makes no mention of what happened to his treasury after the many plunders of Israel following her Babylonian captivity. Not until the Dead Sea Scrolls were found in the caves at Qumran after World Warn, did the world realize that Solomon's wealth may still be intact.

The Dead Sea Scrolls were deciphered at Manchester University in 1955-1956. One scroll makes "explicit reference to great quantities of bullion, sacred vessels, additional unspecified material, and 'treasure' of an indeterminate kind. It cites twenty-four different hoards buried beneath [Solomon's] temple itself."[1936]

The authors of *Holy Blood, Holy Grail* believe that during the Crusades the Knights Templar discovered Solomon's treasure and carried it to southern France.[1937] Following the 14th century inquisitions of the Templars by the Priory of Sion kings and popes, the wealth apparently came into the possession of Sion, and some of it (if not all) may have been taken to England. or possibly to Switzerland, the strongbox for the Merovingian kings.

At any rate, the Priory of Sion pretends to know the whereabouts of this legendary treasure. In 1981 the authors of *The Messianic Legacy* questioned Pierre Plantard, Grand Master of the Priory of Sion, about the lost Temple treasury. His reply indicated possession: "It will be returned to Israel when the time is right."[1938]

Two years following Plantard's remark, English Freemasonry was implicated in an attempt to locate the Holy of Holies beneath the Temple Mount at Jerusalem. The exposure began on Sunday, February 27, 1983, by United Press International - Washington. Articles across the nation screamed headlines, *Israeli Scholar Claims Temple Discovery.*

Supposedly Dr. Asher Kaufman, a professor of physics at Hebrew University, for 15 years had been tunnelling beneath the Temple Mount to locate the Holy of Holies. He claims to have found it "330 feet north of the Dome of the Rock."[1939]

On November 5,1984, *Newsweek* reported that the backer for Kaufman's "dig" was the Temple Mount Foundation. Eighteen months earlier on April 26, 1983 the *Executive Intelligence Review*, in a "Special Report confirmed: "The Jerusalem Temple [Mount] Foundation was established for one objective: to rebuild the Temple of Solomon in Jerusalem. It was set up, and its objective defined, on the recommendation of Freemasonic

---

[1935] Church 78.
[1936] Baigent et al, *Holy Blood, Holy Grail* 88.
[1937] Baigent 91.
[1938] Baigent et al, *Messianic Legacy* XIII.
[1939] *The Knoxville News-Sentinel* 27 Feb.1983: A-7.

circles in England... The monarchist Freemasonic lodges, in particular the Quatuor Coronati lodge," have arranged the alliance.[1940]

If this venture matures, the implications are enormous. Daniel 9:27, 11:31, 12:11 and Matthew 24:15 indicate that the third Temple must be built before the middle of the Tribulation so that the Beast can set up his image in the Holy of Holies. The orthodox Jews believe, however, that the third Temple will be built by the Messiah.[1941] If so, their Messiah cannot be Jesus Christ, for the third Temple (Tribulation Temple) must be built before the Jews recognize Christ as Messiah. According to Zechariah 13:8-9 and 14:1-9, the Jews will not accept our Savior in that capacity until the end of the Tribulation. Therefore, the messiah of the Jews who will build the Tribulation Temple will be a false messiah.

Isaiah 28:15-18, when compared with Daniel 9:27, appears to confirm that the Jews will accept Antichrist (the Apocalyptic Beast) as the messiah. Oddly, Isaiah's descriptive terminology of the Beast is suggestive of Freemasonry, to which the Jews will apparently attach themselves by treaty in the last days: "We [Jews] have made a covenant with death," says Isaiah, "and with hell are we at agreement; when the overflowing scourge shall pass through, it shall not come unto us: for we have made *lies* our refuge, and under falsehood have we hid ourselves."

God's judgement against Freemasonry is also pronounced by Isaiah in carpenter's terminology: "Judgement also will I lay to the [measuring] *line*, and righteousness to the *plummet:* and the hail shall sweep away the refuge of lies, and the waters shall overflow the *hiding place* [Masonic Lodge]. And your [Israel's] covenant with death shall be disannulled, and your agreement with hell shall not stand..." (When we recall that the Apocalyptic Beast is given the names Death and Hell in Revelation 6:7-8, we can clearly see that the covenant Israel makes with Death and Hell is a covenant with the Beast.)

Daniel 9:27 gives the duration of, and purpose for Israel's covenant:

It is a seven year treaty that will first permit the Jews to build the tribulation Temple and then to reinstate animal sacrifice. (Perhaps, at this time the Priory of Sion will return Solomon's treasures to the Temple.) The treaty, however, will be broken in the middle of the seven years, when the Templar Beast places his own image in the Temple.[1942]

What are the current signs that Israel may rebuild its temple for the third time? We know that contemporary Jewish rabbis are looking for the appearance of their Messiah. We know they have already rejected Christ. The question is, who will they accept as Messiah? Obviously a person, or a nation, or an organization (such as Freemasonry) that will guarantee them the opportunity to rebuild their Temple. And if that entity should suddenly return to the nation of Israel Solomon's vast treasury, the Jews will fall headlong into worshiping that entity as their Messiah.

Arthur Crawford, Bible teacher and pastor of Riverside Bible Church of Columbus, Ohio, confirms that "'Two rabbis have suggested that as far as they are concerned, Messiah could be a set of nations, a world power that guaranteed their integrity, an

---

[1940] Nancy Coker and Al Douglas, "Flirting with Armageddon: the Jerusalem Temple Foundation," *Executive Intelligence Review* (26 Apr.1983): 19-20, 72.

[1941] CNN News 9 Oct.1990.

[1942] Pilgrim, footnote to Daniel 9:24. That image of the Beast, which will be placed in the Temple at Jerusalem in the middle of the Tribulation, may be the All-Seeing Eye of Freemasonry, for "image" in Greek means "resemblance" (Strong, Greek 1504), and the "resemblance" of the "seven eyes of the Lord," which was made by the same mystery religion in Zechariah 5:6, was in fact defined as a "singular eye" in Hebrew (Strong, Hebrew 5869 and 5870).

individual or organization - they don't care. Any of those [say the rabbis] would meet the Biblical prophecies of Messiah."[1943]

> *"The merchants of the earth are [made]rich through [her weaith]"*
> *Revelation 18:3*

If London has controlled the wealth of Solomon since the 14th century, estimated to be worth $14 billion, one can only imagine what that treasury is worth today, after being invested for over 700 years.

These investments certainly would make the merchants of the earth rich. The treasury would also make London the financial center of the world, as Revelation 18 suggests Mystery Babylon must be. According to the *Encyclopaedia Britannica*, "The United Kingdom has one of the world's oldest, most extensive, and most highly developed financial systems, and for many purposes London is still the financial centre of the Western world."[1944]

According to British journalist Stephen Knight, this wealthy city is dominated by Freemasonry. He informs us that London is divided into twenty-five wards, ten of which have their own lodges. "Every ward, without exception, has at least one Freemason among its representatives."[1945]

The twenty-five wards of London are run by a city corporation called the Corporation of the City of London, which has elected representatives. However, the main salaried officers of the Corporation are Masons. "Indeed," says Knight, "it is virtually impossible to reach a high position in Guildhall without being an active Brother... The Corporation of the City of London is so strongly masonic [sic] that many connected with it, some Masons included, think of it as virtually an arm of Grand Lodge. But it must not be forgotten that the City is first and foremost a financial centre."[1946]

Knight confirms statistically that English Freemasonry is capitalistic, monopolistic, and in control of world finance. The result is the accumulation of vast wealth by a few "merchants of the earth":

> *According to confidential statistics, from Great Queen Street, there are 1,677 Lodges in London... Between the hours of eight in the morning and six at night when the City's residential population of about 4,000 swells to 345,000 with the influx of commuters, the Square Mile has the highest density of Freemasons anywhere in Britain.*
>
> *The Royal Exchange, the Corn Exchange, the Baltic Exchange, the Metal Exchange, the Bank of England, the merchant banks, the insurance companies, the mercantile houses, the Old Bailey, the Inns of Court, the Guildhall, the schools and colleges, the ancient markets, all of them have Freemasons in significant positions. Among the institutions with their own lodges are the Baltic Exchange (Baltic Lodge No.3006 which has its own temple actually in the Exchange in St. Mary Axe); the Bank of England (Bank of England Lodge No.253); and Lloyd's (Black Horse of Lombard Street Lodge No. 4255).[1947]*

[1943] Arthur Crawford, *Riverside Bible Church Tape Ministry* (Rev.13:8) tape #64.
[1944] "United Kingdom: Finance," *Encyclopaedia Britannica:Macropaedia*.
[1945] Knight, *The Brotherhood* 224.
[1946] Knight 225.
[1947] Knight 223.

Martin Short, author *of Inside The Brotherhood* (1989), after saying that "Freemasonry's strength in the London HQs of England's clearing banks is more than matched in the regions," builds on the Masonic statistics begun by Stephen Knight. The Midland Bank and Trust Company has its own lodge, the Holden No.2946. There is at least one lodge for members of the Stock Exchange, the Verity No.2739. And nothing can happen at Lloyd's Bank or Lloyd's of London says Short, "without the Lutine Lodge knowing about it."[1948]

A non-Mason working in a British commonwealth bank wrote to Short saying:

> I was in a first hand position to observe [the Masons'] activities and was mesmerized by their blatant self-promotion. I saw people totally unqualified for responsible posts being promoted beyond their ability, to the chagrin and bewilderment of officials who had every right to expect the posts themselves. In the peculiarly school-like methods of assessing bank staff ability, I saw the appalling substandard work of brotherhood members receive all the plaudits while the sterling efforts of more worthwhile staff went unremarked. When promotion openings arose, their nameswere far ahead. Independent assessments of two of these execu- tives...stated they had already been promoted greatly in excess of their ability. Both are now making a frightful mess of their appointments and losing shareholders' funds.[1949]

Short sounds the alarm to why the banking industry is in such a mess. His investigations into court cases involving Masonic bankers who have diverted company funds to crooked brethren prompted him to suggest that "The commercial survival of a company, even a nation, could thus be subverted by Masonic insider-trading."[1950]

The biggest business in London is banking. Revelation 18 states that Mystery Babylon is the financial center of the world. The financial center of the Western world is London, and its banks are controlled by English Freemasonry. The financial center of the Eastern world is Hong Kong, also controlled by London bankers.

According to Rev. Church, the land on which London's financial district is located is owned by the Knights Templar, English Freemasonry's adversary. This fact may be the literal truth of the symbol of Scarlet sitting on the Templar Beast.

THE WHORE OF BABYLON SITS ON SEVEN MOUNTAINS

> I saw a woman sit upon a scarlet coloured beast, full of names of blasphemy, having seven heads and ten horns... The seven heads are seven mountains, on which the woman sitteth... And the woman which thou sawest is that great city, which reigneth over the kings of the earth (Revelation 17:3, 9, & 18).

The Whore of Babylon has often been identified with the Roman Catholic Church, in part because Rome is literally built on seven hills. Bible prophecy scholars have often taken this Scripture literally, look. mg to Rome as the seat of the Whore of Babylon. Rev. Hislop's book, *The Two Babylons*, was partially based upon this premise.

Biblical commentators English and Bower give us another understanding of the word "mountain," however. Commenting on Psalms 72:3, they state that "[t]he word *mountain*

[1948] Short 358-369.
[1949] Short 366.
[1950] Short 367.

in the Scriptures often speaks of political and governmental powers and kingdoms; *hills* are lesser powers, small states."[1951]

With this understanding of *mountains and hills*, we can look at this passage of Scripture in a new light. According to Revelation 17:9, the seven mountains on which the Whore sits are not literal mountains, but are the same seven heads (or world powers) of the Beast. William Goetz, in *Apocalypse Next*, identifies six of them as historic world powers: Egypt, Assyria, Babylon, Persia, Greece, and Rome.[1952] All six empires had a profound, yet singular effect on Israel.

At the time of John's vision (90 A.D.), the seventh head or power had not yet come into being. Revelation 17:10-11 gives us a clue as to when the seventh will arise: "And there are seven kings: five are fallen, and one is, and the other is not yet come; and when he cometh, he must continue a short space. And the beast that was, and is not, even he is the eighth, and is of the seven..."

Of the seven kings here mentioned by John, the "one (king that] is" is the existing empire of his time: Rome. Rome, then is the sixth head or power. What, then, is the seventh world power that "must continue a short space"? Clearly, the eighth head, and not the seventh, is the Apocalyptic Beast. The prophet Daniel (in chapters 2, 7, and 8) saw the Beast as revived Rome. Therefore, the seventh head cannot be revived Rome, for revived Rome is reserved for the Beast's eighth head.

The phrase "[the seventh] must continue a short space," indicates that the seventh world power must rise and fall rapidly, sometime between the sixth (old Rome) and the eighth (new Rome). To discover what nation the seventh world power is, we must look at the distinctive features of the previous six, for all seven have the same characteristics.

First, the six were controlled by sun-worshipping Mystery Babylon (Revelation 17:9). Second, each had a profound, yet singular effect on Israel. John adds two more distinctions for identifying the seventh. In Revelation 17:10 he informs us that the seventh must be short-lived.

And in Revelation 12:13 & 18, John indicates that Israel must be reconstituted a nation before the eighth (the Beast) can arise.

Israel was reconstituted a nation in 1948. Therefore, the seventh head had to have been a nation that (1) rose and fell rapidly sometime before 1948; (2) worshipped the sun-god; (3) was controlled by modern Mystery Babylon (English Freemasonry); and (4) had a profound effect on the Jews.

Clearly, the seventh head or world power is Nazi Germany, for Germany under Nazism fits the above-mentioned criteria. It rose and fell rapidly before 1948. It worshipped an occult ideology and figure whose emblem was the swastika, which we have seen is an eastern occult symbol of the sun. Germany and Hitler were supported and raised up by the powers and personages of English Freemasonry. And it conducted systematic genocide against the Jews.

Listed below are the seven historic world powers, their sun gods and the profound, yet singular effect of each on Israel:

World Power Sun god Effect on Israel

    1. Egypt Osiris The Exodus about 1400 B.C
    2. Assyria Baal Scattered the ten northern tribes in 721 B.C.
    3. Babylon Marduk Took Judah and Benjamin captive in 606 B.C.
    4. Persia Zoroaster Sent a remnant back to Jerusalem in 536 B.C.
    5. Greece Zeus Prepared the Jews for the first coming of the Messiah.
    6. Rome Jupiter Scattered the Jews among the Gentile nations in 70 A.D

[1951] Pilgrim, footnote to Psalms 72:3.
[1952] Goetz 188-190.

7. Nazi Germany Swastika, Holocaust forced Jews symbol of the sun. to resurrect Israel in 1948.

THE SEVEN HEADS AS HISTORIC AND END-TIME

And I stood upon the sand of the sea, and saw a beast rise up out of the sea, having seven heads and ten horns, and upon his horns ten crowns... And the beast which I saw was like unto a leopard, and his feet were as the feet of a bear, and his mouth as the mouth of a lion...

And here is the mind which hath wisdom. The seven heads are seven mountains, on which the woman sitteth.

Revelation 13:1-2 & 17:9

The body of the seven-headed and ten-horned Beast consists of a leopard, a bear and a lion. The composite nature of the Beast may represent three regions of the world. The seven heads are historically identifiable nations by the time the Beast, the eighth horn, rises to power. Yet, Revelation 17:9 appears to indicate that the seven heads are also seven end-time nations, for the Whore of Babylon "sitteth" (present tense) on seven mountains.

There are several prophecies in Scripture which (like Revelation 17:9) set a dual prophetic precedence. One is found in Daniel 11, where the prophet is foretelling the rise and fall of the Grecian empire. According to English and Bower, verse 21 is a prophecy of the rise of Antiochus Epiphanes, who ruled Syria three centuries later (around 175 B.C.). As Daniel's vision unfolds, the commentators state that it is evident Antiochus becomes a type of the Tribulation Beast.[1953] Thus, Daniel's one prophecy covered two future events - one 300 years from his time and one to occur at the end-time. Likewise, the seven heads on the Beast in Revelation 17:9 appear to refer to historic nations as well as to nations existing at the end-time.

THE SEVEN-NATION TRILATERAL COMMISSION

Ancient Mystery Babylon sat on, or controlled, six historic world powers. Modern Mystery Babylon - English Freemasonry - sat on, that is, funded and controlled, the seventh, Nazi Germany. Likewise, English Freemasonry is today in control of the contemporary seven-nation Trilateral Commission (TC).

The Trilateral Commission is a third generation offspring of English Freemasonry. The first generation offspring is the Round Table. The second generation consists of the three Round Table Groups: the Council on Foreign Relations (CFR), the Royal Institute of International Affairs (RIIA), and the Institute of Pacific Relations (IPR). From the Round Table Groups sprang the third generation in 1973, the Trilateral Commission, which was then given the task of implementing English Freemasonry's concept of one-world idealism.[1954]

The "Tri" of trilateral of course refers to three regions of the world: North America, Western Europe and Japan. This division may also correlate with the three-part body of the Beast. "Commission" bespeaks the function given the Trilateral Commission by English Freemasonry: "to foster closer cooperation among [these] three regions..."[1955]

[1953] Pilgrim, footnote to Daniel 11:21.

[1954] Antony C. Sutton and Patrick M. Wood, *Trilaterals Over Washington* (Scottsdale, AZ: The August Corp., 1978) 2.

[1955] Sutton 1.

The nation members of the Trilateral Commission are the seven most potent industrial powers in the world: the United States of America, Canada, Great Britain, France, Germany, Italy and Japan. Membership also includes the heads of major oil companies, multinational corporations and international banks. Aristocrats and politicians are members as well, including our past President, George Bush. Our current President, Bill Clinton, is a member of the Bilderbergers, which we know is a cover for English Freemasonry's Round Table. And as a Rhodes Scholar, Clinton is an Anglophile (See Masonic details about President Clinton in Appendix 10).

Since its founding the Trilateral Commission has met annually to discuss solutions to common problems that hinder English Freemasonry's goal of controlling world government. A few months following each annual meeting, the heads of State of the seven industrial powers hold a Summit to work out a strategy for implementing the solutions - a strategy that often involves each nation's legislature. Of course, the subversive law makers are Anglophile politicians groomed by the Round Table Groups to assure passage of any bill that would serve the special one-world interest of English Freemasonry.

Indeed, John's "seven mountains, on which the woman sitteth," appear to be the seven-nation Trilateral Commission, on which English Freemasonry "sitteth."

JEREMIAH INDICATES THAT MODERN BABYLON IS LONDON

Babylon was the dominant world power when Jeremiah prophesied. Some of his prophecies were pronounced and carried out upon the Babylon of his day. Others were directed at a future Babylon, which name describes an entity, not a literal city of Babylon. We should not, for instance, be looking for the literal city of Babylon in modern Iraq to be rebuilt to fulfill Jeremiah's end-time prophecy.

Jeremiah 51:13 describes the location of the end-time spiritual Babylon: "O you who dwell by many waters, Abundant in treasures, Your end is come, The measure of your end."[1956]

Taken literally, this cannot mean modern Iraq, since Iraq is not surrounded by "many waters," nor "Abundant in treasures." Great Britain, however, is "Abundant in treasures." She is also completely surrounded "by many waters" - the Atlantic Ocean to the west, the North Sea to the north and east, and the English Channel to the south.

In verse 42, Jeremiah says, "The sea has come up over Babylon; She has been engulfed with its tumultuous waves." Taken figuratively, "sea" means peoples, as in Revelation 17:15: "The waters which you saw where the harlot sits, are peoples and multitudes and nations and tongues."[1957] London boasts of having every nationality within its city limits.

FREEMASONRY HAS NAMED QUEEN ELIZABETH "QUEEN OF BABYLON"

An interesting Scripture concerning the Mother of Harlots is found in Revelation 18:7. It reads, "How much she hath glorified herself, and lived deliciously, so much torment and sorrow give her: for she saith in her heart, I sit a queen, and am no widow, and shall see no sorrow."

[1956] Bible, New American Standard.
[1957] Bible, New American Standard.

Could this Scripture signify the seat of Mystery Babylon, as well as allude to an actual queen sitting on the modern Babylonian throne? Consider Queen Elizabeth II of England. As head of State she is Patroness of English Freemasonry and head of the Church of England. Her consort, Prince Philip, 3rd Duke of Edinburgh, is a Mason. The Grand Master of the British Brotherhood is the Duke of Kent, the Queen's cousin.[1958]

In January 1983 the Queen and her consort toured the United States. There seemed to be no apparent reason for her visit, other than the honor bestowed on her by the Bohemian Club of California during the last evening of her stay. It was quite an extravaganza.

The Bohemian Club is a West Coast center for the inner elite of Templar Scottish Rite Freemasonry in the United States. Some of its members are Senator Alan Cranston, former FBI and CIA Director William Webster, former Secretaries of State George Shultz and Henry Kissinger.[1959]

On February 3, 1983, a five minute segment of the Bohemian Club's extravaganza in honor of Queen Elizabeth was aired on all three television networks. The event began with a view of the Queen sitting slightly high in the middle of the auditorium, as if on top a pyramid. Two dancers entered the stage wearing huge hats hanging from cable. The cone of the first hat was representative of a walled city with a pyramid, or ziggurat towering in the middle. Obviously, it portrayed ancient Babylon. At the base of the pyramid two doors continuously flapped open and shut displaying inside a large picture of Prince Charles, successor to the British throne, and his wife, Princess Diana. As the dancer and hat moved stage right the second dancer entered from stage left. The cone on the second hat portrayed the city of London, with Big Ben towering in the center. When both dancers centered themselves, with the brims of the huge hats reaching from one end of the stage to the other, a voice bellowed, "Oh Queen, you have traversed the ages from Babylon to London!" Ever so slightly, and without a smile, Queen Elizabeth nodded as if in agreement to the statement.[1960]

That night the Bohemian Club, an arm of Templar Scottish Rite Freemasonry, acknowledged London as the seat of Mystery Babylon. Queen Elizabeth accepted that acknowledgment. If London is the city that the Apostle John saw in his vision, Queen Elizabeth's life and nation will be short-lived if Jesus Christ does not tarry - for who knows better the headquarters of its rival than the ruthless French Knights Templar Scottish Rite of Freemasonry.

THE END-TIME DESTRUCTION OF MYSTERY BABYLON

There will come a time when God will no longer tolerate the sins of Mystery Babylon and will destroy her. Before that happens, however, God in His mercy warns His people to sever their relationship with the Whore of Babylon. In Revelation 18:4-5, God warns: "Come out of her, my people, that ye be not partakers of her sins, and that ye receive not of her plagues. For her sins have reached unto heaven, and God hath remembered her iniquities."

Revelation 17:12-18, and all of Revelation 18, record the end-time destruction of Mystery Babylon. The holocaust is so rapid and complete that it can only be accomplished by modern nuclear weaponry. Revelation 18:10-11 describes the financial depression that this destruction will bring upon the whole earth: "Alas, alas that great city Babylon, that

---

[1958] Knight, *The Brotherhood* 26, 211, 215.

[1959] *Investigative Leads* 25 Feb.1983: 5 and Brian Lanze, White Paper for *IL* (13 Jan.1982): 8.

[1960] When this five minute newscast came on television I was stunned, so stunned I obviously had no time to record it. I have told the story as I recalled it. My mother, residing in another part of the country, saw the same newscast. We verified our stories.

mighty city! for in one hour is thy judgment come. And the merchants of the earth shall weep and mourn over her; for no man buyeth their merchandise any more."

The headquarters of Mystery Babylon cannot be Rome. It should be obvious that if Rome were obliterated by a nuclear bomb today, the world economic system would not suffer. Conversely, if London, the financial capital of the world, were likewise destroyed, the world economic system would suddenly halt, as indicated in the Scripture above.

English Freemasonry is the Mother of Harlots. London is Mystery Babylon. "Ground Zero" is at 10 Duke Street, St. James's, London, England SWI - the 33rd degree Supreme Council Headquarters of English Freemasonry.[1961]

[1961] Knight, *The Brotherhood* 40.

26. IN SEARCH OF THE BEAST EMPIRE

And there are seven kings: five are fallen, and one is, and the other is not yet come; and when he cometh, he must continue a short space. And the beast that was, and is not, even he is the eighth, and is of the seven, and go eth into perdition. And the ten horns which thou sawest are ten kings, which have received no kingdom as yet; but receive power as kings one hour with the beast. These have one mind and give their power and strength unto the beast... these shall hate the whore, and shall make her desolate...

Revelation 17:9-13, 16

Scripture sometimes expresses the Beast as a nation and at other times as a person. As a person the Beast is so integrated with his empire that Beast and empire become one. In our search for the Beast, whether man or empire, it is significant to understand that Scripture teaches that the Beast will sign a treaty with Israel, guaranteeing her seven years of peace. With that guarantee the Jews will accept the Beast as Messiah.[1962]

It is worthwhile to recall again the statement made by Arthur Crawford, pastor and Bible teacher from Riverside Bible Church in Columbus, Ohio, on the who or what of the Beast-Messiah: "Two rabbis have suggested that as far as they are concerned, Messiah could be a set of nations, a world power that guaranteed their integrity, an individual, or organization - they don't care. Any of those [according to the rabbis] would meet the Biblical prophecies of Messiah."[1963]

In our search for the Beast, we are looking only for the empire and not the man.

We learned in the previous chapter that the seven heads of the Beast are (at the writing of this book) historic world powers - Nazi Germany being the seventh. Revelation 17:11 states that the eighth is the Beast empire. In Daniel 7:7, the prophet says that this Beast is different "from all the beasts that were before it." In Daniel 11:36-39 the prophet explains how the end-time Beast shall differ from all other previous gods, tyrants, and evil-doers:

And the king [end-time Beast] shall do according to his will; and he shall exalt himself, and magnify himself above every god, and shall speak marvellous things against the God of gods, and shall prosper till the indignation [his image in the Jewish Temple] be accomplished: for that that is determined shall be done. Neither shall he regard the God of his fathers, nor the desire of women, nor regard any god: for in his estate shall he honour the God of forces: and a god whom his fathers knew not shall he honour with gold, and silver, and with precious stones, and pleasant things. Thus shall he do in the most strong holds with a strange god, whom he shall acknowledge and increase with glory.[1964]

That the Beast disregards traditional gods suggests that he will take his government out from under the mystic control of the Whore of Babylon (English Freemasonry). He

---

[1962] Bible, Pilgrim Edition, Daniel 9:27 and footnote to Daniel 9:24 and Revelation 13:14.

[1963] Arthur Crawford, Revelation 13:8, audio cassette, rec. Riverside Bible Church, Worthington, OH., tape (II) #64.

[1964] Bible, Pilgrim Edition, footnote to Daniel 11:21. This is a prophecy of Antiochus Epiphanes, the king who ruled Syria approximately 175 B.C. As the prophecy unfolds, Epiphanes becomes a type of the Apocalyptic Beast.

will replace the traditional gods with "a strange god" called "the God of forces," whom he "increase[s] with glory."

What does the prophet Daniel mean by the phrase "the God of forces"? The Hebrew word *for forces* literally means "fortified place, fortress, or strength." Figuratively it means "defense."[1965] The word *strange* means "to respect."[1966] The Beast will "increase" this god "with glory." The word *increase* means to "build up."[1967] And, the word glory means "riches."[1968]

With these definitions in mind, we can interpret the passage as follows:

> *Daniel is revealing that the god of the end-time Beast will be an awesome "defense" force that the world "respects" - a defense force that is "built up" with "riches." We know that today's military armament is promoted as "defense," and that, ironically, military budgets are called "defense budgets." Revelation 13:4 confirms the awesome defense capability of the Beast: "Who is like unto the beast? Who is able to make war with him?"*

Confirmation that we are living in the days prophesied by John and Daniel is also found in the world's monetary outlay on armament On June 10, 1991, Reuters news syndicate reported in newspapers across our nation that during the decade of the 1980s, "global spending on arms approached $1 trillion." In 1990 alone, says Reuters, "world spending on the military was about $900 billion." This amounts to spend. mg almost $2 million a minute on war and the weapons of war - an unprecedented amount in the annals of history.

THE BEAST SHALL ARISE OUT OF FRENCH FREEMASONRY

Scripture indicates that the Beast will rely on military might to gain and maintain power. We have in the course of this book seen how all French Masonic-backed revolutions have used military might, violence and terror to achieve their ends. We can conclude that the Beast will be a nation that, with the help of French Freemasonry, will cast out by revolution the horn of a monarchy and form a new nation. When this new nation matures, it will become a mighty nation with an awesome defense force - a nation that will, with one exception, have the same characteristics of ancient Rome.

The exception? The Beast will not follow the Mystery Babylonian religion of English Freemasonry, but will instead follow the atheist-humanist tradition of French Freemasonry.

The allegiance of the Beast to French Freemasonry is confirmed in Scripture. You recall that French Freemasonry declared in 1877 that there is no God. It proclaimed its secular humanism in the motto, "To the Glory of Humanity." Likewise, the Beast regards no god. And like French Freemasonry, which made a god of humanity, the Beast then "exault[s] himself, and magnif[ies] himself above every god..."

Is there further Scriptural evidence to support this interpretation of the nature of the Beast? Dr. Alfred Rehwinkel in his book *The Flood* (1952) says Jesus prophesied an end-time world of atheist-humanists. In Matthew 24:37 Christ tells His disciples that the last days will be as it was in the days of Noah. Rehwinkel says that "The generation before

---

[1965] Strong, *Hebrew* #4581.
[1966] Strong, *Hebrew* #5236 from prim. root 5234.
[1967] Strong, *Hebrew* #7235.
[1968] Strong, *Hebrew* #3515 from prim. root 3513.

the Flood was not a pagan or idolatrous race."[1969] He says they were godless Rehwinkel points to archaeological evidence which supports Scripture and his thesis, quoting Sir Charles Leonard Wooley, a British archaeologist, who has noted, "'In no single [prehistoric] grave has there been any figure of a god, any symbol or ornament that strikes one as being of a religious nature."[1970]

The Old Testament offers further insight into the atheistic, amoral humanism of the Beast and his antediluvian precursors. Genesis 6:4 informs us what antediluvian humanity was like: "There were giants in the earth in those days; and also after that, when the sons of God came in unto the daughters of men, and they bare children to them, the same became mighty men which were of old, men of renown."

Rehwinkel unravels the enigmas of this passage from Genesis and applies it to the atheistic humanists of our day and world:

> The Hebrew word [nephilim] means more than what we understand by the term "giant." It means those that fall upon others, brigands, thugs, tyrants. These nephilim were famous in that world. They had made a great name for themselves through their acts of violence, lawlessness, and corruption. They were known by all, and their statues were probably found in the antediluvian shrines of honor.
>
> There are nephilim, or giants, in the world today. They are the men who rule this world. They hold their councils in secret They dispose of countries and millions of human beings as so many figures on a chessboard. They confiscate property that does not belong to them and condemn millions of innocent people to a horrible death of misery and starvation. They blot out whole cities of men, women, and children, with hell-born missiles of death, but they are applauded as great men and renowned, and their portraits and statues are given a place of honor in the halls of fame in our world today.[1971]

Rehwinkel suggests that the "sons of God" were not supernatural beings, but powerful men who considered themselves as gods a humanistic philosophy which follows atheism.[1972] Likewise, we see that Daniel's Beast is atheistic because he "regards no god." The Beast reveals his humanist face when he declares himself as god. If the Beast-god arises out of French Freemasonry, it is understandable why (according to Revelation 17:16) he will destroy his competitor, English Freemasonry, which believes in many gods.

The apostle John also suggests that the Beast kingdom will come out of French Freemasonry. In Revelation 13:1, he saw the Beast "rise up out of the sea." The *sea* here is a figure of speech for the mass of people upon the earth, as Revelation 17:15 explains: "The waters which thou sawest... are peoples, and multitudes, and nations, and tongues." The French Masonic revolutions sprangfrom the grass roots of mass movements, and these movements then created democratic republics run by the people and for the people.

Unlike English Freemasonry, which wants a world government run by an elite aristocracy, French Freemasonry is working feverishly toward a Universal Democratic Republic run by the people. If the Beast arises out of French Freemasonry, naturally the Beast's empire will be a democratic republic, as was ancient Rome.

[1969] Alfred M. Rehwinkel, *The Flood* (St. Louis, MO: Concordia Publishing House, 1951) 53.

[1970] Rehwinkel.

[1971] Rehwinkel 349-350.

[1972] Rehwinkel 344-346.

ARE THE TEN CROWNS ON THE SEVENTH HEAD, OR THE EIGHTH?

Clarence Larkin, in *The Book of Revelation* (1919), pictures the Beast as having seven heads with ten crowned horns on the seventh head.[1973] At first reading this would appear to be the description in Revelation 13:1: "And I stood upon the sand of the sea, and saw a beast rise up out of the sea, having seven heads and ten horns, and upon his horns ten crowns...

Revelation, however, does not specifically state that the ten horns are on the seventh head. Which head the crowned horns are on is a matter of interpretation. It could be that the ten horns are actually the eighth head in Revelation 17:10-11: "And there are seven kings: five are fallen, and one is, and the other [the seventh] is not yet come; and when he cometh, he must continue a short space. And the beast that was, and is not, even he is the eighth, and is of the seven...

In Revelation 13:3 we learn that one of the Beast's heads seemed to 'have a mortal wound, but its mortal wound was healed."[1974] By interpreting the wounded and healed head in this passage as the seventh and eighth heads in Revelation 17:11, Larkin pictures the two as being one. He does this by changing the word "seven" to "seventh." He writes, "even he is the eighth, and is of the seventh..."[1975]

Since he was writing in 1919, Larkin's interpretation is understandable; he wrote before the rise of Nazi Germany, the seventh head. Larkin agrees with Scripture that the Beast is the eighth head. But it is a matter of interpretation whether the Beast actually came out of the "seven[th]" head or out of one of the "seven."

Since 1919 we have been given almost three-quarters of a century of history to be illumined by Bible prophecy. We can hold this history up to Scripture and see what, from these years, is a possible fulfillment of prophecy. We can now see that the eighth head is not "of the *seven[th]*" for John describes his visions of the eighth head as if he himself were contemporary with the end times: "And the beast that was [sixth head of old Rome], and is not [slain head, or demise of old Rome], even he is the eighth [healed head, or revived Rome]..." Notice that John skips the seventh head, which we believe is Nazi Germany.

Our hypothesis is that the ten crowns (ten kings) are on the eighth head. This understanding is further strengthened by verse 12, where it is written that the Beast gives power to the ten kings, and by verse 13 where we are told "These [ten kings] have one mind, and shall give their power and strength unto the beast [eighth head]."

FRENCH FREEMASONRY PLACES THE TEN CROWNS ON THE HEAD OF THE BEAST

Who or what are the "ten crowns" or kings that will adorn the head of the Beast? Prophecy scholars believe that the ten kings in Revelation 17:12 will be ten of the twelve member nations which make up the European Economic Community (EEC), or European Common Market. These scholars view the Common Market as the revived Roman empire, since the Common Market encompasses the western territory of the old Roman

---

[1973] Clarence Larkin, *The Book of Revelation* (Philadelphia: Clarence Larkin Estate, 1919) 103.
[1974] Bible, RSV.
[1975] Larkin 122.

empire. They believe the EEC is the embryo of the Beast, the eighth world power recorded by John.

Grand Orient Freemasonry was the force behind the Treaty of Rome, which formed the EEC in 1957. Every president of the EEC has since been a Grand Orient Mason. Its current head (1993) is France's president, Francois Mitterrand[1976], the most powerful 33rd degree Grand Orient Mason in Europe.

In 1957 the original signatories of the Treaty of Rome were six nations: France, West Germany, Italy, Belgium, The Netherlands, and Luxembourg. Their intent is eventually to unite Europe, a desire of French Freemasonry as far back as Napoleon Bonaparte, and that emerged again in 1848 when the Grand Orient first mentioned by name the idea of inaugurating the United States of Europe.

Dr. Walter Hallstein, 33rd degree Grand Orient Mason and past president of the EEC, detailed the vision of a United Europe in a speech in the 1960s:

> *Three phases of the European unification are to be noted. First, the customs union, second, the economic union, third, the political union... what we have created on the way to uniting Europe is a mighty economic-political union of which nothing may be sacrificed for any reason. Its value exists not only in what it is, but more in what it promises to become... We may fully expect the great fusion of all economic, military, and political communities together into the United States of Europe.[1977]*

Charles de Gaulle, president of France from 1958 to 1969, used the EEC as an instrument in the service of French interests, attempting once in 1963 to unite Europe under its banner, with France the leader. De Gaulle failed when opposed by West Germany.[1978]

De Gaulle did, however, successfully oppose in 1958 and 1963 two attempts by Great Britain to join the EEC. For economic survival, London organized in 1959 the seven-nation European Free Trade Association (EFTA) with Austria, Norway, Portugal, Sweden, Switzerland, Finland, and Iceland. The purpose of the EFTA was to reduce tariffs on imports received from member countries.[1979]

As described in Revelation 17:9, this combination of seven nations could be considered the Whore of Babylon (English Freemasonry) sitting on seven heads. The EFTA, however, ceased operation when England, Denmark, and Ireland were allowed to join the European Common Market in 1973, the same year the seven-nation Trilateral Commission was founded by the Anglophile CFR.

In 1981 Greece joined the Common Market, increasing the total to ten. Bible prophecy scholars were ecstatic. Since then Spain and Portugal have joined. The EEC, however, is still considered by prophecy scholars as part of the future revived Roman Empire, which entity, if this interpretation is correct, will in God's time consist of ten nations.

The EEC inaugurated the United States of Europe (USE) on December 31, 1992 - seven years to the day of year 2000. Ten of the twelve nations voted to accept the Eurodollar as common currency. The two holdouts were England and Ireland. In July 1993, both nations voted to accept the European currency. Although there are still twelve

---

[1976] "The prophetic truth about Eastern Europe," *The Gospel Truth*,30.12 (Dec.1989): 3.

[1977] Goetz 116.

[1978] "Gaulle, Charles de," *Encyclopaedia Britannica: Macropaedia*.

[1979] "Economic History Since 1500: Internationalism. The Common Market," *Encyclopaedia Britannica: Macropaedia* and "European Free Trade Association (EFTA), *Encyclopaedia Britannica: Micropaedia*.

nations in the EEC, when the Beast burns London, Ireland will fall too, and there will be ten nations.

THE VISION OF THE BEAST EMPIRE IS CONFUSING TO THE PROPHETS

The struggle between English and French Freemasonry has produced such a convoluted body of entangled nations, with so many conflicting interests, that it can only be described as a Beast. For example, four of the nations in French Freemasonry's European Common Market are also members of English Freemasonry's seven-nation Trilateral Commission - England, France, Germany, and Italy.

In looking at this convoluted mess, the prophet Daniel could hardly describe what he saw. He recorded in Daniel 7:7 that it was "dreadful and terrible, and strong exceedingly... and it was diverse from all the beasts that were before it..."

The apostle John appears to have had the same problem in his description. His account of the seven heads as seven nations and ten crowns as ten kings leave the reader asking where the crowns are located on the body of the Beast. John did not specifically mention on which of the seven heads (or eight) the ten horns were mounted. Although we believe they are on the eighth head, the debate continues among Bible prophecy scholars to this day.

The Beast's body, according to Revelation 13:2, is made up of a leopard, the head (or teeth) of a lion and the feet of a bear. Interestingly, the national emblems of England and Russia are the lion and the bear respectively. What nation the leopard represents is not yet clear. One fact is for certain, the ten European nations, or ten crowns in Revelation 17:12, are not the body of the Beast. The ten crowns are separate, as described in John's vision. Likewise, Daniel 7:7-8 reveals the same ten-plus-one Beast: "After this I saw in the night visions, and behold a fourth beast... and it had ten horns. I considered the horns, and, behold, there came up among them another little horn..."

Bible commentators English and Bower state that the "little horn" is the same as the Beast, or the eighth world kingdom mentioned in Revelation 17:11.[1980] John said the Beast comes out of the seven, which means the Beast kingdom may come from both the historical seven empires and the end-time seven-nation Trilateral Commission. Daniel said the Beast comes up from among the ten, which means it may come from one of the twelve Common Market nations. By placing the three groups of nations side by side, we should be able to determine which kingdom or nation is the Beast kingdom by focusing on the one listed in all three groups:

Historic Seven	Trilateral Commission	Common Market
1. Egypt	1. United States	1. France
2. Assyria	2. Canada	2. Belgium
3. Babylon	3. England	3. Netherlands
4. Medo-Persia	4. Japan	4. Luxembourg
5. Greece	5. France	5. England
6. Rome	6. Italy (Rome)	6. Ireland
7. Nazi Germany	7. Germany	7. Denmark
		8. Greece
		9. Spain
		10. Portugal
		11. Italy (Rome)
		12. Germany

[1980] Bible, Pilgrim Edition, footnote to Daniel 7:8.

Two nations are in all three columns - Rome and Germany. Many Bible prophecy scholars believe the Beast's headquarters will be based at Rome, especially those who view the Roman Church as Mystery Babylon. This would make the Beast and the Whore reign from the same city, which is unlikely if, as Revelation 17:16-17 says, the Beast permits the ten kings to burn the city of the Whore. In the process he would permit the burning of his own headquarters.

If the headquarters of the Whore of Babylon is not Rome, but London, then Rome could be a candidate for the headquarters of the Beast.

A revived political Rome does not, however, have to be ruled from old Rome. Daniel says the Beast or "little horn" - which means "new nation" or "young nation" - "came up [from] among" the ten European nations. Therefore, Rome, or any one of the other nine nations could have the same characteristics of ancient Rome. Or the Beast could be an eleventh nation, as the "little horn" suggests. Therefore, the Beast could be a young nation that was born, or "came up [from] among" the ten nations. More accurately stated, the Beast nation is a young nation whose population came from the territory of the ten European nations.

To identify the "little horn," which is revived Rome, we must consider the makeup of ancient Rome. Ancient Rome had 14 basic characteristics before its division by Constantine: (1) it was a democratic republic; (2) it had a divided balance of power; (3) it was based upon specific laws; (4) it protected the rights of Roman citizens; (5) it enforced an international law that all Roman citizens are equal; (6) it had a sordid history of slavery; (7) it operated under a capitalist system; (8) it authorized abortions; (9) it loved what we would call R-rated entertainment; (10) it offered state welfare programs funded by taxes; (11) it had a thriving business in lawsuits; (12) it was the melting-pot of the world; (13) it promoted sports as its favorite pastime; and (14) it displayed as its national emblem the single-headed Eagle with wings spread. After the division, the eagle became doubleheaded.[1981]

GERMANY AS REVIVED ROME

Since the reign of Charlemagne as the first Holy Roman Emperor, German kings have been the most influential rulers in the Holy Roman Empire.[1982] As such, they became the new Caesars, or Kaisers in German. As Rev. Church says, "It seems that Germany plays a far more important role in the fulfillment of Bible prophecy than one might think at first glance. The thought that the future Antichrist could have his roots in Germany becomes more plausible when one considers the historical roots of the empire."[1983]

Germany's historic roots fit many of the requirements of revived Rome. Today Germany is a democratic republic, has a divided balance of power, is based upon specific laws, protects the rights of its citizens, operates under a capitalist system, and has a sordid history of slavery under Nazism.

Germany's most significant historic symbol, and resemblance to ancient Rome, is its national emblem, adopted from Constantine. When Constantine came to power in 306 A.D., he moved his headquarters from Rome to Constantinople in Asia Minor. His Eastern empire became known as the Byzantine Empire, or "the Second Rome." To symbolize the divided empire, Constantine transformed the Roman eagle from a single-head to a double-head. According to *Mackey's Encyclopedia of Freemasonry*, "Upon the

---

[1981] Randy Shupe, *Is America Mystery Babylon the Great?* (Arvada,CO: *The Way, the Truth and the Life Fellowship*, 1990) 93-98.
[1982] Church 82.
[1983] Church 67.

dissolution of that empire, the emperors of Germany, who claimed their empire to be the representative of ancient Rome, assumed the double-headed eagle as their symbol...[1984]

Another reason that Germany could be revived Rome is found in Revelation 13:3. John says of the Beast, "And I saw one of his heads as it were wounded to death; and his deadly wound was healed..."

As we have seen, the seventh head was Nazi Germany. The dividing of Germany into east and west after World War H may indicate the wounding of the seventh head. The "head healed" may refer to the recent reunification of both Germanys in October, 1990.

Germany, however, must be disqualified as revived Rome for two important reasons. First, Revelation 13:4 states that the Beast will be a military power second to none. At present Germany is not that military power, but that could change rapidly. Second, as a member of the European Common Market, Germany is one of the "ten horns," whereas Revelation 17:12 describes the Beast as being separate from the ten. Likewise, Daniel 7:8 describes the Beast, not as the ten horns, but as the "little horn" that "came up [from] among" the ten.

As stated earlier, the "little horn" implies a "young nation." Germany is millenniums old. And the phrase, "came up [from] among [the ten horns]," indicates that this "young nation" will be populated from the territory of the ten nations of the old Roman empire. Again, this cannot mean Germany, for Germany is still primarily populated strictly and proudly by Germanic races.

RUSSIA AS REVIVED ROME

Russia could also be a candidate for the Beast. Under the czars and the Soviets, Russia had a sordid history of slavery. Under the Soviets, Russia was a socialist republic, also with a large gulag slave population. Since December 1991, when the Soviet Union was dissolved, Russia became a democratic republic, and therefore can be considered a young nation (little horn). Moreover, Russia is attempting to operate under a capitalist system, as did old Rome.

Russia's most significant resemblance to old Rome goes back to the fall of Constantinople (the Second Rome) in 1453, when the Turks took that city. From that date, Russia has considered itself as the Third Rome.

In 1472, Ivan Ill was the first Russian emperor to call himself Czar, which is Russian for Caesar.[1985] *Mackey's Encyclopedia of Freemasonry* reports how Russia adopted the double-headed eagle as its emblem: "It was taken by Ivan III as his device on his marriage with Zoe Palaeologa (Sophia), daughter of Thomas of Morea, claimant to the imperial throne of Byzantium... [Ivan III] claimed to be the successor of the Eastern [Roman] Emperors."[1986]

If we are to consider Russia as revived Rome, it must share all the characteristics of ancient Rome. Russia, however, has a long history of failing to protect the rights of her citizens and she certainly is not the melting-pot of the world today. Furthermore, according to the description given in Revelation 13 and 17, the headquarters of the Beast must be in a powerful nation with a strong economic, political and military base, identical to that of ancient Rome. When the Whore's city (London) is destroyed, the economy of the world can quickly be transferred to the headquarters of the Beast kingdom, where it will be controlled by his mark -666. This cannot be Russia. Modern Russia is a nation

---

[1984] "Eagle, Double-Headed," *Mackey's Encyclopedia of Freemasonry*, vol.1.
[1985] "The Cult of Moscow, The Third Rome," *New Solidarity* (19 July 1985): Supplement C.
[1986] "Eagle, Double-Headed."

whose economic stability for three quarters of a century has depended upon financial infusions from the West.

The most significant reason that Russia cannot be the Beast kingdom is that she is not one of the seven historic or contemporary heads of the Beast, as Revelation 17:11 demands. Nor was her nation populated by emigrants from the territory of the old Roman Empire, as Daniel 7:8 requires. Furthermore, Ezekiel 38 and 39 indicates that Russia will be destroyed before the Beast kingdom can have military preeminence.

FRANCE AS REVIVED ROME

France today, under the leadership of 33rd degree Grand Orient Freemason Francois Mitterrand, is preparing for the coming of Antichrist to head the long-awaited French Masonic United States of Europe founded on December 31, 1992. In 1983 Mitterrand hired a Japanese architect, I.M. Pei, to transform the courtyard of the old royal castle into a pyramid. The location of the pyramid is cynically symbolic of Masonry's triumph over both Christianity and the monarchical rule of France. Pei's pyramid is made of triangular glass windowpanes. The weekly *Insight* magazine, July 3, 1989 tells the story:

> *The number of windowpanes in Pei's pyramid - said to be 666- and the form of the pyramid itself are reflections of the president's [Mitterrand] passion for Masonic symbols, not to speak of his fondness of communing with the spirits of Earth that leads him every year, druid-like, to celebrate the spring equinox by pounding a wooden stick on a certain hill called Roche de Soultre in central France.[1987]*

France, however, cannot be revived Rome, because it does not have all fourteen characteristics of ancient Rome. For example, France is not the melting-pot of the world, nor does she display the Eagle as her national emblem.

THE UNITED NATIONS AS REVIVED ROME

In Revelation 17 the Beast is initially controlled by the Whore of Babylon, for she is riding on the back of the Beast. We have shown in chapter 24 that the United Nations is currently controlled by English Freemasonry, the modern Whore of Babylon. Moreover, both Free- masonries are allied politically in the United Nations, as they initially appear to be in the Beast. A problem of numbers, however, eliminates the United Nations at the present time as the kingdom of the Beast. The lack of distinct divisions of "ten nations" and "seven nations" in the General Assembly or the Security Council of the U.N. would suggest it is not the Beast.

Furthermore, the United Nations has no real military strength of its own, as the Beast must have. If the United Nations has any significance at all, it is by virtue of the nation on which soil it resides, and nothing more. The U.N.'s strength as a world power exists only because of the military might of the United States of America, and not because of its own power. The limits of U. N. power was effectively demonstrated in the recent war with Iraq - old Babylon. Had it not been for the dominant presence of U.S. armed forces,

---

[1987] Helle Bering-Jensen, "Glass Tips atop a National Treasure," *Insight* (3 July 1989): 58-59.

the U.N. would not have had the military might to back up its demands that Iraq leave Kuwait.

THE UNITED STATES OF EUROPE AS REVIVED ROME

To build a solid case for identifying the Beast kingdom, we must consider more recent developments in Europe, which may cause the European Economic Community (Common Market) to dissolve. The four primary structural organs of the EEC include the Commission, the Council of Ministers, the Court of Justice, and the European Parliament.[1988] The European Parliament inaugurated the United States of Europe on December 31, 1992, exactly seven years to the day from the year 2000, the figure seven being a significant and prophetic number of years.

The United States of Europe, a phrase first coined in 1848 by French Freemasonry, is the much touted precursor to French Freemasonry's world government, and may itself be the ten horns on the head of the revived Roman Empire instead of ten of the twelve Common Market nations. This, of course, would exclude England and Ireland. The fulfillment of the prophecy in Revelation 17:12-13, and 16, indicates how this might happen. In this passage we see that the ten kings in the United States of Europe shall hate the Whore (London) and pledge their allegiance to the Beast. When the Beast gives the ten kings permission to burn London, Ireland will fall too.

THE ULTIMATE TEST WILL IDENTIFY REVIVED ROME

Scripture gives us the required wisdom with which we can irrefutably identify the Beast and his kingdom. This wisdom comes from under-standing the mark of the Beast. Revelation 13:16-18 explains:

> And he [the Beast) causeth all, both small and great, rich and poor, free and bond, to receive a mark in their right hand or in their foreheads: And that no man might buy or sell, save he that had the mark, or the name of the beast, or the number of his name. Here is wisdom. Let him that hath understanding count the number of the beast; for it is the number of a man; and his number is Six hundred threescore and six.

The clue for identifying the Beast nation is found in a series of numbers that are listed as a triad of two numbers each (600 + 60 + 6), which adds up to 666. *Strong's Concordance* informs us that 666 is a Roman numeral.[1989]

Roman numerals, therefore, give the clue of how to identify the mark of the Beast. When the New Testament was written, Rome used a combination of six alphabet letters to make up all its numbers. The letters are: D C L X V I. (The letter "M" representing 1000 is a more recent invention. Originally it was CIC, with the right-hand C turned

---

[1988] "European Economic Community," *Encyclopaedia Britannica:Micropaedia*.
[1989] Strong, *Greek* #5516.

backwards. By connecting the two "C's" to the "I" in the middle, it gradually evolved into "M").[1990] The six original Roman numerals and their numerical values are:

**D - 500 **
I- 600
C - 100 /
**L - 50 **
I - 60
X - 10 /
**V -5 **
I - 6
I - 1 /
Total 666

When we group each of the letters above in order of two's we discover the exact fulfillment of Revelation 13:18. DC equals 600; LX equals 60; and VI equals 6 - "Six hundred threescore and six."

Applying this Scriptural wisdom we discover that the kingdom of the beast will be a revival of the old Roman Empire. Whatever nation this kingdom is, the ultimate test for identification comes from understanding his mark, or symbol, which is 666 in Roman numerals. Scripture says it will be tied to the medium of exchange.

[1990] Shupe 33."M" originally consisted of the letters DC, with the second "C" turned around to face the "I." The combination of these three Roman numerals became an "M" when the two "Cs" were connected to the "I" at the top.

27. HEADQUARTERS OF THE BEAST EMPIRE

> *The world will be at ease - banquets and parties and weddings -just as it was in Noah's time before the sudden coming of the flood: people wouldn't believe what was going to happen until the flood actually arrived and took them all away. So shall my coming be.*
>
> Matthew 24:37-39[1991]

THE ATLANTIS LEGEND

Every ancient culture tells the story of a prehistoric civilization destroyed by flood. Apart from the Biblical account of Noah's flood, the most renowned is the legend of the sinking of Atlantis. Ignatius Donnally, in *Atlantis; The Antediluvian World*, compares the Biblical account with this Greek legend:

> *The [Biblical] Deluge plainly refers to the destruction of Atlantis, and agrees in many important particulars with the account given by Plato. The people destroyed were, in both instances, the ancient race that had created civilization; they had formerly been in a happy and sinless condition; they had become great and wicked; they were destroyed for their sins - they were destroyed by water.[1992]*

The earliest of secret societies were obsessed with the legend of Atlantis. Freemasonry is no exception. William Still, in *New World Order*, informs us that "[a]ccording to Masonic sources, the most important mystery of secret societies is an ancient plan, passed down for thou-sands of years by oral tradition, for the establishment of a world government - a 'universal democracy' - a 'New Atlantis.'"[1993]

Old Atlantis was believed by Freemasonry to have been a democracy. Legend states that it was also an advanced scientific society. In fact, it is reputed to have been the center of learning. Still explains:

> *Secret societies believe that in Atlantis stood a great university where most of the arts and sciences originated. The structure that housed this university was an immense pyramid with many galleries and corridors, with an observatory for the study of the stars sitting on its immense apex.[1994]*

[1991] Bible, Living Bible edition.

[1992] William T. Still, *New World Order: The Ancient Plan of Secret Societies* (Lafayette, LA: Huntington House, 1990) 42; quoting Ignatius Donnally, *Atlantis: The Antediluvian World* (1976) 192.

[1993] Still 41.

[1994] Still 67.

Mackey's Encyclopedia of Free masonry says that from this legend "developed a long-lasting tale of a continent in the Atlantic, somewhere west of the Straits of Gibraltar, once covered with civilization, which sank suddenly under the waves."[1995]

Explorers have searched for "lost Atlantis" in the Mediterranean, west and south of Africa, South America, and off the east coast of the United States. In 1932 Edgar Cayce (1877-1945), a psychic from Kentucky, reportedly pinpointed Atlantis. To no one's surprise Cayce said it was where Plato had located it, in the Atlantic Ocean, though Cayce did not specify exactly where in that great watery expanse somewhere between the Mediterranean and the Gulf of Mexico. Then, he made another prediction that Atlantis would one day rise up out of the sea near the Caribbean island of Bimini.[1996]

Can we find any connection between the Atlantis of ancient legend and the location of the Beast empire? Surprisingly, the apostle John gives a description similar to Cayce's of the Beast empire in Revelation 13:1: "And I stood upon the sand of the sea, and saw a beast rise up out of the sea, having seven heads and ten horns, and upon his horns ten crowns...

The numbers seven and ten from this verse in Revelation correlate with the Atlantean legend. Still states that "some 10,000 years before the Greek civilization, Atlantis was ruled in complete harmony by a cooperative commonwealth of ten kings, known as the Atlantic League. Seven of these kings ruled over the seven islands that actually made up what was called the 'continent of Atlantis.' The other three kings of the Atlantean kingdom ruled over the other three known continents: Europe, Asia, and Africa."[1997]

The legend states that these ten kings were brothers, which may mean they belonged to a brotherhood similar to Freemasonry. Freemasonry believes the number "10" is significant when applied to government. Manly P. Hall, a 33rd degree Mason, explains:

> *The league of ten kings is the cooperative commonwealth of mankind, the natural and proper form of human government. Atlantis, therefore, is the archetype or the pattern of government, which existed in ancient days but was destroyed...[1998]*

Like the Biblical story, the legend of Atlantis states that its destruction was due in large part to its passion for limitless luxury. No longer did the Atlanteans value goodness above material wealth. Plato says, "The portion of divinity within them was now becoming faint and weak through being ofttimes blended with a large measure of mortality."[1999]

Loving their possessions above all else, the Atlanteans had lost their virtue. And now the seven kings of the seven isles of Atlantis amassed a great army to conquer the three continents. Because of their greed for power, the father of the gods (Zeus) caused the seven islands (seven heads) of Atlantis, with its population, to sink beneath the waves.[2000]

Freemason Hall states that when Atlantis died, so did the "ideal pattern of government." According to Hall, the "league of ten kings" is part of the "Secret Doctrine" preserved by secret societies through their oral traditions. Hall believes that when the unifying force of the ten kings was broken, destruction automatically followed. "So complete was this destruction," he writes, "that men forgot there is a better way of life, and accepted the evils of war and crime and poverty as inevitable... The old Atlantis is

---

[1995] "Atlantis, Lost Continent of," *Mackey's Encyclopedia of Freemasonry,* vol.111.
[1996] "Atlantis: The Eternal Quest," *Mystic Places* (Alexandria, VA: Time-Life Books, 1987) 30-33.
[1997] Still 43.
[1998] Still 44; quoting Manly P. Hall, *The Secret Destiny of America* (1944) 59.
[1999] "Paradise Lost," *Mystic Places* 12.
[2000] "Paradise Lost."

gone, dissolved in a sea of human doubts. But the Philosophical empire would come again, as a democracy of wise men."[2001]

Freemasonry planned long ago to philosophically raise Atlantis out of the sea, and in this new land, reestablish democracy as a New World Order. Masonic author George H. Steinmetz confirms in *Freemasonry: Its Hidden Meaning* that the democratic philosophy of Freemasonry "has been traced back to the 'Lost Continent of Atlantis.'"[2002] He attempts to prove that Atlantis was a Masonic society by suggesting that the destroyed temples of upper Egypt are all part of that Atlantean destruction: "There [in Egypt] we find their ruined temples which, compared with our lodge rooms, have similar floor plans, the same 'dark north,' and many of the same emblems."[2003] Finally Steinmetz says that one cannot understand the universality of Freemasonry without accepting the Atlantean account.[2004]

Hall concurs: "Masonry is a university, teaching the liberal arts and sciences of the soul to all who will attend to its words. It is a shadow of the great Atlantean Mystery School, which stood with all its splendor in the ancient City of the Golden Gates, where now the turbulent Atlantic rolls in unbroken sweep."[2005]

Hall suggests that the antediluvian civilization was democratic, that Freemasonry planned over three centuries ago to recreate a universal democratic society that will philosophically "rise up out of the sea," and like Atlantis, join with ten kings to lead mankind in the pursuit of universal happiness. He says that the Christian Church has delayed the search for the "New Atlantis." And he alludes to the ancient Roman empire as the last attempt at resurrection of the Atlantean project and states that another attempt would be made.[2006]

We can see how Freemasonry's planned resurrection of Atlantis correlates with Daniel's prophecy of a revived Roman empire. Likewise, John's vision of the Beast with ten horns (representing ten kings) is more significant in this regard given the fact that Freemasonry calls for its one-world government to be patterned after the "Atlantean League" often kings. Therefore, to locate the headquarters of Freemasonry's "New Philosophical Atlantis," Daniel's revived Roman empire, and John's Beast, we must search for a land that meets the following requirements:

1. *If old Atlantis was democratic, then New Atlantis will be democratic and most likely be born of Templar French Freemasonry, the father of modern democracy.*

2. *John's Beast and Freemasonry's "Philosophical Atlantis" will figuratively rise up out of the sea in the Atlantic Ocean, somewhere west of the Straits of Gibraltar where old Atlantis was alleged to have sunk.*

3. *If resurrected west of the Straits of Gibraltar, Daniel's revived Rome will be a new land in a new world populated from the territory of the old Roman empire.*

4. *Daniel's uncivilized Beast will be born in an uncivilized western land bordered by water - from Daniel's vantage point at Babylon - a land in the extreme west.*

5. *John's Beast will eventually unite with ten kings as did old Atlantis.*

[2001] Still 43; quoting Hall, *Secret Destiny* 63.

[2002] George H. Steinmetz, *Freemasonry: Its Hidden Meaning* (1948; Richmond, VA: Macoy Masonic Publishing, 1976) 33.

[2003] Steinmetz 33.

[2004] Steinmetz 35.

[2005] Manly P. Hall, *The Lost Keys of Freemasonry* (1923; Richmond, VA: Macoy, 1976) XXI.

[2006] Still 44; quoting Hall, *Secret Destiny* 72.

Unlike Edgar Cayce, Hall is not looking for ancient Atlantis to literally rise out of the sea, but rather, looks to America as the nation that will represent "Philosophical Atlantis." In *America's Assignment With Destiny*, he writes, "The explorers who opened the New World operated from a master plan and were agents of re-discovery rather than discoverers."[2007] In a second book, *The Secret Destiny of America*, Hall claims that the unifying goal of ancient secret societies was to create a "New Atlantis" beyond the Atlantic Ocean, in what is now called America. "The bold resolution," he said, "was that this western continent should become the site of the philosophic empire."[2008]

Still explains that "America, according to this Great Plan, was to become the first nation to begin to establish a 'universal democracy,' or 'world commonwealth of nations.' This quest was said to be the most noble pursuit to which a man could devote himself."[2009]

AMERICA: THE NEW ATLANTIS

The first modern philosopher to promote America as the New Atlantis was Sir Francis Bacon (1561-1626), an English lord and Sionist-Rosicrucian. As an occultist well-versed in the "Great Plan," Bacon concealed the "Secret Doctrine" in a novel entitled *New Atlantis*, in which he laid out the plan for a utopian society to be built on this newly discovered continent. Masonic authors Marie Bauer Hall and Manly P. Hall respectively say of Bacon:

> [Bacon] is the Founder of Free Masonry... the guiding light of the Rosicrucian Order, the members of which kept the torch of true universal knowledge, the Secret Doctrine of the ages, alive during the dark night of the Middle-Ages.[2010]
>
> Bacon had been initiated into the new liberalism represented throughout Europe by secret societies of intellectuals dedicated to civil and religious freedom... Later, when the moment was propitious, he threw the weight of his literary group with the English colonization plan for America... cherishing as he did the dream of a great commonwealth in the New Atlantis.[2011]

Still says, "Baconian scholar and Masonic enthusiast Marie Bauer Hall believes this Great Plan has been perpetuated by an international group of only the highest initiates of the secret societies."[2012]

We have seen how this international group has changed its name many times to conceal the Great Plan. Bacon was the first of modern philosophers to reveal this plan as a Masonic blueprint for America. The hierarchy in his day was the Priory of Sion, operating through the Order of Rose-Croix, and later the Royal Society. It was then usurped by the Knights Templar, who initially operated through the Illuminati, then the Palladian, and now through Lucis mist.

Rosicrucian Sir Walter Raleigh, a member of a secret society named after Bacon (the Baconian Circle), began the British exploration in America in 1585, settling off the coast of North Carolina on Roanoke Island. His colony failed and England did not attempt colonization again for a generation.

[2007] Still 36; quoting Hall, *America's Assignment With Destiny* 49.
[2008] Still 36; quoting Hall, *Secret Destiny* 25.
[2009] Still 36.
[2010] Still 47; quoting Marie B. Hall, *Collections of Emblems* 10.
[2011] Still 47; quoting Manly Hall, *America's Assignment* 59-60.
[2012] Still 49.

Meanwhile, in 1603 the Priory of Sion lost Great Britain to the Templars when James Stuart VI of Scotland ascended the British throne as King James I. German Rosicrucians immediately went into action, founding Rosicrucian Freemasonry in England, then backing Cromwell to dethrone the Templar Stuarts. Many Protestants joined Cromwell's cause. Finally, in 1717 the Stuarts, with their Templar Freemasonry, were deported to France.

During the on-and-off English revolution that spanned the latter half of the 17th century, the New World was colonized by British and European Protestants fleeing persecution. In 1733 English Freemasonry entered America, founding St. John's Lodge at Boston. Boston, in effect, became the Masonic capital of Britain's transatlantic colonies. Between 1733 and 1737, Grand Lodge England chartered additional provincial lodges in Massachusetts, New York, Pennsylvania and South Carolina. These lodges contained only three degrees.

Templar Freemasonry, having been weakened by exile to France, had no strength to establish a base in America. Unimpeded, English Freemasonry planned to inaugurate the Great Plan contained within her Secret Doctrine. Happily for America, most of the settlers were Christian, hence, the Great Plan was forced to operate more slowly from within the newly organized English lodges.

THE TEMPLARS IN AMERICA

One of the requirements of the Beast empire is that it be a democratic nation born of Templar French Freemasonry, the father of modern democracy.

Michael Baigent, co-author of *The Temple and The Lodge,* has traced the movement of the Templars to America. He discovered that Sionist English Freemasonry reigned supreme in Boston until a higher degree Templar lodge was warranted in 1756 by Grand Lodge Scotland. "There were thus two rival Provincial Grand Lodges in Boston," says Baigent, "St. John's, under the aegis of the Grand Lodge of England, and St. Andrew's, under the aegis of Grand Lodge of Scotland... And on 28 August 1769, St. Andrew's conferred, for the first time anywhere in the world, a new Freemasonic degree - specifically called the Knights Templar Degree."[2013]

Shortly thereafter another form of Templar Freemasonry came to America. The quasi-Jacobite Grand Lodge of York warranted lodges in Virginia.[2014] York Rite Freemasonry created additional degrees in the New World until it reached the 13th and final degree, known as the Knights Templar degree.

Thirteen-degree Templar York Rite Masonry, having ceased operation in England after establishing its base in the New World, exists today only in North America. Michael Baigent was able to trace the westward migration of the Templars by following their esoteric number "13." As you recall, the original Templar order consisted of thirteen degrees. The number "13" also commemorates Friday the 13th, 1307, the day persecution of the Templars began. In 1314, Jacques de Molay, the Grand Master of the Knights Templar, was burned at the stake. Only in America, says Baigent, has the Templar Grand Master received his most flattering and lavish public homage, in the form of a youth organization sponsored by Freemasonry, the Order of DeMolay.

TEMPLAR MILITARY LODGES

[2013] Baigent and Leigh, *The Temple and The Lodge* 222.
[2014] Baigent and Leigh 203.

The Templars also stealthily entered America through military lodges. Of particular significance are those chartered by the Irish Grand Lodge, which offered the higher degrees of Jacobite Masonry. Later these lodges incorporated the French Templar Scottish Rite degrees, further dividing colonial America between two rival forms of Freemasonry. While British politics in the colonies was dominated by English Masons in the Northeast, her military was under the influence of French Templar Field Lodges throughout the colonies - not a stable union for governing "13" rebellious colonies.[2015]

EUROPEAN TEMPLARS SETTLE AMERICA

Another identifying characteristic of the Beast's revived Roman empire, according to our analysis of Daniel 7:7-8 in chapter 26, is that it must be populated by immigrants from the territory governed by the old Roman empire. Of course colonial America was populated by peoples from a Europe shaped by ancient Rome and later by the Holy Roman Empire. Templar influence in America began after Prince Charles Edward, the Young Stuart Pretender, failed to regain his British throne. As you recall, in 1746 he was soundly defeated, forever dashing the hopes of Scottish Templars recapturing England. As a result, many Irish and Scottish Templar Jacobites who had fought with Charles Stuart fled to America. Those who returned to France with the Prince founded the Scottish Rite of Freemasonry.

Between 1745 and 1753, the British and European Templar population in the New World had increased dramatically. In 1754 Benjamin Franklin attempted to relieve population pressure by proposing a plan for the union of all 13 colonies. The British government rejected Franklin's proposal, fearing a united America would be difficult to control. Subsequently, the exploding population was forced to move west into French territory, which precipitated the French and Indian War in America, a phase of the Seven Years War on the continent of Europe. During this war the French military brought to the New World the Templar Scottish Rite, first setting up base at Boston, then Charleston, S.C.[2016] Michael Baigent, in *The Temple and The Lodge*, explains:

Prior to the Seven Years War, most of the Freemasonry in North America was orthodox pro- Hanoverian, warranted by Grand Lodge [London]. During the Seven Years War, however, "higher degree" [Templar] Freemasonry, by means of regimental field lodges, was transplanted on a large scale to the American colonies and quickly took root. Boston - the soil from which the American Revolution was to spring - exemplifies the process of transplantation and the friction that sometimes arose from it.[2017]

BENJAMIN FRANKLIN: TEMPLAR SPY MASTER

Benjamin Franklin became a Mason in February 1731 and Provincial Grand Master of Pennsylvania in 1734, and again in 1749. In 1756 he was inducted into the Royal Society in absensia. (The Royal Society, you may recall, was an English Masonic front organization for the Rosicrucian Priory of Sion.)

Between 1757 and 1762, and again between 1764 and 1775, Franklin spent considerable time in England and France. While in England, he discovered English

---

[2015] Baigent and Leigh 204.Templar Jacobite Freemasonry, you recall, sided with the deposed Scottish Stuart royalty who were exiled to France following Great Britain's Glorious Revolution. Sionist English Freemasonry backed the new Hanoverian royalty.

[2016] Baigent and Leigh 207.

[2017] Baigent and Leigh 221.

Freemasonry's "Secret Doctrine" for America. Franklin was in London in 1775 when he was made aware that war between the colonies and Great Britain might break out at any moment, so in March he returned to Philadelphia. Later that year he attended the Second Continental Congress, through which he helped draft the Declaration of Independence. In 1776 he was sent to Paris where he came in contact with the Illuminati. Franklin learned of the esoteric significance of the number "13" and the Illuminati plan for the "13" American colonies. He stayed in Paris only a short while, returning to America with this important information. On the afternoon of July 4, 1776, he, with two other Masons, were appointed by the Continental Congress to design the Great Seal of the United States of America, which would include the Seal of the Illuminati.

Baigent suggests that Franklin favored the Illuminati plan to create a New World democracy, a "Philosophical Atlantis," over the British plan for an oligarchic expansion of empire. When Franklin was in France, he began to build a spy network in preparation for America's independence from England. Baigent gives us the details:

> On 9 November [1777], a special committee - the "Committee of Congress for Secret Correspondence" - was appointed to establish a network of contacts among "our friends abroad." This committee consisted of Robert Morris, John Jay, Benjamin Harrison, John Dickinson and Benjamin Franklin. It was to operate extensively through Freemasonic channels and to lead to the creation of an elaborate spy network. At the same time, and quite coincidentally, it was to overlap a British spy network which ran parallel to it and also operated through Freemasonic channels. Both networks were to be based primarily in Paris, which became the centre for a vast web of espionage, intrigue and shifting allegiances.[2018]

Spying was not foreign to Franklin. As Deputy Postmaster General for the American colonies from the 1750s until 1775, he became particularly friendly with his British counterpart, Sir Francis Dashwood, who moved in Jacobite Masonic circles. Dashwood also had Masonic friends who were staunch supporters of Charles Edward Stuart. While in England Franklin stayed at Dashwood's estate. Michael Baigent gives us more details about the "traditional" role of spymaster incumbent upon Postmasters-General:

> Because it afforded access to virtually all letters, all communications, the position of Postmaster-General was also traditionally that of spymaster. And during the American War for Independence, their experience as Postmasters-General was to stand both Dashwood and Franklin in good stead.
> In his dual role of spymaster and colonial ambassador to France, Franklin established his centre of operations in Paris. He was accompanied here by two other appointees of the Con- gressional Committee for Secret Correspondence, Silas Deane and Arthur Lee. Lee's brother was based in London. So, too, was Franklin's sister, who is also believed to have been engaged in espionage.[2019]

Franklin's sister introduced Franklin to the Howe brothers, one a General in the British Army, the other an Admiral, both of whom belonged to Templar military lodges in the colonial theater of operation. As Templars they were favorable to the rebellion.

[2018] Baigent and Leigh 233.
[2019] Baigent and Leigh 235-236.

And in fact in 1781 the Howe brothers were accused of "belonging to a 'faction' which conspired to facilitate the colonists' bid for independence."[2020]

Franklin's Templar Masonic friends in the postal service and in the military also had Templar sympathizers in the British Parliament. These traitors to the British Crown clandestinely raised money for the Colonial Continental Army and remitted it to Franklin in Paris. Franklin passed it on to North America, or used it in France to purchase arms and material.

In 1778 Franklin joined the Illuminati lodge "Neuf Soeurs" (Nine Sisters), assisting in the initiation of Voltaire. Later he became Grand Master of the Lodge. In 1782 Franklin joined a more elusive and mysterious Freemasonic conclave, the Royal Lodge of Commanders of the Temple West.

As stated earlier, the British spy network in Paris was also Masonic. Its agents had penetrated Franklin's operation by joining his Nine Sisters' Lodge. Thus, "the British government was kept apprised not only of the colonists' activities, but also of French plans for entering the war."[2021]

British knowledge of the impending colonial revolt did not, however, reach ears in America, because the British colonial high command in charge of the Crown's army and navy in the New World (namely the Howe brothers) were Templar Freemasons solidly in the camp of Franklin. To guarantee the success of the American Revolution, the Howe brothers displayed dilatory conduct throughout the war.

A TEMPLAR AMERICAN REVOLUTION

The war for American independence was a continuation of the battle between English and French Freemasonry. The conflict over the control of "New Atlantis" originated in Boston between two adversarial lodges, Sionist St. John's and Templar St. Andrew's. Among the members of St. Andrew's were John Hancock and Paul Revere. To the south in Virginia were two other Templar Masons, Patrick Henry and Richard Henry Lee, who in 1769 prompted the Virginia Assembly to formally condemn the British government. Events swiftly accelerated toward open conflict between England and her American colonies. In 1770 the famous Boston Massacre occurred when British sentries killed five rioters. In 1771 thirteen rebels were executed for treason in North Carolina. In 1772 two prominent Freemasons, John Brown and Abraham Whipple, had attacked a customs ship off Rhode Island and burned it. In 1773 the British government increased the tax on tea to keep the British East India Company solvent. In retaliation, Templar Masons from St. Andrew's Lodge dressed as Mohawk Indians, boarded the *Dartmouth* in Boston harbor and dumped its tea overboard. This was the famous "Boston Tea Party" that is said to have triggered the American Revolution.[2022]

It took three months for the news of the "Boston Tea Party" to reach London, whereupon the British Parliament declared Massachusetts to be in a state of rebellion. Not realizing the significance of the Masonic division in the colonies, the Crown's action was swift and misguidedly drastic. The "Boston Port Bill," which placed an embargo on all trade with Boston, for example, effectively closed the port[2023], and stiffened colonial resolve against the Crown.

On September 5, 1774, the First Continental Congress convened in Philadelphia to plan action against the British. The Congress was under the presidency of Templar

---

[2020] Baigent and Leigh 236.
[2021] Baigent and Leigh 237.
[2022] Baigent and Leigh 223.
[2023] Baigent and Leigh 225.

Freemason Peyton Randolph, a prominent attorney and Provincial Grand Master of Virginia. Boston delegates included Samuel Adams and Paul Revere. In February 1775, the Massachusetts Provincial Congress met and announced plans for armed resistance. Within a month Templar Freemason Patrick Henry made his famous speech - "Give me liberty, or give me death" - to Virginia's Provincial Assembly. On April 18, 1775, 700 British troops were dispatched outside Boston. Templar Freemason Paul Revere made his famous ride, announcing "The Red Coats are coming!" The Templar bid to take America from Rosicrucian England had begun.[2024]

THE TEMPLARS AND PUBLIC OPINION

Englishman Thomas Paine joined Grand Orient Freemasonry while living in Paris. Shortly before the American Revolution, he returned to England and founded several Grand Orient lodges in that country.

Paine was in London when the Boston Tea Party ignited the American Revolution. In 1774 he embarked for Philadelphia. From the City of Brotherly Love, Paine published Common *Sense*, which "did much to polarize attitudes and convert many hitherto loyal colonists to the principle of independence from the mother country."[2025]

THE TEMPLARS AND THE COLONIAL MILITARY

Before the War of Independence began, the Second Continental congress was still under Templar control with the presidency of Peyton Randolph. When Randolph died, John Hancock of St. Andrew's Lodge became president. On May 10, 1775, the Templar-controlled Congress made its move to control the Colonial military by authorizing the raising of a full-fledged Continental army. George Washington, a prominent Templar Mason under the Virginia Grand Mastership of Randolph, was appointed commander-in-chief of the army. Baigent writes, "Indeed, during the early days of the war, the high command of the Continental Army was dominated by Freemasons."[2026]

Virtually all the military generals under Washington were Templar Masons, most of whom were more qualified than he. Richard Montgomery was a prominent Jacobite Mason from Ireland. David Wooster organized the Templar Hiram Lodge No.1 in New Haven, Connecticut, in 1750. Hugh Mercer of the rebel Jacobite army of Charles Edward Stuart had escaped to Philadelphia in 1746. Arthur St. Clair was descended from the Templar Sinclairs in Scotland. Horatio Gates, a Templar Mason, was one of Washington's closest friends. And Israel Putnam was a member of a Templar military lodge.[2027]

The list could go on. John Dixon, Joseph Frye, William Maxwell, and Elias Dayton. All were Templar Freemasons. Yet, of the many generals more qualified than Washington - generals who could have resented his appointment as commander-in-chief - only one did, Freemason Benedict Arnold. His resentment led to treason.

These American generals repeatedly went against tremendous odds. Each time the British generals backed off, as if they wanted the rebels to win their independence. Baigent gives several examples of how the Howe brothers were slothful in the manner in which they fought the colonists:

[2024] Baigent and Leigh 226.
[2025] Baigent and Leigh 239.
[2026] Baigent and Leigh 227.
[2027] Baigent and Leigh 227-228.

> *It is significant that during the following year (1776) - the year of Washington's most severe defeats - he, not Howe, was on the offensive. Howe did not seek him out; he sought out Howe. When he did, Howe reacted cursorily - almost like a man swatting away a fly and going back to sleep.*
>
> *Thus, on 26 December 1776, Washington made his famous crossing of the Delaware and fell in a surprise attack on a detachment of Hessians at Trenton. Eluding the main British force under Cornwallis, he then, on 3 January 1777, won a second victory at Princeton against a smaller contingent. Instead of responding, however, Howe, whose army was vastly superior in both numbers and supplies, simply abandoned New Jersey and moved into Pennsylvania. On 11 September, he brushed aside Washington's assault at Brandywine. Instead of pursuing, however, he proceeded to occupy Philadelphia whence the Continental Congress had hastily fled - and established winter quarters. Three weeks later, on 4 October, Washington attacked again, at Germantown. Again, Howe repulsed him, this time inflicting particularly heavy casualties. His army plagued by disease, desertion, low morale and lack of supplies, Washington withdrew into his own winter quarters at Valley Forge. With gentlemanly good sportsmanship, Howe left him alone to lick his wounds and rebuild his shattered army.[2028]*

When the Howe brothers were accused of facilitating the colonists' bid for independence, the accusation was also extended to George Washington. Baigent quotes an open letter by one "Cicero" as saying, "'Washington's whole conduct demonstrated a confidence which could arise from nothing short of certain knowledge."[2029]

TEMPLARS AND THE NEW MASONIC REPUBLIC

The severe winter of 1776 took its toll on Washington's army. In the spring of 1777 he began to rebuild. By then word had spread through the Continental lodges in Europe that America was experiencing the world's first Templar Masonic Revolution. Response was overwhelming. Baigent gives us brief details:

> *In this process of rebuilding the [American] Continental Army, Freemasonry was to play a particularly significant role. Lured by the dreams which Freemasonry had helped to inculcate, professional soldiers from abroad crossed the Atlantic and rallied to the colonists' cause. There was, for example, Baron Friedrich von Steuben, a Prussian veteran recruited by Franklin and Deane, who became Washington's drill-master. Bringing with him the discipline and professionalism of Frederick the Great's army, Steuben, almost single-handedly, turned the raw colonial recruits into an efficient fighting force. There was also the Frenchman Johann de Kaib, another veteran of European battlefields, who was to become perhaps the most competent and reliable of Washington's subordinate commanders.*
>
> *There was Casimir Pulaski, a passionately committed Pole, destined to die of his wounds at the Siege of Savannah. From Poland, too, came Tadeusz Kosciuszko, who constructed the elaborate fortifications for West Point and became the colonists' leading military architect and engineer. Finally, of course, there was the twenty-year-old Marquis de Lafayette, whose status and*

[2028] Baigent and Leigh 240-241.
[2029] Baigent and Leigh 236.

> *charismatic personality compensated for his lack of military experience and had*
> *a dramatic effect on morale, while his diplomatic activity was to prove crucial.*
> *Indeed, he was probably more responsible than anyone else for bringing France*
> *into the war, and this, in turn, made possible the final victory at Yorktown. With*
> *the exception of Kosciuszko, on whom no relevant information survives, all of*
> *these men were known or probable [Templar] Freemasons. Lafayette and*
> *Steuben in particular saw themselves as contributing to the foundation of the*
> *ideal Freemasonic republic.*[2030]

Templar Masons occupied every dominant position that either ran or protected the fledgling nation. The 1951 Masonic edition of the Holy Bible reports that "twenty-four of George Washington's major generals were Masons, as were thirty of his thirty-three brigadier generals. Of fifty-six signers of the Declaration of Independence, fifty-three were Master Masons."[2031] Freemason Manly P. Hall says, "all but five were Masons"[2032] - still, an overwhelming majority.

Moreover, on February 4, 1789, George Washington, while Grand Master of Alexandria Lodge No.22 in Virginia, was elected first President of the United States. Freemason John Adams was his Vice President The Oath of Office was administered by Robert Livingston, Grand Master of New York's Grand Lodge. The Marshall of the day was Freemason General Jacob Morton. Freemason General Morgan Lewis was Washington's escort. The Bible used for the oath was a Masonic Edition from St. John's Lodge No.1 of New York.[2033]

From the time Ben Franklin made contact with the Illuminati in Paris, to the election of our first President, Templar Freemasonry was in total control of American politics. A century later Professor Charles Eliott Norton of Harvard spoke the following words to his history students:

"Not only were many of the founders of the United States Government Masons, but they received aid from a secret and august body [the Illuminati] existing in Europe, which helped them to establish this country for a peculiar and particular purpose known only to the initiated few."[2034]

Today we know what that "peculiar and particular purpose" was. According to Masonic authority already quoted, the United States of America was Freemasonry's "Philosophical Atlantis" resurrected from the "sea" to establish a democratic nation in the New World that would set the standard for the Old World. Included in this "Great Plan," as we shall soon learn from analysing the meaning of The Great Seal of the United States, was a reuniting of the two adversaries, the Priory of Sion and the Knights Templar. America's system of government was to be a harbinger of things to come - a world of democracy built by Templar Freemasonry, under the watchful eye of the Priory of Sion.

To the Atlanteans, America had philosophically risen "up out of the sea" and had become the new utopia of the world, as envisioned by Sir Francis Bacon. The Illuminati, however, had discarded Great Britain and her English Freemasonry in favor of the United States of America as the new protector of the Priory of Sion. The Knights Templar would begin to build the New World Order in America under Sion's watchful "eye."

[2030] Baigent and Leigh 241.

[2031] Still 61.

[2032] Still 61; quoting Hall in *America's Assignment* 96-97.

[2033] Baigent and Leigh 261.

[2034] Mustafa El-Amin, *Freemasonry, Ancient Egypt and the Islamic Destiny* (Jersey City, NJ: New Mind Productions 1988) 10.

THE UNITED STATES IN BIBLE PROPHECY?

This author was educated at university by Bible prophecy teachers who taught that the United States of America was not in prophecy. They claimed that the Bible remains strangely silent on this issue. Why? Because America will be short-lived - unworthy of mention in prophecy.

It is unlikely that Bible prophecy would remain silent on a 200-year-old America because it is short-lived, when we learned in chapter 26 that the seventh head of the Beast was prophesied to be short-lived - and may have been 10-year-old Nazi Germany. Accepting for the moment that America is not mentioned in prophecy by location, and remembering that America was established by Freemasonry, perhaps Scripture sheds light on America's future, not by location, but by Masonic intrigue and symbols - the same intrigue and symbols understood and used in all mystery religions during Bible times. The author found this to be the case.

In Daniel 2 and 7 the prophet had a vision of four world empires, which, in order, are Babylon, Persia, Greece, and Rome. Daniel's vision shows Rome eventually dividing East and West (2:41), then dividing still further into ten toes (2:42). The ten toes represent ten end-time kings who will be crushed by a "Stone" (2:44-45). The Stone is Jesus Christ.[2035] Daniel describes this end-time power in 7:7-8 as a Beast with ten horns:

> *After this I saw in the night visions, and behold a fourth beast, dreadful and terrible, and strong exceedingly; and it had great iron teeth; it devoured and brake in pieces, and stamped the residue with the feet of it; and it was diverse from all the beasts that were before it; and it had ten horns. I considered the horns, and, behold, there came up among them another little horn, before whom there were three of the first horns plucked up by the roots: and, behold, in this horn were eyes like the eyes of a man, and a mouth speaking great things.*

This fourth Beast represents both old Rome and revived Rome. Verse 7 is the former and verse 8 is the latter. That the ten horns are mentioned in both verses, suggests they are ten European nations that existed in the old Roman empire, and exist in the revived Roman empire as well. The ten horns or nations are not the same as the Beast, for Revelation 17:12-13 states that the ten horns will become subservient to the Beast.

The "little horn" that "came up [from] among" the ten horns represents the birth of revived Rome, a nation that is not one of the ten, but an eleventh nation that "came up [from]" the ten. It appears to be a new nation founded in the latter days by a few people from the territory of the ten, for Daniel 11:23 speaks of it maturing: "he [the little horn] shall work deceitfully: for he shall come up, and shall become strong with a small [few] people."

Before the "little horn," or young nation, matures, it plucks up three of the ten European horns by the roots. The phrase "plucked up by the roots" in Hebrew means "to hamstring."[2036] The little horn "with a small [few] people" is strong enough to hamstring the three, but not mighty enough to destroy them. After a time, however, the little horn builds strength and becomes the Beast, incorporating the ten horns in its empire.

Most prophecy teachers are still looking to the future for the birth of the "little horn." One, however, writes: "We will not find in the future what has already transpired in

---

[2035] Bible, Pilgrim Edition, footnote to Dan. 2:45.
[2036] Strong, *Hebrew* #6132.

history."[2037] Randy Shupe, author of the mistitled book, *Is America Mystery Babylon the Great?*, believes young America is the "little horn." Of the three horns plucked up by their roots, he says, "All had colonial roots planted in America. Through the revolutionary war England was 'plucked up' [eastern third]. France sold out rather than facing war with 'little America' [central third]. Spain was the last to be 'plucked up' through the provoked war with Mexico in 1847. By 1848 Mexico had been defeated and conceded its remaining holdings in America [western third]."[2038]

Young America did not destroy these nations, but rather, as prophecy states, "hamstrung" them. In Daniel 8:25 we read how the Beast matured: "And through his policy [wisdom] also he shall cause craft [deceit] to prosper in his hand; and he shall magnify himself in his heart, and by peace [prosperity through safety] shall destroy [decay] many: he shall also stand up against the Prince of princes; but he shall be broken without hand [decay from within, or self-destruct]."

The key words above describe perfectly the cultural, political, economic, criminal and Masonic life in America today. *Policy* means "intelligence, wisdom."[2039] *Craft* means deceiving, fraud, deceit, false, feigned, guile, treachery."[2040] *Peace* means "security, abundance, peace, prosperity, secure or successful, prosper in safety."[2041] *Destroy* means "to decay, corrupt, or spoil."[2042] *Broken* means, both literally and figuratively, "to burst."[2043] It carries the idea of self-destruction when used with the phrase, "broken without hand." *Without hand* means "to disappear, cease to exist, or fail from within."[2044]

We shall now examine how these key words from Daniel's prophecy of the Beast finds fulfillment in contemporary America.

DECEIT AND AMERICA'S WARS

Daniel uses the word *craft* to describe the deceit used by the Beast. The prophet affirms in 11:23 that this deceit makes the Beast a military power: "he shall work deceitfully: for he shall come up, and shall become strong...

Craft is a synonym for Freemasonry and a nickname for witchcraft. The Hebrew meaning in this verse does not convey the idea of a secret society or the use of witchcraft, but does define the deception in Freemasonry. History confirms the same, revealing that England, France and Spain (the three horns "plucked up by their roots") were "hamstrung" by Masonic deception. For example, our Revolutionary War against British control was a deception, for it was secretly organized in our own Masonic lodges. Our negotiations with France in 1803 for the Louisiana Purchase involved four Masons: Thomas Jefferson, Robert Livingston, James Monroe, and Napoleon Bonaparte. America took advantage of, or "hamstrung" Napoleon, who was in desperate need of the miniscule amount paid for the Louisiana Territory.[2045] Our war with Mexico to oust Spain from the western frontier was a Masonic war. The Most Rev. Francis Clement Kelley, in *Blood-*

[2037] Randy Shupe, *Is America Mystery Babylon the Great?* (Armada, CO: The Way, the Truth and the Life Fellowship, 1990) 79.

[2038] Shupe 80.

[2039] Strong, *Hebrew* #7922.

[2040] Strong, *Hebrew* #4820.

[2041] Strong, *Hebrew* #7962 and 7951.

[2042] Strong, *Hebrew* #7843.

[2043] Strong, *Hebrew* #7665.

[2044] Strong, *Hebrew* #657, from 656 and 3027.

[2045] "Louisiana Purchase," *Encyclopaedia Britannica: Micropaedia*.

Drenched Altars, describes in detail the Masonic intrigue that flourished on both sides during that war.[2046]

And finally, our entry into both World Wars, as we have seen, was engineered through Masonic deceit, which wars made us the most powerful military force in the world. As Daniel prophesied in 11:23, "he [the Beast] shall work deceitfully: for he shall come up, and shall become strong..." No political or civil body can stand or survive continuously when deceit becomes its root and branch. This deceit will eventually cause our nation to "be broken without hand" (decay from within), as described by the prophet in Daniel 8:25.

AMERICA'S MILITARY MUSCLE

A recent secular book entitled The Coming Caesars, subtitled A challenging interpretation of America's destiny in the Light of World History, speaks prophetically of America's role as the dominant world power. The dustjacket boasts:

The author of this challenging and controversial interpretation of America's historical and political destiny believes that our Western world, Europe and America, is threatened with the advent of Caesarism on a scale unknown since the Roman Empire... the tremendous increase in the relative power of America... is virtually becoming an American Empire.[2047]

America has the most powerful military force on earth. Daniel says in 11:38 that the Beast shall "increase," that is build up, his military "forces." The decade of the 1980s certainly saw a build- up of American military might. And in the spring of 1991, the world witnessed the awesome military weapons of America during the Gulf War with Iraq.

In Revelation 13:4, John asks, "Who can make war against him [the Beast]?"[2048] In Revelation 13:13 John describes what seems to be a Star Wars weapon used by the Beast: "And he doeth great wonders, so that he maketh fire come down from heaven on the earth in the sight of man. (Our Star Wars program now in development uses laser beam and particle beam weaponry. A charged particle beam shot from a satellite would be similar to a lightning bolt, looking much like fire coming down from heaven.)

POLICY AND AMERICA'S CULTURAL IMPERIALISM

Virtually all Americans are aware of our global ascendancy, military might, and cultural dominance. An excerpt from a story in the August 23, 1990 *Rocky Mountain News* illustrates the height and breadth of this awareness:

We have cultural dominion. The Academy Awards, a glitzy trade show of some California merchants, were watched on television by 1 billion people in 94 countries - which is linked to the fact that for the first time since Babel, there is an emerging universal language. It is American, or if you prefer the archaic term, English.

[2046] Francis Clement Kelley, *Blood-Drenched Altars: A Catholic Commentary on the History of Mexico* (1935; Rockford, IL: Tan Books, 1987) entire.

[2047] Shupe 91-92.

[2048] Bible, New International Version (NIV).

America is the intellectual center of the world. Our universities are the best. That's why so many foreign students study here. America won 48% of the Nobel Prizes in science and medicine in the 1960s. And 55% in the 1970s. And 64% in the 1980s.

Daniel 8:25 says, "And through his [the Beast's] policy..." The word for "policy" in Hebrew means "intelligence, wisdom." In other words, it is the policy of the Beast kingdom to operate with intelligence. America has the brightest minds in the world.

The Rocky Mountain News continues: "From all over, people come here. We take in more legal immigrants than the rest of the world put together. Legislation now moving through Congress will likely raise the number, yielding healthy population growth."

Daniel 2:43 says that the Beast kingdom will be a mixture of people.[2049] Likewise, Revelation 13:1 states that the Beast kingdom will "rise up out of the sea" - *sea* meaning peoples.

"Such cultural influence, prosperity, commercial and military power," continues the *Rocky Mountain News*, "have never before been in the hands of one nation. We stand partially guilty as charged by anti-Americans. We are, indeed, the most potent cultural imperialists in history, although non-coercive on the side of liberty... Our standard of living remains the highest in the world. And, with little notice, American businessmen are buying into Europe at record rates."

Western Europe, which according to Scripture and our analysis will eventually side with the Beast, is presently concerned about American businessmen. On National Public Radio's *All Things Considered* (April 25, 1991), commentators interviewed European government officials, who voiced concern about the United States of America preparing to build an economic bloc against the soon-to-be United States of Europe, citing, for example, the Free Trade negotiations between the U.S.A., Mexico, and Canada. Economic barriers torn down between these three nations, the broadcast said, would mostly benefit the U.S.A., making it economically superior to any nation, or group of nations on earth, even the United States of Europe.

Europe's fear of America is not limited to economic power alone, but to military power as well. In the same broadcast the commentators spoke of the recent imperialistic nature of America in the Persian Gulf Crisis. Before the disintegration of the U.S.S.R., western Europe remained free from war because of the balance of power between the U.S.A. and the Soviet Union, the commentators said. After having observed America's unopposed military might during the pounding the United States gave Iraq, European politicians are in fear that America, if left unrestrained, will revert to military force to resolve international conflicts.

ANCIENT ROME AND THE UNITED STATES: A COMPARISON ROME

Rome	America
From 100-300 A.D. most of pagan Rome converted to Christianity.	When our nation was founded 67 percent of America's population was Christian.
Christians in Rome suffered severe	Christians in America were fleeing

---

[2049] Bible, NIV.

persecution.	European persecution
Rome was the melting-pot of the world.	America is the melting-pot of the world.
Rome was a democracy based upon a two- party system (the Optimates and the Populares).	The U.S.A. is a democracy based upon a two-party system (the Democrats and the Republicans).
Rome had a divided balance of power (Roman Tribune and his Senate).	America has a divided balance of power (the American President and his Congress).
Rome was based on specific laws (Rome's 12 tables).	America is based on specific laws (our Constitution).
Rome protected the rights of its citizens.	America protects the rights of its citizens (Bill of Rights).
In Rome all men were equal (International law of Rome).	In America all men are equal (Declaration of Independence).
Rome had a sordid history of slavery.	America had a sordid history of slavery.
Rome was capitalistic.	America is capitalistic.
Rome practiced abortion as a means of population control.	America practices abortion as a form of birth control.
Rome loved R-rated entertainment (history of Pompeii).	America protects R-rated entertainment under the First Amendment as freedom of speech.
Rome had a welfare program funded by taxes.	America's welfare budget rivals our military budget.
Rome had a thriving business in lawsuits	America has a thriving business in lawsuits.
Sports was Rome's pastime.	In America football dominates fall and winter, basketball winter and spring, and baseball spring and summer.
Ancient Rome's national emblem was the single-headed eagle pointing west	America's national emblem is the singleheaded eagle pointing west
From 300-500 A.D. the Roman Church was weakened spiritually because of pagan infiltration.	After 200 years the Church in America has been weakened spiritually because of

	Masonic infiltration.[2050]

"AMERICA": WHAT'S IN A NAME?

Most historians attribute the name "America" to the explorer Amerigo Vespucci. Freemasonry, however, has a different point of view. According to Freemason and author Manly Hall, the Indians in Central and South America say the name came from their gods, who were peace- loving. For example, the supreme god of the Mayan culture of Central America was known as Quetzalcoatl, a light skinned god who wore a long white robe covered with red crosses. Carved in the stones of his temples were serpents. Quetzalcoatl was known as the peace-loving serpent god.

The same god in Peru was known as Amaru, the god of peace, who was pictured as a plumed serpent. Amaru's territory was known as Amaruca. The 1895 issue of *Lucifer*, a periodical published by Freemason Blavatsky's Theosophical Society, states:

> From the latter comes our word America. Amaruca is, literally translated, "Land of the Plumed Serpent." The Priests of this God of Peace once ruled the Americas. All the Red men who have remained true to the ancient religion are still under his sway.[2051]

According to author William T. Still, "Manly Hall claims that since the serpent is frequently symbolic of Lucifer, it is no exaggeration to extrapolate from this that America may well mean "Land of Lucifer."[2052]

In chapter 14 we learned that the hierarchy in Freemasonry considers Lucifer to be the good, benevolent and peace-loving god. America is known as the good, benevolent, and peace-loving nation. In chapter 5 we learned that the Seal of the Illuminati (the unfinished pyramid, its capstone, and its All-Seeing Eye) represents the kingdom of Lucifer. The image of this Luciferian masterpiece makes up half of "The Great Seal of the United States of America." (See the reverse side of your $1 bill.)

Ezekiel 28:12 tells us that Lucifer was the epitome of beauty. "America, the Beautiful" may therefore be a sinister figure of speech for "Lucifer, the Beautiful!"

IS AMERICA A CHRISTIAN NATION?

Almighty God has always raised up a righteous standard against the enemy. Noah was that standard before God destroyed the earth by water. Shem, which means "the appointed one to make things right,"[2053] was that standard after the Flood. In Old Testament times the nation of Israel was that standard in the East. Today Christianity is that standard in the West.

Isaiah 59 is a prophetic description of the evil that will pervade the world in the last days. Verse 19 in particular is a prophecy of God's Christian standard against evil from the West: "So shall they fear the name of the Lord from the west... When the enemy [referring to the Beast] shall come in like a flood, the Spirit of the Lord shall lift up a standard against him."

[2050] Shupe 93-98.
[2051] Still 45; quoting James Pryse in the Theosophical Society magazine *Lucifer*.
[2052] Still 46.
[2053] Hislop 65.

Isaiah's prophecy suggests that the Beast (the end-time enemy) and the standard against him will both come from the West - more specifically, from the Western Hemisphere, for the Hebrew word for "west" means *extreme west* - "the region of the setting sun."[2054]

History bears record that Christianity has flourished in the West; more specifically, in the United States of America.

Long before "the enemy" of Christianity, which we know today as Freemasonry, came "in like a flood," and founded democracy in America, God had established his standard in this land with a population of Christians fleeing various persecutions in Europe. William Still informs us that "Although secret societies were generally able to guide the course of political change in colonial America, the vast majority of the population was Christian in its religious orientation. In fact, according to Constitutional scholar John W. Whitehead, when the Constitution was adopted in 1787, the population of the United States numbered about 3.25 million, of whom at least two million were Christians."[2055]

Bible scholar and author Clarence Larkin dates the beginning of the Philadelphia Church age to the colonial era of American history. Writing in 1919, he says that the Philadelphia Church "made possible the evangelistic and missionary labors of the past 150 years."[2056]

The greatest missionary movement of all time has been sustained by the United States of America, whose churches have either tradition-ally sent or supported 95 percent of the world's missionaries.[2057] Christ's words of commendation to the Philadelphia Church in Revelation 3:8 have become a cliché in evangelistic America:

> *"I know thy works: behold, I have set before thee an open door, and no man can shut it: for thou hast a little strength, and hast kept my word, and hast not denied my name."*

Perhaps the headquarters of the Philadelphia Church is the United States of America. This, however, does not mean that America is a Christian nation. Christians in America, not the government of the United States, have taken the gospel of God's Son around the world. For this reason America is known as a Christian nation. In this nation - the land from where the end-time Beast will arise - God has set up His righteous standard against the enemy.

Perhaps Christ's promise to the Philadelphia Church in Revelation 3:10 is a promise to Christians in America: "Because thou hast kept the word of my patience, I also will keep thee from the hour of temptation [the tribulation], which shall come upon all the world, to try them that dwell upon the earth."

Perhaps our land has never witnessed foreign invasion because of this promise.

IS DEMOCRACY GODLY?

The activity of Satan in history would suggest that his end-time empire will be tyrannical - much like communism or fascism. That, however, is not to be the case - at

---

[2054] Strong, *Hebrew* #4628.

[2055] Still 62.

[2056] Larkin 26-27.

[2057] Survey conducted in 1975 by the Christian and Missionary Alliance (C&MA) convention.

least, not at first. Satan, the Master Deceiver, has reserved his greatest deception for the end-time. He will gain power by offering peace and prosperity through democracy.

IS DEMOCRACY GODLY IN THE CHURCH?

Many Christians consider democracy and prosperity a God-given blessing. Yet, both have created the last age or period of the Church, the lukewarm Laodicean Church of Revelation 3:14-22. The word *Laodicea* means "the people speak."[2058]

Based upon definition, Laodicea can be seen plainly as the age of the democratic Church, "rich, and increased with goods, and [in] need of nothing," not even in need of Christ, the Head of the Church, Who we vote out. Our Savior stands outside the Laodicean Church door, knocking for reentry (3:20).

IS DEMOCRACY GODLY IN GOVERNMENT?

In Proverbs 11:15, God says, "By me kings reign." Yet, in a democracy man elevates his will above God's. For example, the Preamble to our Constitution begins with, "We the People..."

"We the people" have replaced God-appointed rulers with man-elected rulers. Yet, from time to time our merciful God offers opportunity in a democracy to vote a righteous man into office. We were given that chance in 1988 with the Presidential candidacy of Pat Robertson. Those who watch *The 700 Club* on television have witnessed Robertson pray daily for the healing of the sick and the healing of our nation. He is devoted to evangelizing the world with the gospel of Christ through television. During his presidential campaign, he publicly declared Jesus Christ as Lord of his life. He said that if he were elected President, Christ would be Lord of his Administration.

Did we vote for him? We should have, because Christians in America knew him much better than any other candidate. Instead, we voted for George Bush, a Templar who promotes the Masonic New World Order.

In the most recent election the Republican platform was predominantly a Christian platform. Did we vote for righteousness? Not at all! The majority voted for Clinton and Perot, who both espoused abortion rights.

IS DEMOCRACY GODLY WHEN DIVIDED?

Daniel 2:43 informs us that the revived Roman empire will be rife with division: "And just as you saw the iron mixed with baked clay, so the people will be a mixture and will not remain united, any more than iron mixes with clay."[2059]

Democracy is "iron mixed with baked clay" - the weakest form of government, because it is based on division. For example, in the governmental arena the power is divided among the Executive, Legislative, and Judicial branches. The Legislative is divided between the House and Senate, and further divided between Democrats and Republicans, causing decision-making to bog down. When legislation is passed, the Executive branch may veto it, or the Judicial branch overturn it. And the process begins again. In the political arena the two-party system divides voters. In the ethnic arena we

---

[2058] Bible, Pilgrim Edition, footnote to Rev. 3:14.
[2059] Bible, NIV.

are a mixture of peoples, as Daniel's prophecy declares, dividing ourselves into communities of race and color.

IS DEMOCRACY GODLY IN RELIGION?

Most devastating is the division in religions, commonly called freedom of religion. Mixing religions has been the nemesis of the one true religion throughout history. For example, when Israel permitted false religions equal opportunity, the Jews went whoring after false gods. America is experiencing the same today. As our revived Roman government accepts more and more emigrants, we have become a nation of pagan religions. To make sure we do not offend the new arrivals, Bible reading and prayer have been outlawed in our public schools. Gradually our educational heritage has been replaced with "New Age" rituals.

Now, with the demise of the Soviet Union, we are anticipating a democratic world. The Beast empire will begin as a democratic empire, and the world will worship it. At first the Beast will act benevolently and be a peace-maker. One day, however, he will show his true character and rule with an iron hand, forcing the world to accept his mark and worship him.

Democracy has left us to our own devices. Is it godly?

MARK OF THE BEAST UPON AMERICA

As we previously noted, Michael Baigent has traced the movement of the Knights Templar from its birth a thousand years ago in Jerusalem, to France, to Scotland, to the British throne, back to France, and finally to America. The three symbols which led Baigent half way around the world in search of the present-day headquarters of the Templars are (1) the skull and crossbones; (2) the octagon, an esoteric form of the Templar splayed cross; and (3) the number "13." We will consider each in this order.

SKULL AND BONES

Antony C. Sutton in the 1980s authored several books on the subject of a little known secret society at Yale University. This society, first exposed a century earlier on October 13, 1873, in *The Iconoclast, a* New Haven, CT. newspaper, is known by several names: The Order, the Brotherhood of Death, and Skull and Bones.

Fifteen seniors are permitted membership each year. They are known as Knights during that year, and after graduation are called Patriarchs. Photographs taken of each year's members show 13 standing and two sitting. Resting atop a table between the two sitting Knights is a human skull and crossbones, the symbol of the Knights Templar. For their entire lives, the initiates wear the skull and bones symbol on their breast.

The Order refers to the outside world as Gentiles and vandals, and like Freemasonry, claims to be Jewish. Yet, Yale graduate and Jewish journalist, Ron Rosenbaum, expressed concern in *Esquire* magazine (September 1977) that The Order has some definite anti-Semitic tendencies.

Sutton ties The Order to the Illuminati, both having been founded in Germany - the former soon after the suppression of the latter. In 1833, three years following the death of Adam Weishaupt, a chapter of The Order was opened at Yale. Sutton reports that "over the century and a half span, a group of 20-30 families has emerged to dominate The Order."[2060]

These families fall into two major groups. First are old line American families who arrived on the east coast in the 1600s from various parts of Great Britain when Templar Stuart kings ruled England - during the time Sir Francis Bacon was promoting America as the "New Atlantis." Many of these American families, no doubt, can trace their origins to the old Templar families. They are Whitney, Lord, Phelps, Wadsworth, Allen, Bundy, Adams, etc. The second group are "families who acquired wealth in the last 100 years, sent their sons to Yale and in time became almost old line families, e.g. Harriman, Rockefeller, Payne, Davison."[2061]

To date about 2500 Yale graduates have been initiated into The Order. At any one time about 500-600 are alive and active, most of whom gather annually for a reunion. We find their names listed as directors on boards of major corporations. They specifically dominate non-profit foundations - and they have taken over both the Ford and Carnegie foundations, neither of whose founders were members of The Order. They have penetrated industry, and a dozen members can be linked to the Federal Reserve. Many are members of the Council on Foreign Relation (CFR) and its spin-off, the Trilateral Commission. Some have been Supreme Court Justices politicians at the state and federal levels, and Presidents of the United States.

Members of The Order have founded the American Historical Association, the American Economic Association, the American Chemical Society, and the American Psychological Association. The Order was the forerunner of the League to Enforce the Peace, which developed into the League of Nations, which link ties The Order to Templar Grand Orient Freemasonry, founder of the League of Nations.

The Order has also penetrated communications with members such as Henry Luce of *Time-Life;* William Buckley of *National Review;* Alfred Cowles, president of Cowles Communications, the Des Moines *Register,* and the Minneapolis Star; Emmett Bates of Litton Educational Systems; Richard Ely Danielson of the *Atlantic Monthly;* Russell Wheller Davenport of *Fortune;* and John Chipman Farrar of Farrar, Straus, the publishers.[2062]

"Historically," says Sutton, "operations of The Order have concentrated on society, how to change society in a specific manner towards a specific goal: a New World Order."[2063]

The Order's most famous member today is former President George Bush. It is often said, "He is Skull and Bones to the marrow," the highest compliment one Bonesman can pay another.[2064]

George Bush was the first person in high office to promote publicly the Templar Masonic New World Order. Following are some of his remarks leading up to, and during the U.N.- Iraqi war. The first is an excerpt from his speech to a joint session of Congress, September 11, 1990:

> The crisis in the Persian Gulf, grave as it is, offers a rare opportunity toward
> an historic period of cooperation. Out of these troubled times our fifth objective,
> a New World Order, can emerge. This is the vision I shared with President
> Gorbachev in Helsinki. He, and other leaders from Europe, the Gulf and around

---

[2060] Antony C. Sutton, *An Introduction to THE ORDER* (Vancouver, B.C.: Veritas Publishing, 1984) 10.

[2061] Sutton 11.

[2062] Sutton 33.

[2063] Sutton 36.

[2064] Russell Baker, "Skull & Bones," *The New York Times* (19 May 1991): n.p.

the world understand how we manage this crisis today could shape the future for generations to come.[2065]

Secretary of State James Baker, on his way to Brussels, Belgium, in the fall of 1990, echoed the President's language in his answer to a question about punishing Saddam Hussein for invading Kuwait:

We think that it would set an extremely unfortunate precedent for the New World Order that we hope will result from this first real crisis of the post cold war era if we start out by some- how rewarding aggression.

If we really believe that there's an opportunity here for a New World Order, and many of us do believe that, we can't start out by appeasing aggression.[2066]

On February 6, 1991, at the height of the war, President Bush spoke before the Economic Club of New York City. Peter G. Peterson, current chairman of the Council on Foreign Relations (CFR), and David Rockefeller, member of the CFR and the Lucis mist, and founder of the Trilateral Commission, were both sitting at the head table with George Bush. After his speech the President was asked by a reporter, "You have talked several times about basing the future on a New World Order. Can you give us a definition of a New World Order, and if it depends on the collaboration between the Soviet Union and the United States, how do events in the [then intact] Soviet Union affect this concept?"[2067]

Two truths emerge from Bush's answer: (1) the New World Order is not a Soviet-styled form of government, but a world democracy; and (2) it does not depend on the [now former] Soviet Union. Bush's reply was:

Well, it doesn't depend entirely on it, but it would be greatly enhanced by a Soviet Union that goes down the line with its commitment to market reform, to private ownership of land, to a free economic system, to a system that resists, and does not use force to assure order amongst the republics, that goes farther down the road with elections, and all the openness that I give President Gorbachev credit for... Now, my vision of a New World Order foresees a United Nations with a revitalized peacekeeping function.[2068]

THE OCTAGON, OR TEMPLAR SPLAYED CROSS

The illuminated French Grand Orient engineered and achieved the French Revolution, then in 1801 merged with the Templar Scottish Rite. That same year in Charleston, South Carolina, the Southern Jurisdiction of Templar Scottish Rite Freemasonry created the 33rd degree Supreme Council, adopting the French Masonic constitution as its own. The Templar splayed cross became the Jewel of the 33rd degree. (See Appendix 2, Figs. 6 and 7.)

The Charleston Lodge was immediately established as Sovereign over all Templar Scottish Rite orders throughout the world. In 1833 its school for higher learning became

---

[2065] "Point of View Radio Broadcast," Larry Abraham interviewed by Marlin Maddox, Dallas, TX, 11 Feb.1991.

[2066] "Point of View."

[2067] "Point of View."

[2068] "Point of View."

Yale College. In 1865 Templar Freemasonry's political headquarters were shifted to Washington, D.C.

Moreover, both Washington and Charleston are the most militarily protected cities in America. Surrounding their outskirts are huge silos filled with anti-ballistic missiles. Charleston alone has over 2,000 - twice as many as Washington. No other city but Charleston can boast such protection.

In 1795 our Masonic founding fathers laid out the streets of Washington to form Masonic symbols - the Square, the Compass, the Rule, the Pentagram, the Pentagon and the Octagon. Edward Decker explains the significance of the design of Washington, D.C. in *FREEMASONRY: Satan's Door to America:*

> *Take any good street map of downtown Washington, D.C. and find the Capitol Building. Facing the Capitol from the Mall and using the Capitol as the head or top of the Compass, the left leg is represented by Pennsylvania Ave. and the right leg, Maryland Ave. The Square is found in the usual Masonic position with intersection of Canal St. and Louisiana Ave. The left leg of the Compass stands on the Jefferson Memorial. The circle drive and short streets behind the Capitol form the head and ears of what Satanists call the Goat of Mendes or Goat's head.*
>
> *On top [to the north] of the White House is an inverted 5-pointed star, or Pentagram. The point is facing South in true occult fashion. It sits within the intersections of Connecticut and Vermont Avenues north to Dupont and Logan Circles, with Rhode Island and Massachusetts going to Washington Circle to the West and Mt. Vernon Square on the East.*
>
> *The center of the pentagram is 16th St. where, thirteen blocks due north of the very center of the White House, the Masonic House of The Temple sits at the top of this occult iceberg.*
>
> *The Washington Monument stands in perfect line to the intersecting point of the form of the Masonic square, stretching from the House of the Temple to the Capitol building. Within the hypotenuse of that right triangle sit many of the headquarters buildings for the most powerful departments of government, such as the Justice Dept., U.S. Senate and the Internal Revenue Service.*
>
> *Every key Federal building from the White House to the Capitol Building has had a cornerstone laid in a Masonic ritual and had specific Masonic paraphernalia placed in each one.*
>
> *The Washington Monument actually represents the Phallic Principle upon which Speculative Masonry is based. From above, the monument and its circular drive form the esoteric Masonic "Point within a circle." The Reflecting Pool bears its shadowed image, with the illusion duplicated in the Lincoln Memorial.*[2069]

Michael Baigent notes the final Templar mark: "The Capitol and the White House were each to become focal points of an elaborate geometry governing the layout of the nation's capital city. This geometry, origin-ally devised by an architect named Pierre l'Enfant, was subsequently modified by Washington and Jefferson so as to produce specifically octagonal patterns incorporating the particular cross used as a device by Masonic Templars."[2070]

[2069] Shupe 25.
[2070] Baigent and Leigh 262.

Baigent says, "It is in America that our story comes full circle, for it is there that the Knights Templar have received the most fulsome public homage to be paid them anywhere in the world."[2071]

SION AND TEMPLARS RECONCILE

The Illuminati planned to discard Great Britain as protector of the Priory of Sion after creating a New World Order under Templar protection. Ben Franklin was exposed to this plan while in Paris, where he also learned that peace between Sion and the Temple was to be made in America. Templar Freemasonry was then to build the New World Order in America under the watchful eye of Sion.

The story of the rapprochement between Sion and the Templars is contained in the Seal of the Illuminati, which identifies the Illuminati with both the Knights Templar and the Priory of Sion. (The Seal can be seen on the left-back of a $1 bill.) The Templars are represented by the thirteen steps of the unfinished pyramid and the thirteen letters in the words, *Annuit Coeptis*. The Priory of Sion is represented by the Egyptian form of the All-Seeing Eye atop the unfinished pyramid.

In 1776 Ben Franklin incorporated the Seal of the Illuminati as part of the Great Seal of the United States. He then set up headquarters in Paris from which to direct the American revolution.[2072] Afterwards, Templar America was to lead the world into peace and prosperity under the watchful eye of Sion.[2073]

DANIEL'S VISION:
THE GREAT SEAL OF THE UNITED STATES

E. Raymond Capt, author of *Our Great Seal* (1979), writes: "It was late in the afternoon of July 4, 1776, after the members of the Continental Congress had signed the 'Declaration of Independence' that a resolution was passed: 'Resolved, that Dr. Franklin, Mr. J. Adams and Mr. Jefferson be a committee to prepare a device for a seal of the United States of America.'"[2074]

SEAL OF THE ILLUMINATI

[2071] Baigent and Leigh 266.

[2072] Personal interviews with the Lyndon LaRouche campaign over a period of six years.

[2073] Personal interviews with the Lyndon LaRouche campaign. LaRouche is a Grand Orient Freemason, who claims there are good Masons and bad Masons. Ben Franklin was a good Mason, says LaRouche. LaRouche also recognizes both Freemasonries, and says that the French style is good and the British wicked. He is bent on the destruction of English Freemasonry. See dossier on LaRouche in Appendix 1.

[2074] Raymond E. Capt, *Our Great Seal: The Symbols of our Heritage and our Destiny* (Thousand Oaks, CA: Artisan Sales, 1979) 11.

Franklin and Jefferson were both Templar Masons and members of the Illuminati. Adams was a Mason, but did not become aware of the illuminati influence in America until the end of the 18th century, at which time he became alarmed.[2075]

At the behest of Franklin, the Seal of the Illuminati became part of the Great Seal of the United States. Above and below the Illuminati pyramid are the Latin words *Annuit Oceptis Novus Ordo Seclorum*, meaning "Announcing the Birth of a New Secular Order!" (New Secular Order can also be interpreted as New World Order.)

As the Latin word *seclorum* implies, America was to be a secular nation, divorced from all religion - a harbinger of the Universal Masonic New World Order. The United States was not the New World Order, "but the birth of," or catalyst behind, a new Masonic concept for the world. America was assigned the task of finishing the universal pyramid empire for Templar Freemasonry.

Hovering above the unfinished pyramid is the triangular capstone with rays of the sun shooting from its peak. In the capstone is an eye like the eye of a man.

The capstone signifies the dwelling place of the pagan god. The All-Seeing Eye represents the pagan god. The gods of eastern mystery religions were believed by pagans to have dwelt in the peaks of the highest mountains; therefore, pagans literally worshipped on mountain peaks, called "high places" in Scripture. Where there were no mountains, pyramids were built to represent mountain peaks.

Dr. Merrill F. Unger, in *Archaeology and the Old Testament,* informs us that the pyramids or ziggurats of Mesopotamia were given the names *Mountain of God,* or *Hill of Heaven.*[2076] Like the gods who dwell in the mountain peaks, their gods are said to have dwelt on the peak of these pyramids.

In Eastern mystery religions, the "triangle" is the geometric symbol used to represent the pyramid or high place on mountain peaks. The Egyptians placed inside their triangle a single eye to represent their sun-god, Osiris. This symbol was adopted by the Priory of Sion and then by Freemasonry. The prophet Daniel saw this symbol when he described the Beast nation as the "little horn" in Daniel 7:8:

> I considered the horns, and, behold, there came up among them another little horn, before whom there were three of the first horns plucked up by the roots: and, behold, in this horn were eyes like eyes of man...

Horn in Hebrew literally means *apeak of a mountain, a ray of light.* It comes from a prime root word, which figuratively means *a horn that shoots out rays, shines.*[2077]

What is most astounding about Daniel's vision is his description of what he saw inside the horn, or sun-rayed triangle. He says, "in this horn were eyes like the eyes of man...

For some unknown reason translators have made the Hebrew word for "eyes" plural. In the original, however, it is singular.[2078] What Daniel actually said was, "in this sun-rayed triangle was an eye like the eye of man What Daniel actually saw was the Great Seal of the United States of America - the emblem of revived Rome.

[2075] Kirban 155.

[2076] Merrill F. Unger, *Archaeology and the Old Testament* (Grand Rapids, MI: Zondervan, 1954) 104.

[2077] Strong, *Hebrew* #7162, from 7161, from 7160.

[2078] Strong, *Hebrew* #5870, corresponding to 5869.

JOHN'S VISION: THE BASE OF THE SEAL

Superimposed on the base layer of bricks on the unfinished pyramid are the Roman numerals MDCCLXXVI (1776), representing the founding date of both the Illuminati and the United States of America. The year 1776 is of utmost significance in identifying the birth of revived Rome. It is the only date that arranges the Roman numerals in the exact order spoken of by John in Revelation 13:18: "and his number is Six hundred threescore and six" (600 + 60 + 6 = 666).

To decipher this arrangement, we must understand more about triangle symbology. We mentioned above that the triangle is symbolic of the pagan pyramid temple or high place. Eastern mystery religions also use triangles to symbolize the three planes of creation - heaven, earth, and hell.

The 33rd degree Templar Scottish Rite of Freemasonry recognizes these three planes of creation in its *Jewel*. These triangles also symbolize the three secret societies in Freemasonry: (1) the Blue Lodge, degrees 1-3; (2) the Scottish Rite, degrees 4-32; and (3) the Supreme Council, degree 33.

JEWEL OF THE 33RD DEGREE

The *Jewel* of the 33rd degree consists of three interlaced triangles, signifying the Supreme Council's dominion over the three secret societies within the Scottish Rite, as well as its perceived dominion over the three planes of creation. Notice the double-headed eagle of the Roman empire in the center of the hooped serpent biting its own tail. The hooped serpent represents zero, the evolutionary origin of Freemasonry's serpent god. In the background is the splayed cross of the Knights Templar.

According to Warren Weston in *Father of Lies*, each plane of creation has its own occult trinity represented by the three corners of the triangle - god the father, god the mother, and god the son.[2079] God the father (the highest numerical value) is at the peak of each triangle, god the mother (the next highest value) is at the lower left, and god the son (the lowest value) is at the lower right.

We have separated the three triangles below, placing them in a row to represent the three planes of occult creation. By grouping the nine Roman numerals in the above order of threes, remembering that the old style for "M" was CIC with the right-hand "C" turned backwards, we are able to decipher the mark of the Beast:

Hidden in the Great Seal of the United States of America is the mark of the Beast in the exact numerical order prophesied by John. Revelation 13:16-17 informs us that the number will be tied to the medium of exchange; that it will be carried in the palm of the hand or in the forehead; that no man can buy or sell without it.

In 1934 President Franklin D. Roosevelt, a 32nd-degree Freemason at the time, had the Seal of the Illuminati placed on the reverse side of our $1 bill. Since that time, when we in America buy and sell with the almighty dollar, the mark of the Beast is in the palm of our hand. If we use credit cards, the mark of the Beast is transferred from our hand to our forehead, for the Greek word *for forehead* means to *transfer*.[2080] The Greek also suggests the use of computers by defining *forehead as accompaniment or association*."[2081] For instance, behind the forehead is the brain, or human computer. Synonyms of *accompaniment* and *association* are *companion* and *resemblance*. John's

---

[2079] Weston, plate I.

[2080] Strong, *Hebrew* #3327 and 3329.

[2081] Strong, *Hebrew* #3359, from 3326.

use of the word *forehead*, therefore, may suggest a companion to, or resemblance of the human brain - a computer.

Don't be alarmed. This type of buying and selling is not what John warns us against. His warning is against the ultimate cashless society that the computers are working towards. We are warned against accepting a mandatory private number through which all buying and selling will be controlled. For example, the so called "Smart Card," the size of a credit card, has a chip that can hold 1,600 pp of information. Our new President is proposing to control health care from birth with this card.

REVERSE   OBVERSE

THE GREAT SEAL OF THE UNITED STATES OF AMERICA

The left side of the Great Seal is spiritual. The All-Seeing Eye hovering above the unfinished pyramid represents the Priory of Sion overseeing the Templar task of building a universal New World Order.

The right side of the Great Seal is political. The 13-starred hexagram hovering above the Flying Eagle represents the union of Sion and the Temple brought about by the revived Roman empire.

THE AMERICAN EAGLE: SYMBOL OF REVIVED ROME

The coat of arms for America became known as the Great Seal of the United States. As we have just seen, the visions of both the prophets Daniel and John, prophesied this emblem or symbol of the Beast. On the front side of the two-sided Seal is displayed the so-called American Eagle. William Still explains what the eagle really represents:

EMBLEM OF THE 33RD DEGREE

[T]he small tuft at the back of the head indicates a hybrid combination of an eagle and the mythical phoenix. This is hardly a revolutionary discovery. The eagle was not the original bird pictured on many coins of early America.

[These coins do] not show the rugged, familiar lines of the American bald eagle, but the thin, long-necked, crested profile of the phoenix.[2082]

The phoenix is a legendary bird which according to legend lived 500 years, burned itself to ashes on a pyre, and rose alive from the ashes to live again. It was one of the most familiar symbols in Egyptian and Atlantean cultures. Moreover, the single-headed phoenix-eagle was the national emblem of ancient Rome, before Constantine divided the empire. *Mackey's Encyclopedia of Freemasonry* tells the story: *"The Eagle Displayed,* that is, with extended wings, as if in the act of flying, has always, from the majestic character of the bird, been deemed an emblem of imperial power. Marius, the [Roman] consul, first consecrated the eagle, about eight years before the Christian era, to be the sole Roman standard at the head of every legion, and hence it became the standard of the Roman Empire ever afterward. As the single-headed eagle was thus adopted as the symbol of imperial power, the double-headed eagle naturally became the representative of a double empire; and on the division of the Roman dominions into the eastern and western empire, which were afterward consolidated by the Carolingian race [through which the Merovingian Holy Bloodline survived] into what was ever after called the Holy Roman Empire, the double-headed eagle was assumed as the emblem of this double empire; one head looking, as it were, to the West, or Rome, and the other to the East, or Byzantium."[2083]

To Freemasonry the double-headed eagle represents immortality and resurrection. In this form it becomes the emblem of the 33rd degree Mason. *Mackey's Encyclopedia of Freemasonry* makes one of the most profound statements regarding the double-headed eagle, which statement suggests that the assignment of the Templar Scottish Rite is to revive the Roman empire:

> The double-headed eagle was brought by Crusaders to the Emperors of the East and West... [It] was first introduced as a symbol into Freemasonry in the year 1758. In that year the Body calling itself the Council of Emperors of the East and West was established in Paris... [Its] successors today are the Supreme Council, 33rd degree.[2084]

Mackey subtly hides the Templars in the name "Crusaders," whose plan, after having conquered Jerusalem, was to revive the Roman empire. This "Secret Doctrine" was kept under lock for five centuries until the New World was discovered. In 1801, the year the Templar Scottish Rite Supreme Council of the world was founded at Charleston, the double-headed eagle was adopted by that body, signifying that the Emperors of the East and West transferred their headquarters to America where the Roman empire would be revived.

[2082] Still 65.
[2083] "Eagle, Double-Headed," *Mackey's Encyclopedia of Freemasonry*, vol.1.
[2084] "Eagle, Double-Headed."

THE FLOWING RIBBON

In the beak of the phoenix-eagle is a flowing ribbon inscribed with *E pluribus Unum*, meaning "one out of many." William Still remarks of the slogan: "This has a double meaning: both the unification of the American states into the American nation, and the ultimate goal, a unification of nations into a one world state."[2085]

The slogan, "one out of many, " has prophetic significance in identifing revived Rome. The "one" Roman Empire covered "many" nations - all of Europe and the territory of the old Grecian Empire. "One out of many" also refers to "many nationalities." Rome itself had every nationality living in its city limits. Likewise, America, which was settled by Europeans from the territories of the old Roman Empire, has the distinguishing mark of being a mixed multitude of races. The prophet Daniel spoke of revived Rome in his interpretation of Nebuchadnezzar's dream in Daniel 2:43: "And just as you saw the iron mixed with baked clay, so the people will be a mixture..."

The apostle John affirms the same in Revelation 13:1: "And I stood upon the sand of the sea. and saw a beast rise up out of the sea..."[2086] Literally the United States rose up from between two oceans, the Atlantic and Pacific, and became to the Masonic hierarchy the "New Atlantis," and was prophesied by the prophets Daniel and John as the revived Rome. As we have noted, figuratively "sea" means "a mixture of peoples. or nationalities, or nations." All three are true in America today. Every race and nationality is represented in our citizenry. And 50 nation-states make up the whole of the United States.

TEN KINGS UNITED WITH THE BEAST: RIDDEN IN THE GLORY CLOUD

One day the Beast will cause ten European nations to agree to unite with him. What crisis will initiate this merger can only be a matter of speculation. It could occur as a result of war, or it may be an economic merger. Western Europe is in fear of both.

The unopposed military might of the United States and the economic threat the Americas (Canada, the U.S.A., and Mexico) present to Europe is of paramount concern to the Old World. Moreover, London, "that great city, which reigneth over the kings of the earth," is also considered a threat, because its banking system controls the finances of the world.

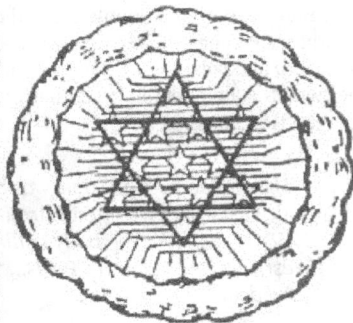

THE GLORY CLOUD

The glory cloud hovering above the hybrid Eagle represents unity between Sion and the Temple. In the glory cloud is the hexagram, or six-pointed star created by a unique arrangement of thirteen pentagrams, or five-pointed stars. E. Raymond Capt, in *Our Great Seal*, states: "This hexagram is composed of two equilateral triangles and in each triangle are exactly ten stars."[2087]

As we have learned, the hexagram is the coat of arms of the Priory of Sion. The thirteen pentagrams (five-pointed stars) represent both the thirteen colonies of America,

---

[2085] Still 67.
[2086] Bible, NIV.
[2087] Capt 54.

and the Knights Templar. They demonstrate the desired unity the United States will bring to Sion and the Temple. The ten pentagrams in the two equilateral triangles represent the perfect unity of government in "New Atlantis," that is, a government ruled over by ten kings, as was old Atlantis. These are the same ten kings who Will be given power for a short time with the Beast.

In the center of the hexagram is a hexagon, within which are seven stars. Thus, the Glory Cloud provides us with the individual numbers "7" and "10", while including the seven with the ten. This correlates with the body of the Beast with seven heads and ten horns. The "7" could represent the seven-nation Trilateral Commission, four of which are members of the European Economic Community, which will eventually consist of ten nations.

THE OLIVE BRANCH OF PEACE

In the right talon of the Eagle is an olive branch with thirteen leaves and thirteen olives. Raymond Capt says, "The official explanation is that it signifies peace."[2088] It has a deeper meaning, however. It represents America holding out the olive branch of peace to the Priory of Sion and the Knights Templar, and ultimately to the world.

THE ARROWS OF MILITARY MIGHT

In the left talon of the Eagle are thirteen arrows, which appear to contradict the olive branch of peace. The official explanation, says Capt, is that "they represent the war power of the country, which is thus shown to be in a state of readiness and preparation." He adds "The Arrows are most appropriately given the secondary or sinister place in the grasp of the Eagle's talon. America prefers peace to war. We offer first, the right hand of friendship. However, we are prepared for conflict."[2089]

The arrows and olive branch also represent the means by which the Beast will maintain peace on earth. The apostle John asks in Revelation 13:4 "Who can make war with him [the Beast]?" Daniel says in 8:25, by peace he shall destroy many. Peace will be maintained by threat of war.

THE SHIELD OF DEFENSE

To complement the arrows of military might and the olive branch of peace is the thirteen-striped *escutcheon,* or shield. "From earliest times," says Capt, "the shieldans been the most honored of defensive arms... Its deep significance has continued to remain among all peoples as the emblem of supreme protection."[2090]

Daniel 11:38 describes the Beast as honoring the god *of forces,* which in Hebrew means *military defense.* The United States of America has the most awesome defense force in the world. Our "Star Wars" program being built in outer space is supposedly for "defense." Our military budget is called a "defense budget."

[2088] Capt 47.
[2089] Capt 49.
[2090] Capt 44.

In Conclusion

The clandestine struggle between English and French Freemasonry is over the control of a one- world government. Christians have lived under every and all forms of government, and may experience living, at the beginning at least, under a one-world government.

This is not a problem, for Christians lived under the one-world government of ancient Rome. The problem is Christians who have billed ranks with Freemasonry - the order that is destined to establish the one-world government of the Antichrist. If you are a Christian in the Lodge, you are contributing to this creation.

Christ pleads with you in Revelation 18:4, "Come out of her, my people, that ye be not partakers of her sins, and that ye receive not of her plagues."

The apostle John completes his prophecy with these words recorded in Revelation 22:20: "He which testified these things said, Surely I come quickly. Amen. Even so, come, Lord Jesus."

AMEN

BIBLIOGRAPHY

It is impossible to investigate the conspiratorial view of history without reading anti-Semitic books. Those that are not anti-Semitic do, however, tie in the Jewish involvement, if not by nationality, by individual names. Because of this, even these books are considered by some to be anti-Semitic.

Appendix 1 contains dossiers of a few conspiracy authors taken from the Bibliography of *Scarlet and the Beast*. They have been considered incredible by some because of their controversial background. To help you understand why and how I have used their publications as source material for my book, I reveal their backgrounds in Appendix 1.

Allen, Gary and Larry Abraham. *None Dare Call It Conspiracy.* Rossmore, CA: Concord Press, 1971.

Allen, Tom. *Rock-n-Roll, the Bible and the Mind.* Beaverlodge, Alberta: Horizon Books, 1982.

"Atlantis: The Eternal Quest." *Mystic Places.* Alexandria, VA: Time-Life Books, 1987.

Amstutz, Wendell. *Exposing and Confronting Satan & Associates.* Rochester, MN: The National Counseling Resource Center, 1990.

Antelman, Marvin S. *To Eliminate the Opiate.* New York: Zahavia, 1974.

Baigent, Michael, Richard Leigh and Henry Lincoln. *Holy Blood, Holy Grail.* New York: Dell, 1982.

Baigent, Michael, Richard Leigh and Henry Lincoln. *Messianic Legacy.* New York: Dell, 1986.

Baigent, Michael and Richard Leigh. *The Temple and the Lodge.* New York: Arcade Publishing, 1989.

Bergmeister, Karl. *The Protocols of the Elders of Zion before the Court in Berne.* 1938. Mettairie, LA: Sons of Liberty, n.d.

Berlitz, Charles. *Dooms-Day 1999 A.D.* New York: Pocket Books, 1981.

Bible. Jerusalem Bible. Wheaton, IL: Tyndale House, 1974. Bible. Living Bible. Grand Rapids, MI: Zondervan, 1981.

Bible. New American Standard Bible. 1901. Chicago: Moody Press, 1963.

Bible. New English Bible. Wheaton, IL: Tyndale House, 1974. Bible. New International Version. Grand Rapids, MI: Zondervan, 1981.

Bible. New King James Version. Nashville, TN: Thomas Nelson Publishers, 1982.

Bible . Phillips Modern English. Wheaton, IL: Tyndale House, 1974

Bible. Pilgrim Edition. New York: Oxford University Press, 1952.

Bible. Revised Standard Version. Grand Rapids, MI: Zondervan, 1981.

Bible. Today's English Version. Wheaton, IL: Tyndale House, 1974.

Billington, James A. *Fire in the Minds of Men.* New York: Basic Books, 1980.

Blanchard, J. *Scottish Rite Masonry illustrated*. Vols. I & II. 1944 Chicago: Powner, 1979.

Booth, Meyrick. *Rudolph Hess: Prisoner of Peace*. Trans. Frau Ilse Hess. Ed. George Pile. Druffel-Verlag, West Germany: n.p., 1954.

Bowen, William. *Globalism, America's Demise*. Shreveport, LA: Huntington House, 1984.

Breasted, James Henry. *Ancient Times, A History Of The Early World*. Boston: Ginn and Company, 1916.

Bresler, Fenton. *The Chinese Mafia*. New York: Stein and Day, 1981.

Buck, J.D. *Symbolism of Mystic Masonry*. 1925. Chicago: Powner, n .d.

Bugliosi, Vincent and Curt Gentry. *Helter Skelter*. Ed. W.W. Norton. 1974. New York: Bantam Books, 1988.

Capell, Frank A. *Henry Kissinger, Soviet Agent*. 1974. Metairie, LA: Sons of Liberty, 1987.

Capt, Raymond E. Our *Great Seal: The Symbols of* our *Heritage* & our *Destiny*. Thousand Oaks, CA: Artisan Sales, 1979

Carr, William Guy. *The Conspiracy to Destroy all Existing Governments and Religions*. Canada: published privately, 1959.

Chaitkin, Anton. *Treason in America*. 2nd ed. New York: New Benjamin Franklin House, 1984.

Church, J.R. *Guardians of the Grail*. Oklahoma City: Prophecy Publications, 1989.

Clarkstown Country Club. *New York: Sales Promotion & Advertising Service*, 1935.

Clausen, Henry C. and Bruce Lee. *Pearl Harbor: Final Judgement*. New York: Crown Publishers. 1992.

Clegg, Robert Ingham. *Mackey's Revised History of Freemasonry*. 1898. New York: The Masonic History Company, 1921.

Commissar, Former Russian. *Trotsky and the Jews behind the Russian Revolution*. 1937. Metairie, LA: Sons of Liberty, 1980.

Congressional Record – Senate. Washington, D.C.: Library of Congress, 9 Sept. 1987.

Corti, Egon Caesar. *The Rise of the House of Rothschild*. 1928. Belmont, MA: Western Islands, 1972.

Council on Foreign Relations 1980 Annual Report. New York: Harold Pratt House, 1980.

Cumbey, Constance. *The Hidden Dangers of the Rainbow*. Shreveport, LA: Huntington House, 1983.

Daniel, John. *Scarlet and the Beast: English Freemasonry, Mother of Modern Cults, vis-a-vis, Mystery Babylon, Mother of Harlots*. vol. 2. Tyler, TX: Jon Kregel, Inc., 1994.

Daniel, John. *Scarlet and the Beast: English Freemasonry, Banks and the Illegal Drug Trade*. vol. 3. Tyler, TX: Jon Kregel, Inc., 1995.

Darrah, Delmar Duane. *History and Evolution of Freemasonry.* 1954. Chicago: Powner, 1979.

Davies, Nigel. *Human Sacrifices in History* and *Today.* New York: William Morrow, 1981.

Decker, Ed and Dave Hunt. *The God Makers.* Eugene, OR: Harvest House, 1984.

Denslow, William R. *10,000 Famous Freemasons.* Vols. 1-4, Trenton, MO: Missouri Lodge of Research, 1957-1961.

De Parrie, Paul. *Unholy Sacrifices of the New Age.* Westchester, lL: Crossway Books, 1988.

De Poncins, Leon. *Freemasonry* and *the Vatican.* Trans. Timothy Tindal-Robertson. N.p.: n.p., 1968.

De Poncins, Leon. *Judaism and the Vatican.* Trans. Timothy Tindal-Robertson. N.p.: n.p., 1967.

De Poncins, Leon. *The Dictatorship of the Occult Powers.* N.p.: n.p., 1932.

De Poncins, Leon. *The Secret Powers Behind Revolution.* 1928. Hawthorne, CA: Christian Book Club of America, n.d.

Dillon, George E. *Grand Orient Freemasonry Unmasked as the Secret Power behind Communism.* 1885. Metairie, LA: Sons of Liberty, n.d.

Dreyfuss, Robert. *Hostage to Khomeini.* New York: New Benjamin Franklin House, 1980.

Durant, Will. *The Story of Civilization: The Reformation.* Vol. VI. New York: Simon and Schuster, 1957.

Durant, Will and Ariel. *The Story of Civilization: The Age of Reason Begins.* Vol. VII. New York: Simon and Schuster, 1961.

Durant, Will and Ariel. *The Story of* Civilization: *The Age of Louis XIV.* Vol. VIII. New York: Simon and Schuster, 1963.

Durant, Will and Ariel. *The Story of Civilization: The Age of Voltaire.* Vol. IX. New York: Simon and Schuster, 1965.

Durant, Will and Ariel. *The Story of Civilization: Rousseau and Revolution.* Vol. X. New York: Simon and Schuster, 1967.

Durant, Will and Ariel. *The Story of Civilization: The Age of Napoleon.* Vol. XI. New York: Simon and Schuster, 1975.

El-Amin, Mustafa. Freemasonry, *Ancient Egypt, and the Islamic Destiny.* Jersey City, NJ: New Mind Production, 1988.

Encyclopedia Americana 1991 ed.

Encyclopaedia Britannica: Macropaedia. 15th edition. 1984.

Encyclopaedia Britannica: Micropaedia. 15th edition. 1984.

Encyclopedia of Jewish History. Ed. Ilana Shamir and Shlomo Shavit. Israel: Massada, 1986.

Epperson, Ralph A. *The New World Order*. Tucson, AZ: Publius Press, 1990.

Epperson, Ralph A. *The Unseen Hand*. Tucson, AZ: Publius Press, 1985.

Fisher, Paul A. *Behind the Lodge* Door. Washington, DC: Shield, 1988.

Foxe, John. *Foxe's Book of Martyrs*. 1569. Chicago: The John C. Winston Co., 1926.

— *Freemasonry: Antichrist Upon Us*. Elon College, NC: Fragments of Truth, late 1950s.

Gentry, Curt. *J. Edgar Hoover: The Man and the Secrets*. New York: Plume, 1991.

Gleick, James. *Chaos: Making a New Science*. New York: Viking, 1987.

Goetz, William R. *Apocalypse Next*. Beaverlodge, Alberta, CD: Horizon House, 1980.

Goff, Kenneth. *The Scarlet Woman of Revelation*. 1952. Metairie, LA: Sons of Liberty, n.d.

Graham, Billy. *Angels: God's Secret Agents*. New York: Doubleday, 1975.

Haggard, Forrest. *The Craft and the Clergy*. Richmond, VA: Macoy, n.d.

Hall, Manly P. *The Lost Keys of Freemasonry*. 1923. Richmond, VA: Macoy Publishing & Masonic Supply Co., 1976.

Halley, Henry H. *Halley's Bible Handbook*. 23rd ed. 1924. Grand Rapids, MI: Zondervan, 1964.

Hammer, Armand. *Hammer*. New York: G.P. Putnam's Sons, 1987.

Harris, Jack. *Freemasonry: The Invisible Cult in our Midst*. Orlando, FL: Daniels Publishing Co., 1983.

Haywood, Harry LeRoy. *The Great Teachings of Masonry*. 1921. Richmond, VA: Macoy, 1971.

Heckethorn, Charles William. *Secret Societies of all Ages and Countries*. Vol. II. London, 1875.

Higham, Charles. *Trading With The Enemy*. New York: Dell, 1983.

Hilton, Stanley E. *Hitler's Secret War in South America, 1939-1945*. New York: Ballantine, 1981.

Hill, Douglas and Pat Williams. *The Supernatural*. New York: Signet Books, 1965.

Hislop, Alexander. *The Two Babylons*. 1916. Neptune, NJ: Loizeaux Brothers, 1959.

History of the Times: 1912-1920. Vol. IV. New York: Macmillan Co 1952.

Hitler, Adolf. *Mein Kampf*. Trans. James Murphy. 1939. Los Angeles: Angriff Press, 1981.

Hogan, Mervin B. "Mormonism and Freemasonry" *Little Masonic Library*. Vol. II. 1946. Richmond, VA: Macoy Publishing & Masonic Supply Co., 1977.

Hubbard, L. Ron. *Dianetics*. Los Angeles: Bridge Publications, 1950.

Infield, Glen B. Secrets *of the* SS. New York: Stein and Day, 1984. *In-Hoc-Signo-Vinces*. New York: Allen Masonic Publishing Co., 1912.

John, Robert. *Behind the Balfour Declaration*. Costa Mesa, CA: The Institute for Historical Review, 1988.

Jung, Carl Gustav. *Memories, Dreams, Reflections*. New York: Vintage Books, 1961.

Kalimtgis, Konstandinos, David Goldman and Jeffrey Steinberg. *Dope*, Inc.: *Britain's* Opium *War against the U.S.* New York: New Benjamin Franklin House, 1978.

Kelley, Francis Clement. *Blood-Drenched Altars*. 1935. Rockford, IL: Tan Books and Publishers, 1987.

Kelly, Clarence. *Conspiracy against God and Man*. Boston: Western Islands, 1974.

Key, William Brian. *Media Sexploitation*. Scarborough, Ont.: Prentice-Hall, 1976.

Kirban, Salem. *Satan's Angels Exposed*. Rossville, GA: Grapevirn Book Distributors, 1980.

Knight, Stephen. *Jack the Ripper: The Final* Solution. 1976. London; Granada, 1977.

Knight, Stephen. *The Brotherhood: The Secret World of The Freemasons*. New York: Stein and Day, 1984.

Knightley, Phillip. *The Master Spy*. New York: Alfred A. Knopf, 1989.

Langguth, A.J. *Patriots: The Men Who Started the American Revolution*. New York: Simon and Schuster, 1988.

Larkin, Clarence. *The Book of Revelation*. 1919. Philadelphia: Clarence Larkin Estate, n.d.

Larson, Bob. *Rock.* Wheaton, IL: Tyndale House, 1983.

Lewis, Harve Spencer. *Rosicrucian Manual*. N.P.: Supreme Grand Lodge of AMORC, 1955.

Lifton, David S. *Best Evidence: Disguise and Deception in the Assassination of John F. Kennedy*. New York: Carroll & Graf, 1988.

Lincoln, Bruce W. *The Romanovs*. New York: Doubleday, 1981.

Lyons, Arthur. *Satan Wants You*. New York: Mysterious Press, 1988.

Mackey, Albert G. *Mackey's Encyclopedia of Freemasonry*. 5th ed. 3 vols. Chicago: The Masonic History Company, 1950.

Mackey, Albert G. *Lexicon of Freemasonry*. Chicago: P.R.C. Publications, n.d.

Mackey, Albert G. *Manual of the Lodge*. Chicago: P.R.C. Publications, n.d.

Mackey, Albert G. *Symbolism of Freemasonry*. Chicago: Powner, 1975.

Mackey, Albert G. *Textbook of Masonic Jurisprudence*. Chicago: P.R.C. Publications, n.d.

Malcolm, James A. *Origins of the Balfour Declaration: Dr. Weizmann's Contribution*. 1944. Torrance, CA: Institute for Historical Review, 1983.

Marsden, Victor E. *Jews in Russia*. Reprint. Metairie, LA: Son's of Liberty, n.d.

Martin, Malachi. *The Decline and fall of the* Roman *Church*. New York: Bantam Books, 1981.

Martin, Malachi. *The Jesuits.* New York: The Linden Press, 1987.

Matthews, E. *What Is Communism?* USA: privately printed, 1937.

McBirnie, William Steuart. *The Search For The Twelve Apostles.* Wheaton, IL: Tyndale House, 1973.

McQuaig, C.F. *The Masonic Report.* Norcross, GA: Answer Books and Tapes, 1976.

Milan, Michael. *The Squad.* New York: Berkley Books, 1992.

Miller, Edith Starr. *Occult Theocrasy.* 1933. Hawthorne, CA: Christian Book Club of America, 1980.

Morris, Robert. *Webb's Monitor.* USA: N.p., n.d.

Morrow, Robert D. *First Hand Knowledge: How I Participated in the CIA-Mafia Murder of President Kennedy.* New York: Shapolsky Publishers, 1992.

Morton, Frederic. *Thunder at Twilight.* New York: Macmillan Publishing Co., 1989.

New Catholic Encyclopedia. Vol. XIII. 1967 ed.

Newton, Joseph Fort. "The Great Light in Masonry" *Little Masonic Library.* Vol. III. 1946. Richmond, VA: Macoy Publishing & Masonic Supply Co., 1977.

Nilus, Sergius. *The Protocols of the meetings of the Learned Elde1 of Zion.* Trans. Victor E. Marsden. London: n.p., 1934.

Noebel, David A. *The Legacy of John Lennon.* Nashville: Thomas Nelson Publishers, 1982.

Noebel, David A. *The Marxist Minstrels.* Tulsa, OK: American Christian College Press, 1974.

"Paradise Lost." *Mystic Places.* Alexandria, VA: Time-Life Books, 1987.

Petersen, William J. *Those Curious New Cults in the 80s.* New Canaan CT: Keats Publishing, 1973.

Pierson, Past Grand Master. *Traditions of Freemasonry.* Chicago Powner, n.d.

Pike, Albert. *Morals and Dogma.* 1871. Richmond, VA: L.H. Jenkins, 1942.

Pinay, Maurice. *The Plot Against The Church.* 1967. Los Angele St. Anthony Press, 1982.

Pipes, Richard. *Russia under the Bolshevik Regime.* New York: Alfred A. Knopf, 1993.

Pool, James and Suzanne. *Who Financed Hitler?* New York: Dial Press, 1978.

Quigley, Carroll. *Tragedy and Hope: A History of the world in our time.* 1966. Los Angeles: Angriff Press, 1974.

Rehwinkel, Alfred M. *The Flood.* St. Louis, MO: Concordia Publishing House, 1951.

Robinson, John J. *Born in Blood, The lost secrets of Freemasonry.* New York: M. Evans & Company, 1989.

Robison, John. *Proofs of a Conspiracy.* 1798. Boston: Western Islands, 1967.

Ronayne, Edmond. *Handbook of Freemasonry.* 1943. Chicago: Powner Co., 1973.

Ronayne, Edmond. *The Master's Carpet.* N.p.: n.p., n.d.

Rodriguez, Cardinal Caro y, Archbishop of Santiago, Chile. *The Mystery of Freemasonry Unveiled.* 1971. Hawthorne, CA: Christian Book Club of America, 1980.

Scheim, David E. *Contract America: The Mafia Murder of President John F. Kennedy.* New York: Zebra Books, 1989.

Scholem, Gershom. *Kabbalah and Its Symbolism.* New York: Schocken Books, 1965.

Schwarzwaller, Wulf. *The Unknown Hitler.* New York: Berkley Books. 1990.

Seidel, Leonard J. *Face the Music.* Springfield, VA: Grace Unlimited Publications, 1988.

Seward, Desmond. *Napoleon and Hitler.* New York: Viking, 1989.

Shaw, Jim and Tom McKenney. *The Deadly Deception.* Lafayette, LA: Huntington House, 1988.

Short, Martin. *Inside The Brotherhood: Further* secrets *of the Freemasons.* New York: Dorset Press, 1989.

Shupe, Randy. *Is America Mystery Babylon the Great?* Arvada, CO: The Way, the Truth and the Life Fellowship, 1990.

Sickles, Daniel. *General Ahiman Rezon.* N.p.: n.p., n.d.

Sklar, Dusty. *The Nazis and the Occult.* New York: Dorset Press, 1977.

Skousen, W. Cleon. *The Naked Capitalist: A review and commentary on Dr. Carroll Quigley's book TRAGEDY AND HOPE.* Salt Lake City: privately printed, 1970.

Southwest Radio Church. *Is the Antichrist in the World Today?* Oklahoma City: Southwest Radio Church, 1982.

Spaulding, Mark. *The Heartbeat of the Dragon: The Occult Roots of Rock & Roll.* Sterling Hts., MI: Light Warrior Press, 1992.

Spenser, Robert Keith. *The Cult Of The All-Seeing Eye.* U.S.A.: Monte Cristo Press, 1964.

Steinmetz, George H. *Freemasonry, Its Hidden Meaning.* Richmond: Macoy, 1976.

Still, William T. *New World Order: The Ancient Plan of Secret Societies.* Lafayette, LA: Huntington House, 1990.

Stoddard, Miss (Inquire Within). *Light-bearers of Darkness.* 1930. Hawthorne, CA: Christian Book Club of America, 1969.

Stoddard, Miss (Inquire Within). *Trail of the Serpent.* 1935. Hawthorne, CA: Christian Book Club of America, n.d.

Stormer, John A. *None Dare Call It Treason – 25 Years Later.* Florissant, MO: Liberty Bell Press, 1990.

Strong, James. *Strong's Exhaustive Concordance of the Bible.*

Sutton, Antony C. *An Introduction to THE ORDER.* Vancouver, BC: Veritas Publishing, 1984.

Sutton, Antony C. and Patrick M. Wood. *Trilaterals overs Washington*. Scottsdale, AZ: The August Corporation, 1978.

Sutton, William Josiah. *The New Age Movement and The Illuminati·666*. U.S.A.: The Institute of Religious Knowledge, 1983.

Tannahill, Reay. *Sex in History*. New York: Stein and Day, 1980.

Terry, Maury. *The Ultimate Evil*. New York: Doubleday, 1987.

— *The Growing Menace of Freemasonry in Britain*. 6th ed. London: n.p., 1936.

Toland, John. *Adolf Hitler*. New York: Ballantine Books, 1976.

Unger, Merrill F. *Archaeology and the Old Testament*. Grand Rapids, MI: Zondervan, 1954.

Voorhis, Harold. *The Story of the Scottish Rite of Freemasonry*. Richmond, VA: Macoy Publishing, 1965.

Wagner, Martin L. *Freemasonry: An Interpretation*. Dayton, OH: privately printed, 1912.

Waite, Arthur Edward. *A New Encyclopaedia of Freemasonry*. 2 vols. New York: Weathervane Books, MCMLXX.

Walker, Charles. *Atlas of Secret Europe*. New York: Dorset Press, 1990.

Webster, Nesta. *Secret Societies* and *Subversive Movements*. 1924. Hawthorne, CA: Christian Book Club of America, 1979.

Webster, Nesta. *The French Revolution*. 1919. Hawthorne, CA: Christian Book Club of America, 1969.

Webster, Nesta. *The Socialist Network*. London: n.p., 1926.

Webster's Ninth New Colleglate Dictionary. Springfield, MA: Merriam-Webster, Inc., 1983.

Weiner, Herbert. *9 1/2 Mystics: The Kabbala Today*. New York: Collier Books, 1969.

Wells, H.G. *Anticipations of the Reaction to Mechanical and Scientific Progress Upon Human Life and Thought*. New York: Harper and Row, 1902.

Wells, H.G. *Experiments in Autobiography*. New York: Macmillan Co., 1934.

Weston, Warren. *Father of Lies*. London: n.p., 1930s.

White, Carol. *The New Dark Ages Conspiracy*. New York: The New Benjamin Franklin House, 1980.

Wigoder, Geoffrey. *The Story of the Synagogue, A Diaspora Museum Book*. Jerusalem: The Domino Press, 1986.

Wilgus, Neal. *The Illuminoids*. 1978. New York: Pocket Books, 1979.

Wilmshurst, W.L. *The Meaning of Masonry*. 1927. New York: Bell Publishing, 1980.

Winrod, Gerald B. *Weishaupt: A Human Devil*. N.p.: n.p., 1935.

Yallop, David A. *In God's Name: An Investigation into the Murder of Pope John Paul I*. New York: Bantam Books, 1984.

Zepp-LaRouche, Helga. *The Hitler Book.* New York: New Benjamin Franklin House, 1984.

Television and Radio Programs

Hour of Power. CBS. KDFW, Dallas. 24 Feb. 1991.

Is the Antichrist in the World today? Inter. Dr. Emil Gaverluk and Constance Cumbey. Southwest Radio Church Broadcast. Oklahoma City, 1982 Transcript show #B-349: 1-39.

Stalin – A time for Judgement. Channel 9 cable. WROC, Rochester, New York. 4 June 1990.

The Devil Worshippers. Corres. Tom Jarriel. Prod. Peter W. Kunhardt and Kenneth Wooden. 20/20. Exec. prod. Av Westin. ABC. 16 May 1985. Transcript show #521.

The New World Order. Point of View. Dallas, TX. 11 Feb. 1991. Marlin Maddox interviews Larry Abraham.

Periodicals, Newspapers, Letters and Unpublished Manuscripts

Associated Press. "Bruises found on Railey's Son." *Longview* (Texas) *Morning Journal.* 13 March 1988: 6-A.

Associated Press. "Interest in occult transformed teen before slaying morn, self." *Longview Daily News.* 13 Jan. 1988: 8-A.

Associated Press. "Satanism linked to killer." *Longview Morning Journal.* 2 Sept. 1985: 14-B.

Association of North American Missions annual report, P.O. Box 9710, Madison, WI 53715. 1985.

"A Strong Delusion." *The Prophecy Newsletter.* 1.5 (?): 5-7.

Baker, Russell. "Skull & Bones." *The New York Times.* 19 May 1991: n.p.

Behar, Richard. "The Thriving Cult of Greed and Power." *Time.* 6 May 1991: 50-57.

Bering-Jensen, Helle. "Glass Tips atop a National Treasure." *Insight.* 3 July 1989: 58-59.

Boswell, Charles. "The Great Fuss and Fume over the Omnipotent OOM." *True.* Jan. 1965: 31-32, 86-91.

CDL Report, P.O. Box 426, Metairie, LA 70004, May-June, 1982.

Chick, Jack. *The Curse of Baphomet.* Chino, CA: Chick Publications, n.d.

Coleman, John. "Special Report from South Africa." *World Economic Review.* July 1987: 3-5, 14-18.

Coleman, John. "The Beast Marks South Africa." *World Economic Review.* October 1986: 4-13.

Coleman, John. "Spy Scandals and Secret Societies." World Economic Review. October 1984: 1-7.

Douglas, Allen. "Solomon's Temple: a pagan crusade against Israel." *Executive Intelligence Review.* 22 May 1984: 22-23.

— "Drugs and Banking." *Executive Intelligence Review.* 7 Sept. 1982: 35.

— *Executive Intelligence Review.* 31 August 1982: 45-46.

Coker, Nancy and Al Douglas. "Flirting with Armageddon: The Jerusalem Temple Foundation." *Executive Intelligence Review.* 26 April 1983: 19-20, 72.

Gerber, Larry. "Helena Navratilova: The assassination that triggered WWI." *Longview Daily News.* 3 July 1984: 9B.

Geyer, Georgie Anne. "After six years, Mikhail Gorbachev left office and achieved greatness." *Longview News Journal.* 1 Jan. 1992: 4A.

Gilman, Richard. "Nazis, Mystics, and Islam: In search of the Nazi-Muslim Connection." *Conspiracy Digest.* Summer 1977: 7.

Gilman, Richard. "The mysterious influence of Edward Bulwer-Lytton." *Conspiracy Digest.* Spring 1978: 1.

Global 2000: Blueprint for Genocide. Special report by the publishers of *Executive Intelligence Review.* August 1982: entire.

Haggard, Forrest D. "Masonry Under Attack." *Texas Mason.* Summer 1990: 5-7.

HRT Newsletter. HRT Ministries, P.O. Box 12, Newtonville, NY 12128-0012. Spring and Summer 1990.

HRT Newsletter. April/May/June 1991.

Intercessors for America. P.O. Box 2639, Reston, VA 22090. Oct. 1988.

Investigative Leads, 304 W. 58th St., NY 10019, February 25, 1983.

Investigative Leads, wihe paper by Brian Lanze, January 13, 1982.

Isaac, Rael Jean. "Do You know where Your Church Offerings Go?" *Reader's Digest.* January 1983: 120-125.

"Is the Antichrist in the world today?" Transcribed interview with Constance Cumbey by Dr. Emil Gaverluk. Oklaoma City: Southwest Radio Church, 1982: entire.

"Is Freemasonry Part Of The New Age Movement?" *Newswatch Magazine.* 7.9. June 1987: 4-10.

"Israel" World Economic Review. Nov. 1986: 13.

"Italian General: Dope Mafia a British Protectorate." *New Solidarity.* Special Report. 20 Sept. 1982: 1.

Lalonde, Peter. "America Health Magazine: Metaphysics Belief on Rise." *Omega-Letter.* 1.12. Dec. 1986: 12.

Lalonde, Pete. *Omega-Letter.* Dec. 1986: 3.

Lalonde, Peter. "A Falling Away First." *Omega-Letter.* March 1988:5.

Marrs, Texe. "Gorbachev and Masonry." *Flashpoint.* Sept. 1990: 1-2.

Matthews, E. *What is Communism?* Unpublished essay, n.d.

— "Muslim Schoolgirl Scarves Banned." *Los Angeles Times.* 7 November 1989: n.p.

— *New Solidarity.* 17 May 1985: Suppplement A and B.

— *NRI Trumpet.* 3.1. July 1989:8.

Peale, Norman Vincent. "Enthousiasm Makes the Difference." *The Scottish Rite Journal.* March 1991: 6.

Reader's Digest. Oct. 1982: 203.

Reader's Digest. Dec. 1991: 200.

Rhodes, Cecil. "Rhodes' 'Confession of Faith' of 1877." *Conspiracy Digest.* Fall 1979: 8.

Rhodes, Cecil. "Rhodes' 'Confession of Faith' of 1877." *Conspiracy Digest.* Winter 1979-80: 8.

"Satanic Worship Reaches New Heights." *World Intelligence Review.* Special Report. May 1989: 3-19.

Schuyler, Montgomery. "To Chief of Staff, Siberia." 9 June 1919. Washington: National Archives, War Records Division.

Smagula, Judy. "Stalker suspect enters pleas." *Longview Daily News.* 2 Sept. 1985: 5-B.

Spivak, John L. "England's Cliveden Set." *Conspiracy Digest.* Fall 1980: 1-3.

— "The Cult of Moscow, The Third Rome." *New Solidarity.* 19 July 1985: Supplement C.

The New Age, Volume XCIII, No. 4, April 1985, The Supreme Council, 33rd degree, Ancient and Accepted Scottish Rite of Freemasonry, Southern Jurisdiction, U.S.A., 1733 Sixteenth street NW., Washington, D.C. 20009.

"The prophetic truth about Eastern Europe." *The Gospel Truth.* Southwest Radio Church, Oklahoma City, OK Dec. 1989:3.

— *The Knoxville News-Sentinel.* 27 Feb. 1983: A-7.

Wilson, Robert Anton. Letter. *Conspiracy Digest.* 3.1. 1978: 8.

"Your Scientology Organizations Across the World." *The Auditor.* 1992: back page.

Cassette Tapes

Coleman, John (former British Intelligence Officer). *King Makers: King Breakers = The Cecils.* rec. 1984. Arabi, LA: Christian Defense League.

Coleman, John. *Secrets of the Kennedy Assassination Revealed.* Part 1 rec. 1983, Part 2 rec. 1990.

Coleman, John. *Witchcraft in Politics Today.* rec. 1984.

Coleman, John. *Update on Secret Societies.* rec. 1984.

Coleman, John. *The Future of Latin America.* rec. 1984.

Coleman, John. *Black Nobility Unmasked.* rec. 1984.

Coleman, John. *The Drug War Against America.* rec. 1984.

Coleman, John. *The Role of Secret Societies.* rec. 1985.

Coleman, John. *Narcotics Trade From A To Z.* rec. 1986.

Coleman, John. *The Oligarchial & Royal Families.* rec. 1987.

Coleman, John. *Dope International, Ltd.* rec. 1987.

Crawford, Arthur. *Revelation 13:8.* Tape #64. Riverside Bible Church Tape Ministry, Worthington, Ohio.

Fagan, Myron. *The Illuminati.* rec. 1967. In the library of John Daniel.

Maddoux, Marlin. *Magic,* Mormonism & *Masonry,* Point of View tape ministry, #740-Kay Trimble & John Hall; International Christian Media, P.O. Box 30, Dallas, TX 75221.

Shaw, Jim. *Degrees of the Adepts.* Audiotape. Tape Ministry of Rev. Jim Shaw, P.O. Box 884, Silver Springs, FL 32688.

Shaw, Jim. *Kissing Jesus good-bye at the Altar of Baal.* Audiotape.

Shaw, Jim. *Pastors in the National Council of Churches who are in Freemasonry.* Audiotape.

Shaw, Jim. *Testimony of Jim Shaw.* Audiotape.

Shaw, Jim. *Questions and Answers* on *Freemasonry.* Audiotape.

INDEX

A

Abif, *37, 38, 85, 305*

abortion, *74, 166, 237, 238, 240, 245, 248, 249, 561, 564*

AC-DC, *343*

Acheson, *507*

Adam and Eve, *22, 33, 59, 323, 325*

Adams, *144, 145, 316, 554, 556, 566, 569, 570*

Adenauer, *495*

Adler, *407, 447*

Adonay, *316, 320, 322, 326*

Affair of the Diamond Necklace, *222*

agents of change, *207, 247*

Ageston Peter, *379*

agriculture, *98, 412, 413*

Albancelli, *55, 56*

Albert Victor Christian Edward, *424*

Alberto, *182*

Albigensians, *42, 74*

Albrecht, *156, 453*

alchemy, *40, 41, 100, 101, 161, 162, 175*

Aldrich, *507*

Aleksander S. Pushkin, *388*

Aleksandra, *397, 398*

Aleksei, *397*

Alexander I, *262, 264, 266, 387, 388*

Alexander II, *69, 300, 303, 390, 391*

Alexander III, *391*

Alexander Pope, *118, 121*

Alexandria Lodge, *556*

Alfonso XIII, *481*

Alice Cooper, *342*

Alliance Israelite Universelle, *291, 292, 298, 394, 396, 401, 402, 458, 523*

Alliance Sociale Democratique, *300*

Allied Powers, *365, 367, 410*

All-Seeing Eye, *78, 129, 142, 143, 146, 148, 150, 151, 152, 169, 176,* *225, 233, 328, 357, 507, 511, 527, 562, 569, 570, 572, 583*

Alpina, *41, 64, 65, 269, 294, 336*

Amaru, *562*

American Civil Liberties Union, *166, 352*

American Civil War, *276, 316*

American Communist Party, *503*

American Eagle, *15, 145, 572*

American I.G. Chemical Corp, *469*

American Jewish Congress, *166*

American labor unions, *504*

American Protective Association, *192*

American Revolution, *47, 58, 143, 144, 399, 551, 553, 554, 581*

Amnesty International, *357*

Anabaptists, *99*

Anarchists, *273, 300, 523*

Ancient and Primitive Rite of Masonry, *348, 355*

Ancient and Primitive Rite of Memphis, *339, 523*

ancient Rome, *536, 537, 541, 542, 543, 551, 573, 576*

Anderson Constitution, *103*

Andrea, *87, 93, 94*

Andropov, *187, 419*

angel of light, *326*

Anglican Church, *44, 334, 356, 359, 519, 525*

Anglophile Masonic fronts, *431*

Animal Magnetism, *231*

Anthroposophical Society, *49, 355, 523*

anti-abortion, *249*

anti-American, *434*

anti-black, *354*

anti-Bolshevik, *482*

anti-capitalist labor unions, *300*

anti-Catholic, *182, 192, 193, 252, 424*

anti-Christ, *210*

Antichrist, 22, 59, 64, 146, 206, 358,

G

H

Habsburg, *63, 65, 107, 125, 127, 131, 157, 173, 222, 252, 255, 285, 315, 368, 369, 377, 381, 438, 459, 460, 473, 487, 488, 512*
Hagen, *461*
Haggard, *57, 58, 213, 580, 586*
Hague Congress of the International, *391*
Hague Grand Lodge, *469*
Halifax, *404, 405, 475*
Hallstein, *539*
Hammer, *33, 413, 580*
Hancock, *553, 554*
Hanover, *102, 258*
Hapsburg, *107, 126, 439*
Harriman, *444, 566*
Harris, *103, 580*
Harrison, *231, 365, 552*
Hasan Saba, *79*
hashish, *79*
Haskala movement, *163*
Haugwitz, *264, 265*
Haushofer, *452, 453, 462, 466*
Haydn, *157*
Haywood, *38, 136, 137, 225, 374, 580*
Hebrew Lodge, *31*
Heine, *385, 386*
Helmholtz, *156*
Helvetius, *241*
Henry II of Valois, *106*
Henry III, *112, 113*
Henry IV, *109, 112, 113*
Henry VIII, *90, 519*
hermaphrodite, *176*
Hermes, *41, 233*
Hermetic, *41, 64, 87, 106, 137, 157, 159, 175, 331, 337, 338, 348, 349, 450*
Hermetic Brotherhood of Light, *348*
heroin, *48, 159, 277, 329, 339, 341*
Herter, *443, 444*
Herz, *167*
Herzegovina, *370*
Herzen, *275*
Herzl, *288, 289, 401*
Hess, *52, 453, 454, 478, 498, 578*
Hesse, *172, 252, 256, 468*

Heuss, *495*
hexagon, *575*
hexagram, *159, 293, 572, 574, 575*
Heydrich, *499, 503, 504*
Hidden Church of the Holy Grail, *348*
hidden hand, *24, 25, 115, 251, 315*
High Masonry, *8, 126, 175*
High Masons, *30, 54, 57, 258, 275, 310, 488*
high place, *37, 38, 570, 571*
Hill of Heaven, *142, 570*
Himmler, *453, 455, 461, 486, 497, 498, 499, 500, 503*
Hindenburg, *478*
Hinduism, *63, 78, 138, 150, 158, 176, 233, 293, 452*
Hitler, *13, 39, 43, 49, 62, 79, 168, 177, 284, 287, 290, 302, 306, 314, 345, 346, 354, 356, 383, 394, 409, 414, 416, 418, 421, 441, 445, 447, 448, 449, 450, 451, 452, 453, 454, 457, 458, 459, 460, 461, 462, 463, 464, 465, 466, 467, 468, 469, 470, 471, 472, 473, 474, 475, 476, 477, 478, 479, 480, 481, 482, 483, 484, 485, 486, 487, 488, 491, 493, 494, 495, 496, 497, 498, 499, 500, 501, 502, 503, 504, 508, 510, 530, 580, 582, 583, 584, 585*
Hohenzollern, *457, 494*
Holbrook, *320*
Holland, *96, 219, 224, 258, 270, 467, 469, 479, 482, 507*
Holly, *177*
holocaust, *27, 168, 314, 344, 421, 463, 533*
Holy Alliance, *388, 389, 438*
Holy Grail, *5, 6, 13, 43, 62, 63, 64, 65, 66, 67, 68, 69, 70, 76, 77, 78, 80, 81, 83, 84, 85, 93, 94, 95, 100, 101, 104, 106, 108, 109, 122, 124, 125, 126, 130, 146, 147, 157, 161, 167, 181, 184, 185, 256, 257, 258, 291, 307, 311, 312, 313, 347, 425, 448, 450, 454, 459, 460, 524, 525, 526, 577*
Holy of Holies, *526, 527*
Holy Order of Rose Croix, *348*
Holy Roman Emperor, *67, 70, 106,*

M

O

Q

T

OTHER PUBLICATIONS

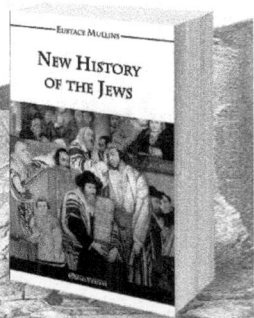

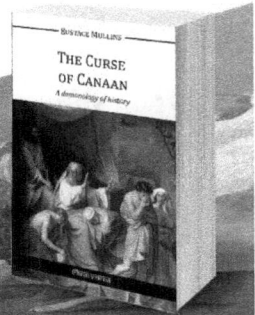